The

Complete Poetry

of alligator sashimi

John Milton

wild fires

post-catharsis

night-blindness

Damocles

Elephant n' Lun

perimeter

Euterpe

cacophony

barbershop medley

Cheese Connoisseur

The Norman Invasion vs
the Dodo Bird
Hawaiian Diamond

bilingl war shop/zeppeln

Helium Torso
Goldust shoes
Houdini

John T. Shawcross received a Ph.D. from New York University and is now professor of English at the University of Kentucky. He is also the author of *With Mortal Voice: The Creation of Paradise Lost*, *John Milton: A Bibliography for the Years 1624–1700*, and *Paradise Regain'd: "Worthy T'Have Not Remain'd So Long Unsung"*.

The
Complete Poetry
of
John Milton

BY
JOHN T. SHAWCROSS

REVISED EDITION

ARRANGED IN CHRONOLOGICAL ORDER

WITH AN INTRODUCTION, NOTES, VARIANTS,

AND LITERAL TRANSLATIONS OF THE

FOREIGN LANGUAGE POEMS

ANCHOR BOOKS

DOUBLEDAY

NEW YORK LONDON TORONTO SYDNEY AUCKLAND

AN ANCHOR BOOK
PUBLISHED BY DOUBLEDAY
a division of Bantam Doubleday Dell Publishing Group, Inc.
1540 Broadway, New York, New York 10036

ANCHOR BOOKS, DOUBLEDAY, and the portrayal
of an anchor are trademarks of Doubleday, a division of
Bantam Doubleday Dell Publishing Group, Inc.

This edition has been especially prepared for Anchor Books
and has never appeared before in book form.

Library of Congress Cataloging-in-Publication Data
Milton, John, 1608–1674.
[Poems]
The complete poetry of John Milton: arranged
in chronological order with an introduction, notes, variants,
and literal translations of the foreign language forms
by John T. Shawcross.—Rev. ed.
    p. cm.
Includes bibliographical references.
I. Shawcross, John T. II. Title.
PR3551.S4   1990   89-77299
821'.4—dc20   CIP

ISBN 0-385-02351-0

Introduction to the Revised Edition

Arranged according to probable date of composition of the verse, this revised edition brings together all original poems and poetic paraphrases written by John Milton. Included therefore are nine poems not published in either of the two collected editions of the minor poems appearing in Milton's lifetime: two verses found with his Commonplace Book, a third poem on Hobson the university carrier possibly by Milton, four sonnets, and two Latin epigrams from two prose works. Poems written in Latin, Greek, and Italian are given in original versions and in new prose translations, which attempt insofar as possible to follow the original lines. Differences from the first edition of this collection include the addition of the foreign language texts and the texts of *Psalms 80–88*, additional notes, a general updating of materials, and some rearrangement of the poems.

I have attempted to narrow the dates of composition as much as is presently possible; when apparent proof of date is missing a question mark is added. But the reader should bear in mind that such dating is open to question and it may be in dispute by scholars. Full discussion of dating will be found in the textual notes. Milton frequently altered poems after he had recorded them in the earliest versions which have survived, but perhaps only *Arcades, A Mask, Samson Agonistes, Paradise Regain'd,* and *Paradise Lost* underwent extensive revisions. Dates for such development are indicated and the poems placed in this arrangement accordingly. *Paradise Regain'd* has been positioned after *Paradise Lost* because the received text is apparently an extensive transformation into epic form of whatever was its early version. *Samson Agonistes* has been rearranged in this revised edition, not because I have altered my belief concerning its date of composition, but because its former position isolated some of the minor poems from others, creating a frankly odd arrangement. It is perhaps best to place the three major poems together, and the standard placement of *Samson Agonistes* last allows one to contrast it effectively with *Paradise Regain'd* in interpretation and form. The dating of the three major poems is, in any case, particularly uncertain and has been frequently challenged.

Explanatory notes present information necessary to an understanding of the poetry for the student and general reader and, hopefully, readings suggestive of structure, biographical contexts, sources of importance, and import for Milton. No attempt has been made to present a history of ideas, a frequent approach to a study of Milton. Textual principles are explained in the introduction to the textual notes. Generally, the basic text is that which seems to be closest to Milton—holograph, then scribal copy, and so forth. Alterations from the basic text are few; and all verbal variants in known significant texts are recorded in the textual notes. All dates for years are given in new style. Milton's prose works are cited from first editions.

The advice and knowledge of Professors J. Max Patrick and William B. Hunter, Jr., have been pervasively instructive in both large matters and small. But the decisions underlying the texts and commentary—and thus the faults—are my own. I am indebted also to William R. Parker for a number of suggestions.

1608

Born (Dec. 9), Bread St., Cheapside, London.

1618 ?–1620 ?

Tutored by Thomas Young.

1620 ?–1624

At St. Paul's School, London, under Alexander Gill. C. 1623 or 1624 family moved to home in St. Martin's-in-the-Fields, Westminster (?).

1625–1632 July

At Christ's College, Cambridge, ostensibly to enter clerical life. Plague closed Cambridge from Apr. 17, 1630, to c. Jan. 1631. C. 1631 family moved to home in Hammersmith.

1625

Admitted to Christ's College (Feb. 12), from which he matriculated on Apr. 9.

1626

Period of rustication (Lent term through spring vacation).

1629

Bachelor's degree conferred (Mar. 26).

1632

Master's degree conferred (July 3).

1632 July–1635 ?

At Hammersmith with parents. "A Mask" ("Comus") performed, Sept. 29, 1634.

1635 ?–1638

At Horton, Bucks, with family. Frequently in London after death of mother, Apr. 3, 1637. Publications: *A Mask* (1637/8 ?); "Lycidas" in *Justa Edovardo King naufrago* (1638).

1638 Apr. ?–1639 Aug. ?

Continental tour to France and Italy.

1639 autumn–1648

Tutoring until c. 1647. Studies continued; prose and poetic writings, some published and others begun. Residence: St. Bride's Church-yard (a few months) and Aldersgate St., London (1640–Sept. ? 1645).

1641

Publications: "Postscript" (?) in Smectymnuus, *An Answer to a Booke entituled, An Humble Remonstrance* (Mar.); *Of Reformation* (May ?); *Of Prelatical Episcopacy* (July ?); *Animadversions upon the Remonstrants Defence, against Smectymnuus* (July).

1642

Publications: *The Reason of Church Government* (Feb. ?); *An Apology against a Pamphlet call'd A Modest Confutation* (Apr.). Married to Mary Powell (May ?), who soon returned to her family's home in Forest Hill (July ?).

1643

Father came to live with Milton (Apr.). Publication: *The Doctrine and Discipline of Divorce* (Ed. 1, c. Aug.).

1644

Publications: *Doctrine and Discipline* (Ed. 2, enlarged, Feb.); *Of Education* (June); *The Judgement of Martin Bucer* (Aug.); *Areopagitica* (Nov.). Sight began noticeably to fail (autumn ?).

1645

Publications: *Tetrachordon* and *Colasterion* (Mar.); *Poems* (Ed. 1, autumn ?). Wife Mary returned home (summer ?). Residence: Barbican (Sept. ?–autumn 1647).

1646

Daughter Anne born (July 29).

1647

Father died (Mar. 13 ?). Residence: High Holborn (autumn–c. Mar. 1649).

1648

Daughter Mary born (Oct. 25).

1649–1660 ?

Period of public service as Secretary for Foreign Tongues to Council of State: appointed Mar. 15, 1649; continued in position until at least Oct. 22, 1659.

1649

Publications: *The Tenure of Kings and Magistrates* (Ed. 1, Feb.); *Observations upon the Articles of Peace* (May); *Eikonoklastes* (Ed. 1, Oct., in answer to *Eikon Basilike*, c. Feb.). Residence: Charing Cross (c. Mar.–Nov.) and Scotland Yard, Whitehall (Nov.–Dec. 1651).

1650

Publications: *Tenure* (Ed. 2, enlarged, Feb.); *Eikonoklastes* (Ed. 2, enlarged). Probably lost sight of left eye.

1651

Publication: *Joannis MiltonI Angli Pro Populo Anglicano Defensio* (Feb., in answer to Salmasius' *Defensio regia pro Carolo I*, which appeared in England by Nov. ? 1649; revision of so-called "Defensio prima" was published in Oct. 1658. Also *Joannis Philippi*

Angli Responsio Ad Apologiam Anonymi, by the younger surviving
son of Milton's sister Anne, published toward end of year in answer
to John Rowland's *Pro Rege et Populo Anglicano Apologia* written
against "Defensio prima.") Son John born (Mar. 16). Became totally
blind before Feb. 1652, and granted assistance in secretaryship.
Residence: Petty France, Westminster (Dec.–Sept. ? 1660).

1652

Daughter Deborah born (May 2); wife Mary died (May 5 ?); and son
John died (June 16 ?). Work on poetry and prose (?) through 1658.

1654

Publication: *Joannis MiltonI Angli Pro Populo Anglicano Defensio
Secunda* (May, in answer to Pierre du Moulin's *Regii Sanguinis
Clamor,* Aug. ? 1652, which attacked the Commonwealth).

1655

Publication: *Joannis MiltonI Angli pro se Defensio* (Aug., in answer to
Alexander More's *Fides Publica,* Oct. ? 1654).

1656

Married to Katherine Woodcock (Nov. 12).

1657

Daughter Katherine born (Oct. 19).

1658

Second wife, Katherine, died (Feb. 3); daughter Katherine died
(Mar. 17). Publication: edited "Sir Walter Ralegh's" *The Cabinet-
Council* (May ?).

1659

Publications and other writings: *A Treatise of Civil Power* (Feb.); *Con-
siderations Touching the likeliest means to remove Hirelings* (Aug.);
*A Letter to a Friend, Concerning the Ruptures of the Common-
wealth* (written Oct. 20, first published by John Toland in 1698);
possible work, "Proposalls of certaine expedients for the preventing

of a civill war now feard, & the settling of a firme government"
(autumn ?, first published in Columbia Milton).

1660

Period of transition between governments, loss of office, and govern-
mental harassment and imprisonment. Publications and other writ-
ings: *The Readie & Easie Way to Establish A Free Commonwealth*
(Mar.; Ed. 2, revised, c. Apr.); *The Present Means, and brief De-
lineation of a Free Commonwealth* ("Letter to General Monk,"
written after Mar. 3, first published by John Toland in 1698); *Brief
Notes Upon a Late Sermon* (Apr.). Residence: Holborn near Red
Lyon Fields (Sept. ?–early 1661). Escaped death penalty under
Act of Oblivion of Aug. 29; in prison, after burning of books written
by him (Oct. ?–Dec. 15).

1661–1674

Period of general retirement; work on poetry and prose.

1661

Residence: Jewin St. (early 1661–1669 ?).

1663

Married to third wife, Elizabeth Minshull (Feb. 24).

1665

Stayed at Chalfont St. Giles, Bucks, to escape plague (June ?–Feb. ?
1666).

1667

Publication: *Paradise Lost* (Ed. 1, Aug. ?; further issues, 1668, 1669).

1669

Publication: *Accedence Commenc't Grammar* (June ?). Residence: Ar-
tillery Walk, Bunhill Fields (c. 1669–74).

1670

Publication: *The History of Britain* (before Nov.).

1671

Publication: *Paradise Regain'd* and *Samson Agonistes* (early in year).

1672

Publication: *Joannis Miltoni Angli, Artis Logicæ Plenior Institutio* (May ?).

1673

Publications: *Of True Religion, Hæresie, Schism, Toleration* (May ?); *Poems* (Ed. 2, enlarged, together with *Of Education*, Ed. 2, Nov. ?).

1674

Publications: *Joannis Miltoni Angli, Epistolarum Familiarium Liber Unus* (with college prolusions, May); *Paradise Lost* (Ed. 2, revised, July); *A Declaration, or Letters Patents* (July ?). Died, apparently of gout (Nov. 8 ?); buried in St. Giles, Cripplegate (Nov. 12).

Posthumous publications: *Literæ Pseudo-Senatûs Anglicani* (Oct. ? 1676; a free and inaccurate English version appeared in 1682); *Mr. John Miltons Character of the Long Parliament* (Apr. ? 1681); *A Brief History of Moscovia* (Feb. ? 1682); *Letters of State* (translated by Edward Phillips, with four sonnets and a biographical memoir, 1694); *Joannis Miltoni Angli De Doctrina Christiana* (1825; translated and published in same year by Charles R. Sumner).

Abbreviations

The following abbreviations, in addition to those which are common-place, those which are standard for books of the Bible, and those which are easily recognizable short forms, will be found in this edition:

Aen.	Aeneid	PQ	Philological Quarterly
Ec.	Virgil, Eclogues	PR	Paradise Regain'd
El.	Elegy	Ps.	Psalm
FQ	Faerie Queene	Rep.	Plato, Republic
HLQ	Huntington Library Quarterly	RES	Review of English Studies
Meta.	Ovid, Metamor-phoses	SA	Samson Agonistes
		SEL	Studies in English Literature
MLN	Modern Language Notes		
		Son.	Sonnet
MLR	Modern Language Review	SP	Studies in Philology
		TLS	Times Literary Supplement
NQ	Notes and Queries		
Od.	Odyssey	TM	Trinity Manuscript
PL	Paradise Lost	UTQ	University of Toronto Quarterly
PMLA	Publications of the Modern Language Association		

Contents

3. POEMS WRITTEN DURING PUBLIC LIFE AND GOVERNMENTAL
   SERVICE (1641–58)

4. THE MAJOR POEMS

PART 1

Poems
Written during School,
College, and University Years
(1624–32)

❋

A Paraphrase on Psalm 114[1]

When the blest seed of *Terah*'s faithfull Son,[2]
After long toil their liberty had won,
And past from *Pharian*[3] fields to *Canaan* Land,
Led by the strength of the Almighties hand,
Jehovah's wonders were in *Israel* shown,   5
His praise and glory was in *Israel* known.
That[4] saw the troubl'd Sea, and shivering fled,
And sought to hide his froth-becurled head
Low in the earth, *Jordans* clear streams recoil,
As a faint host that hath receiv'd the foil.[5]   10
The high, huge-bellied Mountains skip like Rams
Amongst their Ews, the little Hills like Lambs.
Why fled the Ocean? And why skipt the Mountains?
Why turned *Jordan* toward his Crystall Fountains?
Shake earth, and at the presence be agast   15
Of him that ever was, and ay shall last,
That glassy flouds from rugged rocks can crush,
And make soft rills from fiery flint-stones gush.

(1624)

---

[1] Harris Fletcher, analyzing the grammar school lesson of paraphrasing from one language to another, points out that "Milton's effort was cast into eighteen lines, or two more than the original verse divisions called for, and was more or less done in this fashion: lines 2, 4, 8, 10 were really added lines; but in lines 13–14 Milton compressed the four lines of verses 5 and 6 . . ." (*Intellectual Development*, I, 191). Compare the translation of Milton's rendition of this same psalm in Greek.

[2] Abraham; the original cites only Jacob, the blest seed of Abraham.

[3] Egyptian.

[4] "the strength of the Almighties hand," object of "saw."

[5] the sword; therefore, "hath been driven back."

Psalm 136[1]

Let us with a gladsom mind
Praise the Lord, for he is kind.
   For his mercies ay endure,
   Ever faithfull, ever sure.

Let us blaze his Name abroad,   5
For of gods he is the God.
   For, &c.

O let us his praises tell,
That doth the wrathfull tyrants quell.   10
   For, &c.

That with his miracles doth make
Amazed Heav'n and Earth to shake.
   For, &c.   15

That by his wisdom did create
The painted Heav'ns so full of state.
   For, &c.   20

That did the solid Earth ordain
To rise above the watry plain.
   For, &c.

That by his all-commanding might   25
Did fill the new-made world with light.
   For, &c.

And caus'd the Golden-tressed Sun
All the day long his cours to run.   30
   For, &c.

---

[1] Though this paraphrase elaborates upon the Hebrew, its result, unlike that in *Ps.* 114, is relative simplicity of language and image. Phrases have been traced to George Buchanan (in his Latin paraphrases of the psalms) and to Joshua Sylvester (in his translation of DuBartas' *Divine Weeks and Works*). Milton omitted verses 12, 18, and 22 of the original.

The horned Moon to shine by night
Amongst her spangled sisters bright.
   For, *&c.*   35

He with his thunder-clasping hand
Smote the first-born of *Egypt* Land.
   For, *&c.*   40

And in despight of *Pharao* fell,
He brought from thence his *Israel*.
   For, *&c.*

The ruddy waves he cleft in twain,   45
Of the *Erythræan* main.[2]
   For, *&c.*

The floods stood still like Walls of Glass,
While the Hebrew Bands did pass.   50
   For, *&c.*

But full soon they did devour
The Tawny[3] King with all his power.
   For, *&c.*   55

His chosen people he did bless
In the wastfull Wildernes.
   For, *&c.*   60

In bloody battail he brought down
Kings of prowess and renown.
   For, *&c.*

He foild bold *Seon* and his host,   65
That rul'd the *Amorrean* coast.
   For, *&c.*

And large-limb'd *Og* he did subdue,
With all his over-hardy crew.   70
   For, *&c.*

And to his servant *Israel*
He gave their Land therin to dwell.
   For, *&c.*   75

[2] the Red Sea.
[3] dark-complexioned.

He hath with a piteous eye
Beheld us in our misery.
  For, &c.   80

And freed us from the slavery
Of the invading enemy.
  For, &c.

All living creatures he doth feed,   85
And with full hand supplies their need.
  For, &c.

Let us therfore warble forth
His mighty Majesty and worth.   90
  For, &c.

That his mansion hath on high
Above the reach of mortall eye.
  For his mercies ay endure,   95
  Ever faithfull, ever sure.

(1624)

Apologus de Rustico et Hero[1]

Rusticus ex Malo sapidissima poma quotannis
  Legit, et urbano lecta dedit Domino:
Hic incredibili fructûs dulcedine Captus
  Malum ipsam in proprias transtulit areolas.
Hactenus illa ferax, sed longo debilis ævo,   5
  Mota solo assueto, protinùs aret iners.
Quod tandem ut patuit Domino, spe lusus inani,
  Damnavit celeres in sua damna manus.
Atque ait, Heu quantò satius fuit illa Coloni
  (Parva licet) grato dona tulisse animo!   10
Possem Ego avaritiam frœnare, gulamque voracem:
  Nunc periere mihi et fœtus et ipsa parens.

The Fable of the Peasant and the Overlord[1]

Every year a peasant gathered from an appletree the most savory fruit / and gave the choice apples to his overlord who lived in the city. / He, pleased with the unbelievable sweetness of the fruit, / transferred the apple tree itself to his own gardens. / The tree, fruitful up to this time but weak from old age, [5] / when moved from its accustomed soil, instantly withered to inactivity. / When at last it was evident to the overlord that he had been deceived / by a vain hope, he cursed the hands so swift in bringing loss. / And he cried, "Alas, how much more satisfactory it was to receive / with a grateful heart these gifts, although small, from my tenant. [10] / Would I could curb my greed and my voracious gullet: / now both the fruit and its parent are lost to me."

(1624-25)

[1] A version of a popular fable by Aesop, Milton's twelve elegiac lines were derived from ten by Mantuan (*Sylvarum*, Bk. 4).

Carmina Elegiaca[1]

Surge, age, surge, leves, iam convenit, excute somnos,
   Lux oritur; tepidi fulcra relinque tori.
Iam canit excubitor gallus, prænuncius ales
   Solis, et invigilans ad sua quemque vocat;
Flammiger Eois Titan[2] caput exerit undis,   5
   Et spargit nitidum læta per arva iubar.
Daulias[3] argutum modulatur ab ilice carmen
   Edit et excultos mitis alauda modos;
Iam rosa fragrantes spirat silvestris odores;
   Iam redolent violæ luxuriatque seges.   10
Ecce novo campos Zephyritis[4] gramine vestit
   Fertilis, et vitreo rore madescit humus.
Segnes invenias molli vix talia lecto,
   Cum premat imbellis lumina fessa sopor;
Illic languentes abrumpunt somnia somnos,   15
   Et turbant animum tristia multa tuum.

Illic tabifici generantur semina morbi.
   Qui pote torpentem posse valere virum?
Surge, age, surge, leves, iam convenit, excute somnos,
   Lux oritur; tepidi fulcra relinque tori.   20

Elegiac Verses[1]

Arise, up, arise. Now that it is time, shake off slumbers; / light is appear-
ing; leave the props of your languid bed. / Now sings the sentinel cock,
the harbinger bird / of the sun, and, watchful, calls everyone to his own
affairs. / The flaming Titan[2] thrusts his head from the Eastern waves [5]
/ and scatters his glittering splendor through the joyful fields. / The
Daulian[3] modulates her melodious song from the oak / and the gentle
lark pours forth her perfect notes. / Now the wild rose breathes forth its
fragrant perfumes; / now the violets diffuse their scent and the grain
grows rapidly. [10] / Behold, the fruitful consort of Zephyr[4] clothes the
fields with new growth, / and the soil becomes moist with glassy dew. /
Lazy one, you are not likely to find such things in your soft bed, / when
tranquil sleep weighs down your wearied eyes. / There dreams interrupt
dull slumbers [15] / and many griefs disturb your mind. / There the
seeds of a wasting malady are generated. / What strength can a listless
man be capable of? / Arise, up, arise. Now that it is time, shake off slum-
bers; / light is appearing; leave the props of your languid bed. [20]

(*1624–25*)

   [1] These and the following verses were written on a loose sheet found in Mil-
ton's Commonplace Book with only this title given for the first. Grammar school
exercises, they versify a prose theme on early rising found on the reverse of the
sheet: "Mane citus lectum fuge" ("Quick, hasten from your bed in the
morning").
   [2] Hyperion, here identified with the Sun.
   [3] the swallow.
   [4] Chloris, wife of the West Wind.

"Ignavus satrapam dedecet . . ."[1]

Ignavus satrapam dedecet inclytum
Somnus qui populo multifido præest.
Dum Dauni veteris filius armiger[2]
Stratus purpureo procubuit thoro,
Audax Eurialus, Nisus et impiger   5
Invasere cati nocte sub horrida
Torpentes Rutilos castraque Volscia:
Hinc cædes oritur clamor et absonus. . . .

"Slothful sleep . . ."[1]

Slothful sleep is unbecoming to a famous governor / who presides over
people divided into many sections of the land. / While the warlike son
of old Daunas[2] / lay prone on his purple couch, / bold Euryalus and
quick Nisus [5] / cunningly attacked in the frightening night / the sleep-
ing Rutilians and the Volscian camp: / hence slaughter arose and dis-
cordant shout. . . .

(Incomplete; 1624–25)

[1] The meter is the lesser Aesclepiad (an irregular verse form used by Hor-
ace) with a spondee for the first foot.

[2] Turnus, king of the Rutili and leader of the Volscians and other Italian
tribes who resisted Aeneas' invasion. When in a drunken sleep, his army was
attacked by Euryalus and Nisus (*Aen.*, IX, 314–66).

Elegia prima

AD CAROLUM DIODATUM[1]

Tandem, chare, tuæ mihi pervenere tabellæ,
    Pertulit et voces nuntia charta tuas,
Pertulit occiduâ Devæ Cestrensis ab orâ
    Vergivium prono quà petit amne salum.

Multùm crede juvat terras aluisse remotas   5
   Pectus amans nostri, tamque fidele caput,
Quòdque mihi lepidum tellus longinqua sodalem
   Debet, at unde brevi reddere jussa velit.
Me tenet urbs refluâ quam Thamesis alluit undâ,
   Meque nec invitum patria dulcis habet.   10
Jam nec arundiferum mihi cura revisere Camum,
   Nec dudum vetiti me laris angit amor.[2]
Nuda nec arva placent, umbrasque negantia molles,
   Quàm male Phœbicolis convenit ille locus!
Nec duri libet usque minas perferre magistri   15
   Cæteraque ingenio non subeunda meo.
Si sit hoc exilium patrios adiisse penates,
   Et vacuum curis otia grata sequi,
Non ego vel profugi nomen, sortemve recuso,
   Lætus et exilii conditione fruor.   20
O utinam vates nunquam graviora tulisset
   Ille[3] Tomitano flebilis exul agro;
Non tunc Jonio quicquam cessisset Homero
   Neve foret victo laus tibi prima, Maro.[4]
Tempora nam licet hîc placidis dare libera Musis,   25
   Et totum rapiunt me mea vita libri.
Excipit hinc fessum sinuosi pompa theatri,
   Et vocat ad plausus garrula scena suos.[5]
Seu catus auditur senior, seu prodigus hæres,
   Seu procus, aut positâ casside miles adest,   30
Sive decennali fœcundus lite patronus
   Detonat inculto barbara verba foro,
Sæpe vafer gnato succurrit servus amanti,
   Et nasum rigidi fallit ubique Patris;
Sæpe novos illic virgo mirata calores   35
   Quid sit amor nescit, dum quoque nescit, amat.
Sive cruentatum furiosa Tragœdia sceptrum
   Quassat, et effusis crinibus ora rotat,
Et dolet, et specto, juvat et spectasse dolendo,
   Interdum et lacrymis dulcis amaror inest: 40
Seu puer infelix indelibata reliquit
   Gaudia, et abrupto flendus amore cadit,
Seu ferus è tenebris iterat Styga criminis ultor
   Conscia funereo pectora torre movens,
Seu mæret Pelopeia domus, seu nobilis Ili,   45
   Aut luit incestos aula Creontis avos.
Sed neque sub tecto semper nec in urbe latemus,
   Irrita nec nobis tempora veris eunt.

Nos quoque lucus habet vicinâ consitus ulmo
  Atque suburbani nobilis umbra loci.   50
Sæpius hic blandas spirantia sydera flammas
  Virgineos videas præteriisse choros.
Ah quoties dignæ stupui miracula formæ
  Quæ posset senium vel reparare Iovis;
Ah quoties vidi superantia lumina gemmas,
  Atque faces quotquot volvit uterque polus;   55
Collaque bis vivi Pelopis[6] quæ brachia vincant,
  Quæque fluit puro nectare tincta via,
Et decus eximium frontis, tremulosque capillos,
  Aurea quæ fallax retia tendit Amor;   60
Pellacesque genas, ad quas hyacinthina sordet
  Purpura, et ipse tui floris, Adoni, rubor.[7]
Cedite laudatæ toties Heroides[8] olim,
  Et quæcunque vagum cepit amica Jovem.
Cedite Achaemeniæ[9] turritâ fronte puellæ,   65
  Et quot Susa colunt, Memnoniamque Ninon.[10]
Vos etiam Danaæ fasces submittite Nymphæ,
  Et vos Iliacæ, Romuleæque nurus.
Nec Pompeianas Tarpëia Musa columnas[11]
  Jactet, et Ausoniis plena theatra stolis.   70
Gloria Virginibus debetur prima Britannis,
  Extera, sat tibi sit, fœmina, posse sequi.
Tuque urbs Dardaniis Londium structa colonis[12]
  Turrigerum latè conspicienda caput,
Tu nimium felix intra tua mœnia claudis   75
  Quicquid formosi pendulus orbis habet.
Non tibi tot cælo scintillant astra sereno
  Endymioneæ turba ministra deæ,[13]
Quot tibi conspicuæ formáque auróque puellæ
  Per medias radiant turba videnda vias.   80
Creditur huc geminis venisse invecta columbis
  Alma pharetrigero milite cincta Venus,
Huic Cnidon, et riguas Simoentis flumine valles,
  Huic Paphon, et roseam posthabitura Cypron.[14]
Ast ego, dum pueri sinit indulgentia cæci,   85
  Mœnia quàm subitò linquere fausta paro;
Et vitare procul malefidæ infamia Circes
  Atria, divini Molyos usus ope.[15]
Stat quoque juncosas Cami remeare paludes,
  Atque iterum raucæ murmur adire Scholæ.   90
Interea fidi parvum cape munus amici,
  Paucaque in alternos verba coacta modos.[16]

Elegy 1

TO CHARLES DIODATI[1]

At last, dear friend, your letter has reached me / and its news-filled paper conveyed your words, / conveyed them from the western region of the Dee near Chester, / from which with downward flow it seeks the Irish Sea. / I am greatly delighted, believe me, that remote lands have nurtured [5] / a loving heart, and so faithful a head, / and because the far-off region is indebted to me for a charming comrade, / yet from which it is willing to return him in a short while upon command. / The city holds me which the Thames washes with its back-flowing surge, / but my pleasant native home does not keep me against my will. [10] / At this time neither do I care to see the reedy Cam again, / nor does love of my prohibited quarters distress me just now.[2] / Its bare fields are unwelcome, so unyielding are they of mild shadows; / how improperly that place assembles the followers of Phoebus! / It is not pleasant constantly to submit to the threats of a stern tutor [15] / and to other things which are foreign to my nature. / If this be exile, to have gone to the paternal hearth / and, this banishment being free of care, to follow agreeable leisurely pursuits, / neither do I flee that name, nor reject its lot, / and, happy, I delight in the result of exile. [20] / O would that the poet never had borne anything more burdensome, / he, the lamentable exile in the land of Tomis.[3] / Then he would have conceded nothing to Ionian Homer, / nor would the foremost renown be yours, vanquished Maro.[4] / For I am permitted to dedicate my free time to the gentle Muses, [25] / and books—my life—transport me entirely away. / Here the display of the curved theater captivates me, when wearied, / and the talkative stage calls me to its applause.[5] / Sometimes is heard a sly old man, some-

---

[1] The biography of Milton's close friend is related by Donald C. Dorian in *The English Diodatis*. Diodati visited in Chester on the River Dee (from Milton's words in or around the northwestern section of the city) in the spring of 1626. Two Greek letters to Milton are extant in the British Museum (see Yale Prose, I, 336–37).

[2] Milton was suspended in the Lent term of 1626 as a result of a disagreement with his tutor William Chappell. On his return (around April 19), Milton was placed under Nathaniel Tovey.

[3] Ovid, banished in A.D. 8 to Tomis on the Black Sea where the Coralli lived; see *Elegy* 6, l. 19.

[4] Virgil.

[5] These references from his reading which follow (note ll. 26, 47) fit the

times a prodigal heir, / sometimes a suitor, or a soldier appears with his
helmet laid aside, [30] / or an advocate rich from a ten-year lawsuit /
thunders his strange discourse at an uncultivated court. / Often a crafty
slave runs to the aid of a love-sick son / and, everywhere at once, he de-
ceives the stern father under his very nose. / Often a maiden, astonished
by a strange ardor—[35] / she does not know what love is—loves even
while she is ignorant. / Or raging Tragedy tosses her sceptre stained
with blood / and rolls her eyes under dishevelled hair, / and it is painful;
not only do I watch, but I take pleasure in having seen / suffering, and
sometimes sweet bitterness lies in tears: [40] / whether an unhappy
youth left his joys untasted, / and, separated from his love, dies lamen-
tably, / or whether a fierce avenger of crimes returns from the shades
beyond the Styx, / disturbing with his deadly torch hearts conscious of
sin, / or whether the house of Pelops is grieving, or of noble Ilus, [45] /
or the palace of Creon purges its incestuous sires. / But I am not always
living in concealment indoors or in the city, / nor do the hours of spring
hasten by without effect on me. / The wood strewn with close-growing
elm also possesses me / as well as the celebrated shade of a suburban
spot. [50] / Here you may often see bands of maidens, stars / emitting
seductive flames, go dancing by. / Ah, how many times have I been
stunned by the wonders of a becoming figure / which might refresh even
the old age of Jove; / Ah, how many times have I seen eyes surpassing
jewels [55] / and even all the flaming stars which either pole rolls round;
/ and necks which excel the arms of twice-living Pelops,[6] / and in which
flows the vein dyed with pure nectar, / and uncommon grace of brow,
and shaking hair, / by which deceitful Love extends his golden nets,
[60] / and seductive cheeks against which the purple of the hyacinth
seems / of small account, and the blush of your flower, Adonis, as well![7]
/ Yield, Heroides,[8] so often praised in the past, / and every mistress who
subjected capricious Jove. / Yield, Achaemenian[9] maidens with towered
forehead, [65] / and all that dwell in Susa, or Memnonian Nineveh.[10] /

---

comedies of Terence and the tragedies of the Greeks. The house of Pelops is
represented, for example, in Aeschylus' *Agamemnon* and Euripides' *Electra;* the
house of Ilus, in Euripides' *Hecuba* and *Trojan Women;* and the palace of
Creon, in Sophocles' *Oedipus the King* and *Antigone.*
    [6] Pelops, dismembered and offered as food to the Gods, was restored by
Hermes; but the piece of shoulder eaten by Demeter had to be replaced by
ivory.
    [7] The anemone sprang from the blood of Adonis, killed by a boar while
hunting.
    [8] heroines of legend to whom Ovid assigns the letters making up his amatory
poems of this name.
    [9] Persian.
    [10] Susa in southwestern Persia was founded by Memnon's father; Milton's
Latin confusedly connects Memnon with the Assyrian city of Nineveh.

You likewise, Greek maidens, acknowledge your inferiority, / and you women of Troy and of Rome; / nor let the Tarpeian Muse vaunt the Pompeian pillars[11] / or the theaters filled with Italian robes. [70] / The prime honor is due the young women of Britain; / be satisfied, alien womanhood, to be able to follow after. / And you, London, city built by Trojan colonists,[12] / distinguished far and wide for towered height, / exceedingly happy, you enclose with your walls [75] / whatever of beauty the pendant world possesses. / Not so many stars shine down on you from the serene sky, / the ministrant multitude of Endymion's goddess,[13] / as the maidens dazzling to you in their beauty and golden-ness, / the visible throng that shine forth through the trodden ways. [80] / Lofted to this place by her twin-born doves, bountiful Venus is believed / to have come, accompanied by her quiver-bearing soldier; / for this city, she neglects Cnidos and the valleys watered by the river Simois, / for this, Paphos and rosy Cyprus.[14] / But I, while the blind boy's indulgence permits, [85] / am preparing to leave the favorable walled city most quickly; / and to escape from afar the infamous halls of faithless Circe, / preparing with the help of divine moly.[15] / It is de-cided also that I am to return to the rush-filled fens of the Cam / and again to submit to the noise of the raucous school. [90] / Meanwhile accept this small tribute of a loyal friend, / and these few words forced into alternating measures.[16]

(*Apr. 1626*)

---

[11] Ovid lived near the Capitoline hill, where was located the Tarpeian Rock from which criminals met their death. He praised both the theater of Pompey in the Campus Martius and other Italian theaters.

[12] According to legend, England was settled by Brutus, grandson of the Tro-jan Aeneas.

[13] Endymion was beloved by Selene (the Moon), who set him in perpetual sleep, descending each night to embrace him.

[14] Temples to Venus were erected at Cnidos and at Paphos, a city of Cyprus. Paris judged Venus the fairest goddess on the banks of the river Simois. The "quiver-bearing soldier" (l. 82) and the "blind boy" (l. 85) is her son Cupid.

[15] Through the aid of Hermes, Ulysses was able to resist the charms of Circe by eating the herb moly. The enchantress had turned half his followers into swine.

[16] the elegiac couplet, consisting of an hexameter and a pentameter.

Elegia secunda

IN OBITUM PRÆCONIS ACADEMICI CANTABRIGIENSIS[1]

Te, qui conspicuus baculo fulgente solebas
    Palladium toties ore ciere gregem,[2]
Ultima præconum præconem te quoque sæva
    Mors rapit, officio nec favet ipsa suo.
Candidiora licet fuerint tibi tempora plumis   5
    Sub quibus accipimus delituisse Jovem,[3]
O dignus tamen Hæmonio juvensecere succo,
    Dignus in Æsonios vivere posse dies,[4]
Dignus quem Stygiis medicâ revocaret ab undis
    Arte Coronides, sæpe rogante dea.[5]   10
Tu si jussus eras acies accire togatas,
    Et celer a Phœbo[6] nuntius ire tuo,
Talis in Iliacâ stabat Cyllenius[7] aula
    Alipes, æthereâ missus ab arce Patris.
Talis et Eurybates ante ora furentis Achillei   15
    Rettulit Atridæ jussa severa ducis.[8]
Magna sepulchrorum regina, satelles Averni
    Sæva nimis Musis, Palladi sæva nimis,
Quin illos rapias qui pondus inutile terræ?
    Turba quidem est telis ista petenda tuis.   20
Vestibus hunc igitur pullis, Academia, luge,
    Et madeant lachrymis nigra feretra tuis.[9]
Fundat et ipsa modos querebunda Elegëia tristes,
    Personet et totis nænia mœsta scholis.

Elegy 2

ON THE DEATH OF THE BEADLE OF CAMBRIDGE UNIVERSITY[1]

You who, conspicuous with your shining mace, were accustomed / so
often to assemble the Palladian band,[2] / beadle as you were, the last of

---

[1] Richard Ridding, who died in Oct. (?) 1626, as senior beadle, preceded
academic processions bearing the official mace.
[2] Pallas Athena was the goddess of wisdom and the arts.

beadles, fierce Death, / has seized, and does not even favor one in its own service. / Although your temples were whiter than the plumes [5] / under which we understand Jove to have been disguised,[3] / O yet were you worthy to grow young again with a Haemonian potion, / worthy to be able to live to an Aesonian age,[4] / worthy to be one whom Coronides should recall from the Stygian waves / by his curative art, at the frequent entreaty of the goddess.[5] [10] / As whenever you were bidden to fetch the gowned ranks / and to go a swift messenger from your Apollo,[6] / in such manner would wing-footed Cyllenius[7] stand in the court of Ilium, / dispatched from the heavenly vault of his father. / And in like fashion Eurybates before the face of angry Achilles [15] / conveyed the stern order of his chief, Atrides.[8] / Great queen of sepulchers, attendant of Avernus, / too cruel to the Muses, too cruel to Pallas, / why do you not seize those who are useless burdens of the earth? / They are the throng that should be attacked by your darts. [20] / Therefore, mourn for him, Academe, in robes of black, / and moisten with your tears the dark bier,[9] / and let lamenting Elegy itself pour forth its sad measures / and let all the schools resound with its sorrowful dirge.

(Oct. ? 1626)

[3] Jove, in love with the mortal Leda, approached her in the guise of a swan.
[4] Aeson was restored to youth by Medea, whose magic brew was concocted from herbs of the valleys of Haemonia.
[5] At the prayer of Diana, Aesculapius, god of medicine, brought Hippolytus back to life.
[6] the Vice-Chancellor of Cambridge.
[7] Hermes, messenger of the gods, born on Mt. Cyllene in Arcadia, met Priam, king of Ilium, on the plain outside Troy (Iliad, XXIV, 334-57).
[8] Eurybates and other heralds of Agamemnon were sent to Achilles' tent to fetch his concubine Briseis (Iliad, I, 320-25).
[9] Poetic tributes were customarily pinned to the bier.

Elegia tertia

IN OBITUM PRÆSULIS WINTONIENSIS[1]

Mœstus eram, et tacitus nullo comitante sedebam,
  Hærebantque animo tristia plura meo,
Prontinus en subiit funestæ cladis imago
  Fecit in Angliaco quam Libitina[2] solo;
Dum procerum ingressa est splendentes marmore turres   5
  Dira sepulchrali mors metuenda face;

Pulsavitque auro gravidos et jaspide muros,
  Nec metuit satrapum sternere falce greges.
Tunc memini clarique ducis, fratisque verendi
  Intempestivis ossa cremata rogis.[3]   10
Et memini Heroum quos vidit ad æthera raptos,
  Flevit et amissos Belgia tota duces.
At te præcipuè luxi, dignissime præsul,
  Wintoniæque olim gloria magna tuæ;
Delicui fletu, et tristi sic ore querebar,   15
  Mors fera Tartareo diva secunda Jovi,[4]
Nonne satis quod sylva tuas persentiat iras,
  Et quod in herbosos jus tibi detur agros,
Quodque afflata tuo marcescant lilia tabo,
  Et crocus, et pulchræ Cypridi[5] sacra rosa,   20
Nec sinis ut semper fluvio contermina quercus
  Miretur lapsus prætereuntis aquæ?
Et tibi succumbit liquido quæ plurima cælo
  Evehitur pennis quamlibet augur avis,[6]
Et quæ mille nigris errant animalia sylvis,   25
  Et quod alunt mutum Proteos antra pecus.[7]
Invida, tanta tibi cum sit concessa potestas,
  Quid juvat humanâ tingere cæde manus?
Nobileque in pectus certas acuisse sagittas,
  Semideamque animam sede fugâsse suâ?   30
Talia dum lacrymans alto sub pectore volvo,
  Roscidus occiduis Hesperus[8] exit aquis,
Et Tartessiaco[9] submerserat aequore currum
  Phœbus, ab eöo littore mensus iter.
Nec mora, membra cavo posui refovenda cubili,   35
  Condiderant oculos noxque soporque meos;
Cum mihi visus eram lato spatiarier agro,
  Heu nequit ingenium visa referre meum.
Illic puniceâ radiabant omnia luve,
  Ut matutino cum juga sole rubent.   40
Ac veluti cum pandit opes Thaumantia[10] proles,
  Vestitu nituit multicolore solum.
Non dea tam variis ornavit floribus hortos
  Alcinoi, Zephyro Chloris[11] amata levi.
Flumina vernantes lambunt argentea campos,   45
  Ditior Hesperio flavet arena Tago.[12]
Serpit odoriferas per opes levis aura Favoni,[13]
  Aura sub innumeris humida nata rosis.
Talis in extremis terræ Gangetidis oris
  Luciferi[14] regis fingitur esse domus.   50

Ipse racemiferis dum densas vitibus umbras
Et pellucentes miror ubique locos,
Ecce mihi subito præsul Wintonius astat,
Sydereum nitido fulsit in ore jubar;
Vestis ad auratos defluxit candida talos,   55
Infula divinum cinxerat albu caput.
Dumque senex tali incedit venerandus amictu,
Intremuit læto florea terra sono.
Agmina gemmatis plaudunt cælestia pennis,
Pura triumphali personat aethra tubâ.   60
Quisque novum amplexu comitem cantuque salutat,
Hosque aliquis placido misit ab ore sonos;
Nate, veni, et patrii felix cape gaudia regni,
Semper ab hinc duro, nate, labore vaca.[15]
Dixit, et aligeræ tetigerunt nablia turmæ,[16]   65
At mihi cum tenebris aurea pulsa quies.
Flebam turbatos Cephaleiâ pellice[17] somnos,
Talia contingant somnia sæpe mihi.

Elegy 3

ON THE DEATH OF THE BISHOP OF WINCHESTER[1]

I was full of sadness, and I was sitting silent with no companion, / and
many sorrows were clinging to my spirit. / Suddenly, lo, there arose a
vision of the mournful destruction / which Libitina[2] wrought on English
soil; / while dire death, fearful with its sepulchral torch, [5] / entered
the glittering marble palaces of the nobles, / and attacked the walls
laden with gold and jasper, / nor did it hesitate to overthrow hosts of
princes with its scythe. / Then I remembered that illustrious duke, and
his revered brother, / their bones burned on untimely pyres.[3] [10] /
And I remembered the heroes whom the land saw snatched up to the
sky, / and all Belgia mourned the lost leaders. / But I lamented chiefly

[1] Lancelot Andrewes, who died on Sept. 25, 1626.
[2] the Italian goddess of the dead. The plague was severe in London in
1625–26.
[3] often identified as Duke Christian of Brunswick-Wolfenbüttel, who died in
the Low Countries (Belgia) during the Thirty Years' War on June 6, 1626, and
Count Ernest of Mansfeld, who died on Nov. 29. Adherents of the Protestant
cause, they were brothers in arms only. Or perhaps they were King James (died
Mar. 27, 1625) and Maurice, Prince of Orange (died Apr. 23, 1625).

for you, most worthy Bishop, / and once the great glory of your Win-
chester; / I dissolved in weeping, and complained thus with sad words:
[15] / "Savage death, goddess second to Tartarean Jove,[4] / are you
not satisfied that the forest suffers your rages, / that power is given to
you over the grassy fields, / and that the blooming lilies wither from
your pestilence, / and the crocus, and the rose sacred to beautiful
Cypris,[5] [20] / just as you do not allow the oak bordering upon the
river forever / to wonder at the fall of the ebbing water? / And the bird
succumbs to you, although a prophet,[6] / many a one which is lifted
through the liquid air on its pinions, / and the thousand beasts that stray
in the dark forests, [25] / and the dumb herd which the caves of Proteus
sustain.[7] / Envious one, whenever such power is allowed you, / what
delights you to stain your hands with human slaughter? / and to
sharpen your unerring arrows against a noble breast, / and to drive a
half-divine spirit from its residence?" [30] / While, weeping, I medi-
tated such griefs deep in my heart, / dewy Hesperus[8] rose from the
western sea, / and Phoebus sank his chariot in the Tartessian[9] sea, /
after measuring his course from the eastern shore. / With no delay, I lay
down in cavernous bed to refresh my limbs, [35] / and night and sleep
shut my eyes; / when I seemed to be walking in a broad field. / Alas! my
senses cannot relate the things seen. / There all things were shining with
reddish light, / just as the mountain peaks blush with the morning sun.
[40] / But as when the child of Thaumas[10] spreads her riches, / the
earth luxuriated in vestment of many colors. / Chloris,[11] the goddess
beloved by fleet Zephyr, did not adorn / the gardens of Alcinous with
so many various flowers. / Silver rivers washed the verdant field; [45] /
the sand was gilded richer than Hesperian Tagus.[12] / Through the fra-
grant wealth stole the light breath of Favonius,[13] / the dewy breath born
under innumerable roses. / Such, on the distant shores of the land of the
Ganges, / is the home of Lucifer,[14] the king, imagined to be. [50] /
While I myself was marvelling at the dense shades beneath the cluster-

---

[4] Pluto, god of hell and brother of Jove.
[5] Venus.
[6] The belief was the basis of the Roman auspices (*avis spicere*), originally
signs from birds in flight or song, which were prescriptions of conduct and
prayer to determine whether the gods were favorable.
[7] Proteus, the changeable ancient of the sea, herded the seals of Neptune.
[8] the evening star.
[9] Spanish, i.e., western.
[10] Iris, goddess of the rainbow.
[11] goddess of spring and flowers, and wife of the West Wind. The garden of
Alcinous is described in *Od.*, VI, 291–94.
[12] the river in Spain, noted for its golden sand in the reflected sun.
[13] Zephyr.
[14] "bearer of light," the Sun.

ing vines / and the shining regions everywhere, / behold, Winchester's bishop suddenly stood before me, / the splendor of stars shone in his bright face; / a dazzling white robe flowed down to his golden ankles, [55] / a white fillet encircled his divine head. / And while the reverend old man advanced in such fashion, / the flowery earth trembled with happy sound. / The celestial multitudes applaud with jewelled wings, / the pure air resounds with triumphal trumpet. [60] / Everyone salutes the new companion with an embrace and a song, / and one among them uttered these words from his peaceful lips: / "My son, come, and, happy, reap the joys of your father's kingdom; / here rest forever, my son, from harsh labor."[15] / He spoke, and the winged troops touched their harps,[16] [65] / but for me golden sleep was banished with the night. / I wept for the dreams disturbed by the mistress of Cephalus.[17] / May such dreams often befall me! /

(*Oct. ? 1626*)

[15] Rev. xiv. 13: "And I heard a voice from heaven saying unto me: 'Blessed are the dead which die in the Lord from henceforth; Yea, saith the Spirit, that they may rest from their labours; and their works do follow them'."
[16] Rev. xiv. 2: "And I heard a voice from heaven, as the voice of many waters, and as the voice of a great thunder: and I heard the voice of harpers harping with their harps."
[17] Aurora, the dawn.

In obitum Præsulis Eliensis[1]

Adhuc madentes rore squalebant genæ,
    Et sicca nondum lumina
Adhuc liquentis imbre turgebant salis,
    Quem nuper effudi pius,
Dum mæsta charo justa persolvi rogo   5
    Winstoniensis præsulis;[2]
Cum centilinguis Fama (proh semper mali
    Cladisque vera nuntia)
Spargit per urbes divitis Britanniæ,
    Populosque Neptuno[3] satos,   10
Cessisse morti, et ferreis sororibus[4]
    Te, generis humani decus,
Qui rex sacrorum illâ fuisti in insulâ
    Quæ nomen Anguillæ tenet.[5]

Tunc inquietum pectus irâ protinus 15
    Ebulliebat fervidâ,
Tumulis potentem sæpe devovens deam:
    Nec vota Naso[6] in Ibida
Concepit alto diriora pectore,
    Graiusque vates parciùs 20
Turpem Lycambis execratus est dolum,
    Sponsamque Neobolen suam.[7]
At ecce diras ipse dum fundo graves,
    Et imprecor neci necem,
Audisse tales videor attonitus sonos 25
    Leni, sub aurâ, flamine:[8]
Cæcos furores pone, pone vitream
    Bilemque et irritas minas.
Quid temerè violas non nocenda numina,
    Subitoque ad iras percita? 30
Non est, ut arbitraris elusus miser,
    Mors atra Noctis filia,
Erebóve patre creta, sive Erinnye,
    Vastóve nata sub Chao:[9]
Ast illa cælo missa stellato, Dei 35
    Messes ubique colligit;
Animasque mole carneâ reconditas
    In lucem et auras evocat:
Ut cum fugaces excitant Horæ diem
    Themidos Jovisque filiæ;[10] 40
Et sempiterni ducit ad vultus patris;
    At justa raptat impios
Sub regna furvi luctuosa Tartari,
    Sedesque subterraneas.
Hanc ut vocantem lætus audivi, citò 45
    Fœdum reliqui carcerem,
Volatilesque faustus inter milites
    Ad astra sublimis feror:
Vates ut olim raptus ad cœlum senex[11]
    Auriga currus ignei. 50
Non me Boötis terruere lucidi
    Sarraca tarda frigore, aut
Formidolosi Scorpionis brachia,
    Non ensis Orion tuus.[12]
Prætervolavi fulgidi solis globum, 55
    Longéque sub pedibus deam
Vidi triformem,[13] dum coercebat suos
    Frænis dracones aureis.

Erraticorum syderum per ordines,
   Per lacteas vehor plagas,   60
Velocitatem sæpe miratus novam,
   Donec nitentes ad fores
Ventum est Olympi, et regiam Crystallinam, et
   Stratum smaragdis Atrium.[14]
Sed hic tacebo, nam quis effari queat   65
   Oriundus humano patre
Amœnitates illius loci?[15] mihi
   Sat est in æternum frui.

On the death of the Bishop of Ely[1]

As yet my cheeks were not dry with flowing tears, / and eyes not yet
dry, / still were they swollen with the rain of salt liquid, / which lately
I, respectful, poured forth, / while I rendered sorrowful obsequies to
the esteemed bier [5] / of the bishop of Winchester;[2] / when hundred-
tongued Fame (alas always / the true messenger of evil and misfortune)
/ spreads through the cities of affluent Britain / and to the people sprung
from Neptune[3] [10] / that you had yielded to death, and to the cruel
sisters,[4] / you, the ornament of the race of men, / who were the prince
of saints in that island / which retains the name of Eel.[5] / Directly at
that time my restless breast [15] / surged with fervid anger, / frequently
cursing the goddess powerful in the grave: / Ovid[6] in Ibis conceived /
no more ominous vows in the depth of his heart, / and the Greek poet,
more sparing, [20] / cursed the dishonorable deceit of Lycambes, / and
of Neobule, his own betrothed.[7] / But lo! while I pour out these harsh
curses / and invoke death upon death, / astonished, I seem to hear such

[1] Nicholas Felton (1556–1626), Master of Pembroke College, Cambridge,
from 1617 to 1619 when he succeeded Lancelot Andrewes as Bishop of Ely. He
died on Oct. 6.
[2] Lancelot Andrewes, whose death was mourned in El. 3.
[3] See Nov. 5, n. 1.
[4] the three Fates.
[5] the etymological meaning of Ely ("island of eels").
[6] whose poem attacks an unidentified enemy.
[7] Archilochus was in love with Neobule, daughter of Lycambes, who at first
allowed and then forbade their marriage; to avenge himself he wrote such bitter
satires that father and daughter hanged themselves.

sounds as these, [25] / on the gentle breeze beneath the air:[8] / "Put away your blind madness; put away your transparent / melancholy and your ineffectual threats. / Why do you thoughtlessly profane deities unable to be harmed / and roused swift to wrath? [30] / Death is not, as you think, deluded wretch, / the dark daughter of Night, / nor sprung from her father Erebus, nor from Erinys, / nor born under desolate Chaos.[9] / But she, sent from the starry heaven, [35] / gathers the harvest of God everywhere; / and souls hidden by their fleshy bulk / calls forth into light and air, / as when the flying Hours arouse the day, / the daughters of Themis and Jove;[10] [40] / and she leads them into the presence of the eternal Father, / but, just, she sweeps the impious / to the doleful realms of gloomy Tartarus, / to the infernal abodes. / Happy, when I heard her calling, quickly [45] / I left my loathsome prison / and, fortunate, amid the winged warriors / I was borne aloft to the stars, / like the venerable prophet of old,[11] snatched up to heaven, / driver of the fiery chariot. [50] / The wain of shining Boötes did not frighten me, / slow from the cold, nor / the claws of fearsome Scorpion, / not even your sword, Orion.[12] / I flew past the globe of the gleaming sun, [55] / and far below my feet I saw / the triform goddess,[13] whilst she restrained / her dragons with golden reins. / Through rows of wandering stars, / through the milky regions I was conveyed, [60] / often amazed at my strange speed, / until to the shining portals / of Olympus I was come, and the crystalline realm / and the court paved with beryl.[14] / But here I shall be silent, for who is able to proclaim, [65] / descended

---

[8] The following lines, to the end, are spoken by Felton's spirit.

[9] According to Cicero (*De Natura Deorum*, III, xvii, 44), Death is a child of Night by Erebus, offspring of Chaos (the lower world). Erinys was one of the three Furies.

[10] The Hours kept watch at the gates of heaven. Themis personified Justice.

[11] Elijah (2 Kings ii. 11).

[12] In flight he passes three heavenly constellations: Boötes, lying in the north and meaning "ox herder," appears to move slowly; it is near the Great Bear, known as the Wain (wagon). Scorpio, lying in the south, is named for its similarity to a scorpion. Orion, lying on the equator, is in the figure of a hunter with belt and sword.

[13] The moon (Diana) was triform because she was the virgin moon-goddess, the patroness of virginity, and the presider over child-birth, the chase, and nocturnal incantations. The threefold identification rests upon the phases of the moon: increasing, full, and waning. As goddess of nocturnal incantations she was identified with Hecate. As Davis P. Harding shows ("Milton and the Renaissance Ovid" [Harvard Univ. Press, 1946], p. 50), the dragons of the moon were associated with Hecate because they descended to Medea when she invoked the goddess' help to flee from Jason's wrath.

[14] Rev. xxi. 19-21: "And the foundations of the wall of the city were garnished with all manner of precious stones / . . . the eighth, beryl . . . / And the twelve gates were twelve pearls; every several gate was of one pearl: and the street of the city was pure gold, as it were transparent glass."

from human father, / the pleasures of that place?[15] For me / it is enough to enjoy them through eternity."

(*Oct. P 1626*)

[15] 1 Cor. ii. 9: "But it is written, Eye hath not seen, nor ear heard, neither have entered into the heart of man, the things which God hath prepared for them that love him."

In obitum Procancellarii medici[1]

Parére fati discite legibus,
Manusque Parcæ[2] jam date supplices,
 Qui pendulum telluris orbem
  Jäpeti[3] colitis nepotes.
Vos si relicto mors vaga Tænaro[4]   5
Semel vocârit flebilis, heu moræ
 Tentantur incassùm dolique;
  Per tenebras Stygis ire certum est.
Si destinatam pellere dextera
Mortem valeret, non ferus Hercules   10
 Nessi venenatus cruore
  Æmathiâ jacuisset Œtâ.[5]
Nec fraude turpi Palladis invidæ
Vidisset occisum Ilion Hectora,[6] aut
 Quem[7] larva Pelidis peremit   15
  Ense Locro, Jove lacrymante.
Si triste fatum verba Hecatëia[8]
Fugare possint, Telegoni parens[9]
 Vixisset infamis, potentique
  Ægiali soror[10] usa virgâ.   20
Numenque trinum fallere si queant
Artes medentûm, ignotaque gramina,
 Non gnarus herbarum Machaon
  Eurypyli cecidisset hastâ.[11]
Læsisset et nec te, Philyreie,[12]   25
Sagitta echidnæ perlita sanguine,
 Nec tela te fulmenque avitum
  Cæse puer genitricis alvo.[13]
Tuque O alumno major Apolline,
Gentis togatæ cui regimen datum,   30

Frondosa quem nunc Cirrha luget,
   Et mediis Helicon in undis,[14]
Jam præfuisses Palladio gregi
Lætus, superstes, nec sine gloria,
   Nec puppe lustrasses Charontis   35
     Horribiles barathri recessus.
At fila rupit Persephone tua
Irata, cum te viderit artibus
   Succoque pollenti tot atris
     Facibus eripuisse mortis.   40
Colende præses, membra precor tua
Molli quiescant cespite, et ex tuo
   Crescant rosae, calthæque busto,
     Purpureoque hyacinthus ore.
Sit mite de te judicium Æaci,[15]   45
Subrideatque Ætnæa[16] Proserpina,
   Interque felices perennis
     Elysio spatiere campo.

On the death of the Vice-Chancellor, a Physician[1]

Learn to submit to the laws of destiny / and now offer up suppliant hands to the Parca,[2] / descendants of Japetus,[3] who inhabit / the pendulous orb of the earth. / If doleful death, wandering [5] / from abandoned Taenarus,[4] once summon you, alas: delays / and deceptions are essayed in vain; / through the shadows of the Styx one is certain to go. / If the right hand were strong enough / to rout appointed death, the untamed Hercules, [10] / poisoned by the blood of Nessus, / would not have been cast down on Emathian Oeta.[5] / Nor would Troy have seen Hector[6]

---

[1] Dr. John Gostlin, Vice-Chancellor of Cambridge and Regius Professor of Medicine from 1623, died on Oct. 21, 1626.

[2] one of the three Fates; specifically, Morta, who controlled the advent of death.

[3] As father of Atlas, Prometheus, and Epimetheus, he was considered mankind's common progenitor.

[4] the infernal regions.

[5] To win back Hercules' love, his wife Deianira followed the advice of the dying Nessus to smear a robe with his blood, which Hercules was to wear; but since Nessus' blood had been stained with the blood of the hydra, also killed by Hercules, the robe caused fatal poisoning. Hercules had himself placed on a pyre on Mt. Oeta in Macedonia.

[6] Athena, disguised as Hector's brother Deiphobus, urged him to fight with Achilles, in which battle he was slain.

slain / by the shameful deceit of envious Pallas, nor / him[7] whom the
ghost of Achilles killed [15] / with Locrian sword, Jove shedding tears. /
If the incantations of Hecate[8] could put / sad fate to flight, the parent of
Telegonus[9] / would have lived in infamy, and / the sister of Aegialeus[10]
to employ her potent wand. [20] / And if the arts of the physician and
unknown herbs / were able to deceive the triple divinity, / Machaon,
knowing so much of herbs, / would not have fallen by the spear of Eury-
pylus;[11] / neither would the arrow smeared with the hydra's blood [25]
/ have wounded you, son of Philyra,[12] / nor the missiles and thunder-
bolt of your grandfather, you, / boy cut from your mother's womb.[13] /
And you, O greater than your pupil, Apollo, / to whom the government
of our gowned society was given, [30] / and whom now leafy Cirrha
mourns / and Helicon in the midst of its waters,[14] / now you would be
the happy leader to the Palladian troop, / surviving, not without glory;
/ nor in Charon's boat would you traverse [35] / the fearful recesses of
hell. / But Persephone broke your thread of life, / angered, when she
saw you by your arts / and powerful potions snatch so many / from the
black jaws of death. [40] / Reverend Chancellor, I pray your limbs
/ find peace in the gentle soil, and from your grave / spring roses and
marigolds / and the hyacinth with purple face. / May the judgment of
Aeacus[15] be gentle upon you, [45] / and may Sicilian[16] Prosperina
smile, / and forever among the fortunate / may you walk in the Elysian
field.

(*Oct.–Nov. 1626*)

---

[7] Sarpedon, son of Jove, who was slain by Patroclus, wearing Achilles' armor.
[8] goddess of enchantments.
[9] Circe.
[10] Medea, who was learned in magic.
[11] Machaon, surgeon to the Greeks at Troy, was a son of Aesculapius.
[12] Chiron was wounded by one of Hercules' arrows poisoned by the hydra's
blood.
[13] Aesculapius, so delivered by his father Apollo, was killed by Jove, Apollo's
father, because he saved men from death.
[14] In an extravagance Milton has Apollo, god of healing, learning from Gost-
lin, and Cirrha (near Delphi) and Helicon (the haunt of the Muses) equating
Cambridge with its poetic mourners.
[15] a judge of the dead, appointed because of his justice in ruling Aegina.
[16] Sicilian because she was carried off from Enna in Sicily by Pluto.

In proditionem Bombardicam[1]

Cum simul in regem nuper satrapasque Britannos
  Ausus es infandum, perfide Fauxe, nefas,
Fallor? an et mitis voluisti ex parte videri,
  Et pensare malâ cum pietate scelus?
Scilicet hos alti missurus ad atria cæli,   5
  Sulphureo curru flammivolisque rotis.
Qualiter ille[2] feris caput inviolabile Parcis[3]
  Liquit Jördanios turbine raptus agros.

On the Gunpowder Plot[1]

When recently, at the same time against the King and the British lords, /
you attempted, perfidious Fawkes, your unspeakable crime, / am I mis-
taken, or did you wish to seem in part kind / and to compensate for the
heinous deed with wicked piety? / Certainly you would send them to the
courts of high heaven [5] / in a sulphurous chariot with flaming wheels;
/ just as he[2] whose head was inviolable by the cruel Parcae,[3] / carried
off in a whirlwind, disappeared from the plains of the Jordan.

(*Nov. 1626 ?*)

[1] a Roman Catholic conspiracy by Guy Fawkes and others to blow up James
I and the House of Lords on Nov. 5, 1605.
[2] Elijah (2 Kings ii. 11).
[3] Clotho, Lachesis, and Atropos, the Fates who controlled birth and death.

In eandem

Siccine tentasti cælo donâsse Jäcobum
  Quæ septemgemino Bellua monte lates?[1]
Ni meliora tuum poterit dare munera numen,
  Parce precor donis insidiosa tuis.

Ille quidem sine te consortia serus² adivit   5
   Astra, nec inferni pulveris usus ope.
Sic potiùs fœdos in cælum pelle cucullos,³
   Et quot habet brutos Roma profana Deos,
Namque hac aut aliâ nisi quemque adjuveris arte,
   Crede mihi, cæli vix bene scandet iter.   10

On the same

Thus did you strive to vouchsafe James to Heaven, / O Beast, who lurks
on the seven hills?¹ / Unless your divine majesty can bestow better fa-
vors, / spare, I pray, your insidious gifts. / Indeed he has departed ripe
in years,² without your help [5] / and without the employment of in-
fernal powder, to his comrades, the stars. / Thus instead, banish to the
sky your detestable cowls³ / and all the brute gods profane Rome pos-
sesses; / for unless you aid each one firmly in this or some other way, /
believe me, they will hardly mount the path to heaven successfully. [10]

(Nov. 1626 ?)

¹ the Papacy; Rome, built on seven hills, was identified by many Protestants
with the whore of Babylon, who sat on a beast with seven heads (hills) and
ten horns (Rev. xvii. 3–7).
² James died on Mar. 27, 1625.
³ priests.

In eandem

Purgatorem animæ derisit Jäcobus ignem,¹
   Et sine quo superûm non adeunda domus.
Frenduit hoc trinâ monstrum Latiale coronâ²
   Movit et horrificùm cornua dena minax.
Et nec inultus ait, temnes mea sacra, Britanne,   5
   Supplicium spretâ relligione dabis.
Et si stelligeras unquam penetraveris arces,
   Non nisi per flammas triste patebit iter.
O quàm funesto cecinisti proxima vero,
   Verbaque ponderibus vix caritura suis!   10
Nam prope Tartareo³ sublime rotatus ab igni
   Ibat ad æthereas umbra perusta plagas.

On the same

James derided the Purgatorial fire[1] of the soul, / without which there is
no approaching of the celestial mansions. / The Latin monster with triple
crown[2] gnashed its teeth at this / and moved its ten horns with frightful
menace / and, it cried, "You shall not scorn my sacred rites with im-
punity, Englishman; [5] / you shall suffer punishment for your contempt
of religion. / And if ever you enter the starry citadels, / the only way
open is the sad one through the flames." / O how close you came to a
calamitous truth / and only barely were your words deprived of their
consequences, [10] / for he nearly ascended to the eternal regions, /
a scorched ghost, whirled on high by the Tartarean[3] fire.

(Nov. 1626 ?)

[1] James' denial of Purgatory is found in A Premonition to All Most Mightie
Monarches (Works, [Harvard Univ. Press, 1918], p. 125).
[2] the Papacy; the Pope's tiara is a triple crown. Milton thought both of the
beast in Revelation and Daniel's vision of the beast with great iron teeth and
ten horns, which "shall be the fourth kingdom upon earth, . . . and shall de-
vour the whole earth, and shall tread it down, and break it in pieces" (Dan. vii.
7, 23).
[3] Tartarus was the part of the underworld where punishment for sins was
exacted.

In eandem

Quem modò Roma suis devoverat impia diris,[1]
    Et Styge damnarât Tænarioque sinu,[2]
Hunc vice mutatâ jam tollere gestit ad astra,
    Et cupit ad superos evehere usque Deos.

On the same

Whom impious Rome had just marked out for her curses[1] / and condemned to the Styx and the Taenarian gulf,[2] / him, on the contrary, she now desires to lift to the stars / and wishes to elevate even to the higher Gods.

(*Nov. 1626 ?*)

[1] In addition to reimposing recusancy fines in Feb. 1605, James had banished all Roman Catholic priests in Feb. 1604.
[2] the infernal regions.

In inventorem Bombardæ

Japetionidem[1] laudavit cæca vetustas,
    Qui tulit ætheream solis ab axe facem;
At mihi major erit, qui lurida creditur arma,
    Et trifidum fulmen surripuisse Jovi.[2]

On the inventor of Gunpowder

Antiquity in blindness praised the son of Iapetus,[1] / who brought down celestial fire from the chariot of the sun, / but to me he will be greater who is believed to have stolen / the ghastly weapons and threeforked thunderbolt from Jove.[2]

(*Nov. 1626 ?*)

[1] Prometheus.
[2] Compare the description of the Son after the War in Heaven in PL VI, 763–64.

In quintum Novembris

Jam pius extremâ veniens Jäcobus ab arcto
Teucrigenas populos,[1] latéque patentia regna
Albionum tenuit, jamque inviolabile fœdus
Sceptra Caledoniis conjunxerat Anglica Scotis:
Pacificusque novo felix divesque sedebat   5
In solio, occultique doli securus et hostis:
Cum ferus ignifluo regnans Acheronte tyrannus,[2]
Eumenidum pater, æthereo vagus exul Olympo,
Forte per immensum terrarum erraverat orbem,
Dinumerans sceleris socios, vernasque fideles,   10
Participes regni post funera mœsta futuros;
Hic tempestates medio ciet aëre diras,
Illic unanimes odium struit inter amicos,
Armat et invictas in mutua viscera gentes;
Regnaque olivifera vertit florentia pace,   15
Et quoscunque videt puræ virtutis amantes,
Hos cupit adjicere imperio, fraudumque magister
Tentat inaccessum sceleri corrumpere pectus,
Insidiasque locat tacitas, cassesque latentes
Tendit, ut incautos rapiat, ceu Caspia Tigris   20
Insequitur trepidam deserta per avia prædam
Nocte sub illuni, et somno nictantibus astris.
Talibus infestat populos Summanus[3] et urbes
Cinctus cæruleæ fumanti turbine flammæ.
Jamque fluentisonis albentia rupibus arva   25
Apparent, et terra Deo dilecta marino,
Cui nomen dederat quondam Neptunia proles
Amphitryoniaden qui non dubitavit atrocem
Æquore tranato furiali poscere bello,
Ante expugnatæ crudelia sæcula Troiæ.[4]   30
    At simul hanc opibusque et festâ pace beatam
Aspicit, et pingues donis Cerealibus agros,
Quodque magis doluit, venerantem numina veri
Sancta Dei populum, tandem suspiria rupit
Tartareos ignes et luridum olentia sulphur.   35
Qualia Trinacriâ trux ab Jove clausus in Ætna
Efflat tabifico monstrosus ab ore Tiphœus.[5]

Ignescunt oculi, stridetque adamantinus ordo
Dentis, ut armorum fragor, ictaque cuspide cupis.
Atque pererrato solum hoc lacrymabile mundo   40
Inveni, dixit, gens hæc mihi sola rebellis,
Contemtrixque jugi, nostrâque potentior arte.
Illa tamen, mea si quicquam tentamina possunt,
Non feret hoc impune díu, non ibit inulta.
Hactenus; et piceis liquido natat aëre pennis;   45
Quà volat, adversi præcursant agmine venti,
Densantur nubes, et crebra tonitrua fulgent.
Jamque pruinosas velox superaverat alpes,
Et tenet Ausoniæ fines; à parte sinistrâ
Nimbifer Appenninus erat, priscique Sabini,   50
Dextra veneficiis infamis Hetruria, nec non
Te furtiva, Tibris, Thetidi[6] videt oscula dantem;
Hinc Mavortigenæ consistit in arce Quirini.[7]
Reddiderant dubiam jam sera crepuscula lucem,
Cum circumgreditur totam Tricoronifer urbem,   55
Panificosque Deos portat, scapulisque virorum
Evehitur, præeunt summisso poplite reges,
Et mendicantum series longissima fratrum;
Cereaque in manibus gestant funalia cæci,
Cimmeriis nati in tenebris, vitamque trahentes.   60
Templa dein multis subeunt lucentia tædis
(Vesper erat sacer iste Petro) fremitúsque canentum
Sæpe tholos implet vacuos, et inane locorum.
Qualiter exululat Bromius, Bromiique caterva,
Orgia cantantes in Echionio Aracyntho,[8]   65
Dum tremit attonitus vitreis Asopus in undis,
Et procul ipse cavâ responsat rupe Cithæron.
His igitur tandem solenni more peractis,
Nox[9] senis amplexus Erebi taciturna reliquit,
Præcipitesque impellit equos stimulante flagello,   70
Captum oculis Typhlonta, Melanchætemque ferocem,
Atque Acherontæo prognatam patre Siopen
Torpidam, et hirsutis horrentem Phrica capillis.
Interea regum domitor, Phlegetontius hæres,
Ingreditur thalamos (neque enim secretus adulter   75
Producit steriles molli sine pellice noctes);
At vix compositos somnus claudebat ocellos,
Cum niger umbrarum dominus, rectorque silentum,
Prædatorque hominum falsâ sub imagine tectus.
Astitit, assumptis micuerunt tempora canis,   80
Barba sinus promissa tegit, cineracea longo

Syrmate verrit humum vestis, pendetque cucullus
Vertice de raso, et ne quicquam desit ad artes,
Cannabeo lumbos constrinxit fune salaces,
Tarda fenestratis figens vestigia calcëis. 85
Talis, uti fama est, vastâ Franciscus[10] eremo
Tetra vagabatur solus per lustra ferarum,
Sylvestrique tulit genti pia verba salutis
Impius, atque lupos domuit, Lybicosque leones.
  Subdolus at tali Serpens velatus amictu 90
Solvit in has fallax ora execrantia voces;
Dormis, nate? Etiamne tuos sopor opprimit artus?
Immemor O fidei, pecorumque oblite tuorum,
Dum cathedram, venerande, tuam, diademaque triplex
Ridet Hyperboreo gens barbara nata sub axe, 95
Dumque pharetrati spernunt tua jura Britanni;
Surge, age, surge piger, Latius quem Cæsar adorat,
Cui reserata patet convexi janua cæli,
Turgentes animos, et fastus frange procaces,
Sacrilegique sciant, tua quid maledictio possit, 100
Et quid Apostolicæ possit custodia clavis;
Et memor Hesperiæ disjectam ulciscere classem,
Mersaque Iberorum lato vexilla profundo,
Sanctorumque cruci tot corpora fixa probrosæ,
Thermodoontéa nuper regnante puella.[11] 105
At tu si tenero mavis torpescere lecto
Crescentesque negas hosti contundere vires,
Tyrrhenum implebit numeroso milite Pontum,
Signaque Aventino[12] ponet fulgentia colle:
Relliquias veterum franget, flammisque cremabit, 110
Sacraque calcabit pedibus tua colla profanis,
Cujus gaudebant soleïs dare basia reges.
Nec tamen hunc bellis et aperto Marte lacesses,
Irritus ille labor, tu callidus utere fraude,
Quælibet hæreticis disponere retia fas est; 115
Jamque ad consilium extremis rex magnus ab oris
Patricios vocat, et procerum de stirpe creatos,
Grandævosque patres trabeâ, canisque verendos;
Hos tu membratim poteris conspergere in auras,
Atque dare in cineres, nitrati pulveris igne 120
Ædibus injecto, quà convenere, sub imis.
Prontinus ipse igitur quoscumque habet Anglia fidos
Propositi, factique mone, quisquámne tuorum
Audebit summi non jussa facessere Papæ?
Perculsosque metu subito, casúmque stupentes 125

Invadat vel Gallus atrox, vel sævus Iberus.
Sæcula sic illic tandem Mariana[13] redibunt,
Tuque in belligeros iterum dominaberis Anglos.
Et nequid timeas, divos divasque secundas
Accipe, quotque tuis celebrantur numina fastis.   130
Dixit et adscitos ponens malefidus amictus
Fugit ad infandam, regnum illætabile, Lethen.
   Jam rosea Eoas pandens Tithonia portas
Vestit inauratas redeunti lumine terras;
Mæstaque adhuc nigri deplorans funera nati[14]   135
Irrigat ambrosiis montana cacumina guttis;
Cum somnos pepulit stellatæ janitor[15] aulæ
Nocturnos visus, et somnia grata revolvens.
   Est locus æternâ septus caligine noctis
Vasta ruinosi quondam fundamina tecti,   140
Nunc torvi spelunca Phoni, Prodotæque bilinguis
Effera quos uno peperit Discordia partu.
Hic inter cæmenta jacent præruptaque saxa,
Ossa inhumata virûm, et trajecta cadavera ferro;
Hic Dolus intortis semper sedet ater ocellis,   145
Jurgiaque, et stimulis armata Calumnia fauces,
Et Furor, atque viæ moriendi mille videntur
Et Timor, exanguisque locum circumvolat Horror,
Perpetuosque leves per muta silentia Manes
Exululant, tellus et sanguine conscia stagnat.   150
Ipsi etiam pavidi latitant penetralibus antri
Et Phonos, et Prodotes, nulloque sequente per antrum,
Antrum horrens, scopulosum, atrum feralibus umbris.
Diffugiunt sontes, et retrò lumina vortunt;
Hos pugiles Romæ per sæcula longa fideles   155
Evocat antistes Babylonius,[16] atque ita fatur.
Finibus occiduis circumfusum incolit æquor
Gens exosa mihi, prudens natura negavit
Indignam penitùs nostro conjungere mundo;
Illuc, sic jubeo, celeri contendite gressu,   160
Tartareoque leves difflentur pulvere in auras
Et rex et pariter satrapæ, scelerata propago
Et quotquot fidei caluere cupidine veræ
Consilii socios adhibete, operisque ministros.
Finierat, rigidi cupidè paruere gemelli.   165
   Interea longo flectens curvamine cælos
Despicit æthereâ dominus qui fulgurat arce,
Vanaque perversæ ridet conamina turbæ,[17]
Atque sui causam populi volet ipse tueri.

Esse ferunt spatium, quà distat ab Aside terra 170
Fertilis Europe, et spectat Mareotidas undas;
Hic turris posita est Titanidos ardua Famæ[18]
Ærea, lata, sonans, rutilis vicinior astris
Quàm superimpositum vel Athos vel Pelion Ossæ.[19]
Mille fores aditusque patent, totidemque fenestræ, 175
Amplaque per tenues translucent atria muros;
Excitat hic varios plebs agglomerata susurros;
Qualiter instrepitant circum mulctralia bombis
Agmina muscarum, aut texto per ovilia junco,
Dum Canis[20] æstivum cœli petit ardua culmen. 180
Ipsa quidem summâ sedet ultrix matris in arce,
Auribus innumeris cinctum caput eminet olli,
Queis sonitum exiguum trahit, atque levissima captat
Murmura, ab extremis patuli confinibus orbis.
Nec tot, Aristoride[21] servator inique juvencæ 185
Isidos, immiti volvebas lumina vultu,
Lumina non unquam tacito nutantia somno,
Lumina subjectas late spectantia terras.
Istis illa solet loca luce carentia sæpe
Perlustrare, etiam radianti impervia soli. 190
Millenisque loquax auditaque visaque linguis
Cuilibet effundit temeraria, veráque mendax
Nunc minuit, modò confictis sermonibus auget.
Sed tamen a nostro meruisti carmine laudes
Fama, bonum quo non aliud veracius ullum, 195
Nobis digna cani, nec te memorasse pigebit
Carmine tam longo, servati scilicet Angli
Officiis, vaga diva, tuis, tibi reddimus æqua.
Te Deus æternos motu qui temperat ignes,
Fulmine præmisso alloquitur, terrâque tremente: 200
Fama siles? an te latet impia Papistarum
Conjurata cohors in meque meosque Britannos,
Et nova sceptrigero cædes meditata Jäcobo?
Nec plura, illa statim sensit mandata Tonantis,
Et satis antè fugax stridentes induit alas, 205
Induit et variis exilia corpora plumis;
Dextra tubam gestat Temesæo[22] ex ære sonoram.
Nec mora, jam pennis cedentes remigat auras,
Atque parum est cursu celeres prævertere nubes,
Jam ventos, jam solis equos post terga reliquit: 210
Et primò Angliacas solito de more per urbes
Ambiguas voces, incertaque murmura spargit,
Mox arguta dolos, et detestabile vulgat

Proditionis opus, nec non facta horrida dictu,
Authoresque addit sceleris, nec garrula cæcis   215
Insidiis loca structa silet; stupuere relatis,
Et pariter juvenes, pariter tremuere puellæ,
Effætique senes pariter, tantæque ruinæ
Sensus ad ætatem subitò penetraverat omnem.
Attamen interea populi miserescit ab alto   220
Æthereus pater, et crudelibus obstitit ausis
Papicolûm; capti pœnas raptantur ad acres;
At pia thura Deo, et grati solvuntur honores;
Compita læta focis genialibus omnis fumant;
Turba choros juvenilis agit: Quintoque Novembris   225
Nulla Dies toto occurrit celebratior anno.

On the fifth of November

Now the devout James coming from the remote north / ruled over the
Troy-descended people[1] and the wide-stretching realms / of the English,
and now an inviolable covenant / had joined the English kingdoms with
Caledonian Scots: / and the peace-maker, happy and rich, was seated
[5] / on his new throne, untroubled by secret conspiracy or foe: / when
the cruel tyrant[2] reigning over Acheron, which flows with fire, / the
father of the Eumenides, the wandering outcast from celestial Olympus,
/ by chance strayed through the vast circle of the earth, / enumerating
the companions of his wickedness and his faithful slaves, [10] / future
participants of his rule after their woeful deaths. / Here he stirs ominous
tempests in middle air; / there he contrives hatred among harmonious
friends, / and arms invincible nations against mutual cordiality, / and
turns flourishing kingdoms from olive-bearing peace; [15] / and what-
ever lovers of pure virtue he spies, / those he seeks to add to his empire,
and master of guile, / he tries to corrupt the heart inaccessible to sin /
and lays silent plots and stretches unseen snares, / so that he may assault
the incautious, as the Caspian tigress [20] / pursues her anxious prey
through the waste wildernesses / in the moonless night and under the

---

[1] See *El.* 1, n. 12. Albion (ll. 27–28), son of Neptune, gave his name to the
island and its inhabitants.
[2] Pluto, king of hell and father of the avenging spirits. Acheron and Phlege-
thon (l. 74) were rivers of hell. Pluto's likeness to Satan in these lines has been
noted by most editors since Warton.

stars winking in their drowsiness. / With like fears does Summanus[3] harass the people and the cities, / he, wreathed with a smoking tornado of blue flames. / And now the white coasts with their wave-resounding cliffs [25] / appear, and the land highly esteemed by the sea god, / to which Neptune's son gave his name so long ago, / who, having sailed across the sea, did not hesitate to challenge / fierce Hercules with furious battle / before the unmerciful times of conquered Troy.[4] [30] /

But as soon as he beholds this land blessed with wealth / and joyful peace, and with fields rich in the gifts of Ceres, / and, what pained him more, a people revering the sacred divinity / of the true god, at length he breaks into sighs / emitting Tartarean fires and ghastly sulphur. [35] / Such sighs does grim and monstrous Typhoeus,[5] enclosed by Jove / under Sicilian Aetna, breathe from his destructive mouth. / His eyes flash and his inflexible row of teeth / hisses like the crash of arms and the blow of spear against spear. / And then, "Throughout the travelled world I found this worthy of tears only," [40] / he said; "this nation alone is rebellious toward me, / and contemptuous of my yoke and stronger than my art. / Yet if my attempts have power over anyone, it / shall not endure thus with impunity for long; it shall not go unavenged." / No further did he speak, but floats away on pitch-black wings through [45] / the liquid air; wherever he flies adverse winds precede in a mass, / clouds are thickened, and repeated thunderbolts flash. /

And now his speed has surmounted the frosty Alps, / and he reaches the borders of Italy; on his left side / was the stormy Apennine range and the ancient Sabines; [50] / on his right Etruria with its infamous magic potions, and besides / he sees the furtive kisses which you are giving to Thetis,[6] O Tiber; / next he stands still on the citadel of Quirinus, born of Mars.[7] / Already had evening twilight bestowed uncertain light, / when the wearer of the triple crown walks around the entire city, [55] / and carries the gods made of bread, and on men's shoulders / is elevated; kings precede him on bended knee, / and a most lengthy train of mendicant brothers; / and unable to see, they bear wax candles in their hands, / those born and enduring life in Cimmerian darkness. [60] / Next they enter the temples glittering with many torches / (it was that eve sacred to St. Peter) and the noise of those

---

[3] an ancient god of nightly storms, identified with Pluto.

[4] Albion was killed aiding his brother Lestrygon, who was fighting in Gaul against Hercules, son of Amphitryon's wife.

[5] a giant, whom Jove struck with a thunderbolt and buried under Sicily; his head lay beneath Mt. Etna, whose eruptions he spewed forth.

[6] a sea-nymph. The Tiber empties into the Tyrrhene Sea through a delta.

[7] That is, Satan arrives in Rome. The Pope, whose tiara consists of three crowns, in procession with other church dignitaries, carried the Host through the streets to St. Peter's Cathedral on the eve of St. Peter's Day, June 28.

singing / often fills the hollow domes and the void of those places. /
How Bacchus howls, and the followers of Bacchus, / chanting their
orgies on Theban Aracynthus,[8] [65] / while astonished Asopus trembles
under the glassy waves, / and afar off Cithaeron itself echoes from its
hollow rock. /

Then at last, these things performed in a solemn fashion, / silent
Night[9] left the embraces of old Erebus, / and now drives her headlong
horses with a goading whip—[70] / blind Typhlos and spirited Mel-
anchaetes, / torpid Siope, sprung from an infernal father, / and shaggy
Phrix with bristly hair. / Meanwhile the tamer of kings, the heir of hell,
/ enters his chambers (for the secret adulterer [75] / does not spend
sterile nights without a gentle concubine); / but sleep was scarcely clos-
ing his ready eyes, / when the dark lord of the shadows, the ruler of
the dead, / the plunderer of man stood before him, concealed by a false
shape. / His temples flashed with the gray hairs he had assumed; [80]
/ a long beard covered his breast; his ash-colored attire / swept the
ground with a long train; and his hood hung down / from his shaven
crown; and so that none might be absent from his frauds / he bound
his lustful loins with hempen rope, / thrusting his slow feet into open
sandals. [85] / In like manner, as rumor has it, Francis[10] used to wan-
der alone / in the vast, loathsome desert through the haunts of wild
beasts; / he carried the pious word of salvation to the people of the
wood, / himself impious, and tamed the wolves and the Libyan lions. /

But clothed in such garb, the cunning serpent, [90] / deceitful, sep-
arated his accursed lips with these words: / "Are you sleeping, my son?
Does slumber still overpower your limbs? / O negligent of faith and
neglectful of your flocks! / while a barbarous nation born under the
northern sky / ridicules your throne and triple diadem, O venerable one,
[95] / and while the quivered English contemn your laws! / Arise, up,
arise, lazy one, whom the Roman emperor adores, / and for whom the
unlocked gate of arched heaven lies open; / crush their swelling pride
and insolent arrogance, / and let the sacrilegious know what your curse
may be capable of, [100] / and what custody of the Apostolic key may
avail; / and remember to avenge the scattered armada of the Spanish
/ and the banners of the Iberians swallowed up by the broad deep, /
and the bodies of so many saints hanged on infamous gallows / recently
by the reigning Amazonian virgin.[11] [105] / But if you prefer to become
indolent in your soft bed / and refuse to crush the increasing strength

---

[8] a mountain in Boeotia. Asopus is a river, and Cithaeron, a range of hills
lying nearby.
[9] Night and her brother Erebus (primeval darkness) were the parents of Day.
The names of her team were created by Milton.
[10] St. Francis of Assisi.
[11] Elizabeth.

of the foe, / he will fill the Tyrrhene Sea with a vast army / and set his glittering standards on the Aventine hill:[12] / he will destroy and burn with flames the remains of the ancients, [110] / and with profane feet will trample upon your sacred neck, / you whose shoes kings were glad to give their kisses. / Yet you will not challenge him to wars and open conflict; / such would be useless labor; you are shrewd to use deception, / of which any kind is fitting in order to spread traps for heretics; [115] / and now the great king calls the nobles with foreign speech / to council, and those sprung from the stock of celebrated men / and old venerable sires with their robe of state and gray hairs. / You will be able to scatter them limb by limb throughout the air / and to give them up to cinders, by the fire of nitrous [120] / powder exploded beneath the last chambers where they have assembled. / Immediately therefore advise whatever faithful there are in England / of the proposed deed; will any of your followers / dare not dispatch the commands of the supreme Pope? / And instantly may the fierce Gaul and the savage Spaniard [125] / invade them, smitten with dread and stupefied by calamity. / Thus at last the Marian era[13] will return to that land / and you will rule again over the warlike English. / And, so you fear nothing, accept the gods and subordinate goddesses, / as many deities as are honored on your feast days." [130] / The deceiver spoke, and laying his disguise aside, / he fled to Lethe, his abominable, gloomy kingdom. /

Now rosy dawn, throwing open the eastern gates, / dresses the gilded world with returning light; / and hitherto grieving for the sad death of her swarthy son,[14] [135] / she sprinkles the mountain tops with ambrosial tears, / then the keeper[15] of the starry court banished sleep, / repeating his nocturnal visions and delightful dreams. /

There is a place enclosed in the eternal darkness of night, / once the vast foundation of a ruined dwelling, [140] / now the den of savage Murder and double-tongued Treason, / whom fierce Discord bore at one birth. / Here among the unhewn stones and broken rock lie / the unburied bones of men and corpses pierced by steel; / here malicious Deceit sits forever with distorted eyes, [145] / and Contentions and Calumny, its jaws armed with fangs, / Fury and a thousand ways of dying are seen, / and Fear and pale Horror hasten around the place, / and nimble ghosts howl perpetually through the mute silences, / and the conscious earth stagnates with blood. [150] / Besides, Murder and Treason themselves lie hid, quaking, / in the inmost depths of the cave with no one pursuing them through it, / the rough cave, full of

12 one of Rome's seven hills.
13 meaning both a Catholic age (from Mary) and an age of civil war (from Marius, who fought Sulla in 83–82 B.C.).
14 Memnon, son of the goddess of dawn and Tithonus, was slain by Achilles.
15 the Pope.

rocks, dark with deathly shadows. / The guilty ones disperse and run away with backward glance; / these defenders of Rome, faithful through the long ages, [155] / the Babylonian high-priest[16] summons, and thus he speaks: / "A race odious to me lives on the western limits / in the surrounding sea; prudent nature has thoroughly denied / that unworthy people to join our world. / Thither, so I command, journey with swift pace, [160] / and may the king and his nobles together, that impious race, / be blown into thin air by the Tartarean powder, / and whoever for true faith have glowed with love / invite as partners of the plot and accomplices of the deed." / He ended, and the stern twins obeyed with eagerness. [165] /

Meanwhile turning the heavens in a spacious arc, / the Lord, who shines forth from his ethereal height, looks down / and laughs at the efforts of the evil crew,[17] / and orders the defense of his people to be upheld. /

They say there is a section where fertile Europe is separated [170] / from Asian land, and looks toward Mareotidan waters; / here is situated the lofty tower of Titanean Fame,[18] / brazen, broad, resounding, closer to the glowing stars / than Athos or Pelion piled on Ossa.[19] / A thousand doors and entrances lie open, and as many windows, [175] / and spacious courts shine through the thin walls; / here the accumulated people raise various whispers; / how the swarms of flies make noise about the milk pails / by buzzing, or through the sheepfolds of woven reed, / when the lofty Dog Star[20] assails the summer height of the sky. [180] / Indeed Fame herself, avenger of her mother, sits in her topmost fortress; / her head, girt with innumerable ears, projects out from that place, / attracting the faintest sound and seizing the lightest / murmur from the farthest limits of the wide world. / And you, O Argus,[21] unjust guardian

---

[16] See n. 1. to the poem on the Gunpowder Plot, beginning "Thus did you strive . . . ."

[17] Psalm ii. 4: "He that sitteth in the heavens shall laugh: the Lord shall have them in derision."

[18] Ovid's description of Fame (*Meta.*, XII, 39–63) furnished most of the details here. She is called a Titaness by Virgil (*Aen.*, IV, 173–87) because she is the daughter of Earth, who is often abused by men (see l. 181). The Tower of Fame seems to stand in Egypt, for Lake Mareotis was in Lower Egypt near Alexandria. However, this may be an error for "Maeotidas undas" (the waters near Lake Maeotis), which lay between Europe and Asia, at the mouth of the Tanais River (Lucan, III, 272–78).

[19] The giants Otus and Ephialtes piled Mt. Pelion on Mt. Ossa (in Thessaly) in their attempt to overthrow the gods. Mt. Athos was in Macedonia, opposite Lemnos.

[20] Sirius; see *Lycidas*, n. 31.

[21] Jealous Juno had hundred-eyed Argus guard Io after she had been changed into a heifer by Jove.

of the heifer [185] / Io, did not roll so many eyes in your fierce face, / eyes never faltering in silent sleep, / eyes gazing over the adjacent lands far and wide. / With them is Fame accustomed always to survey places deprived of light, / and even those impervious to the radiant sun. [190] / And with a thousand tongues the blabbing one pours out / things heard and seen to anyone who chances by, and now lying, she lessens / the truth, and now she increases it with fabricated rumors. / Nevertheless, Fame, you deserved the praises of my song, / for one good deed than which no other speaks more truly, [195] / worthy to be sung by me, nor shall I repent having commemorated you / at such length in my song. To be sure, we unharmed English / bestow on you what is just for your services, O inconstant goddess. / God who restrains the eternal fires from their agitation / with his dispatched thunderbolt, the earth trembling, exhorts you: [200] / "Fame, are you silent? or does the impious throng of Papists / hide you, conspired against me and my English, / and a new massacre designed against scepter-bearing James?" / No more said, she discerned at once the Thunderer's commands, / and swift enough before, she puts on strident wings, [205] / and clothes her slender body with variegated feathers; / in her right hand she carries a loud trumpet of Temesan[22] brass. / With no delay, she now oars on her wings through the yielding air, / and seems not content to outrun the swift clouds by her flight; / now the winds, now the horses of the sun she leaves behind her back. [210] / But first, in her usual way, through the English cities / she spreads ambiguous rumors and uncertain whispers; / directly, in clear voice, she divulges the deceits and the detestable / work of treason, and likewise deeds frightful when spoken, / and she adds the authors of the crime, nor, being garrulous, is she silent [215] / about the places prepared for secret ambush; men are stunned by the reports, / and youths as well as maidens and weak old men / tremble, and the significance of such great ruin / has penetrated quickly to every age. / But meanwhile the heavenly Father from on high has compassion [220] / on his people, and thwarts the cruel and daring attempts / of the Papists; the captives are dragged to fierce punishments; / but pious incense and grateful honors are paid to God; / all the happy streets smoke with genial bonfires; / the youthful throng moves in dancing groups: and throughout the whole year [225] / no day occurs that is more celebrated than the fifth of November.

(Nov. 1626)

---

[22] Temesa, a town in Italy, was famous for copper mines.

Elegia quarta

AD THOMAM JUNIUM, PRÆCEPTOREM SUUM, APUD MERCATORES
ANGLICOS HAMBURGÆ AGENTES PASTORIS MUNERE FUNGENTEM[1]

Curre per immensum subitò, mea littera, pontum,
  I, pete Teutonicos læve per æquor agros,
Segnes rumpe moras, et nil, precor, obstet eunti,
  Et festinantis nil remoretur iter.
Ipse ego Sicanio frænantem carcere ventos   5
  Æolon,[2] et virides sollicitabo Deos;
Cæruleamque suis comitatam Dorida Nymphis,[3]
  Ut tibi dent placidam per sua regna viam.
At tu, si poteris, celeres tibi sume jugales,
  Vecta quibus Colchis[4] fugit ab ore viri;   10
Aut queis Triptolemus[5] Scythicas devenit in oras
  Gratus Eleusinâ missus ab urbe puer.
Atque ubi Germanas flavere videbis arenas
  Ditis ad Hamburgæ mœnia flecte gradum,
Dicitur occiso quæ ducere nomen ab Hamâ,[6]   15
  Cimbrica quem fertur clava dedisse neci.
Vivit ibi antiquæ clarus pietatis honore
  Præsul Christicolas pascere doctus oves;
Ille quidem est animæ plusquam pars altera nostræ,
  Dimidio vitæ vivere cogor ego.   20
Hei mihi, quot pelagi, quot montes interjecti
  Me faciunt aliâ parte carere mei!
Charior ille mihi quam tu, doctissime Graium,
  Cliniadi,[7] pronepos qui Telamonis erat;
Quámque Stagirites[8] generoso magnus alumno,   25
  Quem peperit Libyco Chaonis alma Jovi.
Qualis Amyntorides, qualis Philyrëius Heros
  Myrmidonum regi,[9] talis et ille mihi.
Primus ego Aonios illo præeunte recessus
  Lustrabam, et bifidi sacra vireta jugi,[10]   30
Pieriosque hausi latices, Clioque favente,
  Castalio sparsi læta ter ora mero.
Flammeus at signum ter viderat arietis Æthon,
  Induxitque auro lanea terga novo,

Bisque novo terram sparsisti, Chlori, senilem 35
  Gramine, bisque tuas abstulit Auster opes:
Necdum ejus licuit mihi lumina pascere vultu,
  Aut linguæ dulces aure bibisse sonos.[11]
Vade igitur, cursuque Eurum[12] præverte sonorum,
  Quàm sit opus monitis res docet, ipsa vides. 40
Invenies dulci cum conjuge forte sedentem,
  Mulcentem gremio pignora chara suo,
Forsitan aut veterum prælarga volumina patrum
  Versantem, aut veri biblia sacra Dei,
Cælestive animas saturantem rore tenellas, 45
  Grande salutiferæ religionis opus.
Utque solet, multam sit dicere cura salutem,
  Dicere quam decuit, si modo adesset, herum.
Hæc quoque paulum oculos in humum defixa modestos,
  Verba verecundo sis memor ore loqui: 50
Hæc tibi, si teneris vacat inter prælia[13] Musis,
  Mittit ab Angliaco littore fida manus.
Accipe sinceram, quamvis sit sera, salutem
  Fiat et hoc ipso gratior illa tibi.
Sera quidem, sed vera fuit, quam casta recepit 55
  Icaris a lento Penelopeia viro.[14]
Ast ego quid volui manifestum tollere crimen,
  Ipse quod ex omni parte levare nequit?
Arguitur tardus meritò, noxamque fatetur,
  Et pudet officium deseruisse suum. 60
Tu modò da veniam fasso, veniamque roganti,
  Crimina diminui, quæ patuere, solent.
Non ferus in pavidos rictus diducit hiantes,
  Vulnifico pronos nec rapit ungue leo.
Sæpe sarissiferi crudelia pectora Thracis[15] 65
  Supplicis ad mœstas delicuere preces.
Extensæque manus avertunt fulminis ictus,
  Placat et iratos hostia parva Deos.
Jamque diu scripsisse tibi fuit impetus illi,
  Neve moras ultra ducere passus Amor. 70
Nam vaga Fama refert, heu nuntia vera malorum!
  In tibi finitimis bella tumere locis,
Teque tuàmque urbem truculento milite cingi,
  Et jam Saxonicos arma parasse duces.
Te circum latè campos populatur Enyo, 75
  Et sata carne virum jam cruor arva rigat.
Germanisque suum concessit Thracia Martem,
  Illuc Odrysios Mars pater egit equos.

Perpetuóque comans jam deflorescit oliva,
    Fugit et ærisonam Diva[16] perosa tubam,   80
Fugit io terris, et jam non ultima virgo
    Creditur ad superas justa volasse domos.
Te tamen intereà belli circumsonat horror,
    Vivis et ignoto solus inópsque solo;
Et, tibi quam patrii non exhibuere penates   85
    Sede peregrinâ quæris egenus opem.
Patria, dura parens, et saxis sævior albis
    Spumea quæ pulsat littoris unda tui,
Siccine te decet innocuous exponere fœtus,
    Siccine in externam ferrea cogis humum,   90
Et sinis ut terris quærant alimenta remotis
    Quos tibi prospiciens miserat ipse Deus,
Et qui læta ferunt de cælo nuntia, quique
    Quæ via post cineres ducat ad astra, docent?[17]
Digna quidem Stygiis quæ vivas clausa tenebris,   95
    Æternâque animæ digna perire fame!
Haud aliter vates terræ Thesbitidis[18] olim
    Pressit inassueto devia tesqua pede,
Desertasque Arabum salebras, dum regis Achabi
    Effugit atque tuas, Sidoni dira, manus.   100
Talis et horrisono laceratus membra flagello,
    Paulus[19] ab Æmathiâ pellitur urbe Cilix.
Piscosæque ipsum Gergessæ civis Jësum
    Finibus ingratus jussit abire suis.[20]
At tu sume animos, nec spes cadat anxia curis   105
    Nec tua concutiat decolor ossa metus.
Sis etenim quamvis fulgentibus obsitus armis,
    Intententque tibi millia tela necem,
At nullis vel inerme latus violabitur armis,
    Deque tuo cuspis nulla cruore bibet.   110
Namque eris ipse Dei radiante sub ægide[21] tutus,
    Ille tibi custos, et pugil ille tibi;
Ille Sionææ qui tot sub mœnibus arcis
    Assyrios fudit nocte silente viros;[22]
Inque fugam vertit quos in Samaritidas oras   115
    Misit ab antiquis prisca Damascus agris,[23]
Terruit et densas pavido cum rege cohortes,
    Aëre dum vacuo buccina clara sonat,
Cornea pulvereum dum verberat ungula campum,
    Currus arenosam dum quatit actus humum,   120
Auditurque hinnitus equorum ad bella ruentûm,
    Et strepitus ferri, murmuraque alta virûm.

Et tu (quod superest miseris) sperare memento,
Et tua magnanimo pectore vince mala.
Nec dubites quandoque frui melioribus annis,   125
Atque iterum patrios posse videre lares.

Elegy 4

TO THOMAS YOUNG, HIS TUTOR, DISCHARGING THE DUTY OF PASTOR
AMONG THE ENGLISH MERCHANTS IN BUSINESS IN HAMBURG[1]

Quickly, my letter, run through the boundless deep; / go, seek Teutonic
lands through the smooth sea; / break off dilatory delays, and let noth-
ing, I pray, thwart your voyage, / and let nothing obstruct the path of
your hastening. / I myself Aeolus[2] bridling the winds in his Sicanian
cave [5] / will exhort, and the vigorous gods, / and cerulian Doris, at-
tended by her nymphs,[3] / to give you a peaceful journey through their
realms. / But you, if you are able, arrogate for yourself the swift team, /
borne by which the Colchian[4] fled from the face of her husband, [10] /
or that by which Triptolemus[5] reached the Scythian borders, / the be-
loved boy sent from the Eleusinian city. / But when you see the German
sands become golden, / turn your steps to the walls of affluent Hamburg,

---

[1] Young (1587?-1655) was Milton's tutor in 1618-20(?). By 1620 he was in
Hamburg, visiting England in Mar.-July 1621 and again sometime in Jan.-Apr.
1625 (see ll. 33-38); he returned sometime between Jan. and Mar. 1628. On
Mar. 27, 1628, he became vicar of St. Peter and St. Mary in Stowmarket, Suf-
folk. Familiar Letter 1 was written Mar. 26, 1627, to accompany this elegy,
which it mentions; a further letter (No. 4), dated July 21, 1628, also survives.
Young was the "TY" of "SMECTYMNUUS," the composite name of the five
divines who in 1641 attacked episcopacy with An Answer to a Book entituled
"An Humble Remonstrance," to which was added A Postscript, probably written
by Milton (see Wolfe, Yale Prose, I, 961-65). Barker (MLR, XXXII, 1937,
517-26) suggests that Young was the friend to whom Of Reformation was writ-
ten, and Parker (TLS, May 16, 1936, p. 420) believes him the unknown friend
of the letter in TM.
[2] god of the winds; the land of the Sicanians was Sicily.
[3] Wife of the river-god Nereus, Doris was the mother of fifty sea-nymphs.
[4] Medea fled from Jason in a chariot drawn by dragons, after murdering their
children.
[5] a son of Celeus, king of Eleusis, whom Ceres sent in her dragon-drawn
chariot to sow wheat throughout the earth (including far Scythia). Ovid like-
wise wished for the chariots of Medea and Triptolemus to return him from exile
(Tristia, III, viii, 1-4).

/ which is said to derive its name from slain Hama,[6] [15] / who it is told was brought to violent death by a Cimbrian club. / Here, renowned for his honor of the primitive faith, lives / a minister well-versed in feeding the sheep that worship Christ; / he, truly, is more than the other half of my soul: / I am constrained to live but half of my life without him. [20] / Alas for me, how many seas, how many mountains intervening / render me cut off from the other half of myself! / Dearer to me is he than you, most learned of Greeks, / to Cliniades,[7] who was the great-grandson of Telamon; / than the lofty Stagirite[8] to his noble pupil [25] / whom the genial daughter of Chaonia bore to Libyan Jove. / What the son of Amyntor, what the heroic son of Philyra / were to the king of the Myrmidons,[9] such is he to me. / I first surveyed the Aonian retreats through his guiding, / and the sacred lawns of the twin-peaked mountain,[10] [30] / and the Pierian water I drank, and by favor of Clio, / I thrice moistened my happy lips with pure Castalian wine. / But thrice has fiery Aethon seen the sign of the ram, / and overspread his woolly back with new gold, / and twice, Chloris, have you bestrewn the old earth with new [35] / grass, and twice Auster removed your wealth; / and yet I have not been allowed to feast my eyes on his countenance / or the sweet sounds of his speech to be drunk in by my ears.[11] / Speed, therefore, and outrun noisy Eurus[12] by your course. / How great is the need of my admonitions, circumstance shows; you yourself perceive.

---

[6] D. T. Starnes (A Tribute to G. C. Taylor, 1952, p. 39) shows that Milton could have learned this legend from entries in Charles Stephanus' Dictionarium. Hama was a Saxon champion reputedly killed by Starchatar, a Danish (Cimbrian) giant.

[7] Alcibiades; one of Plato's dialogues bears his name.

[8] Aristotle, born in Stagira in Macedonia. His famous pupil was Alexander the Great, son of Olympias (of Chaonia in Epirus) and, in legend, of Ammon, as Jove was known in Libya.

[9] Achilles, pupil of Phoenix (son of Amyntor) and Chiron (son of Philyra).

[10] Mt. Parnassus, the haunt of the Muses, in Aonia. The waters that flowed in Castalia, a spring on Mt. Parnassus, afforded poetic inspiration by the bestowal of the Muses, who were born in Pieria. The Muse Clio, as Simonides tells us (Frag. 56), was the "overseer of the pure lustration-water, receiver of the prayers of many a pitcher-carrier." What Milton says is that Young introduced him to the glories of the arts, and that, while under Young's guidance and as a result of the talents given him by Clio, he had thrice been poetically inspired. These early poems are apparently not extant.

[11] Because Aethon, one of the sun's horses, has entered the zodiacal sign of the Ram (Mar. 21–Apr. 19) three times and because Chloris, goddess of flowers here signifying spring, and Auster, the south wind here signifying autumn, have visited the earth twice, Milton must not have seen Young since early 1625.

[12] the east wind, named because Milton was writing to Germany at the time of year that it blows.

[40] / Perhaps you will find him sitting with his sweet wife, / stroking their dear children on his lap; / or perhaps meditating the copious volumes of the old fathers, / or the Holy Bible of the true God, / saturating the delicate souls with celestial dew, [45] / the sublime work of health-bearing religion. / As is the custom, be careful to deliver a hearty greeting, / to speak as would befit your master, if only he were present. / May you be mindful to cast your discreet eyes down a little on the ground / and to speak these words with modest mouth: [50] / These verses to you, if there is time for the delicate Muses between battles,[13] / a devoted hand sends from the English shore. / Accept this sincere wish for your welfare, though it be late, / and may it be the more pleasing to you for that reason. / Late indeed, but genuine it was as that which [55] / the chaste Penelope, daughter of Icarius, received from her dilatory husband.[14] / But why did I consent to cancel a manifest fault / which he himself is utterly unable to discharge? / He is justly reproved as tardy, and confesses his offence, / and is ashamed to have forsaken his duty. [60] / Do only you grant forgiveness to him confessed, and to him begging forgiveness; / crimes which lie exposed are wont to be destroyed. / No beast separates its jaws in fearful openings, / nor does the lion tear those lying prone with his wounding claw. / Often the cruel hearts of Thracian[15] lance-bearers [65] / have melted at the melancholy pleas of a suppliant, / and extended hands avert the stroke of the thunderbolt, / and a small sacrifice pacifies the angry gods. / Now for a long while was there the impulse to write to you in that place, / and love would not endure to suffer further delays; [70] / for wandering rumor imparts—alas the truthful messager of calamities— / that in places neighboring upon you wars burst forth, / that you and your city are surrounded by fierce troops, / and that now the Saxon leaders have procured arms. / Everywhere around you Enyo is devastating the fields, / [75] / and now blood soaks the land sown with the flesh of men. / And Thrace has yielded its Mars to the Germans; / father Mars has driven his Odrysian horses thither. / And now the ever-crested olive fades, / and

---

[13] The conflicts of the Thirty Years' War threatened Hamburg particularly after Christian IV of Denmark (a Protestant leader) was defeated by Tilly, general of the Catholic Holy League, in Western Germany on Aug. 27, 1626. See also ll. 71–76, where reference is made to Bernard, William, and Frederick, Dukes of Saxe-Weimar, who were preparing attacks against Tilly and Wallenstein. Hamburg tried to remain neutral. Enyo (l. 75), a goddess of war, was noted for destruction of cities.

[14] Ulysses, disguised, revealed himself to his wife Penelope several days after his return from the Trojan War and his ensuing travels.

[15] Thrace (Odrysia, l. 78) was the home of Mars.

the goddess[16] detesting the brazen-sounding trumpet has fled, [80] / look, has fled the earth, and now it is believed / the just maid was not the last to fly to the mansions on high. / Nevertheless in the meanwhile the horror of war resounds around you, / and you live alone and destitute on the unfamiliar soil; / and in your foreign residence, indigent, you seek the sustenance [85] / which the hearth of your forefathers does not tender you. / Fatherland, hard parent, and more cruel than the white cliffs / which the spuming wave of your coast beats, / do you think it right thus to expose your innocent children? / To a strange soil thus do you drive them with hard-heartedness? [90] / and do you suffer them to seek livelihood in remote lands / whom provident God himself has sent to you, / and who bring joyous messages from heaven, and who / teach the way which leads beyond the grave to the stars?[17] / Indeed, deservedly, may you, O Fatherland, live enclosed in Stygian darkness, [95] / and deservedly perish by the eternal hunger of the soul! / Just as the Tishbite prophet[18] in days gone by / walked the lonely deserts of the earth with unaccustomed step / and the harsh wastes of Arabia, when he fled / from the hands of King Ahab and yours, Sidonian Fury, [100] / and in such fashion, with limbs lacerated by the dreadful-sounding whip, / was Cilician Paul[19] driven from the Emathian city; / and the ungrateful citizen of fishy Gergessa / bade Jesus himself depart from his coasts.[20] / But you, my tutor, take heart; let not your anxious hope fall from griefs, [105] / nor pale dread terrify your bones. / Although you may be covered over by shining arms / and a thousand spears threaten you with death, / assuredly your unarmed side shall not be violated by any weapon / and no lance will drink your blood. [110] / For you yourself will be safe under the radiant aegis of God.[21] / He

---

[16] Astraea; see *Fair Infant*, n. 9. The olive (l. 79) is the symbol of peace; it and truth are meant as perhaps forsaking earth later than justice.

[17] Lines 87–94 allude to the probable reason for Young's removal to Hamburg: the requirement that ministers subscribe not only to articles concerning faith and the sacraments in the Thirty-nine Articles, but also to those concerning rites and ceremonies. The "you" of l. 95 are those church and governmental officials responsible for Young's exile.

[18] Elijah, who fled into the wilderness from the anger of Ahab's wife Jezebel, daughter of the king of Sidon (1 Kings xix. 1–4).

[19] Paul, who came from Tarsus in Cilicia, was beaten by the multitude of Philippi in Macedonia, or Emathia (Acts xvi. 22–23).

[20] Matt. viii. 28–34 relates how Jesus cast out the devils of two possessed only to have the citizens seek his departure because their swine had perished along with the devils.

[21] Though Milton refers to Young's ministry under the Christian God, he fuses with it the pagan image of Jove's protective shield, borne by Athena, with its Gorgon head warding off all attackers.

will be guardian to you, and he will be champion to you; / he who under the walls of Sion's fortress / vanquished so many Assyrian soldiers in the silent night,[22] / and turned in flight those whom venerable Damascus [115] / sent to the borders of Samaria from her ancient plains,[23] / and affrighted the thronging cohorts with their terrified king / when the glorious trumpet sounded in the empty air, / when the horny hoof scourged the dusty plain, / when the driven chariot shook the sandy ground, [120] / and the neighing of horses rushing into battle was heard, / and the clanking of iron swords, and the deep roar of men. / And you (because it still remains for the sick at heart) remember to hope / and conquer these misfortunes by your magnanimous heart. / And do not doubt at one time or other to enjoy more fortunate years [125] / and to be able to see again your native home.

(*Mar. ? 1627*)

[22] the routing of Sennacherib and his Assyrian host at Jerusalem by the angel of God (2 Kings xix. 35).

[23] The besieging of Samaria by the Damascans under Ben-Hadad is told in 1 and 2 Kings; the flight here described is found in 2 Kings vii. 6–7.

On the Death of a Fair Infant Dying of a Cough[1]

I

O Fairest flower no sooner blown but blasted,
Soft silken Primrose fading timelessly,
Summers chief honour if thou hadst out-lasted
Bleak winters force that made thy blossom drie;
For he being amorous on that lovely die   5
    That did thy cheek envermeil, thought to kiss
But kill'd alas, and then bewayl'd his fatal bliss.

[1] Anne, daughter of Milton's sister Anne and Edward Phillips, was baptized Jan. 12, 1626, and was buried Jan. 22, 1628. The stanza employed here, like that of the induction to the *Nativity Ode*, is perhaps derived from Phineas Fletcher.

II

For since grim *Aquilo*[2] his charioter
By boistrous rape th' *Athenian* damsel got,
He thought it toucht his Deitie full neer,   10
If likewise he some fair one wedded not,
Thereby to wipe away th' infamous blot   *The Northwind*
  Of long-uncoupled bed, and childless eld,[3]
Which 'mongst the wanton gods a foul reproach was held.

III

So mounting up in icy-pearled carr,   *He gets in his chariot*   15
Through middle empire of the freezing air
He wanderd long, till thee he spy'd from farr,
There ended was his quest, there ceast his care.
Down he descended from his Snow-soft chair,
  But all unwares with his cold-kind embrace   20
Unhous'd thy Virgin Soul from her fair biding place.

IV

Yet art thou not inglorious in thy fate;
For so *Apollo*, with unweeting[4] hand
Whilom[5] did slay his dearly-loved mate
Young *Hyacinth* born on *Eurotas* strand,   25
Young *Hyacinth* the pride of *Spartan* land;
  But then transform'd him to a purple flower;[6]
Alack that so to change thee winter had no power.

V

Yet can I not perswade me thou art dead
Or that thy corse corrupts in earths dark womb,   30
Or that thy beauties lie in wormie bed,
Hid from the world in a low delved tomb;
Could Heav'n for pittie thee so strictly doom?
  Oh no! for something in thy face did shine
Above mortalitie that shew'd thou wast divine.   35

---

[2] the northeast wind who stole away the Athenian princess Orithyia.
[3] old age.
[4] "unaware" of the consequences.
[5] formerly.
[6] Compare *Lycidas*, 106.

VI

Resolve me then oh Soul most surely blest
(If so it be that thou these plaints dost hear)
Tell me bright Spirit where e're thou hoverest
Whether above that high first-moving Sphear[7]
Or in th' Elisian fields (if such there were).   40
    Oh say me true if thou wert mortal wight
And why from us so quickly thou didst take thy flight.

VII

Wert thou some Starr which from the ruin'd roof
Of shak't Olympus by mischance didst fall;
Which carefull *Jove* in natures true behoof   45
Took up, and in fit place did reinstall?
Or did of late earths Sons[8] besiege the wall
    Of sheenie Heav'n, and thou some goddess fled
Amongst us here below to hide thy nectar'd head?

VIII

Or wert thou that just Maid[9] who once before   50
Forsook the hated earth, O tell me sooth
And cam'st again to visit us once more?
Or wert thou Mercy that sweet smiling Youth?
Or that crown'd Matron sage white-robed truth?
    Or any other of that heav'nly brood   55
Let down in clowdie throne to do the world some good?

IX

Or wert thou of the golden-winged hoast,
Who having clad thy self in human weed
To earth from thy prefixed[10] seat didst poast,
And after short abode flie back with speed,   60
As if to shew what creatures Heav'n doth breed,
    Thereby to set the hearts of men on fire
To scorn the sordid world, and unto Heav'n aspire?

---

[7] The primum mobile, which lay farthest away from the earth of all other spheres of heavenly bodies, imparted motion to each succeeding inner shell.

[8] the Giants, who waged war against Jove.

[9] Astraea, goddess of justice, the last of the divinities to forsake mankind at the beginning of the Bronze Age because of its impious and wicked conduct.

[10] ordained.

X

But oh why didst thou not stay here below
To bless us with thy heav'n-lov'd innocence,   65
To slake his wrath whom sin hath made our foe
To turn Swift-rushing black perdition hence,
Or drive away the slaughtering pestilence,[11]
    To stand 'twixt us and our deserved smart?
But thou canst best perform that office where thou art.   70

XI

Then thou the mother of so sweet a child
Her false imagin'd loss cease to lament,
And wisely learn to curb thy sorrows wild;
Think what a present thou to God hast sent,
And render him with patience what he lent;   75
    This if thou do he will an off-spring give,[12]
That till the worlds last-end shall make thy name to live.[13]

(Jan.–Mar. 1628)

[11] the plague.
[12] an allusion to the imminent birth of another child; Milton's niece Elizabeth
was baptized on Apr. 9, 1628, at St. Martin's-in-the-Fields.
[13] Isa. lvi. 5: "Even unto them will I give in mine house and within my walks
a place and a name better than of sons and of daughters: I will give them an
everlasting name, that shall not be cut off."

At a Vacation Exercise in the Colledge, part Latin, *part* English.
The Latin *speeches ended, the* English *thus began.*[1]

Hail native Language, that by sinews weak
Didst move my first endeavouring tongue to speak,
And mad'st imperfect words with childish trips,
Half unpronounc't, slide through my infant-lips,
Driving dumb silence from the portal dore,   5

[1] The Latin speeches earlier in this exercise at Cambridge and the English
prose following are lost; immediately preceding these verses was the sixth pro-
lusion ("Sportive Exercises on occasion are not inconsistent with philosophical
Studies"), in which Milton had "thither packt the worst." This poetical frag-
ment illustrates his topic well, for the basis of this humor is satire on scholastic
logic. The midsummer frolic for which these verses were written consisted of
numerous skits and recitals; perhaps Milton's fellow performers were the "late
fantasticks" of l. 20.

Where he had mutely sate two years before:
Here I salute thee and thy pardon ask
That now I use thee in my latter task:
Small loss it is that thence can come unto thee,
I know my tongue but little Grace can do thee: 10
Thou needst not be ambitious to be first,
Believe me I have thither packt the worst:
And, if it happen as I did forecast,
The daintiest dishes shall be serv'd up last.
I pray thee then deny me not thy aid   15
For this same small neglect that I have made:
But haste thee strait to do me once a Pleasure,
And from thy wardrope bring thy chiefest treasure;
Not those new fangled toys, and trimming slight
Which takes our late fantasticks with delight,   20
But cull those richest Robes, and gay'st attire
Which deepest Spirits, and choicest Wits desire:
I have some naked thoughts that rove about
And loudly knock to have their passage out;
And wearie of their place do only stay   25
Till thou hast deck't them in thy best array;
That so they may without suspect or fears
Fly swiftly to this fair Assembly's ears;
Yet I had rather, if I were to chuse,
Thy service in some graver subject use,   30
Such as may make thee search thy coffers round,
Before thou cloath my fancy in fit sound:
Such where the deep transported mind may soar
Above the wheeling poles, and at Heav'ns dore
Look in, and see each blissful Deitie   35
How he before the thunderous throne doth lie,
Listening to what unshorn *Apollo*[2] sings
To th' touch of golden wires, while *Hebe* brings
Immortal Nectar to her Kingly Sire:[3]
Then passing through the Sphears of watchful fire,   40
And mistie Regions of wide air next under,
And hills of Snow and lofts of piled Thunder,
May tell at length how green-ey'd *Neptune* raves,
In Heav'ns defiance mustering all his waves;[4]
Then sing of secret things that came to pass   45

[2] god of music, usually represented with long hair to indicate his youth.
[3] Jove.
[4] Neptune defied the gods in seeking revenge on Ulysses for the blinding of his son.

When Beldam Nature in her cradle was;
And last of Kings and Queens and Heroes old,
Such as the wise *Demodocus* once told
In solemn songs at King *Alcinous* feast,[5]
While sad *Ulisses* soul and all the rest   50
Are held with his melodious harmonie
In willing chains and sweet captivitie.
But fie my wandring Muse how thou dost stray!
Expectance calls thee now another way,
Thou know'st it must be now thy only bent   55
To keep in compass of thy Predicament:[6]
Then quick about thy purpos'd business come,
That to the next I may resign my Room.

Then Ens *is represented as Father of the Predicaments his ten Sons,*
   whereof the Eldest stood for Substance *with his Canons, which* Ens
   thus speaking, explains.[7]

Good luck befriend thee Son; for at thy birth
The Fairy Ladies daunc't upon the hearth;[8]   60
Thy drowsie Nurse hath sworn she did them spie
Come tripping to the Room where thou didst lie;
And sweetly singing round about thy Bed
Strew all their blessings on thy sleeping Head.
She heard them give thee this, that thou should'st still   65
From eyes of mortals walk invisible;[9]
Yet there is something that doth force my fear,
For once it was my dismal hap to hear
A *Sybil* old, bow-bent with crooked age,

---

[5] See *Od.*, VIII, 499–522.

[6] Though he puns on the meaning of the word in logic (see next note), Milton means both the classification of subject assigned him and the plight imposed by not writing what he would prefer.

[7] Milton appeared as Ens, the Aristotelian principle of Absolute Being, father of the ten categories (or predicaments) into which all knowledge can be reduced (*Organon*, Part 1). In addition to the eldest son Substance, these are: Quantity, Quality, Relation, Place, Time, Posture, Possession, Action, and Passion. The canons are the fundamental principles or properties which are common to Substance; e.g., Substance supports the other predicaments (or accidents) and keeps them together.

[8] Thus Substance has been imbued with good fortune.

[9] invisible because Substance cannot be perceived except through the other nine categories (the accidents of Substance). Milton puns on "accident" in l. 74, and the literal meaning of "Substance" ("stands under") in ll. 74–80.

That far events full wisely could presage,   70
And in times long and dark Prospective Glass
Fore-saw what future dayes should bring to pass;
Your Son, said she (nor can you it prevent),
Shall subject be to many an Accident.
O're all his Brethren he shall Reign as King,[10]   75
Yet every one shall make him underling,
And those that cannot live from him asunder
Ungratefully shall strive to keep him under;
In worth and excellence he shall out-go them,
Yet being above them, he shall be below them;   80
From others he shall stand in need of nothing,
Yet on his Brothers shall depend for Cloathing.
To find a Foe it shall not be his hap,[11]
And peace shall lull him in her flowry lap;
Yet shall he live in strife, and at his dore   85
Devouring war[12] shall never cease to roar:
Yea it shall be his natural property
To harbour those that are at enmity.[13]
What power, what force, what mighty spell, if not
Your learned hands, can loose this Gordian knot?[14]   90

The next, Quantity *and* Quality, *spake in Prose, then* Relation *was call'd
   by his Name.*

Rivers[15] arise; whether thou be the Son
Of utmost *Tweed*, or *Oose*, or gulphie *Dun*,
Or *Trent*, who like some earth-born Giant spreads
His thirty Armes along th' indented Meads,
Or sullen *Mole* that runneth underneath,   95
Or *Severn* swift, guilty of Maidens[16] death,
Or rockie *Avon*, or of sedgie *Lee*,
Or coaly *Tine*, or antient hallow'd *Dee*,[17]

[10] Perhaps Edward King, subject of *Lycidas*, enacted the role of Substance.
[11] There is no opposite to Substance.
[12] the change of substance bitterly disputed in the Eucharist.
[13] Though the accidents make up the whole (lulling peace), some are end-lessly opposed (e.g., Action and Passion).
[14] a complicated situation, difficult to undo.
[15] Not only does Milton catalogue English rivers in the remaining lines, but he puns: George or Nizell Rivers apparently was Relation.
[16] Sabrina's; see *A Mask*, ll. 824-32.
[17] The Dee was considered divine since its fluctuations predicted success or failure to the early Britons.

Or *Humber* loud that keeps the *Scythians* Name,[18]
Or *Medway* smooth, or Royal Towred *Thame*.   100

The rest was Prose.

(July 1628)

[18] Spenser tells the story of Humber, a Scythian king driven into the river
where he drowned (*FQ*, II, x, 14–16; IV, xi, 38).

Elegia quinta

IN ADVENTUM VERIS

In se perpetuo Tempus revolubile gyro
    Jam revocat Zephyros vere tepente novos.
Induiturque brevem Tellus reparata juventam,
    Jamque soluta gelu dulce virescit humus.
Fallor? an et nobis redeunt in carmina vires,   5
    Ingeniumque mihi munere veris adest?
Munere veris adest, iterumque vigescit ab illo
    (Quis putet?) atque aliquod jam sibi poscit opus.
Castalis[1] ante oculos, bifidumque cacumen oberrat,
    Et mihi Pyrenen[2] somnia nocte ferunt.   10
Concitaque arcano fervent mihi pectora motu,
    Et furor, et sonitus me sacer intùs agit.
Delius ipse venit, video Penëide lauro
    Implicitos crines, Delius ipse venit.[3]
Jam mihi mens liquidi raptatur in ardua cœli,   15
    Perque vagas nubes corpore liber eo.
Perque umbras, perque antra feror pentralia vatum,
    Et mihi fana patent interiora Deûm.
Intuiturque animus toto quid agatur Olympo,
    Nec fugiunt oculos Tartara cæca meos.   20
Quid tam grande sonat distento spiritus ore?
    Quid parit hæc rabies, quid sacer iste furor?
Ver mihi, quod dedit ingenium, cantabitur illo;
    Profuerint isto reddita dona modo.
Jam, Philomela,[4] tuos foliis adoperta novellis   25
    Instituis modulos, dum silet omne nemus.

Urbe ego, tu sylvâ simul incipiamus utrique,
    Et simul adventum veris uterque canat.
Veris io rediere vices, celebremus honores
    Veris, et hoc subeat Musa perennis opus.   30
Jam sol Æthiopas fugiens Tithoniaque arva,
    Flectit ad Arctöas aurea lora plagas.[5]
Est breve noctis iter, brevis est mora noctis opacæ,
    Horrida cum tenebris exulat illa suis.
Jamque Lycaonius plaustrum cæleste Boötes[6]   35
    Non longâ sequitur fessus ut ante viâ,
Nunc etiam solitas circum Jovis atria toto
    Excubias agitant sydera rara polo.
Nam dolus, et cædes, et vis cum nocte recessit,
    Neve Giganteum[7] Dii timuere scelus.   40
Forte aliquis scopuli recubans in vertice pastor,
    Roscida cum primo sole rubescit humus,
Hac, ait, hac certè caruisti nocte puellâ,
    Phœbe, tuâ, celeres quæ retineret equos.
Læta suas repetit sylvas, pharetramque resumit   45
    Cynthia,[8] Luciferas ut videt alta rotas,
Et tenues ponens radios gaudere videtur
    Officium fieri tam breve fratris ope.
Desere, Phœbus ait, thalamos, Aurora, seniles,
    Quid juvat effœto procubuisse toro?[9]   50
Te manet Æolides[10] viridi venator in herba,
    Surge, tuos ignes altus Hymettus[11] habet.
Flava verecundo dea crimen in ore fatetur,
    Et matutinos ocyus urget equos.
Exuit invisam Tellus rediviva senectam,   55
    Et cupit amplexus, Phœbe, subire tuos;
Et cupit, et digna est, quid enim formosius illâ,
    Pandit ut omniferos luxuriosa sinus,
Atque Arabum spirat messes, et ab ore venusto
    Mitia cum Paphiis fundit amoma rosis?   60
Ecce coronatur sacro frons ardua luco,
    Cingit ut Idæam pinea turris Opim;[12]
Et vario madidos intexit flore capillos,
    Floribus et visa est posse placere suis.
Floribus effusos ut erat redimita capillos   65
    Tænario placuit diva Sicana Deo.[13]
Aspice, Phœbe, tibi faciles hortantur amores,
    Mellitasque movent flamina verna preces.
Cinnameâ Zephyrus leve plaudit odorifer alâ,
    Blanditiasque tibi ferre videntur aves.   70

Nec sine dote tuos temeraria quærit amores
   Terra, nec optatos poscit egena toros;
Alma salutiferum medicos tibi gramen in usus
   Præbet, et hinc titulos adjuvat ipsa tuos.[14]
Quòd si te pretium, si te fulgentia tangunt   75
   Munera (muneribus sæpe coemptus Amor),
Illa tibi ostentat quascunque sub æquore vasto,
   Et superinjectis montibus abdit opes.
Ah quoties cum tu clivoso fessus Olympo
   In vespertinas præcipitaris aquas,   80
Cur te, inquit, cursu languentam, Phœbe, diurno
   Hesperiis recipit cærula mater aquis?
Quid tibi cum Tethy?[15] Quid cum Tartesside lymphâ?
   Dia quid immundo perluis ora salo?
Frigora, Phœbe, meâ melius captabis in umbrâ,   85
   Huc ades, ardentes imbue rore comas.
Mollior egelidâ veniet tibi somnus in herbâ,
   Huc ades, et gremio lumina pone meo.
Quáque jaces circum mulcebit lene susurrans
   Aura per humentes corpora fusa rosas.   90
Nec me (crede mihi) terrent Semelëia[16] fata,
   Nec Phäetontéo fumidus axis equo;
Cum tu, Phœbe, tuo sapientius uteris igni,
   Huc ades et gremio lumina pone meo.
Sic Tellus lasciva suos suspirat amores;   95
   Matris in exemplum cætera turba ruunt.
Nunc etenim toto currit vagus orbe Cupido,
   Languentesque fovet solis ab igne faces.
Insonuere novis lethalia cornua nervis,
   Triste micant ferro tela corusca novo.   100
Jamque vel invictam tentat superasse Dianam,
   Quæque sedet sacro Vesta pudica foco.
Ipsa senescentem reparat Venus annua formam,
   Atque iterum tepido creditur orta mari.
Marmoreas juvenes clamant Hymenæe per urbes,   105
   Littus io Hymen, et cava saxa sonant.
Cultior ille venit tunicâque decentior aptâ,
   Puniceum redolet vestis odora crocum.
Egrediturque frequens ad amœni gaudia veris
   Virgineos auro cincta puella sinus.   110
Votum est cuique suum, votum est tamen omnibus unum,
   Ut sibi quem cupiat, det Cytherea virum.
Nunc quoque septenâ modulatur arundine pastor,
   Et sua quæ jungat carmina Phyllis habet.

Navita nocturno placat sua sydera cantu,   115
   Delphinasque leves ad vada summa vocat.[17]
Jupiter ipse alto cum conjuge ludit Olympo,
   Convocat et famulos ad sua festa Deos.
Nunc etiam Satyri cum sera crepuscula surgunt,
   Pervolitant celeri florea rura choro,   120
Sylvanusque suâ Cyparissi fronde revinctus,
   Semicaperque Deus, semideusque caper.
Quæque sub arboribus Dryades latuere vetustis
   Per juga, per solos expatiantur agros.
Per sata luxuriat fruticetaque Mænalius Pan,   125
   Vix Cybele mater, vix sibi tuta Ceres,
Atque aliquam cupidus prædatur Oreada Faunus,
   Consulit in trepidos dum sibi Nympha pedes,
Jamque latet, latitansque cupit male tecta videri,
   Et fugit, et fugiens pervelit ipsa capi.   130
Dii quoque non dubitant cælo præponere sylvas,
   Et sua quisque sibi numina lucus habet.
Et sua quisque diu sibi numina lucus habeto,
   Nec vos arboreâ, dii, precor ite domo.
Te referant miseris te, Jupiter, aurea terris   135
   Sæcla, quid ad nimbos aspera tela redis?
Tu saltem lentè rapidos age, Phœbe, jugales
   Quà potes, et sensim tempora veris eant.
Brumaque productas tardè ferat hispida noctes,
   Ingruat et nostro serior umbra polo.   140

Elegy 5

ON THE COMING OF SPRING

In his perpetual cycle Time, rolling back, / now recalls fresh zephyrs, with warming spring. / And the restored earth is covered with brief youth / and now the ground, free from frost, is becoming delightfully green. / Am I mistaken? or are powers returning to my songs, [5] / and is inspiration present in me by the favor of spring? / It is present by the favor of spring, and again begins to flourish from it / (who may suspect?) and even now demands some work for itself. / The cleft Castalian peak[1] hovers before my eyes / and dreams transport Pyrene[2] to me in

1 See *El.* 4, n. 10.
2 a fountain at Corinth.

the night. [10] / And my excited breast enflames me with its strange emotion, / and I am made delirious, and a divine sound agitates me from within. / Apollo himself appears—I see his locks entwined / with Daphne's laurel—Apollo himself is descended.[3] / Now my mind is snatched from me into the heights of the liquid sky, [15] / and through the wandering clouds I fly, free from my body. / And through shadows and through caves, the sanctuaries of the poets, / I am borne, and to me the secret temples of the gods are accessible. / My spirit observes all that is done on Olympus, / and the hidden infernal regions do not escape my eyes. [20] / What does my soul sing so sublimely from its full mouth? / What does this madness bring forth, what this sacred rage? / Spring which has furnished me inspiration shall be sung through it; / her returned gifts may have been profitable in this way. / Already, Philomela,[4] you are beginning your modulations, hidden [25] / by the young leaves, while all the grove is still. / I in the city, you in the wood, let us both begin together / and together let each sing the coming of spring. / Ho! changes of spring have returned; let us celebrate the hours / of spring, and let the unfailing Muse take this task upon herself. [30] / Now the sun, fleeing the Ethiopians and the fields of Tithonus, / directs his golden reins toward Arctos' lands.[5] / Brief is the journey of night, brief is the delay of dark night; / that dreadful one lives in exile with her shadows. / And now Lycaonian Boötes,[6] wearied, does not follow [35] / in his celestial wain over the course as before; / now even few stars keep their accustomed watch / about the courts of Jove throughout the entire sky. / For deceit and slaughter and violence retired with the night; / neither have the gods feared the wickedness of the giants.[7] [40] / Perhaps some shepherd, reclining on the top of a cliff / while the dewy earth reddens with the first sunlight, / asserts, "Then, certainly on this night were you deprived, / Apollo, of your love who would delay your swift steeds." / Delighted, Cynthia[8] returns to her forests, and resumes her quiver, [45] / when she sees on high the wheels of Lucifer, / and setting down her feeble beams she seems to be happy / that her task is made short by her brother's power. / Abandon, Apollo says, your aged wedlock, Aurora; / What is pleasing in hav-

[3] Pursued by Apollo, Daphne was turned into a laurel at her own entreaty; thereafter, the leaves of the tree became a symbol of his patronage of poetry and music.
[4] the nightingale, whose song in spring portends success in love.
[5] the vernal equinox. Ethiopia was considered all Africa south of Egypt; Tithonus, loved by Aurora, the dawn, stands for the east; and Arctos, the double constellation of the Great and Lesser Bears, is the north.
[6] See Ely, n. 12. Lycaon, the son of Callisto (the Wain) and Jove, is the Lesser Bear.
[7] See Fair Infant, n. 8.
[8] the moon; Lucifer is the sun.

ing lain stretched out on an impotent bed?[9] [50] / Aeolides,[10] the
hunter, awaits you on the green lawn. / Arise; high Hymettus[11] enjoys
your fires. / With modest face the blushing goddess confesses her guilt,
/ and drives her morning horses more swiftly. / The reviving earth
shakes off her hated old age [55] / and wishes to submit to your em-
braces, Apollo. / Not only does she wish them, but she is worthy of
them; for what is / more beautiful than she, as, voluptuous, she bares
her all-bearing breasts / and breathes the harvests of Arabia, and from
her elegant mouth / pours gentle fragrances with Paphian roses? [60]
/ Behold, her lofty brow is crowned by a sacred wood / just as a piny
tower encompasses Idaean Ops,[12] / and she twines her dewy locks with
various bloom / and with her flowers she is seen able to please, / just as
the Sicilian goddess, wreathed round her flowing locks with flowers, [65]
/ was pleasing to the Taenarian god.[13] / Look, Apollo, facile loves are
calling you / and vernal winds blow honey-sweet pleas. / Odor-bearing
Zephyrus gently claps his cinnamon-scented wings / and the birds seem
to carry their flatteries to you. [70] / The thoughtless earth does not
seek your loves without dowry, / nor does she beg desired marriage, as
if in need; / bounteous, she offers you health-bearing grain for medical
uses / and hence she herself supports your titles.[14] / Because if money,
if glittering gifts impress you [75] / (love is often bought with gifts), /
she holds out to you whatever wealth conceals / under the broad sea
and under the overthrown mountains. / Ah, how often when, wearied
by steep Olympus, / you would sink into the western seas, [80] / does
she say, Why should the blue mother receive you, / Apollo, fainting
from your daily course into her Hesperian waters? / What have you to
do with Tethys?[15] with Tartessian streams? / Why do you bathe your
divine face in the filthy brine? / You will entrap coolness much better
in my shadow, Apollo. [85] / Come hither, moisten your glittering locks
in the dew; / a gentler sleep will come to you in the chill grass. / Come
hither and place your rays on my bosom; / wheresoever you lie about,
a gently murmuring breeze will soothe / our bodies spread on humid
roses. [90] / A destiny like Semele's[16] (believe me) does not frighten

---

[9] Jove made her beloved Tithonus immortal but not eternally youthful.
[10] While hunting, Cephalus, also beloved by Aurora, unwittingly killed his
jealous wife Procis.
[11] a mountain overlooking Athens.
[12] goddess of crops, identified with Earth and Cybele, the Great Mother, who
was worshipped on Mt. Ida.
[13] See Vice-Chancellor, n. 16.
[14] Apollo was god of healing.
[15] consort of Oceanus and mother of rivers. Hesperia was the west, and Tar-
tessus, a maritime city of Spain.
[16] Juno, in anger, persuaded her to entreat Jove to visit her, a mortal, as a
god, for Juno knew that she would be consumed by his lightning.

me, / nor the axle smoking from Phaeton's horse. / When you, Apollo, use your fire more wisely, / come hither and place your rays on my bosom. / Thus wanton Earth breathes out her loves; [95] / her remaining throng rush to ruin by example of the mother. / For now wandering Cupid runs through all the world, / and sustains his dying torches by the flame of the sun. / The lethal horns of his bow resound with new strings, / the tremulous arrows glitter severely with new iron. [100] / And now he attempts to subdue even the invincible Diana, / whoever sits in the sacred hearth by the chaste Vesta. / Venus herself annually refreshes her aging form, / and is believed sprung anew from the warm sea. / Through the marble cities the youth cry aloud, Hymen; [105] / the shore and hollow rocks echo, Io, Hymen. / He appears more elegant and more becoming in proper dress; / his odorous attire diffuses the perfume of purple crocus. / And many a girl with her virgin breasts encircled with gold / comes forth to the inward joys of lovely spring. [110] / Each is her own vow; one vow of all is the same, / that Cytherea will give her the man whom she desires. / Now also the shepherd is making music on his sevenfold reed pipe / and Phyllis has songs which she joins to his. / The sailor calms his stars with nocturnal song [115] / and calls the swift dolphins to the surface of the shallows.[17] / Jove sports himself on high Olympus with his spouse / and assembles the servile gods to his feast. / Now even the satyrs, when the evening shadows rise, / flit about through the flowery fields in a swift dance, [120] / and Sylvanus girded with his cypress foliage, / and the god half-goat and the goat half-god. / The Dryads who have lurked under the ancient trees / wander through the mountains and the lonely fields. / Maenalian Pan revels through the crops and the thickets; [125] / hardly mother Cybele, hardly Ceres is safe from him; / and lustful Faunus ravishes some Oread, / while the nymph reflects to herself on trembling feet. / And now she lies hidden, and lurking she wishes to be seen poorly concealed, / and she flees, and fleeing she may wish herself to be made captive. [130] / The gods also do not hesitate to prefer the woods to heaven, / and every grove possesses its own deities. / Long may every grove possess its own deities; / ye gods, I pray, do not go from your arboreal home! / May the golden age restore you, Jove, to a wretched world! [135] / Why do you come back with your cruel weapons in the clouds? / At least drive your swift team, Apollo, as leisurely / as you can, and may the time of spring pass slowly; / and may foul winter bring prolonged nights tardily, / and may shadow attack later within our heavens. [140]

(*spring 1629*)

[17] alluding to the myth of Arion.

On the Morning of Christs Nativity[1]

I

This is the Month, and this the happy morn
Wherin the Son of Heav'ns eternal King,
Of wedded Maid, and Virgin Mother[2] born, ~paradox~
Our great redemption from above did bring;
For so the holy sages once did sing,   5
    That he our deadly forfeit should release,
And with his Father work us a perpetual peace.

II

That glorious Form, that Light unsufferable,
And that far-beaming blaze of Majesty,
Wherwith he wont at Heav'ns high Councel-Table,   10
To sit the midst of Trinal Unity, ~paradox~
He laid aside;[3] and here with us to be,
    Forsook the Courts of everlasting Day,
And chose with us a darksom House of mortal Clay.

---

[1] The theme is the celebration of Christ's harmonizing of all life by becoming mortal man. This gift of praise for the birthday of Christ has been divided into a pattern of creative sun or silence (I–VIII), the concord which is the essence of music (IX–XVIII), and the conquest and reconciliation of discordant paganism (XIX–XXVI). The return to silence in the last stanza rounds out the pattern drawn by Arthur Barker in *UTQ*, X (1941), 167–81. Don C. Allen (*The Harmonious Vision*) emphasizes the conflict between Milton's aesthetic and intellectual daemons (p. 25), but concludes that the timelessness, immutable Nature, and harmony of God unify the poem (p. 29). The symbolic darkness in the later stanzas, seen against the intermingled and identified light and music of the earlier ones, is dispersed, as Rosemond Tuve reminds us in *Images and Themes*, p. 71, by the heavenly love, described in XXVII in images of brightness, which will work a perpetual peace. The fullest annotation will be found in Albert S. Cook's notes on the ode in *Trans. of the Connecticut Acad. of Arts and Sciences*, XV (1909), 307–68. See Maren-Sofie Røstvig's numerological analysis in *The Hidden Sense and Other Essays* (Oslo, 1963) for the contrast between the earthly concepts of the proem and the regenerative aspects of the hymn itself.
[2] The reversed combinations "wedded Maid" and "Virgin Mother" create a chiasmus, or X, the sign of Christ.
[3] Christ's *kenosis* or emptying himself of his godhead (Phil. ii. 6–8).

III

Say Heav'nly Muse, shall not thy sacred vein   15
Afford a present to the Infant God?
Hast thou no vers, no hymn, or solemn strein,
To welcom him to this his new abode,
Now while the Heav'n by the Suns team untrod,
    Hath took no print of the approaching light,   20
And all the spangled host keep watch in squadrons bright?

IV

See how from far upon the Eastern rode
The Star-led Wisards[4] haste with odours sweet:
O run, prevent[5] them with thy humble ode,
And lay it lowly at his blessed feet;   25
Have thou the honour first, thy Lord to greet,
    And joyn thy voice unto the Angel Quire,
From out his secret Altar toucht with hallow'd fire.[6]

The Hymn

I

It was the Winter wild,
While the Heav'n-born-child,   30
    All meanly wrapt in the rude manger lies;
Nature in aw to him
Had doff't her gawdy trim,
    With her great Master so to sympathize:
It was no season then for her   35
To wanton with the Sun, her lusty Paramour.

---

[4] the three Wise Men.
[5] anticipate.
[6] Isa. vi. 6–7: "Then flew one of the seraphims unto me, having a live coal in his hand, which he had taken with the tongs from off the altar: And he laid it upon my mouth, and said, Lo, this hath touched thy lips."

II

Onely with speeches fair
She woos the gentle Air
   To hide her guilty front with innocent Snow,
And on her naked shame,   40
Pollute[7] with sinfull blame,
   The Saintly Vail of Maiden white to throw,[8]
Confounded, that her Makers eyes
Should look so neer upon her foul deformities.

III

But he her fears to cease,   45
Sent down the meek-ey'd Peace;
   She crown'd with Olive green,[9] came softly sliding
Down through the turning sphear[10]
His ready Harbinger,
   With Turtle wing the amorous clouds dividing,   50
And waving wide her mirtle wand,
She strikes a universall Peace through Sea and Land.

IV

No War, or Battails sound
Was heard the World around:[11]
   The idle spear and shield were high up hung;   55
The hooked Chariot stood
Unstain'd with hostile blood,
   The Trumpet spake not to the armed throng,
And Kings sate still with awfull eye,
As if they surely knew their sovran Lord was by.   60

[7] polluted.
[8] Rev. iii. 18: "I counsel thee to buy of me gold tried in the fire, that thou mayest be rich; and white raiment, that thou mayest be clothed, and that the shame of thy nakedness do not appear; and anoint thine eyes with eyesalve, that thou mayest see."
[9] The dove Peace (the "turtledove" of l. 50) brought an olive branch to the ark as a sign of harmony with nature; the reference suggests the descent of the dove (the Spirit of God) at Christ's baptism. The myrtle wand, sacred to Venus, emphasizes the Love which has created Peace on Earth.
[10] the heavens.
[11] No war took place in the Roman Empire for some years before Jesus' birth.

V

But peacefull was the night
Wherin the Prince of light
   His raign of peace upon the earth began:
The Winds with wonder whist,[12]
Smoothly the waters kist,   65
   Whispering new joyes to the mild Ocean,
Who now hath quite forgot to rave,
While Birds of Calm[13] sit brooding on the charmed wave.

VI

The Stars with deep amaze
Stand fixt in stedfast gaze,   70
   Bending one way their pretious influence,[14]
And will not take their flight,
For all the morning light,
   Or *Lucifer*[15] that often warn'd them thence;
But in their glimmering Orbs did glow,   75
Untill their Lord himself bespake, and bid them go.

VII

And though the shady gloom
Had given day her room,
   The Sun himself with-held his wonted speed,
And hid his head for shame,   80
As his inferiour flame,
   The new-enlight'n'd world no more should need;
He saw a greater Sun appear
Then his bright Throne, or burning Axletree[16] could bear.

VIII

The Shepherds[17] on the Lawn,   85
Or ere the point of dawn,
   Sate simply chatting in a rustick row;

[12] hushed.
[13] the halcyons, which were supposed to breed only when the sea is calm;
the waves are thought of as under a spell. The halcyon, or kingfisher, was a
symbol of Christ. Compare *PL* I, 19–22; VII, 233–37.
[14] The stars, shining toward Bethlehem, are exerting all their power of good
fortune on the Christ-child.
[15] the morning star.
[16] the axle of the sun's chariot.
[17] Compare Luke ii. 8–20.

Full little thought they than,
That the mighty *Pan*[18]
 Was kindly[19] com to live with them below;   90
Perhaps their loves, or els their sheep,
Was all that did their silly[20] thoughts so busie keep.

IX

When such musick sweet   *a band of angels came to sing*
Their hearts and ears did greet,
 As never was by mortall singer strook,   95
Divinely-warbled voice
Answering the stringed noise,
 As all their souls in blisfull rapture took:
The Air such pleasure loth to lose,
With thousand echoes still prolongs each heav'nly close.[21]   100

X

Nature that heard such sound
Beneath the hollow round
 Of *Cynthia's* seat,[22] the Airy region thrilling,
Now was almost won
To think her part was don,   105
 And that her raign had here its last fulfilling;
She knew such harmony[23] alone
Could hold all Heav'n and Earth in happier union.

XI

At last surrounds their sight
A Globe of circular light,   110
 That with long beams the shame-fac't night array'd,
The helmed Cherubim
And sworded Seraphim
 Are seen in glittering ranks with wings displaid,
Harping in loud and solemn quire,   115
With unexpressive[24] notes to Heav'ns new-born Heir.

[18] Christ, the Good Shepherd.
[19] both "in kindness" and "in kinship" as man.
[20] simple.
[21] cadence.
[22] orb of the moon.
[23] in the union both of nature and of divine and human natures in the Incarnation.
[24] inexpressible.

XII

Such Musick (as 'tis said)[25]
Before was never made,
  But when of old the sons of morning sung,
While the Creator Great   120
His constellations set,
  And the well-ballanc't world on hinges hung,
And cast the dark foundations deep,
And bid the weltring waves their oozy channel keep.

XIII

Ring out ye Crystall sphears,[26]   125
Once bless our human ears,
  (If ye have power to touch our senses so)
And let your silver chime
Move in melodious time;
  And let the Base of Heav'ns deep Organ blow,   130
And with your ninefold harmony
Make up full consort[27] to th' Angelick symphony.

XIV

For if such holy Song
Enwrap our fancy long,
  Time will run back, and fetch the age of gold,[28]   135
And speckl'd[29] vanity
Will sicken soon and die,
  And leprous sin will melt from earthly mould,
And Hell it self will pass away,
And leave her dolorous mansions to the peering[30] day.   140

---

[25] Job xxxviii. 6–7: "Whereupon are the foundations thereof fastened? . . .
When the morning stars sang together, and all the sons of God shouted for joy?"
  [26] The music of the nine spheres (the ninth being the Crystalline) resulted
from the harmony of single tones uttered by each of the sirens as she traveled
about the earth on her allotted sphere (*Rep.*, X, 616–17). Pythagoreans believed
that only the sinless could hear this "silver chime."
  [27] concert, group.
  [28] the early age when Saturn ruled the world. It was an age of innocent hap-
piness when men lived without strife, labor, or injustice.
  [29] polluted, abominable. The phrase may translate Horace's "maculosum
nefas" (*Odes*, IV, v, 22) with reference to Ecclesiastes.
  [30] appearing, scrutinizing, equalizing.

XV

Yea Truth, and Justice then
Will down return to men,
    Orb'd in a Rain-bow;[31] and like glories wearing
Mercy will sit between,
Thron'd in Celestiall sheen,   145
    With radiant feet the tissued clouds down stearing,
And Heav'n as at som festivall,
Will open wide the Gates of her high Palace Hall.

XVI

But wisest Fate sayes no,
This must not yet be so,   150
    The Babe lies yet in smiling Infancy,
That on the bitter cross
Must redeem our loss;
    So both himself and us to glorifie:
Yet first to those ychain'd in sleep,[32]   155
The wakefull trump of doom must thunder through the deep.[33]

XVII

With such a horrid clang
As on mount *Sinai* rang
    While the red fire, and smouldring clouds out brake:[34]
The aged Earth agast   160
With terrour of that blast,
    Shall from the surface to the center shake,
When at the worlds last session,
The dreadfull Judge in middle Air shall spread his throne.

Christ

---

[31] See *Mask*, n. 12. The collocation of Truth, Justice, and Mercy comes from Ps. lxxxv. 10; they are the so-called daughters of God, representing the three persons of the Holy Trinity (Father, Holy Spirit, and Son), who combined constitute the fourth daughter, Peace (see ll. 45–52).

[32] death.

[33] 1 Thess. iv. 16: "For the Lord himself shall descend from heaven with a shout, with the voice of the archangel, and with the trump of God: and the dead in Christ shall rise first."

[34] The giving of the ten commandments (Exod. xix. 18–19: "And mount Sinai was altogether on a smoke, because the Lord descended upon it in fire: and the smoke thereof ascended as the smoke of a furnace, and the whole mount quaked. And when the voice of the trumpet sounded long, and waxed louder and louder, Moses spoke . . .") is related to Judgment Day when "The heavens being on fire shall be dissolved, and the elements shall melt with fervent heat" (2 Peter iii. 12).

XVIII

And then at last our bliss   165
Full and perfect is,
  But now begins; for from this happy day
Th' old Dragon[35] under ground
In straiter limits bound,
  Not half so far casts his usurped sway,   170
And wroth to see his Kingdom fail,
Swindges[36] the scaly Horrour of his foulded tail.

XIX

The Oracles are dumm,[37]
No voice or hideous humm
  Runs through the arched roof in words deceiving.   175
Apollo from his shrine
Can no more divine,
  With hollow shreik the steep of Delphos leaving.
No nightly trance, or breathed spell,
Inspires the pale-ey'd[38] Priest from the prophetic cell.   180

XX

The lonely mountains o're,
And the resounding shore,
  A voice of weeping heard, and loud lament;[39]
From haunted spring, and dale
Edg'd with poplar pale,   185
  The parting Genius[40] is with sighing sent;
With flowr-inwov'n tresses torn
The Nimphs in twilight shade of tangled thickets mourn.

XXI

In consecrated Earth,
And on the holy Hearth,   190

[35] Rev. xx. 2–3: "And he laid hold on the dragon, that old serpent, which is the Devil, and Satan, and bound him a thousand years, And cast him into the bottomless pit, and shut him up, ..."
[36] beats, shakes (his coiled tail).
[37] The birth of Christ begins the destruction of the pagan divinities, extending through XXV, by stilling the false oracles of the heathen.
[38] perhaps "paled with fear," derived from the Latin usage of "palleò."
[39] Matt. ii. 18: "In Rama was there a voice heard, lamentation, and weeping, and great mourning . . . ."
[40] the spirit presiding over any particular place, such as a wood.

The *Lars*, and *Lemures*[41] moan with midnight plaint;
In Urns, and Altars round,
A drear, and dying sound
Affrights the *Flamins* at their service quaint;
And the chill Marble seems to sweat,[42]   195
While each peculiar power forgoes his wonted seat.

XXII

Peor,[43] and *Baalim*,
Forsake their Temples dim,
  With that twise batter'd god of *Palestine*,
And mooned *Ashtaroth*,   200
Heav'ns Queen and Mother both,
  Now sits not girt with Tapers holy shine,
The Libyc *Hammon* shrinks his horn,
In vain the *Tyrian* Maids their wounded *Thamuz* mourn.

XXIII

And sullen *Moloch* fled,   205
Hath left in shadows dred
  His burning Idol all of blackest hue;
In vain with Cymbals ring,
They call the grisly king,
  In dismall dance about the furnace blue;   210
The brutish gods of *Nile* as fast,
Isis and *Orus*, and the Dog *Anubis* hast.

---

[41] gods presiding over the home and spirits of the dead. "*Flamins*," l. 194, were Roman priests.
[42] foreboding ill (see *Georgics*, I, 480).
[43] The pagan divinities put to rout (XXII–XXV) are: *Peor*, the Phoenician sun god; *Baalim*, local Phoenician deities concerned with flocks; the Philistine fish god *Dagon*, whose statue was cast down twice because the people of Ashdod had taken the ark of God (1 Sam. v. 3–4); *Ashtaroth*, a Phoenician female divinity, identified with Astarte and Venus; *Ammon*, the North African name for Jove, who as tender of flocks was represented as a ram; *Thammuz*, the Phoenician Adonis, who was killed by a wild boar and revered as a vegetation god (compare Ezek. viii. 14: "behold, there sat women weeping for Tammuz"); *Moloch*, a Semitic deity, represented by a hollow idol filled with fire to consume sacrificed children whose cries were drowned out by cymbals and trumpets; the Egyptian deities *Isis*, the earth goddess, with the head of a cow (thus "brutish"); *Horus*, the hawk-headed sun god; *Anubis*, guide of the dead with the head of a jackal; and *Osiris*, the chief god and judge of the dead, identified with Apis, the Sacred Bull, which was buried in the temple of Serapis at Memphis; and *Typhon*, a hundred-headed serpent who killed Osiris, scattering truth to the four winds (*Areo.*, p. 29).

XXIV

Nor is *Osiris* seen
In *Memphian* Grove, or Green,
   Trampling th' unshowr'd[44] Grass with lowings loud: 215
Nor can he be at rest
Within his sacred chest,
   Naught but profoundest Hell can be his shroud;
In vain with Timbrel'd Anthems dark
The sable-stoled Sorcerers bear his worshipt Ark.[45]   220

XXV

He feels from *Juda*'s Land
The dredded Infants hand,
   The rayes of *Bethlehem* blind his dusky eyn;
Nor all the gods beside,
Longer dare abide,   225
   Not *Typhon* huge ending in snaky twine:
Our Babe to shew his Godhead true,
Can in his swadling bands[46] controul the damned crew.

XXVI

So when the Sun in bed,   *not sunset/sunrise*
Curtain'd with cloudy red,   230
   Pillows his chin upon an Orient wave,
The flocking shadows pale
Troop to th' infernall jail,[47]
   Each fetter'd Ghost slips to his severall grave,
And the yellow-skirted *Fayes*   235
Fly after the Night-steeds, leaving their Moon-lov'd maze.

XXVII

But see the Virgin blest,
Hath laid her Babe to rest.
   Time is our tedious[48] Song should here have ending:

[44] referring to the aridity of Egypt.
[45] Osiris' "sacred chest" borne by his black-robed priests to a temple, accompanied by the sound of tambourines.
[46] Compare Luke ii. 7. The line glances at the legend of the strength of the infant Hercules.
[47] Evil spirits return at morning to their graves or to hell.
[48] wearying (since lengthy).

Heav'ns youngest teemed Star[49] 240
Hath fixt her polisht Car,
  Her sleeping Lord with Handmaid Lamp attending,
  And all about the Courtly Stable,
Bright-harnest[50] Angels sit in order serviceable.

(*Dec. 1629*)

[49] The star of Bethlehem, latest born, has taken position to shine its light on Christ the King.
[50] wearing bright armor.

Elegia sexta

AD CAROLUM DIODATUM RURI COMMORANTEM[1]

*Qui cum idibus Decemb. scripsisset, et sua carmina excusari postulasset
  si solito minus essent bona, quòd inter lautitias quibus erat ab amicis
  exceptus, haud satis felicem operam Musis dare se posse affirmabat,
  hunc habuit responsum.*

Mitto tibi sanam non pleno ventre salutem,
  Quâ tu distento forte carere potes.
At tua quid nostram prolectat Musa camoenam,
  Nec sinit optatas posse sequi tenebras?
Carmine scire velis quàm te redamémque colámque, 5
  Crede mihi vix hoc carmine scire queas.
Nam neque noster amor modulis includitur arctis,
  Nec venit ad claudos integer ipse pedes.[2]
Quàm bene solennes epulas, hilaremque Decembrim
  Festaque cœlifugam[3] quæ coluere Deum, 10
Deliciasque refers, hyberni gaudia ruris,
  Haustaque per lepidos Gallica musta focos.
Quid quereris refugam vino dapibusque poesin?
  Carmen amat Bacchum, Carmina Bacchus amat.[4]
Nec puduit Phœbum virides gestasse corymbos, 15
  Atque hederam lauro præposuisse suæ.[5]
Sæpius Aoniis clamavit collibus Euœ
  Mista Thyonêo turba novena choro.[6]
Naso Corallæis[7] mala carmina misit ab agris:
  Non illic epulæ non sata vitis erat. 20

Quid nisi vina, rosasque racemiferumque Lyæum
  Cantavit brevibus Tëia Musa[8] modis?
Pindaricosque inflat numeros Teumesius Euan,
  Et redolet sumptum pagina quæque merum;
Dum gravis everso currus crepat axe supinus,   25
  Et volat Eléo pulvere fuscus eques.
Quadrimoque madens Lyricen Romanus[9] Jaccho
  Dulce canit Glyceran, flavicomamque Chloen.
Jam quoque lauta tibi generoso mensa paratu,
  Mentis alit vires, ingeniumque fovet.   30
Massica[10] fœcundam despumant pocula venam,
  Fundis et ex ipso condita metra cado.
Addimus his artes, fusumque per intima Phœbum
  Corda, favent uni Bacchus, Apollo, Ceres.[11]
Scilicet haud mirum tam dulcia carmina per te   35
  Numine composito tres peperisse Deos.
Nunc quoque Thressa[12] tibi cælato barbitos auro
  Insonat argutâ molliter icta manu;
Auditurque chelys suspensa tapetia circum,
  Virgineos tremulâ quæ regat arte pedes.   40
Illa tuas saltem teneant spectacula Musas,
  Et revocent, quantum crapula pellit iners.
Crede mihi dum psallit ebur, comitataque plectrum
  Implet odoratos festa chorea tholos,
Percipies tacitum per pectora serpere Phœbum,   45
  Quale repentinus permeat ossa calor,
Perque puellares oculos digitumque sonantem
  Irruet in totos lapsa Thalia[13] sinus.
Namque Elegía levis multorum cura deorum est,
  Et vocat ad numeros quemlibet illa suos;   50
Liber adest elegis, Eratoque, Ceresque, Venusque,
  Et cum purpureâ matre tenellus Amor.
Talibus inde licent convivia larga poetis,
  Sæpius et veteri commaduisse mero.
At qui bella refert, et adulto sub Jove cælum,   55
  Heroasque pios, semideosque duces,
Et nunc sancta canit superum consulta deorum,
  Nunc latrata fero regna profunda cane,[14]
Ille quidem parcè Samii pro more magistri[15]
  Vivat, et innocuos præbeat herba cibos;   60
Stet prope fagineo pellucida lympha catillo,
  Sobriaque è puro pocula fonte bibat.
Additur huic scelerisque vacans, et casta juventus,
  Et rigidi mores, et sine labe manus.

Qualis veste nitens sacrâ, et lustralibus undis   65
  Surgis ad infensos augur iture Deos.
Hoc ritu vixisse ferunt post rapta sagacem
  Lumina Tiresian, Ogygiumque Linon,[16]
Et lare devoto profugum Calchanta, senemque
  Orpheon edomitis sola per antra feris;   70
Sic dapis exiguus, sic rivi potor Homerus
  Dulichium vexit per freta longa virum,
Et per monstrificam Perseiæ Phœbados[17] aulam,
  Et vada fœmineis insidiosa sonis,
Perque tuas, rex ime, domos, ubi sanguine nigro   75
  Dicitur umbrarum detinuisse greges.
Diis etenim sacer est vates, divûmque sacerdos,
  Spirat et occultum pectus, et ora Jovem.
At tu siquid agam, scitabere (si modò saltem
  Esse putas tanti noscere siquid agam)   80
Paciferum canimus cælesti semine regem,[18]
  Faustaque sacratis sæcula pacta libris,
Vagitumque Dei, et stabulantem paupere tecto
  Qui suprema suo cum patre regna colit;
Stelliparumque polum, modulantesque æthere turmas,   85
  Et subitò elisos ad sua fana Deos.
Dona quidem dedimus Christi natalibus illa,
  Illa sub auroram lux mihi prima tulit.
Te quoque pressa manent patriis meditata cicutis,
  Tu mihi, cui recitem, judicis instar eris.   90

Elegy 6

TO CHARLES DIODATI, SOJOURNING IN THE COUNTRY[1]

*Who, when he wrote on the thirteenth of December and asked that his
verses be excused if they were less estimable than usual, being in
the midst of the splendors with which he had been received by his
friends, declared himself to be able to produce by no means suffi-
ciently auspicious work for the Muses, thus had this answer.*

On an empty stomach I send you a wish for health, / which you, stuffed
full, can perhaps do without. / But why does your Muse provoke mine,

---

[1] For Diodati, see *El.* 1, n. 1.

/ and not permit it to be able to pursue its chosen obscurity? / You would like to know by song how I return your love and revere you; [5] / believe me, you can scarcely learn this from song, / for my love is not confined by brief measures, / nor does it itself proceed unimpaired on halting feet.[2] / How well you report the customary sumptuous feasts and jovial December / and festivals that have honored the heaven-fleeing god,[3] [10] / the sports and pleasures of winter in the country, / and the French wines consumed beside agreeable fires. / Why do you complain that poetry is a fugitive from wine and feasts? / Song loves Bacchus, Bacchus loves songs.[4] / Nor did it shame Apollo to wear the green leaves of ivy [15] / and to prefer ivy to his own laurel.[5] / On the Aonian hills the assembled ninefold band / has often evoked Euoe from the Thyonean troop.[6] / Ovid sent poor verses from the Corallian fields;[7] / in that land there were no banquets, nor had the grape been planted. [20] / What but wine and roses and Lyaeus wreathed with clusters / did the Teian poet[8] sing in his shortened measures? / And Teumasian Euan inspires Pindaric odes, / and every page is redolent of the consumed wine, / while the laden chariot clatters on its back from an upset axle, [25] / and the horseman speeds on, darkened with Elean dust; / and the Roman lyricist,[9] wet with four-year-old wine, / sang of sweet Glycera and golden-haired Chloe. / Indeed your table bathed in generous provision also / nourishes the powers of your mind and encourages your genius. [30] / The Massican[10] cups foam out productive strength, / and you decant your verses contained within the wine-flask itself. / To this we add the arts and outpouring of Apollo through your inmost / heart; Bacchus, Apollo, Ceres together are favorable.[11] / No wonder then that it is not doubted, for the three gods [35] / through you have created their delightful songs with combined divinity. / Now also for you the Thracian lyre[12] with inlaid gold / is sounding, gently plucked by a melodious hand; / and the lyre is heard about the hanging tapestries, / which rules the maiden feet by its rhythmic art. [40] / At the

---

2 the elegiac couplet.
3 that is, becoming man on earth.
4 As god of wine, who loosens care, Bacchus inspired music and poetry.
5 See *El.* 5, n. 3.
6 See *El.* 4, n. 10. Thyoneus is Bacchus, also called Lyaeus (l. 21), meaning "deliverer from care," and Teumesian Euan (l. 23), "Euoe" being a shout heard at his festivals.
7 See *El.* 1, n. 3. Reference is to *Epistles from Pontus*, IV, viii, 80–83.
8 Anacreon.
9 Horace in his *Odes*.
10 Mt. Massicus in Campania, which was celebrated for its excellent wine.
11 Bacchus because of the wine-filled festivals, Apollo because Diodati was preparing for a medical career, and Ceres because of the feasts.
12 referring to Orpheus.

least let these scenes detain your Muses / and recall whatever sluggish
intoxication drives away. / Believe me, while the ivory plays on and the
lyre / regales the perfumed halls with attendant festive dance, / you
will feel silent Apollo creep through your breast [45] / like a sudden
heat that permeates to the bones; / and through maiden eyes and sound-
ing finger / gliding Thalia[13] will invade all bosoms. / For gay Elegy is
the concern of many gods / and she calls those whom she wishes to her
measures; [50] / Liber gives attention to elegiac verse, and Erato,
Ceres, and Venus, / and with his rosy mother is delicate Love. / For
such poets thereafter great banquets are allowed / and often to become
soft with old wine. / But who records wars and heaven under mature
Jove, [55] / and pious heroes and half-divine leaders, / and now who
sings the sacred counsels of the supreme gods, / now the infernal realms
bayed by the fierce dog,[14] / let him live indeed frugally in the fashion /
of the Samian teacher,[15] and let herbage furnish his harmless food.
[60] / Let the clear water near at hand stand in its bowl of beech wood,
/ and let him drink nonintoxicating potions from the pure spring. / His
youth void of crime and chaste is joined to this / by stern morals and
without stain of hand. / With like nature, shining with sacred vestment
and lustral waters, [65] / does the priest rise to go to the hostile gods.
/ By this rule it is said wise Tiresias lived / after his eyes were put out,
and Ogygian Linus,[16] / and Calchas fugitive from his appointed house,
and old / Orpheus with the vanquished beasts among the forsaken
caves. [70] / Thus the one poor of feast, thus Homer, drinker of water,
/ carried the man of Ithaca through the vast seas / and through the
monster-making palace of the daughter[17] of Perseis and Apollo, / and
shallows dangerous with Siren songs, / and through your mansions, in-
fernal king, where by dark blood [75] / he is said to have engaged the
trooping shades. / For truly the poet is sacred to the gods, and priest of
the gods, / and his hidden heart and lips breathe Jove. / But if you will
know what I am doing (if only at least / you consider it to be important
to know whether I am doing anything) [80] / I am singing the King,
bringer of peace by his divine origin,[18] / and the blessed times promised

[13] Muse of comedy and bucolic poetry; Erato (l. 51) is the Muse of lyric and
amatory poetry. Liber, a god of vine-growers, was identified with Bacchus; but
he also was a spirit of creativeness.
[14] Cerberus, guardian of Hades.
[15] Pythagoras and his school practised asceticism, particularly in eating.
[16] The Theban Linus instructed Orpheus and Hercules on the lyre; Calchas
(l. 69) was the Greek seer at Troy.
[17] Circe.
[18] the *Nativity Ode*, written in English ("on my native pipes," l. 89) around
Christmas 1629.

in the sacred books, / and the crying of our God and his stabling under
the meagre roof, / who with his Father inhabits the heavenly realms; /
and the heavens insufficient of stars and the hosts singing in the air,
[85] / and the gods suddenly destroyed in their temples. / I dedicate
these gifts in truth to the birthday of Christ, / gifts which the first light
of dawn brought to me. / For you these thoughts formed on my native
pipes are also waiting; / you, when I recite them, will be the judge for
me of their worth. [90]

(*Dec. 1629*)

The Passion[1]

I

Ere-while of Musick, and Ethereal mirth,
Wherwith the stage of Ayr and Earth did ring,
And joyous news of heav'nly Infants birth,
My muse with Angels did divide[2] to sing;
But headlong joy is ever on the wing,   5
    In Wintry solstice like the short'n'd light
Soon swallow'd up in dark and long out-living night.

II

For now to sorrow must I tune my song,
And set my Harp to notes of saddest wo,
Which on our dearest Lord did sease e're long   10
Dangers, and snares, and wrongs, and worse then so,
Which he for us did freely undergo:
    Most perfect *Heroe*,[3] try'd in heaviest plight
Of labours huge and hard, too hard for human wight.

---

[1] Intended as a kind of sequel to the *Nativity Ode,* which is mentioned in the
first stanza, these verses seem to be only an induction to the main subject, Jesus'
suffering and crucifixion. An appended note indicates why the poem was not
completed: "This Subject the Author finding to be above the yeers he had, when
he wrote it, and nothing satisfi'd with what was begun, left it unfinisht."
[2] a musical term meaning to make musical divisions (measures); but perhaps
"divide into parts between them."
[3] Here Christ is paralleled with Hercules.

III

He sov'ran Priest stooping his regall head 15
That dropt with odorous oil down his fair eyes,[4]
Poor fleshly Tabernacle entered,
His starry front low-rooft beneath the skies;
O what a Mask[5] was there, what a disguise!
    Yet more; the stroke of death he must abide, 20
Then lies him meekly down fast by his Brethrens side.

IV

These latter scenes confine my roving vers,
To this Horizon is my *Phœbus*[6] bound;
His Godlike acts, and his temptations fierce,
And former sufferings other where are found; 25
Loud o're the rest *Cremona's* Trump[7] doth sound;
    Me softer airs befit, and softer strings
Of Lute, or Viol still, more apt for mournful things.

V

Befriend me night, best Patroness of grief,
Over the Pole thy thickest mantle throw, 30
And work my flatter'd fancy to belief,
That Heav'n and Earth are colour'd with my wo;
My sorrows are too dark for day to know:
    The leaves should all be black wheron I write,
And letters where my tears have washt a wannish white.[8] 35

VI

See, see the Chariot, and those rushing wheels
That whirl'd the Prophet[9] up at *Chebar* flood;
My spirit som transporting Cherub feels,
To bear me where the Towers of *Salem*[10] stood,

---

[4] "Christ being come an high priest of good things to come, by a greater and more perfect tabernacle" was by God "anointed with the oil of gladness above his fellows" (Heb. ix. 11, i. 9).

[5] the *persona* of the drama, used for the person of the Incarnation.

[6] Muse.

[7] the *Christiad*, an epic on the life of Christ by Marco Girolamo Vida, native of Cremona, which Milton praises over similar religious works.

[8] A Jacobean printing practice was the use of black title pages with white letters.

[9] Ezekiel (Ezek. i. 1–16).

[10] Jerusalem was the home of sacred poetry, for David, reputed author of the psalms, reigned there thirty-three years (2 Sam. v. 5).

Once glorious Towers, now sunk in guiltles blood;   40
There doth my soul in holy vision sit
In pensive trance, and anguish, and ecstatick fit.

VII

Mine eye hath found that sad Sepulchral rock
That was the Casket of Heav'ns richest store,
And here though grief my feeble hands up-lock,   45
Yet on the soft'n'd Quarry would I score
My plaining vers as lively as before;
    For sure so well instructed are my tears,
    That they would fitly fall in order'd Characters.

VIII

Or should I thence hurried on viewles wing,   50
Take up a weeping on the Mountains wild,[11]
The gentle neighbourhood of grove and spring
Would soon unboosom all thir Echoes mild,
And I (for grief is easily beguil'd)
    Might think th' infection of my sorrows loud   55
    Had got a race of mourners on som pregnant cloud.

(*Unfinished, Mar. 1630*)

[11] Jer. ix. 10: "For the mountains will I take up a weeping and wailing, and
for the habitations of the wilderness a lamentation."

Elegia septima

Nondum blanda tuas leges, Amathusia,[1] norâm,
    Et Paphio vacuum pectus ab igne fuit.
Sæpe cupidineas, puerilia tela, sagittas,
    Atque tuum sprevi maxime, numen, Amor.
Tu puer imbelles, dixi, transfige columbas,   5
    Conveniunt tenero mollia bella duci.
Aut de passeribus tumidos age, parve, triumphos,
    Hæc sunt militiæ digna trophæa tuæ.
In genus humanum quid inania dirigis arma?
    Non valet in fortes ista pharetra viros.   10

Non tulit hoc Cyprius (neque enim Deus ullus ad iras
   Promptior), et duplici jam ferus igne calet.
Ver erat, et summæ radians per culmina villæ
   Attulerat primam lux tibi, Maie, diem:
At mihi adhuc refugam quærebant lumina noctem   15
   Nec matutinum sustinuere jubar.
Astat Amor lecto, pictis Amor impiger alis,
   Prodidit astantem mota pharetra Deum:
Prodidit et facies, et dulce minantis ocelli,
   Et quicquid puero, dignum et Amore fuit.   20
Talis in æterno juvenis Sigeius[2] Olympo
   Miscet amatori pocula plena Jovi;
Aut qui formosas pellexit ad oscula nymphas
   Thiodamantæus Naiade raptus Hylas;[3]
Addideratque iras, sed et has decuisse putares,   25
   Addideratque truces, nec sine felle minas.
Et miser exemplo sapuisses tutiùs, inquit,
   Nunc mea quid possit dextera testis eris.
Inter et expertos vires numerabere nostras,
   Et faciam vero per tua damna fidem.   30
Ipse ego, si nescis, strato Pythone superbum
   Edomui Phœbum, cessit et ille mihi;[4]
Et quoties meminit Peneidos, ipse fatetur
   Certiùs et graviùs tela nocere mea.
Me nequit adductum curvare peritiùs arcum,   35
   Qui post terga solet vincere Parthus eques.[5]
Cydoniusque mihi cedit venator,[6] et ille
   Inscius uxori qui necis author[7] erat.
Est etiam nobis ingens quoque victus Orion,[8]
   Herculeæque manus, Herculeusque comes.[9]   40
Jupiter ipse licet sua fulmina torqueat in me,
   Hærebunt lateri spicula nostra Jovis.
Cætera quæ dubitas meliùs mea tela docebunt,
   Et tua non leviter corda petenda mihi.
Nec te, stulte, tuæ poterunt defendere Musæ,   45
   Nec tibi Phœbæus porriget anguis[10] opem.
Dixit, et aurato quatiens mucrone sagittam,
   Evolat in tepidos Cypridos ille sinus.
At mihi risuro tonuit ferus ore minaci,
   Et mihi de puero non metus ullus erat.   50
Et modò quà nostri spatiantur in urbe Quirites
   Et modò villarum proxima rura placent.
Turba frequens, faciéque simillima turba dearum
   Splendida per medias itque reditque vias.

Auctaque luce dies gemino fulgore coruscat.   55
    Fallor? an et radios hinc quoque Phœbus habet?
Hæc ego non fugi spectacula grata severus,
    Impetus et quò me fert juvenilis, agor.
Lumina luminibus malè providus obvia misi,
    Neve oculos potui continuisse meos.   60
Unam forte aliis supereminuisse notabam,
    Principium nostri lux erat illa mali.
Sic Venus optaret mortalibus ipsa videri,
    Sic regina Deûm[11] conspicienda fuit.
Hanc memor objecit nobis malus ille Cupido,   65
    Solus et hos nobis texuit antè dolos.
Nec procul ipse vafer latuit, multæque sagittæ,
    Et facis a tergo grande pependit onus.
Nec mora, nunc ciliis hæsit, nunc virginis ori,
    Insilit hinc labiis, insidet inde genis: 70
Et quascunque agilis partes jaculator oberrat,
    Hei mihi, mille locis pectus inerme ferit.
Protinus insoliti subierunt corda furores,
    Uror amans intùs, flammaque totus eram.
Interea misero quæ jam mihi sola placebat,   75
    Ablata est oculis non reditura meis.
Ast ego progredior tacitè querebundus, et excors,
    Et dubius volui sæpe referre pedem.
Findor, et hæc remanet, sequitur pars altera votum,
    Raptaque tàm subitò gaudia flere juvat.   80
Sic dolet amissum proles Junonia[12] cœlum,
    Inter Lemniacos præcipitata focos.
Talis et abreptum solem respexit, ad Orcum
    Vectus ab attonitis Amphiaraus[13] equis.
Quid faciam infelix, et luctu victus? Amores   85
    Nec licet inceptos ponere, neve sequi.
O utinam spectare semel mihi detur amatos
    Vultus, et coràm tristia verba loqui!
Forsitan et duro non est adamante creata,
    Forte nec ad nostras surdeat illa preces.   90
Crede mihi nullus sic infeliciter arsit,
    Ponar in exemplo primus et unus ego.
Parce, precor, teneri cum sis Deus ales amoris,
    Pugnent officio nec tua facta tuo.
Jam tuus O certè est mihi formidabilis arcus,   95
    Nate deâ, jaculis nec minus igne potens:
Et tua fumabunt nostris altaria donis,
    Solus et in superis tu mihi summus eris.

Deme meos tandem, verùm nec deme furores,
  Nescio cur, miser est suaviter omnis amans: 100
Tu modo da facilis, posthæc mea siqua futura est,
  Cuspis amaturos figat ut una duos.

Elegy 7

Not yet did I know your laws, enticing Amathusia,[1] / and my breast was
free from Paphian fire. / Often Cupid's arrows, childish weapons, / and
especially your divine will I contemned, O Love. / You, boy, I said,
pierce peace-loving doves; [5] / gentle battles are becoming to a tender
warrior, / or, over the sparrows, little one, achieve your arrogant tri-
umphs; / these are the suitable trophies of your warfare. / Why do you
aim your vain darts at mankind? / Against strong men that quiver of
yours has no power. [10] / This the Cyprian boy would not bear—and
indeed no god is swifter / to anger—and straightaway fierce he burned
with double fire. / Spring it was, and beaming through the heights of
the village roofs, / the light had brought to you your first day, O May. /
But my eyes still were seeking the vanishing night, [15] / nor could
they endure the morning radiance. / Love stood by my bed, Love the
indefatigable with painted wings; / the moving quiver betrayed the
standing god; / his face betrayed him, and his sweetly menacing little
eyes, / and whatever else was fitting to youth and to Love. [20] / In
like manner did the Sigean youth[2] on everlasting Olympus / mix the
overflowing cups for amorous Jove, / or rather Hylas,[3] who lured the
lovely nymphs to his kisses, / son of Theomadas, carried off by a Naiad.
/ And his anger grew, but you would have thought it to be proper [25]
/ and his harsh threats increased, not without gall. / "Wretch, you might
more safely have learned from example," he said; / "now you shall be
a witness to what my right hand can do. / And you shall be counted
among the men who have experienced my powers, / and as a result of
your penalty, truly, I shall achieve your faithfulness. [30] / I myself, if
you do not know, overcame Apollo, / and he yielded to me, proud from
subduing Python,[4] / and, as often as he remembers Daphne, he ac-

[1] Venus.
[2] the beautiful youth Ganymede.
[3] He was drawn into a spring by the water nymphs who were enamored of
his beauty.
[4] When he killed the dragon of Delphi, Apollo boasted his archery greater
than Cupid's, and so was smitten with unrequited love for Daphne.

knowledges / that my arrows harm more surely and more gravely. / The Parthian horseman who is wont to conquer behind his back[5] [35] / cannot draw his taut bow more skillfully than I. / And the Cydonian hunter[6] yields to me, and he / who was the unwitting author[7] of his wife's death. / Likewise was prodigious Orion[8] also vanquished by me, / and the powers of Hercules, and the companion of Hercules.[9] [40] / Even if Jove himself hurls his bolts at me / my darts shall hold fast to the side of Jove. / Whatever else you doubt my arrows shall more surely instruct / and your own heart will not be lightly assaulted by me. / Neither will your Muses be able to protect you, fool, [45] / nor will the serpent of Apollo's son[10] extend help to you." / He spoke, and, shaking an arrow with a golden point, / he flew to the warm bosom of Cypris. / But to me the fierce lad thundered with threatening face laughably, / and to me there was nothing to fear from the boy. [50] / And sometimes places in the city where our inhabitants walk / and sometimes the nearby fields of the villages are pleasing. / A great shining throng resembling the visages of goddesses / come and go through the trodden ways. / And with their added light the day gleams with double splendor. [55] / Am I deceived? or is it from them that Apollo also obtains his rays? / I did not austerely shun these pleasurable sights, / but was guided where the impulse of youth led me. / I sent my glances to meet their looks, / poorly cautious, nor could I have restrained my eyes. [60] / By chance I remarked one surpassing all others; / her radiance was the beginning of my misfortune. / Thus Venus herself might choose to appear to mortals, / thus was the queen of the gods[11] worthy of attention. / That wicked Cupid, remembering, cast her before me, [65] / and he alone has woven these snares in my path. / Not far off the cunning one himself was hiding with his many arrows, / and the burden of his mighty torch weighed down his back. / Without delay, he now was fixed on the eyelids, now on the mouth of the maid. / Then he sprang upon her lips, thereupon he lighted on her cheek, [70] / and wherever the agile dart-thrower flits in his office— / alas for me! he strikes my defenseless breast

---

[5] The successful Parthian method of fighting was to turn one's horse as if in flight after each arrow was discharged.

[6] Cydon in southern Crete was noted for its archers.

[7] Cephalus, who accidentally killed Procris.

[8] The hunter Orion's pursuit of the Pleiades caused them and him to be turned into constellations.

[9] perhaps Theseus, whose marriages to Ariadne, Hippolyta, and Phaedra ended unhappily. Theseus was well known as the only one who stood by Hercules after he had killed his wife and children.

[10] The attribute of Aesculapius was the snake, a symbol of rejuvenescence and thus of healing.

[11] Juno.

in a thousand places. / Forthwith unaccustomed passions assailed my heart; / I burned with love inwardly, and was all in flame. / Meanwhile she who alone now was delighting me with misery [75] / was borne off, never to return to my eyes. / But I went forth silently complaining, and without understanding / and uncertain I often wished to retrace my step. / I am torn apart; part stays behind, the other follows my desire, / and I was happy to weep for pleasures so suddenly snatched away. [80] / Thus lamented Juno's child[12] for his lost heaven, / cast down among the hearths of Lemnos, / and such was Amphiaraus,[13] carried off to Hell by his terrified horses, / when he looked back on the vanished sun. / What should I do, unhappy and by sorrow overcome? Incipient love [85] / one is not permitted to dismiss or to pursue. / O if only it were granted me once to look upon her beloved / features, and to relate my sad words in her presence! / Perhaps she is not made of hard adamant, / perhaps she would not be deaf to my prayers. [90] / Believe me, no one burned so unhappily with love; / I may be considered the foremost and only example. / Spare me, I pray, since you are the winged god of gentle love; / do not let your deeds contend with your duty. / Now O child of the goddess, your fearful bow [95] / is assuredly to me no less powerful than fire / and your altars will smoke with my gifts. / To me you will be the only one and the greatest one among the supreme gods. / Take away, at least, my passions, yet do not take them; / I do not know why, every lover is sweetly wretched. [100] / Only grant, courteous one, if hereafter any maiden is to be mine, / that a single point shall transfix the two in love.

(May 1630)

12 Vulcan.
13 A seer, Amphiaraus foreknew his death in the conflict with the Seven against Thebes.

(Lines appended to Elegia septima)[1]

Hæc ego mente olim lævâ, studioque supino
   Nequitiæ posui vana trophæa meæ.
Scilicet abreptum sic me malus impulit error,
   Indocilisque ætas prava magistra fuit.
Donec Socraticos umbrosa Academia rivos   5
   Præbuit, admissum dedocuitque jugum.

Protinus extinctis ex illo tempore flammis,
  Cincta rigent multo pectora nostra gelu.
Unde suis frigus metuit puer ipse Sagittis,
  Et Diomedéam[2] vim timet ipsa Venus.   10

(*Lines appended to* Elegy 7)[1]

I with foolish mind and heedless zeal formerly / erected these idle monuments to my wantonness. / Undoubtedly mischievous error impelled me, thus carried off, / and my ignorant youth was a perverse teacher, / until the shady Academy proffered its Socratic streams [5] / and untaught the admitted yoke. / Directly, with the flames from that time extinct, / my encircled breast congealed with ice, / from which the boy himself dreaded frigidity for his arrows, / and Venus herself is afraid of my Diomedean[2] strength. [10]

(*1630 ?*)

[1] The study of Plato and his Academy moved Milton to disavow, probably not seriously, the affectation of some of his early verse. The "monuments to my wantonness" are therefore perhaps the various poems in Latin and English dealing with awakening amorousness, although usually only *El. 7* is suggested.
[2] The Greek warrior Diomedes wounded Venus during the Trojan War after she tried to protect Aeneas (*Iliad*, V, 334–46).

Song: On May *Morning*[1]

Now the bright morning Star, Dayes harbinger,
Comes dancing from the East, and leads with her
The Flowry *May*, who from her green lap throws
The yellow Cowslip, and the pale Primrose.
  Hail bounteous *May* that dost inspire   5
  Mirth and youth, and warm desire,

[1] The song itself, ll. 5–8, is in the meter of *Epitaph on the Marchioness*, *L'Allegro*, and *Il Penseroso*.

Woods and Groves are of thy dressing,
Hill and Dale doth boast thy blessing.
Thus we salute thee with our early Song,
And welcom thee, and wish thee long.   10

(*May 1630 ?*)

Sonnet 1[1]

O Nightingale, that on yon bloomy Spray
  Warbl'st at eeve, when all the Woods are still,[2]
  Thou with fresh hope the Lovers heart dost fill,
  While the jolly hours lead on propitious *May;*
Thy liquid notes that close the eye of Day,   5
  First heard before the shallow Cuccoo's bill
  Portend success in love; O if *Jove's* will
  Have linkt that amorous power to thy soft lay,
Now timely sing, ere the rude Bird of Hate
  Foretell my hopeles doom in som Grove nigh: 10
  As thou from yeer to yeer hast sung too late
For my relief; yet hadst no reason why.
  Whether the Muse, or Love call thee his mate,
  Both them I serve, and of their train am I.

(*May 1630 ?*)

[1] In the immediate background is the lyric *The Cuckoo and the Nightingale,*
probably by Thomas Clanvowe though attributed to Chaucer in Milton's day.
  [2] Compare *El.* 5, 25–26.

Sonnet 2

Donna leggiadra, il cui bel nome honora
L'herbosa val di Rheno, e il nobil varco,[1]
Ben è colui d'ogni valore scarco
Qual tuo spirto gentil non innamora,

Che dolcemente mostrasi di fuora   5
  De' suoi atti soavi giamai parco,
  E i don', che son d'amor saette ed arco,
  Là onde l'alta tua virtù s'infiora.
Quando tu vaga parli, o lieta canti
  Che mover possa duro alpestre legno,   10
  Guardi ciascun a gli occhi, ed a gli orecchi
L'entrata, chi di te si truova indegno;
  Gratia sola di sù gli vaglia, inanti
  Che'l disio amoroso al cuor s'invecchi.

Sonnet 2

Charming lady, she whose beautiful name honors / the verdant valley
of Reno, and the illustrious ford,[1] / justly is he of every worth discharged
/ whom your noble soul does not inspire with love, / for it sweetly shows
itself from without, [5] / in its gentle acts never sparing, / and the gifts
which are the arrows and bow of Love, / there where your high virtue
flowers. / When you so sweetly speak or gaily sing / that its power stirs
the obdurate alpine wood, [10] / let everyone who finds himself un-
worthy of you / guard the entrance to the eyes and to the ears; / grace
alone from above enables him to withstand / the amorous desire which
would lodge itself in his heart.

(1630 ?)

  [1] As Smart showed, the lady is one Aemilia, the name of the Italian province
through which flow the Reno and the Rubicon with its famous ford. Her family
name and relationship to Milton remain unknown.

Sonnet 3

Qual in colle aspro, al' imbrunir di sera,
  L'avezza giovinetta pastorella
  Va bagnando l'herbetta strana e bella
  Che mal si spande a disusata spera,

Fuor di sua natía alma primavera,   5
  Così Amor meco insù la lingua snella
Desta il fior novo di strania favella,
Mentre io di te, vezzosamente altera,
Canto, dal mio buon popol non inteso,
E'l bel Tamigi cangio col bel Arno.[1]   10
Amor lo volse, ed io a l'altrui peso
Seppi ch'Amor cosa mai volse indarno.
  Deh! foss'il mio cuor lento e'l duro seno
  A chi pianta dal ciel si buon terreno.

Sonnet 3

As on a rugged mountain at the darkening of evening, / the accustomed youthful shepherdess / goes watering the alien and beautiful little plant / that hardly spreads forth in that strange clime, / away from its native, nourishing spring, [5] / so Love on my alert tongue / awakens the new flower of foreign speech / while I sing of you, gracefully noble lady, / by my good countrymen not understood, / and the fair Thames change with the fair Arno.[1] [10] / Love willed it, and I at the expense of others / know that Love never willed anything in vain. / Oh! were my sluggish heart and hard breast / as good soil for him who plants from heaven.

(1630 ?)

[1] that is, exchange English for Italian. The Arno flows through the province of Tuscany, whose dialect had become standard Italian.

Canzone[1]

Ridonsi donne e giovani amorosi
M'accostandosi attorno, e perche scrivi,
Perche tu scrivi in lingua ignota e strana
Verseggiando d'amor, e come t'osi?
Dinne, se la tua speme sia mai vana,   5
E de' pensieri lo miglior t'arrivi;
Così mi van burlando, altri rivi,

Altri lidi t'aspettan, ed altre onde
Nelle cui verdi sponde
Spuntati ad hor, ad hor a la tua chioma   10
L'immortal guiderdon d'eterne frondi.
Perche alle spalle tue soverchia soma?
 Canzon, dirotti, e tu per me rispondi.
Dice mia Donna, e'l suo dir è il mio cuore,
Questa è lingua di cui si vanta Amore.   15

Canzone[1]

Scoffing, amorous maidens and young men / mill about me, so, "Why write, / why do you write in a language unknown and strange / versifying of love, and how do you dare? / Speak, if your hope is never to be vain, [5] / and of your designs the best is to come to you"; / thus they go ridiculing me, "Other rivers, / other shores await you, and other seas, / on whose green banks / is bursting forth at any hour for your crown [10] / the immortal guerdon of eternal leaves. / Why on your shoulders the excessive burden?" /

 Canzone, I will tell you, and you for me will reply. / My lady says, and her word is my heart, / "This is the language of which Love boasts." [15]

(1630 ?)

[1] a fully rhymed stanza repeated several times, followed by a shorter concluding stanza called the *commiato;* obviously, Milton has used the term loosely.

Sonnet 4

Diodati, e te'l dirò con maraviglia,
 Quel ritroso io, ch'amor spreggiar soléa
 E de' suoi lacci spesso mi ridéa
 Già caddi, ov'huom dabben talhor s'impiglia.

Nè treccie d'oro, nè guancia vermiglia   5
  M'abbaglian sì, ma sotto nova idea
  Pellegrina bellezza che'l cuor bea,
  Portamenti alti honesti, e nelle ciglia
Quel sereno fulgor d'amabil nero,
  Parole adorne di lingua più d'una,   10
  E'l cantar che di mezzo l'hemispero
Traviar ben può la faticosa Luna,
  E degli occhi suoi avventa sì gran fuoco
  Che l'incerar gli orecchi mi fia poco.[1]

Sonnet 4

Diodati, and I will say it to you with wonder, / that stubborn I, who used to contemn love / and frequently scoffed at his snares, / now have fallen where upright man sometimes entangles himself. / No tresses of gold nor vermeil cheeks [5] / deceive me thus, but under a new-found fancy / foreign beauty which blesses my heart, / a look highly virtuous, and in her eyes / that tranquil brightness of amiable black, / speech adorned with more than one language, [10] / and the song that could well mislead the laboring moon / from its course in middle sky, / and from her eyes shoots such great fire / that enwaxing my ears would be little help to me.[1]

(1630 ?)

[1] Milton thought of the Sirens' singing to Ulysses, whose men's ears were sealed to avoid enticement (*Od.*, XII, 39–58).

Sonnet 5

Per certo i bei vostr'occhi, Donna mia,
  Esser non può che non sian lo mio sole
  Sì mi percuoton forte, come ei suole
  Per l'arene di Libia chi s'invia,

Mentre un caldo vapor (nè senti' pria)   5
 Da quel lato si spinge ove mi duole,
 Che forse amanti nelle lor parole
 Chiaman sospir; io non so che si sia:
Parte rinchiusa, e turbida si cela
 Scossomi il petto, e poi n'uscendo poco,   10
 Quivi d'attorno o s'agghiaccia, o s'ingiela;
Ma quanto a gli occhi giunge a trovar loco
 Tutte le notti a me suol far piovose
 Finchè mia Alba rivien colma di rose.

Sonnet 5

In truth your fair eyes, my lady, / could not but be my sun; / they powerfully strike me as the sun him / who dispatches his way through the sands of Libya, / while a fervent steam (not felt before) [5] / from that side proceeds where is my grief, / that perhaps lovers in their words / call a sigh; I know not what it may be: / the hidden part, and turbid thus concealed, / has shaken my breast, and then a bit escaping, [10] / there from being enclosed has either frozen or congealed; / but as much as reaches my eyes to find its place / makes all the nights rainy to me alone / until my dawn returns overflowing with roses.

(*1630 ?*)

Sonnet 6

Giovane piano, e semplicetto amante
 Poi che fuggir me stesso in dubbio sono,
 Madonna, a voi del mio cuor l'humil dono
 Farò divoto; io certo a prove tante
L'hebbi fedele, intrepido, costante,   5
 Di pensieri leggiadro, accorto, e buono;
 Quando rugge il gran mondo, e scocca il tuono,
 S'arma di se, e d'intero diamante,

Tanto del forse, e d'invidia sicuro,
  Di timori, e speranze al popol use,   10
  Quanto d'ingegno, e d'alto valor vago,
E di cetra sonora, e delle muse:
  Sol troverete in tal parte men duro
  Ove Amor mise l'insanabil ago.

Sonnet 6

Young, gentle, and candid lover that I am, / since to fly my self I am in
doubt, / my lady, to you the humble gift of my heart / I shall render
devotedly; I, assured by many trials, / have found it faithful, courageous,
constant, [5] / in thoughts gracious, prudent, and good; / when the wide
world roars and the thunder strikes, / it arms itself from itself, and ada-
mantly from within, / safe to such a degree from the chance and envy, /
from the fears and hopes of common men [10] / as its store of indeter-
minate talent and high courage / and of the sounding lyre and the Muses:
/ only will you discover it in like portion less unyielding / where Love has
sent his incurable dart.

(*1630 ?*)

On Shakespear[1]

What needs my *Shakespear* for his honour'd Bones,
The labour of an age in piled Stones,
Or that his hallow'd reliques should be hid
Under a Star-ypointing[2] *Pyramid?*
Dear son of memory,[3] great heir of Fame,   5
What need'st thou such weak witnes of thy name?
Thou in our wonder and astonishment

[1] first printed in the Second Folio of Shakespeare's plays (1632).
[2] The archaic prefix was correctly used only for the past participle.
[3] Aside from his constancy in our memories, Shakespeare is made a brother
of the Muses, the daughters of Mnemosyne.

Hast built thy self a live-long Monument.[4]
For whilst to th' shame of slow-endeavouring art,
Thy easie numbers flow, and that each heart   10
Hath from the leaves of thy unvalu'd[5] Book
Those Delphick[6] lines with deep impression took,
Then thou our fancy of it self bereaving,
Dost make us Marble with too much conceaving;[7]
And so Sepulcher'd in such pomp dost lie,   15
That Kings for such a Tomb would wish to die.

verse

*The book
is a monument.*

(*1630*)

[4] Compare "I have built me a monument more lasting than bronze, / A pyramid higher than a kingly tomb" (Horace, *Odes*, III, xxx, 1–2).
[5] priceless.
[6] inspired by Apollo, patron of poetry, whose abode was Delphi.
[7] Shakespeare's readers are an everlasting monument to his greatness with his lines engraved on their hearts.

Naturam non pati senium[1]

Heu quàm perpetuis erroribus acta fatiscit
Avia mens hominum, tenebrisque immersa profundis
Œdipodioniam volvit sub pectore noctem![2]
Quæ vesana suis metiri facta deorum
Audet, et incisas leges adamante perenni   5
Assimilare suis, nulloque solubile sæclo
Consilium fati perituris alligat horis.
  Ergóne marcescet sulcantibus obsita rugis
Naturæ facies, et rerum publica mater[3]
Omniparum contracta uterum sterilescet ab ævo?   10
Et se fassa senem malè certis passibus ibit
Sidereum tremebunda caput? num tetra vetustas
Annorumque æterna fames, squalorque situsque
Sidera vexabunt? an et insatiabile Tempus
Esuriet Cælum, rapietque in viscera patrem?   15
Heu, potuitne suas imprudens Jupiter arces
Hoc contra munisse nefas, et Temporis isto
Exemisse malo, gyrosque dedisse perennes?
Ergo erit ut quandoque sono dilapsa tremendo
Convexi tabulata ruant, atque obvius ictu   20

Stridat uterque polus, superâque ut Olympius aulâ
Decidat, horribilisque retectâ Gorgone Pallas.[4]
Qualis in Ægæam proles Junonia[5] Lemnon
Deturbata sacro cecidit de limine cæli.
Tu quoque, Phœbe, tui casus imitabere nati[6]   25
Præcipiti curru, subitáque ferere ruinâ
Pronus, et extinctâ fumabit lampade Nereus,[7]
Et dabit attonito feralia sibila ponto.
Tunc etiam aërei divulsis sedibus Hæmi[8]
Dissultabit apex, imoque allisa barathro   30
Terrebunt Stygium dejecta Ceraunia Ditem
In superos quibus usus erat, fraternaque bella.
 At Pater omnipotens fundatis fortius astris
Consuluit rerum summæ, certoque peregit
Pondere fatorum lances, atque ordine summo   35
Singula perpetuum jussit servare tenorem.
Volvitur hinc lapsu mundi rota prima[9] diurno;
Raptat et ambitos sociâ vertigine cælos.
Tardior haud solito Saturnus, et acer ut olim
Fulmineùm rutilat cristatâ casside Mavors.   40
Floridus æternùm Phœbus juvenile coruscat,
Nec fovet effœtas loca per declivia terras
Devexo temone Deus; sed semper amicá
Luce potens eadem currit per signa rotarum.
Surgit[10] odoratis pariter formosus ab Indis   45
Æthereum pecus albenti qui cogit Olympo
Mane vocans, et serus agens in pascua cæli,
Temporis et gemino dispertit regna colore.
Fulget, obitque vices alterno Delia[11] cornu,
Cæruleumque ignem paribus complectitur ulnis.   50
Nec variant elementa fidem, solitóque fragore
Lurida perculsas jaculantur fulmina rupes.
Nec per inane furit leviori murmure Corus,[12]
Stringit et armiferos æquali horrore Gelonos[14]
Trux Aquilo,[13] spiratque hyemem, nimbosque volutat.   55
Utque solet, Siculi diverberat ima Pelori
Rex maris,[15] et raucâ circumstrepit æquora conchâ
Oceani Tubicen,[16] nec vastâ mole minorem
Ægæona[17] ferunt dorso Balearica cete.
Sed neque, Terra, tibi sæcli vigor ille vetusti   60
Priscus abest, servatque suum Narcissus[18] odorem;
Et puer ille suum tenet et puer ille decorem,
Phœbe tuusque et Cypri tuus,[19] nec ditior olim
Terra datum sceleri celavit montibus aurum

Conscia, vel sub aquis gemmas. Sic denique in ævum   65
Ibit cunctarum series justissima rerum,
Donec flamma orbem populabitur ultima, latè
Circumplexa polos, et vasti culmina cæli;
Ingentique rogo flagrabit machina mundi.[20]

Nature does not suffer decay[1]

Alas how the wandering mind of man grows weak, driven / by persistent errors, and immersed in profound darkness / it breathes Oedipean night beneath his breast![2] / Unsound it dares measure the deeds of the gods / by its own, and to laws engraved on eternal adamant [5] / compare its own, and the forever immutable / plan of fate it binds to the passing hours. /

Therefore shall the face of Nature wither, covered over with the wrinkles / of ploughings, and the common mother of things,[3] / contracted of her all-bearing womb, become sterile from old age? [10] / And herself acknowledged old, shall she move with erroneously / certain steps, her starry head trembling? Shall foul old age / and the endless greed of years, and squalor and mold / plague the heavens? Or shall insatiable time / devour heaven and ravage his father's very organs? [15] / Alas, could not unforeseeing Jupiter fortify / his citadels against this execration, and banish / such an evil of time, and yield eternal circuits? / Therefore it shall come to pass that at some time, collapsing with / a

---

[1] That nature does not decay was the philosophic conclusion of both George Hakewell in *An Apologie or Declaration of the Power and Providence of God in the Government of the World* (1627) and other "optimists," as Tillyard calls them (*Elizabethan World Picture*, N.Y., 1944, p. 33). Fink (*Classical Republicans*, pp. 91–122) sees evidence that Milton came to accept the theory of deterioration by 1642, but Joseph A. Bryant, Jr. (*SAMLA Studies in Milton*, pp. 1–19), argues that he maintained the position taken here without even occasional misgiving. Though commonplace, the concept is due to Milton's faith in God: since these things come from God, providence is immutable, matter incorruptible, and nature undegenerate. Hanford, in "Youth of Milton," p. 17, calls this early position "significant in its consistency both with his humanistic inheritance and with his later attitude in theology, politics, and education."

The poem has frequently been identified as the verses which were "ghostwritten" for a Fellow of the college and alluded to as printed in a letter to Alexander Gill, dated July 2, 1628.

[2] Man, like Sophocles' Oedipus, is blind of his own doing; he presumes against God and his laws by seeing them in relation to his own imperfect concepts.

[3] Earth.

tremendous noise, the vaulted floors of heaven will crash down and even
[20] / each exposed pole will rattle with the collision, and Olympian
Jove / will fall from his celestial court, and fearful Athena with her
Gorgon / shield revealed,[4] as for example the child of Juno[5] on Aegean
Lemnos / fell, cast from the sacred threshold of heaven. / You also,
Phoebus, shall copy the misfortune of your son[6] [25] / in your head-
long chariot, and shall be carried in sudden ruin / downward, and
Nereus[7] shall steam at your extinguished light / and issue funereal hisses
from the astonished deep. / Then furthermore the destruction of the
foundations of Haemus[8] / will burst from its summit asunder, and in-
deed, dashed to the lowest depths, [30] / the Ceraunian mountains,
which he had used against the upper regions / in fraternal wars, cast
down, will terrify Stygian Dis. /

But the omnipotent Father, with the stars fixed more steadfastly, /
has taken care of the greatest of things, and with certainty / has trans-
fixed in balance the scales of the fates, and even [35] / commanded each
individual thing in the great order to preserve / its uninterrupted course
perpetually. / Therefore the Prime Wheel[9] of the world turns in its daily
flight / and hastens with kindred whirling motion the encircled heavens.
/ Saturn, as is his wont, is by no means impeded, and as violent as for-
merly, / Mars flashes red lightning from his crested helmet. [40] / Bright
Phoebus gleams forever youthful, / nor does the God warm the ex-
hausted lands throughout the sloping regions / with his down-slanting
chariot; but always strong in his friendly / light he runs onward the same
through the signs of the spheres. / He[10] rises equally beautiful from
the fragrant Indies, [45] / who drives at dawn the heavenly flock from
the sky, / calling the morning, and driving them at evening into the pas-
tures of heaven, / and who divides the kingdoms of time with its twin
hues. / Delia[11] waxes and wanes by turns with alternating horn, / and
she embraces the blue flame which is the sky with constant arms. [50] /
Nor do the elements vary in faithfulness, and with accustomed crash /
the lurid lightning-bolts strike the shattered rocks. / Nor through the

[4] Perseus beheaded the Gorgon Medusa, who turned all who looked upon
her to stone. Pallas Athena placed the head in her shield as a protective figure.
[5] Vulcan.
[6] Phaeton, hurled into the river Eridanus for endangering earth when he
drove the chariot of the sun.
[7] the Old Man of the sea.
[8] a mountain in Thrace. The Ceraunian Mountains (l. 31) were in Epirus.
[9] See Fair Infant, n. 7.
[10] Venus, known as Lucifer when the morning star and as Hesperus when the
evening star.
[11] the moon.

void does Corus[12] rage with milder roar, / and harsh Aquilo[13] draws
the armed Gelonians[14] together / with similar chill, and breathes winter,
and blows the clouds along. [55] / And even the king of the sea,[15] as
is his custom, cleaves the depths / of Sicilian Peloros, and the trum-
peter[16] of Oceanus / clamors his grating conch through the level sea,
/ nor an Aegaeon[17] of less vast bulk / do the Balearic whales carry on
their back. / On the contrary, Earth, the ancient vigor of that former age
[60] / is not removed from you; and Narcissus[18] retains his fragrance;
/ that youth still possesses his beauty, and that lad / of yours, Apollo,
and yours too, Cypris,[19] nor in former times / did knowing Earth more
abundantly conceal the golden gift of mountains, / which leads to crime,
not even the gems beneath the seas. Thus, in short, [65] / into eternity
the most just sequence of all things shall proceed, / until the final flame
shall devastate the world, far and wide / encompassing the poles and
the summits of the deserted sky; / and the frame of the universe shall
burn up in a vast funeral pyre.[20]

(*June 1631 ?*)

---

[12] the northwest wind.

[13] the northeast wind.

[14] a tribe of Scythia.

[15] Neptune, whose waves beat upon Pelorus, the northeastern promontory
of Sicily.

[16] the merman Triton.

[17] a giant with a hundred arms. The Balearic Islands lie in the western Medi-
terranean Sea off Spain.

[18] Narcissus was changed into a flower when he died for love of his own
reflection.

[19] For Hyacinthus (beloved of Apollo), see *Fair Infant*, 25–27; for Adonis
(beloved of Venus), see *El.* 1, n. 7.

[20] This was also the prediction of Hakewell. Compare 2 Peter iii. 10: "the
day of the Lord will come . . . in the which the heavens shall pass away with
a great noise, and the elements shall melt with fervent heat, the earth also and
the works that are therein shall be burned up." See *PL* XII, 547–51.

De Idea Platonica quemadmodum Aristoteles intellexit[1]

Dicite, sacrorum præsides nemorum deæ,[2]
Tuque O noveni perbeata numinis
Memoria mater, quæque in immenso procul
Antro recumbis otiosa Æternitas,

Monumenta servans, et ratas leges Jovis,   5
Cælique fastos atque ephemeridas Deûm,
Quis ille primus cujus ex imagine
Natura sollers finxit humanum genus,
Æternus, incorruptus, æquævus polo,
Unusque et universus, exemplar Dei?   10
Haud ille Palladis gemellus innubæ
Interna proles insidet menti Jovis;[3]
Sed quamlibet natura sit communior,
Tamen seorsùs extat ad morem unius,
Et, mira, certo stringitur spatio loci;   15
Seu sempiternus ille syderum comes
Cæli pererrat ordines decemplicis,[4]
Citimúmve terris incolit Lunæ globum:
Sive inter animas corpus adituras sedens
Obliviosas torpet ad Lethes aquas:[5]   20
Sive in remotâ forte terrarum plagâ
Incedit ingens hominis archetypus gigas,
Et diis tremendus erigit celsum caput
Atlante major portitore syderum.[6]
Non cui profundum cæcitas lumen dedit   25
Dircæus augur[7] vidit hunc alto sinu;
Non hunc silenti nocte Plëiones nepos[8]
Vatum sagaci præpes ostendit choro;
Non hunc sacerdos novit Assyrius, licet
Longos vetusti commemoret atavos Nini,[9]   30
Priscumque Belon, inclytumque Osiridem.
Non ille trino gloriosus nomine
Ter magnus Hermes[10] (ut sit arcani sciens)
Talem reliquit Isidis cultoribus.
At tu perenne ruris Academi[11] decus   35
(Hæc monstra si tu primus induxti scholis)
Jam jam pöetas urbis exules tuæ
Revocabis, ipse fabulator maximus,
Aut institutor ipse migrabis foras.

On the Platonic Idea as Aristotle understood it[1]

Say, goddesses, guardians of the sacred groves,[2] / and you O Memory, most fortunate mother / of the ninefold deity, and you Eternity, / who recline at leisure in a boundless cave far away, / keeping watch over the records and unalterable laws of Jove, [5] / and the calendars of heaven as well as the daybooks of the gods, / say who was that first man from whose likeness / skillful Nature fashioned the human race, / eternal, incorruptible, coeval with the heavens, / and unique yet universal, the image of God? [10] / Certainly he is not seated, an internal offspring, / the twin of the virgin Athena, in the mind of Jove;[3] / but although his nature be commonplace, / yet he exists separate unto himself by habit, / and, strange it is, is confined by regions in fixed space; [15] / or, the comrade of the imperishable stars, / he roams through the tenfold spheres[4] of the sky, / or inhabits the nearest to the earth, the moon: / or perhaps he is motionless, sitting by the waters of Lethe / among the oblivious souls waiting to enter a body:[5] [20] / or perhaps in a far-off region of the world / the archetype of man casually advances, a prodigious giant, / and, terrifying creature, to the gods raises his lofty head / higher than Atlas, the bearer of the stars.[6] / The Dircean seer,[7] to whom blindness yielded a profound light, [25] / did not discern him in his deep hiding-place; / the swift grandson of Pleione[8] in the silent night did not / behold him in the wise company of prophets; / the Assyrian priest had no knowledge of him, although / he was mindful of the long ancestry of aged Ninus[9] [30] / and primitive Belus, and renowned

---

[1] Milton satirizes Aristotle's criticism of Plato's archetypal man in *Metaphysics* by raising unimaginative and insensible objections such as a matter-of-fact Aristotelian might do. It is evident, however, that he favors Plato's theory of ideas (or archetypes), of which existing things are but imperfect copies. Compare the second prolusion, "On the Harmony of the Spheres."

[2] the nine Muses whose mother was Mnemosyne (Memory).

[3] Pallas Athena sprang full-grown from the head of Jove.

[4] in the Ptolemaic system, the ten revolving spherical transparent shells, with earth as center, in which the heavenly bodies were set.

[5] Plato often referred to transmigration of souls (e.g., *Phaedo*, 70–72); the waters of Lethe were drunk to induce forgetfulness before reincarnation.

[6] As punishment, Atlas held up the heavens with his head and hands.

[7] Tiresias.

[8] Hermes, god of dreams.

[9] Ninus was reputedly the founder of Assyria; Belus and Osiris were principal deities of Assyria and Egypt, respectively. Isis (l. 34) was the sister and wife of Osiris.

Osiris. / Even thrice-great Hermes,[10] that one glorious for his triple name / (granting his esoteric knowledge), / did not bequeath the like to the worshippers of Isis. / But you, eternal glory of the Academy of the fields[11] [35] / (if you first introduced these marvels into schools), / now will recall the poets, exiles of your city, / since you yourself are the greatest fabler, / or else, creator, you shall quit that state yourself.

(June 1631 ?)

[10] the Egyptian god Thoth, identified with Hermes by the Neoplatonists. Milton uses a variant of this third name, Hermes Trismegistus. He was supposedly author of magical, astrological, and alchemical works.

[11] Plato, whose Academy was in a grove near Athens. One of his reflections was that poets must be exiled from the ideal state because they corrupt men's natures by encouragement of the lower elements of the soul at the expense of the higher (*Rep.*, III, 395–98; X, 595–607).

On the University Carrier who sick'n'd in the time of his vacancy, being forbid to go to London, *by reason of the Plague*[1]

Here lies old *Hobson,* Death hath broke his girt,
And here alas, hath laid him in the dirt,
Or els the ways being foul, twenty to one,
He's here stuck in a slough, and overthrown.
'Twas such a shifter, that if truth were known,   5
Death was half glad when he had got him down;
For he had any time this ten yeers full,
Dodg'd with him, betwixt *Cambridge* and the Bull.
And surely, Death could never have prevail'd,
Had not his weekly cours of carriage fail'd;   10
But lately finding him so long at home,
And thinking now his journeys end was come,
And that he had tane up his latest Inn,
In the kind office of a Chamberlin[2]

[1] Thomas Hobson, a coachman whose circuit lay between Cambridge and the Bull Inn in Bishopsgate Street, London, died at eighty-seven on Jan. 1, 1631, after being forced by the plague to discontinue his weekly trips. "Hobson's choice," a choice without an alternative, refers to his practice of requiring a customer seeking a horse to take the one nearest the door or none at all.

[2] Death is represented as an attendant ushering Hobson to his room in the inn where he will perpetually sleep.

Shew'd him his room where he must lodge that night,   15
Pull'd off his Boots, and took away the light:
If any ask for him, it shall be sed,
Hobson has supt, and's newly gon to bed.

(*early 1631*)

Another on the same

Here lieth one who did most truly prove
That he could never die while he could move,
So hung his destiny never to rot
While he might still jogg on, and keep his trot,
Made of sphear-metal,[1] never to decay   5
Untill his revolution was at stay.
Time numbers[2] motion, yet (without a crime
'Gainst old truth) motion number'd out his time;
And like an Engin mov'd with wheel and waight,
His principles being ceast, he ended strait.   10
Rest that gives all men life, gave him his death,
And too much breathing put him out of breath;
Nor were it contradiction to affirm
Too long vacation hast'n'd on his term.
Meerly to drive the time away he sick'n'd,   15
Fainted, and di'd, nor would with Ale be quick'n'd;
Nay, quoth he, on his swooning bed outstretch'd,
If I may not carry, sure Ile ne're be fetch'd,
But vow though the cross Doctors all stood hearers,
For one Carrier put down to make six bearers.   20
Ease was his chief disease, and to judge right,
He di'd for heavines that his Cart went light.
His leasure told him that his time was com,
And lack of load made his life burdensom,
That even to his last breath (ther be that say't)   25
As he were prest to death, he cry'd more waight;[3]
But had his doings lasted as they were,

[1] the indestructible material of which heavenly bodies are made.
[2] measures.
[3] that is, to hasten death and end his misery. The pun with the lightness of his cart is typical of the witty opposites on which the humor of the poem is built.

He had bin an immortall Carrier.
Obedient to the Moon he spent his date
In cours reciprocal, and had his fate 30
Linkt to the mutual flowing of the Seas,
Yet (strange to think) his wain[4] was his increase:
His Letters are deliver'd all and gon,
Onely remains this superscription.

(early 1631)

[4] Another involved pun: his "wain" (cart) was his "increase" (continued accumulation of years and of wealth); and his "wane" (diminishing as of the moon to which he was obedient, or ebbing of life) was his "increase" (waxing of the moon, or passing into another state).

Hobsons Epitaph[1]

Here *Hobson* lies amongst his many betters,
A man not learned, yet of many letters:[2]
The Schollers well can testify as much
That have receiv'd them from his pregnant pouch.
His carriage was well known; oft hath he gon 5
In Embassy 'twixt father and the son.[3]
In *Cambridge* few (in good time be it spoken)
But well remembreth him by som good token.
From thence to *London* rode he day by day,
Till death benighting him, he lost his way. 10
No wonder is it, that he thus is gone,
Since most men knew he long was drawing on.
His Team was of the best, nor could he have
Bin mir'd in any ground, but in the grave:
And here he sticks indeed, still like to stand, 15
Until some Angell lend his helping hand.
So rest in peace thou ever-toyling swain,
And supream Waggoner, next to Charls-wain.[4]

(early 1631)

[1] Milton's authorship of this poem is not certain; see *Textual Notes*.
[2] Hobson carried the mails, but he had no academic degrees.
[3] primarily to deliver requests for money and infrequent compliances.
[4] the Big Dipper, punning on his cart and his dying and ascending to the heavens.

An Epitaph on
the Marchioness of Winchester[1]

7 syllable line

This rich Marble doth enterr
The honour'd Wife of *Winchester,*
A Vicounts daughter, an Earls heir,
Besides what her vertues fair
Added to her noble birth,   5
More then she could own from Earth.
Summers three times eight save one
She had told, alas too soon,
After so short time of breath,
To house with darknes, and with death,   10
Yet had the number of her days
Bin as compleat as was her praise,
Nature and fate had had no strife
In giving limit to her life.
Her high birth, and her graces sweet   15
Quickly found a lover meet;
The Virgin quire for her request
The God that sits at marriage feast;[2]
He at their invoking came
But with a scarce-well-lighted flame;   20
And in his Garland as he stood,
Ye might discern a Cipress bud.
Once had the early Matrons run
To greet her of a lovely son,[3]
And now with second hope she goes,   25
And calls *Lucina*[4] to her throws;

---

[1] Jane, wife of John Paulet, the Marquis of Winchester (a Roman Catholic), died in childbirth, with her child, on Apr. 15, 1631, at the age of twenty-three. Her father was Thomas, Viscount of Rock-Savage, and through her mother, she was heir of Lord Darcy, Earl of Rivers.

[2] Hymen; his "scarce-well-lighted flame" indicates brevity of marriage, and the "Cipress bud" the imminency of death. His torch was usually made from white hawthorn, signifying simultaneous joy and pain. Milton knew that the Paulets had been married in 1622, as ll. 15–23 in the manuscript version show (see *Textual Notes*).

[3] Charles, later first Duke of Bolton, was born in 1629. The matrons of Rome held a festival called the Matralia on June 11, which celebrated childbirth.

[4] goddess of childbirth.

But whether by mischance or blame
Atropos[5] for *Lucina* came;
And with remorsles cruelty,
Spoil'd at once both fruit and tree: 30
The haples Babe before his birth
Had burial, yet not laid in earth,
And the languisht Mothers Womb
Was not long a living Tomb.
So have I seen som tender slip   35
Sav'd with care from Winters nip,
The pride of her carnation train,
Pluck't up by som unheedy swain,
Who onely thought to crop the flowr
New shot up from vernall showr;   40
But the fair blossom hangs the head
Side-ways as on a dying bed,
And those Pearls of dew she wears
Prove to be presaging tears
Which the sad morn had let fall   45
On her hast'ning funerall.
Gentle Lady may thy grave
Peace and quiet ever have;
After this thy travail sore
Sweet rest sease thee evermore,   50
That to give the world encrease,
Short'n'd hast thy own lives lease;
Here besides the sorrowing
That thy noble House doth bring,
Here be tears of perfect moan   55
Wept for thee in *Helicon*,[6]
And som Flowers, and som Bays,
For thy Hears to strew the ways,
Sent thee from the banks of *Came*,[7]
Devoted to thy vertuous name;   60
Whilst thou bright Saint high sit'st in glory,
Next her much like to thee in story,
That fair *Syrian* Shepherdess,[8]

[5] the Fate who cut the thread of life.
[6] the mountain haunt of the Muses. Poems were written by the students of Cambridge to accompany her hearse (ll. 55–58); among other tributes is one by Ben Jonson.
[7] the river which flows by Cambridge.
[8] Rachel, who died in childbirth of Benjamin; the story of her husband Jacob referred to here is found in Gen. xxix–xxxvii.

Who after yeers of barrennes
The highly favour'd *Joseph* bore   65
To him that serv'd for her before,
And at her next birth much like thee,
Through pangs fled to felicity,
Far within the boosom bright
Of blazing Majesty and Light;   70
There with thee, new welcom Saint,
Like fortunes may her soul acquaint,
With thee there clad in radiant sheen,
No Marchioness, but now a Queen.

(Apr. 1631)

L'Allegro[1]

Hence loathed Melancholy
    Of *Cerberus*,[2] and blackest midnight born,
In *Stygian* Cave forlorn
    'Mongst horrid shapes, and shreiks, and sights unholy.
Find out som uncouth[3] cell,   5
    Wher brooding darknes spreads his jealous wings,
And the night-Raven sings;
    There under *Ebon* shades, and low-brow'd Rocks,
As ragged as thy Locks,
    In dark *Cimmerian* desert ever dwell.   10

---

[1] "The joyful man" delights in the pleasures of day and light, and in those happy activities of night which are enjoyed with others. Its companion and structurally parallel poem, *Il Penseroso*, "the contemplative man," presents images of pensiveness and darkness, and thus of aloneness and primarily night. Notable is the strong Platonic element.

The contrasting first ten lines of each poem have been traced to a number of literary sources for metrics and subject matter. The antithetic subjects of the twin poems were probably conceived as a kind of scholastic exercise such as produced the first and seventh prolusions, "Whether Day or Night Is the More Excellent" and "Learning Makes Men Happier than Ignorance."

[2] the watchdog of Hades; "Stygian," l. 3, refers to one of the rivers flowing through Hell.

[3] unfamiliar.

But com thou Goddes fair and free,
In Heav'n yclept[4] *Euphrosyne,*

spring/sunshine

And by men, heart-easing Mirth,

gladness, laughter

Whom lovely *Venus* at a birth
With two sister Graces more

*Venus + Bacchus
& 3 sister graces
including Euphrosyne*   15

To Ivy-crowned *Bacchus* bore;
Or whether (as som Sager[5] sing)
The frolick Wind that breathes the Spring,

*or Zephir + Aurora
Euphrosyne*

Zephir with *Aurora* playing,
As he met her once a-Maying, *May day*   20
There on Beds of Violets blew,
And fresh-blown Roses washt in dew,
Fill'd her with thee a daughter fair,
So bucksom, blith, and debonair.
Haste thee nymph, and bring with thee   25
Jest and youthful Jollity,
Quips and Cranks, and wanton Wiles,
Nods, and Becks, and Wreathed Smiles,
Such as hang on *Hebe's*[6] cheek,
And love to live in dimple sleek;   30
Sport that wrincled Care derides,
And Laughter holding both his sides.
Com, and trip it as ye go
On the light fantastick toe,
And in thy right hand lead with thee   35
The Mountain Nymph, sweet Liberty;
And if I give thee honour due,
Mirth, admit me of thy crew

(mirth)

To live with her, and live with thee,
In unreproved pleasures free;   40
To hear the Lark begin his flight,
And singing startle the dull night,
From his watch-towr in the skies,
Till the dappled dawn doth rise;
Then to com in spight of sorrow,   45
And at my window bid good morrow
Through the Sweet-Briar, or the Vine,
Or the twisted Eglantine.
While the Cock with lively din

rooster

---

[4] called. The sister Graces (l. 15) are Aglaia (Brilliance) and Thalia (Bloom).
[5] probably meaning "some who are Sager."
[6] goddess of youth.

Scatters the rear of darknes thin,   50
And to the stack, or the Barn dore,
Stoutly struts his Dames before,
Oft list'ning how the Hounds and horn,
Chearly rouse the slumbring morn,
From the side of som Hoar[7] Hill,   55
Through the high wood echoing shrill.
Som time walking not unseen[8]
By Hedge-row Elms, or Hillocks green,
Right against the Eastern gate,
Wher the great Sun begins his state,[9]   60
Rob'd in flames, and Amber light,
The clouds in thousand Liveries dight,
While the Plowman neer at hand
Whistles o're the Furrow'd Land,
And the Milkmaid singeth blithe,   65
And the Mower whets his sithe,
And every Shepherd tells his tale
Under the Hawthorn in the dale.
Streit mine eye hath caught new pleasures
Whilst the Lantskip round it measures   70
Russet Lawns, and Fallows gray,
Where the nibling flocks do stray,
Mountains on whose barren brest
The labouring clouds do often rest:
Meadows trim with Daisies pide,[10]   75
Shallow Brooks, and Rivers wide.
Towers, and Battlements it sees
Boosom'd high in tufted Trees,
Wher perhaps som beauty lies,
The Cynosure of neighbouring eyes.   80
Hard by, a Cottage chimney smokes,
From betwixt two aged Oaks,
Where *Corydon* and *Thyrsis*[11] met
Are at their savory dinner set
Of Hearbs, and other Country Messes,   85
Which the neat-handed *Phillis* dresses;
And then in haste her Bowr she leaves,

[7] light gray (at dawn).
[8] out in the open.
[9] stately progress.
[10] spotted.
[11] commonplace rustic names as are "Phillis" (l. 86) and "Thestylis" (l. 88).

With *Thestylis* to bind the Sheaves;
Or if the earlier season lead
To the tann'd Haycock in the Mead,   90
Som times with secure[12] delight
The up-land Hamlets will invite,
When the merry Bells ring round,
And the jocond rebecks sound
To many a youth, and many a maid,   95
Dancing in the Chequer'd shade;
And young and old com forth to play
On a Sunshine Holyday,
Till the live-long day-light fail,
Then to the Spicy Nut-brown Ale,   100
With stories told of many a feat,
How *Faery Mab* the junkets eat;
She[13] was pincht, and pull'd she sed,
And he by Friars Lanthorn[14] led
Tells how the drudging *Goblin* swet,   105
To earn his Cream-bowl duly set,
When in one night, ere glimps of morn,
His shadowy Flail hath thresh'd the Corn
That ten day-labourers could not end,
Then lies him down the Lubbar Fend,   110
And stretch'd out all the Chimney's length,
Basks at the fire his hairy strength;
And Crop-full out of dores he flings,
Ere the first Cock his Mattin rings.
Thus don the Tales, to bed they creep,   115
By whispering Winds soon lull'd asleep.
Towred Cities please us then,
And the busie humm of men,
Where throngs of Knights and Barons bold,
In weeds of Peace high triumphs[15] hold,   120
With store of Ladies, whose bright eies
Rain influence, and judge the prise
Of Wit, or Arms, while both contend
To win her Grace, whom all commend.
There let *Hymen*[16] oft appear   125

[12] free from care.
[13] one of the tellers of tales, as is "he," l. 104.
[14] *ignis fatuus*, a misleading light; probably the Friar is identical with the "Goblin," l. 105, and "Lubbar Fend," l. 110 (Robin Goodfellow).
[15] festivals.
[16] god of marriage, a frequent character in court masques.

In Saffron robe, with Taper clear,
And pomp, and feast, and revelry,
With mask, and antique Pageantry,
Such sights as youthfull Poets dream
On Summer eeves by haunted stream.   130
Then to the well-trod stage anon,
If *Jonsons* learned Sock[17] be on,
Or sweetest *Shakespear* fancies[18] child,
Warble his native Wood-notes wild,
And ever against eating Cares,   135
Lap me in soft *Lydian* Aires,
Married to immortal verse
Such as the meeting soul may pierce
In notes, with many a winding bout
Of linked sweetnes long drawn out,   140
With wanton heed, and giddy cunning,
The melting voice through mazes running;
Untwisting all the chains that tie
The hidden soul of harmony.
That *Orpheus*[19] self may heave his head   145
From golden slumber on a bed
Of heapt *Elysian* flowrs, and hear
Such streins as would have won the ear
Of *Pluto*, to have quite set free
His half-regain'd *Eurydice*.   150
These delights, if thou canst give,
Mirth with thee I mean to live.[20]

(1631 ?)

[17] low-heeled slippers worn by actors in comedy; hence, when one of Jonson's comedies is being played.
[18] imagination's.
[19] Orpheus sought to recover his wife Eurydice from Pluto's realm of death; his wondrous music gained his wish for him on the condition that he not look back as she followed. But he failed as they neared the upper world and Eurydice vanished.
[20] Compare Marlowe's: "If these delights thy mind may move, Then live with me, and be my love."

Il Penseroso

Hence vain deluding joyes,
  The brood of folly without father bred,
How little you bested,
  Or fill the fixed mind with all your toyes;
Dwell in som idle brain,   5
  And fancies fond[1] with gaudy shapes possess,
As thick and numberless
  As the gay motes that people the Sun Beams,
Or likest hovering dreams
  The fickle Pensioners of *Morpheus* train.[2]   10

But hail thou Goddes, sage and holy,
Hail divinest Melancholy,
Whose Saintly visage is too bright
To hit the Sense of human sight;
And therfore to our weaker view,   15
O're laid with black staid Wisdoms hue.
Black, but such as in esteem,
Prince *Memnons*[3] sister might beseem,
Or that Starr'd *Ethiope* Queen[4] that strove
To set her beauties praise above   20
The Sea Nymphs, and their powers offended.
Yet thou art higher far descended,
Thee bright-hair'd *Vesta*[5] long of yore,
To solitary *Saturn* bore;
His daughter she (in *Saturns* raign,   25
Such mixture was not held a stain)
Oft in glimmering Bowrs, and glades
He met her, and in secret shades

[1] foolish.
[2] attendants upon the god of dreams.
[3] an Ethiopian prince, known for his handsomeness.
[4] Cassiopeia boasted that her daughter Andromeda was more beautiful than the Nereids, for which she was made a constellation.
[5] Goddess of the hearth, Vesta was the virgin daughter of Saturn. Although the genealogy of Melancholy was apparently made up by Milton, the relation between Saturn and the "pensive nun" may have been suggested by the supposed gravity of those born under the sign of Saturn.

Of woody *Ida*'s inmost grove,
While yet there was no fear of *Jove*.[6]   30
Com pensive Nun, devout and pure,
Sober, stedfast, and demure,
All in a robe of darkest grain,
Flowing with majestick train,
And sable stole of *Cipres* Lawn,[7]   35
Over thy decent shoulders drawn.
Com, but keep thy wonted state,
With eev'n step, and musing gate,
And looks commercing with the skies,
Thy rapt soul sitting in thine eyes: 40
There held in holy passion still,
Forget thy self to Marble, till
With a sad[8] Leaden downward cast,
Thou fix them on the earth as fast.
And joyn with thee calm Peace, and Quiet,   45
Spare Fast, that oft with gods doth diet,
And hears the Muses in a ring,
Ay round about *Joves* Altar sing.
And add to these retired leasure,
That in trim Gardens takes his pleasure;   50
But first, and chiefest, with thee bring
Him that yon soars on golden wing,
Guiding the fiery-wheeled throne,[9]
The Cherub Contemplation,[10]
And the mute Silence hist along,   55
'Less *Philomel*[11] will daign a Song,
In her sweetest, saddest plight,
Smoothing the rugged brow of night,
While *Cynthia* checks her Dragon yoke,[12]
Gently o're th' accustom'd Oak;   60
Sweet Bird that shunn'st the noise of folly,
Most musicall, most melancholy!
Thee Chauntress oft the Woods among,

[6] son of Saturn, who overthrew his father's rule of the heavens.
[7] a fine, black fabric.
[8] firmly established.
[9] drawn from Ezekiel's vision (Ezek. i, x) of the fiery wheels and the throne above the cherubim.
[10] The cherubim had the faculty of knowledge and contemplation of divine things.
[11] the nightingale.
[12] See *Ely*, n. 13.

I woo to hear thy eeven Song;
And missing thee, I walk unseen 65
On the dry smooth-shaven Green,
To behold the wandring Moon,
Riding neer her highest noon,
Like one that had bin led astray
Through the Heav'ns wide pathles way; 70
And oft, as if her head she bow'd,
Stooping through a fleecy cloud.
Oft on a Plat of rising ground,
I hear the far-off Curfew sound,
Over som wide-water'd shoar, 75
Swinging slow with sullen roar;
Or if the Ayr will not permit,
Som still removed place will fit,
Where glowing Embers through the room
Teach light to counterfeit a gloom, 80
Far from all resort of mirth,
Save the Cricket on the hearth,
Or the Belmans[13] drousie charm,
To bless the dores from nightly harm:
Or let my Lamp at midnight hour, 85
Be seen in som high lonely Towr,
Where I may oft out-watch the *Bear*,[14]
With thrice great *Hermes*, or unsphear
The spirit of *Plato* to unfold
What Worlds, or what vast Regions hold 90
Th' immortal mind that hath forsook
Her mansion in this fleshly nook:
And of those *Dæmons*[15] that are found
In fire, air, flood, or under ground,
Whose power hath a true consent 95
With Planet, or with Element.
Som time let Gorgeous Tragedy
In Scepter'd Pall com sweeping by,
Presenting *Thebes*, or *Pelops* line,

[13] the town's night-watchman.
[14] The northern constellation of the Great Bear, since it never sets, was regarded by Hermes Trismegistus (for whom see *Idea*, n. 10) as a kind of perfection. "Il Penseroso," reading Hermes, will thus study and think through the full night.
[15] Neoplatonic deities of the four elements in the next line.

Or the tale of *Troy* divine,[16]   100
Or what (though rare) of later age,
Ennobled hath the Buskind stage.
But, O sad Virgin, that thy power
Might raise *Musæus*[17] from his bower,
Or bid the soul of *Orpheus* sing   105
Such notes as warbled to the string,
Drew Iron tears down *Pluto*'s cheek,
And made Hell grant what Love did seek.[18]
Or call up him[19] that left half told
The story of *Cambuscan* bold,   110
Of *Camball*, and of *Algarsife*,
And who had *Canace* to wife,
That own'd the vertuous Ring and Glass,
And of the wondrous Hors of Brass,
On which the *Tartar* King did ride;   115
And if ought els, great Bards beside,
In sage and solemn tunes have sung,
Of Turneys and of Trophies hung;
Of Forests, and inchantments drear,
Where more is meant then meets the ear.   120
Thus night oft see me in thy pale career,[20]
Till civil-suited[21] Morn appeer,
Not trickt and frounc't as she was wont,
With the Attick Boy[22] to hunt,
But Cherchef't in a comly Cloud,   125
While rocking Winds are Piping loud,
Or usher'd with a shower still,
When the gust hath blown his fill,
Ending on the russling Leaves,
With minute drops from off the Eaves.   130
And when the Sun begins to fling
His flaring beams, me Goddes bring
To arched walks of twilight groves,

---

[16] He seems to contemplate such plays as those dealing with the Oedipean dynasty, the house of Atreus, and Euripedes' *Trojan Women* and *Hecuba*. Tragic actors wore high-heeled boots (buskins).

[17] a legendary Greek poet praised by Plato.

[18] See *L'Allegro*, n. 19.

[19] Chaucer, whose unfinished "Squire's Tale" tells this story. The ring and glass gave special powers of achievement to their owner.

[20] course.

[21] unshowily dressed.

[22] Cephalus; see *El.* 5, n. 10.

And shadows brown that *Sylvan*[23] loves
Of Pine, or monumental Oak,   135
Where the rude Ax with heaved stroke,
Was never heard the Nymphs to daunt,
Or fright them from their hallow'd haunt.
There in close covert by som Brook,
Where no profaner eye may look,   140
Hide me from Day's garish eie,
While the Bee with Honied thigh,
That at her flowry work doth sing,
And the Waters murmuring
With such consort[24] as they keep,   145
Entice the dewy-feather'd Sleep;
And let som strange mysterious dream
Wave at his Wings in Airy stream,
Of lively protrature display'd,
Softly on my eye-lids laid.   150
And as I wake, sweet musick breath
Above, about, or underneath,
Sent by som spirit to mortals good,
Or th' unseen Genius of the Wood.
But let my due feet never fail   155
To walk the studious Cloysters pale,[25]
And love the high embowed Roof,
With antick Pillars massy proof,[26]
And storied Windows richly dight,
Casting a dimm religious light.   160
There let the pealing Organ blow
To the full voic'd Quire below,
In Service high, and Anthems cleer,
As may with sweetnes, through mine ear,
Dissolve me into extasies,   165
And bring all Heav'n before mine eyes.
And may at last my weary age
Find out the peacefull hermitage,
The Hairy Gown and Mossy Cell,
Where I may sit and rightly spell,[27]   170
Of every Star that Heav'n doth shew,

23 Sylvanus, god of forests.
24 harmony.
25 the bounds of the cloister.
26 grotesque pillars so massive as to prevent the roof from falling.
27 ponder.

And every Herb that sips the dew;
Till old experience do attain
To somthing like Prophetic strain.
These pleasures *Melancholy* give,   175
And I with thee will choose to live.

(*1631 ?*)

PART 2

Poems
Written During
Studious Retirement
or Associated with the
European Trip
(1632–40)

✳

Sonnet 7

How soon hath Time the suttle theef of youth,
  Stoln on his wing my three and twentith yeer!
  My hasting dayes fly on with full career,[1]
  But my late spring no bud or blossom shew'th.[2] *he hasn't shown himself yet.*
Perhaps my semblance might deceave the truth   5
  That I to manhood am arriv'd so neer,
  And inward ripenes doth much less appear,
  That som more timely-happy spirits[3] indu'th.[4]
Yet be it[5] less or more, or soon or slow,
  It shall be still[6] in strictest measure eev'n[7]   10
  To that same lot, however mean or high,
Toward which Time leads me, and the will of Heav'n;
  All is, if I have grace to use it so,
  As ever in my great task-maisters eye.[8]

(*Dec. 1632*)

---

[1] speed.

[2] It is unlikely that any specific vocation is referred to here, though some have interpreted the line in terms of poetry.

[3] those who have matured as one might normally expect. Milton remarks his lack of accomplishment to date, the point made in a letter to a friend, to which he attached this sonnet: "I am somtyme suspicious of my selfe, & doe take notice of a certaine belatednesse in me" (TM, p. 6).

[4] invests.

[5] inward ripening.

[6] always.

[7] level, equivalent.

[8] "All things are, as they always have been, foreseen by God, my great task-master, just as long as I have the grace to use my inward ripeness as He wishes." As pointed out by Lewis Campbell (*Classical Review*, VIII, 1894, 349), the lines may owe something to Pindar (*Nemean Odes*, IV, 41–43): "Whatsoever excellence Lord Destiny assigned me, well I know that the lapse of time will bring it to its appointed perfection." Yet they are Biblical too; Exod. xxxiii. 13: "Now therefore, I pray thee, if I have found grace in thy sight, shew me now thy way, that I may know thee, that I may find grace in thy sight"; and Rom. xii. 3, 6: "For I say, through the grace given unto me, to every man that is among you, not to think of himself more highly than he ought to think; but to think soberly, according as God hath dealt to every man the measure of faith . . . . Having then gifts differing according to the grace that is given to us . . . ."

Arcades[1]

Part of an entertainment presented to the Countess Dowager of Darby[2]
at Harefield, *by som Noble persons of her Family, who appear
on the Scene in pastoral habit, moving toward the seat of State,*[3]
with this Song.

1. SONG

Look Nymphs, and Shepherds look,
What sudden blaze of majesty
Is that which we from hence descry
Too divine to be mistook:
   This this is she   5
To whom our vows[4] and wishes bend,
Heer our solemn search hath end.

Fame that her high worth to raise
Seem'd erst so lavish and profuse,
We may justly now accuse   10
Of detraction from her praise,
   Less then half we find exprest,
   Envy bid conceal the rest.

Mark what radiant state she spreds
In circle round her shining throne,   15
Shooting her beams like silver threds.
This this is she alone,
   Sitting like a Goddes bright
   In the center of her light.

[1] natives of Arcadia, an area of Peloponnesus, whose rivers were Alpheus
(l. 30) and Ladon (l. 97) and whose mountains were Lycaeus (l. 98), Cyllene
(l. 98), Erymanthus (l. 100), and Maenalus (l. 102).
[2] Alice Spencer, widow of Ferdinando Stanley, Lord Strange and fifth Earl
of Derby, who married Sir Thomas Egerton in 1600. Her daughter Frances mar-
ried his son Sir John Egerton, later Earl of Bridgewater, whose children Alice,
John, and Thomas may have taken part in the entertainment. The occasion and
thus the date of the presentation are uncertain.
[3] where the Countess sits on "her shining throne."
[4] prayers.

Might she the wise *Latona*[5] be   20
Or the towred *Cybele*,[6]
Mother of a hunderd gods;
Juno dares not give her odds;[7]
   Who had thought this clime had held
   A deity so unparalel'd?   25

As they com forward, the Genius of the Wood[8] appears, and turning toward them, speaks.

  Gen. Stay gentle[9] Swains, for though in this disguise,
I see bright honour sparkle through your eyes.
Of famous *Arcady* ye are, and sprung
Of that renowned flood so often sung,
Divine *Alphéus*, who by secret sluse,   30
Stole under seas to meet his *Arethuse;*[10]
And ye the breathing Roses of the Wood,
Fair silver-buskin'd Nymphs as great and good,
I know this quest of yours, and free intent[11]
Was all in honour and devotion ment   35
To the great Mistres of yon princely shrine,
Whom with low reverence I adore as mine,
And with all helpfull service will comply
To furder this nights glad solemnity;
And lead ye where ye may more neer behold   40
What shallow-searching *Fame* hath left untold;
Which I full oft amidst these shades alone
Have sate to wonder at, and gaze upon:
For know by lot[12] from *Jove* I am the powr
Of this fair Wood, and live in Oak'n bowr,   45
To nurse the Saplings tall, and curl the grove
With Ringlets quaint, and wanton windings wove.

---

[5] Leto, mother of Apollo and Diana.

[6] the Great Mother, whose crown indicated her guidance to men in fortifying their cities (see *Aen.*, X, 252–53).

[7] "dares not wager with her" since the odds (advantage) are in her favor.

[8] See *Nativity Ode*, n. 40. Henry Lawes (see *Mask* and *Son.* 13) probably enacted this role and wrote music for the entertainment.

[9] of gentlemanly rank.

[10] The river-god Alpheus fell in love with the nymph Arethuse as she bathed. She fled to Ortygia (an island off Sicily) where Diana transformed her into a fountain, but Alpheus flowed beneath the sea ("by secret sluse") to be united with her.

[11] lavish intention.

[12] allotment.

And all my Plants I save from nightly ill
Of noisom winds, or blasting vapours chill,
And from the Boughs brush off the evil dew,[13]   50
And heal the harms of thwarting[14] thunder blew
Or what the cross dire-looking Planet[15] smites,
Or hurtfull Worm[16] with canker'd venom bites.
When Eev'ning gray doth rise, I fetch[17] my round
Over the mount, and all this hallow'd ground,   55
And early ere the odorous breath of morn
Awakes the slumbring leaves, or tassel'd horn[18]
Shakes the high thicket, hast I all about,
Number my ranks,[19] and visit every sprout
With puissant words, and murmurs made to bless,[20]   60
But els in deep of night when drowsines
Hath lockt up mortal sense, then listen I
To the celestial *Sirens* harmony,
That sit upon the nine enfolded Sphears,[21]
And sing to those that hold the vital shears,[22]   65
And turn the Adamantine spindle round,
On which the fate of gods and men is wound.
Such sweet compulsion doth in musick lie,
To lull the daughters of *Necessity*
And keep unsteddy Nature to her Law,   70
And the low world in measur'd motion draw
After the heav'nly tune, which none can hear
Of human mould with gross unpurged ear;
And yet such musick worthiest were to blaze
The peerles height of her immortal praise,   75
Whose lustre leads us, and for her most fit,
If my inferior hand or voice could hit
Inimitable sounds, yet as we go,
What ere the skill of lesser gods can show,

---

[13] hoarfrost (frozen dew).
[14] traversing (the sky).
[15] Saturn; see *Damon*, n. 13.
[16] the injurious cankerworm.
[17] take.
[18] the huntsman's horn, adorned with tassels.
[19] count my rows (of plants).
[20] with prayers for growth.
[21] See *Nativity Ode*, n. 26.
[22] The Fates, the daughters of Necessity, were Clotho, who held the spindle of life, on which the spheres turned; Lachesis, who drew off the thread; and Atropos, who cut it short with her shears.

I will assay,[23] her worth to celebrate,   80
And so attend ye toward her glittering state;
Where ye may all that are of noble stemm
Approach, and kiss her sacred vestures hemm.

2. SONG

O're the smooth enamel'd green
Where no print of step hath been,   85
  Follow me as I sing,
  And touch the warbled string.
Under the shady roof
Of branching Elm Star-proof,
  Follow me;   90
I will bring you where she sits,
Clad in splendor as befits
  Her deity.
  Such a rural Queen
All *Arcadia* hath not seen.   95

3. SONG

Nymphs and Shepherds dance no more
By sandy *Ladons* lillied banks.
On old *Lycæus* or *Cyllene* hoar,
  Trip no more in twilight ranks,
Though *Erymanth* your loss deplore,   100
  A better soyl shall give ye thanks.
From the stony *Mænalus*
Bring your Flocks, and live with us.
  Heer ye shall have greater grace
  To serve the Lady of this place.   105
  Though *Syrinx*[24] your *Pans* Mistres were,
  Yet *Syrinx* well might wait on her.
    Such a rural Queen
  All *Arcadia* hath not seen.

$$(1633-34\ ?)$$

[23] attempt.
[24] a nymph, unsuccessfully wooed by Pan.

A Mask[1]

THE PERSONS

The attendant Spirit afterwards in the habit of *Thyrsis*
Comus with his crew
The Lady
1 Brother
2 Brother
Sabrina the Nymph

*The first scene discovers a wild wood. The attendant Spirit descends or
enters.*

Before the starry threshold of *Joves* court
My mansion is,[2] where those immortal shapes
Of bright aëreal spirits live insphear'd
In regions mild of calm and serene air,
Above the smoak and stirr of this dim spot,   5
Which men call Earth, and with low-thoughted care
Confin'd and pester'd in this pinfold heer,
Strive to keep up a frail and feavourish beeing

---

[1] Written originally in celebration of the Earl of Bridgewater's election as
Lord President of Wales, *A Mask* was presented on Sept. 29, 1634, at Ludlow
Castle, with his three children enacting the Lady and her brothers. Thyrsis was
played by Henry Lawes, music tutor to the Bridgewater family and composer
of the music for the masque. As a masque, the work employs songs, dances,
ideal and unreal characters and powers; but its length and dramatic action cre-
ate a play unlike most other masques. Its more usual name of "Comus" is the
result of its popularity in the eighteenth century as a play with music by
Thomas Arne, into which frequently were interpolated passages from *L'Allegro*.
But this title gives a false impression, for Milton's emphasis is not on evil but on
the positive virtue of Temperance, on the dynamic purity of Chastity, as Wood-
house and others have argued. Basically the masque is a temptation in a wil-
derness involving Comus' proffer of drink, his admonition that the earth's riches
and beauty must not be hoarded, and his immobilizing the Lady in alabaster,
which nonetheless cannot immanacle her mind "while Heav'n sees good." What
overcomes Comus' glozing words is Virtue, which "may be assail'd but never
hurt."

[2] John xiv. 2: "In my Father's house are many mansions."

Unmindfull of the crown that vertue gives[3]
After this mortal change to her true servants   10
Amongst the enthron'd gods on sainted seats.
Yet som there be that by due steps aspire
To lay thir just hands on that golden key
That opes the palace of Eternity:
To such my errand is, and but for such,   15
I would not soil these pure ambrosial weeds[4]
With the rank vapours of this sin-worn mould.
    But to my task. *Neptune* besides the sway
Of every salt flood and each ebbing stream
Took in by lot 'twixt high, and neather *Jove*[5]   20
Imperial rule of all the sea-girt Iles
That like to rich and various gems inlay
The unadorned bosom of the deep,
Which he to grace his tributary gods
By course commits to severall government   25
And gives them leave to wear thir saphire crowns
And weild thir little tridents, but this Ile
The greatest and the best of all the main
He quarters to his blu-hair'd deities,
And all this tract[6] that fronts the falling sun   30
A noble peer of mickle[7] trust and power
Has in his charge, with temper'd aw to guide
An old and haughty nation proud in Arms:
Where his fair ofspring nurs't in princely lore
Are comming to attend thir fathers state   35
And new-entrusted Scepter, but thir way
Lies through the perplext paths of this drear wood,
The nodding horror of whose shady brows
Threats the forlorn and wandring passinger.
And heer thir tender age might suffer perill,   40
But that by quick command from Soveran *Jove*
I was dispatcht for thir defence, and guard;
And listen why, for I will tell you now

[3] 1 Cor. ix. 25: "And every man that striveth for the mastery is temperate in all things. Now they do it to obtain a corruptible crown; but we an incorruptible"; and Rev. ii. 10: "be thou faithful unto death, and I will give thee a crown of life."
[4] immortal garments.
[5] Pluto.
[6] Wales, whose Lord President was the Earl of Bridgewater; the celebration of his "new-entrusted Scepter" awaits the arrival of his children through "this drear wood"—the story background for the masque.
[7] great.

What never yet was heard in tale or song
From old or modern Bard in hall, or bowr.   45
  Bacchus, that first from out the purple grape
Crush't the sweet poyson of mis-used wine
After the *Tuscan* mariners transform'd[8]
Coasting the *Tyrrhene* shore, as the winds listed
On *Circe*'s Iland[9] fell (who knows not *Circe*   50
The daughter of the Sun? whose charmed cup
Whoever tasted lost his upright shape
And downward fell into a groveling swine)
This nymph that gaz'd upon his clustring locks
With ivy berries wreath'd, and his blith youth   55
Had by him ere he parted thence, a son
Much like his father, but his mother more,
Whom therfore she brought up, and *Comus* nam'd,
Who ripe and frolick of his full grown age,
Roaving the *Celtick*, and *Iberian* feilds,[10]   60
At last betakes him to this ominous wood,
And in thick shelter of black shade imbowr'd,
Excells his mother at her mighty art,
Offring to every weary travailer
His orient liquor in a crystal glass   65
To quench the drouth of *Phœbus*, which as they tast
(For most do tast through fond intemperate thirst)
Soon as the potion works, thir human countnance,
Th' express resemblance of the gods, is chang'd
Into som brutish form of wolf or bear   70
Or Ounce,[11] or tiger, hog, or bearded goat,
All other parts remaining as they were,
And they, so perfect is thir misery,
Not once perceave thir foul disfigurement,
But boast themselves more comely then before   75
And all thir freinds and native home forget
To roul with pleasure in a sensual stie.
Therfore when any favour'd of high *Jove*
Chances to pass through this adventrous glade,
Swift as the sparkle of a glancing star   80
I shoot from Heav'n to give him safe convoy
As now I do: but first I must put off

---

[8] Bacchus, carried off by pirates, changed them into dolphins.
[9] Aeaea where the enchantress transformed Ulysses' men to swine.
[10] French and Spanish lands, known for their wine.
[11] lynx.

These my sky robes spun out of *Iris* woof[12]
And take the weeds and likenes of a swain
That to the service of this house belongs,   85
Who with his soft pipe and smooth-dittied song
Well knows to still the wild winds when they roar,[13]
And hush the waving woods, nor of less faith,
And in this office of his mountain watch,
Likeliest and neerest to the present aid   90
Of this occasion, but I hear the tread
Of hatefull steps, I must be veiwles now.

*Comus enters with a charming rod in one hand, his glass in the other,
with him a rout of monsters headed like sundry sorts of wild beasts,
but otherwise like men and women, their apparell glistring; they
com in making a riotous and unruly noise, with torches in their
hands.*

    Comus. The star that bids the shepherd fold,[14]
Now the top of Heav'n doth hold,
And the gilded car of day   95
His glowing axle doth allay[15]
In the steep *Atlantick* stream,
And the slope sun his upward beam
Shoots against the dusky pole,
Pacing toward the other goal   100
Of his chamber in the East.
Mean while welcom Joy and feast,
Midnight shout, and revelry,
Tipsie dance, and jollity.
Braid your locks with rosie twine   105
Dropping odours, dropping wine.
Rigor now is gon to bed,
And Advice with scrupulous head,
Strict age, and sowr severity
With thir grave saws in slumber lie.   110
We that are of purer fire
Imitate the starry quire,[16]
Who in thir nightly watchfull sphears
Lead in swift round the months and years.

[12] material of a rainbow, "the bow in the cloud" of Noah (Gen. ix. 11–17).
[13] Milton praises Lawes (the "swain" of l. 84) by comparison with Orpheus.
[14] The evening star, Hesperus, rising, is a sign to gather sheep into their fold
for the night.
[15] cool.
[16] those creating the music of the spheres.

The sounds and seas with all thir finny drove   115
Now to the moon in wavering morrice[17] move,
And on the tawny sands and shelves
Trip the pert fairies, and the dapper elves.
By dimpled brook and fountain brim,
The wood nymphs deckt with daysies trim   120
Thir merry wakes[18] and pastimes keep:
What hath night to do with sleep?
Night has better sweets to prove,
Venus now wakes, and wak'ns Love.
Com let us our rights begin,   125
'Tis only daylight that makes sin
Which these dun shades will ne're report.
Hail goddess of nocturnal sport,
Dark-vaild Cotytto,[19] t' whom the secret flame
Of midnight torches burns; mysterious Dame   130
That ne're art call'd, but when the dragon womb
Of Stygian darknes spitts her thickest gloom
And makes one blot of all the air,
Stay thy cloudy ebon chair,
Wherin thou rid'st with *Hecat'*,[20] and befreind   135
Us thy vow'd preists till utmost end
Of all thy dues be don and none left out,
Ere the blabbing eastern scout,
The nice morn on th' *Indian* steep
From her cabin'd loop hole peep,   140
And to the tell-tale sun discry
Our conceal'd solemnity.
Com, knit hands, and beat the ground,
In a light fantastick round.

The Measure.

Break off, break off, I feel the different pace   145
Of som chast footing neer about this ground,
Run to your shrouds within these brakes and trees,
Our number may affright. Som virgin sure
(For so I can distinguish by mine art)
Benighted in these woods. Now to my charms,   150

[17] a rustic dance.
[18] night revels.
[19] a Thracian goddess of nightly pleasure.
[20] goddess of the moon (her team was three dragons, l. 131) and of witch-craft.

And to my wily trains;[21] I shall e're long
Be well stock't with as fair a herd as graz'd
About my mother *Circe*. Thus I hurl
My dazling spells into the spungy air,
Of power to cheat the eye with blear illusion   155
And give it false presentments, lest the place
And my quaint habits breed astonishment
And put the damsel to suspicious flight,
Which must not be, for that's against my course;
I under fair pretence of freindly ends   160
And well-plac't words of glozing[22] courtesie
Baited with reasons not unplausible
Wind me into the easie-hearted man,
And hugg him into snares. When once her eye
Hath met the vertue of this magick dust,   165
I shall appear som harmles villager
Whom thrift keeps up about his country gear,
But heer she comes, I fairly step aside
And hearken, if I may, her buisness heer.

The Lady enters.

Lady. This way the noise was, if mine ear be true,   170
My best guide now; me thought it was the sound
Of riot and ill-manag'd merriment,
Such as the jocond flute or gamesom pipe
Stirrs up amongst the loose unletter'd hinds,
When for thir teeming flocks, and granges full   175
In wanton dance they praise the bounteous *Pan*[23]
And thank the gods amiss. I should be loath
To meet the rudeness and swill'd insolence
Of such late wassailers; yet O where els
Shall I inform my unacquainted feet   180
In the blind maze of this tangl'd Wood?
My brothers when they saw me wearied out
With this long way, resolving heer to lodge
Under the spreading favour of these pines,
Stept, as they sed, to the next thicket side   185
To bring me berries, or such cooling fruit
As the kind hospitable woods provide.
They left me then, when the gray-hooded Eev'n

[21] tricks.
[22] flattering.
[23] here the god of shepherds.

Like a sad votarist in palmers weeds[24]
Rose from the hindmost wheels of *Phœbus* wain.   190
But where they are and why they came not back
Is now the labour of my thoughts; 'tis likeliest
They had ingag'd thir wandring steps too far,
And envious darknes, e're they could return,
Had stoln them from me; els O theevish night   195
Why shouldst thou, but for som fellonious end,
In thy dark lantern[25] thus close up the stars
That nature hung in Heav'n, and fill'd thir lamps
With everlasting oil, to give due light
To the misled and lonely travailer?   200
This is the place, as well as I may guess,
Whence eev'n now the tumult of loud mirth
Was rife and perfet in my list'ning ear,
Yet nought but single darknes do I find.
What might this be? A thousand fantasies   205
Begin to throng into my memory
Of calling shapes, and beckning shadows dire,
And airy tongues, that syllable mens names
On sands, and shoars, and desert wildernesses.
These thoughts may startle well, but not astound   210
The vertuous mind, that ever walks attended
By a strong siding champion conscience——
O welcom pure-ey'd Faith, white-handed Hope,
Thou flittering Angel girt with golden wings,
And thou unblemish't form of Chastity,   215
I see ye visibly, and now beleeve
That he, the supreme good, t' whom all things ill
Are but as slavish officers of vengeance,
Would send a glistring guardian if need were
To keep my life and honour unassail'd.   220
Was I deceav'd, or did a sable cloud
Turn forth her silver lining on the night?
I did not err, there does a sable cloud
Turn forth her silver lining on the night
And casts a gleam over this tufted grove.   225
I cannot hallow to my brothers, but
Such noise as I can make to be heard fardest
Ile venter, for my new-enliv'n'd spirits
Prompt me; and they perhaps are not far off.

[24] a serious religious devotee whose dress shows that he has kept his vow of a pilgrimage to the Holy Land.
[25] one with a slide by which the light can be concealed. Since Fawkes had used one in the Gunpowder Plot, the image had become nefarious.

SONG

Sweet Echo, sweetest nymph that liv'st unseen   230
          Within thy airy cell
     By slow Mæander's[26] *margent green,*
And in the violet-imbroider'd vale
Where the love-lorn nightingale
Nightly to thee her sad song mourneth well.   235
Canst thou not tell me of a gentle pair
     That likest thy Narcissus *are?*[27]
          O if thou have
     Hid them in som flowry Cave,
          Tell me but where   240
Sweet Queen of Parly, Daughter of the Sphear,
So maist thou be translated to the skies,
And give resounding grace to all Heav'ns harmonies.

Comus. Can any mortal mixture of Earths mould
Breath such divine inchanting ravishment?   245
Sure somthing holy lodges in that brest,
And with these raptures moves the vocal air
To testifie his hidd'n residence;
How sweetly did they float upon the wings
Of silence, through the empty-vaulted night,   250
At every fall[28] smoothing the raven down
Of darknes till she smil'd: I have oft heard
My Mother *Circe* with the Sirens three,
Amidst the flowry-kirtl'd *Naiades*
Culling thir potent hearbs, and balefull drugs,   255
Who as they sung, would take the prison'd soul,
And lap it in *Elysium; Scylla*[29] wept,
And chid her barking waves into attention,
And fell *Charybdis* murmur'd soft applause:
Yet they in pleasing slumber lull'd the sense,   260
And in sweet madnes rob'd it of it self,
But such a sacred, and home-felt delight,
Such sober certainty of waking bliss
I never heard till now. Ile speak to her

[26] a winding river.
[27] The Lady likens her brothers to a beautiful youth beloved by Echo.
[28] musical cadence.
[29] rocks lying opposite the whirlpool Charybdis, which Ulysses had to pass, personified as a woman with six heads that barked like dogs.

And she shall be my Queen. Hail forren wonder   265
Whom certain these rough shades did never breed
Unless the Goddes that in rurall shrine
Dwell'st heer with *Pan* or *Silvan*, by blest song
Forbidding every bleak unkindly fog
To touch the prosperous growth of this tall wood.   270
   Lady. Nay gentle shepherd, ill is lost that praise
That is addrest to unattending ears,
Not any boast of skill, but extreme shift
How to regain my sever'd company
Compell'd me to awake the courteous Echo   275
To give me answer from her mossie couch.
   Comus. What chance good Lady, hath bereft you thus?
   Lady. Dim darknes, and this leavy Labyrinth.
   Comus. Could that divide you from neer-ushering guides?
   Lady. They left me weary on a grassie terf.   280
   Comus. By falshood, or discourtesie or why?
   Lady. To seek i'th valley som cool freindly spring.
   Comus. And left your fair side all unguarded Lady?
   Lady. They were but twain, and purpos'd quick return.
   Comus. Perhaps fore-stalling night prevented them.   285
   Lady. How easie my misfortune is to hit!
   Comus. Imports thir loss, beside the present need?
   Lady. No less then if I should my brothers loose.
   Comus. Were they of manly prime, or youthfull bloom?
   Lady. As smooth as *Hebe*'s thir unrazor'd lips.   290
   Comus. Two such I saw, what time the labour'd ox
In his loose traces from the furrow came,
And the swink't[30] hedger at his supper sate;
I saw 'em under a green mantling vine
That crawls along the side of yon small hill,   295
Plucking ripe clusters from the tender shoots,
Thir port was more then human, as they stood;
I took it for a faery vision
Of som gay creatures of the element
That in the colours of the rainbow live   300
And play i'th plighted[31] clouds. I was aw-strook,
And as I past, I worshipt; if those you seek
It were a journey like the path to Heav'n,
To help you find them.

   [30] wearied.
   [31] pleated.

Lady.   Gentle villager
What readiest way would bring me to that place?   305
Comus. Due west it rises from this shrubby point.
Lady. To find out that, good shepherd, I suppose,
In such a scant allowance of star-light,
Would overtask the best land-pilots art,
Without the sure guess of well-practiz'd feet.   310
Comus. I know each lane, and every alley green
Dingle, or bushy dell of this wide wood,
And every bosky bourn[32] from side to side
My dayly walks and ancient neighbourhood,
And if your stray attendance be yet lodg'd,   315
Or shroud within these limits, I shall know
Ere morrow wake, or the low-roosted lark
From her thach't pallat rowse, if otherwise
I can conduct you Lady, to a low
But loyal cottage, where you may be safe   320
Till furder quest.
Lady.   Shepherd I take thy word,
And trust thy honest offer'd courtesie,
Which oft is sooner found in lowly sheds
With smoaky rafters, then in tapstry halls
And courts of princes, where it first was nam'd,   325
And yet is most pretended: In a place
Less warranted then this, or less secure
I cannot be, that I should fear to change it;
Eye me blest providence, and square my triall
To my proportion'd strength. Shepherd lead on.—   330

The two Brothers.

Elder Brother. Unmuffle ye faint stars, and thou fair moon
That wontst to love the travailers benizon,
Stoop thy pale visage through an amber cloud,
And disinherit *Chaos,* that raigns heer
In double night of darknes, and of shades;   335
Or if your influence be quite damm'd up
With black usurping mists, som gentle taper
Though a rush[33] candle from the wicker hole
Of som clay habitation visit us
With thy long levell'd rule of streaming light,   340

[32] stream lined with bushes.
[33] a reed made into a candle by dipping in tallow.

And thou shalt be our star of *Arcady,*
Or *Tyrian* Cynosure.[34]
   2 *Brother.*   Or if our eyes
Be barr'd that happines, might we but hear
The folded flocks pen'd in thir watled cotes,
Or sound of pastoral reed with oaten stops,   345
Or whistle from the lodge, or village cock
Count the night watches to his feathery Dames,
'Twould be som solace yet, som little chearing
In this close dungeon of innumerous bows.
But O that haples virgin our lost sister,   350
Where may she wander now, whether betake her
From the chill dew, amongst rude burrs and thistles?
Perhaps som cold bank is her boulster now
Or 'gainst the rugged bark of som broad Elm
Leans her unpillow'd head fraught with sad fears.   355
What if in wild amazement, and affright,
Or while we speak within the direfull grasp
Of Savage hunger, or of Savage heat?
   Elder Brother. Peace brother, be not over-exquisite[35]
To cast the fashion of uncertain evils;   360
For grant they be so, while they rest unknown,
What need a man forestall his date of grief,
And run to meet what he would most avoid?
Or if they be but false alarms of Fear,
How bitter is such self-delusion?   365
I do not think my sister so to seek,
Or so unprincipl'd in vertues book,
And the sweet peace that goodnes bosoms ever,
As that the single want of light and noise
(Not being in danger, as I trust she is not)   370
Could stir the constant mood of her calm thoughts,
And put them into misbecomming plight.
Vertue could see to do what vertue would
By her own radiant light, though sun and moon
Were in the flat sea sunk. And wisdoms self   375
Oft seeks to sweet retired solitude,
Where with her best nurse Contemplation
She plumes her feathers, and lets grow her wings

---

  [34] the Great Bear and the pole star of the Lesser Bear, by which, respectively, Greek and Phoenician sailors set their course.
  [35] over-precise.

That in the various bustle of resort
Were all to[36] ruffl'd, and somtimes impair'd.   380
He that has light within his own cleer brest
May sit i'th center,[37] and enjoy bright day,
But he that hides a dark soul, and foul thoughts
Benighted walks under the midday sun;
Himself is his own dungeon.   385
   2 *Brother.*   Tis most true
That musing meditation most affects[38]
The Pensive secrecy of desert cell,
Far from the cheerfull haunt of men, and herds,
And sits as safe as in a Senat house,
For who would rob a Hermit of his weeds,   390
His few books, or his beads, or maple dish,
Or do his gray hairs any violence?
But beauty like the fair Hesperian Tree
Laden with blooming gold, had need the guard
Of dragon watch with uninchanted[39] eye,   395
To save her blossoms and defend her fruit
From the rash hand of bold incontinence.[40]
You may as well spred out the unsun'd heaps
Of misers treasure by an outlaws den,
And tell me it is safe, as bid me hope   400
Danger will wink on opportunity,
And let a single helpless maiden pass
Uninjur'd in this wild surrounding wast.
Of night, or lonelines it recks me not,[41]
I fear the dred events that dog them both,   405
Lest som ill greeting touch attempt the person
Of our unowned[42] sister.
   Elder Brother.   I do not, brother,
Inferr, as if I thought my sisters state
Secure without all doubt, or controversie:
Yet where an equall poise of hope and fear   410

[36] probably a prefix meaning "very."
[37] the earth.
[38] likes.
[39] unenchantable.
[40] The golden apples of the tree had been given to Hera (queen of the gods) by Gaia (goddess of the earth) upon her marriage to Jove (God). See ll. 981–93 and n.
[41] does not matter to me.
[42] unaccompanied.

Does arbitrate th' event, my nature is
That I encline to hope, rather then fear,
And banish gladly squint suspicion.
My sister is not so defenceless left
As you imagine, she has a hidden strength   415
Which you remember not.
   2 Brother.   What hidden strength,
Unless the strength of Heav'n, if you mean that?
   Elder Brother. I mean that too, but yet a hidden strength
Which if Heav'n gave it, may be term'd her own:
'Tis chastity, my brother, chastity: 420
She that has that, is clad in compleat steel,
And like a quiver'd nymph[43] with arrows keen
May trace huge forests, and unharbour'd heaths,
Infamous hills, and sandy perilous wilds,
Where through the sacred rayes of chastity,   425
No savage feirce, bandite, or mountaneer
Will dare to soyl her virgin purity;
Yea there, where very desolation dwells
By grots, and caverns shag'd with horrid shades,
She may pass on with unblench't majesty,   430
Be it not don in pride, or in presumption.
Som say no evil thing that walks by night
In fog, or fire, by lake, or moorie fen,
Blue meager hag, or stubborn unlaid ghost,
That breaks his magick chains at curfew time,   435
No goblin, or swart faery of the mine,
Has hurtfull power o're true virginity.
Do ye beleeve me yet, or shall I call
Antiquity from the old schools of *Greece*
To testifie the arms of chastity?   440
Hence had the huntress *Dian* her dred bow,
Fair silver-shafted Queen for ever chaste,
Wherwith she tam'd the brinded lioness
And spotted mountain pard,[44] but set at naught
The frivolous bolt of *Cupid;* gods and men   445
Fear'd her stern frown, and she was queen o'th woods.
What was that snaky-headed *Gorgon* sheild
That wise *Minerva* wore,[45] unconquer'd virgin,
Wherwith she freez'd her foes to congeal'd stone?

[43] like Diana, goddess of the hunt and of chastity.
[44] panther.
[45] See *El.* 4, n. 21.

But rigid looks of chast austerity,   450
And noble grace that dash't brute violence
With sudden adoration, and blank aw.
So dear to Heav'n is saintly chastity,
That when a soul is found sincerely so,
A thousand liveried angels lackey her,   455
Driving far off each thing of sin and guilt,
And in cleer dream, and solemn vision
Tell her of things that no gross ear can hear,
Till oft convers with heav'nly habitants
Begin to cast a beam on th' outward shape,   460
The unpolluted temple of the mind,
And turns it by degrees to the souls essence,
Till all be made immortal: but when lust
By unchast looks, loose gestures, and foul talk,
But most by lewd and lavish act of sin,   465
Lets in defilement to the inward parts,
The soul grows clotted by contagion,
Imbodies, and imbrutes,[46] till she quite loose
The divine property of her first being.
Such are those thick and gloomy shadows damp   470
Oft seen in charnel vaults, and sepulchers
Hovering, and sitting by a new made grave,
As loath to leave the body that it lov'd,
And link't it self by carnal sensualty
To a degenerate and degraded state.   475
    2 Brother. How charming is divine philosophy!
Not harsh, and crabbed as dull fools suppose,
But musical as is Apollo's lute,
And a perpetual feast of nectar'd sweets,
Where no crude surfet raigns.   480
    Elder Brother.   List, list, I hear
Som far off hallow break the silent Air.
    2 Brother. Me thought so too; what should it be?
    Elder Brother.   For certain
Either som one like us night-founder'd[47] heer,
Or els som neighbour woodman, or at worst,
Som roaving robber calling to his fellows.   485
    2 Brother. Heav'n keep my sister! Agen, agen and neer,[48]
Best draw, and stand upon our guard.

[46] becomes sensual and brutish.
[47] led helplessly astray by night.
[48] nearer.

Elder Brother.   Ile hallow,
If he be freindly he comes well, if not,
Defence is a good cause, and Heav'n be for us.

The attendant Spirit habited like a Shepherd.

That hallow I should know, what are you? speak;   490
Com not too neer, you fall on iron stakes[49] else.
Spirit. What voice is that, my young Lord? speak agen.
2 Brother. O brother, 'tis my fathers shepherd sure.
Elder Brother. Thyrsis? Whose artfull strains have oft delaid
The huddling[50] brook to hear his madrigal,   495
And sweeten'd every muskrose of the dale,
How cam'st thou heer good Swain? hath any ram
Slip't from his fold, or young Kid lost his dam,
Or straggling weather the pen't flock forsook?
How couldst thou find this dark sequester'd nook?   500
Spirit. O my lov'd maisters heir, and his next joy,
I came not heer on such a trivial toy
As a stray'd ewe, or to pursue the stealth
Of pilfering wolf, not all the fleecy wealth
That doth enrich these downs, is worth a thought   505
To this my errand, and the care it brought.
But O my virgin Lady, where is she?
How chance she is not in your company?
Elder Brother. To tell thee sadly shepherd, without blame,
Or our neglect, we lost her as we came.   510
Spirit. Ay me unhappy! then my fears are true.
Elder Brother. What fears good *Thyrsis?* Prethee breifly shew.
Spirit. Ile tell you. Tis not vain, or fabulous,
(Though so esteem'd by shallow ignorance)
What the sage poets taught by th' heav'nly Muse,   515
Storied of old in high immortal vers
Of dire *Chimera*'s and inchanted Iles,
And rifted rocks whose entrance leads to hell,
For such there be, but unbeleif is blind.
Within the navil[51] of this hideous wood,   520
Immur'd in cypress shades a sorcerer dwells
Of *Bacchus* and of *Circe* born, great *Comus*,
Deep skill'd in all his mothers witcheries,

[49] swords.
[50] rushing forward in confusion.
[51] center.

And heer to every thirsty wanderer
By sly enticement gives his banefull cup,   525
With many murmurs mixt, whose pleasing poison
The visage quite transforms of him that drinks,
And the inglorious likenes of a beast
Fixes instead, unmoulding reasons mintage[52]
Character'd in the face; this have I learn't   530
Tending my flocks hard by i'th hilly crofts
That brow this bottom glade, whence night by night
He and his monstrous rout are heard to howl
Like stabl'd wolves, or tigers at thir prey,
Doing abhorred rites to *Hecate*   535
In thir obscured haunts of inmost bowrs.
Yet have they many baits, and guilefull spells
T' inveigle and invite th' unwary sense
Of them that pass unweeting[53] by the way.
This evening late by then the chewing flocks   540
Had tane thir supper on the savoury herb
Of Knot-grass dew-besprent, and were in fold,
I sate me down to watch upon a bank
With ivy canopied, and interwove
With flaunting honiesuckle, and began   545
Wrapt in a pleasing fit of melancholy[54]
To meditate my rural minstrelsie,
Till fancy had her fill, but ere a close[55]
The wonted roar was up amidst the woods,
And fill'd the air with barbarous dissonance,   550
At which I ceas't, and listen'd them a while,
Till an unusuall stop of sudden silence
Gave respit to the drowsie frighted steeds
That draw the litter of close-curtain'd sleep.
At last a soft and solemn breathing sound   555
Rose like a steam of rich distill'd perfumes
And stole upon the air, that even silence
Was took e're she was ware, and wish't she might
Deny her nature, and be never more
Still to be so displac't. I was all ear,   560
And took in strains that might create a soul
Under the ribs of Death, but O ere long

[52] removing the look of reason in one's face.
[53] unaware.
[54] pensiveness, which here leads to Thyrsis' playing his pipe until his imagination has vented his thoughts.
[55] completion of the music.

Too well I did perceave it was the voice
Of my most honour'd Lady, your dear sister.
Amaz'd I stood, harrow'd with greif and fear,   565
And O poor hapless nightingale thought I,
How sweet thou sing'st, how neer the deadly snare!
Then down the lawns I ran with headlong hast
Through paths and turnings oft'n trod by day,
Till guided by mine ear I found the place   570
Where that damn'd wisard hid in sly disguise
(For so by certain signs I knew) had met
Already, ere my best speed could prevent,[56]
The aidless innocent Lady his wisht prey,
Who gently askt if he had seen such two,   575
Supposing him som neighbour villager;
Longer I durst not stay, but soon I gues't
Ye were the two she meant; with that I sprung
Into swift flight, till I had found you heer,
But furder know I not.   580
    2 Brother.   O night and shades,
How are ye joyn'd with hell in triple knot
Against th' unarmed weakness of one virgin
Alone, and helpless! Is this the confidence
You gave me brother?
    Elder Brother.   Yes, and keep it still,
Lean on it safely, not a period[57]   585
Shall be unsaid for me: against the threats
Of malice or of sorcery, or that power
Which erring men call chance, this I hold firm,
Vertue may be assail'd, but never hurt,
Surpris'd by unjust force, but not enthrall'd,   590
Yea even that which mischeif meant most harm
Shall in the happy trial prove most glory.
But evil on it self shall back recoyl,
And mix no more with goodness, when at last
Gather'd like scum, and setl'd to it self   595
It shall be in eternal restless change
Self-fed, and self-consum'd; if this fail,
The pillar'd firmament is rott'nness,
And earths base built on stubble. But com let's on.
Against th' opposing will and arm of Heav'n   600
May never this just sword be lifted up,

[56] outrun (their meeting).
[57] sentence.

But for that damn'd magician, let him be girt
With all the greisly legions that troop
Under the sooty flag of *Acheron,*
Harpies and *Hydras,* or all the monstrous buggs[58]   605
'Twixt *Africa* and *Inde.* Ile find him out,
And force him to restore his purchase[59] back,
Or drag him by the curls and cleave his scalp
Down to the hipps.
    Spirit.   Alas good ventrous youth,
I love thy courage yet, and bold emprise,[60]   610
But heer thy sword can do thee little stead;
Farr other arms and other weapons must
Be those that quell the might of hellish charms,
He with his bare wand can unthred thy joynts,
And crumble all thy sinews.   615
    Elder Brother.   Why prethee shepherd,
How durst thou then thy self approach so neer
As to make this relation?
    Spirit.   Care and utmost shifts
How to secure the Lady from surprisal
Brought to my mind a certain shepherd lad
Of small regard to see to, yet well skill'd   620
In every vertuous[61] plant and healing herb
That spreds her verdant leaf to th' morning ray;
He lov'd me well, and oft would beg me sing,
Which when I did, he on the tender grass
Would sit and hearken ev'n to extasie,   625
And in requitall ope his leathern scrip,
And shew me simples[62] of a thousand names
Telling thir strange and vigorous faculties;
Amongst the rest a small unsightly root,
But of divine effect, he cull'd me out;   630
The leaf was darkish, and had prickles on it,
But in another country, as he said,
Bore a bright golden flowr, but not in this soyl:
Unknown, and like esteem'd, and the dull swayn
Treads on it dayly with his clouted shoon,[63]   635
And yet more med'cinal is it then that *Moly*

[58] bugbears, bogies.
[59] prey.
[60] enterprise.
[61] health-giving.
[62] medicinal plants.
[63] shoes heavy with nails.

Which *Hermes* once to wise *Ulysses* gave;[64]
He call'd it *Hæmony*, and gave it me,
And bad me keep it as of sovran use
'Gainst all inchantments, mildew blast, or damp   640
Or gastly Furies apparition;
I purs't it up, but little reck'ning made,
Till now that this extremity compell'd,
But now I find it true; for by this means
I knew the foul inchanter though disguis'd   645
Enter'd the very lime-twigs[65] of his spells,
And yet came off: if you have this about you
(As I will give you when we go) you may
Boldly assault the necromancers hall;
Where if he be, with dauntless hardihood,   650
And brandish't blade rush on him, break his glass,
And shed the lushious liquor on the ground
But sease his wand; though he and his curst crew
Feirce sign of battail make, and menace high,
Or like the sons of *Vulcan* vomit smoak,[66]   655
Yet will they soon retire, if he but shrink.
    Elder Brother. Thyrsis lead on apace, Ile follow thee,
And som good angel bear a sheild before us.[67]

*The scene changes to a stately Palace, set out with all manner of deli-
    ciousness: soft Musick, Tables spred with all dainties.* Comus *ap-
    pears with his rabble, and the Lady set in an inchanted Chair, to
    whom he offers his Glass; which she puts by, and goes about to rise.*

    Comus. Nay Lady sit; if I but wave this wand,
Your nervs are all chain'd up in alablaster   660
And you a statue; or as *Daphne* was
Root-bound, that fled *Apollo*.[68]
    Lady.   Fool do not boast,
Thou canst not touch the freedom of my mind
With all thy charms, although this corporal rind
Thou hast immanacl'd, while Heav'n sees good.   665
    Comus. Why are you vext Lady? why do you frown?
Heer dwell no frowns, nor anger, from these gates
Sorrow flies farr: See here be all the pleasures

[64] to ward off Circe's charms.
[65] snares.
[66] They were conceived as lying beneath volcanoes.
[67] The attendant spirit as Thyrsis is doing just that.
[68] See *El.* 5, n. 3.

That fancy can beget on youthfull thoughts,
When the fresh blood grows lively, and returns   670
Brisk as the *April* buds in primrose season.
And first behold this cordial Julep heer
That flames, and dances in his crystal bounds
With spirits of balm, and fragrant syrops mixt.
Not that *Nepenthes*[69] which the wife of *Thone*   675
In *Egypt* gave to *Jove*-born *Helena*
Is of such power to stir up joy as this,
To life so freindly, or so cool to thirst.
Why should you be so cruel to your self,
And to those dainty limms which nature lent   680
For gentle usage, and soft delicacy?
But you invert the cov'nants of her trust,
And harshly deal like an ill borrower
With that which you receav'd on other terms,
Scorning the unexempt condition   685
By which all mortal frailty must subsist,
Refreshment after toil, ease after pain,
That have bin tir'd all day without repast,
And timely rest have wanted, but fair Virgin,
This will restore all soon.   690
    Lady.   'Twill not false traitor,
'Twill not restore the truth and honesty
That thou hast banisht from thy tongue with lies;
Was this the cottage, and the safe abode
Thou toldst me of? What grim aspects are these,
These oughly-headed monsters? Mercy guard me!   695
Hence with thy brew'd inchantments, foul deceaver;
Hast thou betrai'd my credulous innocence
With visor'd falshood and base forgeries
And wouldst thou seek again to trap me heer
With lickerish[70] baits fit to ensnare a brute?   700
Were it a draft for *Juno* when she banquets,
I would not taste thy treasonous offer; none
But such as are good men can give good things,
And that which is not good is not delicious
To a well-govern'd and wise appetite.   705
    Comus. O foolishnes of men! that lend thir ears
To those budge[71] doctors of the stoick furr,

[69] an opiate. Reference is *Od.*, IV, 221.
[70] lustful.
[71] a fur used on scholars' gowns; hence, solemn, austere.

And fetch thir precepts from the cynick tub,[72]
Praising the lean and sallow abstinence.
Wherfore did nature powr her bounties forth   710
With such a full and unwithdrawing hand,
Covering the earth with odours, fruits, and flocks,
Thronging the seas with spawn innumerable,
But all to please and sate the curious taste?
And set to work millions of spinning worms   715
That in thir green shops weave the smooth-hair'd silk
To deck her sons, and that no corner might
Be vacant of her plenty, in her own loyns
She hutch't[73] th' all-worshipt ore and precious gems
To store her children with; if all the world   720
Should in a pet of temperance feed on pulse,
Drink the clear stream, and nothing wear but freise,[74]
Th' all-giver would be unthank't, would be unprais'd,
Not half his riches known, and yet dispis'd,
And we should serve him as a grudging maister,   725
As a penurious niggard of his wealth,
And live like natures bastards, not her sons,
Who would be quite surcharg'd with her own waight
And strangl'd with her wast fertility;
Th' earth cumber'd, and the wing'd air dark't with plumes,   730
The herds would over-multitude thir Lords,
The sea o'refraught would swell, and th' unsought diamonds
Would so emblaze the forhead of the deep[75]
And so bestudd with stars that they below
Would grow inur'd to light, and com at last   735
To gaze upon the sun with shameless brows.
List Lady be not coy, and be not cozen'd[76]
With that same vaunted name virginity;
Beauty is natures coyn, must not be hoorded,
But must be currant, and the good therof   740
Consists in mutual and partak'n bliss,
Unsavoury in th' injoyment of it self.
If you let slip time, like a neglected rose
It withers on the stalk with languish't head.

[72] Diogenes renounced luxury by living in a tub.
[73] closed up.
[74] a shaggy woolen fabric.
[75] the earth.
[76] deluded.

Beauty is natures brag, and must be shown   745
In courts, at feasts, on high solemnities
Where most may wonder at the workmanship;
It is for homely features to keep home,
They had thir name thence; course complexions
And cheeks of sorry grain[77] will serve to ply   750
The sampler, or to teize[78] the huswifes wooll.
What need a vermeil-tinctur'd lip for that,
Love-darting eyes, or tresses like the morn?
There was another meaning in these guifts,
Think what, and be advis'd, you are but young yet.   755
    Lady. I had not thought to have unlockt my lips
In this unhallow'd air, but that this jugler
Would think to charm my judgement, as mine eyes
Obtruding false rules pranckt in reasons garb.
I hate when vice can bolt[79] her arguments,   760
And vertue has no tongue to check her pride:
Impostor, do not charge most innocent nature,
As if she would her children should be riotous
With her abundance; she good cateress,
Means her provision only to the good   765
That live according to her sober laws
And holy dictate of spare temperance:
If every just man that now pines with want
Had but a moderate and beseeming share
Of that which lewdly-pamper'd Luxury   770
Now heaps upon som few with vast excess,
Natures full blessings would be well dispens't
In unsuperfluous eev'n proportion,
And she no whit encumber'd with her store,
And then the giver would be better thankt,   775
His praise due paid, for swinish gluttony
Ne're looks to Heav'n amidst his gorgeous feast,
But with besotted base ingratitude
Cramms, and blasphemes his feeder. Shall I go on?
Or have I said anough? To him that dares   780
Arm his profane tongue with contemptuous words
Against the Sun-clad power of Chastity,
Fain would I somthing say, yet to what end?

---

[77] pale color.
[78] comb.
[79] pick and choose.

Thou hast nor Ear, nor Soul to apprehend
The sublime notion, and high mystery[80]   785
That must be utter'd to unfold the sage
And serious doctrine of Virginity,
And thou art worthy that thou shouldst not know
More happines then this thy present lot.
Enjoy your deer Wit, and gay Rhetorick   790
That hath so well been taught her dazling fence,[81]
Thou art not fit to hear thy self convinc't;
Yet should I try, the uncontrouled worth
Of this pure cause would kindle my rapt spirits
To such a flame of sacred vehemence,   795
That dumb things would be mov'd to sympathize,
And the brute Earth would lend her nerves, and shake,
Till all thy magick structures rear'd so high,
Were shatter'd into heaps o're thy false head.
   Comus. She fables not, I feel that I do fear   800
Her words set off by som superior power;
And though not mortal, yet a cold shuddring dew
Dips me all o're, as when the wrath of *Jove*
Speaks thunder, and the chains of *Erebus*[82]
To som of *Saturns* crew. I must dissemble,   805
And try her yet more strongly. Com, no more,
This is meer moral babble, and direct
Against the canon laws of our foundation;
I must not suffer this, yet 'tis but the lees
And setlings of a melancholy blood;   810
But this will cure all streight, one sip of this
Will bath the drooping spirits in delight
Beyond the bliss of dreams. Be wise and tast.

*The brothers rush in with Swords drawn, wrest his Glass out of his hand,
   and break it against the ground; his rout make sign of resistance,
   but are all driven in. The attendant Spirit comes in.*

   Spirit. What, have you let the false enchanter scape?
O ye mistook, ye should have snatcht his wand   815
And bound him fast; without his rod revers't
And backward mutters of dissevering power,

[80] The word combines a meaning of something beyond Comus' comprehension and a religious article of faith known only to the initiated.
[81] fencing, i.e., debating.
[82] that is, when Jove dooms to hell those who during his rebellion followed his father Saturn.

We cannot free the Lady that sits heer
In stony fetters fixt and motionless;
Yet stay, be not disturb'd, now I bethink me,   820
Som other means I have which may be us'd,
Which once of *Melibæus*[83] old I learnt
The soothest shepherd that e're pip't on plains.
   There is a gentle Nymph not farr from hence
That with moist curb sways the smooth Severn stream,   825
Sabrina is her name, a virgin pure;
Whilom she was the daughter of *Locrine,*
That had the scepter from his father *Brute.*
She guiltless damsell, flying the mad pursuit
Of her enraged stepdam *Guendolen,*   830
Commended her fair innocence to the flood
That stay'd her flight with his cross-flowing course.[84]
The water nymphs that in the bottom plaid
Held up thir pearled wrists and took her in,
Bearing her strait to aged *Nereus*[85] hall,   835
Who piteous of her woes, rear'd her lank head,
And gave her to his daughters to imbath
In nectar'd lavers strew'd with Asphodil,[86]
And through the porch and inlet of each sense
Dropt in Ambrosial oils till she reviv'd   840
And underwent a quick immortal change,
Made goddess of the river; still she retains
Her maid'n gentlenes, and oft at eeve
Visits the herds along the twilight meadows,
Helping all urchin blasts, and ill luck signs   845
That the shrewd medling elf delights to make,
Which she with pretious viold liquors heals.
For which the shepherds at thir festivals
Carrol her goodnes loud in rustick layes,
And throw sweet garland wreaths into her stream   850
Of pancies, pinks, and gaudy daffadils.
And, as the old swain said, she can unlock
The clasping charm, and thaw the numming spell,
If she be right invok't in warbled song,

[83] Spenser; see *FQ,* II, x, 19.
[84] Milton altered Geoffrey of Monmouth's account of the murder of Estrildis
and her illegitimate daughter Sabrina by Locrine's jealous wife Gwendolen.
[85] a sea-god.
[86] a flower yielding immortality.

For maid'nhood she loves, and will be swift   855
To aid a virgin, such as was her self
In hard besetting need; this will I try
And add the power of som adjuring verse.

SONG

Sabrina fair
    Listen where thou art sitting   860
Under the glassie, cool, translucent wave,
    In twisted braids of Lillies knitting
The loose train of thy amber-dropping hair,
    Listen for dear honours sake,
    Goddess of the silver lake,   865
        Listen and save.

Listen and appear to us
In name of great *Oceanus*,[87]
By th' earth-shaking *Neptunes* mace,
And *Tethys* grave majestick pace,   870
By hoary *Nereus* wrincled look,
And the *Carpathian* wizards hook,
By scaly *Tritons* winding shell,
And old sooth-saying *Glaucus* spell,
By *Leucothea*'s lovely hands,   875
And her son that rules the strands,
By *Thetis* tinsel-slipper'd feet,
And the songs of *Sirens* sweet,
By dead *Parthenope*'s dear tomb,
And fair *Ligéa*'s golden comb,   880
Wherwith she sits on diamond rocks
Sleeking her soft alluring locks,
By all the *Nymphs* that nightly dance
Upon the streams with wily glance,
Rise, rise, and heave thy rosie head   885
From thy coral-pav'n bed,
And bridle in thy headlong wave,
Till thou our summons answer'd have.
                    Listen and save.

[87] The sea deities include Tethys, wife of Oceanus and mother of rivers; Proteus, who lived in the Carpathian Sea and was known for changing his appearance; Triton, Neptune's herald; Glaucus, an immortal fisherman; Leucothea (or Ino) who escaped her husband's insanity with her son Melicertes by throwing herself into the sea; Thetis, a Nereid; and the Sirens Parthenope and Ligea.

Sabrina rises, attended by water-nymphs, and sings.

By the rushy-fringed bank,   890
  Where grows the willow and the osier dank,
My sliding chariot stayes,
Thick set with agat, and the azurn sheen
  Of turkis[88] blew, and emrauld green
    That in the channell strayes,   895
  Whilst from off the waters fleet
  Thus I set my printless feet
    O're the Cowslips Velvet head
    That bends not as I tread.

Gentle swain at thy request   900
I am heer.
  Spirit. Goddess dear
We implore thy powerful hand
To undoe the charmed band
Of true virgin heer distrest,   905
Through the force, and through the wile
Of unblest inchanter vile.
  Sabrina. Shepherd 'tis my office best
To help insnared chastity;
Brightest Lady look on me,   910
Thus I sprinkle on thy brest
Drops that from my fountain pure,
I have kept of pretious cure,
Thrice upon thy fingers tip,
Thrice upon thy rubied lip;   915
Next this marble venom'd seat
Smear'd with gumms of glutenous heat
I touch with chast palms moist and cold,
Now the spell hath lost his hold;
And I must hast ere morning howr   920
To wait in *Amphitrite's*[89] bowr.

Sabrina descends, and the Lady rises out of her seat.

  Spirit. Virgin, daughter of *Locrine*
Sprung of old *Anchises* line,
May thy brimmed waves for this
Thir full tribute never miss   925

[88] turquoise.
[89] the wife of Neptune.

From a thousand petty rills
That tumble down the snowy hills:
Summer drouth, or singed air
Never scorch thy tresses fair,
Nor wet *Octobers* torrent flood   930
Thy molten crystal fill with mudd;
May thy billows rowl ashoar
The beryl and the golden ore,
May thy lofty head be crown'd
With many a towr and terrace round,[90]   935
And heer and there thy banks upon
With groves of myrrhe, and cinnamon.

Com Lady while Heav'n lends us grace,
Let us fly this cursed place,
Lest the sorcerer us intice   940
With som other new device.
Not a wast or needless sound
Till we com to holier ground,
I shall be your faithfull guide
Through this gloomy covert wide,   945
And not many furlongs thence
Is your Fathers residence,
Where this night are met in state
Many a freind to gratulate
His wish't presence, and beside   950
All the swains that there abide,
With Jiggs and rural dance resort.
We shall catch them at thir sport,
And our sudden comming there
Will double all thir mirth and chere;   955
Com let us hast, the stars grow high,
But night sits monarch yet in the mid sky.

The scene changes presenting Ludlow *Town and the Presidents Castle,
then com in country-dancers, after them the attendant Spirit, with
the two brothers and the Lady.*

SONG

    *Spirit. Back shepherds, back, anough your play,
    Till next sunshine holiday,
    Heer be without duck or nod   960
    Other trippings to be trod*

[90] Compare "the towred Cybele" (*Arcades*, 21, and n. 6).

Of lighter toes, and such court guise
As Mercury *did first devise*[91]
With the mincing Dryades
On the lawns, and on the leas.   965

This second Song presents them to their father and mother.

Noble Lord and Lady bright,
I have brought ye new delight,
Heer behold so goodly grown
Three fair branches of your own.
Heav'n hath timely[92] *tri'd thir youth,*   970
Thir faith, thir patience, and thir truth.
And sent them heer through hard assays
With a crown of deathless praise,
*   To triumph in victorious dance*
O're sensual folly, and intemperance.   975

The dances ended, the Spirit Epiloguizes.

Spirit. To the Ocean now I fly,
And those happy climes that lie
Where day never shuts his eye,
Up in the broad feilds of the sky:
There I suck the liquid air   980
All amidst the gardens fair
Of *Hesperus* and his daughters three
That sing about the golden tree:[93]
Along the crisped[94] shades and bowrs
Revels the spruce and jocond Spring,   985
The Graces, and the rosie-boosom'd Howrs,[95]
Thither all thir bounties bring,
That there eternal Summer dwells,
And west winds, with musky wing
About the cedarn alleys fling   990
Nard, and *Cassia's* balmy smells.

[91] Besides having wings on his sandals, indicating his swiftness, Mercury invented the lyre.

[92] early.

[93] The Hesperian tree with its golden apples, guarded by a dragon, symbolized the Tree of Life, whose fruit yielded immortality; the dragon, here and in ll. 393–97, is identified with the cherubic watch with flaming swords placed there by God (*PL* XI, 118–25).

[94] quivering.

[95] goddesses of the seasons.

Iris there with humid bow[96]
Waters the odorous banks that blow
Flowers of more mingled hew
Then her purfl'd[97] scarf can shew,   995
And drenches with *Elysian* dew
(List mortals, if your ears be true)
Beds of hyacinth and roses
Where young *Adonis* oft reposes,
Waxing well of his deep wound   1000
In slumber soft, and on the ground
Sadly sits th' *Assyrian* Queen;[98]
But farr above in spangled sheen
Celestial *Cupid* her fam'd Son advanc't
Holds his dear *Psyche*[99] sweet intranc't   1005
After her wandring labours long,
Till free consent the gods among
Make her his eternal bride,
And from her fair unspotted side
Two blissful twins are to be born,   1010
Youth and Joy; so *Jove* hath sworn.
    But now my task is smoothly don,
I can fly, or I can run
Quickly to the green earths end,
Where the bow'd welkin slow doth bend,   1015
And from thence can soar as soon
To the corners[100] of the Moon.
    Mortals that would follow me,
Love vertue, she alone is free,
She can teach ye how to clime   1020
Higher then the spheary chime;[101]
Or if Vertue feeble were,
Heav'n it self would stoop to her.

(*1634, before Sept. 29;
revised, autumn–winter 1637*)

[96] See n. 12; in the following lines the water imagery indicates eternal life in contrast with Noah's flood of death.
[97] embroidered along the edge.
[98] Venus, whose lover Adonis had been gored by a wild boar.
[99] The myth points to Milton's allegory: life and heavenly bliss are the off-spring of the legitimate union of heart and soul. The mere appetite of Venus' love causes Adonis to languish and her to sit sadly far below the celestial heavens.
[100] horns.
[101] the music of the spheres.

Psalm 114

Ἰσραὴλ ὅτε παῖδες, ὅτ' ἀγλαὰ φῦλ' Ἰακώβου
Αἰγύπτιον λίπε δῆμον, ἀπεχθέα, βαρβαρόφωνον,
Δὴ τότε μοῦνον ἔην ὅσιον γένος υἷες Ἰούδα.
Ἐν δὲ θεὸς λαοῖσι μέγα κρείων βασίλευεν.
Εἶδε, καὶ ἐντροπάδην φύγαδ' ἐρρώησε θάλασσα,   5
Κύματι εἰλυμένη ῥοθίῳ, ὁ δ' ἄρ' ἐστυφελίχθη
Ἱρὸς Ἰορδάνης ποτὶ ἀργυροειδέα πηγήν.
Ἐκ δ' ὅρεα σκαρθμοῖσιν ἀπειρέσια κλονέοντο,
Ὡς κριοὶ σφριγόωντες εὐτραφερῷ ἐν ἀλωῇ.
Βαιότεραι δ' ἅμα πᾶσαι ἀνασκίρτησαν ἐρίπναι,   10
Οἷα παραὶ σύριγγι φίλη ὑπὸ μητέρι ἄρνες.
Τίπτε σύ γ' αἰνὰ θάλασσα πέλωρ φυγάδ' ἐρρώησας,
Κύματι εἰλυμένη ῥοθίῳ; τί δ' ἄρ' ἐστυφελίχθης
Ἱρὸς Ἰορδάνη ποτὶ ἀργυροειδέα πηγήν;
Τίπτ' ὅρεα σκαρθμοῖσιν ἀπειρέσια κλονέεσθε   15
Ὡς κριοὶ σφριγόωντες εὐτραφερῷ ἐν ἀλωῇ;
Βαιότεραι τί δ' ἄρ' ὕμμες ἀνασκιρτησατ' ἐρίπναι,
Οἷα παραὶ σύριγγι φίλη ὑπὸ μητέρι ἄρνες,
Σείεο, γαῖα, τρέουσα θεὸν μεγάλ' ἐκτυπέοντα,
Γαῖα, θεὸν τρείουσ' ὕπατον σέβας Ἰσσακίδαο   20
Ὅς τε καὶ εκ σπιλάδων ποταμοὺς χέε μορμύροντας
Κρήνην τ' ἀέναον πέτρης ἀπὸ δακρυοέσσης.

Psalm 114

When the children of Israel, when the noble tribes of Jacob / left behind the land of Egypt, hated, barbarous of speech, / already at that time the only chosen race was the sons of Judah. / But among the people God ruled, a mighty Lord. / The sea saw, and turning back, made the fugitive strong, [5] / its roaring waves folded beneath, and straightaway was / the sacred Jordan thrust back upon its silvery sources. / The boundless mountains rushed wildly thither, skipping / as well-filled rams in a thriving garden. / At the same time all the strange little crags leaped up [10] / as lambs to the shepherd's pipe about their dear mother. /

Why then, dread monster sea, did you make the fugitive strong, / your roaring waves folded beneath? Why then were you, / sacred Jordan, thrust back upon your silvery sources? / Why did the boundless mountains rush wildly, skipping [15] / as well-filled rams in a thriving garden? / Why then did you, strange little crags, leap up / as lambs to the shepherd's pipe about your dear mother? / Tremble, Earth, and fear the Lord, doer of mighty works; / Earth, fear the Lord, the highest majesty of the seed of Isaac, [20] / who poured forth both the roaring streams out of the rocks / and the ever-flowing fountain down from the weeping crags.

(*Nov. 1634*)

*Philosophus ad regem quendam qui eum ignotum &
insontem inter reos forte captum inscius damnaverat*
τήν ἐπὶ θανάτῳ πορευόμενος, *hæc subito misit*.[1]

'Ω ἄνα εἰ ὀλέσῃς με τὸν ἔννομον, οὐδέ τιν' ἀνδρῶν
Δεινὸν ὅλως δράσαντα, σοφώτατον ἴθί κάρηνον
Ρηϊδίως ἀφέλοιο, τὸ δ'ὕστερον αὖθι νοήσεις,
Μαψ αὔτως δ' ἀρ' ἔπειτα χρόνῳ μάλα πολλὸν ὀδύρῃ,
Τοιόνδ' ἐκ πόλεως περιώνυμον ἄλκαρ ὀλέσσας.   5

*A philosopher on his way to his death suddenly sent
this message to a certain king who had unawares
condemned him, unrecognized and innocent,
when he was seized by chance among criminals.*[1]

O king, if you make an end of me, a lawful person / and a doer of utterly no harm to man, you easily take away / one of the wisest of heads,

[1] Though these verses sound like a paraphrase of a classic epigram, no source has been determined. If they are the result of encouragement from Alexander Gill to try further Greek composition, the subject may have been chosen, as Parker suggests ("Notes," p. 129), to "allude to Gill's unfortunate clash with Laud and the Star Chamber, and his subsequent pardon by King Charles (November 30, 1630) . . . ." Two years before, Gill had toasted the health of John Felton, assassin of the king's minister, the Duke of Buckingham.

but later you will perceive / just as before; surely at last, you will grieve
vainly and exceedingly / because you have destroyed such a greatly
renowned bulwark from out of the city. [5]

(*Dec. 1634 ?*)

On Time

Fly envious Time,[1] till thou run out thy race,
Call on the lazy leaden-stepping howrs,
Whose speed is but the heavy plummets[2] pace;
And glut thy self with what thy womb devours,
Which is no more then what is false and vain,   5
And meerly mortal dross;
So little is our loss,
So little is thy gain.
For when as each thing bad thou hast entomb'd,
And last of all thy greedy self consum'd,   10
Then long Eternity shall greet our bliss
With an individual[3] kiss;
And Joy shall overtake us as a flood,
When every thing that is sincerely good
And perfectly divine,   15
With Truth, and Peace, and Love shall ever shine
About the supreme Throne
Of him t' whose happy-making sight alone,
When once our heav'nly-guided soul shall clime,
Then all this Earthy grosnes quit,   20
Attir'd with Stars, we shall for ever sit,
    Triumphing over Death, and Chance, and thee O Time.

(*1633–37 ?*)

[1] Cronos was jealous of even his own children (Hesiod, *Theogony*, 453 ff.).
[2] the weight which by gravity moved the wheels of the clock and in turn its
hands. The poem originally was to be "set on a clock case."
[3] usually interpreted as "undividable," that is, "everlasting"; however, O. B.
Hardison, Jr. (*Texas Studies in Lit. and Lang.*, III, 1961, 107–22) argues
cogently for the simpler reading: "Eternity shall greet us individually with a
kiss."

Upon the Circumcision[1]

Ye flaming Powers,[2] and winged Warriours bright
That erst with musick, and triumphant song
First heard by happy watchfull Shepherds ear,
So sweetly sung your joy the clouds along
Through the soft silence of the list'ning night,   5
Now mourn, and if sad share with us to bear
Your fiery essence can distill no tear,[3]
Burn in your sighs, and borrow
Seas wept from our deep sorrow.
He who with all Heav'ns heraldry whilere   10
Enter'd the world, now bleeds to give us ease;
Alas, how soon our sin
    Sore doth begin
His infancy to sease!
   O more exceeding love or law more just?[4]   15
Just law indeed, but more exceeding love!
For we by rightfull doom remediles
Were lost in death till he that dwelt above
High-thron'd in secret bliss, for us frail dust
Emptied his glory,[5] ev'n to nakednes;   20
And that great Cov'nant[6] which we still transgress
Intirely satisfi'd,
    And the full wrath beside
Of vengefull Justice bore for our excess,

---

[1] This poem of two fourteen-line verses, with single original lines 13–14 and 27–28, "reproduces as closely as possible the stanza used by Petrarch in his *canzone* to the Blessed Virgin" (Prince, p. 61). The Feast of the Circumcision of Christ, eight days after birth in accord with Mosaic law, is Jan. 1.

[2] The Powers were sixth in the celestial hierarchy, and the "winged Warriours" are the "helmed Cherubim" and "sworded Seraphim" of the *Nativity Ode*, 112–13; but Milton uses the terms to represent all the angels whose song Luke (ii. 13–14) quotes.

[3] Besides the conceit of opposites, the line refers to the opinion that angels were incapable of performing such bodily functions.

[4] This second stanza is an early statement of the high justice of God the Father and the mercy of the Son, who became man for man's salvation (see *PL* III, 80–344; XII, 393–419).

[5] Christ's *kenosis;* see Phil. ii. 6–8.

[6] that everlasting covenant made with Abraham when the rite of circumcision was instituted (Gen. xvii. 7, 10); it implies obedience to God's will.

And seals obedience first with wounding smart   25
This day, but O ere long
   Huge pangs and strong
Will peirce more neer his heart.

(1633–37 ?)

At a solemn Musick

Blest pair of *Sirens*, pledges of Heav'ns joy,
Sphear-born, harmonious sisters, Voice, and Vers,[1]
Wed your divine sounds, and mixt power employ
Dead things with inbreath'd sense able to peirce
And to our high-rais'd phantasie present   5
That undisturbed Song of pure concent[2]
Ay sung before the saphire-colour'd throne
To him that sits theron
With saintly shout, and solemn Jubily,
Where the bright Seraphim in burning row   10
Thir loud up-lifted Angel trumpets blow,
And the Cherubick hoast in thousand quires
Touch thir immortal harps of golden wires
With those just Spirits that wear victorious Palms,
Hymns devout and holy Psalms   15
Singing everlastingly;
That we on Earth with undiscording voice
May rightly answer that melodious noise
As once we did, till disproportion'd sin
Jarr'd against natures chime, and with harsh din   20
Broke the fair musick that all creatures made
To thir great Lord, whose love thir motion sway'd
In perfect Diapason,[3] whilst they stood
In first obedience, and thir state of good.

---

[1] The nine celestial sirens assigned to the nine spheres of the universe (see *Nativity Ode*, n. 26) were identified with the Muses, here specifying Polyhymnia, the muse of sacred song, and Erato, the muse of lyric poetry. Milton fuses the harmonious music of the spheres and the song of the multitude with palms in their hands before the throne of God (Rev. vii. 9).
[2] harmony.
[3] consonance of the entire compass of tones in an octave, thus referring to the harmonious song of "all creatures" regardless of relative position in the chain of being.

O may we soon again renew that Song,   25
And keep in tune with Heav'n, till God e're long
To his celestial consort[4] us unite
    To live with him, and sing in endles morn of light.

(*1637*)

[4] both fellowship and company of music makers ("concert"). There is also
a hint of wordplay on the meaning "marital association" ("consortium") with
Christ the Bridegroom.

Lycidas[1]

*In this Monody the Author bewails a learned Freind,[2] unfortunatly
drown'd in his passage from* Chester *on the* Irish Seas, *1637. And by
occasion foretells the ruin of our corrupted Clergy then in their
height.*

Yet once more, O ye Laurels, and once more
Ye Myrtles brown, with Ivy never sere,
I com to pluck your berries harsh and crude,[3]
And with forc't fingers rude
Shatter your leaves before the mellowing year.   5
Bitter constraint, and sad occasion dear
Compells me to disturb your season due:

---

[1] Built on verse paragraphs of varying lengths, the poem is irregularly rhymed
(including ten unrhymed lines) with key lines linking groups of rhymes, and
ends in *ottava rima*. The two so-called digressions (ll. 64–84 and 103–31),
which French sees as the core of the poem (*SP*, L, 1953, 485–90), are preceded
by passages concerned with death by water and followed by a passage in which
water becomes the source of new life. The vernal flowers which strew Lycidas'
hearse contrast with the dying vegetation in ll. 37–49, recalling the rebirth of
Orpheus and such vegetation gods. As Wayne Shumaker shows (*PMLA*, LXVI,
1951, 485–94), the apotheosis (ll. 165–85), which presents the poet-priest-
shepherd as still living, gives hope and courage and reconciliation to destiny
and the physical world.
[2] Edward King, who attended Christ's College, Cambridge, was drowned on
Aug. 10, 1637, when his ship capsized (despite good weather, according to
Milton, though not according to King's brother Henry). He had planned to en-
ter the clergy and had attempted some occasional verse; his pastoral name is
that used by Virgil for a shepherd-poet (*Ec.* ix). The poem appears last in a
collection of less distinguished Latin, Greek, and English obsequies, *Justa Edo-
vardo King naufrago* (1638).
[3] unripe.

For *Lycidas* is dead, dead ere his prime
Young *Lycidas*, and hath not left his peer:
Who would not sing for *Lycidas?* he well knew   10
Himself to sing, and build the lofty rime.
He must not flote upon his watry bear
Unwept, and welter to the parching wind
Without the meed of som melodious tear.
    Begin then, Sisters of the sacred well[4]   15
That from beneath the seat of *Jove* doth spring,
Begin, and somwhat loudly sweep the string.
Hence with denial vain, and coy excuse,
So may som gentle muse
With lucky[5] words favour my destin'd urn,   20
And as he passes, turn
And bid fair peace be to my sable shroud.
For we were nurst upon the self-same hill,
Fed the same flock by fountain, shade, and rill.
    Together both ere the high Lawns appear'd   25
Under the opening eyelids of the morn,
We drove afeild, and both together heard
What time the gray fly winds her sultry[6] horn,
Batning[7] our flocks with the fresh dews of night,
Oft till the star[8] that rose in Evning bright   30
Toward Heav'ns descent had sloapt his westring wheel.
Mean while the rurall ditties were not mute,
Temper'd to th' oaten flute:
Rough Satyrs danc't, and Fauns with clov'n heel
From the glad sound would not be absent long,   35
And old *Damœtas*[9] lov'd to hear our song.
    But O the heavy change now thou art gone,
Now thou art gon, and never must return!
Thee shepherd, thee the woods and desert caves
With wild Thyme, and the gadding vine o'regrown,   40
And all thir echoes mourn.
The willows, and the hazel copses green
Shall now no more be seen,

[4] the Muses; see *El.* 4, n. 10.
[5] propitious or, George O. Marshall suggests (*Explicator*, XVII, 1959, item 66), "having an unstudied felicity."
[6] warm from midday heat.
[7] feeding.
[8] Hesperus.
[9] apparently a tutor at Cambridge.

Fanning thir joyous leavs to thy soft layes.
As killing as the canker to the rose,   45
Or taint-worm to the weanling herds that graze,
Or frost to flowrs that thir gay wardrope wear,
When first the white thorn blows;
Such, *Lycidas*, thy loss to shepherds ear.

    Where were ye nymphs when the remorseless deep   50
Clos'd o're the head of your lov'd *Lycidas?*
For neither were ye playing on the steep,
Where your old bards the famous Drüids lie,
Nor on the shaggy top of *Mona*[10] high,
Nor yet where *Deva*[11] spreds her wisard stream: 55
Ay me, I fondly dream!
Had ye bin there, for what could that have don?
What could the Muse[12] her self that *Orpheus* bore,
The Muse her self for her inchanting son
Whom universal nature did lament,   60
When by the rout that made the hideous roar
His goary visage down the stream was sent,
Down the swift *Hebrus* to the *Lesbian* shoar.

    Alas! What boots it[13] with incessant care
To tend the homely slighted shepherds trade   65
And strictly meditate the thankless muse?
Were it not better don as others use,
To sport with *Amaryllis* in the shade,
Or with the tangles of *Neæra*'s hair?
Fame is the spur that the clear spirit doth raise   70
(That last infirmity of noble mind)
To scorn delights, and live laborious dayes;
But the fair guerdon[14] when we hope to find
And think to burst out into sudden blaze,
Comes the blind *Fury*[15] with th' abhorred shears   75
And slits the thin-spun life. But not the praise,
Phœbus repli'd, and touch't my trembling ears; stopped him
Fame is no plant that grows on mortal soil, goes beyond earth
Nor in the glistering foil[16]

[10] the isle of Anglesey.
[11] the river Dee.
[12] Calliope; Orpheus was torn to pieces by drunken followers of Bacchus, and his head floated down the Hebrus to the island of Lesbos.
[13] of what advantage is it?
[14] reward.
[15] Atropos, one of the Fates.
[16] a thin leaf of metal used as a background to enhance a gem.

Set off to th' world, nor in broad rumor lies,   80
But lives and spreds aloft by those pure eyes
And perfet witness of all-judging *Jove*
As he pronounces lastly on each deed,
Of so much fame in Heav'n expect thy meed.

   O Fountain *Arethuse*[17] and thou honour'd flood,   85
Smooth-sliding *Mincius*, crown'd with vocall reeds,
That strain I heard was of a higher mood:
But now my oat[18] proceeds
And listens to the Herald of the Sea[19]
That came in *Neptunes* plea,   90
He askt the waves, and askt the fellon winds,
What hard mishap hath doom'd this gentle swain?
And question'd every gust of rugged wings
That blows from off each beaked promontory,
They knew not of his story,   95
And sage *Hippotades*[20] thir answer brings,
That not a blast was from his dungeon straid,
The air was calm, and on the levell brine
Sleek *Panope* with all her sisters[21] plaid.
It was that fatall and perfidious bark   100
Built in th' eclipse, and rigg'd with curses dark,
That sunk so low that sacred head of thine.

   Next *Camus*,[22] reverend Sire, went footing slow,
His mantle hairy, and his bonnet sedge,
Inwraught with figures dim, and on the edge   105
Like to that sanguine flowr[23] inscrib'd with woe.
Ah! who hath reft, quoth he, my dearest pledge?
Last came and last did goe
The Pilot of the *Galilean* lake,[24]
Two massy keys he bore of mettalls twain   110
(The golden opes, the iron shuts amain),
He shook his mitr'd locks and stern bespake,
How well could I have spar'd for thee, young swain,
Anow of such as for thir bellies sake

---

[17] See *Arcades*, n. 10.
[18] pastoral song.
[19] Triton, who pleads the innocence of the sea in causing King's death.
[20] god of the winds.
[21] water-nymphs.
[22] god of the river Cam, representing Cambridge University.
[23] the hyacinth, named for the youth accidentally killed by Apollo; the inscription was the Greek word for "alas."
[24] St. Peter, wearing a bishop's miter and bearing the keys of heaven.

Creep and intrude, and clime into the fold?   115
Of other care they little reckning make
Then how to scramble at the shearers feast
And shove away the worthy bidden guest.
Blind mouths! that scarse themselves know how to hold
A sheephook, or have learn't ought els the least   120
That to the faithfull herdsmans art belongs!
What recks it them? What need they? They are sped;[25]
And when they list, thir lean and flashy songs
Grate on thir scrannel[26] pipes of wretched straw,
The hungry sheep look up and are not fed,   125
But swoln with wind, and the rank mist they draw,
Rot inwardly, and foul contagion spred:
Besides what the grim wolf[27] with privy paw
Dayly devours apace, and little sed,
But that two-handed engine[28] at the dore   130
Stands ready to smite once and smite no more.
    Return *Alphéus*, the dred voice is past
That shrunk thy streams; return *Sicilian* Muse,[29]
And call the vales and bid them hither cast
Thir bells, and flowrets of a thousand hues.   135
Ye valleys low where the mild whispers use,
Of shades and wanton winds, and gushing brooks,
On whose fresh lap the swart star[30] sparely looks,
Throw hither all your quaint enamel'd eyes
That on the green terf suck the honied showrs   140
And purple all the ground with vernal flowrs.
Bring the rathe[31] primrose that forsaken dies,
The tufted crowtoe and pale Gessamine,

---

[25] What does it matter to them? What do they need? They have fared well.
[26] feeble.
[27] perhaps the Anglican church, headed by Archbishop Laud.
[28] Whatever the specific reference, the meaning seems clear: the corrupted clergy will be punished finally and absolutely. 1 Sam. xxvi. 8: "let me smite him . . . with the spear even to the earth at once, and I will not smite him the second time." Probably intended, however, is the avenging sword of the Archangel Michael ("the great vision of the guarded mount," l. 161); see *PL* VI, 249–53, 278.
    Compare the passage with John x. 1–13, from which it is drawn, and Ezek. xxxiv.
[29] that of Theocritus and others who wrote pastorals.
[30] the blackening Dog Star (at its height when summer heat scorches vegetation).
[31] early.

The white pink, and the pansie freakt[32] with jet,
The glowing violet,   145
The musk rose and the well-attir'd woodbine,
With cowslips wan that hang the pensive head,
And every flower that sad imbroidrie wears:
Bid *Amaranthus*[33] all his beauties shed
And daffadillies fill thir cups with tears   150
To strew the laureat herse where *Lycid'* lies.
For so to interpose a little ease,
Let our frail thoughts dally with false surmise
Ay me! whilst thee the shoars and sounding seas
Wash far away, where ere thy bones are hurl'd,   155
Whether beyond the stormy *Hebrides*
Where thou perhaps under the whelming tide
Visit'st the bottom of the monstrous[34] world;
Or whether thou to our moist vows deni'd
Sleep'st by the fable of *Bellerus*[35] old   160
Where the great vision of the guarded mount[36]
Looks toward *Namancos*, and *Bayona*'s hold;
Look homeward Angel now and melt with ruth
And O ye *Dolphins*, waft the hapless youth.[37]
    Weep no more, wofull shepherds weep no more,[38]   165
For *Lycidas* your sorrow is not dead,
Sunk though he be beneath the watry floar,
So sinks the day star[39] in the Ocean bed
And yet anon repairs his drooping head
And tricks his beams, and with newspangled ore   170
Flames in the forehead of the morning sky:
So *Lycidas* sunk low but mounted high
Through the dear might of him[40] that walkt the waves:

---

[32] spotted.
[33] a flower supposedly yielding immortality.
[34] full of sea monsters.
[35] a mythical Cornish giant.
[36] Off Land's End in Cornwall, a large rock, traditionally guarded by the archangel Michael, points toward Namancos, a mountain range, and Bayona, a city, in Spain.
[37] as in the legend they carried Arion, who was born on Lesbos; compare ll. 57–63. They also rescued the dead body of Melicartes, who became the sea-god Palaemon. The dolphin is a symbol of Christ.
[38] Lines 165–81 are perhaps said by Michael, the redeeming voice, as William G. Madsen argues in *SEL*, III (1963), 1–7.
[39] the sun.
[40] Christ.

Where other groves and other streams along
With nectar pure his oozy locks he laves   175
And hears the unexpressive[41] nuptiall song
In the blest kingdoms meek of joy and love.
There entertain him all the Saints above
In solemn troops, and sweet societies
That sing, and singing in thir glory move   180
And wipe the tears for ever from his eyes.[42]
Now *Lycidas*, the shepherds weep no more;
Henceforth thou art the Genius of the shoar
In thy large recompence, and shalt be good
To all that wander in that perilous flood.   185
    Thus sang the uncouth swain to th' oaks and rills,
While the still morn went out with sandals gray;
He toucht the tender stops of various quills,
With eager thought warbling his *Dorick*[43] lay:
And now the Sun had stretcht out all the hills,   190
And now was dropt into the western bay;
At last he rose and twitcht his mantle blew:
To morrow to fresh woods and pastures new.

(Nov. 1637)

[41] inexpressible.
[42] Rev. xxi. 4: "And God shall wipe away all tears from their eyes; and there shall be no more death, neither sorrow, nor crying, neither shall there be any more pain; for the former things are passed away."
[43] pastoral.

Ad Patrem

Nunc mea Pierios[1] cupiam per pectora fontes
Irriguas torquere vias, totumque per ora
Volvere laxatum gemino de vertice rivum;
Ut tenues oblita sonos audacibus alis
Surgat in officium venerandi Musa parentis.   5
Hoc utcunque tibi gratum, pater optime, carmen
Exiguum meditatur opus, nec novimus ipsi
Aptiùs à nobis quæ possint munera donis
Respondere tuis, quamvis nec maxima possint
Respondere tuis, nedum ut par gratia donis   10
Esse queat, vacuis quæ redditur arida verbis.

Sed tamen hæc mostros ostendit pagina census,
Et quod habemus opum chartâ numeravimus istâ,
Quæ mihi sunt nullæ, nisi quas dedit aurea Clio[2]
Quas mihi semoto somni peperere sub antro,   15
Et nemoris laureta sacri Parnassides umbræ.
  Nec tu vatis opus divinum despice carmen,
Quo nihil æthereos ortus, et semina cæli,
Nil magis humanam commendat origine mentem,
Sancta Promethéæ retinens vestigia flammæ.   20
Carmen amant superi, tremebundaque Tartara carmen
Ima ciere valet, divosque ligare profundos,
Et triplici duros Manes adamante coercet.
Carmine sepositi retegunt arcana futuri
Phœbades, et tremulæ pallentes ora Sibyllæ;[3]   25
Carmina sacrificus sollennes pangit ad aras
Aurea seu sternit motantem cornua taurum;
Seu cùm fata sagax fumantibus abdita fibris
Consulit, et tepidis Parcam scrutatur in extis.
Nos etiam patrium tunc cum repetemus Olympum,   30
Æternæque moræ stabunt immobilis ævi,
Ibimus auratis per cæli templa coronis,
Dulcis suaviloquo sociantes carmina plectro,
Astra quibus, geminique poli convexa sonabunt.
Spiritus[4] et rapidos qui circinat igneus orbes,   35
Nunc quoque sydereis intercinit ipse choreis
Immortale melos, et inenarrabile carmen;
Torrida dum rutilus compescit sibila serpens,[5]
Demissoque ferox gladio mansuescrit Orion;
Stellarum nec sentit onus Maurusius Atlas.   40
Carmina regales epulas ornare solebant,
Cum nondum luxus, vastæque immensa vorago
Nota gulæ, et modico spumabat cœna Lyæo.[6]
Tum de more sedens festa ad convivia vates
Æsculeâ intonsos redimitus ab arbore crines,   45
Heroumque actus, imitandaque gesta canebat,
Et chaos, et positi latè fundamina mundi,
Reptantesque Deos, et alentes numina glandes,[7]
Et nondum Ætnæo quæsitum fulmen ab antro.[8]
Denique quid vocis modulamen inane juvabit,   50
Verborum sensusque vacans, numerique loquacis?
Silvestres decet iste choros, non Orphea cantus,
Qui tenuit fluvios et quercubus addidit aures
Carmine, non cithârâ, simulachraque functa canendo
Compulit in lacrymas; habet has à carmine laudes.   55

Nec tu perge precor sacras contemnere Musas,
Nec vanas inopesque puta, quarum ipse peritus
Munere, mille sonos numeros componis ad aptos,
Millibus et vocem modulis variare canoram
Doctus, Arionii[9] meritò sis nominis hæres.   60
Nunc tibi quid mirum, si me genuisse poëtam
Contigerit, charo si tam propè sanguine juncti
Cognatas artes, studiumque affine sequamur?
Ipse volens Phœbus[10] se dispertire duobus,
Altera dona mihi, dedit altera dona parenti,   65
Dividuumque Deum genitorque puerque tenemus.
Tu tamen ut simules teneras odisse camœnas,
Non odisse reor, neque enim, pater, ire jubebas
Quà via lata patet, quà pronior area lucri,
Certaque condendi fulget spes aurea nummi: 70
Nec rapis ad leges, malè custoditaque gentis
Jura, nec insulsis damnas clamoribus aures.
Sed magis excultam cupiens ditescere mentem,
Me procul urbano strepitu, secessibus altis
Abductum Aoniæ[11] jucunda per otia ripæ   75
Phœbæo lateri comitem finis ire beatum.
Officium chari taceo commune parentis,
Me poscunt majora. Tuo, pater optime, sumptu
Cùm mihi Romuleæ patuit facundia linguæ,
Et Latii veneres, et quæ Jovis ora decebant   80
Grandia magniloquis elata vocabula Graiis,
Addere suasisti quos jactat Gallia flores,
Et quam degeneri novus Italus ore loquelam
Fundit, Barbaricos testatus voce tumultus,
Quæque Palæstinus loquitur mysteria vates.[12]   85
Denique quicquid habet cælum, subjectaque cœlo
Terra parens, terræque et cœlo interfluus aer,
Quicquid et unda tegit, pontique agitabile marmor,
Per te nosse licet, per te, si nosse libebit.
Dimotàque venit spectanda scientia nube,   90
Nudaque conspicuous inclinat ad oscula vultus,
Ni fugisse velim, ni sit libâsse molestum.
I nunc, confer opes quisquis malesanus avitas
Austriaci gazas, Perüanaque regna præoptas.
Quæ potuit majora pater tribuisse, vel ipse   95
Jupiter, excepto, donâsset ut omnia, cœlo?
Non potiora dedit, quamvis et tuta fuissent,
Publica qui juveni commisit lumina nato

Atque Hyperionios currus, et fræna diei,
Et circùm undantem radiatâ luce tiaram.   100
Ergo ego jam doctæ pars quamlibet ima catervæ
Victrices hederas inter, laurosque sedebo,
Jamque nec obscurus populo miscebor inerti,
Vitabuntque oculos vestigia nostra profanos.
Este procul, vigiles curæ, procul este querelæ,   105
Invidiæque acies transverso tortilis hirquo,
Sæva nec anguiferos extende, Calumnia, rictus;
In me triste nihil fœdissima turba potestis,
Nec vestri sum juris ego; securaque tutus
Pectora, vipereo gradiar sublimis ab ictu.   110
   At tibi, chare pater, postquam non æqua merenti
Posse referre datur, nec dona rependere factis,
Sit memorâsse satis, repetitaque munera grato
Percensere animo, fidæque reponere menti.
   Et vos, O nostri, juvenilia carmina, lusus,   115
Si modo perpetuos sperare audebitis annos,
Et domini superesse rogo, lucemque tueri,
Nec spisso rapient oblivia nigra sub Orco,
Forsitan has laudes, decantatumque parentis
Nomen, ad exemplum, sero servabitis ævo.   120

To my Father

Now I long for the Pierian[1] fountains / to whirl their watery paths
through my breast and to roll / through my mouth the entire stream
released from the twin peaks / so that my Muse, her trifling songs forgot-
ten, might rise / on spirited wings in courtesy of my revered father. [5]
/ However, this grateful song she is meditating for you, dear father, /
is a poor attempt; yet I do not know myself / what gifts from me could
more aptly / repay your gifts, although my greatest ones could never /
repay yours, for by no means can barren gratitude which is paid [10] /
with empty words be equal to your gifts. / But notwithstanding, this
page exhibits mine, / and I have reckoned up on this paper whatever I
possess of abilities, / which to me are insignificant, save those which
golden Clio[2] has given, / those which to me slumbers have begotten in

1 See *El.* 4, n. 10.
2 See *El.* 4, n. 10.

the remote cave [15] / and the laurel groves of the sacred wood, Parnassian shadows. /

You should not despise the poet's task, divine song, / than which nothing commends more completely the offspring of heaven / to their ethereal origins, or the human mind to its lineage, / for song preserves a holy spark of Promethean fire. [20] / The gods love song, and song has power to stir / the trembling depths of Tartarus, and to bind the lower gods; / and it restrains the stern shades with triple adamant. / By song the priestesses of Apollo and the pale lips of the fearful Sibyl[3] / disclose the mysteries of the distant future. [25] / The sacrificial priest composes songs at altars, / both when he strews about the altar pieces of the bull which shakes its golden horns / and when, sagacious, he consults hidden destinies / in the steaming entrails and seeks out the Fate in the warm viscera. / Besides, when finally we return to our native Olympus [30] / and the everlasting ages of immutable eternity are established, / we shall walk with golden crowns through the temples of heaven, / with a sweet lyre uniting us in soft songs, / to which the stars and the vault of heaven will resound from the twin poles. / And the fiery spirit[4] that circles the swift planets [35] / even now himself is singing with heavenly verses / his immortal melody and indescribable song; / while the glittering serpent[5] checks his burning hisses / and with lowered sword fierce Orion becomes gentle, / and Mauretanian Atlas no longer suffers his burden of stars. [40] / Songs were used to embellish regal banquets, / luxury and the boundless depths of an enormous appetite / were not yet known, and the dinner table foamed forth for temperate Lyaeus;[6] / then according to custom a poet, sitting at festal banquets, / his unshorn tresses crowned with a garland from the oak, [45] / sang deeds of heroes and emulable achievements / and chaos and the foundations of the far-reaching earth, / the creeping gods and deities feeding on acorns,[7] / and the thunderbolt not yet sought from the cavern of Etna.[8] / And lastly what will support the melody of a petty voice, [50] / empty of words and sense, and of expressive rhythm? / Such music is suitable for forest choruses, not for Orpheus, / who restrained the rivers and gave ears to the oaks / by his song, not by his cithara, and singing stirred / the shades of the dead to tears; that fame he owes to his song. [55] /

Do not continue, I beg, to contemn the sacred Muses, / and do not

---

[3] the Sibyls at Delphi, and the Cumaean Sibyl who prophesied Aeneas' wars in Latium and led him through the world of the dead (*Aen.*, VI).

[4] Apollo, the Sun, god of poetry and music.

[5] For the Serpent (Scorpio) and Orion, see *Ely*, n. 12; for Atlas, see *Idea*, n. 6.

[6] See *El.* 6, n. 6.

[7] the Titans who had not yet learned agriculture.

[8] The Cyclops forged Jove's thunderbolt below Mt. Etna.

deem them fruitless and contemptible, by whose favor / you yourself, skillful, compose a thousand sounds to apt numbers, / and are trained to vary the melodious voice with countless modulations, / so that you are deservedly the heir of Arion's name.[9] [60] / Now since it has fallen to me to have been born a poet, / why is it strange to you that we, so closely joined by dear blood, / should follow related arts and kindred endeavor? / Apollo,[10] wishing to disperse himself between the two, / gave to me certain gifts, to my father others, [65] / and father and son, we possess the divided god. /

Although you may maintain that you hate the similar Muses of poetry, / I believe you do not. For, father, you did not bid me go / where the way lies broad, where the field of wealth is easier / and the golden hope of amassing money glitters sure; [70] / neither do you force me to the laws and the courts of the people, / so poorly overseen, nor do you doom my ears to insipid noises. / But wishing more completely to enrich my cultivated mind, / you permit me to walk by Apollo's side, his blessed companion, / removed far from city din to high retreats, [75] / for the sake of the pleasant leisures of the Aonian stream.[11] / I do not recount an esteemed father's usual kindness; / greater things demand my pen. When at your expense, most honored father, / I was exposed to the eloquence of the language of Romulus / and to the charms of Latin, and the lofty names of the magniloquent Greeks, [80] / which are fitting for the sublime lips of Jove, / you advised me to add the flowers which France boasts / and the language which the modern Italian pours from his / degenerate mouth, witness by his speech to the barbarian wars, / and the mysteries which the Palestinian prophet pronounces.[12] [85] / And finally all that heaven holds and earth, our parent, / bordering upon the sky, and the air flowing between the earth and sky, / and whatever water covers, and the surface of the restless sea, / through you I am allowed to know, through you, if I will be so disposed to know. / From a separated and observing cloud knowledge appears [90] / and, naked, she bends her conspicuous features to my kisses, / unless I should wish to flee, unless it be lamentable to taste. /

Go now, gather riches, fool, you who prefer / the ancient treasures of Austria and the Peruvian lands. / What father could bestow a greater gift, or Jove himself, [95] / with the exception of heaven, if he had given all? / He bestowed no more preferable gifts, however many might have been prudent, / who trusted to his young son the common light,

[9] the semi-legendary poet saved from drowning by a dolphin, who was charmed by his song. Milton's father had contributed music to various song collections, including settings for psalms.
[10] that is, since Apollo was god of both poetry and music.
[11] See *El.* 4, n. 10.
[12] in the Old Testament.

/ the chariot of Hyperion, the reins of day, / and the tiara waving about with radiant brightness. [100] / Therefore, now that I am a part of the learned company, however humble, / I shall sit among the ivy and the laurels of the victor. / And now I shall no longer mingle unknown with the indolent rabble / and my steps shall shun profane eyes. / Begone, sleepless cares; begone, complaints, [105] / and the twisted gaze of envy with oblique goatish leer. / And do not open your serpentine jaws, fell Calumny; / you can do nothing disagreeable to me, O most detestable band, / nor am I under your authority, and with heart secure / I shall walk, lifted high from your viperous stroke. [110] /

But to you, dear father, since it is not granted me to be able / to return gifts equal to your due or to repay for your deeds, / let it be enough to have remembered, and with a grateful mind / to enumerate your repeated offices and preserve them in a loyal heart. /

And you, O my juvenile songs and amusements, [115] / if only you dare to hope for immortality / and to remain after your master's death, and to gaze upon the light, / and if dark oblivion does not carry you beneath dense Orcus, / perhaps you will preserve these praises and the name of the father / sung again and again, as an example to a future generation. [120]

(*Mar. 1638 ?*)

Ad Salsillum poetam Romanum ægrotantem[1]

O Musa gressum quæ volens trahis claudum,[2]
Vulcanioque[3] tarda gaudes incessu,
Nec sentis illud in loco minus gratum,
Quàm cùm decentes flava Dëiope[4] suras
Alternat aureum ante Junonis lectum,   5
Adesdum et hæc s'is verba pauca Salsillo
Refer, camœna nostra cui tantum est cordi,
Quamque ille magnis prætulit immeritò divis.[5]
Hæc ergo alumnus ille Londini Milto,
Diebus hisce qui suum linquens nidum   10
Polique tractum (pessimus ubi ventorum,
Insanientis impotensque pulmonis
Pernix anhela sub Jove exercet flabra),
Venit feraces Itali soli ad glebas,
Visum superbâ cognitas urbes famâ   15
Virosque doctæque indolem juventutis,

Tibi optat idem hic fausta multa, Salsille,
Habitumque fesso corpori penitùs sanum;
Cui nunc profunda bilis infestat renes,
Præcordiisque fixa damnosùm spirat.   20
Nec id pepercit impia quòd tu Romano
Tam cultus ore Lesbium condis melos.⁶
O dulce divûm munus, O salus, Hebes⁷
Germana! Tuque Phœbe, morborum terror
Pythone cæso, sive tu magis Pæan   25
Libentur audis,⁸ hic tuus sacerdos est.
Querceta Fauni, vosque rore vinoso
Colles benigni, mitis Evandri sedes,⁹
Siquid salubre vallibus frondet vestris,
Levamen ægro ferte certatim vati.   30
Sic ille charis redditus rursùm Musis
Vicina dulci prata mulcebit cantu.
Ipse inter atros emirabitur lucos
Numa, ubi beatum degit otium æternum,
Suam reclivis semper Ægeriam spectans.¹⁰   35
Tumidusque et ipse Tibris hinc delinitus
Spei favebit annuæ colonorum:
Nec in sepulchris ibit obsessum reges
Nimiùm sinistro laxus irruens loro:
Sed fræna melius temperabit undarum,   40
Adusque curvi salsa regna Portumni.¹¹

To Salzilli, a Roman poet, being ill¹

O Muse who willingly drags along with a limping step² / and is pleased
with a halting gait like Vulcan's,³ / and who perceives that in its fitting
place it is no less gratifying / than when the flaxen-haired Deiope⁴ with
well-formed calves / dances before the golden couch of Juno, come
hither, [5] / if it pleases you, and carry back these few words to Salzilli,
/ by whom our poetry is prized so cordially, / and who preferred it, un-

---

¹ Giovanni Salzilli, a minor poet, contributed eleven sonnets and four other
poems to *Poesie de' Signori Accademici Fantastici* (1637). The two poets met
while Milton was touring Italy in 1638–39.
² Labelled "Scazontes," these iambic verses employ a reversed final foot (a
trochee or spondee), thus producing a "limping" effect.
³ Vulcan was lame from birth.
⁴ one of Juno's nymphs.

deservedly, before that of the divine poets.[5] / These things, therefore, that same Milton, brought up in London, / speaks forth, who lately forsaking his nest [10] / and that region of the northern skies (where the worst of the winds, / with raging and violent lungs, / the one that is so brisk, lets forth his gasping blasts beneath the heavens) / came alone to the fertile soil of Italy / to see its cities known to proud fame [15] / and its men and the talents of its learned youth, / to you that same Milton, Salzilli, wishes many blessings / and a healthy constitution deep within for your weakened body; / whose reins now an excessive bile impairs / and, firmly settled, emits its poison from its seat beneath your heart. [20] / Nor has the accursed thing had mercy although you, / so very cultivated, fashion Lesbian melody[6] with your Roman mouth. / O sweet gift of the gods, O health, Hebe's[7] / sister! And you, Phoebus, terror of diseases / as a result of slain Python, or Paean if you more [25] / willingly give ear,[8] this man is your priest. / Oak forests of Faunus, and yon hills rich / with wine-tasting dew, the seats of kindly Evander,[9] / if any healthful plant grows in your valleys, / let it eagerly speed relief to the ailing poet. [30] / Thus restored anew to his dear Muses he / will delight the neighboring meadows with his sweet song. / Numa himself will marvel among the gloomy woods / where he spends blessed, eternal leisure, / leaning backwards, gazing always at his Egeria.[10] [35] / And the swelling Tiber itself, from this time calmed, / will favor the annual hope of the farmers: / nor will it run, slackened on its left rein / in excess filled, rushing over kings in their tombs; / but it will better control the bridle of its waves [40] / even to the salt realms of curving Portumnus.[11]

(Nov. ? 1638)

---

[5] Salzilli's commendatory epigram printed in the 1645 edition asserts that Milton should be crowned with the triple laurel of poetry, for he surpasses the Greek, Latin, and Etruscan (Italian) poets.

[6] poetry apparently imitative of the lyrics of Alcaeus and Sappho, both of Lesbos.

[7] goddess of youth.

[8] The invocation "Ie Paion" was a part of a song of healing addressed to Apollo, who had slain the dragon Python, personification of the evils of the underworld.

[9] The woodland deity Faunus, guardian of crops and king of Latium, the Roman hills, and Evander, founder of a colony on the banks of the Tiber, are called upon since Salzilli lies ill in Rome.

[10] Numa, legendary king of Rome, attributed with having written many books on sacred law, would be amazed at a restored Salzilli. Egeria, goddess of fountains, counseled Numa by a sacred spring.

[11] The Tiber frequently inundated surrounding areas, particularly those on the lower left bank. Portumnus, the god of harbors, is perhaps called "curving" because of the location of ports at shore indentations and because of the sinuousness of the Italian coast where the Tiber empties into the Tyrrhenian Sea.

Mansus

Joannes Baptista Mansus, Marchio Villensis, vir ingenii laude, tum literarum studio, nec non et bellicâ virtute apud Italos clarus in primis est. Ad quem Torquati Tassi dialogus extat de Amicitiâ scriptus; erat enim Tassi amicissimus; ab quo etiam inter Campaniæ principes celebratur, in illo poemate cui titulus Gerusalemme conquistata, lib. 20.

> *Fra cavalier magnanimi, è cortesi*
> *Risplende il Manso—*

Is authorem Neapoli commorantem summâ benevolentiâ prosecutus est, multaque ei detulit humanitatis officia. Ad hunc itaque hospes ille antequam ab eâ urbe discederet, ut ne ingratum se ostenderet, hoc carmen misit.

Hæc quoque, Manse, tuæ meditantur carmina laudi
Pierides,[1] tibi, Manse choro notissime Phœbi,
Quandoquidem ille alium haud æquo est dignatus honore,
Post Galli cineres, et Mecænatis Hetrusci.[2]
Tu quoque si nostræ tantùm valet aura Camœnæ,   5
Victrices hederas inter, laurosque sedebis.
Te pridem magno felix concordia Tasso
Junxit, et æternis inscripsit nomina chartis.
Mox tibi dulciloquum non inscia Musa Marinum[3]
Tradidit, ille tuum dici se gaudet alumnum,   10
Dum canit Assyrios divûm prolixus amores;
Mollis et Ausonias stupefecit carmine nymphas.
Ille itidem moriens tibi soli debita vates
Ossa tibi soli, supremaque vota reliquit.
Nec manes pietas tua chara fefellit amici,   15
Vidimus arridentem operoso ex ære poetam.
Nec satis hoc visum est in utrumque, et nec pia cessant
Officia in tumulo, cupis integros rapere Orco,
Quà potes, atque avidas Parcarum eludere leges:
Amborum genus, et variâ sub sorte peractam   20
Describis vitam, moresque, et dona Minervæ;[4]
Æmulus illius Mycalen qui natus ad altam
Rettulit Æolii vitam facundus Homeri.[5]
Ergo ego te Cliûs[6] et magni nomine Phœbi,

Manse pater, jubeo longum slavere per ævum　　　　　　25
Missus Hyperboreo[7] juvenis peregrinus ab axe.
Nec tu longinquam bonus aspernabere Musam,
Quæ nuper gelidâ vix enutrita sub Arcto
Imprudens Italas ausa est volitare per urbes.
Nos etiam in nostro modulantes flumine cygnos　　　　　　30
Credimus obscuras noctis sensisse per umbras,
Quà Thamesis latè puris argenteus urnis
Oceani glaucos perfundit gurgite crines.
Quin et in has quondam pervenit Tityrus[8] oras.
Sed neque nos genus incultum, nec inutile Phœbo,　　　　　　35
Quà plaga septeno mundi sulcata Trione
Brumalem patitur longâ sub nocte Boöten.[9]
Nos etiam colimus Phœbum, nos munera Phœbo
Flaventes spicas, et lutea mala canistris,
Halantemque crocum (perhibet nisi vana vetustas)　　　　　　40
Misimus, et lectas Druidum de gente choreas.
(Gens Druides antiqua sacris operata deorum
Heroum laudes imitandaque gesta canebant)
Hinc quoties festo cingunt altaria cantu
Delo in herbosâ Graiæ de more puellæ　　　　　　45
Carminibus lætis memorant Corineïda Loxo,
Fatidicamque Upin, cum flavicomâ Hecaërge
Nuda Caledonio variatas pectora fuco.[10]
Fortunate senex,[11] ergo quacunque per orbem
Torquati decus, et nomen celebrabitur ingens,　　　　　　50
Claraque perpetui succrescet fama Marini,
Tu quoque in ora frequens venies plausumque virorum,
Et parili carpes iter immortale volatu.
Dicetur tum sponte tuos habitasse penates
Cynthius, et famulas venisse ad limina Musas:　　　　　　55
At non sponte domum tamen idem, et regis adivit
Rura Pheretiadæ cælo fugitivus Apollo;[12]
Ille licet magnum Alciden susceperat hospes;
Tantùm ubi clamosos placuit vitare bubulcos,
Nobile mansueti cessit Chironis[13] in antrum,　　　　　　60
Irriguos inter saltus frondosaque tecta
Peneium prope rivum: ibi sæpe sub ilice nigrâ
Ad citharæ strepitum blandâ prece victus amici
Exilii duros lenibat voce labores.
Tum neque ripa suo, barathro nec fixa sub imo,　　　　　　65
Saxa stetere loco, nutat Trachinia rupes,
Nec sentit solitas, immania pondera, silvas,

Emotæque suis properant de collibus orni,
Mulcenturque novo maculosi carmine lynces.
Diis dilecte senex, te Jupiter æquus oportet   70
Nascentem, et miti lustrarit lumine Phœbus,
Atlantisque nepos;[14] neque enim nisi charus ab ortu
Diis superis poterit magno favisse poetæ.
Hinc longæva tibi lento sub flore senectus
Vernat, et Æsonios[15] lucratur vivida fusos,   75
Nondum deciduos servans tibi frontis honores,
Ingeniumque vigens, et adultum mentis acumen.
O mihi si mea sors talem concedat amicum
Phœbæos decorâsse viros qui tam bene norit,
Si quando indigenas revocabo in carmina reges,   80
Arturumque etiam sub terris bella moventem;
Aut dicam invictæ sociali fœdere mensæ,
Magnanimos Heroas, et (O modo spiritus adsit)
Frangam Saxonicas Britonum sub Marte phalanges.
Tandem ubi non tacitæ permensus tempora vitæ,   85
Annorumque satur cineri sua jura relinquam,
Ille mihi lecto madidis astaret ocellis,
Astanti sat erit si dicam, sim tibi curæ;
Ille meos artus liventi morte solutos
Curaret parvâ componi molliter urnâ.   90
Forsitan et nostros ducat de marmore vultus,
Nectens aut Paphiâ myrti aut Parnasside lauri[16]
Fronde comas, at ego securâ pace quiescam.
Tum quoque, si qua fides, si præmia certa bonorum,
Ipse ego cælicolûm semotus in æthera divûm,   95
Quò labor et mens pura vehunt, atque ignea virtus,
Secreti hæc aliquâ mundi de parte videbo
(Quantum fata sinunt) et totâ mente serenùm
Ridens purpureo suffundar lumine vultus
Et simul æthereo plaudam mihi lætus Olympo.   100

Manso

*John Baptista Manso, Marquis of Villa, man of genius, well-praised al-
ready for his study of literature and also for his martial courage, is
renowned in the foremost ranks among Italians. A dialogue on friend-
ship written to him by Torquato Tasso is extant; for he was most
friendly to Tasso; by whom likewise he is honored among the Cam-
panian princes, in that poem which is titled* Jerusalem Conquered,
Book 20:

> *Among magnanimous and courteous cavaliers
> Manso is resplendent.*

*He honored the author sojourning in Naples with the greatest kindness,
and granted him many courteous attentions. To whom accordingly
before he left that city, the visitor, so that he would not show him-
self ungrateful, sent this poem.*

These verses also, Manso, the Pierides[1] are meditating / in your praise;
for you, Manso, well-known among the choir of Apollo, / since indeed
after the death of Gallus and of Etruscan Maecenas,[2] / he deems no
other equally worthy in honor. / You also, if the breath of my Muse has
power to such a degree, [5] / will sit among the victorious ivy and lau-
rels. / Happy friendship joined you to the great Tasso / long ago, and
has inscribed your names in everlasting scrolls. / Soon afterwards the
Muse, not without wisdom, committed to you / the sweet-tongued
Marini;[3] he was pleased to be called your foster-son, [10] / when, prolix,
he sang the Assyrian loves of the gods; / and, gentle, he benumbed the
Ausonian nymphs with his song. / So that poet, dying, bequeathed his
indebted remains to you alone / and his last wishes to you alone. / And
your dear affection has not disappointed your friend's shade; [15] / we
have seen the poet smiling from his artfully wrought bronze. / But this
was not perceived sufficiently in each one, and your tender services / did
not end in the tomb; you wish to seize them unharmed from Orcus, / as
well as you can, and to elude the greedy laws of the Fates: / you write

[1] the Muses.
[2] Cornelius Gallus (69–26 B.C.) established the elegy as a main form of
Latin poetry; Gaius Maecenas was patron of a literary circle which included
Virgil, Horace, Propertius, and Varius.
[3] Giambattista Marini (1569–1625) was author of *Adone* (1623), which re-
counts the love of Venus for Adonis, the sun-god of the Assyrians (l. 11). "Au-
sonian," l. 12, means Italian.

the ancestry of both and each one's life, achieved [20] / under change-
able fortune, their traits, and their gifts from Athena;[4] / eloquent rival
of that man born in high Mycale / who recounted the life of Aeolian
Homer.[5] / Therefore, in the name of Clio[6] and great Apollo, / father
Manso, I bid you be well through a long life, [25] / a young pilgrim
sent from an Hyperborean[7] clime. / You, good man will not scorn a re-
mote Muse, / who, hardly nourished under the frozen Bear, ignorant, /
has recently ventured to fly to and fro through the Italian cities. / Fur-
thermore I believe that in the dark shadows of night I have heard [30]
/ the swans singing on our river / where the silvery Thames with pure
urns / widely bathes her gleaming tresses in the abyss of the ocean. /
And of a truth Tityrus[8] long ago attained these shores. / But we, neither
an uncultivated race nor one unserviceable to Apollo, [35] / in the region
of the world which is furrowed by the sevenfold Triones, / endure in the
long night wintry Boötes.[9] / We therefore worship Apollo; we have sent
presents to him, / golden ears of grain, and yellow apples in baskets, /
and fragrant crocus (unless antiquity bestows vain things), [40] / and
choice dances from the race of the Druids. / (The ancient Druid nation,
experienced in the sacred rites of the gods, / used to sing the praises of
heroes and their emulable deeds.) / So often as the Greek maidens en-
circle with festive music / the altars in grassy Delos, according to their
custom, [45] / they celebrate with happy songs Corinedian Loxo / and
prophetic Upis, with flaxen-haired Hecaerge, / painted diversely to their
naked breasts with Caledonian dye.[10] / Fortunate old man![11] therefore,
wherever through the world / the glory and the great name of Torquato
shall be celebrated [50] / and the illustrious fame of immortal Marini
shall grow anew, / you shall also spring repeatedly into the mouths and
applause of men, / and with equal swiftness you shall tread upon the
road of immortality. / It shall be said then that Apollo dwelled in your
house of his own accord, / and that the Muses came as attendants to
your doors: [55] / and yet not freely did that same Apollo, fugitive from

---

[4] Manso wrote a biography of Tasso, but one of Marini is unknown except for
this reference. The gifts of Athena are wisdom and intellectual pursuits.

[5] Herodotus, supposedly born in Mycale, a promontory of Asia Minor.

[6] the Muse of history.

[7] northern.

[8] Chaucer, whom Spenser represented thus in *Shepheardes Calendar*, Feb.,
92; June, 81; Dec., 4. Spenser sang of the swans on the Thames in *Prothalamion*,
37 ff.

[9] See *Ely*, n. 12. The Triones (ploughing oxen) were the seven principal
stars in each of the Bears.

[10] Loxo, Upis, and Hecaerge—names for Diana, who was born on Delos—are
northern (Corinedian, British) maidens in Callimachus' *Hymn to Delos*, 291–94.

[11] In Milton's mind was Virgil's *Ec.* I, 46, praising one retired to his farm.

heaven, / approach the rural home of King Admetus,[12] / although he had been host to great Hercules; / when he wished so much to escape the noisy ploughmen, / he retired to the renowned cave of the gentle Chiron[13] [60] / among the moist woodlands and leafy abodes / near the river Peneus: there often under the dark ilex, / to the sound of the cithara, won by his friend's soft plea, / he would lighten the hard labors of exile by his voice. / Then neither bank nor rocks fixed under the lowest abyss [65] / would stay in place; the Trachinian cliff tottered, / and no longer felt the vast weight in its accustomed forests, / and displaced mountain-ashes hastened from their hills, / and the spotted lynxes were soothed by the strange song. / Old man, beloved of the gods, favorable Jove must have been present [70] / at your birth, and Phoebus must have purified you with his mellow light, / and the grandson of Atlas;[14] for no one, unless favored from birth / by the heavenly gods, could have befriended a great poet. / Therefore to you old age blooms with lasting flower, / and, vigorous, gains the spindles of Aeson,[15] [75] / preserving the honors of brow not yet falling to you, / and esteeming your talents and mature power of mind. / O if my lot might grant me such a friend, / one who so well knows how to honor the devotees of Apollo, / if ever I shall recall our native kings in songs, [80] / and likewise Arthur waging wars under the earth; / or proclaim the magnanimous heroes of the invincible table / with their convenant of companionship, and (O only let the spirit be present) / shatter the Saxon phalanxes under British Mars. / And when at last, having traversed the hours of a not silent life, [85] / and full of years, I bequeath to the ashes their due, / he should stand by my couch with tearful eyes, / it shall be enough if I might say to him standing there, Would I were in your care; / he would be solicitous for my limbs, relaxed by livid death, / gently to be gathered in a little urn. [90] / And perhaps he might fashion my features from marble, / fastening my locks with a garland of either Paphian myrtle / or Parnassian laurel,[16] so I should rest in untroubled peace. / Then also, if to that degree faithful, if certain of the rewards of the good, / I myself, far removed in the upper air of the heaven-dwelling gods, [95] / where labor and a pure mind and fervid virtue lead, / shall see these things from some part of the secret world / (as many as the fates allow), and with my whole heart, / smiling, shall be suffused with brilliant light on my serene

[12] Apollo, exiled for vengeance on the Cyclops, served as a serf with Admetus, king of Pherae, for a year. For the visit of Hercules, see *Son. 23*, n. 2.
[13] the centaur, who lived in Thessaly; the Trachinian cliff (l. 66) is Mt. Oeta.
[14] Hermes, inventor of the lyre.
[15] Aeson was restored to youth by his daughter-in-law Medea, thus reversing the spindles of the Fates.
[16] from Paphos, sacred to Venus, and Mt. Parnassus, sacred to the Muses.

face / and at the same time I shall congratulate myself, full of joy, on ethereal Olympus. [100]

(*Dec. 1638*)

Ad Leonoram Romæ canentem[1]

Angelus unicuique suus (sic credite gentes)
  Obtigit æthereis ales ab ordinibus.
Quid mirum, Leonora, tibi si gloria major?
  Nam tua præsentem vox sonat ipsa Deum.
Aut Deus, aut vacui certè mens tertia cœli[2]   5
  Per tua secretò guttura serpit agens;
Serpit agens, facilisque docet mortalia corda
  Sensim immortali assuescere posse sono.
Quòd si cuncta quidem Deus est, per cunctaque fusus,
  In te unâ loquitur, cætera mutus habet.   10

To Leonora singing in Rome[1]

Each person's own particular angel (so believe, nations) / from the heavenly orders protects us with his wings. / What wonder, Leonora, if a greater glory be yours? / Certainly your voice itself pours forth the presence of God. / Either God or certainly a third mind from the empty skies[2] [5] / secretly winds through your throat effectively; / winds effectively and willingly teaches mortal hearts / how they may gradually become accustomed to immortal sounds. / But if God is all things in truth, and through all things diffused, / in you alone he speaks, and holds all others mute. [10]

(*Feb. ? 1639*)

---

[1] the Neapolitan singer Leonora Baroni, whom Milton may have heard in the palace of Cardinal Barberini in Rome.
[2] perhaps the Holy Ghost, third person of the Trinity.

Ad eandem

Altera Torquatum cepit Leonora Poëtam,
  Cujus ab insano cessit amore furens.[1]
Ah miser ille tuo quantò feliciùs ævo
  Perditus, et propter te, Leonora, foret!
Et te Pieriâ sensisset voce canentem   5
  Aurea maternæ fila movere lyræ![2]
Quamvis Dircæo torsisset lumina Pentheo[3]
  Sævior, aut totus desipuisset iners,
Tu tamen errantes cæcâ vertigine sensus
  Voce eadem poteras composuisse tuâ;   10
Et poteras ægro spirans sub corde quietem
  Flexanimo cantu restituisse sibi.

To the same

Another Leonora captured the poet Torquato, / from excessive love of
whom he went mad.[1] / Ah, unfortunate man, how much more happily
in your age / he might have been ruined, and for you, Leonora! / And
he would have heard you singing with Pierian voice [5] / to set in mo-
tion the golden strings of your mother's lute.[2] / Although he had rolled
his eyes more furiously than Dircean Pentheus,[3] / or raved to total im-
mobility, / you still could have quieted his wandering senses / in their
blind giddiness by your voice; [10] / and you, breathing peace beneath
his suffering heart, / could have restored him to himself with your heart-
moving song.

(Feb. ? 1639)

[1] Torquato Tasso had spells of derangement for many years before his death
in 1595; his love for Leonora d'Este, sister of his patron Alfonso, Duke of Fer-
rara, was romantically given as the cause.
[2] Adriana Baroni, an accomplished musician and lutist. Pierian refers to the
Muses.
[3] a king of Thebes, who was torn to pieces by followers of Bacchus.

Ad eandem

Credula quid liquidam Sirena, Neapoli, jactas,
  Claraque Parthenopes[1] fana Achelöiados,
Littoreamque tuâ defunctam Naiada ripâ
  Corpora Chalcidico sacra dedisse rogo?
Illa quidem vivitque, et amœnâ Tibridis undâ   5
  Mutavit rauci murmura Pausilipi.[2]
Illic Romulidûm studiis ornata secundis,
  Atque homines cantu detinet atque Deos.

To the same

Why, credulous Naples, do you vaunt your clear-voiced Siren / and the
famous temple of Parthenope,[1] daughter of Achelous, / and your shore-
Naiad, perished on the coast, / her consecrated body to be dedicated on
a Chalcidian pyre? / In truth she lives and, for the delightful surge of
the Tiber, [5] / has exchanged the roaring of raucous Pausilipus.[2] /
There, honored by the favorable zeal of the sons of Romulus, / she de-
tains both men and gods with her song.

(Feb. ? 1639)

[1] a siren, who, after drowning herself because of Ulysses' escape, was washed
ashore in the bay of Naples, an area settled by Greeks from Chalcis.
[2] a mountain northwest of Naples, through which a much travelled road
passed. Leonora, now in Rome, has left the noise of Naples behind.

Epitaphium Damonis[1]

ARGUMENTUM

Thyrsis et Damon ejusdem viciniæ Pastores, eadem studia sequuti a pue-
ritiâ amici erant, ut qui plurimùm. Thyrsis animi causâ profectus
peregrè de obitu Damonis nuncium accepit.[2] Domum postea rever-
sus, et rem ita esse comperto, se, suamque solitudinem hoc carmine
deplorat. Damonis autem sub personâ hîc intelligitur Carolus Deo-
datus ex urbe Hetruriæ Luca paterno genere oriundus, cætera An-
glus; ingenio, doctrina, clarissimisque cæteris virtutibus, dum viveret,
juvenis egregius.

Himerides[3] nymphæ (nam vos et Daphnin et Hylan,
Et plorata diu meministis fata Bionis)
Dicite Sicelicum Thamesina per oppida carmen:
Quas miser effudit voces, quæ murmura Thyrsis,
Et quibus assiduis exercuit antra querelis,   5
Fluminaque, fontesque vagos, nemorumque recessus,
Dum sibi præreptum queritur Damona, neque altam
Luctibus exemit noctem loca sola pererrans.
Et jam bis[4] viridi surgebat culmus arista,
Et totidem flavas numerabant horrea messes,   10
Ex quo summa dies tulerat Damona sub umbras,
Nec dum aderat Thyrsis; pastorem scilicet illum
Dulcis amor Musæ Thusca retinebat in urbe.
Ast ubi mens expleta domum, pecorisque relicti[5]
Cura vocat, simul assuetâ sedítque sub ulmo,   15
Tum vero amissum tum denique sentit amicum,
Cœpit et immensum sic exonerare dolorem.
    Ite domum impasti, domino jam non vacat, agni.
Hei mihi! quæ terris, quæ dicam numina cœlo,
Postquam te immiti rapuerunt funere, Damon;   20
Siccine nos linquis, tua sic sine nomine virtus
Ibit, et obscuris numero sociabitur umbris?
At non ille,[6] animas virgâ qui dividit aureâ,
Ista velit, dignumque tui te ducat in agmen,
Ignavumque procul pecus arceat omne silentum.   25
    Ite domum impasti, domino jam non vacat, agni.
Quicquid erit, certè nisi me lupus antè videbit,[7]
Indeplorato non comminuere sepulcro,
Constabitque tuus tibi honos, longúmque vigebit

Inter pastores: Illi tibi vota secundo   30
Solvere post Daphnin, post Daphnin dicere laudes
Gaudebunt, dum rura Pales, dum Faunus amabit:[8]
Si quid id est, priscamque fidem coluisse, piúmque,
Palladiásque artes, sociúmque habuisse canorum.
 Ite domum impasti, domino jam non vacat, agni.   35
Hæc tibi certa manent, tibi erunt hæc præmia, Damon,
At mihi quid tandem fiet modò? quis mihi fidus
Hærebit lateri comes, ut tu sæpe solebas
Frigoribus duris, et per loca fœta pruinis,
Aut rapido sub sole, siti morientibus herbis?   40
Sive opus in magnos fuit eminùs ire leones
Aut avidos terrere lupos præsepibus altis;
Quis fando sopire diem, cantuque solebit?
 Ite domum impasti, domino jam non vacat, agni.
Pectora cui credam? quis me lenire docebit   45
Mordaces curas, quis longam fallere noctem
Dulcibus alloquiis, grato cùm sibilat igni
Molle pyrum, et nucibus strepitat focus, at malus auster
Miscet cuncta foris, et desuper intonat ulmo.
 Ite domum impasti, domino jam non vacat, agni.   50
Aut æstate, dies medio dum vertitur axe,
Cum Pan æsculeâ somnum capit abditus umbrâ,
Et repetunt sub aquis sibi nota sedilia nymphæ,
Pastoresque latent, stertit sub sæpe colonus,
Quis mihi blanditiásque tuas, quis tum mihi risus,   55
Cecropiosque sales[9] referet, cultosque lepores?
 Ite domum impasti, domino jam non vacat, agni.
At jam solus agros, jam pascua solus oberro,
Sicubi ramosæ densantur vallibus umbræ,
Hic serum expecto, supra caput imber et Eurus[10]   60
Triste sonant, fractæque agitata crepuscula silvæ.
 Ite domum impasti, domino jam non vacat, agni.
Heu quàm culta mihi priùs arva procacibus herbis
Involvuntur, et ipsa situ seges alta fatiscit!
Innuba neglecto marcescit et uva racemo,   65
Nec myrteta juvant; ovium quoque tædet, at illæ
Mœrent, inque suum convertunt ora magistrum.
 Ite domum impasti, domino jam non vacat, agni.
Tityrus ad corylos vocat, Alphesibœus ad ornos,
Ad salices Ægon, ad flumina pulcher Amyntas,[11]   70
Hic gelidi fontes, hîc illita gramina musco,
Hic Zephyri, hîc placidas interstrepit arbutus undas;
Ista canunt surdo, frutices ego nactus abibam.
 Ite domum impasti, domino jam non vacat, agni.

Mopsus[12] ad hæc, nam me redeuntem forte notârat   75
(Et callebat avium linguas, et sydera Mopsus)
Thyrsi quid hoc? dixit, quæ te coquit improba bilis?
Aut te perdit amor, aut te malè fascinat astrum,
Saturni[13] grave sæpe fuit pastoribus astrum,
Intimaque obliquo figit præcordia plumbo.   80
    Ite domum impasti, domino jam non vacat, agni.
Mirantur nymphæ, et quid te, Thyrsi, futurum est?
Quid tibi vis? ajunt, non hæc solet esse juventæ
Nubila frons, oculique truces, vultusque severi,
Illa choros, lususque leves, et semper amorem   85
Jure petit, bis ille miser qui serus amavit.
    Ite domum impasti, domino jam non vacat, agni.
Venit Hyas, Dryopéque, et filia Baucidis Ægle
Docta modos, citharæque sciens, sed perdita fastu,
Venit Idumanii Chloris vicina fluenti;[14]   90
Nil me blanditiæ, nil me solantia verba,
Nil me, si quid adest, movet, aut spes ulla futuri.
    Ite domum impasti, domino jam non vacat, agni.
Hei mihi quam similes ludunt per prata juvenci,
Omnes unanimi secum sibi lege sodales,   95
Nec magis hunc alio quisquam secernit amicum
De grege, sic densi veniunt ad pabula thoes,
Inque vicem hirsuti paribus junguntur onagri;
Lex eadem pelagi, deserto in littore Proteus[15]
Agmina phocarum numerat, vilisque volucrum   100
Passer habet semper quicum sit, et omnia circum
Farra libens volitet, serò sua tecta revisens,
Quem si fors letho objecit, seu milvus adunco
Fata tulit rostro, seu stravit arundine fossor,
Protinus ille alium socio petit inde volatu.   105
Nos durum genus, et diris exercita fatis
Gens, homines, aliena animis, et pectore discors,
Vix sibi quisque parem de millibus invenit unum,
Aut si sors dederit tandem non aspera votis,
Illum inopina dies quâ non speraveris horâ   110
Surripit, æternum linquens in sæcula damnum.
    Ite domum impasti, domino jam non vacat, agni.
Heu quis me ignotas traxit vagus error in oras
Ire per aëreas rupes, Alpemque nivosam!
Ecquid erat tanti Romam vidisse sepultam?   115
Quamvis illa foret, qualem dum viseret olim,
Tityrus[16] ipse suas et oves et rura reliquit;
Ut te tam dulci possem caruisse sodale,
Possem tot maria alta, tot interponere montes,

Tot sylvas, tot saxa tibi, fluviosque sonantes?   120
Ah certè extremum licuisset tangere dextram,
Et bene compositos placidè morientis ocellos,
Et dixisse vale, nostri memor ibis ad astra.
   Ite domum impasti, domino jam non vacat, agni.
Quamquam etiam vestri nunquam meminisse pigebit,   125
Pastores Thusci, Musis operata juventus,
Hic Charis, atque Lepos; et Thuscus tu quoque Damon,
Antiquâ genus unde petis Lucumonis ab urbe.
O ego quantus eram, gelidi cum stratus ad Arni
Murmura, populeumque nemus, quà mollior herba,   130
Carpere nunc violas, nunc summas carpere myrtos,
Et potui Lycidæ certantem audire Menalcam.
Ipse etiam tentare ausus sum,[17] nec puto multûm
Displicui, nam sunt et apud me munera[18] vestra
Fiscellæ, calathique et cerea vincla cicutæ,   135
Quin et nostra suas docuerunt nomina fagos
Et Datis, et Fancinus, erant et vocibus ambo
Et studiis noti, Lydorum[19] sanguinis ambo.
   Ite domum impasti, domino jam non vacat, agni.
Hæc mihi tum læto dictabat roscida luna,   140
Dum solus teneros claudebam cratibus hœdos.
Ah quoties dixi, cùm te cinis ater habebat,
Nunc canit, aut lepori nunc tendit retia Damon,
Vimina nunc texit, varios sibi quod sit in usus;
Et quæ tum facili sperabam mente futura   145
Arripui voto levis, et præsentia finxi,
Heus bone numquid agis? nisi te quid forte retardat,
Imus? et argutâ paulùm recubamus in umbra,
Aut ad aquas Colni,[20] aut ubi jugera Cassibelauni?
Tu mihi percurres medicos, tua gramina, succos,   150
Helleborúmque, humilésque crocos, foliûmque hyacinthi,
Quasque habet ista palus herbas, artesque medentûm.
Ah pereant herbæ, pereant artesque medentûm,
Gramina, postquam ipsi nil profecere magistro.
Ipse etiam, nam nescio quid mihi grande sonabat   155
Fistula, ab undecimâ jam lux est altera nocte,[21]
Et tum forte novis admôram labra cicutis,
Dissiluere tamen rupta compage, nec ultra
Ferre graves potuere sonos, dubito quoque ne sim
Turgidulus, tamen et referam, vos cedite silvæ.   160
   Ite domum impasti, domino jam non vacat, agni.
Ipse ego Dardanias Rutupina per æquora puppes
Dicam,[22] et Pandrasidos regnum vetus Inogeniæ,
Brennúmque Arviragúmque duces, priscúmque Belinum,

Et tandem Armoricos Britonum sub lege colonos;   165
Tum gravidam Arturo fatali fraude Jögernen,
Mendaces vultus, assumptáque Gorlöis arma,
Merlini dolus. O mihi tum si vita supersit,
Tu procul annosa pendebis fistula pinu
Multùm oblita mihi, aut patriis mutata camœnis   170
Brittonicum strides, quid enim? omnia non licet uni
Non sperasse uni licet omnis, mi satis ampla
Merces, et mihi grande decus (sim ignotus in ævum
Tum licet, externo penitúsque inglorius orbi)
Si me flava comas legat Usa, et potor Alauni,   175
Vorticibúsque frequens Abra, et nemus omne Treantæ,
Et Thamesis meus ante omnes, et fusca metallis
Tamara, et extremis me discant Orcades undis.²³
    Ite domum impasti, domino jam non vacat, agni.
Hæc tibi servabam lentâ sub cortice lauri,   180
Hæc, et plura simul, tum quæ mihi pocula²⁴ Mansus,
Mansus Chalcidicæ²⁵ non ultima gloria ripæ
Bina dedit, mirum artis opus, mirandus et ipse,
Et circùm gemino cælaverat argumento:
In medio rubri maris unda, et odoriferum ver,   185
Littora longa Arabum, et sudantes balsama silvæ,
Has inter Phœnix divina avis, unica terris
Cæruleùm fulgens diversicoloribus alis
Auroram vitreis surgentem respicit undis.
Parte alia polus omnipatens, et magnus Olympus,   190
Quis putet? hic quoque Amor,²⁶ pictæque in nube pharetræ,
Arma corusca faces, et spicula tincta pyropo;
Nec tenues animas, pectúsque ignobile vulgi
Hinc ferit, at circùm flammantia lumina torquens
Semper in erectum spargit sua tela per orbes   195
Impiger, et pronos nunquam collimat ad ictus,
Hinc mentes ardere sacræ, formæque deorum.
    Tu quoque in his, nec me fallit spes lubrica, Damon,
Tu quoque in his certè es, nam quò tua dulcis abiret
Sanctáque simplicitas, nam quò tua candida virtus?   200
Nec te Lethæo fas quæsivisse sub orco,²⁷
Nec tibi conveniunt lacrymæ, nec flebimus ultrà,
Ite procul lacrymæ, purum colit æthera Damon,
Æthera purus habet, pluvium pede reppulit arcum;
Heroúr.que animas inter, divósque perennes,   205
Æthereos haurit latices et gaudia potat
Ore Sacro. Quin tu cœli post jura recepta
Dexter ades, placidúsque fave quicúnque vocaris,
Seu tu noster eris Damon, sive æquior audis

Diodatus, quo te divino nomine[28] cuncti   210
Cœlicolæ norint, sylvísque vocabere Damon.
Quòd tibi purpureus pudor, et sine labe juventus
Grata fuit, quòd nulla tori libata voluptas,
En etiam tibi virginei servantur honores;[29]
Ipse caput nitidum cinctus rutilante corona,   215
Lætáque frondentis gestans umbracula palmæ
Æternùm perages immortales hymenæos;
Cantus ubi, choreisque furit lyra mista beatis,
Festa Sionæo bacchantur et Orgia Thyrso.[30]

Damon's Epitaph[1]

ARGUMENT

Thyrsis and Damon, shepherds of the same neighborhood, were friends from childhood, since for the most part they had followed the same studies. Thyrsis received the news concerning Damon's death, travelling abroad for the sake of amusement.[2] Afterwards having returned home and upon having ascertained this to be so, he bewailed himself and his loneliness in this song. Moreover Charles Diodati as seen here in the person of Damon, descended through paternal forebears from the Etrurian city of Lucca, in other respects an Englishman; a youth distinguished while he lived by genius, learning, and the other most honorable virtues.

Nymphs of Himera[3]—for you remember Daphnis and Hylas / and the long-lamented fate of Bion— / proclaim your Sicilian song through the towns of the Thames: / what cries the mournful Thyrsis poured forth, what murmurings, / and with what incessant complaints he vexed the

---

[1] In addition to likenesses to the pastoral elegies and idyls of Theocritus, Bion, and Moschus, *Damon* frequently echoes Virgil (e.g., the refrain from *Ec.*, VII, 44, and the similarity of form to *Ec.*, X) and Castiglione's *Alcon;* see T. P. Harrison, Jr., *PMLA*, L (1935), 480–93. But Dorian (*English Diodatis*, pp. 177–78) points out the break with tradition: *Damon* is devoid of real mourners other than Milton. "And because of this concentration on the emotional problem of his personal bereavement, it tells considerably less than do most pastoral elegies of the shepherd who is gone."

[2] Charles Diodati (Damon) was buried at St. Anne's, Blackfriars, London, on Aug. 27, 1638, while Milton (Thyrsis) was abroad. Milton was probably informed of his death (from the plague?) when he reached Venice around Apr. 1639 (see n. 4 below). See also *El.* 1, n. 1, for material about Diodati.

[3] A nymph of the Sicilian river Himera punished Daphnis for refusing her love (Theocritus, *Idyl* 1); and Bion was mourned by the Sicilian poet Moschus. For Hylas, see *El.* 7, n. 3.

caves [5] / and rivers, the wandering streams and recesses of the woods, / when to himself he lamented Damon, prematurely borne away, nor did he / banish the deep night with his griefs, wandering through lonely places. / And now twice[4] was the stalk with its green ear rising, / and twice were the yellow harvests being counted in the barns, [10] / since the last day had swept Damon beneath the shadows, / and still Thyrsis was not present; namely, love of the sweet Muse / was keeping that shepherd in the Tuscan city. / But when his mind was full and the care of the flock / left behind[5] called him home, and as soon as he sat under the accustomed elm, [15] / then truly, then at last, he felt the loss of his friend, / and began to disburden his great sorrow thus: /

Go home unfed, your master has no time now, my lambs. / Ah me! what on earth, what divinities in heaven shall I affirm, / since they have torn you away to inexorable death, Damon? [20] / Thus do you forsake us, thus shall your virtue go below without a name, / and be joined to the troop of unknown shades? / But he[6] who divides the souls with his golden wand / would not wish this, and he would lead you into a multitude worthy of you, / and would keep at a distance the entire slothful, silent herd. [25] /

Go home unfed, your master has no time now, my lambs. / Whatever will be, assuredly, unless a wolf sees me first,[7] / you shall not crumble to dust in an unwept sepulchre; / your repute will endure and flourish long / among the shepherds. To you they shall be glad to pay their vows [30] / second after Daphnis, after Daphnis to sing praises, / while Pales, while Faunus loves the fields:[8] / if there is any worth in having cultivated the ancient faith and piety / and the arts of Pallas, and in having possessed a comrade of songs. /

Go home unfed, your master has no time now, my lambs. [35] / These certainly await you, for you these rewards will exist, Damon. / But what at length will become of me now? what faithful companion / will cling to my side, as you often were wont / in the hard winters and through the regions full of snows, / or under the fierce sun, with herbs dying from thirst, [40] / whether the task was to advance on great lions from a distance / or to frighten hungry wolves away from the high sheepfolds. / Who will be wont to lull my time with speaking and singing? /

[4] referring to Italian, not English, agriculture; both winter and spring wheat are harvested in the Arno valley. The imperfect tenses of ll. 9–13 imply that Milton did not learn of Diodati's death until after his second stay in Florence, the Tuscan city, in Mar. 1639.
[5] possibly Milton's nephews Edward and John Phillips, who joined his household shortly after his return.
[6] Hermes, who led the dead to the nether world.
[7] Seen by a wolf first, a man became dumb.
[8] Pales was a tutelary of shepherds and flocks; Faunus, of crops and herds.

Go home unfed, your master has no time now, my lambs. / To whom shall I confide my heart? Who will teach me to assuage [45] / my mordant cares, who to deceive the long night / with pleasant conversations, while the delicate pear hisses / before the grateful fire, and the hearth crackles with nuts, as the evil / southwind rattles all the doors, and whistles in the elm above. /

Go home unfed, your master has no time now, my lambs. [50] / Or in summer, when the day is turned to noon, / when Pan enjoys sleep, hidden in the shade of an oak, / and the nymphs return to their well-known haunts beneath the waters, / and the shepherds lie concealed, the farmer snores under a hedge, / who will bring back to me your flatteries, who then [55] / your laughter and Attic salt,[9] your cultured graces? /

Go home unfed, your master has no time now, my lambs. / But now alone in the fields, now alone in the pastures I roam / wherever the branching shadows are made dense by the valleys, / there I await the evening; overhead the rain and the southeast wind[10] [60] / sorrowfully resound, and in the restless twilight of the buffeted wood. /

Go home unfed, your master has no time now, my lambs. / Alas, how entangled with insolent weeds are my once cultivated / fields, and the tall grain itself is drooping with neglect, / the unmarried grape withers on its slighted vine, [65] / nor do myrtle groves delight; my sheep also offend, but they / mourn and turn their faces to their master. /

Go home unfed, your master has no time now, my lambs. / Tityrus calls to the hazels, Alphesiboeus to the mountain ashes, / Aegon to the willows, handsome Amyntas to the rivers:[11] [70] / Here are the icy springs, here the pastures spread with moss, / here the zephyrs, here the arbutus sounds amidst the quiet waters. / They sing to deaf ears; having stumbled on them, I vanished into the shrubs. /

Go home unfed, your master has no time now, my lambs. / Mopsus[12] came after them, for he had marked me by chance returning, [75] / and truly Mopsus did understand the songs of birds and the stars: / Thyrsis, what now? he said, what excessive bile torments you? / Either love is destroying you or a star is wickedly bewitching you. / Saturn's star[13] has often been painful to shepherds, / and it pierces the inmost heart with its slanting leaden bullet. [80] /

Go home unfed, your master has no time now, my lambs. / The

[9] poignant and delicate wit.
[10] The southeast wind and the rain suggest composition of *Damon* in autumn (around Oct.).
[11] All are shepherds of idyllic literature and appear in Virgil's *Eclogues*.
[12] a fusion of the Greek seer and of Virgil's shepherd (*Ec.*, V, VIII). For the relation of birds to prophecy, see *El.* 3, n. 6.
[13] The planet Saturn, alchemically the name for lead, was known for its gloomy and sullen aspect.

nymphs are amazed, and they speak, What is to become of you, Thyrsis? / What do you wish for yourself? that brow of youth is not wont to be / melancholy, nor its eyes grim, nor its countenance severe; / these things justly desire dances and nimble sports [85] / and always love; twice miserable he who loved late. /

Go home unfed, your master has no time now, my lambs. / Hyas came, and Dryope, and Aegle, the daughter of Baucis, / well-versed in melodies and skilled with the harp, but ruined by pride; / Chloris, a neighbor of the Idumanian river, came.[14] [90] / Neither flatteries nor consoling words, / nothing moves me, if anything appears, nor any hope of the future. /

Go home unfed, your master has no time now, my lambs. / Ah me, alas! how similarly the young bullocks play through the meadows, / all comrades together under a law harmonious to themselves, [95] / and none parts a friend from one more than from another / of the herd; thus the wolves come to their food in packs, / and the shaggy asses are joined with their mates in turn; / the law of the sea is the same, on the deserted shore Proteus[15] / counts his hosts of seals, and least valuable of birds, [100] / the sparrow always has someone with whom he may be, and to all the grains / flies about free, returning late to his own nest; / if chance has delivered him to death, or a kite has brought him misfortune / with its hooked beak, or a peasant has brought him down with an arrow, / forthwith that bird seeks another for companion flight. [105] / We men are an insensible race, and driven on by detestable fate, / a nation hostile in our minds and discordant in our heart, / scarcely does anybody find one equal to himself in a thousand, / or if a destiny not unkind were granted at last to our prayers, / an unexpected hour, as far as you will have trusted time, [110] / steals that one, leaving behind an eternal loss to future ages. /

Go home unfed, your master has no time now, my lambs. / Alas! what wandering fancy carried me into unknown climes / to pass through airy rocks and the snow-capped Alps? / Was it of such worth to have seen buried Rome? [115] / although it were such as he viewed it when long ago / Tityrus[16] himself left his sheep and fields, / that I could have been absent from you, from so dear a companion, / that I could set between you so many deep seas, so many mountains, / so many forests, so many rocky lands and roaring rivers? [120] / Ah, surely I would have been

[14] The mourners seem to be one of the Hyades, nymphs of rain, who were changed into stars; Dryope, who was changed into a lotus tree; Aegle, one of the Heliades, who was changed into a poplar tree; and Chloris, goddess of flowers. Baucis probably means an old woman. The Idumanian river is the Chelmer, leading into Blackwater Bay in Essex.

[15] See *El.* 3, n. 7.

[16] in Virgil's *Ec.,* I.

permitted to touch his right hand at the last / and his calmed eyes dying
very peacefully, / and to have said, Farewell! you will go to the stars
remembering me. /

Go home unfed, your master has no time now, my lambs. / And even
though I never shall repent to remember you, [125] / Tuscan shepherds,
youths devoted to the Muses, / here was grace and charm; and you also
Damon were a Tuscan, / from whom you claim your descent from the
ancient city of Lucca. / O how great I was when stretched beside / the
murmurings of the cool Arno and the poplar-grove, where was the softer
grass, [130] / I could pluck now violets, now the tallest myrtles, / and
hear Menalcas contending with Lycidas! / And even I myself dared to
compete,[17] nor do I suppose that I much / displeased, for your gifts[18]
are still with me, / the baskets of twigs, those of wicker, and the shepherd
pipes with waxen bonds. [135] / Indeed Dati and Francini taught their
beech trees my name / and both were noted for their songs / and learn-
ing, both of Lydian blood.[19] /

Go home unfed, your master has no time now, my lambs. / These
things the dewy moon spoke to me, then full of joy, [140] / when alone
I shut the tender kids in their wattled folds. / Ah, how often did I say,
when dark ashes possessed you, / Now Damon is singing or now he is
stretching out his nets for a hare, / now he is weaving osiers for him-
self although it be for various uses. / And then what future I was hoping
for with my affable mind [145] / I snatched from my trivial desire and
supposed my present circumstances. / Hark, good friend! are you doing
anything? unless anything detain you by accident, / let us go and lie for
a while in the clear shade, / either beside the waters of the Colne[20]
or where lie the lands of Cassivelaunas. / You shall run through your
medicinal potions for me, your herbs, [150] / and your hellebore, hum-
ble crocuses, and leaf of hyacinth, / and what plants that marsh holds,
and the arts of the physicians. / Ah! let the plants perish, let the arts of
the physicians perish, / and the herbs, since they themselves have ac-
complished nothing for their master. / Even I—for I do not know what
my pipe was pouring forth [155] / loudly—now daylight is present after
the eleventh night—[21] / perhaps I was then directing my lips to my

---

[17] referring to *Idyl 7* of Theocritus and Milton's poetical performances at the
Svogliati Academy in Florence.

[18] poems and books of verse from his Italian friends, among whom were Carlo
Dati and Antonio Francini.

[19] Lydians were supposed to have founded an early colony in Italy.

[20] the river near Horton. Cassivelaunas was an early British military leader.

[21] signifying the beginning of the latest possible time, under the concept of
twelve, to bemoan his loss. The twelfth day becomes the epiphany, or mani-
festation of divinity, of Diodati. Compare Matt. xx. 6: "And about the eleventh
hour he went out, and found others standing idle, and saith unto them, Why
stand ye here all the day idle?"

new pipes, / yet they have burst asunder with their binding broken, and no further / have they been able to carry the grave notes; I question also that I may not be / vain, and yet that I may recite; depart, you woods. [160] /

Go home unfed, your master has no time now, my lambs. / I myself shall celebrate[22] the Dardanian ships through the Rutupian sea, / and the ancient kingdom of Inogene, daughter of Pandrasus, / the chieftains Brennus and Arviragus, and old Belinus, / and the Armorican colonists at last under the law of the Britons; [165] / then Igraine pregnant with Arthur by fatal deception, / Gorlois' counterfeit features and assumed arms, / the guile of Merlin. O then if life remain to me, / you, my pipe, will hang far off on an aged pine tree / quite forgotten by me, or changed, you shall shrill a tale of Britain [170] / to your native Muses! What then? one can not do everything, / one can not hope to do everything. For me it is sufficiently ample / reward, and to me great glory—even if I be unknown forever / and utterly inglorious to the outside world— / if blonde Ouse read me under her locks and the drinker of the Alne [175] / and the Humber well-filled with whirlpools, and every wood along the Trent, / and before all my Thames, and the Tamar blackened by mines, / and if the Orkneys in their distant seas become acquainted with me.[23] /

Go home unfed, your master has no time now, my lambs. / These things I was keeping for you in the tough bark of the laurel, [180] / these and more besides; moreover the two cups[24] which Manso / gave me, Manso, not the least glory of the Chalcidian shore,[25] / these a marvellous work of art, and he himself singular, / and he had engraved them around with a twofold theme. / In the middle are the waves of the Red Sea, and odor-bearing spring, [185] / the far-reaching shores of Arabia, and

---

[22] Subjects for English epical works included the invasion of England by Brutus (son of Aeneas), and the Trojan colony; the conquests of Gaul and Rome by the British kings Brennus and Belinus; the military engagements in Rome of Arviragus, son of Cymbeline; the settlement of the Britons, fleeing the Saxons, in Armorica (Brittany); the begetting of Arthur through Merlin's magic of making Uther Pendragon appear to Igraine as her husband Gorlois; and perhaps a further but different epic on a British theme. Dardanus was the progenitor of the royal race of Troy; Rutupiae was a part of Kent; and Inogene was Brutus' wife.

[23] The rivers Ouse, Alne, Humber, Trent, and Tamar (in a valley famous for mines) cover much of England, and the Orkneys signify Scotland; Milton's reward will be enough if the British Isles read and know his work.

[24] Michele de Filippis' suggestion that Milton is referring to books, Manso's *Erocallia* and *Poesie Nomiche* (see *PMLA*, LI, 1936, 745–56), is supported by Donald C. Dorian (*PMLA*, LIV, 1939, 612–13), since the same simile of cups for books is found in Pindar's seventh Olympian Ode.

[25] the Bay of Naples.

the woods exuding balsam gums; / among those woods the Phoenix, divine bird, unique on earth, / gleaming cerulean with diversely colored wings, / watches Aurora rising over the glassy waters. / In another part are the wide-extending sky and mighty Olympus. [190] / Who would imagine? here also Love,[26] his quiver painted against a cloud, / his gleaming arms, his torches and darts stained with gold-bronze; / from this place he does not smite trifling spirits or the ignoble heart / of the rabble, but, whirling around with flaming eyes, / he endlessly scatters his darts aloft through the spheres, [195] / unwearied, and never aims toward downward shots. / Hence holy minds and the images of the gods have taken fire. /

You also are among these—for no uncertain hope deceives me, Damon— / you also are among these certainly; for where else might your sweet / and holy simplicity have gone, for where else your radiant virtue? [200] / It would not be proper to have sought you in Lethean Orcus,[27] / neither do tears for you befit, nor shall I shed them more. / Away, my tears; Damon lives in the pure air, / the air he so pure possesses: he rejected the rainbow with his foot. / Among the souls of heroes and immortal gods, [205] / he consumes the heavenly draughts and drinks their joys / with his sacred mouth. But you, since having received the privilege of heaven, / are on the right hand; and peaceful, favor me, however you may be called, / whether you will be our Damon, or hearken more favorably to / Diodati, by which divine name[28] the whole [210] / of heaven will know you, and you will be called Damon in the woods. / Because blushing modesty and youth without blemish / were dear to you, because the delight of marriage was tasted not at all, / lo! likewise the rewards of virginity are reserved for you.[29] / You, encircled around your glorious head with a shining crown [215] / and riding in happy bowers entwined with palm leaves, / shall pursue eternally the immortal marriage / where song and mingled lyre rage with blessed dances, / and festal orgies revel under the thyrsus of Sion.[30]

(*autumn 1639*)

[26] the Platonic Heavenly Eros.
[27] See *Idea*, n. 5.
[28] literally, "god-given."
[29] alluding to Rev. xiv. 4: "These are they which were not defiled with women; for they are virgins. These are they which follow the Lamb whithersoever he goeth."
[30] Diodati is envisioned as joining the heavenly host (Rev. vii. 9) in Bacchic dance of ecstasy under the thyrsus (a staff twined with ivy and vine shoots borne by Bacchantes) of Sion (the heavenly city of God).

PART 3

Poems
Written During Public Life
and Governmental Service
(1641–58)

✳

Sonnet 8

Captain or Colonel, or Knight in Arms,
  Whose chance on these defenceless dores may sease,[1]
  If ever deed of honour did thee please,
  Guard them, and him within protect from harms.
He can requite thee, for he knows the charms   5
  That call Fame on such gentle acts as these,
  And he can spread thy name o're lands and seas,
  What ever clime the suns bright circle warms.
Lift not thy spear against the Muses bowr:[2]
  The great *Emathian* Conqueror[3] bidd spare   10
  The house of *Pindarus,* when temple and towr
Went to the ground: and the repeated air
  Of sad *Electra's* poet[4] had the power
  To save th' *Athenian* walls from ruin bare.

(Nov. 1642)

---

[1] During the earlier days of the First Civil War the Royalist army, after success at Edgehill on Oct. 23, 1642, advanced toward London but retreated Nov. 12–13. Milton's home in Aldersgate Street was just beyond the London city gate; the MS title indicated (in jest) that the sonnet was to be tacked on his door.

[2] Despite the mocking tone of the thin spear raised against the undefended door, Milton is seriously comparing the far-reaching powers of poetry with the inglorious limitations of war.

[3] Alexander the Great of Macedonia (Emathia). Thebes was attacked in 335 B.C. for revolt against Macedonia; the Congress of Corinth decreed that the city was to be razed.

[4] Euripides. The first chorus of that play (ll. 167 ff.) reputedly dissuaded the Spartans from sacking Athens in 404 B.C.

Sonnet 9

Ladie, that in the prime of earliest youth
  Wisely hast shun'd the broad way and the green[1]
  And with those few art eminently seen
  That labour up the hill of heav'nly Truth,[2]
The better part with *Mary* and with *Ruth*[3]   5
  Chosen thou hast, and they that overween
  And at thy growing vertues fret thir spleen
  No anger find in thee, but pitty and ruth.
Thy care is fixt and zealously attends
  To fill thy odorous lamp with deeds of light   10
  And Hope that reaps not shame. Therfore be sure[4]
Thou, when the Bridegroom with his feastfull freinds
  Passes to bliss at the midd howr of night,
  Hast gain'd thy entrance, Virgin wise and pure.[5]

(*1643–45*)

---

[1] The unidentified lady is commended for her steadfast and virtuous life: unlike the Bride who unwisely and unsuccessfully sought her Lord "in the broad ways" (S. of Sol. iii. 2), the lady will attain the kingdom of Heaven because she has followed Jesus' admonition: "Enter ye at the strait gate: for wide is the gate, and broad is the way, that leadeth to destruction, . . . and narrow is the way, which leadeth unto life" (Matt. vii. 13, 14). The green way of the impatient and complaining comes from Job viii. 12–13, 16: "Whilst it is yet in his greenness, and not cut down, it withereth before any other herb. So are the paths of all that forget God; and the hypocrite's hope shall perish: . . . He is green before the sun. . . ."

[2] God's holy hill is gained through perseverance of the virtuous life, for Jesus had said, "I am the way, the truth, and the life: no man cometh unto the Father, but by me" (John xiv. 6). Compare Hesiod's Hill of Virtue (*Works and Days*, 287).

[3] Mary, who steadfastly sat at Jesus' feet to hear his word, had "chosen that good part, which shall not be taken away from her" (Luke x. 42). Ruth, known to the people to be a steadfast and virtuous woman (Ruth i. 18, iii. 11), chose to follow Naomi and her advice, thus becoming a progenitor of Joseph, husband of Jesus' mother, through her marriage to Boaz.

[4] be assured.

[5] The wise virgins, who had filled their lamps in preparation for the time that the kingdom of Heaven would be at hand, were ready when at midnight the Bridegroom came (Matt. xxv. 1–13). As Brooks and Hardy note (p. 160), "it was at midnight too . . . that Boaz awakened to find Ruth at his feet, and when he lay down he had just come from a feast" (Ruth iii. 7–8).

Sonnet 10

Daughter to that good Earle,¹ once President
Of *Englands* Counsel, and her Treasury,
Who liv'd in both, unstain'd with gold or fee,
And left them both, more in himself content,
Till the sad breaking of that Parlament   5
Broke him,² as that dishonest victory
At *Chæronéa*, fatal to liberty
Kill'd with report that Old man eloquent,³
Though later born then to have known the daies
Wherin your Father flourisht, yet by you   10
Madam, me thinks I see him living yet;
So well your words his noble Vertues praise,
That all both judge you to relate them true
And to possess them, Honourd *Margaret*.

(*1643–45*)

¹ Sir James Ley, Earl of Marlborough, Lord Chief Justice, Lord High Treasurer, and Lord President of the Council of State under Charles I. The subject of the sonnet was Lady Margaret, wife of Captain John Hobson.
² Charles' Third Parliament was dissolved by him on Mar. 10, 1629, primarily because of the intractable opposition of Commons to tonnage and poundage; Marlborough died four days later. The next parliament (the Short Parliament) was not called until Apr. 13, 1640.
³ Isocrates. Philip of Macedonia's defeat of Thebes and Athens at Chaeronea in 338 B.C., ending Greek independence, reputedly caused the well-known orator to commit suicide four days later. Like this shameful victory, Charles' thwarting of the people's will was a curtailment of liberty.

In Effigiei Ejus Sculptorem¹

'Αμαθεῖ γεγράφθαί χειρὶ τήνδε μὲν εἰκόνα
Φαίης τάχ' ἄν, πρὸς εἶδος αὐτοφυὲς βλέπων·
Τὸν δ' ἐκτυπωτὸν οὐκ ἐπιγνόντες, φίλοι,
Γελᾶτε φαύλου δυσμίμημα ζωγράφου.

On the Engraver of His Likeness[1]

This image was drawn by an untaught hand, / you might perhaps say, looking at the form of the original. / But since here you do not recognize the modelled face, friends, / laugh at a bad imitation by a worthless artist.

(1645)

[1] A poorly drawn portrait served as a frontispiece in the 1645 edition of the poems; these lines appeared beneath. The engraver was William Marshall.

Sonnet 11[1]

I did but prompt the age to quit thir clogs
  By the known rules of ancient liberty,[2]
  When strait a barbarous noise environs me
  Of Owls and cuckoes, asses, apes and dogs.
As when those hinds that were transform'd to frogs   5
  Rail'd at *Latona's* twin-born progeny
  Which after held the Sun and Moon in Fee.[3]
  But this is got by casting pearl to hogs;[4]

---

[1] See the *Textual Notes* for numbering.

[2] The twin divorce tracts *Tetrachordon* and *Colasterion* were published Mar. 4, 1645; to Milton his work on divorce was part of his contribution to true liberty (*Defensio secunda*, pp. 90–91). In *Tetrachordon* he justified divorce through exposition of Deut. xxiv. 1, 2. Among the published detractions of *Tetrachordon* was Ephraim Pagitt's *Heresiography*, the second edition (1645), which remarks Milton's recourse to scripture to maintain his opinion (p. 142).

[3] The twin children of Latona and Jove were Apollo, god of the sun, and Diana, goddess of the moon. The Lycian peasants who refused Latona and her children drink were turned into frogs by Jove. As Parker has noted (*Explicator,* VIII, 1949, item 3) the fact that Milton's derided pamphlets were published together recalled this image of the twin gods.

[4] Adapted from Matt. vii. 6: "Give not that which is holy unto the dogs, neither cast ye your pearls before swine, lest they trample them under their feet, and turn again and rend you."

That bawl for freedom in thir senseles mood,
    And still⁵ revolt when Truth would set them free.   10
    Licence they mean, when they cry liberty,
For who loves that, must first be wise, and good;
    But from that mark how farr they roav, we see
    For all this wast of wealth, and loss of blood.⁶

(autumn 1645 ?)

⁵ nevertheless.
⁶ The image likens the people who think they aim at liberty by means of Civil
War to wasteful archers whose arrows (rovers) miss their mark and merely
wound their prey.

Sonnet 13

Harry,¹ whose tunefull and well-measur'd song
    First taught our English Music how to span
    Words with just note and accent, not to scan
    With *Midas* eares,² committing short and long,
Thy worth and skill exempts thee from the throng,   5
    With praise anough for Envy to look wan;
    To after-age thou shalt be writt the man
    That with smooth air couldst humor best our tongue.
Thou honourst Vers, and Vers must lend her wing
    To honour thee, the Preist of *Phœbus* quire   10
    That tun'st thir happiest lines in hymn, or story.³

¹ Henry Lawes (1596–1662), who wrote the music for *Mask* (and probably
for *Arcades*), enacted the attendant spirit, and was instrumental in having the
work published. The sonnet was prefixed to *Choice Psalmes put into Musick
For Three Voices* (1648); Milton's nephews, Edward and John Phillips, con-
tributed commendatory lyrics to Lawes' *Ayres* (1653). The standard biography
is Willa M. Evans' *Henry Lawes, Musician and Friend to Poets* (New York,
1941).
² Apollo changed Midas' ears to those of an ass for his obtuseness in declaring
Pan a superior flutist to Apollo. Milton is praising Lawes' faithful attention to
lyrics, in distinction to some lesser seventeenth-century composers' practice of
altering them to fit their music.
³ referring to Lawes' setting of William Cartwright's *The Complaint of
Ariadne.*

Dante shall give Fame leav to set thee higher
Then his *Casella*,[4] whom he woo'd to sing
Met in the milder shades of Purgatory.

(*Feb. 1646*)

[4] a Florentine musician and friend of Dante. When Dante arrived in Purgatory from Hell, he spied Casella, who sang the second canzone of Dante's *Convitio* (*Purgatorio*, II, 76–123).

Sonnet 14[1]

When Faith and Love which parted from thee never,
    Had rip'n'd thy just soul to dwell with God,
    Meekly thou didst resigne this earthy load
Of death, call'd life; which us from life doth sever.
Thy Works and Almes, and all thy good Endeavor   5
    Staid not behind, nor in the grave were trod;
    But as Faith pointed with her golden rod,
Follow'd thee up to joy and bliss for ever.
Love led them on, and Faith who knew them best
    Thy handmaids, clad them o're with purple beames   10
    And azure wings, that up they flew so drest,
And spake the truth of thee in glorious theames[2]
    Before the Judge, who thenceforth bidd thee rest,
    And drink thy fill of pure immortal streames.

(*Dec. 1646*)

[1] Mrs. Catharine Thomason, wife of the book collector George Thomason, was buried on Dec. 12, 1646. The poem is a tissue of Biblical allusions, such as the Christian armor of Faith and Love (Eph. vi. 13–24), the just who shall live by faith (Gal. iii. 11), the meek who inherit the earth (Matt. v. 5), the judgment according to one's faith and works (James ii. 22, 24), the ascent of alms to God (Acts x. 4), the river of immortality (Rev. xxii. 1).

[2] As Grierson pointed out (*TLS*, Jan. 15, 1925, p. 40), the term is musical; it is a song before the throne of God (Rev. xiv. 2–3).

Ad Joannem Roüsium

OXONIENSIS ACADEMIÆ BIBLIOTHECARIUM

De libro poëmatum amisso, quem ille sibi denuò mitti postulabat, ut cum aliis nostris in Bibliotheca publica reponeret, Ode.[1]

STROPHE 1

Gemelle cultu simplici gaudens liber,[2]
Fronde licet geminâ,
Munditiéque nitens non operosâ,
Quam manus attulit
Juvenilis olim,   5
Sedula tamen haud nimii poetæ,
Dum vagus Ausonias[3] nunc per umbras
Nunc Britannica per vireta lusit
Insons populi, barbitóque devius
Indulsit patrio, mox itidem pectine Daunio[4]   10
Longinquum intonuit melos
Vicinis, et humum vix tetigit pede.

ANTISTROPHE

Quis te, parve liber, quis te fratribus
Subduxit reliquis dolo?
Cum tu missus ab urbe,   15
Docto jugiter obsecrante amico,
Illustre tendebas iter
Thamesis[5] ad incunabula
Cærulei patris,
Fontes ubi limpidi   20
Aonidum,[6] thyasusque sacer
Orbi notus per immensos
Temporum lapsus redeunte cælo,
Celeberque futurus in ævum?

STROPHE 2

Modò quis deus, aut editus deo   25
Pristinam gentis miseratus indolem
(Si satis noxas luimus priores
Mollique luxu degener otium)

Tollat nefandos civium tumultus,[7]
Almaque revocet studia sanctus   30
Et relegatas sine sede Musas
Jam penè totis finibus Angligenûm;
Immundasque volucres
Unguibus imminentes
Figat Apollineâ pharetrâ,   35
Phinéamque abigat pestem procul amne Pegaséo?[8]

ANTISTROPHE

Quin tu, libelle, nuntii licet malâ
Fide, vel oscitantiâ
Semel erraveris agmine fratrum,
Seu quis te teneat specus,
Seu qua te latebra, forsan unde vili   40
Callo teréris institoris insulsi,
Lætare felix, en iterum tibi
Spes nova fulget posse profundam
Fugere Lethen, vehique superam   45
In Jovis aulam remige pennâ,

STROPHE 3

Nam te Roüsius sui
Optat peculî, numeróque justo
Sibi pollicitum queritur abesse,
Rogatque venias ille cujus inclyta   50
Sunt data virûm monumenta curæ:
Téque adytis etiam sacris
Voluit reponi quibus et ipse præsidet
Æternorum operum custos fidelis,
Quæstorque gazæ nobilioris,   55
Quàm cui præfuit Iön
Clarus Erechtheides
Opulenta dei per templa parentis[9]
Fulvosque tripodas, donaque Delphica,
Iön Actæâ genitus Creüsâ.   60

ANTISTROPHE

Ergo tu visere lucos
Musarum ibis amœnos,
Diamque Phœbi rursùs ibis in domum
Oxoniâ quam valle colit

Delo posthabitâ,   65
Bifidóque Parnassi jugo:
Ibis honestus,
Postquam egregiam tu quoque sortem
Nactus abis, dextri prece sollicitatus amici.
Illic legéris inter alta nomina   70
Authorum, Graiæ simul et Latinæ
Antiqua gentis lumina, et verum decus.

EPODOS

Vos tandem haud vacui mei labores,
Quicquid hoc sterile fudit ingenium.
Jam serò placidam sperare jubeo   75
Perfunctam invidiâ requiem, sedesque beatas
Quas bonus Hermes[10]
Et tutela dabit solers Roüsi,
Quò neque lingua procax vulgi penetrabit, atque longè
Turba legentum prava facesset;   80
At ultimi nepotes,
Et cordatior ætas
Judicia rebus æquiora forsitan
Adhibebit integro sinu.
Tum livore sepulto,   85
Siquid meremur, sana posteritas sciet
Roüsio favente.

(Ode tribus constat strophis, totidémque antistrophis unâ demùm epodo
clausis; quàs, tametsi omnes nec versuum numero nec certis ubique
colis exactè respondeant, ita tamen secuimus, commodè legendi potius,
quàm ad antiquos concinendi modos, rationem spectantes. Alioquin hoc
genus rectiùs fortasse dici monstrophicum debuerat. Metra partim sunt
κατὰ σχέσιν, partim ἀπολελυμένα. Phaleucia quæ sunt, spondæum tertio
loco bis admittunt, quod idem in secundo loco Catullus ad libitum fecit.)[11]

To John Rouse

LIBRARIAN OF OXFORD UNIVERSITY

An Ode concerning a lost volume of poems which he requested be sent to him a second time, so that it might be put back with my others in the public library.[1]

STROPHE 1

Two-part book rejoicing in single garb,[2] / although with double leaf, / and glittering with no painstaking elegance, / which a hand once / young wrought, [5] / a careful hand, yet by no means too great a poet's, / while, unsettled, now through the Ausonian[3] shades, / now through British lawns he dallied, / innocent of people and out of touch with life, / he indulged his native lute, soon afterwards in like manner [10] / with Daunian[4] lyre he resounded his foreign air / to those around him, and barely touched the soil with his foot.

ANTISTROPHE

Who, little book, who with evil intent / withdrew you from your remaining brothers? / when, dispatched from the city, [15] / immediately upon request by my learned friend, / you were travelling the distinguished road / to the birthplace of the Thames,[5] / the blue father, / where are the limpid fountains [20] / of the Aonides,[6] and the sacred Bacchic dance / known to the world through endless / ages, fallen away under the revolving heavens, / but celebrated to eternity?

[1] Complying with Rouse's request, Milton sent to the Bodleian Library a second copy of his 1645 *Poems*, in which today the manuscript of this ode is found. The eleven prose tracts published to date (c. 1646) had been sent, with an autograph inscription, with the first copy.

[2] The *Poems* were published with separate title pages and pagination ("gemina fronde") for the English and the Latin poems; copies of the Latin poems without the English poems are extant.

[3] Italian.

[4] Italian.

[5] Oxford.

[6] See *El.* 4, n. 10; l. 66 is also explained by this note.

STROPHE 2

Today what god or lofty creature of god, [25] / having pity on the primitive nature of my nation, / (if we have atoned sufficiently for our former offences / and the base idleness of our unmanly extravagance) / will remove forever the execrable civil wars of its citizenry,[7] / and what sainted man will call back the nourishing studies [30] / and the banished Muses without abode / now in nearly all the bounds of England; / and who will pierce with Apollo's quiver / the foul birds / with menacing talons, [35] / and drive the pest of Phineus far from Pegasus' stream?[8]

ANTISTROPHE

But, little book, though by the bad faith of the messenger / or his negligence, / you have wandered once from the company of your brothers, / whether some den holds you fast [40] / or some hidden recess, perhaps wherein / you are rubbed by the vile, calloused hand of a tasteless huckster, / be cheered, fortunate one; behold! again / a new hope shines to enable you / to avoid the abyss of Lethe, and be conveyed [45] / to the supreme court of Jove on oaring wing,

STROPHE 3

for Rouse selects you / for his own property, and from the rightful collection / promised, complains you to be removed, / and he requests you return to him, to whose care [50] / are the glorious monuments of men assigned: / and indeed in the sacred sanctuaries / over which he himself presides he has wished you to be preserved, / a faithful custodian of immortal works / and a guardian of treasure nobler [55] / than the golden tripods, and the Delphic gifts, / which Ion protects, / the honorable grandson of Erechtheus, / in the rich temple of the god, his father,[9] / Ion, born of Actaean Creusa. [60]

[7] reference primarily to the Civil Wars and a former extravagant life.

[8] Apollo was god of archery. The Harpies (as noisome, ravenous birds) were sent to steal or defile the food of Phineus. Pegasus, the winged horse, had created the fountain Hippocrene, sacred to the Muses, by the stamp of his foot, and with his aid Bellerophon had destroyed the Chimaera and attempted to fly to heaven. Oxford is thus likened to Pegasus because of its cultivation of the Muses, its dispelling of ignorance, and its attempt at high achievement. The surrender of royalist Oxford to the Parliamentarians occurred six months before Milton wrote in June 1646.

[9] Apollo's temple at Delphi.

ANTISTROPHE

Therefore you shall fly to see / the delightful groves of the Muses, / and again you shall find your way to the divine home of Phoebus / in the Oxford valley, which he frequents / in preference to Delos [65] / and the cleft peak of Parnassus: / You shall go full of honor, / since you also depart possessed of / a distinguished lot, invited by the prayer of a fortunate friend. / There you shall be read among the august names [70] / of authors, the ancient lights and true glory / both of the Greek and the Latin people.

EPODE

You at last my labors have not been in vain, / whatever that sterile genius has brought forth. / Now I bid you hope for placid rest [75] / discharged from envy in a later age, in the blessed abodes / which the good Hermes[10] gives / and the expert protection of Rouse, / where never shall penetrate the insolent speech of the multitude and even / the vicious throng of readers shall retire far off; [80] / but our distant descendants, / and a more prudent age / will perhaps exercise a fairer judgment / of things from its unbiassed breast. / Then with envy entombed, [85] / a rational posterity will know if I deserve any merit, / thanks to Rouse.

(The ode consists of three strophes, and the same number of antistrophes, closed at last by one epode; although all do not correspond exactly in the number of verses or in fixed parts where there are cola, nevertheless I have divided them thus in order to observe convenience in reading rather than respect to ancient rules of versifying. In other respects this type more correctly should probably have been called monostrophic. The meters are partly regularly patterned, partly free. There are two Phaleucian lines which admit a spondee in the third foot, which same practice Catullus freely employed in the second foot.)[11]

(*Jan. 1647*)

[10] god of learning.
[11] Milton's concern in drawing attention to his prosodic experiment should be read alongside remarks accompanying the *Fifth Ode* and *Psalms* 80–88 and alongside the metrics of *SA*. Prefacing the drama is the similar verse description: "call'd by the Greeks *Monostrophic*, or rather *Apolelymenon*, without regard had to *Strophe, Antistrophe* or *Epod*." The Phaleucian consisted of a spondee, a dactyl, and three trochees. Catullus is thought of here primarily because he employed the hendecasyllabic line so frequently.

The Fifth Ode of Horace. Book I.

Quis multa gracilis te puer in rosa render'd almost word for word without rime according to the Latin Measure, as near as the Language will permit.[1]

What slender Youth bedew'd with liquid odours
Courts thee on Roses in some pleasant Cave,
  Pyrrha? for whom bindst thou
  In wreaths thy golden Hair,
Plain in thy neatness? O how oft shall he   5
On Faith and changed Gods complain: and Seas
  Rough with black winds and storms
  Unwonted shall admire:
Who now enjoyes thee credulous, all Gold,
Who alwayes vacant, alwayes amiable   10
  Hopes thee; of flattering gales
  Unmindfull. Hapless they
To whom thou untry'd seem'st fair. Me in my vow'd
Picture the sacred wall declares t' have hung
  My dank and dropping weeds   15
  To the stern God of Sea.

(1646–48 ?)

[1] Milton aimed at reproducing Horace's quantitative meters, and so subjoined the Latin text to allow the reader to evaluate his rendition. Perhaps this translation, along with *Ps.* 80–88, which also emphasize the nature of the rendering, was intended as an exercise of prosodic discipline.

Ad Pyrrham. Ode V

Horatius ex Pyrrhae illecebris tanquam e naufragio enataverat, cujus amore irretitos, affirmat esse miseros.

Quis multa garcilis te puer in rosa
Perfusus liquidis urget odoribus,
  Grato, *Pyrrha*, sub antro?
  Cui flavam religas comam

Simplex munditie? heu quoties fidem   5
Mutatosque deos flebit, et aspera
  Nigris æquora ventis
  Emirabitur insolens,
Qui nunc te fruitur credulus, aurea:
Qui semper vacuam, semper amabilem   10
  Sperat, nescius auræ
  Fallacis. miseri quibus
Intentata nites. me tabula sacer
Votiva paries indicat uvida
  Suspendisse potenti   15
  Vestimenta maris Deo.

Sonnet 12

A book was writt of late call'd *Tetrachordon*,[1]
  And wov'n close both matter, form, and stile,
  The subject new; it walk'd the town a while,
  Numbring good intellects; now seldom por'd on.
Cries the stall-reader, bless us! what a word on   5
  A title page is this! and som in file
  Stand spelling fals, while one might walk to Mile-
  End Green.[2] Why is it harder, Sirs, then Gordon,[3]
Colkitto, or Macdonnell, or Galasp?[4]
  Those rugged names to our like mouths grow sleek   10
  That would have made *Quintilian*[5] stare and gasp.

---

[1] Milton's pamphlet confirming his *Doctrine and Discipline of Divorce* was published Mar. 4, 1645. The four "tones" on which Milton's tetrachord is built are Gen. i. 27–28, Deut. xxiv. 1–2, Matt. v. 31–32, and 1 Cor. vii. 10–16, "the foure chief places in Scripture, which treat of Mariage, or nullities in Mariage."
[2] the intersection of Cambridge Heath Road and Whitechapel Road, which is one measured mile along the latter thoroughfare from Aldgate.
[3] James Gordon, Lord Aboyne, influential, though vacillating, adherent of the Scots Royalist James Graham, Marquis of Montrose; at the battle of Auldearn, May 8–9, 1645, he aided MacDonnell in routing the Parliamentary army.
[4] The three names all refer to Alexander MacDonnell, known as MacColkitto and MacGillespie, Montrose's major-general. For his victory at Auldearn, Mac-Donnell is famed in Gaelic legend; he was knighted by Montrose in 1645. Milton contrasts the repute of these two enemies of the Parliamentarians in mid-1645 and the concurrent derision of advocates of true liberty like himself.
[5] the Roman rhetorician, whose *Institutio Oratoria* ("The Education of an Orator") warned of the corruptions of language from foreign sources and of the need for the study of Greek.

Thy age, like ours, O Soul of Sir *John Cheek*,[6]
Hated not learning wors then toad or Asp,
When thou taught'st *Cambridge,* and King *Edward* Greek.[7]

(*Jan. 1647 ?*)

---

[6] First professor of Greek at Cambridge, Cheke introduced "Erasmian" pronunciation, rejecting the identical sounding of various vowels and diphthongs. He became tutor to Prince Edward in 1544, continuing after the accession, and was one of seven divines appointed to draw up a body of laws for church administration.

[7] The final five lines are concerned with (1) the lack of learning and of appreciation of learning in Milton's age, which is contrasted with the humanism of Cheke's "reformative age" when Quintilian's concept that education should produce men of high character and culture prevailed; and (2) a comparison between the reception of his efforts and of the work by Cheke and other divines to enact relaxations of church laws of divorce (discussed on p. 97 of *Tetrachordon*). Only Edward VI's untimely death prevented establishment of these divorce laws by Parliament.

On the Forcers of Conscience[1]

Because you have thrown off your Prelate Lord
And with stiff vows renounc'd his Liturgie[2]
To seise the widow'd whore Plurality[3]
From them whose sin ye envi'd, not abhorr'd,
Dare ye for this adjure the civill sword   5
To force our Consciences that Christ set free,
And ride us with a classic Hierarchy[4]

---

[1] The "new" forcers of conscience as they were called in the 1673 printing of this tailed sonnet may be those who in the last months of 1646 particularly demanded immediate legislation for the repression of heresy and error and who tried to effect Presbyterian organization throughout England. In January 1647 Clarendon commented on the intolerant measures which were provoking revolt among the Independents and the army (see *State Papers,* Nos. 2396, 2405).

[2] In Aug. 1645 the House of Commons forbade public and private use of the *Book of Common Prayer.*

[3] Although prelates who held multiple posts were "thrown off" when episcopacy was formally abolished in July 1643, the Presbyterian system supported the same kind of pluralism.

[4] Presbyterian administration was built on the classis (or synod), which was composed of all ministers and elders of a district; it thus had control over the clergy and religious affairs in that district. Provinces were to be established throughout England, according to the Westminster Assembly, which in turn were to be subdivided into classes.

Taught ye by meer *A.S.*[5] and *Rotherford?*[6]
Men whose life, learning, faith and pure intent
  Would have bin held in high esteem with *Paul*   10
Must now be nam'd and printed Hereticks
By shallow *Edwards*[7] and Scotch what d'ye call;[8]
But we doe hope to find out all your tricks,
Your plots and packings wors then those of *Trent,*[9]
            That so the Parlament   15
May with their wholsom and preventive sheares
Clip your Phylacteries[10] though bauk your eares
            And succour our just feares
When they shall read this cleerly in your charge
New Presbyter is but old Preist writt large.[11]   20

(*early 1647 ?*)

_____

[5] Adam Stewart, a Scot who, using only initials, pamphleteered for orthodox Presbyterianism; he was a member of both Assembly and Parliament.
[6] Samuel Rutherford (1600?–1661), author of *Plea for Presbytery* (1642) and Scots member of the Assembly from 1643 through 1647.
[7] Thomas Edwards (1599–1647), author of *Gangraena* (1646), subtitled, "a Catalogue and Discovery of many of the Errours, Heresies, Blasphemies and pernicious Practices of the Sectaries of this time," and of *The Casting down of the last Stronghold of Satan, or a Treatise against Toleration and pretended Liberty of Conscience* (1647).
[8] Robert Baillie (1599–1662), another Scots member of the Assembly (until 1646), who directed his attacks against the Independents.
[9] The Council of Trent, opened in 1545, undertook the reform of the Church in three separate synods through 1563, but any hope of reconciliation with the Protestants was thwarted by dogmatic decisions and a voting procedure which packed the Council in the Pope's favor.
[10] square leather boxes containing scriptural passages, worn by Jews at prayer. But they became symbols of hypocrisy since they were worn openly by the Pharisees only to impress others (Matt. xxiii. 5). However, such ministers as Milton indicts will not be removed from future service to the Church—the meaning of the image of not cutting off (bauking) their ears (see Donald C. Dorian, *MLN*, LVI, 1941, 63). William Prynne, who is referred to in the original version of this line in the TM, had both ears cut off in 1637 for his attack against episcopacy.
[11] "Preist" and the longer "Presbyter" both derive from the Greek *presbyteros*.

Psalm 80[1]

1 Thou Shepherd that dost Israel *keep*
  Give ear *in time of need,*
  Who leadest like a flock of sheep
  Thy loved Josephs seed,
  That sitt'st between the Cherubs *bright*   5
  Between their wings out-spread,
  Shine forth, *and from thy cloud give light,*
  And on our foes thy dread.
2 In Ephraims view and Benjamins,
  And in Manasse's sight   10
  Awake [a] thy strength, come, and *be seen*   [a] *Gnorera.*
  To save us *by thy might.*
3 Turn us again, *thy grace divine*
  To us O God *vouchsafe;*
  Cause thou thy face on us to shine   15
  And then we shall be safe.
4 Lord God of Hosts, how long wilt thou,
  How long wilt thou declare
  Thy [b] smoaking wrath, *and angry brow*   [b] *Gnashanta.*
  Against thy peoples praier?   20
5 Thou feed'st them with the bread of tears,
  Their bread with tears they eat,
  And mak'st them [c] largely drink the tears   [c] *Shalish.*
  Wherwith their cheeks are wet.
6 A strife thou mak'st us *and a prey*   25
  To every nieghbour foe,
  Among themselves they [d] laugh, they [d] play,
  And [d] flouts at us they throw.   [d] *Jilgnagu.*

---

[1] In accord with usual practice in printing biblical texts, Milton pointed out
that "all but what is in a different Character [i.e., italicized] are the very words
of the Text, translated from the Original." The nine psalms were rendered in the
common measure (ballad stanza) of standard psalters (e.g., Sternhold and Hop-
kins), paraphrasing rather than translating, and expanding or compressing origi-
nal verses as desired. Marginal notes cite the Hebrew (or a more literal
translation). Written during the civil wars, the subject matter and tone of the
psalms may reflect Milton's dejection from the course of events and his hope for
the future under enlightened leadership. See also the discussion by William B.
Hunter, Jr., in *PQ*, XL (1961), 485–94.

7 Return us, *and thy grace divine,*
   O God of Hosts *vouchsafe;*   30
  Cause thou thy face on us to shine,
   And then we shall be safe.
8 A Vine from Ægypt thou hast brought,
   Thy free love made it thine,
  And drov'st out Nations *proud and haut*   35
   To plant this *lovely* Vine.
9 Thou did'st prepare for it a place
   And root it deep and fast
  That it *began to grow apace,*
   And fill'd the land *at last.*   40
10 With her *green* shade *that* cover'd *all,*
   The Hills were *over-spread,*
  Her Bows as *high as* Cedars tall
   Advanc'd their lofty head.
11 Her branches *on the western side*   45
   Down to the Sea she sent,
  And *upward* to that river *wide*
   Her other branches *went.*
12 Why hast thou laid her Hedges low
   And brok'n down her Fence,   50
  That all may pluck her, as they go,
   With rudest violence?
13 The *tusked* Boar out of the wood
   Up turns it by the roots,
  Wild Beasts there brouze, and make their food   55
   Her Grapes and tender Shoots.
14 Return now, God of Hosts, look down
   From Heav'n, thy Seat divine,
  Behold *us, but without a frown,*
   And visit this *thy* Vine.   60
15 Visit this Vine, which thy right hand
   Hath set, and planted *long,*
  And the young branch, that for thy self
   Thou hast made firm and strong.
16 But now it is consum'd with fire,   65
   And cut *with Axes* down.
  They perish at thy dreadfull ire,
   At thy rebuke and frown.
17 Upon the man of thy right hand
   Let thy *good* hand be *laid,*
  Upon the Son of Man, whom thou   70
   Strong for thy self hast made.

18 So shall we not go back from thee
   To wayes of sin and shame,
   Quick'n us thou, then *gladly* wee   75
   Shall call upon thy Name.
19 Return us, *and thy grace divine*
   Lord God of Hosts voutsafe,
   Cause thou thy face on us to shine,
   And then we shall be safe.   80

(*Apr. 1648*)

Psalm 81

1 To God our strength sing loud, *and clear*
   Sing loud to God *our King,*
   To Jacobs God, *that all may hear*
   Loud acclamations ring.
2 Prepare a Hymn, prepare a Song,   5
   The Timbrel hither bring,
   The *cheerfull* Psaltry bring along
   And Harp *with* pleasant *string.*
3 Blow, *as is wont,* in the new Moon
   With Trumpets *lofty sound,*   10
   Th' appointed time, the day wheron
   Our solemn Feast *comes round.*
4 This was a Statute *giv'n of old*
   For Israel *to observe,*
   A Law of Jacobs God, *to hold*   15
   From whence they might not swerve.
5 This he a Testimony ordain'd
   In Joseph, *not to change,*
   When as he pass'd through Ægypt land;
   The Tongue I heard was strange.   20
6 From burden, *and from slavish toyl*
   I set his shoulder free;
   His hands from pots, *and mirie soyl*
   Deliver'd were *by me.*
7 When trouble did thee sore assail,   25
   On me then didst thou call,

And I to free thee *did not fail,*
  And led thee out of thrall.
I answer'd thee in ^a thunder deep   ^a *Besether ragnam.*
  With clouds encompass'd round;   30
I tri'd thee at the water *steep*
  Of Meriba *renown'd.*
8 Hear O my people, *heark'n well,*
  I testifie to thee
Thou antient stock of Israel,   35
  If thou wilt list to mee,
9 Throughout the land of thy abode
  No alien God shall be,
Nor shalt thou to a forein God
  In honour bend thy knee.   40
10 I am the Lord thy God which brought
  Thee out of Ægypt land;
Ask large enough, and I, *besought,*
  Will grant thy full demand.
11 And yet my people would not *hear,*   45
  Nor hearken to my voice;
And Israel *whom I lov'd so dear*
  Mislik'd me for his choice.
12 Then did I leave them to their will
  And to their wandring mind;   50
Their own conceits they follow'd still
  Their own devises blind.
13 O that my people would *be wise*
  To serve me *all their daies,*
And O that Israel would *advise*   55
  To walk my *righteous* waies.
14 Then would I soon bring down their foes
  That now so proudly rise,
And turn my hand against *all those*
  That are their enemies.   60
15 Who hate the Lord should *then be fain*
  To bow to him and bend,
But *they, his People, should remain,*
  Their time should have no end.
16 And we would feed them *from the shock*   65
  With flour of finest wheat,
And satisfie them from the rock
  With Honey *for their Meat.*

(*Apr. 1648*)

Psalm 82

1 God in the ^a great ^a assembly stands   ^a *Bagnadath-el.*
   Of Kings and lordly States,
  Among the gods ^b on both his hands   ^b *Bekerev.*
   He judges and debates.
2 How long will ye ^c pervert the right   ^c *Tishphetu*   5
   With ^c judgment false and wrong,   *gnavel.*
  Favouring the wicked *by your might,*
   Who thence grow bold and strong?
3 ^d Regard the ^d weak and fatherless,   ^d *Shiphtu-*
   ^d Dispatch the ^d poor mans cause,   *dal.*   10
  And ^e raise the man in deep distress
   By ^e just and equal Laws.   ^e *Hatzdiku.*
4 Defend the poor and desolate,
   And rescue from the hands
  Of wicked men the low estate   15
   Of him *that help demands.*
5 They know not nor will understand,
   In darkness they walk on,
  The Earths foundation all are ^f mov'd
   And ^f out of order gon.   ^f *Jimmotu.*   20
6 I said that ye were Gods, yea all
   The Sons of God most high.
7 But ye shall die like men, and fall
   As other Princes *die.*
8 Rise God, ^g judge thou the earth *in might,*   25
   This *wicked* earth ^g redress,   ^g *Shiphta.*
  For thou art he who shalt by right
   The Nations all possess.

(Apr. 1648)

Psalm 83

1 Be not thou silent *now at length*
O God hold not thy peace,
Sit not thou still O God of *strength*,
We cry and do not cease.

2 For lo thy *furious* foes *now* ᵃ swell   5
And ᵃ storm outrageously,   ᵃ *Jehemajun.*
And they that hate thee *proud and fell*
Exalt their heads full high.

3 Against thy people they ᵇ contrive   ᵇ *Jagnarimu.*
ᶜ Their Plots and Counsels deep,   ᶜ *Sod.*   10
ᵈ Them to ensnare they chiefly strive   ᵈ *Jithjagnatsu*
ᵉ Whom thou dost hide and keep.   *gnal.*
4 Come let us cut them off, say they,   ᵉ *Tsephuneca.*
Till they no Nation be,
That Israels name for ever may   15
Be lost in memory.

5 For they consult ᶠ with all their might,   ᶠ *Lev jachdau.*
And all as one in mind
Themselves against thee they unite
And in firm union bind.   20

6 The tents of Edom, and the brood
Of *scornful* Ishmael,
Moab, with them of Hagars blood
That in the Desart dwell,

7 Gebal and Ammon *there conspire,*   25
And *hateful* Amalec,
The Philistims, and they of Tyre
Whose bounds the Sea doth check.

8 With them *great* Asshur also bands
And doth confirm the knot,
All these have lent their armed hands   30
To aid the Sons of Lot.

9 Do to them as to Midian *bold*
That wasted all the Coast,
To Sisera, and as *is told*   35
Thou didst to Jabins *hoast,*

When at the brook of Kishon *old*
   They were repulst and slain,
10 At Endor quite cut off, and rowl'd
   As dung upon the plain.   40
11 As Zeb and Oreb evil sped
   So let their Princes speed,
  As Zeba, and Zalmunna *bled*
   So let their Princes *bleed.*
12 *For they amidst their pride* have said   45
   By right now shall we seize
  Gods houses, and *will now invade*
   ᵍ Their stately Palaces.   ᵍ *Neoth Elohim*
13 My God, oh make them as a wheel,   *bears both.*[1]
   No quiet let them find,   50
  Giddy and *restless* let *them reel*
   Like stubble from the wind.
14 As *when* an *aged* wood takes fire
   Which on a sudden straies,
  The *greedy* flame runs higher and higher   55
   Till all the mountains blaze,
15 So with thy whirlwind them pursue,
   And with thy tempest chase;
16 ʰ And till they ʰ yield thee honour due,   ʰ *They seek thy*
   Lord fill with shame their face.   *Name,* Heb. 60
17 Asham'd and troubl'd let them be,
   Troubl'd and sham'd for ever,
  Ever confounded, and so die
   With shame, *and scape it never.*
18 Then shall they know that thou whose name   65
   Jehova is alone,
  Art the most high, *and thou the same*
   O're all the earth *art one.*

(*Apr. 1648*)

---

[1] That is, both "Gods houses" and "Their stately Palaces."

Psalm 84

1 How lovely are thy dwellings fair!
    O Lord of Hoasts, how dear
The *pleasant* Tabernacles are
    Where thou dost dwell so near!
2 My Soul doth long and almost die   5
    Thy Courts O Lord to see,
My heart and flesh aloud do crie,
    O living God, for thee.
3 There ev'n the Sparrow *freed from wrong*
    Hath found a house of *rest,*   10
The Swallow there, to lay her young
    Hath built her *brooding* nest,
Ev'n *by* thy Altars Lord of Hoasts
    They find their safe abode,
And home they fly from round the Coasts   15
    Toward thee, My King, my God.
4 Happy, who in thy house reside
    Where thee they ever praise,
5 Happy, whose strength in thee doth bide,
    And in their hearts thy waies.   20
6 They pass through Baca's *thirstie* Vale,
    That dry and barren ground
As through a fruitfull watry Dale
    Where Springs and Showrs abound.
7 They journey on from strength to strength   25
    With joy and gladsom cheer
Till all before *our* God *at length*
    In Sion do appear.
8 Lord God of Hoasts hear *now* my praier,
    O Jacobs God give ear,   30
9 Thou God our shield look on the face
    Of thy anointed *dear.*
10 For one day in thy Courts *to be*
    Is better, *and more blest*
Then *in the joyes of Vanity,*   35
    A thousand daies *at best.*

    I in the temple of my God
      Had rather keep a dore
    Then dwell in Tents, *and rich abode*
      With Sin *for evermore*.   40
11 For God the Lord both Sun and Shield
      Gives grace and glory *bright*,
    No good from them shall be with-held
      Whose waies are just and right.
12 Lord *God* of Hoasts *that raign'st on high*,   45
      That man is *truly* blest,
    Who *only* on thee doth relie,
      And in thee only rest.

(Apr. 1648)

Psalm 85

1 Thy Land to favour graciously
      Thou hast not Lord been slack,
    Thou hast from *hard* Captivity
      Returned Jacob back.
2 Th' iniquity thou didst forgive   5
      That wrought thy people woe,
    And all their Sin *that did thee grieve*
      Hast hid *where none shall know*.
3 Thine anger all thou hadst remov'd,
      And *calmly* didst return   10
    From thy ᵃ fierce wrath which we had prov'd ᵃ Heb. *The*
      Far worse then fire to burn.   *burning heat of*
4 God of our saving health and peace,   *thy wrath.*
      Turn us, and us restore,
    Thine indignation cause to cease   15
      Toward us, *and chide no more*.
5 Wilt thou be angry without end,
      For ever angry thus?
    Wilt thou thy frowning ire extend
      From age to age on us?   20
6 Wilt thou not ᵇ turn, and *hear our voice* ᵇ Heb. *Turn to*
    And us again ᵇ revive,   *quicken us.*
    That so thy people may rejoyce
      By thee preserv'd alive.

7 Cause us to see thy goodness Lord,   25
  To us thy mercy shew,
Thy saving health to us afford
  And life in us renew.
8 *And now* what God the Lord will speak
  I will *go strait and* hear,   30
For to his people he speaks peace
  And to his Saints *full dear,*
To his dear Saints he will speak peace,
  But let them never more
Return to folly, *but surcease*   35
  To trespass as before.
9 Surely to such as do him fear
  Salvation is at hand
And glory shall *ere long appear*
  To dwell within our Land.   40
10 Mercy and Truth *that long were miss'd*
  Now *joyfully* are met;
Sweet Peace and Righteousness have kiss'd
  And hand in hand are set.
11 Truth from the earth *like to a flowr*   45
  Shall bud and blossom *then,*
And Justice from her heav'nly bowr
  Look down *on mortal men.*
12 The Lord will also then bestow
  Whatever thing is good;   50
Our Land shall forth in plenty throw
  Her fruits *to be our food.*
13 Before him Righteousness shall go
  His Royal Harbinger,
Then c will he come, and not be slow,   c Heb. *He will set*   55
  His footsteps cannot err.   *his steps to the way.*

(*Apr. 1648*)

Psalm 86

1 Thy *gracious* ear, O Lord, encline,
  O hear me *I thee pray,*
For I am poor, and almost pine
  With need, *and sad decay.*

2 Preserve my soul, for ^a I have trod
    Thy waies, and love the just;
    Save thou thy servant O my God
    Who *still* in thee doth trust.
3 Pitty me Lord for daily thee
    I call; *4* O make rejoyce
    Thy Servants Soul; for Lord to thee
    I lift my soul *and voice,*
5 For thou art good, thou Lord art prone
    To pardon, thou to all
    Art full of mercy, thou *alone*
    To them that on thee call.
6 Unto my supplication Lord
    Give ear, and to the crie
    Of my *incessant* praiers afford
    Thy hearing graciously.
7 I in the day of my distress
    Will call on thee *for aid;*
    For thou wilt *grant* me *free access*
    And answer, *what I pray'd.*
8 Like thee among the gods is none
    O Lord, nor any works
    Of all that other gods have done
    Like to thy *glorious* works.
9 The Nations all whom thou hast made
    Shall come, *and all shall frame*
    To bow them low before thee Lord,
    And glorifie thy name.
10 For great thou art, and wonders great
    By thy strong hand are done,
    Thou *in thy everlasting Seat*
    Remainest God alone.
11 Teach me O Lord thy way *most right,*
    I in thy truth will bide,
    To fear thy name my heart unite
    So shall it never slide.
12 Thee will I praise O Lord my God
    Thee honour, and adore
    With my whole heart, and blaze abroad
    Thy name for ever more.
13 For great thy mercy is toward me,
    And thou hast free'd my Soul,
    Eev'n from the lowest Hell set free
    From deepest darkness foul.

^a Heb. *I am* 5
good, loving, a
doer of good
and holy
things. 10

15

20

25

30

35

40

45

14 O God the proud against me rise
    And violent men are met   50
    To seek my life, and in their eyes
      No fear of thee have set.
15 But thou Lord art the God most mild
      Readiest thy grace to shew,
    Slow to be angry, and *art stil'd*   55
      Most mercifull, most true.
16 O turn to me *thy face at length,*
      And me have mercy on,
    Unto thy servant give thy strength,
      And save thy hand-maids Son.   60
17 Some sign of good to me afford,
      And let my foes *then* see
    And be asham'd, because thou Lord
      Dost help and comfort me.

(*Apr. 1648*)

Psalm 87

1 Among the holy Mountains *high*
      Is his foundation fast,
    There seated in his Sanctuary,
      His Temple there is plac't.
2 Sions *fair* Gates the Lord loves more   5
      Then all the dwellings *fair*
    Of Jacobs *Land, though there be store,*
      And all within his care.
3 City of God, most glorious things
      Of thee *abroad* are spoke;   10
4 I mention Egypt, *where proud Kings*
      Did our forefathers yoke,
    I mention Babel to my friends,
      Philistia *full of scorn,*
    And Tyre with Ethiops *utmost ends,*   15
      Lo this man there was born:
5 But *twise that praise shall in our ear*
      Be said of Sion *last*
    This and this man was born in her,
      High God shall fix her fast.   20

6 The Lord shall write it in a Scrowl
   That ne're shall be out-worn
When he the Nations doth enrowl
   That this man there was born.
7 Both they who sing, and they who dance   25
   With sacred Songs are there,
In thee *fresh brooks, and soft streams glance*
   And all my fountains *clear.*

(*Apr. 1648*)

Psalm 88

1 Lord God that dost me save and keep,
      All day to thee I cry;
   And all night long before thee *weep,*
      Before thee *prostrate lie.*
2 Into thy presence let my praier   5
      With sighs devout ascend,
   And to my cries, that *ceaseless are,*
      Thine ear with favour bend.
3 For cloy'd with woes and trouble store
      Surcharg'd my Soul doth lie,   10
   My life *at deaths uncherful dore*
      Unto the grave draws nigh.
4 Reck'n'd I am with them that pass
      Down to the *dismal* pit;
   I am a ᵃ man, but weak alas   ᵃ Heb. *A man*   15
      And for that name unfit.   *without manly*
5 From life discharg'd and parted quite *strength.*
      Among the dead *to sleep,*
   And like the slain *in bloody fight*
      That in the grave lie *deep,*   20
   Whom thou rememberest no more,
      Dost never more regard;
   Them from thy hand deliver'd o're
      Deaths hideous house hath barr'd.
6 Thou in the lowest pit *profound*   25
      Hast set me *all forlorn,*

Where thickest darkness *hovers round,*
In horrid deeps *to mourn.*
7 Thy wrath *from which no shelter saves*
Full sore doth press on me;   30
ᵇ Thou break'st upon me all thy waves,   ᵇ *The* Hebr. *bears*
ᵇ And all thy waves break me.   *both.*¹
8 Thou dost my friends from me estrange,
And mak'st me odious,
Me to them odious, *for they change,*   35
And I here pent up thus.
9 Through sorrow, and affliction great
Mine eye grows dim and dead,
Lord all the day I thee entreat,
My hands to thee I spread.   40
10 Wilt thou do wonders on the dead,
Shall the deceas'd arise
And praise thee *from their loathsom bed*
With pale and hollow eyes?
11 Shall they thy loving kindness tell   45
On whom the grave *hath hold,*
Or they *who* in perdition *dwell*
Thy faithfulness *unfold?*
12 In darkness can thy mighty *hand*
Or wondrous acts be known,   50
Thy justice in the *gloomy* land
Of *dark* oblivion?
13 But I to thee O Lord do cry
E're yet my life be spent,
ˋ And *up to thee* my praier *doth hie*   55
Each morn, and thee prevent.
14 Why wilt thou Lord my soul forsake,
And hide thy face from me,
15 That am already bruis'd, and ᶜ *shake*   ᶜ Heb. *Præ*
With terror sent from thee;   *Concussione.* 60
Bruz'd, and afflicted and *so low*
As ready to expire,
While I thy terrors undergo
Astonish'd with thine ire.
16 Thy fierce wrath over me doth flow   65
Thy threatnings cut me through.
17 All day they round about me go,
Like waves they me persue.

¹ That is, both l. 31 and l. 32.

18 Lover and friend thou hast remov'd
    And sever'd from me far.   70
  They *fly me now* whom I have lov'd,
    And as in darkness are.

(*Apr. 1648*)

Sonnet 15

Fairfax,[1] whose name in armes through *Europe* rings,
  Filling each mouth with envy, or with praise,
  And all her jealous monarchs with amaze,
  And rumors loud, that daunt remotest kings,
Thy firm unshak'n vertue ever brings   5
  Victory home, though new rebellions raise
  Thir Hydra heads, and the fals *North*[2] displaies
  Her brok'n league, to imp her serpent wings,
O yet a nobler task awaits thy hand;[3]
  For what can Warrs[4] but endless warr still breed,   10
  Till Truth, and Right from Violence be freed,
And Public Faith cleard from the shamefull brand
  Of Public Fraud. In vain doth Valour bleed
  While Avarice, and Rapine share the land.

(*Aug. 1648*)

---

[1] Sir Thomas Fairfax (1612–1671), commander in chief of the Parliamentarian army, who, amongst other victories, captured Colchester on August 27, 1648, after a seventy-five day siege, at the end of the Second Civil War.

[2] Scotland. After having entered into the Solemn League and Covenant with Parliament on Sept. 25, 1643, the Scots broke the League by invading England in August under James, Duke of Hamilton. Since joining the Parliamentarians had impaired her usually serpentine wings, Milton is saying, Scotland has now imped them (repaired them by inserting new feathers) through a return to treacherous action.

[3] However, Fairfax resigned his military command in June 1650 because of unwillingness to attack Scotland unless provoked by invasion.

[4] that is, specifically, the current Civil Wars.

Verse from Pro Populo Anglicano defensio

Quis expedivit Salmasio[1] suam Hundredam,[2]
Picámque *docuit nostra verba conari?*
Magister artis venter, et Jacobæi[3]
Centum, exulantis viscera marsupii regis.
Quòd si dolosi spes refulserit nummi,   5
Ipse Antichristi qui modò primatum Papæ[4]
Minatus uno est dissipare sufflatu,
Cantabit ultrò Cardinalitium[5] *melos.*

Verse from Pro Populo Anglicano defensio

Who released to Salmasius[1] his "hundred"[2] / and taught the magpie
to presume our words? / Master of art, the belly, and the hundred /
Jacobuses,[3] the inwards of the purse of the exiled king, led him. / Be-
cause if a hope of deceitful coin glistened, [5] / this fellow, who lately
threatened to demolish the supremacy / of the Pope,[4] the Antichrist,
with a single puff, / would gratuitously sing the song of the Cardinals.[5]

(*1650*)

---

[1] Claude de Saumaise (1588–1653), who condemned the English regicides
in *Defensio regia pro Carolo I ad Serenissimum Magnæ Britanniæ regem Caro-
lum II* (1649); *Pro Populo Anglicano defensio* was written as a reply.

[2] a subdivision of an English shire. Salmasius attempted to turn English terms
into Latin (here "Hundreda"); Milton is ridiculing his spurious knowledge of
English law.

[3] The Jacobus, named for James I, was a gold coin worth about twenty-two
shillings. Salmasius was reputed to be persuaded to write *Defensio regia* for a
hundred Jacobuses; this is denied in *Claudii Salmasii Ad Johannem Miltonum
Responsio* (1660), p. 270.

[4] Salmasius had attacked the supremacy of the Pope in *De primatu papæ*
(1645).

[5] the ecclesiastical officers.

Sonnet 16

Cromwell, our cheif of men, who through a cloud
  Not of warr onely, but detractions rude,
  Guided by faith and matchless Fortitude
  To peace and truth thy glorious way hast plough'd,[1]
And on the neck of crowned Fortune proud   5
  Hast reard Gods Trophies and his work pursu'd,
  While *Darwen* stream with blood of Scots imbru'd,
  And *Dunbarr* feild resounds thy praises loud,
And *Worcesters* laureat wreath;[2] yet much remains
  To conquer still; peace hath her victories   10
  No less renown'd then warr, new foes arise
Threatning to bind our souls with secular chains:[3]
  Help us to save free Conscience from the paw
  Of hireling wolves whose Gospell is their maw.[4]

(*May 1652*)

---

[1] Luke ix. 62: "And Jesus said unto him, No man, having put his hand to the plow, and looking back, is fit for the kingdom of God."

[2] Cromwell was victorious against the Scots at the battle near Preston on the Darwen, Aug. 17–20, 1648; at Dunbar, Scotland, Sept. 3, 1650; and at Worcester, Sept. 3, 1651.

[3] Fifteen proposals were offered in Mar. 1652 to the Committee for the Propagation of the Gospel by some of its members, recommending that the clergy be supported by the State. Spiritual matters ("our souls") would thus be subject to "secular chains." To maintain freedom of moral action, Milton believed, no excess or undue manner of giving or taking recompense can exist in the church (*Hirelings*, p. 8). The gospel should not be used for remuneration, nor should we listen to those who are thinking only of their own stomachs and pleasures.

[4] John x. 12: "But he that is an hireling, and not the shepherd, whose own the sheep are not, seeth the wolf coming, and leaveth the sheep, and fleeth: and the wolf catcheth them, and scattereth the sheep."

Sonnet 17

Vane,[1] young in yeares, but in sage counsell old,
  Then whom a better Senator ne're held
  The helm of *Rome*, when gowns not armes repell'd
  The feirce *Epeirot* and th' *African* bold,[2]
Whether to settle peace or to unfold   5
  The drift of hollow states[3] hard to be spell'd,
  Then to advise how warr may best, upheld,
  Move by her two main nerves, Iron and Gold[4]
In all her equipage; besides to know
  Both spirituall power and civill, what each means,   10
  What severs each thou hast learnt, which few have don.
The bounds of either sword[5] to thee we ow.
  Therfore on thy firm hand religion leans
  In peace, and reck'ns thee her eldest son.

(June ? 1652)

---

[1] Sir Henry Vane the Younger (1613–1662), councillor of state, one of the commissioners who settled the union with Scotland and its civil government (Dec. 1651–Mar. 1652), and committeeman appointed to establish relations and alliances with European powers.

[2] The Roman Senate rejected peace with Pyrrhus of Epeirus despite his victories at Heraclea (280 B.C.) and Ausculam (279 B.C.), and rallied the people in 216 B.C. to stave off Hannibal, the Carthaginian leader, after his successes in 218–217.

[3] the United Provinces (the Netherlands); Milton puns on the name "Holland" with its low-lying land and on its alleged insincerity. The Navigation Act of Oct. 1651, aiming at breaking Dutch maritime supremacy, precipitated the first Anglo-Dutch War in 1652. Vane endeavored to maintain peace, but ended negotiations in June when it became evident that the Dutch did not really want peace. Like the Epeirots and the Carthaginians, the Dutch were initially successful.

[4] Among others Cicero (*Philippics*, V, 2) called money the nerves of war, and Machiavelli (*Discourses*, II, x) compared armed force as iron sinew. The lines allude to Vane's activities as member of the committee of defence and as treasurer of the navy.

[5] the spiritual sword and the civil sword. Vane advocated broad religious tolerance, arguing against the proposals of the committee for the propagation of faith; in this he showed awareness of the limits and the separation of these powers. His example not followed, it was necessary to counsel Richard Cromwell and Parliament further in 1659: "both commonwealth and religion will at length, if ever, flourish in Christendom, when either they who govern discern between civil and religious, or they only who so discern shall be admitted to govern" (*Treatise of Civil Power*, p. A5ʳ).

Psalm 1[1]

Blest is the man who hath not walk'd astray
In counsel of the wicked, and i'th way
Of sinners hath not stood, and in the seat
Of scorners hath not sate. But in the great
Jehovahs Law is ever his delight,   5
And in his Law he studies day and night.
He shall be as a tree which planted grows
By watry streams, and in his season knows
To yield his fruit, and his leaf shall not fall,
And what he takes in hand shall prosper all.   10
Not so the wicked, but as chaff which fann'd
The wind drives, so the wicked shall not stand
In judgment, or abide their tryal then,
Nor sinners in th' assembly of just men.
For the Lord knows th' upright way of the just,   15
And the way of bad men to ruin must.

(*Aug. 7 ?, 1653*)

---

[1] The following eight psalms experiment with various meters, rhyme schemes, and rhythms, perhaps as exercises prefatory to renewed poetic activity. It is probably significant that their run-on lines and frequent full medial stops move close to the continuity of rhythm in the blank verse of *PL;* Hunter ("Sources," p. 143) remarks that "their syllabic nature is the same as that of *PL.*" These translations were undoubtedly important in the full development of reversed feet (e.g., in No. 7) and the displaced caesura (e.g., in No. 2) which characterize Milton's mature poetry. Milton makes no attempt in these close translations to maintain the verse structure of either the Hebrew originals or standard English renditions.

Parker ("Date of *SA,*" pp. 161 ff.) calls attention to the anguished entreaty and sense of God's protection in these psalms, which may reflect personal afflictions.

Psalm 2[1]

Why do the Gentiles tumult, and the Nations
  Muse a vain thing, the Kings of th' earth upstand
  With power, and Princes in their Congregations
Lay deep their plots together through each Land,
  Against the Lord and his Messiah dear.   5
  Let us break off, say they, by strength of hand
Their bonds, and cast from us, no more to wear,
  Their twisted cords: he who in Heav'n doth dwell
  Shall laugh, the Lord shall scoff them, then severe
Speak to them in his wrath, and in his fell   10
  And fierce ire trouble them; but I saith hee
  Anointed have my King (though ye rebell)
On Sion my holi'hill. A firm decree
  I will declare; the Lord to me hath said
  Thou art my Son; I have begotten thee   15
This day; ask of me, and the grant is made;
  As thy possession I on thee bestow
  Th' Heathen, and as thy conquest to be sway'd
Earths utmost bounds: them shalt thou bring full low
  With Iron Scepter bruis'd, and them disperse   20
  Like to a potters vessel shiver'd so.
And now be wise at length ye Kings averse
  Be taught ye Judges of the earth; with fear
  Jehovah serve, and let your joy converse
With trembling; kiss the Son least he appear   25
  In anger and ye perish in the way
  If once his wrath take fire like fuel sere.
Happy all those who have in him their stay.

(Aug. 8, 1653)

[1] Here Milton used Dante's *terza rima* or, as he labeled these stanzas, *terzetti*, but the lines are not end-stopped.

Psalm 3

When he fled from Absalom.

Lord how many are my foes,
    How many those
   That in arms against me rise.
    Many are they
That of my life distrustfully thus say,   5
No help for him in God there lies.
But thou Lord art my shield my glory,
    Thee through my story
   Th' exalter of my head I count;
    Aloud I cry'd   10
Unto Jehovah, he full soon reply'd
And heard me from his holy mount.
I lay and slept, I wak'd again,
    For my sustain
   Was the Lord. Of many millions   15
    The populous rout
   I fear not though incamping round about
They pitch against me their Pavillions.
Rise Lord, save me my God for thou
    Hast smote ere now   20
   On the cheek-bone all my foes,
    Of men abhorr'd
   Hast broke the teeth. This help was from the Lord;
Thy blessing on thy people flows.

(Aug. 9, 1653)

Psalm 4

Answer me when I call
God of my righteousness;
In straits and in distress
Thou didst me disinthrall

And set at large; now spare,   5
  Now pity me, and hear my earnest praier.
Great ones how long will ye
My glory have in scorn,
How long be thus forborn
Still to love vanity,   10
To love, to seek, to prize
  Things false and vain and nothing else but lies?
Yet know the Lord hath chose,
Chose to himself apart
The good and meek of heart   15
(For whom to chuse he knows);
Jehovah from on high
  Will hear my voyce what time to him I crie.
Be aw'd, and do not sin,
Speak to your hearts alone,   20
Upon your beds, each one,
And be at peace within.
Offer the offerings just
  Of righteousness and in Jehovah trust.
Many there be that say   25
Who yet will shew us good?
Talking like this worlds brood;
But Lord, thus let me pray,
On us lift up the light,
  Lift up the favour of thy count'nance bright.   30
Into my heart more joy
And gladness thou hast put
Then when a year of glut
Their stores doth over-cloy
And from their plenteous grounds   35
  With vast increase their corn and wine abounds.
In peace at once will I
Both lay me down and sleep
For thou alone dost keep
Me safe where ere I lie: 40
As in a rocky Cell
  Thou Lord alone in safety mak'st me dwell.

(*Aug. 10, 1653*)

Psalm 5

Jehovah to my words give ear
   My meditation waigh,
The voyce of my complaining hear
My King and God for unto thee I pray.
   Jehovah thou my early voyce   5
      Shalt in the morning hear,
   I'th morning I to thee with choyce
Will rank my praiers, and watch till thou appear.
   For thou art not a God that takes
      In wickedness delight,   10
   Evil with thee no biding makes
Fools or mad men stand not within thy sight.
   All workers of iniquity
      Thou hat'st; and them unblest
   Thou wilt destroy that speak a lie;   15
The bloodi' and guileful man God doth detest.
   But I will in thy mercies dear,
      Thy numerous mercies go
   Into thy house; I in thy fear
Will towards thy holy temple worship low.   20
   Lord lead me in thy righteousness,
      Lead me because of those
   That do observe if I transgress,
Set thy wayes right before, where my step goes.
   For in his faltring mouth unstable   25
      No word is firm or sooth;
   Their inside, troubles miserable;
An open grave their throat, their tongue they smooth.
   God, find them guilty, let them fall
      By their own counsels quell'd;   30
   Push them in their rebellions all
Still on; for against thee they have rebell'd;
   Then all who trust in thee shall bring
      Their joy, while thou from blame
   Defend'st them, they shall ever sing   35
And shall triumph in thee, who love thy name.

For thou Jehovah wilt be found
    To bless the just man still,
As with a shield thou will surround
Him with thy lasting favour and good will.   40

(*Aug. 12, 1653*)

Psalm 6

Lord in thine anger do not reprehend me
    Nor in thy hot displeasure me correct;
Pity me Lord for I am much deject,
    Am very weak and faint; heal and amend me,
For all my bones, that even with anguish ache,   5
    Are troubled, yea my soul is troubled sore;
And thou O Lord how long? turn Lord, restore
    My soul, O save me for thy goodness sake
For in death no remembrance is of thee;
    Who in the grave can celebrate thy praise?   10
Wearied I am with sighing out my dayes,
    Nightly my Couch I make a kind of Sea;
My Bed I water with my tears; mine Eie
    Through grief consumes, is waxen old and dark
I'th midst of all mine enemies that mark.   15
    Depart all ye that work iniquitie.
Depart from me, for the voice of my weeping
    The Lord hath heard, the Lord hath heard my praier
My supplication with acceptance fair
    The Lord will own, and have me in his keeping.   20
Mine enemies shall all be blank and dash't
    With much confusion; then grow red with shame,
They shall return in hast the way they came
    And in a moment shall be quite abash't.

(*Aug. 13, 1653*)

Psalm 7

Upon the words of Chush *the* Benjamite *against him.*

Lord my God to thee I flie,
Save me and secure me under
Thy protection while I crie,
Least as a Lion (and no wonder)
He hast to tear my Soul asunder   5
Tearing and no rescue nigh.

Lord my God if I have thought
Or done this, if wickedness
Be in my hands, if I have wrought
Ill to him that meant me peace,   10
Or to him have render'd less,
And not freed my foe for naught;

Let th' enemy pursue my soul
And overtake it, let me tread
My life down to the earth and roul   15
In the dust my glory dead,
In the dust and there outspread
Lodge it with dishonour foul.

Rise Jehovah in thine ire
Rouze thy self amidst the rage   20
Of my foes that urge like fire;
And wake for me, their furi' asswage;
Judgment here thou didst ingage
And command which I desire.

So th' assemblies of each Nation   25
Will surround thee, seeking right,
Thence to thy glorious habitation
Return on high and in their sight.
Jehovah judgeth most upright
All people from the worlds foundation.   30

Judge me Lord, be judge in this
According to my righteousness
And the innocence which is
Upon me: cause at length to cease
Of evil men the wickedness   35
And their power that do amiss.

But the just establish fast,
Since thou art the just God that tries
Hearts and reins. On God is cast
My defence, and in him lies,   40
In him who both just and wise
Saves th' upright of heart at last.

God is a just Judge and severe,
And God is every day offended;
If th' unjust will not forbear,   45
His Sword he whets, his Bow hath bended
Already, and for him intended
The tools of death, that waits him near.

(His arrows purposely made he
For them that persecute.) Behold   50
He travels big with vanitie,
Trouble he hath conceav'd of old
As in a womb, and from that mould
Hath at length brought forth a lie.

He dig'd a pit, and delv'd it deep,   55
And fell into the pit he made;
His mischief that due course doth keep,
Turns on his head, and his ill trade
Of violence will undelay'd
Fall on his crown with ruin steep.   60

Then will I Jehovah's praise
According to his justice raise
And sing the Name and Deitie
Of Jehovah the most high.

(*Aug. 13, 1653*)

Psalm 8

O Jehovah our Lord, how wondrous great
  And glorious is thy name through all the earth!
So as above the Heav'ns thy praise to set
  Out of the tender mouths of latest birth,

Out of the mouths of babes and sucklings thou   5
  Hast founded strength because of all thy foes
To stint th' enemy, and slack th' avengers brow
  That bends his rage thy providence t'oppose.

When I behold thy Heav'ns, thy Fingers art,
  The Moon and Starrs which thou so bright hast set   10
In the pure firmament, then saith my heart,
  O what is man that thou remembrest yet,

And think'st upon him; or of man begot
  That him thou visit'st and of him art found;
Scarce to be less then Gods, thou mad'st his lot,   15
  With honour and with state thou hast him crown'd.

O're the works of thy hand thou mad'st him Lord,
  Thou hast put all under his lordly feet,
All Flocks, and Herds, by thy commanding word,
  All beasts that in the field or forrest meet.   20

Fowl of the Heav'ns, and Fish that through the wet
  Sea-paths in shoals do slide. And know no dearth.
O Jehovah our Lord, how wondrous great
  And glorious is thy name through all the earth.

(*Aug. 14, 1653*)

Verse from Defensio secunda

Gaudete Scombri, et quicquid est piscium salo,
Qui frigidâ hyeme incolitis algentes fretal
Vestrûm misertus ille Salmasius eques[1]
Bonus amicire nuditatem cogitat;
Chartæque largus apparat papyrinos   5
Vobis cucullos præferentes Claudii
Insignia nomenque et decus Salmasii,
Gestetis ut per omne cetarium forum
Equitis clientes, scriniis mungentium
Cubito[2] virorum, et capsulis gratissimos.   10

Verse from Defensio secunda

Rejoice, mackerel, and whosoever is of the fish in the deep, / who may inhabit through the winter the frigid, chilling seasl / That good knight Salmasius[1] in pity meditates / to enwrap your nudity; / and abounding in paper he is furnishing for you [5] / paper garments exhibiting the arms / and name and honor of Claudius Salmasius, / so that through all the fish-market you may deport yourselves / the knight's followers, in cases right for papers and in little boxes, / most pleasing to men wiping their noses on their sleeve.[2] [10]

(1654 ?)

[1] For Salmasius, see note to the verse from *Defensio prima*. The likeness of his name to Latin *salmo* (the salmon) and his presentation with the indiscriminately conferred Order of St. Michael by Louis XIII made Salmasius the target of a punning sneer.

[2] "A cant appellation among the Romans for fishmongers," according to Thomas Warton.

Sonnet 18

Avenge O Lord thy slaughter'd Saints,[1] whose bones
  Lie scatter'd on the *Alpine* mountains cold,[2]
  Ev'n them who kept thy truth so pure of old
  When all our Fathers worship't Stocks and Stones,[3]
Forget not: in thy book[4] record their groans   5
  Who were thy Sheep and in their antient fold
  Slain by the bloody *Piemontese* that roll'd
  Mother with Infant down the Rocks.[5] Their moans
The Vales redoubl'd to the Hills, and they
  To Heav'n. Their martyr'd blood and ashes sow[6]   10

---

[1] Rev. vi. 9–10: "And when he had opened the fifth seal, I saw under the altar the souls of them that were slain for the word of God, and for the testimony which they held: And they cried with a loud voice, saying, How long, O Lord, holy and true, dost thou not judge and avenge our blood on them that dwell on the earth?"

[2] The "slaughter'd Saints" were the Vaudois (descendants of the Waldenses) who lived in the foothills of the Alps. The Waldenses, followers of Peter Waldo, around 1179 broke with the Papacy over dogmas and practices which in their judgment had developed after Apostolic times. Like them, the Vaudois believed the Bible to be the sole guide to salvation. In an effort to stamp out rising heresies and thus win papal favor, the Duke of Savoy ordered the Vaudois to repudiate their dissent, thereby inspiring a fanatic army of Savoyards, French, and Irish to an attack on them on Apr. 24, 1655. Among the Miltonic state papers are letters from Cromwell requesting the cooperation of Sweden, the United Provinces, the Swiss Cantons, and others in putting an end to the persecution, which continued through October.

[3] As David S. Berkeley pointed out (*Explicator*, XV, 1957, item 58), Milton thought of the idolaters in Jer. ii. 27, who say "to a stock, Thou art my father; and to a stone, Thou hast brought me forth."

[4] Rev. xx. 12: "And I saw the dead, small and great, stand before God; and the books were opened: and another book was opened, which is the book of life: and the dead were judged out of those things which were written in the books, according to their works."

[5] Sir Samuel Morland, Cromwell's representative to Savoy, detailed such charges in *The History of the Evangelical Churches of the Valleys of Piemont* (1658). See also Jer. li. 24–25: "And I will render unto Babylon and to all the inhabitants of Chaldea all their evil that they have done in Zion in your sight, saith the Lord. Behold, I am against thee, O destroying mountain, saith the Lord, which destroyest all the earth; and I will stretch out mine hand upon thee, and roll thee down from the rocks, and will make thee a burnt mountain."

[6] "Blood of martyrs is the seed of the Church" (Tertullian, *Apologeticus*, 50). The whore of Babylon (which Milton and other Protestants identified with

O're all th' *Italian* fields where still doth sway
The triple Tyrant:[7] that from these may grow
A hunderd-fold,[8] who having learnt thy way
Early may fly the *Babylonian* wo.[9]

(May ? 1655)

---

the Roman Catholic Church) is "drunken with the blood of the saints, and with the blood of the martyrs of Jesus" (Rev. xvii. 6).

[7] the Pope; compare the poem on the Gunpowder Plot beginning "James derided," n. 2.

[8] To the parable of the sower, whose seed "bringeth forth, some an hundred-fold" (Matt. xiii. 3–23), suggests Kester Svendsen (*Shakespeare Ass'n. Bulletin,* XX, 1945, p. 155, n. 12), Milton added the legend of Cadmus, who sowed dragon's teeth from which sprang up armed warriors. It is interesting to note that this is the hundredth word in the sonnet. The eleven words that complete the poem suggest regeneration and thus salvation.

[9] The fall and desolation of Babylon is described in Jer. li and Rev. xviii; in its fall will be "found the blood of prophets, and of saints, and all that were slain upon the earth" (Rev. xviii. 24).

Sonnet 19

When I consider how my light is spent,
    E're half my days[1] in this dark world and wide,
    And that one Talent which is death to hide
    Lodg'd with me useless, though my Soul more bent
To serve therewith my Maker, and present   5
    My true account, least he returning chide,[2]

---

[1] that is, probably before he had reached the age of fifty. If so, Milton may have thought of the Lord's words after the scourging and purifying of Israel: "There shall be no more thence an infant of days, nor an old man that hath not filled his days; for the child shall die an hundred years old but the sinner being a hundred years old shall be accursed" (Isa. lxv. 20). The phrase has frequently been interpreted in terms of normal life span and the Biblical three score and ten years, requiring an earlier date of composition. Maurice Kelley reviews the external evidence for dating in 1655 in *Seventeenth-Century News,* XI (1953), 29.

[2] The use of the parable of the talents (Matt. xxv. 14–30) emphasizes both Milton's service despite blindness and his single-purposed ability "to reason against that man" who has brought oppression to God's children (*Reason,* p. 35). In a letter to a friend in the TM, Milton also mentioned "that command in the gospel set out by the terrible seasing of him that hid the talent"; and in *Reason* (p. 35) he spoke of "those few talents which God at that present had lent me." He who did not employ his one talent had it taken away and given to the servant having ten.

Doth God exact day labour, light deny'd,[3]
I fondly[4] ask; but patience to prevent
That murmur, soon replies, God doth not need
Either man's work or his own gifts, who best   10
Bear his mild yoak,[5] they serve him best, his State
Is Kingly. Thousands at his bidding speed
And post o're Land and Ocean without rest:
They also serve who only stand[6] and wait.

(Oct. ? 1655)

---

[3] In the letter to a friend he remarked "that the day is at hand wherin Christ commands all to labour while there is light" (John ix. 4); with this command Jesus turned to heal the blind man. Behind the play of "light" and "dark" are the further words of Jesus: "Yet a little while is the light with you. Walk while ye have the light, lest darkness come upon you" (John xii. 35).

[4] foolishly.

[5] Harry F. Robins (*RES*, VII, 1956, 360–66) first noted the pertinency of Christ's answer to those who would be righteous: "Come unto me, all ye that labour and are heavy laden . . . Take my yoke upon you, and learn of me . . . For my yoke is easy and my burden is light" (Matt. xi. 28–30).

[6] The word indicates that Milton is attentively ready to serve God; he is not sitting down. Compare *PL* III, 648–53, and *PR* IV, n. 49.

Sonnet 20[1]

Lawrence of vertuous Father vertuous Son,[2]
    Now that the Fields are dank, and ways are mire,
    Where shall we sometimes meet, and by the fire
    Help wast a sullen day; what may be won
From the hard Season gaining: time will run   5
    On smoother, till *Favonius*[3] re-inspire
    The frozen earth; and cloth in fresh attire
    The Lillie and Rose, that neither sow'd nor spun.[4]

[1] Milton's note of invitation to conversation and a "neat repast" unites the verse epistle and sonnet in a gentle admonition to those who would allow no lightness in their lives. The echoes of Horace's invitations in *Odes*, I, iv, and I, xi, for example, underline the aptness of style here and in *Son.* 21.

[2] Edward Lawrence, who died in 1657, was a member of Parliament; his father was Henry Lawrence, Lord President of Cromwell's Council of State (1653–1659). The line imitates Horace's "O matre pulchra filia pulchrior" (*Odes*, I, xvi, 1).

[3] the west wind (Zephyr), husband of Chloris, goddess of spring.

[4] "Consider the lilies of the field, how they grow; they toil not, neither do they spin" (Matt. vi. 28).

What neat repast shall feast us, light and choice,
Of Attick tast,[5] with wine, whence we may rise   10
To hear the lute well toucht, or artfull voice
Warble immortal notes and *Tuskan*[6] air?
He who of those delights can judge, and spare[7]
To interpose them oft, is not unwise.

(*Oct.–Nov. 1655*)

[5] explained by "light and choice."
[6] Italian.
[7] "spare time" as Fraser Neiman (*PMLA*, LXIV, 1949, 480–83) and Elizabeth Jackson (*PMLA*, LXV, 1950, 328–29) illustrate. The source of the lines is *Catonis Disticha*, III, 6: "Interpose occasionally enjoyment amidst your care / that you may be able to bear in your mind whatever toil you find."

Sonnet 21

Cyriack,[1] whose Grandsire on the Royal Bench
Of Brittish *Themis*, with no mean applause
Pronounc't and in his volumes taught our Laws,[2]
Which others at their Barr so often wrench;
To day deep thoughts resolve with me to drench   5
In mirth, that after no repenting draws;
Let *Euclid* rest and *Archimedes* pause,
And what the *Swede* intends and what the *French*.[3]

---

[1] Cyriack Skinner (1627–1700), Milton's student at Aldersgate Street and probable amanuensis, was a lawyer from Lincoln's Inn. Parker (*TLS*, Sept. 13, 1957, p. 547) argues that he is the author of the so-called Anonymous Life which was written by the scribe of the copies of this sonnet and No. 22 in TM.

[2] Skinner's grandfather Sir Edward Coke (1552–1634), Chief Justice of the King's Bench, was influential in reaching decisions unfavorable to James I concerning constitutional questions. His *Reports* and *The Institutes of the Law of England* are compendia still important to modern-day jurisprudence. Themis was the Greek personification of Justice.

[3] Line 7 refers to mathematical and scientific interests. The current First Northern War against Poland aimed at Swedish annexation of southeastern Baltic areas; the Treaty of Westminster (Oct. 12, 1655) between England and France did not settle Mazarin's relations with Spain as Cromwell wished.

J. H. Finley, Jr. (*Harvard Studies in Class. Philo.*, XLVIII, 1937, 64–67), reviews the echoes of Horace (such as *Odes*, II, xi, 1–6, to which should be added *Epistles*, I, xi, 22); these lead to Biblical admonitions of moderation (Eccl. iii. 1–9).

To measure life learn thou betimes, and know
  Toward solid good what leads the nearest way;   10
  For other things mild Heav'n a time ordains,
And disapproves that care, though wise in show,
  That with superfluous burden loads the day,
  And when God sends a cheerfull hour, refrains.

(Oct.–Nov. 1655)

Sonnet 22

Cyriack, this three years day these eyes, though clear
  To outward view of blemish or of spot,[1]
  Bereft of light thir seeing have forgot,
  Nor to thir idle orbs doth sight appear
Of Sun or Moon or Starr throughout the year,[2]   5
  Or man, or woman. Yet I argue not
  Against heav'ns hand or will, nor bate a jot
  Of heart or hope; but still bear up and steer
Right onward. What supports me dost thou ask?
  The conscience, Friend, t' have lost them overply'd   10
  In liberties defence,[3] my noble task,
  Of which all Europe talks from side to side.
  This thought might lead me through the worlds vain mask
  Content though blind, had I no better guide.[4]

(Dec. 1655)

[1] A similar description is found in Defensio secunda, p. 42 ("from without they are unimpaired, clear and bright without a cloud").

[2] Eccl. xii. 2: "while the sun, or the light, or the moon, or the stars, be not darkened, nor the clouds return after the rain."

[3] referring to Pro Populo Anglicano defensio, the writing of which he said (Defensio secunda, p. 47) hastened his loss of sight.

[4] Perhaps the line owes something to Luke i. 79: God on high shines forth "To give light to them that sit in darkness and in the shadow of death, to guide our feet into the way of peace."

Sonnet 23

Mee thought I saw my late espoused saint[1]
Brought to me like *Alcestis* from the grave
Whom *Joves* great son to her glad husband gave
Rescu'd from death by force though pale and faint.[2]
Mine as whom washt from spot of child-bed taint   5
Purification in th' old law did save,[3]
And such, as yet once more I trust to have
Full sight of her in heav'n without restraint,
Came vested all in white,[4] pure as her mind:
Her face was vail'd, yet to my fancied sight   10
Love, sweetness, goodness in her person shin'd
So clear, as in no face with more delight.
But O as to imbrace me she enclin'd,
I wak'd, she fled, and day brought back my night.

(1656–58 ?)

---

[1] traditionally considered to be Milton's second wife Katherine Woodcock, whom he married Nov. 12, 1656, but W. R. Parker suggests his first wife Mary Powell (*RES*, XXI, 1945, 235–38). Argument for Mary depends upon the interpretation of ll. 5–9; argument for Katherine depends upon Milton's unsentimental references to Mary in the nuncupative will, interpretation of "late espoused" and ll. 5–9, 10–12, the lack of evidence of the scribe's employment before Jan. 14, 1658, and the etymology of "Katherine." All arguments are reviewed in *NQ*, n.s. III (1956), 202–3. T. B. Stroup (*PQ*, XXXIX, 1960, 125–26) suggests a likeness between Mary and Aeneas' vision of Creusa. Considering the real subject a heavenly vision, Leo Spitzer (*Hopkins Review*, IV, Summer 1951, 17–25) analyzes the organization of the sonnet as a tripartite crescendo drawn from the pagan, the Jewish, and the Christian traditions. Thomas Wheeler (*SP*, LVIII, 1961, 510–15) believes Milton portrays his ideal mate rather than either wife.

[2] Through Apollo's intervention, Admetus was allowed longer life when his wife, Alcestis, consented to die at his destined time. Hercules, considered Jove's son, learning of her noble death, intercepted Thanatos to restore the veiled Alcestis to her husband.

[3] Lev. xii. 5: "But if she bear a maid child, then she shall be unclean two weeks, as in her separation: and she shall continue in the blood of her purifying three score and six days." Mary died about May 5, 1652, after giving birth to Milton's daughter Deborah a few days earlier. Katherine died Feb. 3, 1658, after giving birth to a daughter Katherine on Oct. 19, 1657.

[4] Rev. vii. 13–14: "And one of the elders answered, saying unto me, What are these which are arrayed in white robes? and whence came they? And I said unto them, Sir, thou knowest. And he said to me, These are they which came out of great tribulation, and have washed their robes, and made them white in the blood of the lamb."

PART 4

The
Major
Poems

❊

Paradise Lost[1]

The Measure is *English* Heroic Verse without Rime, as that of *Homer* in *Greek*, and of *Virgil* in *Latin;* Rime being no necessary Adjunct or true Ornament of Poem or good Verse, in longer Works especially, but the Invention of a barbarous Age, to set off wretched matter and lame

---

[1] The ten books of the epic in the 1667 edition became twelve in the second edition (1674) by the division of VII into VII and VIII, and of X into XI and XII. The early books (I, II, IV) emphasize the nature of the fall from grace and the nature of evil; the means of regaining grace is expounded in III, in Raphael's discussion of free will and the revolt of Satan in V, and in the war in heaven in VI. At first evil seems to dominate (a strong cause for the former critical judgment of Satan as hero), but the victory over Satan counsels Man against the "terrible Example . . . of disobedience" (VI, 910–11). The later books relate the actual fall of Adam and Eve and its consequences for Man and his history thereafter. The poem, beginning classically in the middle of the action, goes both forward and backward, Raphael bringing the action up to date and Michael foretelling the future. The dramatic climax occurs with the defeat of the rebellious angels in the War in Heaven; see VI, 762, and n. The poem ascends and descends repeatedly, the first fall (of Satan and his cohorts) occurring in Heaven, and the second fall (of Adam and Eve) occurring on Earth. But the latter as a *felix culpa* allows for ascent.

The "message" of the epic is that true freedom lies in obedience—and obedience is not bondage. Man has free will to choose although his choices may be limited. Obedience requires faith in God and God's omniscience. The fall has thus been considered "fortunate" since it points to the need for obedience to God's will.

The universe depicted by Milton is complex and reflects the astronomical theories of his age, including four of the most important ones (compare VIII, 12–168). Basically, however, the created universe with earth as center consists of ten spheres: those of the seven planets and the fixed stars, the Crystalline Sphere, and the outermost primum mobile. Surrounding the universe is boundless Chaos (II, 890–967), in which is found Hell (II, 570–628). The middle layer of air (frequently referred to), which lies between earth and the first sphere of the moon, is the region in which clouds, winds, rains, snow, thunder, etc., are generated.

The poem, a compendium of the scientific, metaphysical, political, moral, and theological doctrines of the times, adheres to the theory of accommodation: because actual knowledge of God is beyond the comprehension of man, He "accommodates" or adjusts what He reveals to the limited, finite understanding of mankind and to the inadequacies of human vocabulary. He conveys His truths in words, images, parables, etc., which are accurate and complete to the extent that human intellect is capable of grasping them. The Bible, as the foremost revelation of God, is cited throughout for its "types" or "shadows" of God, God's acts and will, and God's accommodation. The most significant references to the Bible are given.

Meeter; grac't indeed since by the use of some famous modern Poets, carried away by Custom, but much to thir own vexation, hindrance, and constraint to express many things otherwise, and for the most part worse then else they would have exprest them. Not without cause therefore some both *Italian*[2] and *Spanish*[3] Poets of prime note have rejected Rime both in longer and shorter Works, as have also long since our best *English* Tragedies, as a thing of it self, to all judicious ears, triveal and of no true musical delight; which[4] consists only in apt Numbers, fit quantity of Syllables, and the sense variously drawn out from one Verse into another, not in the jingling sound of like endings, a fault avoyded by the learned Ancients both in Poetry and all good Oratory. This neglect then of Rime so little is to be taken for a defect, though it may seem so perhaps to vulgar Readers, that it rather is to be esteem'd an example set, the first in *English*, of ancient liberty recover'd to Heroic Poem from the troublesom and modern bondage of Riming.

[2] e.g., Trissino and Tasso.
[3] identified as Gaoncalo Perez (translator of the *Odyssey*, 1550) and Juan de Jáuregni (translator of Tasso's *Aminta*, c. 1607) by Carl W. Cobb in *PQ*, XLII (1963), 264–67. The introduction to *Aminta* defended the use of blank verse.
[4] that is, true musical delight.

BOOK I

THE ARGUMENT

This first Book proposes, first in brief, the whole Subject, Mans disobedience, and the loss thereupon of Paradise wherein he was plac't: *Then touches* the prime cause of his fall, the Serpent, or rather *Satan* in the Serpent; who revolting from God, and drawing to his side many Legions of Angels, was by the command of God driven out of Heaven with all his Crew into the great Deep. *Which action past over, the Poem hasts into the midst of things, presenting* Satan with his Angels now fallen into Hell, *describ'd here,* not in the Center (*for Heaven and Earth may be suppos'd as yet not made, certainly not yet accurst*) but in a place of utter darkness, fitliest call'd *Chaos:* Here *Satan* with his Angels lying on the burning Lake, thunder-struck and astonisht, after a certain space recovers, as from confusion, calls up him who next in Order and Dignity lay by him; they confer of thir miserable fall. *Satan* awakens all his Legions, who lay till then in the same manner confounded; they rise, thir Numbers, array of Battel, thir chief Leaders nam'd, according to the Idols known afterwards in *Canaan* and the Countries adjoyning. To these *Satan* directs his Speech, comforts them with hope yet of regaining Heaven, but tells them lastly of a new World and new kind of Creature to be created, according to an ancient Prophesie or report in Heaven; *for*

*that Angels were long before this visible Creation, was the opinion of
many ancient Fathers.* To find out the truth of this Prophesie, and what
to determin thereon he refers to a full Councel. What his Associates
thence attempt. *Pandemonium* the Palace of *Satan* rises, suddenly built
out of the Deep: The infernal Peers there sit in Councel.

Of Mans First Disobedience, and the Fruit
Of that Forbidden Tree, whose mortal[5] tast
Brought Death into the World, and all our woe,
With loss of *Eden*, till one greater Man[6]
Restore us, and regain the blissful Seat,   5
Sing Heav'nly Muse,[7] that on the secret top
Of *Oreb*, or of *Sinai*, didst inspire
That Shepherd,[8] who first taught the chosen Seed,
In the Beginning how the Heav'ns and Earth
Rose out of *Chaos*: Or if *Sion* Hill[9]   10
Delight thee more, and *Siloa*'s Brook that flow'd
Fast by the Oracle of God;[10] I thence
Invoke thy aid to my adventrous Song,
That with no middle flight intends to soar[11]
Above th' *Aonian* Mount,[12] while it pursues   15
Things unattempted yet in Prose or Rime.
And chiefly Thou O Spirit, that dost prefer
Before all Temples th' upright heart and pure,[13]
Instruct me, for Thou know'st; Thou from the first
Wast present, and with mighty wings outspread   20
Dove-like satst brooding on the vast Abyss[14]
And mad'st it pregnant:[15] What in me is dark

---

[5] playing on its derivation from *mors* ("death").
[6] Christ.
[7] Urania, but see VII, 1, and n.
[8] Moses.
[9] a reference to David as King.
[10] the temple in Jerusalem, the site of divine revelation. John ix. 7: As Jesus
heals the blind man, he says, "Go, wash in the pool of Siloam. . . . He went his
way therefore, and came seeing."
[11] Compare *Orlando Furioso*, I, ii, 2.
[12] a mountain sacred to the muses: probably Mount Parnassus; see *El. 4*,
n. 10. Milton is going to soar above the level of Nature and the pagan muses to
treat revealed truths.
[13] Compare Ps. xv. 1–2 and 1 Cor. iii. 16.
[14] Compare Matt. iii. 16, Mark i. 10, Luke iii. 22, and John i. 2.
[15] The lines equate the concept of the fortunate fall: out of the abyss of
darkness (and evil) the Spirit of God (the dove being an emblem of the Holy
Spirit) creates the universe, but what is more important, other dove-like be-
ings, Man. "Brooding" means producing young (see *Nativity Ode*, n. 13), with,
however, a glance here at the sad way in which such creatures must be pro-

Illumin, what is low raise and support;
That to the highth of this great Argument
I may assert Eternal Providence,   25
And justifie the wayes of God to men.
    Say first, for Heav'n hides nothing from thy view
Nor the deep Tract of Hell, say first what cause
Mov'd our Grand Parents in that happy State,
Favour'd of Heav'n so highly, to fall off   30
From thir Creator, and transgress his Will
For one restraint, Lords of the World besides?
Who first seduc'd them to that foul revolt?
Th' infernal Serpent; he it was, whose guile
Stird up with Envy and Revenge, deceiv'd   35
The Mother of Mankind, what time his Pride
Had cast him out from Heav'n, with all his Host
Of Rebel Angels, by whose aid aspiring
To set himself in Glory above his Peers,
He trusted to have equal'd the most High,   40
If he oppos'd; and with ambitious aim
Against the Throne and Monarchy of God
Rais'd impious War in Heav'n and Battel proud
With vain attempt. Him the Almighty Power
Hurld headlong flaming from th' Ethereal Skie   45
With hideous ruin and combustion down
To bottomless perdition, there to dwell
In Adamantine Chains and penal Fire,
Who durst defie th' Omnipotent to Arms.
Nine times the Space that measures Day and Night[16]   50
To mortal men, he with his horrid crew
Lay vanquisht, rowling in the fiery Gulf
Confounded though immortal: But his doom
Reserv'd him to more wrath; for now the thought
Both of lost happiness and lasting pain   55
Torments him; round he throws his baleful eyes
That witness'd huge affliction and dismay
Mixt with obdurate pride and stedfast hate:
At once as far as Angels kenn[17] he views
The dismal Situation waste and wild,   60
A Dungeon horrible, on all sides round
As one great Furnace flam'd, yet from those flames

---

duced. Compare VII, 233–35. In the background is the myth that Chaos and
Night were the parents of Day.
    [16] Compare the Titans in Hesiod's *Theogony*, 720 ff.
    [17] perhaps a noun meaning "range of sight."

No light, but rather darkness visible
Serv'd only to discover sights of woe,
Regions of sorrow, doleful shades, where peace   65
And rest can never dwell, hope never comes
That comes to all; but torture without end
Still urges, and a fiery Deluge, fed
With ever-burning Sulphur unconsum'd:
Such place Eternal Justice had prepar'd   70
For those rebellious, here thir Prison ordain'd
In utter darkness, and thir portion set
As far remov'd from God and light of Heav'n
As from the Center thrice to th' utmost Pole.[18]
O how unlike the place from whence they fell!   75
There the companions of his fall, o'rewhelm'd
With Floods and Whirlwinds of tempestuous fire,
He soon discerns, and weltring by his side
One next himself in power, and next in crime,
Long after known in *Palestine*, and nam'd   80
Beëlzebub. To whom th' Arch-Enemy,
And thence in Heav'n call'd Satan,[19] with bold words
Breaking the horrid silence thus began.
   If thou beest he; but O how fall'n! how chang'd[20]
From him, who in the happy Realms of Light   85
Cloth'd with transcendent brightness didst outshine
Myriads though bright: If he whom mutual league,
United thoughts and counsels, equal hope
And hazard in the Glorious Enterprize,
Joynd with me once, now misery hath joynd   90
In equal ruin: into what Pit thou seest
From what highth fall'n, so much the stronger prov'd
He with his Thunder: and till then who knew
The force of those dire Arms? yet not for those,
Nor what the Potent Victor in his rage   95
Can else inflict, do I repent or change,
Though chang'd in outward lustre; that fixt mind
And high disdain, from sence of injur'd merit,
That with the mightiest rais'd me to contend,
And to the fierce contention brought along   100
Innumerable force to Spirits arm'd

[18] The distance between hell and heaven is three times that between earth and the primum mobile, or outermost sphere.
[19] literally, "adversary." "Beelzebub" means "god of flies."
[20] Isa. xiv. 12: "How art thou fallen from Heaven, O Lucifer, son of the morning!"

That durst dislike his reign, and me preferring,
His utmost power with adverse power oppos'd
In dubious[21] Battel on the Plains of Heav'n,
And shook his throne. What though the field be lost?   105
All is not lost; th' unconquerable Will,
And study of revenge, immortal hate,
And courage never to submit or yield:
And what is else not to be overcome?
That Glory never shall his wrath or might   110
Extort[22] from me. To bow and sue for grace
With suppliant knee, and deifie his power,
Who from the terrour of this Arm so late
Doubted[23] his Empire, that were low indeed,
That were an ignominy and shame beneath   115
This downfall; since by Fate the strength of Gods
And this Empyreal substance cannot fail,
Since through experience of this great event
In Arms not worse, in foresight much advanc't,
We may with more successful hope resolve   120
To wage by force or guile eternal Warr
Irreconcileable, to our grand Foe,
Who now triumphs, and in th' excess of joy
Sole reigning holds the Tyranny of Heav'n.
      So spake th' Apostate Angel, though in pain,   125
Vaunting aloud, but wrackt with deep despair:
And him thus answer'd soon his bold Compeer.
      O Prince, O Chief of many Throned Powers,[24]
That led th' imbattell'd Seraphim to Warr
Under thy conduct, and in dreadful deeds   130
Fearless, endanger'd Heav'ns perpetual King;
And put to proof his high Supremacy,
Whether upheld by strength, or Chance, or Fate,
Too well I see and rue the dire event,
That with sad overthrow and foul defeat   135
Hath lost us Heav'n, and all this mighty Host
In horrible destruction laid thus low,
As far as Gods and Heav'nly Essences
Can perish: for the mind and spirit remains

[21] meaning that they were uncertain of the outcome, but also that any battle with God is futile.
[22] Note throughout the choice of words assigned to Satan: they ascribe his own evil motives and actions to others, here to God.
[23] feared for.
[24] one of the orders of angels, but Milton uses the names of those orders to signify all the angels.

Invincible, and vigour soon returns,   140
Though all our Glory extinct, and happy state
Here swallow'd up in endless misery.
But what if he our Conquerour (whom I now
Of force believe Almighty, since no less
Then such could have orepow'rd such force as ours),   145
Have left us this our spirit and strength intire
Strongly to suffer and support our pains,
That we may so suffice his vengeful ire,
Or do him mightier service as his thralls
By right of Warr, what e're his business be   150
Here in the heart of Hell to work in Fire,
Or do his Errands in the gloomy Deep;
What can it then avail though yet we feel
Strength undiminisht, or eternal being
To undergo eternal punishment?   155
Whereto with speedy words th' Arch-fiend reply'd.
   Fall'n Cherub, to be weak is miserable
Doing or Suffering: but of this be sure,
To do aught good never will be our task,
But ever to do ill our sole delight,   160
As being the contrary to his high will
Whom we resist. If then his Providence
Out of our evil seek to bring forth good,
Our labour must be to pervert that end,
And out of good still to find means of evil;   165
Which oft times may succeed, so as perhaps
Shall grieve him, if I fail not, and disturb
His inmost counsels from thir destind aim.
But see the angry Victor hath recall'd
His Ministers of vengeance and pursuit   170
Back to the Gates of Heav'n: the Sulphurous Hail
Shot after us in storm, oreblown hath laid
The fiery Surge, that from the Precipice
Of Heav'n receiv'd us falling, and the Thunder,
Wing'd with red Lightning and impetuous rage,   175
Perhaps hath spent his shafts, and ceases now
To bellow through the vast and boundless Deep.
Let us not slip th' occasion, whether scorn,
Or satiate fury yield it from our Foe.
Seest thou yon dreary Plain, forlorn and wild,   180
The seat of desolation, voyd of light,
Save what the glimmering of these livid flames
Casts pale and dreadful? Thither let us tend
From off the tossing of these fiery waves,

There rest, if any rest can harbour there,   185
And reassembling our afflicted[25] Powers,
Consult how we may henceforth most offend
Our Enemy, our own loss how repair,
How overcome this dire Calamity,
What reinforcement we may gain from Hope,   190
If not what resolution from despair.
   Thus Satan talking to his neerest Mate
With Head up-lift above the wave, and Eyes
That sparkling blaz'd, his other Parts besides
Prone on the Flood, extended long and large   195
Lay floating many a rood, in bulk as huge
As whom the Fables name of monstrous size,
Titanian,[26] or Earth-born, that warr'd on Jove,
Briareos or Typhon, whom the Den
By ancient Tarsus held, or that Sea-beast   200
Leviathan,[27] which God of all his works
Created hugest that swim th' Ocean stream:
Him haply slumbring on the Norway foam
The Pilot of some small night-founder'd Skiff,
Deeming some Island, oft, as Sea-men tell,   205
With fixed Anchor in his skaly rind
Moors by his side under the Lee, while Night
Invests the Sea, and wished Morn delayes:
So stretcht out huge in length the Arch-fiend lay
Chain'd on the burning Lake, nor ever thence   210
Had ris'n or heav'd his head, but that the will
And high permission of all-ruling Heav'n
Left him at large to his own dark designs,
That with reiterated crimes he might
Heap on himself damnation, while he sought   215
Evil to others, and enrag'd might see
How all his malice serv'd but to bring forth
Infinite goodness, grace and mercy shewn
On Man by him seduc't, but on himself
Treble confusion, wrath and vengeance[28] pour'd.   220
Forthwith upright he rears from off the Pool
His mighty Stature; on each hand the flames
Drivn backward slope thir pointing spires, and rowl'd

25 overthrown.
26 the goddess Earth, whose sons, including hundred-armed Briareus, were
giants. Typhon was a giant with a hundred heads. The assault on Jove (see
Nov. 5, n. 19) is a "type" of the rebellion against God.
27 a whale-like monster, often called a serpent and identified with Satan.
28 being antithetical to truth, mercy, and justice dispensed to man.

In billows, leave i' th' midst a horrid Vale.
Then with expanded wings he stears his flight   225
Aloft, incumbent on the dusky Air
That felt unusual weight, till on dry Land
He lights, if it were Land that ever burn'd
With solid, as the Lake with liquid fire;
And such appear'd in hue,[29] as when the force   230
Of subterranean wind transports a Hill
Torn from *Pelorus*,[30] or the shatter'd side
Of thundring *Ætna*, whose combustible
And fewel'd entrails thence conceiving Fire,
Sublim'd[31] with Mineral fury, aid the Winds,   235
And leave a singed bottom all involv'd
With stench and smoak: Such resting found the sole
Of unblest feet. Him followed his next Mate,
Both glorying to have scap't the *Stygian* flood
As Gods, and by thir own recover'd strength,   240
Not by the sufferance of supernal Power.
    Is this the Region, this the Soil, the Clime,
Said then the lost Arch-Angel, this the seat
That we must change for Heav'n, this mournful gloom
For that celestial light? Be it so, since he   245
Who now is Sovran can dispose and bid
What shall be right: fardest from him is best
Whom reason hath equald, force hath made supream
Above his equals. Farewel happy Fields
Where Joy for ever dwells: Hail horrours, hail   250
Infernal world, and thou profoundest Hell
Receive thy new Possessor: One who brings
A mind not to be chang'd by Place or Time.
The mind is its own place, and in it self
Can make a Heav'n of Hell, a Hell of Heav'n.   255
What matter where, if I be still the same,
And what I should be, all but less than he
Whom Thunder hath made greater? Here at least
We shall be free; th' Almighty hath not built
Here for his envy, will not drive us hence: 260
Here we may reign secure, and in my choyce
To reign is worth ambition though in Hell:
Better to reign in Hell, then serve in Heav'n.

[29] form, appearance.
[30] a promontory of Sicily near Mt. Etna, whose eruption is described; compare *Nov.* 5, 31–39, and n. 5.
[31] refined.

But wherefore let we then our faithful friends,
Th' associates and copartners of our loss   265
Lye thus astonisht on th' oblivious Pool,[32]
And call them not to share with us their part
In this unhappy Mansion, or once more
With rallied Arms to try what may be yet
Regaind in Heav'n, or what more lost in Hell?   270
  So *Satan* spake, and him *Beëlzebub*
Thus answer'd. Leader of those Armies bright,
Which but th' Omnipotent none could have foyl'd,
If once they hear that voyce, thir liveliest pledge
Of hope in fears and dangers, heard so oft   275
In worst extreams, and on the perilous edge
Of battel when it rag'd, in all assaults
Thir surest signal, they will soon resume
New courage and revive, though now they lye
Groveling and prostrate on yon Lake of Fire,   280
As we erewhile, astounded and amaz'd,
No wonder, fall'n such a pernicious highth.
  He scarce had ceas't when the superiour Fiend
Was moving toward the shoar; his ponderous shield
Ethereal temper, massy, large and round,   285
Behind him cast; the broad circumference
Hung on his shoulders like the Moon, whose Orb
Through Optic Glass the *Tuscan* Artist[33] views
At Ev'ning from the top of *Fesole*,
Or in *Valdarno*, to descry new Lands,   290
Rivers or Mountains in her spotty Globe.
His Spear, to equal which the tallest Pine
Hewn on *Norwegian* hills, to be the Mast
Of some great Ammiral,[34] were but a wand,
He walkt with to support uneasie steps   295
Over the burning Marl, not like those steps
On Heavens Azure, and the torrid Clime
Smote on him sore besides, vaulted with Fire;
Nathless he so endur'd, till on the Beach
Of that inflamed Sea, he stood and call'd   300
His Legions, Angel Forms, who lay intrans't
Thick as Autumnal Leaves that strow the Brooks
In *Vallombrosa*,[35] where th' *Etrurian* shades

[32] Lethe, infernal river of forgetfulness.
[33] Galileo, who lived in Fiesole above the valley of the Arno.
[34] the flagship of a fleet.
[35] near Florence.

High overarch't imbowr; or scatterd sedge
Afloat, when with fierce Winds *Orion*[36] arm'd   305
Hath vext the Red-Sea Coast, whose waves orethrew
Busiris and his *Memphian* Chivalry,
While with perfidious hatred they pursu'd
The Sojourners of *Goshen,* who beheld
From the safe shore thir floating Carkases   310
And broken Chariot Wheels, so thick bestrown
Abject and lost lay these, covering the Flood,
Under amazement of thir hideous change.
He call'd so loud, that all the hollow Deep
Of Hell resounded. Princes, Potentates,   315
Warriers, the Flowr of Heav'n, once yours, now lost,
If such astonishment as this can sieze
Eternal spirits; or have ye chos'n this place
After the toyl of Battel to repose
Your wearied vertue, for the ease you find   320
To slumber here, as in the Vales of Heav'n?
Or in this abject posture have ye sworn
T' adore the Conquerour? who now beholds
Cherub and Seraph rowling in the Flood
With scatter'd Arms and Ensigns, till anon   325
His swift pursuers from Heav'n Gates discern
Th' advantage, and descending tread us down
Thus drooping, or with linked Thunderbolts
Transfix us to the bottom of this Gulf.
Awake, arise, or be for ever fall'n.   330
   They heard, and were abasht, and up they sprung
Upon the wing, as when men wont to watch
On duty, sleeping found by whom they dread,
Rouse and bestir themselves ere well awake.
Nor did they not perceave the evil plight   335
In which they were, or the fierce pains not feel;
Yet to thir Generals Voyce they soon obeyd
Innumerable. As when the potent Rod
Of *Amrams* Son[37] in *Egypts* evill day
Wav'd round the Coast, up call'd a pitchy cloud   340
Of *Locusts,* warping[38] on the Eastern Wind,
That ore the Realm of impious *Pharaoh* hung

---

[36] the equatorial constellation associated with winter storms. Busiris, an Egyptian king who persecuted foreigners, was mistakenly identified with Pharaoh who pursued the Israelites across the Red Sea.
[37] Moses; see Exod. x. 12–15.
[38] moving forward.

Like Night, and darken'd all the Land of *Nile:*
So numberless were those bad Angels seen
Hovering on wing under the Cope of Hell   345
'Twixt upper, nether, and surrounding Fires;
Till, as a signal giv'n, th' uplifted Spear
Of thir great Sultan waving to direct
Thir course, in even ballance down they light
On the firm brimstone, and fill all the Plain;   350
A multitude, like which the populous North
Pour'd never from her frozen loyns, to pass
Rhene or the *Danaw,*[39] when her barbarous Sons
Came like a Deluge on the South, and spread
Beneath *Gibralter* to the *Lybian* sands.[40]   355
Forthwith from every Squadron and each Band
The Heads and Leaders thither hast where stood
Thir great Commander; Godlike shapes and forms
Excelling human, Princely Dignities,
And Powers that earst in Heaven sat on Thrones;   360
Though of thir Names in heav'nly Records now
Be no memorial blotted out and raz'd
By thir Rebellion, from the Books of Life.[41]
Nor had they yet among the Sons of *Eve*
Got them new Names, till wandring ore the Earth,   365
Through Gods high sufferance for the tryal of man,
By falsities and lyes the greatest part
Of Mankind they corrupted to forsake
God thir Creator, and th' invisible
Glory of him that made them, to transform   370
Oft to the Image of a Brute, adorn'd
With gay Religions full of Pomp and Gold,
And Devils to adore for Deities:
Then were they known to men by various Names,
And various Idols through the Heathen World.   375
Say, Muse, thir Names then known, who first, who last,
Rous'd from thir slumber, on that fiery Couch,
At thir great Emperors call, as next in worth
Came singly where he stood on the bare strand,
While the promiscuous croud stood yet aloof?   380
The chief were those who from the Pit of Hell
Roaming to seek thir prey on earth, durst fix
Thir Seats long after next the Seat of God,

[39] Rhine or the Danube.
[40] The Vandals invaded Spain and thence North Africa.
[41] Rev. iii. 5: "I will not blot out his name out of the book of life."

Thir Altars by his Altar, Gods ador'd
Among the Nations round, and durst abide   385
Jehovah thundring out of *Sion*, thron'd
Between the Cherubim; yea, often plac'd
Within his Sanctuary it self thir Shrines,
Abominations; and with cursed things
His holy Rites, and solemn Feasts profan'd,   390
And with thir darkness durst affront his light.
First *Moloch*,[42] horrid King besmear'd with blood
Of human sacrifice, and parents tears,
Though for the noyse of Drums and Timbrels loud
Thir childrens cries unheard, that past through fire   395
To his grim Idol. Him the *Ammonite*
Worshipt in *Rabba* and her watry Plain,
In *Argob* and in *Basan*, to the stream
Of utmost *Arnon*. Nor content with such
Audacious neighbourhood, the wisest heart   400
Of *Solomon* he led by fraud to build
His Temple right against the Temple of God
On that opprobrious Hill,[43] and made his Grove
The pleasant Vally of *Hinnom*, *Tophet* thence
And black *Gehenna* call'd, the Type of Hell.   405
Next *Chemos*,[44] th' obscene dread of *Moabs* Sons,
From *Aroar* to *Nebo*, and the wild
Of Southmost *Abarim;* in *Hesebon*
And *Horonaim*, *Seons*[45] Realm, beyond
The flowry Dale of *Sibma* clad with Vines,   410
And *Eleale* to th' *Asphaltick* Pool.[46]
Peor his other Name, when he entic'd
Israel in *Sittim* on thir march from *Nile*
To do him wanton rites, which cost them woe.
Yet thence his lustful Orgies he enlarg'd   415
Ev'n to that Hill of scandal, by the Grove
Of *Moloch* homicide, lust hard by hate;
Till good *Josiah* drove them thence to Hell.
With these came they, who from the bordring flood
Of old *Euphrates* to the Brook[47] that parts   420

[42] literally, "king"; see *Nativity Ode*, n. 43. He was worshipped by the Ammonites.
[43] the Mount of Olives (2 Kings xxiii. 13); called also "that Hill of scandal" (l. 416).
[44] the god of the Moabites, whose lands are cited in the following lines.
[45] Sihon's.
[46] the Dead Sea.
[47] the Besor.

Egypt from *Syrian* ground, had general Names
Of *Baalim* and *Ashtaroth*,[48] those male,
These Feminine. For Spirits when they please
Can either Sex assume, or both; so soft
And uncompounded is thir Essence pure,   425
Not ti'd or manacl'd with joynt or limb,
Nor founded on the brittle strength of bones,
Like cumbrous flesh; but in what shape they choose
Dilated or condens't, bright or obscure,
Can execute thir aerie purposes,   430
And works of love or enmity fulfill.
For these the Race of *Israel* oft forsook
Thir living strength, and unfrequented left
His righteous Altar, bowing lowly down
To bestial Gods; for which thir heads as low   435
Bow'd down in Battel, sunk before the Spear
Of despicable foes. With these in troop
Came *Astoreth*, whom the *Phœnicians* call'd
Astarte, Queen of Heav'n, with crescent Horns;
To whose bright Image nightly by the Moon   440
Sidonian Virgins paid thir Vows and Songs,
In *Sion* also not unsung, where stood
Her Temple on th' offensive Mountain, built
By that uxorious King,[49] whose heart though large,
Beguil'd by fair Idolatresses, fell   445
To Idols foul. *Thammuz*[50] came next behind,
Whose annual wound in *Lebanon* allur'd
The *Syrian* Damsels to lament his fate
In amorous ditties all a Summers day,
While smooth *Adonis* from his native Rock   450
Ran purple to the Sea, suppos'd with blood
Of *Thammuz* yearly wounded: the Love-tale
Infected *Sions* daughters with like heat,
Whose wanton passions in the sacred Porch
Ezekiel saw, when by the Vision led   455
His eye survay'd the dark Idolatries
Of alienated *Judah*.[51] Next came one
Who mourn'd in earnest, when the Captive Ark
Maim'd his brute Image, head and hands lopt off
In his own Temple, on the grunsel[52] edge,   460

[48] plural forms of the Phoenician male and female chief gods.
[49] Solomon.
[50] identified with Adonis; see *Nativity Ode*, n. 43.
[51] See Ezek. viii. 13–14.
[52] threshold.

Where he fell flat, and sham'd his Worshipers:
Dagon[53] his Name, Sea Monster, upward Man
And downward Fish: yet had his Temple high
Rear'd in *Azotus*, dreaded through the Coast
Of *Palestine*, in *Gath* and *Ascalon*   465
And *Accaron* and *Gaza's* frontier bounds.
Him follow'd *Rimmon*, whose delightful Seat
Was fair *Damascus*, on the fertil Banks
Of *Abbana* and *Pharphar*, lucid streams.
He also against the house of God was bold: 470
A Leper[54] once he lost and gain'd a King,
Ahaz his sottish Conquerour, whom he drew
Gods Altar to disparage and displace
For one of *Syrian* mode, whereon to burn
His odious offrings, and adore the Gods   475
Whom he had vanquisht. After these appear'd
A crew who under Names of old Renown,
Osiris, Isis, Orus[55] and thir Train
With monstrous shapes and sorceries abus'd
Fanatic *Egypt* and her Priests, to seek   480
Thir wandring Gods disguis'd in brutish forms
Rather then human. Nor did *Israel* scape
Th' infection when thir borrow'd Gold compos'd
The Calf[56] in *Oreb:* and the Rebel King[57]
Doubl'd that sin in *Bethel* and in *Dan*,   485
Lik'ning his Maker to the Grazed Ox,
Jehovah, who in one Night when he pass'd
From *Egypt* marching, equal'd with one stroke
Both her first born and all her bleating Gods.[58]
Belial[59] came last, then whom a Spirit more lewd   490
Fell not from Heaven, or more gross to love
Vice for it self: To him no Temple stood
Or Altar smoak'd; yet who more oft then hee
In Temples and at Altars, when the Priest
Turns Atheist, as did *Ely's* Sons, who fill'd   495
With lust and violence the house of God.[60]
In Courts and Palaces he also Reigns

[53] god of the Philistines, whose chief cities are listed; see *Nativity Ode*, n. 43.
[54] Naaman; see 2 Kings v.
[55] See *Nativity Ode*, n. 43.
[56] identified with the Egyptian Apis, a sacred bull.
[57] Jeroboam; see 1 Kings xii. 25–33.
[58] See Exod. xii. 29.
[59] The name means worthlessness.
[60] See 1 Sam. ii. 12–17.

And in luxurious Cities, where the noyse
Of riot ascends above thir loftiest Towrs,
And injury and outrage: And when Night   500
Darkens the Streets, then wander forth the Sons
Of *Belial*, flown with insolence and wine.
Witness the Streets of *Sodom*, and that night
In *Gibeah*, when th' hospitable door
Expos'd a Matron to avoid worse rape.[61]   505
These were the prime in order and in might;
The rest were long to tell, though far renown'd,
Th' *Ionian* Gods, of *Javans*[62] Issue held
Gods, yet confest[63] later then Heav'n and Earth
Thir boasted Parents; *Titan*[64] Heav'ns first born   510
With his enormous brood, and birthright seis'd
By younger *Saturn*, he from mightier *Jove*
His own and *Rhea*'s Son like measure found;
So *Jove* usurping reign'd: these first in *Creet*
And *Ida* known, thence on the Snowy top   515
Of cold *Olympus* rul'd the middle Air
Thir highest Heav'n; or on the *Delphian* Cliff,[65]
Or in *Dodona*, and through all the bounds
Of *Doric* Land; or who with *Saturn* old
Fled over *Adria*[66] to th' *Hesperian* Fields,   520
And ore the *Celtic* roam'd the utmost Isles.
All these and more came flocking; but with looks
Down cast and damp, yet such wherein appear'd
Obscure som glimps of joy, to have found thir chief
Not in despair, to have found themselves not lost   525
In loss it self; which on his count'nance cast
Like doubtful hue: but he his wonted pride
Soon recollecting, with high words, that bore
Semblance of worth, not substance, gently rais'd
Thir fainting courage, and dispel'd thir fears.   530
Then strait commands that at the warlike sound
Of Trumpets loud and Clarions be upreard
His mighty Standard; that proud honour claim'd
Azazel as his right, a Cherub tall:
Who forthwith from the glittering Staff unfurld   535
Th' Imperial Ensign, which full high advanc't

---

[61] See Judges xix. 22–28.
[62] Ion, his issue being the Ionian Greeks, but identified with Japheth's son.
[63] that is, faith was placed in them.
[64] the eldest Titan; his brother Saturn seized his inheritance.
[65] Mt. Parnassus.
[66] the Adriatic, then the western lands (Italy, France, the British Isles).

Shon like a Meteor streaming to the Wind
With Gemms and Golden lustre rich imblaz'd,
Seraphic arms and Trophies: all the while
Sonorous mettal blowing Martial sounds: 540
At which the universal Host upsent
A shout that tore Hells Concave, and beyond
Frighted the Reign of *Chaos* and old Night.[67]
All in a moment through the gloom were seen
Ten thousand Banners rise into the Air   545
With Orient Colours waving: with them rose
A Forrest huge of Spears: and thronging Helms
Appear'd, and serried Shields in thick array
Of depth immeasurable: Anon they move
In perfect *Phalanx* to the *Dorian* mood   550
Of Flutes and soft Recorders; such as rais'd
To highth of noblest temper Hero's old
Arming to Battel, and in stead of rage
Deliberate valour breath'd, firm and unmov'd
With dread of death to flight or foul retreat,   555
Nor wanting power to mitigate and swage
With solemn touches, troubl'd thoughts, and chase
Anguish and doubt and fear and sorrow and pain
From mortal or immortal minds. Thus they
Breathing united force with fixed thought   560
Mov'd on in silence to soft Pipes that charm'd
Thir painful steps o're the burnt soyl; and now
Advanc't in view they stand, a horrid Front
Of dreadful length and dazling Arms, in guise
Of Warriers old with order'd Spear and Shield,   565
Awaiting what command thir mighty Chief
Had to impose: He through the armed Files
Darts his experienc't eye, and soon traverse
The whole Battalion views, thir order due,
Thir visages and stature as of Gods,   570
Thir number last he summs. And now his heart
Distends with pride, and hardning in his strength
Glories: For never since created man,
Met such imbodied force, as nam'd with these
Could merit more then that small infantry[68]   575
Warr'd on by Cranes: though all the Giant brood
Of *Phlegra* with th' Heroic Race were joyn'd

[67] the area ruled by Chaos and Erebus.
[68] "that Pigmean Race Beyond the *Indian* Mount" (ll. 780–81); see *Iliad*,
III, 1–5, for the battle, and Pliny (VII, vii) for the pygmies' abode.

That fought at *Thebes* and *Ilium*, on each side
Mixt with auxiliar Gods; and what resounds
In Fable or *Romance* of *Uthers* Son[69]   580
Begirt with *British* and *Armoric*[70] Knights;
And all who since, Baptiz'd or Infidel
Jousted in *Aspramont* or *Montalban*,
Damasco, or *Marocco*, or *Trebisond*,
Or whom *Biserta* sent from *Afric* shore   585
When *Charlemain* with all his Peerage fell
By *Fontarabbia*.[71] Thus far these beyond
Compare of mortal prowess, yet observ'd
Thir dread commander: he above the rest
In shape and gesture proudly eminent   590
Stood like a Towr; his form had yet not lost
All her Original brightness, nor appear'd
Less then Arch Angel ruind, and th' excess
Of Glory obscur'd: As when the Sun new ris'n
Looks through the Horizontal misty Air   595
Shorn of his Beams, or from behind the Moon
In dim Eclips disastrous twilight sheds
On half the Nations, and with fear of change
Perplexes Monarchs. Dark'n'd so, yet shon
Above them all th' Arch Angel: but his face   600
Deep scars of Thunder had intrencht, and care
Sat on his faded cheek, but under Brows
Of dauntless courage, and considerate Pride
Waiting revenge: cruel his eye, but cast
Signs of remorse and passion to behold   605
The fellows of his crime, the followers rather
(Far other once beheld in bliss) condemn'd
For ever now to have thir lot in pain,
Millions of Spirits for his fault amerc't[72]
Of Heav'n, and from Eternal Splendors flung   610
For his revolt, yet faithfull how they stood,
Thir Glory witherd. As when Heavens Fire
Hath scath'd the Forrest Oaks, or Mountain Pines,
With singed top thir stately growth though bare
Stands on the blasted Heath. He now prepar'd   615
To speak; whereat thir doubl'd Ranks they bend

[69] Arthur.
[70] of Brittany.
[71] References are scenes in romantic epics: one called *Aspramont, Orlando Furioso* (among others), Marino's *Il Collvandro Fedele*, and the *Song of Roland*.
[72] punished.

From wing to wing, and half enclose him round
With all his Peers: attention held them mute.
Thrice he assayd, and thrice in spight of scorn,
Tears such as Angels weep, burst forth: at last   620
Words interwove with sighs found out thir way.
   O Myriads of immortal Spirits, O Powers
Matchless, but with th' Almighty, and that strife
Was not inglorious, though th' event[73] was dire,
As this place testifies, and this dire change   625
Hateful to utter: but what power of mind
Foreseeing or presaging, from the Depth
Of knowledge past or present, could have fear'd,
How such united force of Gods, how such
As stood like these, could ever know repulse?   630
For who can yet beleeve, though after loss,
That all these puissant Legions, whose exile
Hath emptied Heav'n,[74] shall fail to re-ascend
Self-rais'd, and repossess thir native seat?
For mee be witness all the Host of Heav'n,   635
If counsels different, or danger shun'd
By mee, have lost our hopes. But he who reigns
Monarch in Heav'n, till then as one secure
Sat on his Throne, upheld by old repute,
Consent or custom, and his Regal State   640
Put forth at full, but still his strength conceal'd,
Which tempted our attempt, and wrought our fall.
Henceforth his might we know, and know our own
So as not either to provoke, or dread
New warr, provok't; our better part remains   645
To work in close design, by fraud or guile
What force effected not: that he no less
At length from us may find, who overcomes
By force, hath overcome but half his foe.
Space may produce new Worlds; whereof so rife   650
There went a fame[75] in Heav'n that he ere long
Intended to create, and therein plant
A generation, whom his choice regard
Should favour equal to the Sons of Heav'n:
Thither, if but to pry, shall be perhaps   655
Our first eruption, thither or elsewhere:
For this Infernal Pit shall never hold

[73] outcome.
[74] Satan misrepresents: both Death (II, 692) and Raphael (V, 710) tell us
it was a third.
[75] rumor.

Cælestial Spirits in Bondage, nor th' Abyss
Long under darkness cover. But these thoughts
Full Counsel must mature: Peace is despaird,   660
For who can think Submission? Warr then, Warr
Open or understood must be resolv'd.

He spake: and to confirm his words, out-flew
Millions of flaming swords, drawn from the thighs
Of mighty Cherubim; the sudden blaze   665
Far round illumin'd hell: highly they rag'd
Against the Highest, and fierce with grasped Arms
Clash'd on thir sounding Shields the din of war,
Hurling defiance toward the Vault of Heav'n.

There stood a Hill not far whose griesly top   670
Belch'd fire and rowling smoak; the rest entire
Shon with a glossie scurff, undoubted sign
That in his womb was hid metallic Ore,
The work of Sulphur. Thither wing'd with speed
A numerous Brigad hasten'd. As when Bands   675
Of Pioners with Spade and Pickax arm'd
Forerun the Royal Camp, to trench a Field,
Or cast a Rampart. *Mammon*[76] led them on,
Mammon, the least erected Spirit that fell
From heav'n, for ev'n in heav'n his looks and thoughts   680
Were always downward bent, admiring more
The riches of Heav'ns pavement, trod'n Gold,
Then aught divine or holy else enjoy'd
In vision beatific: by him first
Men also, and by his suggestion taught,   685
Ransack'd the Center, and with impious hands
Rifl'd the bowels of thir mother Earth
For Treasures better hid. Soon had his crew
Op'nd into the Hill a spacious wound
And dig'd out ribs of Gold. Let none admire   690
That riches grow in Hell; that soyl may best
Deserve the precious bane. And here let those
Who boast in mortal things, and wondring tell
Of *Babel,*[77] and the works[78] of *Memphian* Kings
Learn how thir greatest Monuments of Fame,   695
And Strength and Art are easily outdone
By Spirits reprobate, and in an hour
What in an age they with incessant toyl

[76] literally, "wealth."
[77] capital of the tyrant Nimrod, which is compared with the pyramids.
[78] the Pyramids.

And hands innumerable scarce perform.
Nigh on the Plain in many cells prepar'd,   700
That underneath had veins of liquid fire
Sluic'd from the Lake, a second multitude
With wondrous Art founded the massie Ore,
Severing each kind, and scum'd the Bullion dross:
A third as soon had form'd within the ground   705
A various mould, and from the boyling cells
By strange conveyance fill'd each hollow nook,
As in an Organ from one blast of wind
To many a row of Pipes the sound-board breaths.
Anon out of the earth a Fabrick huge   710
Rose like an Exhalation, with the sound
Of Dulcet Symphonies and voices sweet,
Built like a Temple, where *Pilasters* round
Were set, and Doric pillars overlaid
With Golden Architrave; nor did there want   715
Cornice or Freeze, with bossy[79] Sculptures grav'n,
The Roof was fretted Gold. Not *Babilon*,
Nor great *Alcairo*[80] such magnificence
Equal'd in all thir glories, to inshrine
Belus or *Serapis*[81] thir Gods, or seat   720
Thir Kings, when *Ægypt* with *Assyria* strove
In wealth and luxurie. Th' ascending pile
Stood fixt her stately highth, and strait the dores
Op'ning thir brazen foulds discover wide
Within, her ample spaces, o're the smooth   725
And level pavement: from the arched roof
Pendant by suttle Magic many a row
Of Starry Lamps and blazing Cressets fed
With *Naphtha* and *Asphaltus* yeilded light
As from a sky. The hasty multitude   730
Admiring enter'd, and the work some praise
And some the Architect: his hand was known
In Heav'n by many a Towred structure high,
Where Scepter'd Angels held thir residence,
And sat as Princes, whom the supreme King   735
Exalted to such power, and gave to rule,
Each in his Hierarchie, the Orders bright.
Nor was his name unheard or unador'd

[79] embossed.
[80] Memphis, near modern Cairo.
[81] Baal or Osiris.

In ancient *Greece;* and in *Ausonian*[82] land
Men call'd him *Mulciber;*[83] and how he fell   740
From Heav'n, they fabl'd, thrown by angry *Jove*
Sheer o're the Chrystal Battlements: from Morn
To Noon[84] he fell, from Noon to dewy Eve,
A Summers day; and with the setting Sun
Dropt from the Zenith like a falling Star,   745
On *Lemnos* th' *Ægæan* Ile: thus they relate,
Erring; for he with this rebellious rout
Fell long before; nor aught avail'd him now
To have built in Heav'n high Towrs; nor did he scape
By all his Engins, but was headlong sent   750
With his industrious crew to build in hell.
Mean while the winged Haralds by command
Of Sovran power, with awful Ceremony
And Trumpets sound throughout the Host proclaim
A solemn Councel forthwith to be held   755
At *Pandæmonium*,[85] the high Capitol
Of Satan and his Peers: thir summons call'd
From every Band and squared Regiment
By place or choice the worthiest; they anon
With hunderds and with thousands trooping came   760
Attended: all access was throng'd, the Gates
And Porches wide, but chief the spacious Hall
(Though like a cover'd field, where Champions bold
Wont ride in arm'd, and at the Soldans chair
Defi'd the best of *Paynim*[86] chivalry   765
To mortal combat or carreer with Lance)
Thick swarm'd, both on the ground and in the air,
Brusht with the hiss of russling wings. As Bees
In spring time, when the Sun with *Taurus*[87] rides,
Pour forth thir populous youth about the Hive   770
In clusters; they among fresh dews and flowers
Flie to and fro, or on the smoothed Plank,
The suburb of thir Straw-built Cittadel,
New rub'd with Baum, expatiate[88] and confer
Thir State affairs. So thick the aerie crowd   775

[82] Italian.
[83] Vulcan, whose fall is recounted in *Iliad*, I, 588–95.
[84] The ambiguous meaning "midnight" (compare *Il Penseroso*, 67–68) lurks
in the background with its evil connotations.
[85] "all the spirits" and then pejoratively "all the demons."
[86] pagan, Mohammedan.
[87] the Zodiacal sign for Apr. 20–May 20.
[88] walk about.

Swarm'd and were strait'n'd; till the Signal giv'n.
Behold a wonder! they but now who seemd
In bigness to surpass Earths Giant Sons
Now less than smallest Dwarfs, in narrow room
Throng numberless, like that Pigmean Race   780
Beyond the *Indian* Mount, or Faerie Elves,
Whose midnight Revels, by a Forrest side
Or Fountain some belated Peasant sees,
Or dreams he sees, while over-head the Moon
Sits Arbitress, and neerer to the Earth   785
Wheels her pale course, they on thir mirth and dance
Intent, with jocond Music charm his ear;
At once with joy and fear his heart rebounds.
Thus incorporeal Spirits to smallest forms
Reduc'd thir shapes immense, and were at large,   790
Though without number still amidst the Hall
Of that infernal Court. But far within
And in thir own dimensions like themselves
The great Seraphic Lords and Cherubim
In close recess and secret conclave sat   795
A thousand Demy-Gods on golden seats,
Frequent[89] and full. After short silence then
And summons read, the great consult began.

[89] crowded.

BOOK II

THE ARGUMENT

The Consultation begun, *Satan* debates whether another Battel be to be
hazarded for the recovery of Heaven: some advise it, others dissuade:
A third proposal is prefer'd, mention'd before by *Satan,* to search the
truth of that Prophesie or Tradition in Heaven concerning another world,
and another kind of creature equal or not much inferiour to themselves,
about this time to be created: Thir doubt who shall be sent on this diffi-
cult search: *Satan* thir chief undertakes alone the voyage, is honourd
and applauded. The Councel thus ended, the rest betake them several
wayes and to several imployments, as thir inclinations lead them, to en-
tertain the time till *Satan* return. He passes on his Journey to Hell Gates,
finds them shut, and who sat there to guard them, by whom at length
they are op'n'd, and discover to him the great Gulf between Hell and
Heaven; with what difficulty he passes through, directed by *Chaos,* the
Power of that place, to the sight of this new World which he sought.

High on a Throne of Royal State, which far
Outshon the wealth of *Ormus*[1] and of *Ind,*
Or where the gorgeous East with richest hand
Showrs on her Kings *Barbaric* Pearl and Gold,[2]
Satan exalted sat, by merit rais'd   5
To that bad eminence; and from despair
Thus high uplifted beyond hope, aspires
Beyond thus high, insatiate to pursue
Vain Warr with Heav'n, and by success untaught
His proud imaginations thus displaid.   10
   Powers and Dominions, Deities of Heav'n,
For since no deep within her gulf can hold
Immortal vigor, though opprest and fall'n,
I give not Heav'n for lost. From this descent
Celestial vertues rising, will appear   15
More glorious and more dread then from no fall,
And trust themselves to fear no second fate:
Mee though just right, and the fixt Laws of Heav'n
Did first create your Leader, next, free choice,
With what besides, in Counsel or in Fight,   20
Hath bin achiev'd of merit, yet this loss
Thus farr at least recover'd, hath much more
Establisht in a safe unenvied Throne
Yeilded with full consent. The happier state
In Heav'n, which follows dignity, might draw   25
Envy from each inferior; but who here
Will envy whom the highest place exposes
Formost to stand against the Thunderers aim
Your bulwark, and condemns to greatest share
Of endless pain? where there is then no good   30
For which to strive, no strife can grow up there
From Faction; for none sure will claim in Hell
Precedence, none, whose portion is so small
Of present pain, that with ambitious mind
Will covet more. With this advantage then   35
To union, and firm Faith, and firm accord,
More then can be in Heav'n, we now return
To claim our just inheritance of old,
Surer to prosper then prosperity
Could have assur'd us; and by what best way,   40
Whether of open Warr or covert guile,
We now debate; who can advise, may speak.

---

[1] Hormuz, on the Persian gulf, was famous for precious gems.
[2] a custom in eastern empires.

He ceas'd, and next him _Moloc_, Scepter'd King
Stood up, the strongest and the fiercest Spirit
That fought in Heav'n; now fiercer by despair: 45
His trust was with th' Eternal to be deem'd
Equal in strength, and rather then be less
Car'd not to be at all; with that care lost
Went all his fear: of God, or Hell, or worse
He reck'd not, and these words thereafter spake.   50
   My sentence is for open Warr: Of Wiles,
More unexpert, I boast not: them let those
Contrive who need, or when they need, not now.
For while they sit contriving, shall the rest,
Millions that stand in Arms, and longing wait   55
The Signal to ascend, sit lingring here
Heav'ns fugitives, and for thir dwelling place
Accept this dark opprobrious Den of shame,
The Prison of his Tyranny who Reigns
By our delay? no, let us rather choose   60
Arm'd with Hell flames and fury all at once
O're Heav'ns high Towrs to force resistless way,
Turning our Tortures into horrid Arms
Against the Torturer; when to meet the noise
Of his Almighty Engin he shall hear   65
Infernal Thunder, and for Lightning see
Black fire and horror shot with equal rage
Among his Angels; and his Throne it self
Mixt with _Tartarean_ Sulphur, and strange fire,
His own invented Torments. But perhaps   70
The way seems difficult and steep to scale
With upright wing against a higher foe.
Let such bethink them, if the sleepy drench
Of that forgetful Lake benumm not still,
That in our proper motion we ascend   75
Up to our native seat: descent and fall
To us is adverse.[3] Who but felt of late
When the fierce Foe hung on our brok'n Rear
Insulting, and pursu'd us through the Deep,
With what compulsion and laborious flight   80
We sunk thus low? Th' ascent is easie then;
Th' event is fear'd; should we again provoke
Our stronger, some worse way his wrath may find
To our destruction: if there be in Hell
Fear to be worse destroy'd: what can be worse   85

[3] since angels were made of heavenly quintessence.

Then to dwell here, driv'n out from bliss, condemn'd
In this abhorred deep to utter woe;
Where pain of unextinguishable fire
Must exercise us without hope of end
The Vassals of his anger, when the Scourge   90
Inexorably, and the torturing hour
Calls us to Penance? More destroy'd then thus
We should be quite abolisht and expire.
What fear we then? what doubt we to incense
His utmost ire? which to the highth enrag'd,   95
Will either quite consume us, and reduce
To nothing this essential, happier farr
Then miserable to have eternal being:
Or if our substance be indeed Divine,
And cannot cease to be, we are at worst   100
On this side nothing; and by proof we feel
Our power sufficient to disturb his Heav'n,
And with perpetual inrodes to Allarm,
Though inaccessible, his fatal Throne:
Which if not Victory is yet Revenge.   105
    He ended frowning, and his look denounc'd[4]
Desperate revenge, and Battel dangerous
To less then Gods. On th' other side up rose
Belial, in act more graceful and humane;
A fairer person lost not Heav'n; he seemd   110
For dignity compos'd and high exploit:
But all was false and hollow; though his Tongue
Dropt Manna, and could make the worse appear
The better reason, to perplex and dash
Maturest Counsels: for his thoughts were low;   115
To vice industrious, but to Nobler deeds
Timorous and slothful: yet he pleas'd the ear,
And with perswasive accent thus began.
    I should be much for open Warr, O Peers,
As not behind in hate; if what was urg'd   120
Main reason to perswade immediate Warr,
Did not disswade me most, and seem to cast
Ominous conjecture on the whole success:
When he who most excels in fact of Arms,
In what he counsels and in what excels   125
Mistrustful, grounds his courage on despair
And utter dissolution, as the scope
Of all his aim, after some dire revenge.

    [4] proclaimed (an evil).

First, what Revenge? the Towrs of Heav'n are fill'd
With Armed watch, that render all access   130
Impregnable; oft on the bordering Deep
Encamp thir Legions, or with obscure wing
Scout farr and wide into the Realm of night,
Scorning surprize. Or could we break our way
By force, and at our heels all Hell should rise   135
With blackest Insurrection, to confound
Heav'ns purest Light, yet our great Enemy
All incorruptible would on his Throne
Sit unpolluted, and th' Ethereal mould
Incapable of stain would soon expel   140
Her mischief, and purge off the baser fire
Victorious. Thus repuls'd, our final hope
Is flat despair: we must exasperate
Th' Almighty Victor to spend all his rage,
And that must end us, that must be our cure,   145
To be no more; sad cure; for who would loose,
Though full of pain, this intellectual being,
Those thoughts that wander through Eternity,
To perish rather, swallowd up and lost
In the wide womb of uncreated night,   150
Devoid of sense and motion? and who knows,
Let this be good, whether our angry Foe
Can give it, or will ever? how he can
Is doubtful; that he never will is sure.
Will he, so wise, let loose at once his ire,   155
Belike through impotence, or unaware,
To give his Enemies thir wish, and end
Them in his anger, whom his anger saves
To punish endless? wherefore cease we then?
Say they who counsel Warr, we are decreed,   160
Reserv'd and destin'd to Eternal woe;
Whatever doing, what can we suffer more,
What can we suffer worse? is this then worst,
Thus sitting, thus consulting, thus in Arms?
What when we fled amain, pursu'd and strook   165
With Heav'ns afflicting Thunder, and besought
The Deep to shelter us? this Hell then seem'd
A refuge from those wounds: or when we lay
Chain'd on the burning Lake? that sure was worse.
What if the breath that kindl'd those grim fires   170
Awak'd should blow them into sevenfold rage
And plunge us in the flames? or from above
Should intermitted vengeance arm again

His red right hand to plague us?[5] what if all
Her stores were open'd, and this Firmament   175
Of Hell should spout her Cataracts of Fire,
Impendent horrors, threatning hideous fall
One day upon our heads; while we perhaps
Designing or exhorting glorious warr,
Caught in a fierie Tempest shall be hurl'd   180
Each on his rock transfixt,[6] the sport and prey
Of racking whirlwinds, or for ever sunk
Under yon boyling Ocean, wrapt in Chains;
There to converse with everlasting groans,
Unrespited, unpitied, unrepreev'd,   185
Ages of hopeless end; this would be worse.
Warr therefore, open or conceal'd, alike
My voice disswades; for what can force or guile
With him, or who deceive his mind, whose eye
Views all things at one view? he from heav'ns highth   190
All these our motions vain, sees and derides;[7]
Not more Almighty to resist our might
Then wise to frustrate all our plots and wiles.
Shall we then live thus vile, the Race of Heav'n
Thus trampl'd, thus expell'd to suffer here   195
Chains and these Torments? better these then worse
By my advice; since fate inevitable
Subdues us, and Omnipotent Decree,
The Victors will. To suffer, as to doe,
Our strength is equal, nor the Law unjust   200
That so ordains: this was at first resolv'd,
If we were wise, against so great a foe
Contending, and so doubtful what might fall.
I laugh, when those who at the Spear are bold
And vent'rous, if that fail them, shrink and fear   205
What yet they know must follow, to endure
Exile, or ignominy, or bonds, or pain,
The sentence of thir Conquerour: This is now
Our doom; which if we can sustain and bear,
Our Supream Foe in time may much remit   210
His anger, and perhaps thus farr remov'd
Not mind us not offending, satisfi'd
With what is punish't; whence these raging fires

---

[5] Compare the "red Lightning" of I, 175; red was the color of the horse of
war in Rev. vi. 4, which carried a great sword. See also Horace, *Odes*, I, ii, 2–3.
[6] Compare Ajax's punishment (*Aeneid*, I, 44–45; VI, 75).
[7] Ps. ii. 4: "He that sitteth in the heavens shall laugh: the Lord shall have
them in derision."

Will slack'n, if his breath stir not thir flames.
Our purer essence then will overcome   215
Thir noxious vapour, or enur'd not feel,
Or chang'd at length, and to the place conformd
In temper and in nature, will receive
Familiar the fierce heat, and void of pain;
This horror will grow mild, this darkness light,   220
Besides what hope the never-ending flight
Of future dayes may bring, what chance, what change
Worth waiting, since our present lot appeers
For happy though but ill, for ill not worst,
If we procure not to our selves more woe.   225
    Thus *Belial* with words cloath'd in reasons garb
Counsel'd ignoble ease, and peaceful sloath,
Not peace: and after him thus *Mammon* spake.
    Either to disinthrone the King of Heav'n
We warr, if warr be best, or to regain   230
Our own right lost: him to unthrone we then
May hope, when everlasting Fate shall yeild
To fickle Chance, and *Chaos* judge the strife:
The former vain to hope argues as vain
The latter: for what place can be for us   235
Within Heav'ns bound, unless Heav'ns Lord supream
We overpower? Suppose he should relent
And publish Grace to all, on promise made
Of new Subjection; with what eyes could we
Stand in his presence humble, and receive   240
Strict Laws impos'd, to celebrate his Throne
With warbl'd Hymns, and to his Godhead sing
Forc't Halleluiahs; while he Lordly sits
Our envied Sovran, and his Altar breathes
Ambrosial Odours and Ambrosial Flowers,   245
Our servile offerings. This must be our task
In Heav'n, this our delight; how wearisom
Eternity so spent in worship paid
To whom we hate. Let us not then pursue
By force impossible, by leave obtain'd   250
Unacceptable, though in Heav'n, our state
Of splendid vassalage, but rather seek
Our own good from our selves, and from our own
Live to our selves, though in this vast recess,
Free, and to none accountable, preferring   255
Hard liberty before the easie yoke[8]

---

[8] Compare Matt. xi. 30: "For my yoke is easy, and my burden is light."

Of servile Pomp. Our greatness will appear
Then most conspicuous, when great things of small,
Useful of hurtful, prosperous of adverse
We can create, and in what place so e're   260
Thrive under evil, and work ease out of pain
Through labour and indurance. This deep world
Of darkness do we dread? How oft amidst
Thick clouds and dark doth Heav'ns all-ruling Sire
Choose to reside, his Glory unobscur'd,   265
And with the Majesty of darkness round
Covers his Throne; from whence deep thunders roar
Must'ring thir rage, and Heav'n resembles Hell?
As he our darkness, cannot we his Light
Imitate when we please? This Desart soil   270
Wants not her hidden lustre, Gemms and Gold;
Nor want we skill or Art, from whence to raise
Magnificence; and what can Heav'n shew more?
Our torments also may in length of time
Become our Elements, these piercing Fires   275
As soft as now severe, our temper chang'd
Into their temper; which must needs remove
The sensible of pain. All things invite
To peaceful Counsels, and the settl'd State
Of order, how in safety best we may   280
Compose our present evils, with regard
Of what we are and where, dismissing quite
All thoughts of warr: ye have what I advise.
    He scarce had finisht, when such murmur filld
Th' Assembly, as when hollow Rocks retain   285
The sound of blustring winds, which all night long
Had rous'd the Sea, now with hoarse cadence lull
Sea-faring men orewatcht, whose Bark by chance
Or Pinnace anchors in a craggy Bay
After the Tempest: Such applause was heard   290
As Mammon ended, and his Sentence pleas'd,
Advising peace: for such another Field
They dreaded worse then Hell: so much the fear
Of Thunder and the Sword of Michael
Wrought still within them; and no less desire   295
To found this nether Empire, which might rise
By pollicy, and long process of time,
In emulation opposite to Heav'n.
Which when Beëlzebub perceiv'd, then whom,
Satan except, none higher sat, with grave   300
Aspect he rose, and in his rising seem'd

A Pillar of State; deep on his Front engrav'n
Deliberation sat and public care;
And Princely counsel in his face yet shon,
Majestic though in ruin: sage he stood   305
With *Atlantean*[9] shoulders fit to bear
The weight of mightiest Monarchies; his look
Drew audience and attention still as Night
Or Summers Noon-tide air, while thus he spake.

   Thrones and Imperial Powers, off-spring of heav'n,   310
Ethereal Vertues; or these Titles now
Must we renounce, and changing stile be call'd
Princes of Hell? for so the popular vote
Inclines, here to continue, and build up here
A growing Empire; doubtless; while we dream,   315
And know not that the King of Heav'n hath doom'd
This place our dungeon, not our safe retreat
Beyond his Potent arm, to live exempt
From Heav'ns high jurisdiction, in new League
Banded against his Throne, but to remain   320
In strictest bondage, though thus far remov'd,
Under th' inevitable curb, reserv'd
His captive multitude: For he, be sure,
In highth or depth, still first and last will Reign
Sole King, and of his Kingdom loose no part   325
By our revolt, but over Hell extend
His Empire, and with Iron Scepter rule
Us here, as with his Golden those in Heav'n.
What sit we then projecting peace and Warr?
Warr hath determin'd us, and foild with loss   330
Irreparable; tearms of peace yet none
Voutsaf't or sought; for what peace will be giv'n
To us enslav'd, but custody severe,
And stripes, and arbitrary punishment
Inflicted? and what peace can we return,   335
But to our power hostility and hate,
Untam'd reluctance,[10] and revenge though slow,
Yet ever plotting how the Conqueror least
May reap his conquest, and may least rejoyce
In doing what we most in suffering feel?   340
Nor will occasion want, nor shall we need
With dangerous expedition to invade
Heav'n, whose high walls fear no assault or Siege,

[9] referring to Atlas who bore the earth on his shoulders.
[10] revolt.

Or ambush from the Deep. What if we find
Some easier enterprize? There is a place   345
(If ancient and prophetic fame in Heav'n
Err not) another World, the happy seat
Of som new Race call'd *Man*, about this time
To be created like to us, though less
In power and excellence, but favour'd more   350
Of him who rules above; so was his will
Pronounc'd among the Gods, and by an Oath,
That shook Heav'ns whole circumference, confirm'd.
Thither let us bend all our thoughts, to learn
What creatures there inhabit, of what mould,   355
Or substance, how endu'd, and what thir Power,
And where thir weakness, how attempted best,
By force or suttlety: Though Heav'n be shut,
And Heav'ns high Arbitrator sit secure
In his own strength, this place may lye expos'd   360
The utmost border of his Kingdom, left
To their defence who hold it: here perhaps
Som advantagious act may be achiev'd
By sudden onset, either with Hell fire
To waste his whole Creation, or possess   365
All as our own, and drive as we were driv'n,
The punie[11] habitants, or if not drive,
Seduce them to our Party, that thir God
May prove thir foe, and with repenting hand
Abolish his own works. This would surpass   370
Common revenge, and interrupt his joy
In our Confusion, and our Joy upraise
In his disturbance; when his darling Sons
Hurl'd headlong to partake with us, shall curse
Thir frail Originals,[12] and faded bliss,   375
Faded so soon. Advise if this be worth
Attempting, or to sit in darkness here
Hatching vain Empires.[13] Thus *Beëlzebub*
Pleaded his devilish Counsel, first devis'd
By *Satan*, and in part propos'd:[14] for whence,   380
But from the Author of all ill could Spring
So deep a malice, to confound the race
Of mankind in one root, and Earth with Hell

[11] younger, weak.
[12] Adam and Eve.
[13] Compare I, 20–22.
[14] See I, 650–56.

To mingle and involve, done all to spite
The great Creatour? But thir spite still serves   385
His glory to augment. The bold design
Pleas'd highly those infernal States, and joy
Sparkl'd in all thir eyes; with full assent
They vote: whereat his speech he thus renews.
    Well have ye judg'd, well ended long debate,   390
Synod of Gods, and like to what ye are,
Great things resolv'd, which from the lowest deep
Will once more lift us up, in spight of Fate,
Neerer our ancient Seat; perhaps in view
Of those bright confines, whence with neighbouring Arms   395
And opportune excursion we may chance
Re-enter Heav'n; or else in some mild Zone
Dwell not unvisited of Heav'ns fair Light
Secure, and at the brightning Orient beam
Purge off this gloom; the soft delicious Air,   400
To heal the scarr of these corrosive Fires
Shall breath her balm. But first whom shall we send
In search of this new world, whom shall we find
Sufficient? who shall tempt[15] with wandring feet
The dark unbottom'd infinite Abyss   405
And through the palpable obscure find out
His uncouth[16] way, or spread his aerie flight
Upborn with indefatigable wings
Over the vast abrupt, ere he arrive
The happy Ile; what strength, what art can then   410
Suffice, or what evasion bear him safe
Through the strict Senteries and Stations thick
Of Angels watching round? Here he had need
All circumspection, and we now no less
Choice in our suffrage; for on whom we send,   415
The weight of all and our last hope relies.
    This said, he sat; and expectation held
His look suspence, awaiting who appeer'd
To second, or oppose, or undertake
The perilous attempt: but all sat mute,   420
Pondering the danger with deep thoughts; and each
In others count'nance read his own dismay
Astonisht: none among the choice and prime
Of those Heav'n-warring Champions could be found
So hardie as to proffer or accept   425

15 test.
16 unknown.

Alone the dreadful voyage; till at last
Satan, whom now transcendent glory rais'd
Above his fellows, with Monarchal pride
Conscious of highest worth, unmov'd thus spake.
   O Progeny of Heav'n, Empyreal Thrones,   430
With reason hath deep silence and demurr
Seis'd us, though undismaid: long is the way
And hard, that out of Hell leads up to light;
Our prison strong, this huge convex of Fire,
Outrageous to devour, immures us round   435
Ninefold, and gates of burning Adamant
Barr'd over us prohibit all egress.
These past, if any pass, the void profound
Of unessential[17] Night receives him next
Wide gaping, and with utter loss of being   440
Threatens him, plung'd in that abortive gulf.
If thence he scape into whatever world,
Or unknown Region, what remains him less
Then unknown dangers and as hard escape.
But I should ill become this Throne, O Peers,   445
And this Imperial Sov'ranty, adorn'd
With splendor, arm'd with power, if aught propos'd
And judg'd of public moment, in the shape
Of difficulty or danger could deterr
Mee from attempting. Wherefore do I assume   450
These Royalties, and not refuse to Reign,
Refusing to accept as great a share
Of hazard as of honour, due alike
To him who Reigns, and so much to him due
Of hazard more, as he above the rest   455
High honourd sits? Go therfore mighty Powers,
Terror of Heav'n, though fall'n; intend[18] at home,
While here shall be our home, what best may ease
The present misery, and render Hell
More tollerable; if there be cure or charm   460
To respite or deceive, or slack the pain
Of this ill Mansion: intermit no watch .
Against a wakeful Foe, while I abroad
Through all the coasts of dark destruction seek
Deliverance for us all: this enterprise   465
None shall partake with me. Thus saying rose

---

[17] without essence, since it is "abortive" (l. 441) or prematurely brought forth.
[18] direct your thoughts to.

The Monarch, and prevented all reply,
Prudent, least from his resolution rais'd
Others among the chief might offer now
(Certain to be refus'd) what erst they feard;   470
And so refus'd might in opinion stand
His rivals, winning cheap the high repute
Which he through hazard huge must earn. But they
Dreaded not more th' adventure then his voice
Forbidding; and at once with him they rose;   475
Thir rising all at once was as the sound
Of Thunder heard remote. Towards him they bend
With awful reverence prone; and as a God
Extoll him equal to the highest in Heav'n:
Nor fail'd they to express how much they prais'd,   480
That for the general safety he despis'd
His own: for neither do the Spirits damn'd
Loose all thir vertue; least bad men should boast
Thir specious deeds on earth, which glory excites,
Or close ambition varnisht o're with zeal.   485
Thus they thir doubtful consultations dark
Ended rejoycing in thir matchless Chief:
As when from mountain tops the dusky clouds
Ascending, while the North wind sleeps, o'respread
Heav'ns chearful face, the lowring Element   490
Scowls ore the dark'n'd lantskip Snow, or showr;
If chance the radiant Sun with farewell sweet
Extend his ev'ning beam, the fields revive,
The birds thir notes renew, and bleating herds
Attest thir joy, that hill and valley rings.   495
O shame to men! Devil with Devil damn'd
Firm concord holds, men onely disagree
Of Creatures rational, though under hope
Of heav'nly Grace: and God proclaiming peace,
Yet live in hatred, enmity, and strife   500
Among themselves, and levie cruel warrs,
Wasting the Earth, each other to destroy:
As if (which might induce us to accord)
Man had not hellish foes anow besides,
That day and night for his destruction wait.   505
   The *Stygian* Councel thus dissolv'd; and forth
In order came the grand infernal Peers,
Midst came thir mighty Paramount, and seemd
Alone th' Antagonist of Heav'n, nor less
Then Hells dread Emperour with pomp Supream,   510
And God-like imitated State; him round

A Globe of fierie Seraphim inclos'd
With bright imblazonrie, and horrent Arms.
Then of thir Session ended they bid cry
With Trumpets regal sound the great result: 515
Toward the four winds four speedy Cherubim[19]
Put to thir mouths the sounding Alchymie[20]
By Haralds voice explain'd:[21] the hollow Abyss
Heard farr and wide, and all the host of Hell
With deafning shout, return'd them loud acclaim.   520
Thence more at ease thir minds and somwhat rais'd
By false presumptuous hope, the ranged powers
Disband, and wandring, each his several way
Pursues, as inclination or sad choice
Leads him perplext, where he may likeliest find   525
Truce to his restless thoughts, and entertain
The irksom hours, till his great Chief return.
Part on the Plain, or in the Air sublime
Upon the wing, or in swift race contend,
As at th' Olympian Games or *Pythian* fields;   530
Part curb thir fierie Steeds, or shun the Goal
With rapid wheels, or fronted Brigads form.
As when to warn proud Cities warr appears
Wag'd in the troubl'd Skie, and Armies rush
To Battel in the Clouds, before each Van   535
Prick forth the Aerie Knights, and couch thir spears
Till thickest Legions close; with feats of Arms
From either end of Heav'n the welkin burns.
Others with vast *Typhœan*[22] rage more fell
Rend up both Rocks and Hills, and ride the Air   540
In whirlwind; Hell scarce holds the wild uproar.
As when *Alcides*[23] from *Oechalia* Crown'd
With conquest, felt th' envenom'd robe, and tore
Through pain up by the roots *Thessalian* Pines,
And *Lichas* from the top of *Oeta* threw   545
Into th' *Euboic* Sea. Others more mild,
Retreated in a silent valley, sing
With notes Angelical to many a Harp
Thir own Heroic deeds and hapless fall

---

[19] Compare Matt. xxiv. 31: "And he shall send his angels with a great sound
of a trumpet, and they shall gather together his elect from the four winds, from
one end of heaven to the other."
[20] the alloy (brass) of which trumpets were made.
[21] proclaimed.
[22] referring to a hundred-headed giant.
[23] Hercules; see *Vice-Chancellor*, n. 5.

By doom of Battel; and complain that Fate 550
Free Vertue should enthrall to Force or Chance.
Thir song was partial, but the harmony
(What could it less when Spirits immortal sing?)
Suspended Hell, and took with ravishment
The thronging audience. In discourse more sweet 555
(For Eloquence the Soul, Song charms the Sense,)
Others apart sat on a Hill retir'd,
In thoughts more elevate, and reason'd high
Of Providence, Foreknowledge, Will and Fate,
Fixt Fate, free will, foreknowledge absolute, 560
And found no end, in wandring mazes lost.
Of good and evil much they argu'd then,
Of happiness and final misery,
Passion and Apathie, and glory and shame,
Vain wisdom all, and false Philosophie: 565
Yet with a pleasing sorcerie could charm
Pain for a while or anguish, and excite
Fallacious hope, or arm th' obdured brest
With stubborn patience as with triple steel.
Another part in Squadrons and gross²⁴ Bands, 570
On bold adventure to discover wide
That dismal world, if any Clime perhaps
Might yeild them easier habitation, bend
Four ways thir flying March, along the Banks
Of four infernal Rivers that disgorge 575
Into the burning Lake thir baleful streams;
Abhorred *Styx* the flood of deadly hate,
Sad *Acheron* of sorrow, black and deep;
Cocytus, nam'd of lamentation loud
Heard on the ruful stream; fierce *Phlegeton* 580
Whose waves of torrent fire inflame with rage.
Farr off from these a slow and silent stream,
Lethe the River of Oblivion rouls
Her watrie Labyrinth, whereof who drinks,
Forthwith his former state and being forgets, 585
Forgets both joy and grief, pleasure and pain.
Beyond this flood a frozen Continent
Lies dark and wild, beat with perpetual storms
Of Whirlwind and dire Hail, which on firm land
Thaws not, but gathers heap, and ruin seems 590
Of ancient pile; all else deep snow and ice,

²⁴ compact.

A gulf profound as that *Serbonian* Bog[25]
Betwixt *Damiata* and mount *Casius* old,
Where Armies whole have sunk: the parching Air
Burns frore, and cold performs th' effect of Fire.   595
Thither by harpy-footed Furies hail'd,
At certain revolutions all the damn'd
Are brought: and feel by turns the bitter change
Of fierce extreams, extreams by change more fierce,
From Beds of raging Fire to starve[26] in Ice   600
Thir soft Ethereal warmth, and there to pine
Immovable, infixt, and frozen round,
Periods of time, thence hurried back to fire.
They ferry over this *Lethean* Sound
Both to and fro, thir sorrow to augment,   605
And wish and struggle, as they pass, to reach
The tempting stream, with one small drop to loose
In sweet forgetfulness all pain and woe,
All in one moment, and so neer the brink;
But Fate withstands, and to oppose th' attempt   610
Medusa with *Gorgonian* terror guards
The Ford, and of it self the water flies
All taste of living wight, as once it fled
The lip of *Tantalus*.[27] Thus roving on
In confus'd march forlorn, th' adventrous Bands   615
With shuddring horror pale, and eyes agast
View'd first thir lamentable lot, and found
No rest: through many a dark and drearie Vale
They pass'd, and many a Region dolorous,
O're many a frozen, many a fierie Alp,   620
Rocks, Caves, Lakes, Fens, Bogs, Dens, and shades of death,
A Universe of death, which God by curse
Created evil, for evil only good,
Where all life dies, death lives, and nature breeds,
Perverse, all monstrous, all prodigious things,   625
Abominable, inutterable, and worse
Then Fables yet have feign'd, or fear conceiv'd,
Gorgons and *Hydra's*, and *Chimera's* dire.   opponent; enemy
   Mean while the Adversary of God and Man,
Satan with thoughts inflam'd of highest design,   630
Puts on swift wings, and towards the Gates of Hell

[25] in northern Egypt.
[26] to die.
[27] whose punishment in hell was never to clutch the grapes he reached for
or drink from the water in which he stood.

Explores his solitary flight; som times
He scours the right hand coast, som times the left,
Now shaves with level wing the Deep, then soars
Up to the fiery Concave touring high.   635
As when farr off at Sea a Fleet descri'd
Hangs in the Clouds, by *Æquinoctial* Winds
Close sailing from *Bengala*, or the Iles
Of *Ternate* and *Tidore*,[28] whence Merchants bring
Thir spicie Drugs: they on the Trading Flood   640
Through the wide *Ethiopian* to the Cape[29]
Ply stemming[30] nightly toward the Pole. So seem'd
Farr off the flying Fiend: at last appeer
Hell bounds high reaching to the horrid Roof,
And thrice threefold the Gates; three folds were Brass,   645
Three Iron, three of Adamantine Rock,
Impenetrable, impal'd with circling fire,
Yet unconsum'd. Before the Gates there sat
On either side a formidable shape;[31]
The one seem'd Woman to the waste, and fair,   650
But ended foul in many a scaly fould
Voluminous and vast, a Serpent arm'd
With mortal sting: about her middle round
A cry of Hell Hounds never ceasing bark'd
With wide *Cerberean* mouths full loud, and rung   655
A hideous Peal: yet, when they list, would creep,
If aught disturb'd thir noyse, into her woomb,
And kennel there, yet there still bark'd and howl'd,
Within unseen. Farr less abhorr'd then these
Vex'd *Scylla* bathing in the Sea that parts   660
Calabria from the hoarce *Trinacrian*[32] shore:
Nor uglier follow the Night-Hag,[33] when call'd
In secret, riding through the Air she comes
Lur'd with the smell of infant blood, to dance
With *Lapland* Witches, while the labouring Moon   665
Eclipses at thir charms. The other shape,[34]
If shape it might be call'd that shape had none

[28] islands of the Moluccas.
[29] Through the Indian Ocean to the Cape of Good Hope.
[30] making headway despite difficulty.
[31] See James i. 15: "Then when lust hath conceived, it bringeth forth sin: and sin, when it is finished, bringeth forth death."
[32] Sicilian; see *Mask*, n. 29.
[33] Hecate.
[34] The introduction of Death at l. 666 suggests the beast of Revelation (see xiii. 18).

Distinguishable in member, joynt, or limb,
Or substance might be call'd that shadow seem'd,
For each seem'd either; black it stood as Night,   670
Fierce as ten Furies, terrible as Hell,
And shook a dreadful Dart; what seem'd his head
The likeness of a Kingly Crown had on./
Satan was now at hand, and from his seat
The Monster moving onward came as fast   675
With horrid strides, Hell trembled as he strode.
Th'undaunted Fiend what this might be admir'd,
Admir'd, not fear'd; God and his Son except,
Created thing naught valu'd he nor shun'd;
And with disdainful look thus first began.   680
    Whence and what art thou, execrable shape,
That dar'st, though grim and terrible, advance
Thy miscreated Front athwart my way
To yonder Gates? through them I mean to pass,
That be assur'd, without leave askt of thee: 685
Retire, or taste thy folly, and learn by proof,
Hell-born, not to contend with Spirits of Heav'n.
    To whom the Goblin full of wrauth reply'd,
Art thou that Traitor Angel, art thou hee,
Who first broke peace in Heav'n and Faith, till then   690
Unbrok'n, and in proud rebellious Arms
Drew after him the third part of Heav'ns Sons[35]
Conjur'd against the highest, for which both Thou
And they outcast from God, are here condemn'd
To waste Eternal dayes in woe and pain?   695
And reck'n'st thou thy self with Spirits of Heav'n,
Hell-doom'd, and breath'st defiance here and scorn,
Where I reign King, and to enrage thee more,
Thy King and Lord? Back to thy punishment,
False fugitive, and to thy speed add wings,   700
Least with a whip of Scorpions I pursue
Thy lingring, or with one stroke of this Dart
Strange horror seise thee, and pangs unfelt before.
    So spake the grieslie terrour, and in shape,
So speaking and so threatning, grew tenfold   705
More dreadful and deform: on th' other side
Incenst with indignation Satan stood
Unterrifi'd, and like a Comet burn'd,

[35] as cited in Rev. xii. 4: "And his [the great red dragon's] tail drew the third
part of the stars of heaven, and did cast them to the earth. . . ."

That fires the length of *Ophiucus*[36] huge
In th' Artick Sky, and from his horrid hair   710
Shakes Pestilence and Warr. Each at the Head
Level'd his deadly aim; thir fatall hands
No second stroke intend, and such a frown
Each cast at th' other, as when two black Clouds
With Heav'ns Artillery fraught, come rattling on   715
Over the *Caspian,* then stand front to front
Hov'ring a space, till Winds the signal blow
To joyn their dark Encounter in mid air:
So frownd the mighty Combatants, that Hell
Grew darker at thir frown, so matcht they stood;   720
For never but once more was either like
To meet so great a foe:[37] and now great deeds
Had been achiev'd, whereof all Hell had rung,
Had not the Snakie Sorceress that sat
Fast by Hell Gate, and kept the fatal Key,   725
Ris'n, and with hideous outcry rush'd between.
    O Father, what intends thy hand, she cry'd,
Against thy only Son? What fury O Son,
Possesses thee to bend that mortal Dart
Against thy Fathers head? and know'st for whom;   730
For him who sits above and laughs the while
At thee ordain'd his drudge, to execute
What e're his wrath, which he calls Justice, bids,
His wrath which one day will destroy ye both.
    She spake, and at her words the hellish Pest   735
Forbore, then these to her *Satan* return'd:
    So strange thy outcry, and thy words so strange
Thou interposest, that my sudden hand
Prevented spares to tell thee yet by deeds
What it intends; till first I know of thee,   740
What thing thou art, thus double-form'd, and why
In this infernal Vale first met thou call'st
Me Father, and that Fantasm call'st my Son?
I know thee not, nor ever saw till now

[36] a constellation extending into the northern hemisphere; the name means "serpent-bearer." Satan, "Incenst with indignation" at Death, is metaphorically a comet which lights up the northerly regions of Ophiucus (that is, himself as combiner of fire and ice); as comet he challenges Death with the "cold" instruments of death, pestilence and war. A nova (sometimes cited as a comet) appeared in the northern sky in 1618, the year in which the religious Thirty Years' War began.

[37] that is, Jesus who resisted Satan's temptations and who triumphed over death.

Sight more detestable then him and thee.   745
   T' whom thus the Portress of Hell Gate reply'd;
Hast thou forgot me then, and do I seem
Now in thine eye so foul, once deemd so fair
In Heav'n, when at th' Assembly, and in sight
Of all the Seraphim with thee combin'd   750
In bold conspiracy against Heav'ns King,
All on a sudden miserable pain
Surpris'd thee, dim thine eyes, and dizzie swumm
In darkness, while thy head flames thick and fast
Threw forth, till on the left side op'ning wide,   755
Likest to thee in shape and count'nance bright,
Then shining heav'nly fair, a Goddess arm'd
Out of thy head I sprung:[38] amazement seis'd
All th' Host of Heav'n; back they recoild affraid
At first, and call'd me Sin, and for a Sign   760
Portentous[39] held me; but familiar grown,
I pleas'd, and with attractive graces won
The most averse, thee chiefly, who full oft
Thy self in me thy perfect image viewing
Becam'st enamour'd, and such joy thou took'st   765
With me in secret, that my womb conceiv'd
A growing burden. Mean while Warr arose,
And fields were fought in Heav'n; wherein remaind
(For what could else) to our Almighty Foe
Cleer Victory, to our part loss and rout _defeat_   770
Through all the Empyrean: down they fell
Driv'n headlong from the Pitch of Heaven, down
Into this Deep, and in the general fall
I also; at which time this powerful Key
Into my hands was giv'n, with charge to keep   775
These Gates for ever shut, which none can pass
Without my op'ning. Pensive here I sat
Alone, but long I sat not, till my womb
Pregnant by thee, and now excessive grown _condition of
Prodigious motion felt and rueful throes._ _agonizing pain_   780
At last this odious offspring whom thou seest
Thine own begotten, breaking violent way
Tore through my entrails, that with fear and pain

---

[38] alluding to the birth of Athena (goddess of wisdom) from the head of
Jove. Jas. i. 15 cites the procreation of sin and death, but parody of the Trinity
underlies the passage. Eve was created from Adam's left side (VIII, 465); note
also ll. 868–70.
   [39] referring to the Latin meanings "unnatural" and a "portent"; the emphasis
is on her "monstrous" being.

Distorted, all my nether shape thus grew
Transform'd: but he my inbred[40] enemie   785
Forth issu'd, brandishing his fatal Dart
Made to destroy: I fled, and cry'd out *Death;*
Hell trembl'd at the hideous Name, and sigh'd
From all her Caves, and back resounded *Death.*
I fled, but he pursu'd (though more, it seems,   790
Inflam'd with lust then rage) and swifter far,
Mee overtook his mother all dismaid,
And in embraces forcible and foul
Ingendring with me, of that rape begot
These yelling Monsters that with ceasless cry   795
Surround me, as thou sawst, hourly conceiv'd
And hourly born, with sorrow infinite
To me, for when they list into the womb
That bred them they return, and howl and gnaw
My Bowels, thir repast; then bursting forth   800
Afresh with conscious terrours vex me round,
That rest or intermission none I find.
Before mine eyes in opposition sits
Grim *Death* my Son and foe, who sets them on,
And me his Parent would full soon devour   805
For want of other prey, but that he knows
His end with mine involv'd; and knows that I
Should prove a bitter Morsel, and his bane,
When ever that shall be; so Fate pronounc'd.
But thou O Father, I forewarn thee, shun   810
His deadly arrow; neither vainly hope
To be invulnerable in those bright Arms,
Though temper'd heav'nly, for that mortal dint,
Save he who reigns above, none can resist.
    She finish'd, and the suttle Fiend his lore   815
Soon learnd, now milder, and thus answerd smooth.
Dear Daughter, since thou claim'st me for thy Sire,
And my fair Son here showst me, the dear pledge
Of dalliance had with thee in Heav'n, and joys
Then sweet, now sad to mention, through dire change   820
Befall'n us unforeseen, unthought of, know
I come no enemie, but to set free
From out this dark and dismal house of pain,
Both him and thee, and all the heav'nly Host
Of Spirits that in our just pretenses arm'd   825
Fell with us from on high: from them I go

[40] bred physically within and bred incestuously.

This uncouth errand sole, and one for all
My self expose, with lonely steps to tread
Th' unfounded deep, and through the void immense
To search with wandring quest a place foretold   830
Should be, and, by concurring signs, ere now
Created vast and round, a place of bliss
In the Pourlieues of Heav'n, and therein plac't
A race of upstart Creatures, to supply
Perhaps our vacant room, though more remov'd,   835
Least Heav'n surcharg'd with potent multitude
Might hap to move new broils: Be this or aught
Then this more secret now design'd, I haste
To know, and this once known, shall soon return,
And bring ye to the place where Thou and Death   840
Shall dwell at ease, and up and down unseen
Wing silently the buxom[41] Air, imbalm'd
With odours; there ye shall be fed and fill'd
Immeasurably, all things shall be your prey.
He ceas'd, for both seemd highly pleas'd, and Death   845
Grinnd horrible a gastly smile, to hear
His famine should be fill'd, and blest his maw
Destin'd to that good hour: no less rejoyc'd
His mother bad, and thus bespake her Sire.
    The key of this infernal Pit by due,   850
And by command of Heav'ns all-powerful King
I keep, by him forbidden to unlock
These Adamantine Gates; against all force
Death ready stands to interpose his dart,
Fearless to be o'rematcht by living might.   855
But what ow I to his commands above
Who hates me, and hath hither thrust me down
Into this gloom of *Tartarus* profound,
To sit in hateful Office here confin'd,
Inhabitant of Heav'n, and heav'nlie-born,   860
Here in perpetual agonie and pain,
With terrors and with clamors compasst round
Of mine own brood, that on my bowels feed:
Thou art my Father, thou my Author, thou
My being gav'st me; whom should I obey   865
But thee, whom follow? thou wilt bring me soon
To that new world of light and bliss, among
The Gods who live at ease, where I shall Reign
At thy right hand voluptuous, as beseems

[41] pliable.

Thy daughter and thy darling, without end.   870
  Thus saying, from her side the fatal Key,
Sad instrument of all our woe, she took;
And towards the Gate rouling her bestial train,
Forthwith the huge Porcullis high up drew,
Which but her self not all the *Stygian* powers   875
Could once have mov'd; then in the key-hole turns
Th' intricate wards, and every Bolt and Bar
Of massie Iron or sollid Rock with ease
Unfast'ns: on a sudden op'n flie
With impetuous recoil and jarring sound   880
Th' infernal dores, and on thir hinges grate
Harsh Thunder, that the lowest bottom shook
Of *Erebus*.[42] She op'nd, but to shut
Excel'd her power;[43] the Gates wide op'n stood,
That with extended wings a Bannerd Host   885
Under spread Ensigns marching might pass through
With Horse and Chariots rankt in loose array;
So wide they stood, and like a Furnace mouth
Cast forth redounding smoak and ruddy flame.
Before thir eyes in sudden view appear   890
The secrets of the hoarie deep, a dark
Illimitable Ocean without bound,
Without dimension, where length, breadth, and highth,
And time and place are lost; where eldest Night
And *Chaos*, Ancestors of Nature, hold   895
Eternal *Anarchie*, amidst the noise
Of endless Warrs, and by confusion stand.
For hot, cold, moist, and dry,[44] four Champions fierce
Strive here for Maistrie, and to Battel bring
Thir embryon Atoms; they around the flag   900
Of each his Faction, in thir several Clanns,
Light-arm'd or heavy, sharp, smooth, swift or slow,
Swarm populous, unnumber'd as the Sands
Of *Barca* or *Cyrene's*[45] torrid soil,
Levied to side with warring Winds, and poise[46]   905
Thir lighter wings. To whom these most adhere,

[42] primeval darkness, thus hell.
[43] Likewise Eve opens the gates by transgression, but she cannot undo what is
past.
[44] the four qualities of elements and humours—fire, choler: hot and dry; air,
blood: hot and moist; water, phlegm: cold and moist; earth, melancholy: cold
and dry.
[45] desert and a city in Libya.
[46] balance.

Hee[47] rules a moment; *Chaos* Umpire sits,
And by decision more imbroils the fray
By which he Reigns: next him high Arbiter
Chance[48] governs all. Into this wild Abyss,   910
The Womb of nature and perhaps her Grave,
Of neither Sea, nor Shore, nor Air, nor Fire,
But all these in thir pregnant causes[49] mixt
Confus'dly, and which thus must ever fight,
Unless th' Almighty Maker them ordain   915
His dark materials to create more Worlds,
Into this wild Abyss the warie fiend
Stood on the brink of Hell and look'd a while,
Pondering his Voyage; for no narrow frith
He had to cross. Nor was his ear less peal'd   920
With noises loud and ruinous (to compare
Great things with small) then when *Bellona*[50] storms,
With all her battering Engines bent to rase
Som Capital City; or less then if this frame
Of Heav'n were falling, and these Elements   925
In mutinie had from her Axle torn
The stedfast Earth. At last his Sail-broad Vans _wings_
He spreads for flight, and in the surging smoak
Uplifted spurns the ground, thence many a League
As in a cloudy Chair ascending rides   930
Audacious, but that seat soon failing, meets
emptiness _vacuum_ A vast vacuitie: all unawares
Fluttring his pennons vain plumb down he drops
Ten thousand fadom deep, and to this hour
Down had been falling, had not by ill chance   935
The strong rebuff of som tumultuous cloud
Instinct[51] with Fire and Nitre hurried him
As many miles aloft: that furie stay'd,
Quencht in a Boggie *Syrtis*,[52] neither Sea,
Nor good dry Land: nigh founderd on he fares,   940
Treading the crude consistence, half on foot,

[47] one of the champions of l. 898.
[48] The chance of Chaos opposes the providence of God.
[49] The phrase recalls I, 20–22, for the whole passage and underscores the sexual imagery connected with Chaos, Satan, and Adam after the fall, in sharp contrast to the Father's begetting of His Son. The causes are Ramus' forces by which things exist: nothing has been born yet from their confusion but potential birth is imminent. (See VII, 232 ff., and n. 26.)
[50] Roman goddess of war.
[51] charged.
[52] an inlet on the coast of Libya.

Half flying; behoves him now both Oar and Sail.
As when a Gryfon through the Wilderness
With winged course ore Hill or moarie Dale,
Pursues the *Arimaspian*,[53] who by stelth   945
Had from his wakeful custody purloind
The guarded Gold: So eagerly the fiend
Ore bog or steep, through strait, rough, dense, or rare,
With head, hands, wings or feet pursues his way,
And swims or sinks, or wades, or creeps, or flyes: 950
At length a universal hubbub wild
Of stunning sounds and voices all confus'd
Born through the hollow dark assaults his ear
With loudest vehemence: thither he plyes,
Undaunted to meet there what ever power   955
Or Spirit of the nethermost Abyss
Might in that noise reside, of whom to ask
Which way the neerest coast of darkness lyes
Bordering on light; when strait behold the Throne
Of *Chaos*, and his dark Pavilion spread[54]   960
Wide on the wasteful Deep; with him Enthron'd
Sat Sable-vested *Night*, eldest of things,
The Consort of his Reign; and by them stood
Orcus and *Ades*,[55] and the dreaded name
Of *Demogorgon; Rumor* next and *Chance*,   965
And *Tumult* and *Confusion* all imbroild,
And *Discord* with a thousand various mouths.
   T' whom *Satan* turning boldly, thus. Ye Powers
And Spirits of this nethermost Abyss,
Chaos and ancient *Night*, I come no Spy,   970
With purpose to explore or to disturb
The secrets of your Realm, but by constraint
Wandring this darksome Desart, as my way
Lies through your spacious Empire up to light,
Alone, and without guide, half lost,[56] I seek   975
What readiest path leads where your gloomie bounds
Confine with Heav'n; or if som other place
From your Dominion won, th' Ethereal King
Possesses lately, thither to arrive
I travel this profound,[57] direct my course;   980

[53] a Scythian tribe.
[54] Ps. xviii. 11: "He made darkness his secret place; his pavilion round about him were dark waters and thick clouds of the skies."
[55] Hades.
[56] Compare Adam and Eve's expulsion, XII, 632–649.
[57] deep, abyss.

Directed, no mean recompence it brings
To your behoof, if I that Region lost,
All usurpation thence expell'd, reduce
To her original darkness and your sway
(Which is my present journey) and once more   985
Erect the Standard there of ancient *Night;*
Yours be th' advantage all, mine the revenge.
   Thus *Satan;* and him thus the Anarch old
With faultring speech and visage incompos'd[58]
Answer'd. I know thee, stranger, who thou art,   990
That mighty leading Angel, who of late
Made head against Heav'ns King, though overthrown.
I saw and heard, for such a numerous Host
Fled not in silence through the frighted deep
With ruin upon ruin, rout on rout,   995
Confusion worse confounded; and Heav'n Gates
Pourd out by millions her victorious Bands
Pursuing. I upon my Frontiers here
Keep residence; if all I can will serve,
That little which is left so to defend,   1000
Encroacht on still through our intestine broils
Weakning the Scepter of old *Night:* first Hell
Your dungeon stretching far and wide beneath;
Now lately Heav'n and Earth, another World
Hung ore my Realm, link'd in a golden Chain   1005
To that side Heav'n from whence your Legions fell:
If that way be your walk, you have not farr;
So much the neerer danger; go and speed;
Havock and spoil and ruin are my gain.
   He ceas'd; and *Satan* staid not to reply,   1010
But glad that now his Sea should find a shore,
With fresh alacritie and force renew'd
Springs upward like a Pyramid[59] of fire
Into the wild expanse, and through the shock
Of fighting Elements, on all sides round   1015
Environ'd wins his way; harder beset
And more endanger'd, then when *Argo*[60] pass'd
Through *Bosporus* betwixt the justling Rocks:
Or when *Ulysses* on the Larbord shunnd
Charybdis, and by th' other whirlpool[61] steard.   1020

[58] disturbed.
[59] chosen because of the supposed etymological source in "pyre."
[60] the ship of Jason and the Argonauts.
[61] Scylla, seen here to be a symbol of Sin.

So he with difficulty and labour hard
Mov'd on, with difficulty and labour hee;
But hee once past, soon after when man fell,
Strange alteration! Sin and Death amain
Following his track, such was the will of Heav'n,   1025
Pav'd after him a broad and beat'n way
Over the dark Abyss, whose boiling Gulf
Tamely endur'd a Bridge of wondrous length
From Hell continu'd reaching th' utmost Orb
Of this frail World;[62] by which the Spirits perverse   1030
With easie intercourse pass to and fro
To tempt or punish mortals, except whom
God and good Angels guard by special grace.
But now at last the sacred influence
Of light appears, and from the walls of Heav'n   1035
Shoots farr into the bosom of dim Night
A glimmering dawn; here Nature first begins
Her fardest verge, and *Chaos* to retire
As from her outmost works a brok'n foe
With tumult less and with less hostile din,   1040
That *Satan* with less toil, and now with ease
Wafts on the calmer wave by dubious light
And like a weather-beaten Vessel holds
Gladly the Port, though Shrouds and Tackle torn;
Or in the emptier waste, resembling Air,   1045
Weighs his spread wings, at leasure to behold
Farr off th' Empyreal Heav'n, extended wide
In circuit, undetermind square or round,[63]
With Opal Towrs and Battlements adorn'd
Of living Saphire, once his native Seat;   1050
And fast by hanging in a golden Chain
This pendant world,[64] in bigness as a Starr
Of smallest Magnitude close by the Moon.
Thither full fraught with mischievous revenge,
Accurst, and in a cursed hour he hies.   1055

[62] The building of the bridge is described in X, 293–324. The language in these two passages derives from Matt. vii. 13: "for wide is the gate, and broad is the way, that leadeth to destruction."

[63] Compare X, 381, and see Rev. xxi. 16: "And the city lieth foursquare, and the length is as large as the breadth: and he measured the city with the reed, twelve thousand furlongs. The length and the breadth and the height of it are equal."

[64] the whole universe within the Crystalline Sphere.

BOOK III

THE ARGUMENT

God sitting on his Throne sees *Satan* flying towards this world, then newly created; shews him to the Son who sat at his right hand; foretells the success of *Satan* in perverting mankind; clears his own Justice and Wisdom from all imputation, having created Man free and able enough to have withstood his Tempter; yet declares his purpose of grace towards him, in regard he fell not of his own malice, as did *Satan*, but by him seduc't. The Son of God renders praises to his Father for the manifesta- tion of his gracious purpose towards Man; but God again declares, that Grace cannot be extended towards Man without the satisfaction of di- vine Justice; Man hath offended the majesty of God by aspiring to God- head, and therefore with all his Progeny devoted to death must dye, unless some one can be found sufficient to answer for his offence, and undergo his Punishment. The Son of God freely offers himself a Ransom for Man: the Father accepts him, ordains his incarnation, pronounces his exaltation above all Names in Heaven and Earth; commands all the An- gels to adore him; they obey, and hymning to thir Harps in full Quire, celebrate the Father and the Son. Mean while *Satan* alights upon the bar convex of this Worlds outer-most Orb; where wandring he first finds a place since call'd the Lymbo of Vanity; what persons and things fly up thither; thence comes to the Gate of Heaven, describ'd ascending by stairs, and the waters above the Firmament that flow about it: His pas- sage thence to the Orb of the Sun; he finds there *Uriel* the Regent of that Orb, but first changes himself into the shape of a meaner Angel; and pretending a zealous desire to behold the new Creation and Man whom God had plac't here, inquires of him the place of his habitation, and is directed; alights first on Mount *Niphates*.

Hail holy Light, ofspring of Heav'n first-born,
Or of th' Eternal Coeternal beam
May I express thee unblam'd? since God is light,
And never but in unapproached light
Dwelt from Eternitie, dwelt then in thee,   5
Bright effluence of bright essence increate.[1]
Or hear'st thou rather pure Ethereal stream,
Whose Fountain who shall tell? before the Sun,
Before the Heav'ns thou wert, and at the voice
Of God, as with a Mantle didst invest   10
The rising world of waters dark and deep,

[1] not created. Thus the Holy Light is identified with the Son.

Won from the void and formless infinite.
Thee I revisit now with bolder wing,
Escap't the *Stygian* Pool, though long detain'd
In that obscure sojourn, while in my flight   15
Through utter and through middle darkness borne
With other notes then to th' *Orphean*[2] Lyre
I sung of *Chaos* and *Eternal Night*,
Taught by the heav'nly Muse to venture down
The dark descent, and up to reascend,   20
Though hard and rare: thee I revisit safe,
And feel thy sovran vital Lamp; but thou
Revisit'st not these eyes, that rowl in vain
To find thy piercing ray, and find no dawn;
So thick a drop serene[3] hath quencht thir Orbs,   25
Or dim suffusion veild. Yet not the more
Cease I to wander where the Muses haunt
Cleer Spring, or shadie Grove, or Sunnie Hill,
Smit with the love of sacred Song; but chief
Thee Sion and the flowrie Brooks beneath   30
That wash thy hallowd feet, and warbling flow,
Nightly I visit: nor somtimes forget
Those other two equal'd with me in Fate,
So were I equal'd with them in renown,
Blind *Thamyris* and blind *Mæonides*,[4]   35
And *Tiresias* and *Phineus* Prophets old.
Then feed on thoughts, that voluntarie move
Harmonious numbers; as the wakeful Bird
Sings darkling, and in shadiest Covert hid
Tunes her nocturnal Note. Thus with the Year   40
Seasons return, but not to me returns
Day, or the sweet approach of Ev'n or Morn,
Or sight of vernal bloom, or Summers Rose,
Or flocks, or heards, or human face divine;
But cloud in stead, and ever-during[5] dark   45
Surrounds me, from the chearful wayes of men
Cut off, and for the Book of knowledge fair

[2] Orpheus, who descended to Hades, won back his wife by his musical art,
but reascending broke the difficult covenant made with Pluto.
[3] total blindness (*gutta serena*); "Suffusion" is partial blindness. For a reex-
amination of the nature of Milton's blindness, see William B. Hunter, Jr.'s ar-
ticle in *Journal of the History of Medicine and Allied Sciences*, XVII (1962),
333–41.
[4] Homer. Thamyris is mentioned in *Iliad*, II, 595; Phineus, blinded by the
sun, was victimized by the Harpies.
[5] everlasting.

Presented with a Universal blanc
Of Natures works to mee expung'd and ras'd,
And wisdom at one entrance quite shut out.   50
So much the rather thou Celestial light
Shine inward, and the mind through all her powers
Irradiate, there plant eyes, all mist from thence
Purge and disperse, that I may see and tell
Of things invisible to mortal sight.   55
   Now had th' Almighty Father from above,
From the pure Empyrean where he sits
High Thron'd above all highth, bent down his eye,
His own works and their works at once to view:
About him all the Sanctities of Heav'n   60
Stood thick as Starrs, and from his sight receiv'd
Beatitude past utterance; on his right
The radiant image of his Glory sat,
His onely Son; on Earth he first beheld
Our two first Parents, yet the onely two   65
Of mankind, in the happie Garden plac't,
Reaping immortal fruits of joy and love,
Uninterrupted joy, unrivald love
In blissful solitude; he then survey'd
Hell and the Gulf between, and *Satan* there   70
Coasting the wall of Heav'n on this side Night
In the dun Air sublime, and ready now
To stoop with wearied wings, and willing feet
On the bare outside of this World, that seem'd
Firm land imbosom'd without Firmament,   75
Uncertain which, in Ocean or in Air.
Him God beholding from his prospect high,
Wherein past, present, future he beholds,
Thus to his onely Son foreseeing spake.
   Onely begotten Son, seest thou what rage   80
Transports our adversarie, whom no bounds
Prescrib'd, no barrs of Hell, nor all the chains
Heapt on him there, nor yet the main Abyss
Wide interrupt[6] can hold; so bent he seems
On desperat revenge, that shall redound   85
Upon his own rebellious head. And now
Through all restraint broke loose he wings his way
Not farr off Heav'n, in the Precincts[7] of light,

[6] broken widely apart.
[7] The word also retains its etymological meaning of places "encompassed in early times" (by light).

Directly towards the new created World,
And Man there plac't, with purpose to assay 90
If him by force he can destroy, or worse,
By som false guile pervert; and shall pervert;
For man will heark'n to his glozing lyes,
And easily transgress the sole Command,
Sole pledge of his obedience: So will fall 95
Hee and his faithless Progenie: whose fault?
Whose but his own? ingrate, he had of mee
All he could have; I made him just and right,
Sufficient to have stood, though free to fall.
Such I created all th' Ethereal Powers 100
And Spirits, both them who stood and them who faild;
Freely they stood who stood, and fell who fell.
Not free, what proof could they have givn sincere
Of true allegiance, constant Faith or Love,
Where onely what they needs must do, appeard, 105
Not what they would? what praise could they receive?
What pleasure I from such obedience paid,
When Will and Reason (Reason also is choice)
Useless and vain, of freedom both despoild,
Made passive both, had serv'd necessitie, 110
Not mee. They therefore as to right belong'd,
So were created, nor can justly accuse
Thir maker, or thir making, or thir Fate;
As if Predestination over-rul'd
Thir will, dispos'd by absolute Decree 115
Or high foreknowledge; they themselves decreed
Thir own revolt, not I: if I foreknew,
Foreknowledge had no influence on their fault,
Which had no less prov'd certain unforeknown.
So without least impulse or shadow of Fate, 120
Or aught by me immutablie foreseen,
They trespass, Authors to themselves in all
Both what they judge and what they choose; for so
I formd them free, and free they must remain,
Till they enthrall themselves: I else must change 125
Thir nature, and revoke the high Decree
Unchangeable, Eternal, which ordain'd
Thir freedom, they themselves ordain'd thir fall.
The first sort by thir own suggestion fell,
Self-tempted, self-deprav'd: Man falls deceiv'd 130
By the other first: Man therefore shall find grace,
The other none: in Mercy and Justice both,
Through Heav'n and Earth, so shall my glorie excel,

But Mercy first and last shall brightest shine.[8]

   Thus while God spake, ambrosial fragrance fill'd   135
All Heav'n, and in the blessed Spirits elect
Sense of new joy ineffable diffus'd:
Beyond compare the Son of God was seen
Most glorious, in him all his Father shon
Substantially[9] express'd, and in his face   140
Divine compassion visibly appeerd,
Love without end, and without measure Grace,
Which uttering thus he to his Father spake.

   O Father, gracious was that word which clos'd
Thy sovran sentence, that Man should find grace;   145
For which both Heav'n and Earth shall high extoll
Thy praises, with th' innumerable sound
Of Hymns and sacred Songs, wherewith thy Throne
Encompass'd shall resound thee ever blest.
For should Man finally be lost, should Man   150
Thy creature late so lov'd, thy youngest Son
Fall circumvented thus by fraud, though joynd
With his own folly? that be from thee farr,
That farr be from thee, Father, who art Judge
Of all things made, and judgest onely right.   155
Or shall the Adversarie thus obtain
His end, and frustrate thine, shall he fulfill
His malice, and thy goodness bring to naught,
Or proud return though to his heavier doom,
Yet with revenge accomplish't and to Hell   160
Draw after him the whole Race of mankind,
By him corrupted? or wilt thou thy self
Abolish thy Creation, and unmake,
For him, what for thy glorie thou hast made?
So should thy goodness and thy greatness both   165
Be questiond and blaspheam'd without defence.

   To whom the great Creatour thus reply'd.
O Son, in whom my Soul hath chief delight,
Son of my bosom, Son who art alone
My word, my wisdom, and effectual might,   170
All hast thou spok'n as my thoughts are, all
As my Eternal purpose hath decreed:

   [8] Mercy is to be granted through the love of the Son, who will atone for human disobedience and thereby pacify the wrath of the Father, guardian of Divine Justice. C. A. Patrides (*PMLA*, LXXIV, 1959, 7–13) makes clear that the atonement demanded by the Father here was accepted by both contemporary Protestant thinkers and earlier writers.
   [9] in like substance.

Man shall not quite be lost, but sav'd who will,
Yet not of will in him, but grace in me
Freely voutsaft; once more I will renew   175
His lapsed powers, though forfeit and enthrall'd
By sin to foul exorbitant desires;
Upheld by me, yet once more he shall stand
On even ground against his mortal foe,
By me upheld, that he may know how frail   180
His fall'n condition is, and to me ow
All his deliv'rance, and to none but me.
Some I have chosen of peculiar grace
Elect above the rest;[10] so is my will:
The rest shall hear me call, and oft be warnd   185
Thir sinful state, and to appease betimes
Th' incensed Deitie, while offerd grace
Invites; for I will cleer thir senses dark,
What may suffice, and soft'n stonie hearts
To pray, repent, and bring obedience due.   190
To prayer, repentance, and obedience due,
Though but endevord with sincere intent,
Mine ear shall not be slow, mine eye not shut.
And I will place within them as a guide
My Umpire *Conscience*, whom if they will hear,   195
Light after light well us'd they shall attain,
And to the end persisting, safe arrive.[11]
This my long sufferance and my day of grace
They who neglect and scorn, shall never taste;
But hard be hard'n'd, blind be blinded more,   200
That they may stumble on, and deeper fall;
And none but such from mercy I exclude.
But yet all is not don; Man disobeying,
Disloyal breaks his fealtie, and sinns
Against the high Supremacie of Heav'n,   205
Affecting God-head, and so loosing all,
To expiate his Treason hath naught left,
But to destruction sacred and devote,
He with his whole posteritie must die,
Die hee or Justice must; unless for him   210
Som other able, and as willing, pay
The rigid satisfaction, death for death.

[10] a basic doctrine of Calvinism. Although salvation is available to all men, some have special grace. Lines 183–97 indicate Milton's differences from the Calvinist doctrine of the elect.
[11] fundamentally a statement of Arminianism.

Say Heav'nly Powers, where shall we find such love,
Which of ye will be mortal to redeem
Mans mortal crime, and just th' unjust to save,   215
Dwels in all Heaven charitie so dear?
   He ask'd, but all the Heav'nly Quire stood mute,
And silence was in Heav'n: on mans behalf
Patron or Intercessor none appeerd,
Much less that durst upon his own head draw   220
The deadly forfeiture, and ransom set.
And now without redemption all mankind
Must have bin lost, adjudg'd to Death and Hell
By doom severe, had not the Son of God,
In whom the fulness dwels of love divine,   225
His dearest[12] mediation thus renewd.
   Father, thy word is past, man shall find grace;
And shall grace not find means, that finds her way,
The speediest of thy winged messengers,
To visit all thy creatures, and to all   230
Comes unprevented, unimplor'd, unsought,
Happie for man, so coming; he her aid
Can never seek, once dead in sins and lost;
Attonement for himself, or offering meet,
Indebted and undon, hath none to bring: 235
Behold mee then, mee for him, life for life
I offer, on mee let thine anger fall;
Account mee man; I for his sake will leave
Thy bosom, and this glorie next to thee
Freely put off, and for him lastly die   240
Well pleas'd, on me let Death wreck all his rage;
Under his gloomie power I shall not long
Lie vanquisht; thou hast givn me to possess
Life in my self for ever, by thee I live,
Though now to Death I yeild, and am his due   245
All that of me can die, yet that debt paid,
Thou wilt not leave me in the loathsom grave
His prey, nor suffer my unspotted Soul
For ever with corruption there to dwell;
But I shall rise Victorious, and subdue   250
My Vanquisher, spoild of his vanted spoil;
Death his deaths wound shall then receive, and stoop
Inglorious, of his mortall sting disarm'd.
I through the ample Air in Triumph high

---

[12] hardest, most glorious, most loving.

Shall lead Hell Captive maugre[13] Hell, and show   255
The powers of darkness bound. Thou at the sight
Pleas'd, out of Heaven shalt look down and smile,
While by thee rais'd I ruin all my Foes,
Death last, and with his Carcass glut the Grave:
Then with the multitude of my redeemd   260
Shall enter Heav'n long absent, and return,
Father, to see thy face, wherein no cloud
Of anger shall remain, but peace assur'd,
And reconcilement; wrauth shall be no more
Thenceforth, but in thy presence Joy entire.   265
   His words here ended, but his meek aspect
Silent yet spake, and breath'd immortal love
To mortal men, above which only shon
Filial obedience: as a sacrifice
Glad to be offer'd, he attends the will   270
Of his great Father. Admiration seis'd
All Heav'n, what this might mean, and whither tend
Wondring; but soon th' Almighty thus reply'd:
   O thou in Heav'n and Earth the only peace
Found out for mankind under wrauth, O thou   275
My sole complacence! well thou know'st how dear,
To me are all my works, nor Man the least
Though last created, that for him I spare
Thee from my bosom and right hand, to save,
By loosing thee a while, the whole Race lost.   280
Thou therefore whom thou only canst redeem,
Thir Nature also to thy Nature joyn;
And be thy self Man among men on Earth,
Made flesh, when time shall be, of Virgin seed,
By wondrous birth: Be thou in *Adams* room[14]   285
The Head of all mankind, though *Adams* Son.
As in him perish all men, so in thee
As from a second root shall be restor'd,
As many as are restor'd, without thee none.
His crime makes guiltie all his Sons, thy merit   290
Imputed shall absolve them who renounce
Thir own both righteous and unrighteous deeds,
And live in thee transplanted, and from thee
Receive new life. So Man, as is most just,
Shall satisfie for Man, be judg'd and die,   295
And dying rise, and rising with him raise

[13] in spite of.
[14] place.

His Brethren, ransomd with his own dear life.
So Heav'nly love shall outdo Hellish hate,
Giving to death, and dying to redeem,
So dearly to redeem what Hellish hate   300
So easily destroy'd, and still destroyes
In those who, when they may, accept not grace.
Nor shalt thou by descending to assume
Mans Nature, less'n or degrade thine own.
Because thou hast, though Thron'd in highest bliss   305
Equal to God, and equally enjoying
God-like fruition, quitted all to save
A World from utter loss, and hast been found
By Merit more then Birthright Son of God,
Found worthiest to be so by being Good,   310
Farr more then Great or High; because in thee
Love hath abounded more then Glory abounds,
Therefore thy Humiliation shall exalt
With thee thy Manhood also to this Throne;
Here shalt thou sit incarnate, here shalt Reign   315
Both God and Man, Son both of God and Man,
Anointed universal King; all Power
I give thee, reign for ever, and assume
Thy Merits; under thee as Head Supream
Thrones, Princedoms, Powers, Dominions I reduce: 320
All knees to thee shall bow, of them that bide
In Heav'n, or Earth, or under Earth in Hell;
When thou attended gloriously from Heav'n
Shalt in the Sky appeer, and from thee send
The summoning Arch-Angels to proclaim   325
Thy dread Tribunal: forthwith from all Winds
The living, and forthwith the cited dead
Of all past Ages to the general Doom[15]
Shall hast'n, such a peal shall rouse thir sleep.
Then all thy Saints assembl'd, thou shalt judge   330
Bad men and Angels, they arraign'd shall sink
Beneath thy Sentence; Hell her numbers full,
Thenceforth shall be for ever shut. Mean while
The World shall burn, and from her ashes spring[16]
New Heav'n and Earth,[17] wherein the just shall dwell   335
And after all thir tribulations long

[15] the Last Judgment.
[16] The symbol of the phoenix indicated immortality; it is appropriate here in
conjunction with the Son since it was the embodiment of the Egyptian sun-god.
[17] See 2 Peter iii. 12–13, which refers to Isa. lxv. 17–25.

See golden days, fruitful of golden deeds,
With Joy and Love triumphing, and fair Truth.
Then thou thy regal Scepter shalt lay by,
For regal Scepter then no more shall need, 340
God shall be All in All.[18] But all ye Gods,
Adore him, who to compass all this dies,
Adore the Son, and honour him as mee.
    No sooner had th' Almighty ceas't, but all
The multitude of Angels with a shout 345
Loud as from numbers without number, sweet
As from blest voices, uttering joy, Heav'n rung
With Jubilee, and loud Hosanna's filld
Th' eternal Regions: lowly reverent
Towards either Throne they bow, and to the ground 350
With solemn adoration down they cast
Thir Crowns inwove with Amarant and Gold,
Immortal Amarant, a Flowr which once
In Paradise, fast by the Tree of Life
Began to bloom, but soon for mans offence 355
To Heav'n remov'd where first it grew, there grows,
And flowrs aloft shading the Fount of Life,
And where the river of Bliss through midst of Heavn
Rowls o're _Elisian_ Flowrs her Amber stream;
With these that never fade the Spirits Elect 360
Bind thir resplendent locks inwreath'd with beams,
Now in loose Garlands thick thrown off, the bright
Pavement that like a Sea of Jasper shon
Impurpl'd with Celestial Roses smil'd.
Then Crown'd again thir gold'n Harps they took, 365
Harps ever tun'd, that glittering by thir side
Like Quivers hung, and with Præamble sweet
Of charming symphonie they introduce
This sacred Song, and waken raptures high;
No voice exempt, no voice but well could join 370
Melodious part, such concord is in Heav'n.
    Thee Father first they sung Omnipotent,
Immutable, Immortal, Infinite,
Eternal King; thee Author of all being,
Fountain of Light, thy self invisible 375
Amidst the glorious brightness where thou sit'st
Thron'd inaccessible, but when thou shad'st

---

[18] 1 Cor. xv. 28: "And when all things shall be subdued unto him, then shall the Son also himself become subject unto him that put all things under him, that God may be all in all."

The full blaze of thy beams, and through a cloud
Drawn round about thee like a radiant Shrine,
Dark with excessive bright thy skirts appeer,   380
Yet dazle Heav'n, that brightest Seraphim
Approach not, but with both wings veil thir eyes.
Thee next they sang of all Creation first,
Begotten Son, Divine Similitude,
In whose conspicuous count'nance, without cloud   385
Made visible, th' Almighty Father shines,
Whom else no Creature can behold; on thee
Impresst th' effulgence of his Glorie abides,
Transfus'd on thee his ample Spirit rests.
Hee Heav'n of Heav'ns and all the Powers therein   390
By thee created, and by thee threw down
Th' aspiring Dominations: thou that day
Thy Fathers dreadful Thunder didst not spare,
Nor stop thy flaming Chariot wheels, that shook
Heav'ns everlasting Frame, while o're the necks   395
Thou drov'st of warring Angels disarraid.
Back from pursuit thy Powers with loud acclaim
Thee only extoll'd, Son of thy Fathers might,
To execute fierce vengeance on his foes,
Not so on Man; him through their malice fall'n,   400
Father of Mercie and Grace, thou didst not doom
So strictly, but much more to pitie encline:
No sooner did thy dear and onely Son
Perceive thee purpos'd not to doom frail Man
So strictly, but much more to pitie enclin'd,   405
He to appease thy wrauth, and end the strife
Of Mercy and Justice in thy face discern'd,
Regardless of the Bliss wherein hee sat
Second to thee, offerd himself to die
For mans offence. O unexampl'd love,   410
Love no where to be found less then Divine!
Hail Son of God, Saviour of Men, thy Name
Shall be the copious matter of my Song
Henceforth, and never shall my Harp thy praise
Forget, nor from thy Fathers praise disjoin.   415
     Thus they in Heav'n, above the starry Sphear,
Thir happie hours in joy and hymning spent.
Mean while upon the firm opacous[19] Globe
Of this round World, whose first convex divides
The luminous inferior Orbs, enclos'd   420

[19] dark.

From *Chaos* and th' inroad of Darkness old,
Satan alighted walks: a Globe farr off
It seem'd, now seems a boundless Continent
Dark, waste, and wild, under the frown of Night
Starless expos'd, and ever-threatning storms   425
Of *Chaos* blustring round, inclement skie;
Save on that side which from the wall of Heav'n
Though distant farr som small reflection gains
Of glimmering air less vext with tempest loud:
Here walk'd the Fiend at large in spacious field.   430
As when a Vultur on *Imaus*[20] bred,
Whose snowie ridge the roving *Tartar* bounds,
Dislodging from a Region scarce of prey
To gorge the flesh of Lambs or yeanling Kids
On Hills where Flocks are fed, flies toward the Springs   435
Of *Ganges* or *Hydaspes*, *Indian* streams;
But in his way lights on the barren plains
Of *Sericana*, where *Chineses* drive
With Sails and Wind thir canie Waggons light:
So on this windie Sea of Land, the Fiend   440
Walk'd up and down alone bent on his prey,
Alone, for other Creature in this place
Living or liveless to be found was none,
None yet, but store hereafter from the earth
Up hither like Aereal vapours flew   445
Of all things transitorie and vain, when Sin
With vanity had filld the works of men:
Both all things vain, and all who in vain things
Built thir fond hopes of Glorie or lasting fame,
Or happiness in this or th' other life;   450
All who have thir reward on Earth, the fruits
Of painful Superstition and blind Zeal,
Naught seeking but the praise of men, here find
Fit retribution, emptie as thir deeds;
All th' unaccomplisht works of Natures hand,   455
Abortive, monstrous, or unkindly[21] mixt,
Dissolv'd on Earth, fleet hither, and in vain,
Till final dissolution, wander here,
Not in the neighbouring Moon, as some[22] have dreamd;
Those argent Fields more likely habitants,   460

[20] a mountain in the Himalayas.
[21] both in the modern sense and with the meaning "unnatural."
[22] e.g., Ariosto.

Translated Saints,[23] or middle Spirits hold
Betwixt th' Angelical and Human kind:
Hither of ill-joynd Sons and Daughters born
First from the ancient World those Giants came
With many a vain exploit, though then renownd: 465
The builders next of *Babel* on the Plain
Of *Sennaar*, and still with vain designe
New *Babels*, had they wherewithall, would build:
Others came single; he who to be deemd
A God, leap'd fondly into *Ætna* flames,   470
Empedocles, and hee who to enjoy
Plato's Elysium, leap'd into the Sea,
Cleombrotus, and many more too long,
Embryo's and Idiots, Eremits and Friers
White, Black and Grey,[24] with all thir trumperie.   475
Here Pilgrims roam, that stray'd so farr to seek
In *Golgotha* him dead, who lives in Heav'n;
And they who to be sure of Paradise
Dying put on the weeds of *Dominic*,
Or in *Franciscan* think to pass disguis'd;   480
They pass the Planets seven, and pass the fixt,
And that Crystalline Sphear whose ballance weighs
The Trepidation[25] talkt, and that first mov'd;
And now Saint *Peter* at Heav'ns Wicket seems
To wait them with his Keys, and now at foot   485
Of Heav'ns ascent they lift thir Feet, when loe
A violent cross wind from either Coast
Blows them transverse ten thousand Leagues awry
Into the devious Air; then might ye see
Cowls, Hoods and Habits with thir wearers tost   490
And fluttered into Raggs, then Reliques, Beads,
Indulgences, Dispenses, Pardons, Bulls,
The sport of Winds: all these upwhirld aloft
Fly o're the backside of the World farr off
Into a *Limbo* large and broad, since calld   495
The Paradise of Fools, to few unknown
Long after, now unpeopl'd, and untrod;
All this dark Globe the Fiend found as he pass'd,
And long he wanderd, till at last a gleam
Of dawning light turnd thither-ward in haste   500

23 Enoch and Elijah.
24 Carmelites, Dominicans, and Franciscans.
25 Two theories were advanced ("talkt"): the Ptolemaic explained trepida-
tion as the backward motion of the fixed stars which created the equinoxes; the
Copernican classified it as the wobble of the earth rotating on its axis.

His travell'd steps; farr distant he descries
Ascending by degrees magnificent
Up to the wall of Heav'n a Structure high,
At top whereof, but farr more rich appeerd
The work as of a Kingly Palace Gate   505
With Frontispice of Diamond and Gold
Imbellisht, thick with sparkling orient Gemms
The Portal shon, inimitable on Earth
By Model, or by shading Pencil drawn.
The Stairs were such as whereon *Jacob* saw   510
Angels ascending and descending, bands
Of Guardians bright, when he from *Esau* fled
To *Padan-Aram* in the field of *Luz*,
Dreaming by night under the open Skie,
And waking cri'd, *This is the Gate of Heav'n.*[26]   515
Each Stair mysteriously[27] was meant, nor stood
There alwayes, but drawn up to Heav'n somtimes
Viewless, and underneath a bright Sea flow'd
Of Jasper, or of liquid Pearl, whereon
Who after came from Earth, sayling arriv'd,   520
Wafted by Angels, or flew o're the Lake
Rapt in a Chariot drawn by fiery Steeds.[28]
The Stairs were then let down, whether to dare
The Fiend by easie ascent, or aggravate
His sad exclusion from the dores of Bliss.   525
Direct against which op'n'd from beneath,
Just o're the blissful seat of Paradise,
A passage down to th' Earth, a passage wide,
Wider by farr then that of after-times
Over Mount *Sion*, and, though that were large,   530
Over the *Promis'd Land* to God so dear,
By which, to visit oft those happy Tribes,
On high behests his Angels to and fro
Pass'd frequent, and his eye with choice regard
From *Paneas*[29] the fount of *Jordans* flood   535
To *Beërsaba*, where the *Holy Land*
Borders on *Ægypt* and th' *Arabian* shoar;
So wide the op'ning seemd, where bounds were set
To darkness, such as bound the Ocean wave.
Satan from hence now on the lower stair   540

[26] Gen. xxviii. 17.
[27] allegorically; the stairs are Jacob's ladder (Gen. xxviii. 12).
[28] 2 Kings ii. 11: "behold, there appeared a chariot of fire, and horses of fire
. . . and Elijah went up by a whirlwind into heaven."
[29] a city of Dan. The lines survey all of the Holy Land.

That scal'd by steps of Gold to Heav'n Gate
Looks down with wonder at the sudden view
Of all this World at once. As when a Scout
Through dark and desart wayes with peril gone
All night; at last by break of chearful dawn   545
Obtains the brow of some high-climbing Hill,
Which to his eye discovers unaware
The goodly prospect of some forein land
First-seen, or some renown'd Metropolis
With glistering Spires and Pinnacles adornd,   550
Which now the Rising Sun guilds with his beams.
Such wonder seis'd, though after Heaven seen,
The Spirit maligne, but much more envy seis'd
At sight of all this World beheld so fair.
Round he surveys, and well might, where he stood   555
So high above the circling Canopie
Of Nights extended shade; from Eastern Point
Of *Libra* to the fleecie Starr[30] that bears
Andromeda farr off *Atlantic* Seas
Beyond th' *Horizon;* then from Pole to Pole   560
He views in bredth, and without longer pause
Down right into the Worlds first Region throws
His flight precipitant, and winds with ease
Through the pure marble Air his oblique way
Amongst innumerable Starrs, that shon   565
Stars distant, but nigh hand seemd other Worlds,
Or other Worlds they seemd, or happy Iles,
Like those *Hesperian* Gardens fam'd of old,[31]
Fortunate Fields, and Groves and flowrie Vales,
Thrice happy Iles, but who dwelt happy there   570
He stayd not to enquire: above them all
The golden Sun in splendor likest Heav'n
Allur'd his eye: Thither his course he bends
Through the calm Firmament; but up or down
By center, or eccentric,[32] hard to tell,   575
Or Longitude, where the great Luminarie
Alooff the vulgar Constellations thick,
That from his Lordly eye keep distance due,
Dispenses Light from farr; they as they move
Thir Starry dance in numbers that compute   580
Days, months, and years, towards his all-chearing Lamp

[30] Aries, the ram.
[31] See *Mask*, notes 40 and 93.
[32] toward or away from the center (the earth), "hard to tell" because of the varying views of the universe.

Turn swift thir various motions, or are turnd
By his Magnetic beam, that gently warms
The Univers, and to each inward part
With gentle penetration, though unseen, 585
Shoots invisible vertue ev'n to the deep:
So wondrously was set his Station bright.
There lands the Fiend, a spot like which perhaps
Astronomer in the Sun's lucent Orb
Through his glaz'd Optic Tube yet never saw.[33] 590
The place he found beyond expression bright,
Compar'd with aught on Earth, Mettal or Stone;
Not all parts like, but all alike informd[34]
With radiant light, as glowing Iron with fire;
If mettal, part seemd Gold, part Silver cleer; 595
If stone, Carbuncle most or Chrysolite,
Rubie or Topaz, to the Twelve that shon
In *Aarons* Brest-plate, and a stone[35] besides
Imagind rather oft then elsewhere seen,
That stone, or like to that which here below 600
Philosophers in vain so long have sought,
In vain, though by thir powerful Art they bind
Volatil *Hermes,* and call up unbound
In various shapes old *Proteus* from the Sea,
Draind through a Limbec to his Native form. 605
What wonder then if fields and regions here
Breathe forth *Elixir* pure, and Rivers run
Potable Gold, when with one vertuous touch
Th' Arch-chimic Sun so farr from us remote
Produces with Terrestrial Humor mixt 610
Here in the dark so many precious things
Of colour glorious and effect so rare?
Here matter new to gaze the Devil met
Undazl'd, farr and wide his eye commands,
For sight no obstacle found here, nor shade, 615
But all Sun-shine, as when his Beams at Noon

[33] Galileo had discerned sunspots in 1609.
[34] both "given form to" and "made known."
[35] the philosopher's stone (the *"Elixir"* of l. 607) which would turn base metal into gold. An alembic (l. 605) was a vessel in which the "Native" (l. 605) form of a substance was distilled. Mercury ("Volatil *Hermes,*" l. 603) was thought a component of all minerals, and the changeable Proteus was symbolic of basic matter. (See Edgar H. Duncan, *Osiris,* XI, 1954, 386–421.) The sun, thought to produce gold and precious gems, was a true alchemist (ll. 609 ff.). Urim ("radiant") and Thummim in Aaron's breastplate arm the Son when he ascends after the War in Heaven with Victory at his right hand (VI, 760–63). They were considered mediums for the revelation of God's will.

Culminate from th' Æquator, as they now
Shot upward still direct, whence no way round
Shadow from body opaque can fall, and th' Air,
No where so cleer, sharp'n'd his visual ray 620
To objects distant farr, whereby he soon
Saw within kenn a glorious Angel stand,
The same whom *John* saw also in the Sun:[36]
His back was turnd, but not his brightness hid;
Of beaming sunnie Raies, a golden tiar 625
Circl'd his Head, nor less his Locks behind
Illustrious on his Shoulders fledge with wings
Lay waving round; on som great charge imploy'd
He seemd, or fixt in cogitation deep.
Glad was the Spirit impure; as now in hope 630
To find who might direct his wandring flight
To Paradise the happie seat of Man,
His journies end and our beginning woe.
But first he casts to change his proper shape,
Which else might work him danger or delay: 635
And now a stripling Cherub he appeers,
Not of the prime, yet such as in his face
Youth smil'd Celestial, and to every Limb
Sutable grace diffus'd, so well he feign'd;
Under a Coronet his flowing hair 640
In curls on either cheek plaid, wings he wore
Of many a colourd plume sprinkl'd with Gold,
His habit fit for speed succinct, and held
Before his decent[37] steps a Silver wand.
He drew not nigh unheard, the Angel bright, 645
Ere he drew nigh, his radiant visage turnd,
Admonisht by his ear, and strait was known
Th' Arch-Angel *Uriel*,[38] one of the seav'n
Who in Gods presence, neerest to his Throne
Stand ready at command, and are his Eyes[39] 650
That run through all the Heav'ns, or down to th' Earth
Bear his swift errands over moist and dry,
O're Sea and Land: him *Satan* thus accosts.
    Uriel, for thou of those seav'n Spirits that stand
In sight of Gods high Throne, gloriously bright, 655
The first art wont his great authentic will

[36] See Rev. xix. 17.
[37] appropriate.
[38] literally, "the fire of God"; he was the archangel who in Jewish tradition ruled the south.
[39] See Rev. iv. 5 and Zech. iv. 10.

Interpreter through highest Heav'n to bring,
Where all his Sons thy Embassie attend;
And here art likeliest by supream decree
Like honour to obtain, and as his Eye   660
To visit oft this new Creation round;
Unspeakable desire to see, and know
All these his wondrous works, but chiefly Man,
His chief delight and favour, him for whom
All these his works so wondrous he ordaind,   665
Hath brought me from the Quires of Cherubim
Alone thus wandring. Brightest Seraph tell
In which of all these shining Orbs hath Man
His fixed seat, or fixed seat hath none,
But all these shining Orbs his choice to dwell;   670
That I may find him, and with secret gaze,
Or open admiration him behold
On whom the great Creator hath bestowd
Worlds, and on whom hath all these graces powrd;
That both in him and all things, as is meet,   675
The Universal Maker we may praise;
Who justly hath drivn out his Rebell Foes
To deepest Hell, and to repair that loss
Created this new happie Race of Men
To serve him better: wise are all his wayes.   680
    So spake the false dissembler unperceiv'd;
For neither Man nor Angel can discern
Hypocrisie, the only evil that walks
Invisible, except to God alone,
By his permissive will, through Heav'n and Earth: 685
And oft though wisdom wake, suspicion sleeps
At wisdoms Gate, and to simplicitie
Resigns her charge, while goodness thinks no ill
Where no ill seems: Which now for once beguil'd
Uriel, though Regent of the Sun, and held   690
The sharpest sighted Spirit of all in Heav'n;
Who to the fraudulent Impostor foul
In his uprightness answer thus returnd.
Fair Angel, thy desire which tends to know
The works of God, thereby to glorifie   695
The great Work-Maister, leads to no excess
That reaches blame, but rather merits praise
The more it seems excess, that led thee hither
From thy Empyreal Mansion thus alone,
To witness with thine eyes what some perhaps   700
Contented with report hear onely in heav'n:

For wonderful indeed are all his works,
Pleasant to know, and worthiest to be all
Had in remembrance alwayes with delight;
But what created mind can comprehend   705
Thir number, or the wisdom infinite
That brought them forth, but hid thir causes deep.
I saw when at his Word the formless Mass,
This worlds material mould, came to a heap:
Confusion heard his voice, and wild uproar   710
Stood rul'd, stood vast infinitude confin'd;
Till at his second bidding darkness fled,
Light shon, and order from disorder sprung:
Swift to thir several Quarters hasted then
The cumbrous Elements, Earth, Flood, Air, Fire,   715
And this Ethereal quintessence of Heav'n
Flew upward, spirited with various forms,
That rowld orbicular, and turnd to Starrs
Numberless, as thou seest, and how they move;
Each had his place appointed, each his course,   720
The rest in circuit walls this Universe.
Look downward on that Globe whose hither side
With light from hence, though but reflected, shines;
That place is Earth the seat of Man, that light
His day, which else as th' other Hemisphere   725
Night would invade, but there the neighbouring Moon
(So call that opposite fair Starr) her aid
Timely interposes, and her monthly round
Still ending, still renewing through mid Heav'n,
With borrow'd light her countenance triform[40]   730
Hence fills and empties to enlighten th' Earth,
And in her pale dominion checks the night.
That spot to which I point is *Paradise*,
Adams abode, those loftie shades his Bowr.
Thy way thou canst not miss, me mine requires.   735
    Thus said, he turnd, and *Satan* bowing low,
As to superior Spirits is wont in Heav'n,
Where honour due and reverence none neglects,
Took leave, and toward the coast of Earth beneath,
Down from th' Ecliptic, sped with hop'd success,   740
Throws his steep flight in many an Aerie wheel,
Nor staid,[41] till on *Niphates*[42] top he lights.

[40] See *Ely*, n. 13.
[41] ceased such movement.
[42] a mountain in Armenia, near Assyria; see also IV, 126.

BOOK IV

THE ARGUMENT

Satan now in prospect of *Eden*, and nigh the place where he must now attempt the bold enterprize which he undertook alone against God and Man, falls into many doubts with himself, and many passions, fear, envy, and despare; but at length confirms himself in evil; journeys on to Paradise, whose outward prospect and scituation is described, overleaps the bounds, sits in the shape of a Cormorant on the Tree of life, as highest in the Garden to look about him. The Garden describ'd; *Satans* first sight of *Adam* and *Eve;* his wonder at thir excellent form and happy state, but with resolution to work thir fall; overhears thir discourse, thence gathers that the Tree of knowledge was forbidden them to eat of, under penalty of death; and thereon intends to found his Temptation, by seducing them to transgress: then leaves them a while, to know further of thir state by some other means. Mean while *Uriel* descending on a Sunbeam warns *Gabriel,* who had in charge the Gate of Paradise, that some evil spirit had escap'd the Deep, and past at Noon by his Sphere in the shape of a good Angel down to Paradise, discovered after by his furious gestures in the Mount. *Gabriel* promises to find him ere morning. Night coming on, *Adam* and *Eve* discourse of going to thir rest: thir Bower describ'd; thir Evening worship. *Gabriel* drawing forth his Bands of Night-watch to walk the round of Paradise, appoints two strong Angels to *Adams* Bower, least the evill spirit should be there doing some harm to *Adam* or *Eve* sleeping; there they find him at the ear of *Eve*, tempting her in a dream, and bring him, though unwilling, to *Gabriel;* by whom question'd, he scornfully answers, prepares resistance, but hinder'd by a Sign from Heaven, flies out of Paradise.

O for that warning voice,[1] which he who saw
Th' *Apocalyps,* heard cry in Heaven aloud,
Then when the Dragon, put to second rout,
Came furious down to be reveng'd on men,
Wo to th' inhabitants on Earth! that now,   5
While time was, our first Parents had bin warnd
The coming of thir secret foe, and scap'd
Haply so scap'd his mortal snare; for now
Satan, now first inflam'd with rage, came down,
The Tempter ere th' Accuser of man-kind,   10
To wreck on innocent frail man his loss
Of that first Battel, and his flight to Hell:

---

[1] See Rev. xii. 7–13; the voice is that of St. John the Divine.

Yet not rejoycing in his speed, though bold,
Far off and fearless, nor with cause to boast,
Begins his dire attempt, which nigh the birth   15
Now rowling, boils in his tumultuous brest,
And like a devillish Engine back recoils
Upon himself; horror and doubt distract
His troubl'd thoughts, and from the bottom stirr
The Hell within him, for within him Hell   20
He brings, and round about him, nor from Hell
One step no more then from himself can fly
By change of place: Now conscience wakes despair
That slumberd, wakes the bitter memorie
Of what he was, what is, and what must be   25
Worse; of worse deeds worse sufferings must ensue.
Sometimes towards *Eden*² which now in his view
Lay pleasant, his griev'd look he fixes sad,
Sometimes towards Heav'n and the full-blazing Sun,
Which now sat high in his Meridian Towr: 30
Then much revolving, thus in sighs began.
    O thou that with surpassing Glory crownd,
Look'st from thy sole Dominion like the God
Of this new World; at whose sight all the Starrs
Hide thir diminisht heads; to thee I call,   35
But with no friendly voice, and add thy name
O Sun, to tell thee how I hate thy beams
That bring to my remembrance from what state
I fell, how glorious once above thy Sphear;
Till Pride and worse Ambition threw me down   40
Warring in Heav'n against Heav'ns matchless³ King:
Ah wherefore! he deserv'd no such return
From me, whom he created what I was
In that bright eminence, and with his good
Upbraided none; nor was his service hard.   45
What could be less then to afford him praise,
The easiest recompence, and pay him thanks,
How due! yet all his good prov'd ill in me,
And wrought but malice; lifted up so high
I sdeind⁴ subjection, and thought one step higher   50
Would set me highest, and in a moment quit
The debt immense of endless gratitude,
So burthensome still paying, still to ow;

² literally, "pleasure."
³ both "unequaled" and "not to be contested."
⁴ disdained.

Forgetful what from him I still receiv'd,
And understood not that a grateful mind   55
By owing owes not, but still pays, at once
Indebted and discharg'd; what burden then?
O had his powerful Destiny ordaind
Me some inferiour Angel, I had stood
Then happie; no unbounded hope had rais'd   60
Ambition. Yet why not? som other Power
As great might have aspir'd, and me though mean
Drawn to his part; but other Powers as great
Fell not, but stand unshak'n, from within
Or from without, to all temptations arm'd.   65
Hadst thou the same free Will and Power to stand?
Thou hadst: whom hast thou then or what t' accuse,
But Heav'ns free Love dealt equally to all?
Be then his Love accurst, since love or hate,
To me alike, it deals eternal woe.   70
Nay curs'd be thou; since against his thy will
Chose freely what it now so justly rues.
Me miserable! which way shall I flie
Infinite wrauth, and infinite despair?
Which way I flie is Hell; my self am Hell;   75
And in the lowest deep a lower deep
Still threatning to devour me opens wide,
To which the Hell I suffer seems a Heav'n.
O then at last relent: is there no place
Left for Repentance, none for Pardon left?   80
None left but by submission; and that word
Disdain forbids me, and my dread of shame
Among the Spirits beneath, whom I seduc'd
With other promises and other vaunts
Then to submit, boasting I could subdue   85
Th' Omnipotent. Ay me, they little know
How dearly I abide that boast so vain,
Under what torments inwardly I groan:
While they adore me on the Throne of Hell,
With Diadem and Scepter high advanc't   90
The lower still I fall, onely supream
In miserie; such joy Ambition finds.
But say I could repent and could obtain
By Act of Grace my former state; how soon
Would highth recall high thoughts, how soon unsay   95
What feign'd submission swore: ease would recant
Vows made in pain, as violent and void.
For never can true reconcilement grow

Where wounds of deadly hate have peirc'd so deep:
Which would but lead me to a worse relapse,   100
And heavier fall: so should I purchase dear
Short intermission bought with double smart.
This knows my punisher; therefore as farr
From granting hee, as I from begging peace:
All hope excluded thus, behold in stead   105
Of us out-cast, exil'd, his new delight,
Mankind created, and for him this World.
So farwell Hope, and with Hope farwell Fear,
Farwell Remorse: all Good to me is lost;
Evil be thou my Good;[5] by thee at least   110
Divided Empire with Heav'ns King I hold
By thee, and more then half perhaps will reigne;
As Man ere long, and this new World shall know.
    Thus while he spake, each passion dimm'd his face
Thrice chang'd with pale, ire, envie and despair,   115
Which marrd his borrow'd visage, and betraid
Him counterfet, if any eye beheld.
For heav'nly minds from such distempers foul
Are ever cleer. Whereof hee soon aware,
Each perturbation smooth'd with outward calm,   120
Artificer of fraud; and was the first
That practis'd falshood under saintly shew,
Deep malice to conceal, couch't with revenge:
Yet not anough had practis'd to deceive
Uriel once warnd; whose eye pursu'd him down   125
The way he went, and on th' Assyrian mount
Saw him disfigur'd,[6] more then could befall
Spirit of happie sort: his gestures fierce
He mark'd and mad demeanour, then alone,
As he suppos'd, all unobserv'd, unseen.   130
So on he fares, and to the border comes
Of Eden, where delicious Paradise,
Now nearer, Crowns with her enclosure green,
As with a rural mound the champain head[7]
Of a steep wilderness, whose hairie sides   135
With thicket overgrown, grottesque and wild,
Access deni'd; and over head up grew
Insuperable highth of loftiest shade,
Cedar, and Pine, and Firr, and branching Palm,

---

[5] Compare Isa. v. 20: "Woe unto them that call evil good and good evil; that put darkness for light, and light for darkness. . . ."
[6] that is, "saw him lose his former appearance" and "saw him in his ugliness."
[7] plateau.

A Silvan Scene, and as the ranks ascend   140
Shade above shade, a woodie Theatre
Of stateliest view. Yet higher then thir tops
The verdurous wall of Paradise up sprung:
Which to our general Sire gave prospect large
Into his neather Empire neighbouring round.   145
And higher then that Wall a circling row
Of goodliest Trees loaden with fairest Fruit,
Blossoms and Fruit at once of golden hue
Appeerd, with gay enameld colours mixt:
On which the Sun more glad impress'd his beams   150
Then in fair Evening Cloud, or humid Bow,
When God hath showrd the earth; so lovely seemd
That Lantskip: And of pure now purer air
Meets his approach, and to the heart inspires
Vernal delight and joy, able to drive   155
All sadness but despair: now gentle gales
Fanning thir odoriferous wings dispense
Native perfumes, and whisper whence they stole
Those balmie spoils. As when to them who sail
Beyond the *Cape of Hope*, and now are past   160
Mozambic, off at Sea North-East winds blow
Sabean[8] Odours from the spicie shoar
Of *Arabie* the blest, with such delay
Well pleas'd they slack thir course, and many a League
Chear'd with the grateful smell old Ocean smiles.   165
So entertaind those odorous sweets the Fiend
Who came thir bane, though with them better pleas'd
Then *Asmodeus*[9] with the fishie fume,
That drove him, though enamour'd, from the Spouse
Of *Tobits* Son, and with a vengeance sent   170
From *Media* post to *Ægypt,* there fast bound.
   Now to th' ascent of that steep savage[10] Hill
Satan had journied on, pensive and slow;
But further way found none, so thick entwin'd,
As one continu'd brake, the undergrowth   175
Of shrubs and tangling bushes had perplext
All path of Man or Beast that past that way:
One Gate there only was, and that look'd East
On th' other side: which when th' arch-fellon saw
Due entrance he disdaind, and in contempt,   180

[8] of Sheba, part of Arabia Felix.
[9] See Tobit viii.
[10] woody.

At one slight bound high overleap'd all bound
Of Hill or highest Wall, and sheer within
Lights on his feet. As when a prowling Wolf,
Whom hunger drives to seek new haunt for prey,
Watching where Shepherds pen thir Flocks at eeve   185
In hurdl'd Cotes amid the field secure,
Leaps o're the fence with ease into the Fould:
Or as a Thief bent to unhoord the cash
Of some rich Burgher, whose substantial dores,
Cross-barrd and bolted fast, fear no assault,   190
In at the window climbs, or o're the tiles;
So clomb this first grand Thief into Gods Fould:
So since into his Church lewd Hirelings climb.[11]
Thence up he flew, and on the Tree of Life,
The middle Tree and highest there that grew,   195
Sat like a Cormorant;[12] yet not true Life
Thereby regaind, but sat devising Death
To them who liv'd; nor on the vertue thought
Of that life-giving Plant, but only us'd
For prospect, what well us'd had bin the pledge   200
Of immortality. So little knows
Any, but God alone, to value right
The good before him, but perverts best things
To worst abuse, or to thir meanest use.
Beneath him with new wonder now he views   205
To all delight of human sense expos'd
In narrow room Natures whole wealth, yea more,
A Heav'n on Earth: for blissful Paradise
Of God the Garden was, by him in th' East
Of *Eden* planted; *Eden* stretch'd her Line   210
From *Auran*[13] Eastward to the Royal Towrs
Of great *Seleucia,* built by *Grecian* Kings,
Or where the Sons of *Eden* long before
Dwelt in *Telassar:*[14] in this pleasant soil
His farr more pleasant Garden God ordaind;   215
Out of the fertil ground he caus'd to grow
All Trees of noblest kind for sight, smell, taste;
And all amid them stood the Tree of Life,
High eminent, blooming Ambrosial Fruit
Of vegetable Gold; and next to Life   220

[11] The passage is drawn from John x. 1–13.
[12] traditional symbol of greed.
[13] on the Euphrates; Seleucia, founded by one of Alexander's generals, was
on the Tigris.
[14] a city of Eden (2 Kings xix. 12 and Isa. xxxvii. 12).

Our Death the Tree of Knowledge grew fast by,
Knowledge of Good bought dear by knowing ill.
Southward through *Eden* went a River[15] large,
Nor chang'd his course, but through the shaggie hill
Pass'd underneath ingulft, for God had thrown   225
That Mountain as his Garden mould high rais'd
Upon the rapid current, which through veins
Of porous Earth with kindly thirst up drawn,
Rose a fresh Fountain, and with many a rill
Waterd the Garden; thence united fell   230
Down the steep glade, and met the neather Flood,
Which from his darksom passage now appeers,
And now divided into four main Streams,[16]
Runs divers, wandring many a famous Realm
And Country whereof here needs no account,   235
But rather to tell how, if Art could tell,
How from that Saphire Fount the crisped Brooks,
Rowling on Orient Pearl and sands of Gold,
With mazie error[17] under pendant shades
Ran Nectar, visiting each plant, and fed   240
Flowrs worthy of Paradise which not nice Art
In Beds and curious Knots,[18] but Nature boon[19]
Powrd forth profuse on Hill and Dale and Plain,
Both where the morning Sun first warmly smote
The open field, and where the unpierc't shade   245
Imbrownd the noontide Bowrs: Thus was this place,
A happy rural seat of various view;
Groves whose rich Trees wept odorous Gumms and Balm,
Others whose fruit burnisht with Golden Rind
Hung amiable, *Hesperian* Fables true,   250
If true, here only, and of delicious taste:
Betwixt them Lawns, or level Downs, and Flocks
Grasing the tender herb, were interpos'd,
Or palmie hilloc, or the flowrie lap
Of som irriguous Valley spred her store,   255
Flowrs of all hue, and without Thorn the Rose:
Another side, umbrageous Grots and Caves
Of cool recess, o're which the mantling vine
Layes forth her purple Grape, and gently creeps
Luxuriant; mean while murmuring waters fall   260

---

[15] probably the Tigris (see ll. 210–12).
[16] traditionally the Nile, Euphrates, Tigris, and Indus.
[17] wandering.
[18] elaborate flower gardens.
[19] bountiful.

Down the slope hills, disperst, or in a Lake,
That to the fringed Bank with Myrtle crownd,
Her chrystal mirror holds, unite thir streams.
The Birds thir quire apply; aires, vernal aires,
Breathing the smell of field and grove, attune   265
The trembling leaves, while Universal *Pan*
Knit with the *Graces*[20] and the *Hours* in dance
Led on th' Eternal Spring. Not that fair field
Of *Enna*, where *Proserpin* gathring flowrs
Her self a fairer Flowr by gloomie *Dis*   270
Was gatherd,[21] which cost *Ceres* all that pain
To seek her through the world; nor that sweet Grove
Of *Daphne*[22] by *Orontes*, and th' inspir'd
Castalian Spring might with this Paradise
Of *Eden* strive; nor that *Nyseian* Ile[23]   275
Girt with the River *Triton*, where old *Cham*,[24]
Whom Gentiles *Ammon* call and *Lybian Jove*,
Hid *Amalthea* and her Florid Son
Young *Bacchus* from his Stepdame *Rhea's* eye;
Nor where *Abassin*[25] Kings thir issue Guard,   280
Mount *Amara*, though this by som suppos'd
.True Paradise under the *Ethiop* Line[26]
By *Nilus* head, enclos'd with shining Rock,
A whole dayes journey high, but wide remote
From this *Assyrian* Garden, where the Fiend   285
Saw undelighted all delight, all kind
Of living Creatures new to sight and strange:
Two of far nobler shape erect and tall,
Godlike erect, with native Honour clad
In naked Majestie seemd Lords of all,   290
And worthie seemd, for in thir looks Divine
The image of thir glorious Maker shon,
Truth, Wisdom, Sanctitude severe and pure,
Severe, but in true filial freedom plac't;
Whence true autoritie in men; though both   295
Not equal, as thir sex not equal seemd;

[20] The Graces were Aglaia (Brilliance), Euphrosyne (Joy), and Thalia (Bloom); the Hours were the goddesses of the seasons.
[21] See *Vice-Chancellor*, n. 16. Ceres was the mother of Proserpina.
[22] The groves of Daphne on the Orontes in Syria were the site of a temple to Apollo; the spring on Mt. Parnassus inspired great poetry and foretold oracles.
[23] Nysa, in what is now Tunis.
[24] Ham, identified with Ammon.
[25] Abyssinian.
[26] the equator.

For contemplation hee and valour formd,
For softness shee and sweet attractive Grace,
Hee for God only, shee for God in him:
His fair large Front and Eye sublime[27] declar'd   300
Absolute rule; and Hyacinthin Locks
Round from his parted forelock manly hung
Clustring, but not beneath his shoulders broad:
Shee as a vail down to the slender waste
Her unadorned golden tresses wore   305
Dissheveld, but in wanton[28] ringlets wav'd
As the Vine curls her tendrils, which impli'd
Subjection,[29] but requir'd with gentle sway,[30]
And by her yeilded, by him best receiv'd,
Yeilded with coy submission, modest pride,   310
And sweet reluctant amorous delay.
Nor those mysterious parts were then conceald,
Then was not guiltie shame, dishonest[31] shame
Of natures works, honor dishonorable,
Sin-bred, how have ye troubl'd all mankind   315
With shews instead, meer shews of seeming pure,
And banisht from mans life his happiest life,
Simplicitie and spotless innocence.
So pass'd they naked on, nor shund the sight
Of God or Angel, for they thought no ill: 320
So hand in hand[32] they pass'd, the loveliest pair
That ever since in loves imbraces met,
Adam[33] the goodliest man of men since born
His Sons, the fairest of her Daughters *Eve*.[34]
Under a tuft of shade that on a green   325
Stood whispering soft, by a fresh Fountain side
They sat them down, and after no more toil
Of thir sweet Gardning labour then suffic'd
To recommend cool *Zephyr*, and made ease
More easie, wholsom thirst and appetite   330
More grateful, to thir Supper Fruits they fell,

---

[27] upraised.
[28] undisciplined, luxuriant.
[29] both "being under control" (ironically) and their "lying beneath."
[30] both "necessary for gentle undulation" and "demanding of gentle governing." The hair image implies Eve's potential vacillation and her need to be controlled.
[31] unchaste.
[32] Compare IV, 488-89, 689, 739; VIII, 510-11; IX, 385, 1037; XII, 648.
[33] derived from a word meaning "dust," "soil," and thence "man."
[34] derived from a word meaning "live," "be," and thence "Mother of Mankind" (V, 388).

Nectarine Fruits which the compliant boughs
Yeilded them, side-long as they sat recline
On the soft downie Bank damaskt with flowrs:
The savourie pulp they chew, and in the rind   335
Still as they thirsted scoop the brimming stream;
Nor gentle purpose,[35] nor endearing smiles
Wanted, nor youthful dalliance as beseems
Fair couple, linkt in happie nuptial League,
Alone as they. About them frisking playd   340
All Beasts of th' Earth, since wild, and of all chase
In Wood or Wilderness, Forrest or Den;
Sporting the Lion ramp'd, and in his paw
Dandl'd the Kid; Bears, Tygers, Ounces, Pards
Gambold before them, th' unwieldy Elephant   345
To make them mirth us'd all his might, and wreath'd
His Lithe Proboscis; close the Serpent sly
Insinuating,[36] wove with Gordian twine
His breaded train, and of his fatal guile
Gave proof unheeded; others on the grass   350
Coucht, and now fild with pasture gazing sat,
Or Bedward ruminating: for the Sun
Declin'd was hasting now with prone carreer[37]
To th' Ocean Iles,[38] and in th' ascending Scale
Of Heav'n the Starrs that usher Evening rose: 355
When *Satan* still in gaze, as first he stood,
Scarce thus at length faild speech recoverd sad.
    O Hell! what doe mine eyes with grief behold,
Into our room of bliss thus high advanc't
Creatures of other mould, earth-born perhaps,   360
Not Spirits, yet to heav'nly Spirits bright
Little inferior; whom my thoughts pursue
With wonder, and could love, so lively shines
In them Divine resemblance, and such grace
The hand that formd them on thir shape hath pourd.   365
Ah gentle pair, yee little think how nigh
Your change approaches, when all these delights
Will vanish and deliver ye to woe,
More woe, the more your taste is now of joy;
Happie, but for so happie ill secur'd   370

[35] conversation.
[36] with the added meaning "coiling"; his wile ("train") is difficult to un-
tangle ("Gordian"), because it is braided ("breaded"). The spelling implies the
method used for his guile.
[37] a swift course.
[38] the Azores.

Long to continue, and this high seat your Heav'n
Ill fenc't for Heav'n to keep out such a foe
As now is enterd; yet no purpos'd foe
To you whom I could pittie thus forlorn
Though I unpittied: League with you I seek,   375
And mutual amitie so streight, so close,
That I with you must dwell, or you with me
Henceforth; my dwelling haply may not please
Like this fair Paradise, your sense, yet such
Accept your Makers work; he gave it me,   380
Which I as freely give; Hell shall unfold,
To entertain you two, her widest Gates,
And send forth all her Kings; there will be room,
Not like these narrow limits, to receive
Your numerous ofspring; if no better place,   385
Thank him who puts me loath to this revenge
On you who wrong me not for him who wrong'd.
And should I at your harmless innocence
Melt, as I doe, yet public reason just,
Honour and Empire with revenge enlarg'd,   390
By conquering this new World, compels me now
To do what else though damnd I should abhorr.
    So spake the Fiend, and with necessitie,
The Tyrants plea, excus'd his devilish deeds.
Then from his loftie stand on that high Tree   395
Down he alights among the sportful Herd
Of those fourfooted kinds, himself now one,
Now other, as thir shape serv'd best his end
Neerer to view his prey, and unespi'd
To mark what of thir state he more might learn   400
By word or action markt: about them round
A Lion now he stalks with fierie glare,
Then as a Tiger, who by chance hath spi'd
In some Purlieu two gentle Fawns at play,
Strait couches close, then rising changes oft   405
His couchant watch, as one who chose his ground
Whence rushing he might surest seise them both
Grip't in each paw: when *Adam* first of men
To first of women *Eve* thus moving speech,
Turnd him all ear to hear new utterance flow.   410
    Sole partner and sole part of all these joyes,
Dearer thy self then all; needs must the Power
That made us, and for us this ample World
Be infinitly good, and of his good
As liberal and free as infinite,   415

That rais'd us from the dust and plac't us here
In all this happiness, who at his hand
Have nothing merited, nor can perform
Aught whereof hee hath need, hee who requires
From us no other service then to keep   420
This one, this easie charge, of all the Trees
In Paradise that bear delicious fruit
So various, not to taste that onely Tree
Of knowledge, planted by the Tree of Life,
So neer grows Death to Life, what ere Death is,   425
Som dreadful thing no doubt; for well thou knowst
God hath pronounc't it death to taste that Tree,
The only sign of our obedience left
Among so many signes of power and rule
Conferrd upon us, and Dominion giv'n   430
Over all other Creatures that possess
Earth, Air, and Sea. Then let us not think hard
One easie prohibition, who enjoy
Free leave so large to all things else, and choice
Unlimited of manifold delights: 435
But let us ever praise him, and extoll
His bountie, following our delightful task
To prune these growing Plants, and tend these Flowrs,
Which were it toilsom, yet with thee were sweet.
     To whom thus Eve repli'd. O thou for whom   440
And from whom I was formd flesh of thy flesh,
And without whom am to no end, my Guide
And Head, what thou hast said is just and right.
For wee to him indeed all praises owe,
And daily thanks, I chiefly who enjoy   445
So farr the happier Lot, enjoying thee
Præeminent by so much odds, while thou
Like consort to thy self canst no where find.
That day I oft remember, when from sleep
I first awak't, and found my self repos'd   450
Under a shade on flowrs, much wondring where
And what I was, whence thither brought, and how.
Not distant far from thence a murmuring sound
Of waters issu'd from a Cave and spread
Into a liquid Plain, then stood unmov'd   455
Pure as th' expanse of Heav'n; I thither went
With unexperienc't thought, and laid me down
On the green bank, to look into the cleer
Smooth Lake, that to me seemd another Skie.
As I bent down to look, just opposite,   460

A Shape within the watry gleam appeerd
Bending to look on me, I started back,
It started back, but pleas'd I soon returnd,
Pleas'd it returnd as soon with answering looks
Of sympathie and love; there I had fixt   465
Mine eyes till now, and pin'd with vain desire,
Had not a voice thus warnd me, What thou seest,
What there thou seest fair Creature is thy self,
With thee it came and goes: but follow me,
And I will bring thee where no shadow staies[39]   470
Thy coming, and thy soft imbraces, hee
Whose image thou art, him thou shall enjoy
Inseparablie thine, to him shalt bear
Multitudes like thy self, and thence be call'd
Mother of human Race: what could I doe,   475
But follow strait, invisibly thus led?
Till I espi'd thee, fair indeed and tall,
Under a Platan, yet methought less fair,
Less winning soft, less amiablie mild,
Then that smooth watry image; back I turnd,   480
Thou following cryd'st aloud, Return fair *Eve*,
Whom fli'st thou? whom thou fli'st, of him thou art,
His flesh, his bone; to give thee being I lent
Out of my side to thee, neerest my heart
Substantial Life, to have thee by my side   485
Henceforth an individual[40] solace dear;
Part of my Soul I seek thee, and thee claim
My other half: with that thy gentle hand
Seis'd mine, I yeilded, and from that time see
How beauty is excelld by manly grace   490
And wisdom, which alone is truly fair.
    So spake our general Mother, and with eyes
Of conjugal attraction unreprov'd,
And meek surrender, half imbracing leand
On our first Father, half her swelling Breast   495
Naked met his under the flowing Gold
Of her loose tresses hid: he in delight
Both of her Beauty and submissive Charms
Smil'd with superior Love, as *Jupiter*
On *Juno*[41] smiles, when he impregns the Clouds   500
That shed *May* Flowers; and press'd her Matron lip

[39] awaits.
[40] undividable.
[41] i.e., the sun on air.

With kisses pure: aside the Devil turnd
For envie, yet with jealous leer maligne
Ey'd them askance, and to himself thus plaind.
     Sight hateful, sight tormenting! thus these two   505
Imparadis't in one anothers arms
The happier *Eden,* shall enjoy thir fill
Of bliss on bliss, while I to Hell am thrust,
Where neither joy nor love, but fierce desire,
Among our other torments not the least,   510
Still unfulfill'd with pain of longing pines;
Yet let me not forget what I have gain'd
From thir own mouths; all is not theirs it seems:
One fatal Tree there stands of Knowledge call'd,
Forbidden them to taste: Knowledge forbidd'n?   515
Suspicious, reasonless. Why should thir Lord
Envie them that? can it be sin to know,
Can it be death? and do they onely stand
By Ignorance, is that thir happie state,
The proof of thir obedience and thir faith?   520
O fair foundation laid whereon to build
Thir ruin! Hence I will excite thir minds
With more desire to know, and to reject
Envious commands, invented with designe
To keep them low whom knowledge might exalt   525
Equal with Gods; aspiring to be such,
They taste and die: what likelier can ensue?
But first with narrow search I must walk round
This Garden, and no corner leave unspi'd;
A chance but chance may lead where I may meet   530
Some wandring Spirit of Heav'n, by Fountain side,
Or in thick shade retir'd, from him to draw
What further would be learnt. Live while ye may,
Yet happie pair; enjoy, till I return,
Short pleasures, for long woes are to succeed.   535
     So saying, his proud step he scornful turn'd,
But with sly circumspection, and began
Through wood, through waste, o're hill, o're dale his roam.
Mean while in utmost Longitude,[42] where Heav'n
With Earth and Ocean meets, the setting Sun   540
Slowly descended, and with right aspect[43]
Against the eastern Gate of Paradise
Leveld his eevning Rayes: it was a Rock

[42] in the farthest west.
[43] direct look.

Of Alablaster, pil'd up to the Clouds,
Conspicuous farr, winding with one ascent   545
Accessible from Earth, one entrance high;
The rest was craggie cliff, that overhung
Still as it rose, impossible to climb.
Betwixt these rockie Pillars *Gabriel* sat
Chief of th' Angelic Guards, awaiting night;   550
About him exercis'd Heroic Games
Th' unarmed Youth of Heav'n, but nigh at hand
Celestial Armourie, Shields, Helms, and Speares
Hung high with Diamond flaming, and with Gold.
Thither came *Uriel*, gliding through the Eev'n   555
On a Sun beam, swift as a shooting Starr
In *Autumn* thwarts the night, when vapors fir'd
Impress the Air, and shews the Mariner
From what point of his Compass to beware
Impetuous winds: he thus began in haste.   560
  Gabriel, to thee thy cours by Lot hath giv'n
Charge and strict watch that to this happie place
No evil thing approach or enter in;
This day at highth of Noon came to my Sphear
A Spirit, zealous, as he seem'd, to know   565
More of th' Almighties works, and chiefly Man
Gods latest Image: I describ'd his way
Bent all on speed, and markt his Aerie Gate;
But in the Mount that lies from *Eden* North,
Where he first lighted, soon discernd his looks   570
Alien from Heav'n, with passions foul obscur'd:
Mine eye pursu'd him still, but under shade
Lost sight of him; one of the banisht crew
I fear, hath ventur'd from the deep, to raise
New troubles; him thy care must be to find.   575
  To whom the winged Warriour thus returnd:
Uriel, no wonder if thy perfet sight,
Amid the Suns bright circle where thou sitst,
See farr and wide: in at this Gate none pass
The vigilance here plac't, but such as come   580
Well known from Heav'n; and since Meridian hour
No Creature thence: if Spirit of other sort,
So minded, have oreleapt these earthie bounds
On purpose, hard thou knowst it to exclude
Spiritual substance with corporeal barr.   585
But if within the circuit of these walks
In whatsoever shape he lurk, of whom
Thou tellst, by morrow dawning I shall know.

So promis'd hee, and *Uriel* to his charge
Returnd on that bright beam, whose point now rais'd   590
Bore him slope downward to the Sun now fall'n
Beneath th' *Azores;* whither the prime Orb,
Incredible how swift, had thither rowl'd
Diurnal, or this less volubil Earth
By shorter flight to th' East, had left him there   595
Arraying with reflected Purple and Gold
The Clouds that on his Western Throne attend:
Now came still Eevning on, and Twilight gray
Had in her sober Liverie all things clad;
Silence accompanied, for Beast and Bird,   600
They to thir grassie Couch, these to thir Nests
Were slunk, all but the wakeful Nightingale;
She all night long her amorous descant sung;
Silence was pleas'd: now glow'd the Firmament
With living Saphirs: *Hesperus* that led   605
The starrie Host, rode brightest, till the Moon
Rising in clouded Majestie, at length
Apparent Queen unvaild her peerless light,
And o're the dark her Silver Mantle threw.

When *Adam* thus to *Eve:* Fair Consort, th' hour   610
Of night, and all things now retir'd to rest
Mind us of like repose, since God hath set
Labour and rest, as day and night to men
Successive, and the timely dew of sleep
Now falling with soft slumbrous weight inclines   615
Our eye-lids; other Creatures all day long
Rove idle unimploid, and less need rest;
Man hath his daily work of body or mind
Appointed, which declares his Dignitie,
And the regard of Heav'n on all his waies;   620
While other Animals unactive range,
And of thir doings God takes no account.
To morrow ere fresh Morning streak the East
With first approach of light, we must be ris'n,
And at our pleasant labour, to reform   625
Yon flowrie Arbors, yonder Allies green,
Our walk at noon, with branches overgrown,
That mock our scant manuring,[44] and require
More hands then ours to lop thir wanton growth:
Those Blossoms also, and those dropping Gumms,   630
That lie bestrown unsightly and unsmooth,

[44] hand cultivation.

Ask riddance, if we mean to tread with ease;
Mean while, as Nature wills, Night bids us rest.
    To whom thus *Eve* with perfet beauty adornd.
My Author and Disposer, what thou bidst   635
Unargu'd I obey; so God ordains,
God is thy Law, thou mine: to know no more
Is womans happiest knowledge and her praise.
With thee conversing I forget all time,
All seasons[45] and thir change, all please alike.   640
Sweet is the breath of morn, her rising sweet,
With charm[46] of earliest Birds; pleasant the Sun
When first on this delightful Land he spreads
His orient Beams, on herb, tree, fruit, and flowr,
Glistring with dew; fragrant the fertil earth   645
After soft showers; and sweet the coming on
Of grateful Eevning mild, then silent Night
With this her solemn Bird and this fair Moon,
And these the Gemms of Heav'n, her starrie train:
But neither breath of Morn when she ascends   650
With charm of earliest Birds, nor rising Sun
On this delightful land, nor herb, fruit, flowr,
Glistring with dew, nor fragrance after showers,
Nor grateful Eevning mild, nor silent Night
With this her solemn Bird, nor walk by Moon,   655
Or glittering Starr-light without thee is sweet.
But wherfore all night long shine these, for whom
This glorious sight, when sleep hath shut all eyes?
    To whom our general Ancestor repli'd.
Daughter of God and Man, accomplisht[47] *Eve*,   660
Those have thir course to finish, round the Earth,
By morrow Eevning, and from Land to Land
In order, though to Nations yet unborn,
Ministring light prepar'd, they set and rise;
Least total darkness should by Night regain   665
Her old possession, and extinguish life
In Nature and all things, which these soft fires
Not only enlighten, but with kindly heat
Of various influence foment and warm,
Temper or nourish, or in part shed down   670
Thir stellar vertue on all kinds that grow

[45] times of day.
[46] song.
[47] ironically indicating her lack of need of further accouterments such as
those to which she later succumbs.

On Earth, made hereby apter to receive
Perfection from the Suns more potent Ray.
These then, though unbeheld in deep of night,
Shine not in vain, nor think, though men were none,　　　675
That heav'n would want spectators, God want praise;
Millions of spiritual Creatures walk the Earth
Unseen, both when we wake, and when we sleep:
All these with ceasless praise his works behold
Both day and night: how often from the steep　　　　680
Of echoing Hill or Thicket have we heard
Celestial voices to the midnight air,
Sole, or responsive each to others note
Singing thir great Creator: oft in bands
While they keep watch, or nightly rounding walk　　　685
With Heav'nly touch of instrumental sounds
In full harmonic number joind, thir songs
Divide the night,[48] and lift our thoughts to Heav'n.
　　Thus talking hand in hand alone they pass'd
On to thir blissful Bower; it was a place　　　　690
Chos'n by the sovran Planter, when he fram'd
All things to mans delightful use; the roof
Of thickest covert was inwoven shade
Laurel and Mirtle, and what higher grew
Of firm and fragrant leaf; on either side　　　　695
Acanthus, and each odorous bushie shrub
Fenc'd up the verdant wall; each beauteous flowr,
Iris all hues, Roses, and Gessamin
Rear'd high thir flourisht[49] heads between, and wrought
Mosaic; underfoot the Violet,　　　　700
Crocus, and Hyacinth with rich inlay
Broiderd the ground, more colour'd then with stone
Of costliest Emblem:[50] other Creature here
Beast, Bird, Insect, or Worm durst enter none;
Such was thir awe of Man. In shadier Bower　　　705
More sacred and sequesterd, though but feign'd,
Pan or Silvanus never slept, nor Nymph,
Nor Faunus haunted. Here in close recess
With Flowers, Garlands, and sweet-smelling Herbs
Espoused Eve deckt first her Nuptial Bed,　　　　710
And heav'nly Quires the Hymenæan[51] sung,

[48] into the watches of l. 685.
[49] adorned with flowers.
[50] inlaid with precious gems.
[51] marriage song.

What day the genial[52] Angel to our Sire
Brought her in naked beauty more adorn'd,
More lovely than *Pandora*,[53] whom the Gods
Endowd with all thir gifts, and O too like   715
In sad event, when to th' unwiser Son
Of *Japhet* brought by *Hermes,* she ensnar'd
Mankind with her fair looks, to be aveng'd
On him who had stole *Joves* authentic fire.
    Thus at thir shadie Lodge arriv'd, both stood,   720
Both turnd, and under op'n Skie ador'd
The God that made both Skie, Air, Earth and Heav'n
Which they beheld, the Moons resplendent Globe
And starrie Pole: Thou also mad'st the Night,
Maker Omnipotent, and thou the Day,   725
Which we in our appointed work imployd
Have finisht happie in our mutual help
And mutual love, the Crown of all our bliss
Ordaind by thee, and this delicious place
For us too large, where thy abundance wants   730
Partakers, and uncropt falls to the ground.
But thou hast promis'd from us two a Race
To fill the Earth, who shall with us extoll
Thy goodness infinite, both when we wake,
And when we seek, as now, thy gift of sleep.   735
    This said unanimous, and other Rites
Observing none, but adoration pure
Which God likes best, into thir inmost bowr
Handed they went; and eas'd the putting off
These troublesom disguises which wee wear,   740
Strait side by side were laid, nor turnd I ween
Adam from his fair Spouse, nor *Eve* the Rites
Mysterious of connubial Love refus'd:
Whatever Hypocrites austerely talk
Of puritie and place and innocence,   745
Defaming as impure what God declares
Pure, and commands to som, leaves free to all.
Our Maker bids increase, who bids abstain
But our Destroyer, foe to God and Man?
Hail wedded Love, mysterious Law, true sourse   750
Of human ofspring, sole proprietie,

[52] nuptial.
[53] literally, "all-gifted"; through curiosity, she allowed the world's evils to fly
from a magic box, only hope remaining behind. Her husband was Epimethus,
brother of Prometheus, sons of Japetus, who was identified with Noah's son
Japheth.

In Paradise of all things common else.
By thee adulterous lust was driv'n from men
Among the bestial herds to raunge, by thee
Founded in Reason, Loyal, Just, and Pure,   755
Relations dear, and all the Charities
Of Father, Son, and Brother first were known.
Farr be it, that I should write thee sin or blame,
Or think thee unbefitting holiest place,
Perpetual Fountain of Domestic sweets,   760
Whose bed is undefil'd and chast pronounc't,
Present, or past, as Saints and Patriarchs us'd.
Here Love his golden shafts imploies, here lights
His constant Lamp, and waves his purple wings,
Reigns here and revels; not in the bought smile   765
Of Harlots, loveless, joyless, unindeard,
Casual fruition, nor in Court Amours
Mixt Dance, or wanton Mask, or Midnight Ball,
Or Serenate, which the starv'd Lover sings
To his proud fair, best quitted with disdain.   770
These lulld by Nightingales imbracing slept,
And on thir naked limbs the flowrie roof
Showrd Roses, which the Morn repair'd.[54] Sleep on
Blest pair; and O yet happiest if ye seek
No happier state, and know to know no more.]   775
    Now had night measur'd with her shaddowie Cone[55]
Half way up Hill this vast Sublunar Vault,
And from thir Ivorie Port the Cherubim
Forth issuing at th' accustomd hour stood armd
To thir night watches in warlike Parade,   780
When *Gabriel* to his next in power thus spake.
    Uzziel,[56] half these draw off, and coast the South
With strictest watch; these other wheel the North,
Our circuit meets full West. As flame they part
Half wheeling to the Shield,[57] half to the Spear.[58]   785
From these, two strong and suttle Spirits he calld
That neer him stood, and gave them thus in charge.
    Ithuriel and *Zephon*,[59] with wing'd speed
Search through this Garden, leav unsearcht no nook,
But chiefly where those two fair Creatures Lodge,   790

[54] that is, repaired the roof by bringing forth more roses.
[55] the shadow of the earth, shaped like a cone, as the sun descends.
[56] literally, "strength of God."
[57] left.
[58] right.
[59] literally, "discovery of God" and "searcher."

Now laid perhaps asleep secure of harm.
This Eevning from the Sun's decline arriv'd
Who tells of som infernal Spirit seen
Hitherward bent (who could have thought?) escap'd
The barrs of Hell, on errand bad no doubt: 795
Such where ye find, seise fast, and hither bring.
   So saying, on he led his radiant Files,
Daz'ling the Moon; these to the Bower direct
In search of whom they sought: him there they found
Squat like a Toad, close at the ear of *Eve;*   800
Assaying by his Devilish art to reach
The Organs of her Fancie, and with them forge
Illusions as he list, Phantasms and Dreams,
Or if, inspiring venom, he might taint
Th' animal Spirits[60] that from pure blood arise   805
Like gentle breaths from Rivers pure, thence raise
At least distemperd, discontented thoughts,
Vain hopes, vain aimes, inordinate desires
Blown up with high conceits ingendring pride.
Him thus intent *Ithuriel* with his Spear   810
Touch'd lightly; for no falshood can endure
Touch of Celestial temper, but returns
Of force to its own likeness: up he starts
Discoverd and surpriz'd. As when a spark
Lights on a heap of nitrous Powder, laid   815
Fit for the Tun som Magazin to store
Against a rumord Warr, the Smuttie grain
With sudden blaze diffus'd, inflames the Air:
So started up in his own shape the Fiend.
Back stept those two fair Angels half amaz'd   820
So sudden to behold the grieslie King;
Yet thus, unmov'd with fear, accost him soon.
   Which of those rebell Spirits adjudg'd to Hell
Com'st thou, escap'd thy prison, and transform'd,
Why satst thou like an enemie in wait   825
Here watching at the head of these that sleep?
   Know ye not then said *Satan,* fill'd with scorn,
Know ye not mee? ye knew me once no mate
For you, there sitting where ye durst not soar;
Not to know mee argues your selves unknown,   830
The lowest of your throng; or if ye know,
Why ask ye, and superfluous begin

---

[60] Natural spirits imply liver, veins; vital spirits, heart, blood; animal spirits, brain, sense and motion.

Your message, like to end as much in vain?
To whom thus *Zephon*, answering scorn with scorn.
Think not, revolted Spirit, thy shape the same,   835
Or undiminisht brightness, to be known
As when thou stoodst in Heav'n upright and pure;
That Glorie then, when thou no more wast good,
Departed from thee, and thou resembl'st now
Thy sin and place of doom obscure and foul.   840
But come, for thou, be sure, shalt give account
To him who sent us, whose charge is to keep
This place inviolable, and these from harm.
    So spake the Cherub, and his grave rebuke
Severe in youthful beautie, added grace   845
Invincible: abasht the Devil stood,
And felt how awful goodness is, and saw
Vertue in her shape how lovely, saw, and pin'd
His loss; but chiefly to find here observ'd
His lustre visibly impar'd; yet seemd   850
Undaunted. If I must contend, said he,
Best with the best, the Sender not the sent,
Or all at once; more glorie will be wonn,
Or less be lost. Thy fear, said *Zephon* bold,
Will save us trial what the least can doe   855
Single against thee wicked, and thence weak.
    The Fiend repli'd not, overcome with rage;
But like a proud Steed reind, went hautie on,
Chaumping his iron curb: to strive or flie
He held it vain; awe from above had quelld   860
His heart, not else dismai'd. Now drew they nigh
The western Point, where those half-rounding guards
Just met, and closing stood in squadron joind
Awaiting next command. To whom thir Chief
Gabriel from the Front thus calld aloud.   865
    O friends, I hear the tread of nimble feet
Hasting this way, and now by glimps discern
Ithuriel and *Zephon* through the shade,
And with them comes a third of Regal port,
But faded splendor wan; who by his gate   870
And fierce demeanour seems the Prince of Hell,
Not likely to part hence without contest;
Stand firm, for in his look defiance lours.
    He scarce had ended, when those two approach'd
And brief related whom they brought, wher found,   875
How busied, in what form and posture coucht.
    To whom with stern regard thus *Gabriel* spake.

Why hast thou, *Satan*, broke the bounds prescrib'd
To thy transgressions, and disturb'd the charge
Of others, who approve not to transgress 880
By thy example, but have power and right
To question thy bold entrance on this place;
Imploi'd it seems to violate sleep, and those
Whose dwelling God hath planted here in bliss?
   To whom thus *Satan*, with contemptuous brow. 885
Gabriel, thou hadst in Heav'n th' esteem of wise,
And such I held thee; but this question askt
Puts me in doubt. Lives ther who loves his pain?
Who would not, finding way, break loose from Hell,
Though thither doomd? Thou wouldst thy self, no doubt, 890
And boldly venture to whatever place
Farthest from pain, where thou mightst hope to change
Torment with ease, and soonest recompence
Dole with delight, which in this place I sought;
To thee no reason; who knowst only good, 895
But evil hast not tri'd: and wilt object
His will who bound us? let him surer barr
His Iron Gates, if he intends our stay
In that dark durance: thus much what was askt.
The rest is true, they found me where they say; 900
But that implies not violence or harm.
   Thus he in scorn. The warlike Angel mov'd,
Disdainfully half smiling thus repli'd.
O loss of one in Heav'n to judge of wise,
Since *Satan* fell, whom follie overthrew, 905
And now returns him from his prison scap't,
Gravely in doubt whether to hold them wise
Or not, who ask what boldness brought him hither
Unlicenc't from his bounds in Hell prescrib'd;
So wise he judges it to fly from pain 910
However, and to scape his punishment.
So judge thou still, presumptuous, till the wrauth,
Which thou incurr'st by flying, meet thy flight
Seavenfold, and scourge that wisdom back to Hell,
Which taught thee yet no better, that no pain 915
Can equal anger infinite provok't.
But wherefore thou alone? wherefore with thee
Came not all Hell broke loose? is pain to them
Less pain, less to be fled, or thou then they
Less hardie to endure? courageous Chief, 920
The first in flight from pain, had'st thou alledg'd
To thy deserted host this cause of flight,

Thou surely hadst not come sole fugitive.
To which the Fiend thus answerd frowning stern.
Not that I less endure, or shrink from pain,   925
Insulting Angel, well thou knowst I stood
Thy fiercest, when in Battel to thy aid
The blasting volied Thunder made all speed
And seconded thy else not dreaded Spear.
But still thy words at random, as before,   930
Argue thy inexperience what behooves
From hard assaies and ill successes past
A faithful Leader, not to hazard all
Through wayes of danger by himself untri'd.
I therefore, I alone first undertook   935
To wing the desolate Abyss, and spie
This new created World, whereof in Hell
Fame is not silent, here in hope to find
Better abode, and my afflicted Powers
To settle here on Earth, or in mid Air;   940
Though for possession put to try once more
What thou and thy gay Legions dare against;
Whose easier business were to serve thir Lord
High up in Heav'n, with songs to hymn his Throne,
And practis'd distances to cringe, not fight.   945
    To whom the warriour Angel soon repli'd.
To say and strait unsay, pretending first
Wise to flie pain, professing next the Spie,
Argues no Leader, but a lyar trac't,
Satan, and couldst thou faithful add? O name,   950
O sacred name of faithfulness profan'd!
Faithful to whom? to thy rebellious crew?
Armie of Fiends, fit body to fit head;
Was this your discipline and faith ingag'd,
Your military obedience, to dissolve   955
Allegeance to th' acknowledg'd Power supream?
And thou sly hypocrite, who now wouldst seem
Patron of liberty, who more then thou
Once fawn'd, and cring'd, and servilly ador'd
Heav'ns awful Monarch? wherefore but in hope   960
To dispossess him, and thy self to reigne?
But mark what I arreed[61] thee now, avant;
Flie thither whence thou fledst: if from this hour
Within these hallowd limits thou appeer,
Back to th' infernal pit I drag thee chaind,   965

_____
[61] advise.

And Seal t'hee so, as henceforth not to scorn
The facil gates of hell too slightly barrd.
  So threatn'd hee, but *Satan* to no threats
Gave heed, but waxing more in rage repli'd.
  Then when I am thy captive talk of chains,   970
Proud limitarie[62] Cherub, but ere then
Farr heavier load thy self expect to feel
From my prevailing arm, though Heavens King
Ride on thy wings, and thou with thy Compeers,
Us'd to the yoak, draw'st his triumphant wheels   975
In progress through the rode of Heav'n Star-pav'd.
  While thus he spake, th' Angelic Squadron bright
Turnd fierie red, sharpning in mooned horns
Thir Phalanx, and began to hemm him round
With ported Spears, as thick as when a field   980
Of *Ceres* ripe for harvest waving bends
Her bearded Grove of ears, which way the wind
Swayes them; the careful[63] Plowman doubting stands
Least on the threshing floor his hopeful sheaves
Prove chaff. On th' other side *Satan* allarm'd   985
Collecting all his might dilated stood,
Like *Teneriff* or *Atlas*[64] unremov'd:
His stature reacht the Skie, and on his Crest
Sat horror Plum'd; nor wanted in his grasp
What seemd both Spear and Shield: now dreadful deeds   990
Might have ensu'd, nor onely Paradise
In this commotion, but the Starrie Cope
Of Heav'n perhaps, or all the Elements
At least had gon to rack, disturb'd and torn
With violence of this conflict, had not soon   995
Th' Eternal to prevent such horrid fray
Hung forth in Heav'n his golden Scales,[65] yet seen
Betwixt *Astrea* and the *Scorpion* signe,
Wherein all things created first he weigh'd,
The pendulous round Earth with ballanc't Air   1000

---

[62] guarder of boundaries.
[63] anxious.
[64] mountains in the Canary Islands and north Africa.
[65] Libra, which in the Zodiac lies between Virgo and Scorpio; that is, between innocence and evil. In like manner Zeus weighed the fate of the Greeks and the Trojans (*Iliad*, VIII, 69–72) and of Achilles and Hector (*Iliad*, XXII, 209). At the same time Libra becomes Mercy set between Justice and the Truth of Man's failing (compare *Nativity Ode*, 141–48), and the passage comments upon the beginning of Man's fall since the Sun enters Libra at the autumnal equinox, proceeding through evil (Scorpio), wounding (Sagittarius), and lust (Capricorn) before movement toward rebirth (Aries) is begun.

In counterpoise, now ponders all events,
Battels and Realms: in these he put two weights
The sequel each of parting and of fight;
The latter quick up flew, and kickt the beam;
Which *Gabriel* spying, thus bespake the Fiend.   1005
  Satan, I know thy strength, and thou knowst mine,
Neither our own but giv'n; what follie then
To boast what Arms can doe, since thine no more
Then Heav'n permits, nor mine, though doubl'd now
To trample thee as mire: for proof look up,   1010
And read thy Lot in yon celestial Sign
Where thou art weigh'd, and shown how light, how weak,
If thou resist. The Fiend lookt up and knew
His mounted scale aloft: nor more; but fled
Murmuring, and with him fled the shades of night.   1015

BOOK V

THE ARGUMENT

Morning approach't, *Eve* relates to *Adam* her troublesome dream; he
likes it not, yet comforts her: They come forth to thir day labours: Thir
Morning Hymn at the Door of thir Bower. God to render Man inexcusa-
ble sends *Raphael* to admonish him of his obedience, of his free estate,
of his enemy near at hand; who he is, and why his enemy, and whatever
else may avail *Adam* to know. *Raphael* comes down to Paradise, his ap-
pearance describ'd, his coming discern'd by *Adam* afar off sitting at the
door of his Bower; he goes out to meet him, brings him to his lodge, en-
tertains him with the choycest fruits of Paradise got together by *Eve;*
thir discourse at Table: *Raphael* performs his message, minds *Adam* of
his state and of his enemy; relates at *Adams* request who that enemy is,
and how he came to be so, beginning from his first revolt in Heaven,
and the occasion thereof; how he drew his Legions after him to the parts
of the North, and there incited them to rebel with him, perswading all
but only *Abdiel* a Seraph, who in Argument diswades and opposes him,
then forsakes him.

  Now Morn her rosie steps in th' Eastern Clime
Advancing, sow'd the Earth with Orient Pearl,
When *Adam* wak't, so customd, for his sleep
Was Aerie light, from pure digestion bred,
And temperat vapors[1] bland, which th' only sound   5
Of leaves and fuming rills, *Aurora's* fan,

---

[1] exhalations.

Lightly dispers'd, and the shrill Matin Song
Of Birds on every bough; so much the more
His wonder was to find unwak'nd *Eve*
With Tresses discompos'd, and glowing Cheek,   10
As through unquiet rest: he on his side
Leaning half-rais'd, with looks of cordial Love
Hung over her enamour'd, and beheld
Beautie, which whether waking or asleep,
Shot forth peculiar Graces; then with voice   15
Mild, as when *Zephyrus* on *Flora* breathes,
Her hand soft touching, whisperd thus. Awake
My fairest, my espous'd, my latest found,
Heav'ns last best gift, my ever new delight,
Awake, the morning shines, and the fresh field   20
Calls us, we lose the prime, to mark how spring
Our tended Plants, how blows the Citron Grove,
What drops the Myrrh, and what the balmie Reed,[2]
How Nature paints her colours, how the Bee
Sits on the Bloom extracting liquid sweet.   25
      Such whispering wak'd her, but with startl'd eye
On *Adam*, whom imbracing, thus she spake.
      O Sole in whom my thoughts find all repose,
My Glorie, my Perfection, glad I see
Thy face, and Morn return'd, for I this Night,   30
Such night till this I never pass'd, have dream'd,
If dream'd, not as I oft am wont, of thee,
Works of day pass't, or morrows next designe,
But of offence and trouble, which my mind
Knew never till this irksom night; methought   35
Close at mine ear one call'd me forth to walk
With gentle voice, I thought it thine; it said,
Why sleepst thou *Eve*? now is the pleasant time,
The cool, the silent, save where silence yields
To the night-warbling Bird, that now awake   40
Tunes sweetest his love-labor'd song; now reignes
Full Orb'd the Moon, and with more pleasing light
Shadowie sets off the face of things; in vain,
If none regard; Heav'n wakes with all his eyes,
Whom to behold but thee, Natures desire,   45
In whose sight all things joy, with ravishment
Attracted by thy beauty still to gaze.
I rose as at thy call, but found thee not;
To find thee I directed then my walk;

---

[2] the balsam, source of balm.

And on, methought, alone I pass'd through ways   50
That brought me on a sudden to the Tree
Of interdicted Knowledge: fair it seem'd,
Much fairer to my Fancie[3] then by day:
And as I wondring lookt, beside it stood
One shap'd and wing'd like one of those from Heav'n   55
By us oft seen; his dewie locks distill'd
Ambrosia; on that Tree he also gaz'd;
And O fair Plant, said he, with fruit surcharg'd,
Deigns none to ease thy load and taste thy sweet,
Nor God, nor Man; is Knowledge so despis'd?   60
Or envie, or what reserve forbids to taste?
Forbid who will, none shall from me withhold
Longer thy offerd good, why else set here?
This said he paus'd not, but with ventrous Arm
He pluckt, he tasted; mee damp horror chil'd   65
At such bold words voucht with a deed so bold:
But he thus overjoy'd, O Fruit Divine,
Sweet of thy self, but much more sweet thus cropt,
Forbidd'n here, it seems, as onely fit
For Gods, yet able to make Gods of Men: 70
And why not Gods of Men, since good, the more
Communicated, more abundant grows,
The Author not impair'd, but honourd more?
Here, happie Creature, fair Angelic *Eve,*
Partake thou also; happie though thou art,   75
Happier thou mayst be, worthier canst not be:
Taste this, and be henceforth among the Gods
Thy self a Goddess, not to Earth confind,
But sometimes in the Air, as wee, somtimes
Ascend to Heav'n, by merit thine, and see   80
What life the Gods live there, and such live thou.
So saying, he drew nigh, and to me held,
Evn to my mouth of that same fruit held part
Which he had pluckt; the pleasant savourie smell
So quick'nd appetite, that I, methought,   85
Could not but taste. Forthwith up to the Clouds
With him I flew, and underneath beheld
The Earth outstretcht immense, a prospect wide
And various: wondring at my flight and change
To this high exaltation; suddenly   90
My Guide was gon, and I, me thought, sunk down,
And fell asleep; but O how glad I wak'd

[3] Compare IV, 802.

To find this but a dream! Thus *Eve* her Night
Related, and thus *Adam* answerd sad.
   Best Image of my self and dearer half,   95
The trouble of thy thoughts this night in sleep
Affects me equally; nor can I like
This uncouth dream, of evil sprung I fear;
Yet evil whence? in thee can harbour none,
Created pure. But know that in the Soul   100
Are many lesser Faculties that serve
Reason as chief; among these Fansie next
Her office holds; of all external things,
Which the five watchful Senses represent,
She forms Imaginations, Aerie shapes,   105
Which Reason joyning or disjoyning, frames
All what we affirm or what deny, and call
Our knowledge or opinion; then retires
Into her private Cell when Nature rests.
Oft in her absence mimic Fansie wakes   110
To imitate her; but misjoyning shapes,
Wild work produces oft, and most in dreams,
Ill matching words and deeds long past or late.
Som such resemblances methinks I find
Of our last Eevnings talk, in this thy dream,   115
But with addition strange: yet be not sad.
Evil into the mind of God[4] or Man
May come and go, so unapprov'd, and leave
No spot or blame behind: Which gives me hope
That what in sleep thou didst abhorr to dream,   120
Waking thou never wilt consent to do.
Be not disheart'nd then, nor cloud those looks
That wont to be more chearful and serene
Then when fair Morning first smiles on the World,
And let us to our fresh imployments rise   125
Among the Groves, the Fountains, and the Flowrs
That open now thir choicest bosom'd smells
Reserv'd from night, and kept for thee in store.
   So cheard he his fair Spouse, and she was cheard,
But silently a gentle tear let fall   130
From either eye, and wip'd them with her hair;
Two other precious drops that ready stood,
Each in thir chrystal sluce, hee ere they fell
Kiss'd as the gracious signs of sweet remorse

[4] The omniscience of God admits of evil, but the word may mean only "angel."

And pious awe, that feard to have offended.   135
   So all was cleard, and to the Field they haste.
But first from under shadie arborous roof,
Soon as they forth were come to open sight
Of day-spring, and the Sun, who scarce up ris'n
With wheels yet hov'ring o're the Ocean brim,   140
Shot paralel to th' earth his dewie ray,
Discovering in wide Lantskip all the East
Of Paradise and *Edens* happie Plains,
Lowly they bow'd adoring, and began
Thir Orisons, each Morning duly paid   145
In various style, for neither various style
Nor holy rapture wanted they to praise
Thir Maker, in fit strains pronounc't or sung
Unmeditated, such prompt eloquence
Flowd from thir lips, in Prose or numerous[5] Verse,   150
More tuneable then needed Lute or Harp
To add more sweetness, and they thus began.
   These are thy glorious works, Parent of good,
Almightie, thine this universal Frame,
Thus wondrous fair; thy self how wondrous then!   155
Unspeakable, who sitst above these Heav'ns
To us invisible or dimly seen
In these thy lowest works, yet these declare
Thy goodness beyond thought, and Power Divine:
Speak yee who best can tell, ye Sons of light,   160
Angels, for yee behold him, and with songs
And choral symphonies, Day without Night,
Circle his Throne rejoycing, yee in Heav'n,
On Earth joyn all ye Creatures to extoll
Him first, him last, him midst, and without end.   165
Fairest of Starrs,[6] last in the train of Night,
If better thou belong not to the dawn,
Sure pledge of day, that crownst the smiling Morn
With thy bright Circlet, praise him in thy Sphear
While day arises, that sweet hour of Prime.   170
Thou Sun, of this great World both Eye and Soul,
Acknowledge him thy Greater, sound his praise
In thy eternal course, both when thou climb'st,
And when high Noon hast gaind, and when thou fallst.
Moon, that now meetst the orient Sun, now fli'st   175

----

[5] metrical.
[6] Venus (Lucifer as the morning star, Hesperus as the evening star).

With the fixt Starrs, fixt in thir Orb that flies,[7]
And yee five other wandring Fires that move
In mystic Dance not without Song, resound
His praise, who out of Darkness call'd up Light.
Air, and ye Elements the eldest birth   180
Of Natures Womb, that in quaternion[8] run
Perpetual Circle, multiform; and mix
And nourish all things, let your ceasless change
Varie to our great Maker still new praise.
Ye Mists and Exhalations that now rise   185
From Hill or steaming Lake, duskie or grey,
Till the Sun paint your fleecie skirts with Gold,
In honour to the Worlds great Author rise,
Whether to deck with Clouds th' uncolourd[9] skie,
Or wet the thirstie Earth with falling showers,   190
Rising or falling still advance his praise.
His praise ye Winds, that from four Quarters blow,
Breath soft or loud; and wave your tops, ye Pines,
With every Plant, in sign of Worship wave.
Fountains and yee, that warble, as ye flow,   195
Melodious murmurs, warbling tune his praise.
Joyn voices all ye living Souls, ye Birds,
That singing up to Heaven Gate ascend,
Bear on your wings and in your notes his praise;
Yee that in Waters glide, and yee that walk   200
The Earth, and stately tread, or lowly creep;
Witness if I be silent, Morn or Eev'n,
To Hill, or Valley, Fountain, or fresh shade
Made vocal by my Song, and taught his praise.
Hail universal Lord, be bounteous still   205
To give us onely good; and if the night
Have gather'd aught of evil or conceald,
Disperse it, as now light dispels the dark.
    So pray'd they innocent, and to thir thoughts
Firm peace recoverd soon and wonted calm.   210
On to thir mornings rural work they haste
Among sweet dews and flowrs; where any row
Of Fruit-trees overwoodie reach'd too farr
Thir pamperd boughs, and needed hands to check
Fruitless imbraces: or they led the Vine   215

[7] the sphere of fixed stars which circle the earth once every twenty-four hours.
The "wandering Fires" are the planets Mercury, Venus, Mars, Jupiter, and
Saturn.
    [8] the four elements variously combined.
    [9] of one color.

To wed her Elm; she spous'd about[10] him twines
Her mariageable arms, and with her brings
Her dowr th' adopted Clusters, to adorn
His barren leaves. Them thus imploid beheld
With pittie Heav'ns high King, and to him call'd   220
Raphael,[11] the sociable Spirit, that deign'd
To travel with Tobias, and secur'd
His marriage with the seaventimes-wedded Maid.[12]
  Raphael, said hee, thou hear'st what stir on Earth
Satan from Hell scap't through the darksom Gulf   225
Hath rais'd in Paradise, and how disturb'd
This night the human pair, how he designes
In them at once to ruin all mankind.
Go therefore, half this day as friend with friend
Converse with Adam, in what Bowr or shade   230
Thou find'st him from the heat of Noon retir'd,
To respit his day-labour with repast,
Or with repose; and such discourse bring on,
As may advise him of his happie state,
Happiness in his power left free to will,   235
Left to his own free Will, his Will though free,
Yet mutable; whence warn him to beware
He swerve not too secure: tell him withall
His danger, and from whom, what enemie
Late falln himself from Heav'n, is plotting now   240
The fall of others from like state of bliss;
By violence, no, for that shall be withstood,
But by deceit and lies; this let him know,
Least wilfully transgressing he pretend
Surprisal, unadmonisht, unforewarnd.   245
  So spake th' Eternal Father, and fulfilld
All Justice: nor delaid the winged Saint
After his charge receiv'd; but from among
Thousand Celestial Ardors,[13] where he stood
Vaild with his gorgeous wings, up springing light   250
Flew through the midst of Heav'n; th' angelic Quires
On each hand parting, to his speed gave way
Through all th' Empyreal road; till at the Gate
Of Heav'n arriv'd, the gate self-opend wide
On golden Hinges turning, as by work   255
Divine the sov'ran Architect had fram'd.

[10] placed in embracement about, wedded to.
[11] literally, "medicine of God."
[12] See Tobit viii.
[13] angels.

From hence, no cloud, or, to obstruct his sight,
Starr interpos'd, however small he sees,
Not unconform to other shining Globes,
Earth and the Gard'n of God, with Cedars crownd   260
Above all Hills. As when by night the Glass[14]
Of *Galileo*, less assur'd, observes
Imagind Lands and Regions in the Moon:
Or Pilot from amidst the *Cyclades*[15]
Delos or *Samos* first appeering kenns   265
A cloudy spot. Down thither prone[16] in flight
He speeds, and through the vast Ethereal Skie
Sails between worlds and worlds, with steddie wing
Now on the polar winds, then with quick Fann[17]
Winnows the buxom[18] Air; till within soar   270
Of Towring Eagles, to all the Fowls he seems
A *Phœnix*, gaz'd by all, as that sole Bird
When to enshrine his reliques in the Sun's
Bright Temple, to *Ægyptian Thebes* he flies.[19]
At once on th' Eastern cliff of Paradise   275
He lights, and to his proper shape returns
A Seraph wing'd; six wings he wore, to shade
His lineaments Divine; the pair that clad
Each shoulder broad, came mantling o're his brest
With regal Ornament; the middle pair   280
Girt like a Starrie Zone his waste, and round
Skirted his loins and thighs with downie Gold
And colours dipt in Heav'n; the third his feet
Shaddowd from either heel with featherd mail
Skie-tinctur'd grain.[20] Like *Maia's* son[21] he stood,   285
And shook his Plumes, that Heav'nly fragrance filld
The circuit wide. Strait knew him all the Bands
Of Angels under watch; and to his state,
And to his message high in honour rise;
For on som message high they guess'd him bound.   290
Thir glittering Tents he pass'd, and now is come
Into the blissful field, through Groves of Myrrh,

[14] telescope.
[15] Aegean islands.
[16] downward.
[17] wing.
[18] compliant.
[19] The unique and undying Phoenix rose from its own ashes in Heliopolis
("city of the sun") rather than in the neighboring Egyptian city of Thebes,
according to Ovid, *Meta.*, XV, 391–407.
[20] colored blue.
[21] Hermes, whose sandals bore wings.

And flowring Odours, Cassia, Nard, and Balm;
A Wilderness of sweets; for Nature here
Wantond as in her prime, and plaid at will   295
Her Virgin Fancies, pouring forth more sweet,
Wild above Rule or Art; enormous bliss.
Him through the spicie Forrest onward com
Adam discernd, as in the dore he sat
Of his cool Bowr, while now the mounted Sun   300
Shot down direct his fervid Raies to warm
Earths inmost womb, more warmth then *Adam* needs;
And *Eve* within, due at her hour prepar'd
For dinner savourie fruits, of taste to please
True appetite, and not disrelish thirst   305
Of nectarous draughts between, from milkie stream,[22]
Berrie or Grape: to whom thus *Adam* call'd.
    Haste hither *Eve*, and worth thy sight behold
Eastward among those Trees, what glorious shape
Comes this way moving; seems another Morn   310
Ris'n on mid-noon; som great behest from Heav'n
To us perhaps he brings, and will voutsafe
This day to be our Guest. But goe with speed,
And what thy stores contain, bring forth and pour
Abundance, fit to honour and receive   315
Our Heav'nly stranger; well we may afford
Our givers thir own gifts, and large bestow
From large bestowd, where Nature multiplies
Her fertil growth, and by disburd'ning grows
More fruitful, which instructs us not to spare.   320
    To whom thus *Eve. Adam*, earths hallowd mould,
Of God inspir'd, small store will serve, where store,
All seasons, ripe for use hangs on the stalk;
Save what by frugal storing firmness gains
To nourish, and superfluous moist consumes: 325
But I will haste and from each bough and break,
Each Plant and juiciest Gourd will pluck such choice
To entertain our Angel guest, as hee
Beholding shall confess that here on Earth
God hath dispenst his bounties as in Heav'n.   330
    So saying, with dispatchful looks in haste
She turns, on hospitable thoughts intent
What choice to chuse for delicacie best,
What order, so contriv'd as not to mix

[22] fresh water, but implying the milk and honey of the Promised Land; see
also *SA*, 550.

Tastes, not well joynd, inelegant, but bring   335
Taste after taste upheld with kindliest[23] change,
Bestirs her then, and from each tender stalk
Whatever Earth all-bearing Mother yeilds
In *India* East or West,[24] or middle shoar
In *Pontus* or the *Punic* Coast,[25] or where   340
Alcinous reign'd, fruit of all kinds, in coat,
Rough, or smooth rind, or bearded husk, or shell
She gathers, Tribute large, and on the board
Heaps with unsparing hand; for drink the Grape
She crushes, inoffensive moust, and meaths[26]   345
From many a berrie, and from sweet kernels prest
She tempers dulcet creams, nor these to hold
Wants her fit vessels pure, then strews the ground
With Rose and Odours from the shrub unfum'd.[27]
Mean while our Primitive great Sire, to meet   350
His god-like Guest, walks forth, without more train
Accompani'd then with his own compleat
Perfections, in himself was all his state,
More solemn then the tedious pomp that waits
On Princes, when thir rich Retinue long   355
Of Horses led, and Grooms besmeard with Gold
Dazles the crowd, and sets them all agape.
Neerer his presence *Adam* though not awd,
Yet with submiss approach and reverence meek,
As to a superior Nature, bowing low,   360
Thus said. Native of Heav'n, for other place
None can then Heav'n such glorious shape contain;
Since by descending from the Thrones above,
Those happie places thou hast deign'd a while
To want, and honour these, voutsafe with us   365
Two onely, who yet by sov'ran gift possess
This spacious ground, in yonder shadie Bowr
To rest, and what the Garden choicest bears
To sit and taste, till this meridian heat
Be over, and the Sun more cool decline.   370
    Whom thus th' Angelic Vertue answerd mild.
Adam, I therefore came, nor art thou such
Created, or such place hast here to dwell,

[23] most natural.
[24] India and the Indies (East) and America (West).
[25] the Black Sea or the Carthaginian coast. Alcinous' gardens of perpetual spring and harvest were visited by Ulysses (*Od.*, VII, 125 ff.).
[26] unfermented liquor and meads.
[27] unburned; it is natural odor rather than that from incense.

As may not oft invite, though Spirits of Heav'n
To visit thee; lead on then where thy Bowr   375
Oreshades; for these mid-hours, till Eevning rise
I have at will. So to the Silvan Lodge
They came, that like *Pomona's*[28] Arbour smil'd
With flowrets deck't and fragrant smells; but *Eve*
Undeckt, save with her self more lovely fair   380
Then Wood-Nymph, or the fairest Goddess feign'd
Of three[29] that in Mount *Ida* naked strove,
Stood t' entertain her guest from Heav'n; no vail
Shee needed, Vertue-proof, no thought infirm
Alterd her cheek. On whom the Angel *Hail*   385
Bestowd, the holy salutation us'd
Long after to blest *Marie,* second *Eve.*

Hail Mother of Mankind, whose fruitful Womb
Shall fill the World more numerous with thy Sons
Then with these various fruits the Trees of God   390
Have heap'd this Table. Rais'd of grassie terf
Thir Table was, and mossie seats had round,
And on her ample Square from side to side
All *Autumn* pil'd, though *Spring* and *Autumn* here
Danc'd hand in hand. A while discourse they hold;   395
No fear lest Dinner cool; when thus began
Our Authour. Heav'nly stranger, please to taste
These bounties which our Nourisher, from whom
All perfet good unmeasur'd out, descends,
To us for food and for delight hath caus'd   400
The Earth to yeild; unsavourie food perhaps
To spiritual Natures; only this I know,
That one Celestial Father gives to all.

To whom the Angel. Therefore what he gives
(Whose praise be ever sung) to man in part   405
Spiritual, may of purest Spirits be found
No ingrateful food: and food alike those pure
Intelligential substances require
As doth your Rational; and both contain
Within them every lower facultie   410
Of sense, whereby they hear, see, smell, touch, taste,
Tasting concoct,[30] digest, assimilate,
And corporeal to incorporeal turn.
For know, whatever was created, needs

[28] Roman goddess of fruits.
[29] Juno, Minerva, and Venus whose beauty was judged by Paris on Mt. Ida.
[30] begin to digest.

To be sustaind and fed; of Elements   415
The grosser feeds the purer, Earth the Sea,
Earth and the Sea feed Air, the Air those Fires
Ethereal, and as lowest first the Moon;
Whence in her visage round those spots, unpurg'd
Vapours not yet into her substance turnd.[31]   420
Nor doth the Moon no nourishment exhale
From her moist Continent to higher Orbs.
The Sun that light imparts to all, receives
From all his alimental recompence
In humid exhalations, and at Ev'n   425
Sups with the Ocean: though in Heav'n the Trees
Of life ambrosial fruitage bear, and vines
Yeild Nectar, though from off the boughs each Morn
We brush mellifluous Dews, and find the ground
Cover'd with pearly grain:[32] yet God hath here   430
Varied his bounty so with new delights,
As may compare with Heaven; and to taste
Think not I shall be nice. So down they sat,
And to thir viands fell, nor seemingly
The Angel, nor in mist, the common gloss   435
Of Theologians, but with keen dispatch
Of real hunger, and concoctive heat
To transubstantiate; what redounds,[33] transpires
Through Spirits with ease; nor wonder; if by fire
Of sooty coal th' Empiric Alchimist   440
Can turn, or holds it possible to turn
Metals of drossiest Ore to perfet Gold
As from the Mine. Mean while at Table *Eve*
Ministerd naked, and thir flowing cups
With pleasant liquors crown'd: O innocence   445
Deserving Paradise! if ever, then,
Then had the Sons of God excuse t' have bin
Enamour'd at that sight; but in those hearts
Love unlibidinous reign'd, nor jealousie
Was understood, the injur'd Lovers Hell.   450
    Thus when with meats and drinks they had suffic'd,
Not burd'nd Nature, sudden mind arose
In *Adam,* not to let th' occasion pass
Giv'n him by this great Conference to know
Of things above his World, and of thir being   455

[31] Moon spots had been thought to be exhalations from earth.
[32] manna.
[33] overflows.

Who dwell in Heav'n, whose excellence he saw
Transcend his own so farr, whose radiant forms
Divine effulgence, whose high Power so far
Exceeded human, and his wary speech
Thus to th' Empyreal Minister he fram'd.   460
  Inhabitant with God, now know I well
Thy favour, in this honour done to man,
Under whose lowly roof thou hast voutsaf't
To enter, and these earthly fruits to taste,
Food not of Angels, yet accepted so,   465
As that more willingly thou couldst not seem
At Heav'ns high feasts t' have fed: yet what compare?
  To whom the winged Hierarch repli'd.
O *Adam*, one Almightie is, from whom
All things proceed, and up to him return,[34]   470
If not deprav'd from good, created all
Such to perfection, one first matter all,
Indu'd with various forms, various degrees
Of substance, and in things that live, of life;
But more refin'd, more spiritous, and pure,   475
As neerer to him plac't or neerer tending
Each in thir several active Sphears assign'd,
Till body up to spirit work, in bounds
Proportiond to each kind. So from the root
Springs lighter the green stalk, from thence the leaves   480
More aerie, last the bright consummate flowr
Spirits odorous breathes: flowrs and thir fruit
Mans nourishment, by gradual scale sublim'd
To vital Spirits aspire, to animal,
To intellectual, give both life and sense,[35]   485
Fansie and understanding, whence the Soul
Reason receives, and reason is her being,
Discursive, or Intuitive; discourse
Is oftest yours, the latter most is ours,
Differing but in degree, of kind the same.   490
Wonder not then, what God for you saw good
If I refuse not, but convert, as you,
To proper substance; time may come when men
With Angels may participate, and find

[34] referring to the chain of being which tends upward toward its creator.
Man's natural bodily spirits (ll. 483 ff.) are raised to the vital emotional spirits
and then to the intellectual (animal) spirits. Thus man is able to reason, but
his conclusions are those which angels know intuitively.

[35] the vegetative, sensitive, and rational souls of plants, animals, and men
respectively.

No inconvenient Diet, nor too light Fare: 495
And from these corporal nutriments perhaps
Your bodies may at last turn all to Spirit,
Improv'd by tract of time, and wing'd ascend
Ethereal, as wee, or may at choice
Here or in Heav'nly Paradises dwell; 500
If ye be found obedient, and retain
Unalterably firm his love entire
Whose progenie you are. Mean while enjoy
Your fill what happiness this happie state
Can comprehend, incapable of more. 505
  To whom the Patriarch of mankind repli'd.
O favourable spirit, propitious guest,
Well hast thou taught the way that might direct
Our knowledge, and the scale of Nature set
From center to circumference, whereon 510
In contemplation of created things
By steps we may ascend to God. But say,
What meant that caution joind, *if ye be found
Obedient?* can we want obedience then
To him, or possibly his love desert 515
Who formd us from the dust, and plac'd us here
Full to the utmost measure of what bliss
Human desires can seek or apprehend?
  To whom the Angel. Son of Heav'n and Earth,
Attend: That thou art happie, owe to God; 520
That thou continu'st such, owe to thy self,
That is, to thy obedience; therein stand.
This was that caution giv'n thee; be advis'd.
God made thee perfet, not immutable;
And good he made thee, but to persevere 525
He left it in thy power, ordaind thy will
By nature free, not over-rul'd by Fate
Inextricable, or strict necessity;
Our voluntarie service he requires,
Not our necessitated, such with him 530
Finds no acceptance, nor can find, for how
Can hearts, not free, be tri'd whether they serve
Willing or no, who will but what they must
By Destinie, and can no other choose?
My self and all th' Angelic Host that stand 535
In sight of God enthron'd, our happie state
Hold, as you yours, while our obedience holds;
On other suretie none; freely we serve,
Because wee freely love, as in our will

To love or not; in this we stand or fall: 540
And som are fall'n, to disobedience fall'n,
And so from Heav'n to deepest Hell; O fall
From what high state of bliss into what woe!
    To whom our great Progenitor. Thy words
Attentive, and with more delighted ear,   545
Divine instructer, I have heard, then when
Cherubic Songs by night from neighbouring Hills
Aereal Music send: nor knew I not
To be both will and deed created free;
Yet that we never shall forget to love   550
Our maker, and obey him whose command
Single, is yet so just, my constant thoughts
Assur'd me, and still assure: though what thou tellst
Hath past in Heav'n, som doubt within me move,
But more desire to hear, if thou consent,   555
The full relation, which must needs be strange,
Worthy of Sacred silence to be heard;
And we have yet large day, for scarce the Sun
Hath finisht half his journey, and scarce begins
His other half in the great Zone of Heav'n.   560
    Thus *Adam* made request, and *Raphael*
After short pause assenting, thus began.
    High matter thou injoinst me, O prime of men,
Sad task and hard, for how shall I relate
To human sense th' invisible exploits   565
Of warring Spirits; how without remorse
The ruin of so many glorious once
And perfet while they stood; how last unfould
The secrets of another world, perhaps
Not lawful to reveal? yet for thy good   570
This is dispenc't, and what surmounts the reach
Of human sense, I shall delineate so,
By lik'ning spiritual to corporal forms,
As may express them best, though what if Earth
Be but the shaddow of Heav'n,[36] and things therein   575
Each t' other like, more then on earth is thought?
    As yet this world was not, and *Chaos* wild
Reign'd where these Heav'ns now rowl, where Earth now rests
Upon her Center pois'd, when on a day
(For Time, though in Eternitie, appli'd   580

[36] typologically, that is, as a foreshadowing of Heaven, according to William
G. Madsen (*PMLA*, LXXV, 1960, 519–26), rather than Platonically as a simu-
lation of Heaven.

To motion, measures all things durable
By present, past, and future) on such day
As Heav'ns great Year[37] brings forth, th' Empyreal Host
Of Angels by Imperial summons call'd,
Innumerable before th' Almighties Throne   585
Forthwith from all the ends of Heav'n appeerd
Under thir Hierarchs in orders bright;
Ten thousand thousand Ensignes high advanc'd,
Standards, and Gonfalons[38] twixt Van and Rear
Stream in the Air, and for distinction serve   590
Of Hierarchies, of Orders, and Degrees;
Or in thir glittering Tissues bear imblaz'd
Holy Memorials, acts of Zeal and Love
Recorded eminent. Thus when in Orbs
Of circuit inexpressible they stood,   595
Orb within Orb, the Father infinite,
By whom in bliss inbosom'd sat the Son,
Amidst as from a flaming Mount, whose top
Brightness had made invisible, thus spake.
  Hear all ye Angels, Progenie of Light,   600
Thrones, Dominations, Princedoms, Vertues, Powers,
Hear my Decree, which unrevok't shall stand.
This day I have begot[39] whom I declare
My onely Son, and on this holy Hill
Him have anointed, whom ye now behold   605
At my right hand; your Head I him appoint;
And by my Self have sworn to him shall bow
All knees in Heav'n, and shall confess him Lord:
Under his great Vice-gerent Reign abide
United as one individual[40] Soul   610
For ever happie: him who disobeys
Mee disobeys, breaks union, and that day
Cast out from God and blessed vision, falls
Into utter darkness, deep ingulft, his place
Ordaind without redemption, without end.   615
  So spake th' Omnipotent, and with his words
All seemd well pleas'd, all seem'd, but were not all.
That day, as other solemn dayes, they spent
In song and dance about the sacred Hill,

[37] the time it would take a star to complete the equinoctial precession, around 26,000 years.
[38] flags suspended from crosspieces.
[39] not the creation of the Son, but his anointing as king; see Milton's translation of *Ps. 2* (verses 6–7).
[40] undividable.

Mystical dance, which yonder starrie Sphear   620
Of Planets and of fixt in all her Wheels
Resembles nearest, mazes intricate,
Eccentric, intervolv'd, yet regular
Then most, when most irregular they seem:
And in thir motions harmonie Divine   625
So smooths her charming tones, that Gods own ear
Listens delighted. Eevning now approach'd
(For wee have also our Eevning and our Morn,
Wee ours for change delectable, not need)
Forthwith from dance to sweet repast they turn   630
Desirous; all in Circles as they stood,
Tables are set, and on a sudden pil'd
With Angels Food, and rubied Nectar flows:
In Pearl, in Diamond, and massie Gold
Fruit of delicious Vines, the growth of Heav'n.   635
On flowrs repos'd, and with fresh flowrets crownd,
They eat, they drink, and in communion sweet
Quaff immortalitie and joy, secure
Of surfet where full measure onely bounds
Excess, before th' all-bounteous King, who showrd   640
With copious hand, rejoycing in thir joy.
Now when ambrosial Night with Clouds exhal'd
From that high mount of God, whence light and shade
Spring both, the face of brightest Heav'n had chang'd
To grateful Twilight (for Night comes not there   645
In darker veil) and roseat Dews dispos'd
All but th' unsleeping eyes of God to rest,
Wide over all the Plain, and wider farr
Then all this globous Earth in Plain outspred,
(Such are the Courts of God) th' Angelic throng   650
Disperst in Bands and Files thir Camp extend
By living Streams among the Trees of Life,
Pavilions numberless, and sudden reard,
Celestial Tabernacles, where they slept
Fannd with cool Winds, save those who in thir course   655
Melodious Hymns about the sovran Throne
Alternate all night long: but not so wak'd
Satan, so call him now, his former name
Is heard no more in Heav'n; he of the first,
If not the first Arch-Angel, great in Power,   660
In favour and in præeminence, yet fraught
With envie against the Son of God, that day
Honourd by his great Father, and proclaimd
Messiah King anointed, could not bear

Through pride that sight, and thought himself impaird.   665
Deep malice thence conceiving and disdain,
Soon as midnight brought on the duskie hour
Friendliest to sleep and silence, he resolv'd
With all his Legions to dislodge, and leave
Unworshipt, unobey'd the Throne supream   670
Contemptuous, and his next subordinate[41]
Awak'ning, thus to him in secret spake.
　　Sleepst thou Companion dear, what sleep can close
Thy eye-lids? and remembrest what Decree
Of yesterday, so late hath past the lips   675
Of Heav'ns Almightie. Thou to me thy thoughts
Wast wont, I mine to thee was wont t' impart;
Both waking we were one; how then can now
Thy sleep dissent? new Laws thou seest impos'd;
New Laws from him who reigns, new minds may raise   680
In us who serve, new Counsels, to debate
What doubtful may ensue, more in this place
To utter is not safe. Assemble thou
Of all those Myriads which we lead the chief;
Tell them that by command, ere yet dim Night   685
Her shadowie Cloud withdraws, I am to haste,
And all who under me thir Banners wave,
Homeward with flying march where we possess
The Quarters of the North, there to prepare
Fit entertainment to receive our King   690
The great *Messiah*, and his new commands,
Who speedily through all the Hierarchies
Intends to pass triumphant, and give Laws.
　　So spake the false Arch-Angel, and infus'd
Bad influence into th' unwarie brest   695
Of his Associate; hee together calls,
Or several one by one, the Regent Powers,
Under him Regent, tells, as he was taught,
That the most High commanding, now ere Night,
Now ere dim Night had disincumberd Heav'n,   700
The great Hierarchal Standard was to move;
Tells the suggested cause, and casts between
Ambiguous words and jealousies, to sound
Or taint integritie; but all obey'd
The wonted signal, and superior voice   705
Of thir great Potentate; for great indeed
His name, and high was his degree in Heav'n;

[41] Beelzebub.

His count'nance, as the Morning Starr that guides
The starrie flock, allur'd them, and with lyes
Drew after him the third part of Heav'ns Host:[42]   710
Mean while th' Eternal eye, whose sight discerns
Abstrusest thoughts, from forth his holy Mount
And from within the golden Lamps that burn
Nightly before him, saw without thir light
Rebellion rising, saw in whom, how spred   715
Among the sons of Morn, what multitudes
Were banded to oppose his high Decree;
And smiling to his onely Son thus said.
    Son, thou in whom my glory I behold
In full resplendence, Heir of all my might,   720
Neerly it now concerns us to be sure
Of our Omnipotence, and with what Arms
We mean to hold what anciently we claim
Of Deitie or Empire, such a foe
Is rising, who intends t' erect his Throne   725
Equal to ours, throughout the spacious North;
Nor so content, hath in his thought to try
In battel, what our Power is, or our right.
Let us advise, and to this hazard draw
With speed what force is left, and all imploy   730
In our defence, lest unawares we lose
This our high place, our Sanctuarie, our Hill.
    To whom the Son with calm aspect and cleer
Light'ning Divine, ineffable, serene,
Made answer. Mightie Father, thou thy foes   735
Justly hast in derision,[43] and secure
Laugh'st at thir vain designes and tumults vain,
Matter to mee of Glory, whom thir hate
Illustrates, when they see all Regal Power
Giv'n me to quell thir pride, and in event   740
Know whether I be dextrous[44] to subdue
Thy Rebels, or be found the worst in Heav'n.
    So spake the Son, but Satan with his Powers
Farr was advanc't on winged speed, an Host
Innumerable as the Starrs of Night,   745
Or Starrs of Morning, Dew-drops, which the Sun
Impearls on every leaf and every flower.

---

[42] Rev. xii. 4: And the dragon's "tail drew the third part of the stars of
heaven, and did cast them to the earth."
[43] See note to II, 191.
[44] alluding also to his position at the Father's right hand (see l. 606).

Regions they pass'd, the mightie Regencies
Of Seraphim and Potentates and Thrones
In thir triple Degrees,[45] Regions to which   750
All thy Dominion, *Adam,* is no more
Then what this Garden is to all the Earth,
And all the Sea, from one entire globose[46]
Stretcht into Longitude; which having pass'd
At length into the limits of the North   755
They came, and *Satan* to his Royal seat
High on a Hill, far blazing, as a Mount
Rais'd on a Mount, with Pyramids and Towrs
From Diamond Quarries hew'n, and Rocks of Gold,
The Palace of great *Lucifer* (so call   760
That Structure in the Dialect of men
Interpreted), which not long after, he
Affecting all equality with God,
In imitation of that Mount whereon
Messiah was declar'd in sight of Heav'n,   765
The Mountain of the Congregation call'd;
For thither he assembl'd all his Train,
Pretending so commanded to consult
About the great reception of thir King,
Thither to come, and with calumnious Art   770
Of counterfeted truth thus held thir ears.
    Thrones, Dominations, Princedoms, Vertues, Powers,
If these magnific Titles yet remain
Not meerly titular, since by Decree
Another now hath to himself ingross't   775
All Power, and us eclipst under the name
Of King anointed, for whom all this haste
Of midnight march, and hurried meeting here,
This onely to consult how we may best
With what may be devis'd of honours new   780
Receive him coming to receive from us
Knee-tribute yet unpaid, prostration vile,
Too much to one, but double how endur'd,
To one and to his image now proclaim'd?
But what if better counsels might erect   785
Our minds and teach us to cast off this Yoke?
Will ye submit your necks, and chuse to bend

[45] referring to the three divisions of the nine orders of angels, but the order and division seem not to be those of Dionysius, which are: seraphim, cherubim, thrones; dominions, virtues, powers (potentates); principalities, archangels, angels.
[46] sphere.

The supple knee? ye will not, if I trust
To know ye right, or if ye know your selves
Natives and Sons of Heav'n possest before   790
By none, and if not equal all, yet free,
Equally free; for Orders and Degrees
Jarr not with liberty, but well consist.
Who can in reason then or right assume
Monarchie over such as live by right   795
His equals, if in power and splendor less,
In freedom equal? or can introduce
Law and Edict on us, who without law
Err not, much less for this to be our Lord,
And look for adoration to th' abuse   800
Of those Imperial Titles which assert
Our being ordain'd to govern, not to serve?
     Thus farr his bold discourse without controul
Had audience, when among the Seraphim
Abdiel, then whom none with more zeal ador'd   805
The Deitie, and divine commands obei'd,
Stood up, and in a flame of zeal severe
The current of his fury thus oppos'd.
     O argument blasphemous, false and proud!
Words which no ear ever to hear in Heav'n   810
Expected, least of all from thee, ingrate
In place thy self so high above thy Peers.
Canst thou with impious obloquie condemn
The just Decree of God, pronounc't and sworn,
That to his only Son by right endu'd   815
With Regal Scepter, every Soul in Heav'n
Shall bend the knee, and in that honour due
Confess him rightful King? unjust thou saist
Flatly unjust, to bind with Laws the free,
And equal over equals to let Reigne,   820
One over all with unsucceeded power.
Shalt thou give Law to God, shalt thou dispute
With him the points of libertie, who made
Thee what thou art, and formd the Pow'rs of Heav'n
Such as he pleas'd, and circumscrib'd thir being?   825
Yet by experience taught we know how good,
And of our good, and of our dignitie
How provident he is, how farr from thought
To make us less, bent rather to exalt
Our happie state under one Head more neer   830
United. But to grant it thee unjust,
That equal over equals Monarch Reigne:

Thy self though great and glorious dost thou count,
Or all Angelic Nature joind in one,
Equal to him begotten Son, by whom   835
As by his Word the mighty Father made
All things, ev'n thee, and all the Spirits of Heav'n
By him created in thir bright degrees,
Crownd them with Glory, and to thir Glory nam'd
Thrones, Dominations, Princedoms, Vertues, Powers,   840
Essential Powers, nor by his Reign obscur'd,
But more illustrious made, since he the Head
One of our number thus reduc't becomes,
His Laws our Laws, all honour to him done
Returns our own. Cease then this impious rage,   845
And tempt not these; but hast'n to appease
Th' incensed Father, and th' incensed Son,
While Pardon may be found in time besought.
   So spake the fervent Angel, but his zeal
None seconded, as out of season judg'd,   850
Or singular and rash, whereat rejoic'd
Th' Apostat, and more haughty thus repli'd.
That we were formd then saist thou? and the work
Of secondarie hands, by task transferd
From Father to his Son? strange point and new!   855
Doctrin which we would know whence learnt: who saw
When this creation was? rememberst thou
Thy making, while the Maker gave thee being?
We know no time when we were not as now;
Know none before us, self-begot, self-rais'd   860
By our own quick'ning power, when fatal course
Had circl'd his full Orb, the birth mature
Of this our native Heav'n, Ethereal Sons.
Our puissance is our own, our own right hand
Shall teach us highest deeds, by proof to try   865
Who is our equal: then thou shalt behold
Whether by supplication we intend
Address, and to begirt th' Almighty Throne
Beseeching or besieging. This report,
These tidings carrie to th' anointed King;   870
And fly, ere evil intercept thy flight.
   He said, and as the sound of waters deep
Hoarce murmur echo'd to his words applause
Through the infinite Host, nor less for that
The flaming Seraph fearless, though alone   875
Encompass'd round with foes, thus answerd bold.
   O alienate from God, O spirit accurst,

Forsak'n of all good; I see thy fall
Determind, and thy hapless[47] crew involv'd
In this perfidious fraud, contagion spred   880
Both of thy crime and punishment: henceforth
No more be troubl'd how to quit the yoke
Of Gods *Messiah;* those indulgent Laws
Will not be now voutsaf't, other Decrees
Against thee are gon forth without recall;   885
That Golden Scepter which thou didst reject
Is now an Iron Rod to bruise and break
Thy disobedience. Well thou didst advise,
Yet not for thy advise or threats I fly
These wicked Tents devoted,[48] least the wrauth   890
Impendent, raging into sudden flame
Distinguish not: for soon expect to feel
His Thunder on thy head, devouring fire.
Then who created thee lamenting learn,
When who can uncreate thee thou shalt know.   895
     So spake the Seraph *Abdiel* faithful found,
Among the faithless, faithful only hee;
Among innumerable false, unmov'd,
Unshak'n, unseduc'd, unterrifi'd
His Loyaltie he kept, his Love, his Zeal;   900
Nor number, nor example with him wrought
To swerve from truth, or change his constant mind
Though single. From amidst them forth he pass'd,
Long way through hostile scorn, which he susteind
Superior, nor of violence fear'd aught;   905
And with retorted[49] scorn his back he turn'd
On those proud Towrs to swift destruction doom'd.

[47] not only because they cannot have luck, but also because opposition to God does not allow a chance outcome. Thus such opposition as is proposed is a "fraud."
[48] doomed.
[49] turned back.

BOOK VI

THE ARGUMENT

Raphael continues to relate how *Michael* and *Gabriel* were sent forth to battel against *Satan* and his Angels. The first Fight describ'd: *Satan* and his Powers retire under Night: He calls a Councel, invents devilish Engines, which in the second dayes Fight put *Michael* and his Angels to some disorder; but they at length pulling up Mountains overwhelm'd

both the force and Machins of *Satan:* Yet the Tumult not so ending, God
on the third day sends *Messiah* his Son, for whom he had reserv'd the
glory of that Victory: Hee in the Power of his Father coming to the
place, and causing all his Legions to stand still on either side, with his
Chariot and Thunder driving into the midst of his Enemies, pursues
them unable to resist towards the wall of Heaven; which opening,
they leap down with horrour and confusion into the place of punish-
ment prepar'd for them in the Deep: *Messiah* returns with triumph to
his Father.

All night the dreadless Angel unpursu'd
Through Heav'ns wide Champain held his way, till Morn,
Wak't by the circling Hours, with rosie hand
Unbarr'd the gates of Light. There is a Cave
Within the Mount of God, fast by his Throne,   5
Where light and darkness in perpetual round
Lodge and dislodge by turns, which makes through Heav'n
Grateful vicissitude,[1] like Day and Night;
Light issues forth, and at the other dore
Obsequious[2] darkness enters, till her hour   10
To veil the Heav'n, though darkness there might well
Seem twilight here; and now went forth the Morn
Such as in highest Heav'n, arrayd in Gold
Empyreal, from before her vanisht Night,
Shot through with orient Beams: when all the Plain   15
Coverd with thick embatteld Squadrons bright,
Chariots and flaming Armes, and fierie Steeds
Reflecting blaze on blaze, first met his view:
Warr he perceav'd, warr in procinct,[3] and found
Already known what he for news had thought   20
To have reported: gladly then he mixt
Among those friendly Powers who him receav'd
With joy and acclamations loud, that one
That of so many Myriads fall'n, yet one
Returnd not lost: On to the sacred hill   25
They led him high applauded, and present
Before the seat supream; from whence a voice
From midst a Golden Cloud thus mild was heard.
Servant of God,[4] well done, well hast thou fought

---

[1] "change, variety, movement, the mark of vitality and joy characteristic of
both the divine and the human master artist's work" (Joseph H. Summers, *The
Muse's Method*, p. 71).
[2] compliantly following.
[3] readiness.
[4] the literal meaning of Abdiel.

The better fight, who single hast maintaind   30
Against revolted multitudes the Cause
Of Truth, in word mightier then they in Armes;
And for the testimonie of Truth hast born
Universal reproach, far worse to bear
Then violence: for this was all thy care   35
To stand approv'd in sight of God, though Worlds
Judg'd thee perverse: the easier conquest now
Remains thee, aided by this host of friends,
Back on thy foes more glorious to return
Then scornd thou didst depart, and to subdue   40
By force, who reason for thir Law refuse,
Right reason for thir Law, and for thir King
Messiah, who by right of merit Reigns.
Go Michael of Celestial Armies Prince,
And thou in Military prowess next   45
Gabriel, lead forth to Battel these my Sons
Invincible, lead forth my armed Saints
By Thousands and by Millions rang'd for fight;
Equal in number to that Godless crew
Rebellious, them with Fire and hostile Armes   50
Fearless assault, and to the brow of Heav'n
Pursuing drive them out from God and bliss,
Into thir place of punishment, the Gulf
Of Tartarus, which ready opens wide
His fiery Chaos to receave thir fall.   55
   So spake the Sovran voice, and Clouds began
To darken all the Hill, and smoak to rowl
In duskie wreaths, reluctant flames, the signe
Of wrauth awak't: nor with less dread the loud
Ethereal Trumpet from on high gan blow: 60
At which command the Powers Militant,
That stood for Heav'n, in mighty Quadrate[5] joyn'd
Of Union irresistible, mov'd on
In silence thir bright Legions, to the sound
Of instrumental Harmonie that breath'd   65
Heroic Ardor to advent'rous deeds
Under thir God-like Leaders, in the Cause
Of God and his Messiah. On they move
Indissolubly firm; nor obvious[6] Hill,
Nor streit'ning[7] Vale, nor Wood, nor Stream divides   70

[5] (a maneuver in the shape of a) square.
[6] lying in the way.
[7] narrowing.

Thir perfet ranks; for high above the ground
Thir march was, and the passive Air upbore
Thir nimble tread, as when the total kind
Of Birds in orderly array on wing
Came summond over *Eden* to receive   75
Thir names of thee; so over many a tract
Of Heav'n they march'd, and many a Province wide
Tenfold the length of this terrene: at last
Farr in th' Horizon to the North appeer'd
From skirt to skirt a fierie Region, stretcht   80
In battailous aspect, and neerer view
Bristl'd with upright beams innumerable
Of rigid Spears, and Helmets throng'd, and Shields
Various, with boastful Argument[8] portraid,
The banded Powers of *Satan* hasting on   85
With furious expedition; for they weend
That self-same day by fight, or by surprize
To win the Mount of God, and on his Throne
To set the envier of his State, the proud
Aspirer, but thir thoughts prov'd fond and vain   90
In the mid way: though strange to us it seemd
At first, that Angel should with Angel warr,
And in fierce hosting[9] meet, who wont to meet
So oft in Festivals of joy and love
Unanimous, as sons of one great Sire   95
Hymning th' Eternal Father: but the shout
Of Battel now began, and rushing sound
Of onset ended soon each milder thought.
High in the midst exalted as a God
Th' Apostat in his Sun-bright Chariot sate   100
Idol of Majestie Divine, enclos'd
With Flaming Cherubim, and golden Shields;
Then lighted from his gorgeous Throne, for now
'Twixt Host and Host but narrow space was left,
A dreadful intervall, and Front to Front   105
Presented stood in terrible array
Of hideous length: before the cloudie Van,
On the rough edge of battel ere it joyn'd,
Satan with vast and haughtie strides advanc't,
Came towring, armd in Adamant and Gold;   110
Abdiel that sight endur'd not, where he stood
Among the mightiest, bent on highest deeds,

---

[8] inscription.
[9] fighting of hosts (of angels).

THE COMPLETE POETRY OF JOHN MILTON

And thus his own undaunted heart explores.
O Heav'n! that such resemblance of the Highest
Should yet remain, where faith and realtie[10]   115
Remain not; wherfore should not strength and might
There fail where Vertue fails, or weakest prove
Where boldest; though to sight unconquerable?
His puissance, trusting in th' Almightie's aid,
I mean to try, whose Reason I have tri'd[11]   120
Unsound and false; nor is it aught but just,
That he who in debate of Truth hath won,
Should win in Arms, in both disputes alike
Victor; though brutish that contest and foul,
When Reason hath to deal with force, yet so   125
Most reason is that Reason overcome.
     So pondering, and from his armed Peers
Forth stepping opposite, half way he met
His daring foe, at this prevention more
Incens't, and thus securely him defi'd.   130
     Proud, art thou met? thy hope was to have reacht
The highth of thy aspiring unoppos'd,
The Throne of God unguarded, and his side
Abandond at the terror of thy Power
Or potent tongue; fool, not to think how vain   135
Against th' Omnipotent to rise in Arms;
Who out of smallest things could without end
Have rais'd incessant Armies to defeat
Thy folly; or with solitarie hand
Reaching beyond all limit at one blow   140
Unaided could have finisht thee, and whelmd
Thy Legions under darkness; but thou seest
All are not of thy Train; there be who Faith
Prefer, and Pietie to God, though then
To thee not visible, when I alone   145
Seemd in thy World erroneous to dissent
From all: my Sect thou seest, now learn too late
How few somtimes may know, when thousands err.
     Whom the grand foe with scornful eye askance
Thus answerd. Ill for thee, but in wisht hour   150
Of my revenge, first sought for thou returnst
From flight, seditious Angel, to receave
Thy merited reward, the first assay[12]

[10] loyalty.
[11] tested and found.
[12] trial.

Of this right hand provok't, since first that tongue
Inspir'd with contradiction durst oppose   155
A third part of the Gods, in Synod met
Thir Deities to assert, who while they feel
Vigour Divine within them, can allow
Omnipotence to none. But well thou comst
Before thy fellows, ambitious to win   160
From me som Plume, that thy success may show
Destruction to the rest: this pause between
(Unanswerd least thou boast) to let thee know;
At first I thought that Libertie and Heav'n
To heav'nly Souls had bin all one: but now   165
I see that most through sloth had rather serve,
Ministring Spirits, traind up in Feast and Song;
Such hast thou arm'd, the Minstrelsie[13] of Heav'n,
Servilitie with freedom to contend,
As both thir deeds compar'd this day shall prove.   170
    To whom in brief thus *Abdiel* stern repli'd.
Apostat, still thou errst, nor end wilt find
Of erring, from the path of truth remote:
Unjustly thou deprav'st it with the name
Of *Servitude* to serve whom God ordains,   175
Or Nature; God and Nature bid the same,
When he who rules is worthiest, and excells
Them whom he governs. This is servitude,
To serve th' unwise, or him who hath rebell'd
Against his worthier, as thine now serve thee,   180
Thy self not free, but to thy self enthrall'd;
Yet leudly dar'st our ministring upbraid.
Reign thou in Hell thy Kingdom, let mee serve
In Heav'n God ever blest, and his Divine
Behests obey, worthiest to be obey'd,   185
Yet Chains in Hell, not Realms expect: mean while
From mee returnd, as erst thou saidst, from flight,
This greeting on thy impious Crest receive.
    So saying, a noble stroke he lifted high,
Which hung not, but so swift with tempest fell   190
On the proud Crest of *Satan*, that no sight,
Nor motion of swift thought, less could his Shield
Such ruin intercept: ten paces huge
He back recoild; the tenth on bended knee
His massie Spear upstaid; as if on Earth   195
Winds under ground or waters forcing way

[13] the angels who sing God's hymns and whom Satan calls servile.

Sidelong, had push't a Mountain from his seat
Half sunk with all his Pines. Amazement seis'd
The Rebel Thrones, but greater rage to see
Thus foil'd thir mightiest, ours joy fill'd, and shout,   200
Presage of Victorie and fierce desire
Of Battel: whereat *Michael* bid sound
Th' Arch-Angel trumpet; through the vast of Heav'n
It sounded, and the faithful Armies rung
Hosanna to the Highest: nor stood at gaze   205
The adverse Legions, nor less hideous joyn'd
The horrid shock: now storming furie rose,
And clamour such as heard in Heav'n till now
Was never, Arms on Armour clashing bray'd
Horrible discord, and the madding Wheels   210
Of brazen Chariots rag'd; dire was the noise
Of conflict; over head the dismal hiss
Of fiery Darts in flaming volies flew,
And flying vaulted either Host with fire.
So under fierie Cope[14] together rush'd   215
Both Battels main, with ruinous assault
And inextinguishable rage; all Heav'n
Resounded, and had Earth bin then, all Earth
Had to her Center shook. What wonder? when
Millions of fierce encountring Angels fought   220
On either side, the least of whom could weild
These Elements, and arm him with the force
Of all thir Regions: how much more of Power
Armie against Armie numberless to raise
Dreadful combustion warring, and disturb,   225
Though not destroy, thir happie Native seat;
Had not th' Eternal King Omnipotent
From his strong hold of Heav'n high over-rul'd
And limited thir might; though numberd such
As each divided Legion might have seemd   230
A numerous Host, in strength each armed hand
A Legion; led in fight, yet Leader seemd
Each Warriour single as in Chief, expert
When to advance, or stand, or turn the sway
Of Battel, open when, and when to close   235
The ridges[15] of grim Warr; no thought of flight,
None of retreat, no unbecoming deed
That argu'd fear; each on himself reli'd,

[14] canopy of the sky.
[15] lines of warriors.

As onely in his arm the moment[16] lay
Of victorie; deeds of eternal fame   240
Were don, but infinite: for wide was spred
That Warr and various; somtimes on firm ground
A standing fight, then soaring on main wing
Tormented all the Air; all Air seemd then
Conflicting Fire: long time in eeven scale   245
The Battel hung; till *Satan*, who that day
Prodigious power had shewn, and met in Armes
No equal, raunging through the dire attack
Of fighting Seraphim confus'd, at length
Saw where the Sword of *Michael* smote, and fell'd   250
Squadrons at once, with huge two-handed sway
Brandisht aloft the horrid edge came down
Wide wasting; such destruction to withstand
He hasted, and oppos'd the rockie Orb
Of tenfold Adamant, his ample Shield   255
A vast circumference: At his approach
The great Arch-Angel from his warlike toil
Surceas'd, and glad as hoping here to end
Intestine War in Heav'n, th' arch foe subdu'd
Or Captive drag'd in Chains, with hostile frown   260
And visage all enflam'd first thus began.
    Author of evil, unknown till thy revolt,
Unnam'd in Heav'n, now plenteous, as thou seest
These Acts of hateful strife, hateful to all,
Though heaviest by just measure on thy self   265
And thy adherents: how hast thou disturb'd
Heav'ns blessed peace, and into Nature brought
Miserie, uncreated till the crime
Of thy Rebellion? how hast thou instill'd
Thy malice into thousands, once upright   270
And faithful, now prov'd false. But think not here
To trouble Holy Rest; Heav'n casts thee out
From all her Confines. Heav'n the seat of bliss
Brooks not the works of violence and Warr.
Hence then, and evil go with thee along   275
Thy ofspring, to the place of evil, Hell,
Thou and thy wicked crew; there mingle broils,
Ere this avenging Sword begin thy doom,
Or som more sudden vengeance wing'd from God
Precipitate thee with augmented pain.   280
    So spake the Prince of Angels; to whom thus

---

[16] the mechanical tendency to move.

The Adversarie. Nor think thou with wind
Of airie threats to aw whom yet with deeds
Thou canst not. Hast thou turnd the least of these
To flight, or if to fall, but that they rise   285
Unvanquisht, easier to transact with mee
That thou shouldst hope, imperious, and with threats
To chase me hence? err not that so shall end
The strife which thou call'st evil, but wee style
The strife of Glorie: which we mean to win,   290
Or turn this Heav'n it self into the Hell
Thou fablest, here however to dwell free,
If not to reign: mean while thy utmost force,
And join him nam'd *Almighty* to thy aid,
I flie not, but have sought thee farr and nigh.   295
    They ended parle, and both addrest[17] for fight
Unspeakable; for who, though with the tongue
Of Angels, can relate, or to what things
Liken on Earth conspicuous, that may lift
Human imagination to such highth   300
Of Godlike Power: for likest Gods they seemd,
Stood they or mov'd, in stature, motion, arms
Fit to decide the Empire of great Heav'n.
Now wav'd thir fierie Swords, and in the Air
Made horrid Circles; two broad Suns thir Shields   305
Blaz'd opposite, while expectation stood
In horror; from each hand with speed retir'd
Where erst was thickest fight, th' Angelic throng,
And left large field, unsafe within the wind
Of such commotion, such as to set forth   310
Great things by small, if Natures concord broke,
Among the Constellations warr were sprung,
Two Planets rushing from aspect maligne
Of fiercest opposition in mid Skie,
Should combat, and thir jarring Sphears confound.   315
Together both with next t' Almightie Arm,
Uplifted imminent one stroke they aim'd
That might determine,[18] and not need repeat,
As not of power, at once; nor odds[19] appeerd
In might or swift prevention; but the sword   320
Of *Michael* from the Armorie of God
Was giv'n him temperd so, that neither keen

[17] prepared.
[18] (the outcome).
[19] advantage; "prevention" (l. 320) means "anticipation."

Nor solid might resist that edge; it met
The sword of *Satan* with steep force to smite
Descending, and in half cut sheer, not staid,   325
But with swift wheel reverse, deep entring shar'd
All his right side; then *Satan* first knew pain,
And writh'd him to and fro convolv'd; so sore
The griding[20] sword with discontinuous wound
Pass'd through him, but th' Ethereal substance clos'd   330
Not long divisible, and from the gash
A stream of Nectarous humor issuing flow'd
Sanguin, such as Celestial Spirits may bleed,
And all his Armour staind ere while so bright.
Forthwith on all sides to his aid was run   ·   335
By Angels many and strong, who interpos'd
Defence, while others bore him on thir Shields
Back to his Chariot; where it stood retir'd
From off the files of warr; there they him laid
Gnashing for anguish and despite and shame   340
To find himself not matchless, and his pride
Humbl'd by such rebuke, so farr beneath
His confidence to equal God in power.
Yet soon he heal'd; for Spirits that live throughout
Vital in every part, not as frail man   345
In Entrails, Heart or Head, Liver or Reins,
Cannot but by annihilating die;
Nor in thir liquid texture mortal wound
Receive, no more then can the fluid Air:
All Heart they live, all Head, all Eye, all Ear,   350
All Intellect, all Sense, and as they please,
They Limb themselves, and colour, shape or size
Assume, as likes them best, condense or rare.
    Mean while in other parts like deeds deserv'd
Memorial, where the might of *Gabriel* fought,   355
And with fierce Ensignes pierc'd the deep array
Of *Moloc* furious King, who him defi'd,
And at his Chariot wheels to drag him bound
Threat'n'd, nor from the Holie One of Heav'n
Refrein'd his tongue blasphemous; but anon   360
Down clov'n to the waste, with shatterd Armes
And uncouth pain fled bellowing. On each wing
Uriel and *Raphael* his vaunting foe,
Though huge, and in a Rock of Diamond Armd,
Vanquish'd *Adramelec*, and *Asmadai*,   365

[20] cutting, thus "discontinuing" or separating the flesh.

Two potent Thrones, that to be less then Gods
Disdain'd, but meaner thoughts learnd in thir flight,
Mangl'd with gastly wounds through Plate and Mail.
Nor stood unmindful *Abdiel* to annoy
The Atheist crew, but with redoubl'd blow   370
Ariel and *Arioc*, and the violence
Of *Ramiel* scorcht and blasted overthrew.
I might relate of thousands, and thir names
Eternize here on Earth; but those elect
Angels contented with thir fame in Heav'n   375
Seek not the praise of men: the other sort
In might though wondrous and in Acts of Warr,
Nor of Renown less eager, yet by doom
Canceld from Heav'n and sacred memorie,
Nameless in dark oblivion let them dwell.   380
For strength from Truth divided and from Just,
Illaudable, naught merits but dispraise
And ignominie, yet to glorie aspires
Vain glorious, and through infamie seeks fame:
Therfore Eternal silence be thir doom.   385
    And now thir mightiest quell'd, the battel swerv'd,
With many an inrode gor'd; deformed rout
Enter'd, and foul disorder; all the ground
With shiverd armour strown, and on a heap
Chariot and Charioter lay overturnd   390
And fierie foaming Steeds; what stood, recoyld
Orewearied, through the faint Satanic Host
Defensive scarse, or with pale fear surpris'd,
Then first with fear surpris'd and sense of pain
Fled ignominious, to such evil brought   395
By sin of disobedience, till that hour
Not liable to fear or flight or pain.
Far otherwise th' inviolable Saints
In Cubic Phalanx firm advanc't entire,
Invulnerable, impenitrably arm'd: 400
Such high advantages thir innocence
Gave them above thir foes, not to have sinn'd,
Not to have disobei'd; in fight they stood
Unwearied, unobnoxious[21] to be pain'd
By wound, though from thir place by violence mov'd.   405
    Now Night her course began, and over Heav'n
Inducing darkness, grateful truce impos'd,
And silence on the odious dinn of Warr:

[21] not subject to injury.

Under her Cloudie covert both retir'd,
Victor and Vanquisht: on the foughten field   410
Michael and his Angels prevalent[22]
Encamping, plac'd in Guard thir Watches round,
Cherubic waving fires: on th' other part
Satan with his rebellious disappeerd,
Far in the dark dislodg'd, and void of rest,   415
His Potentates to Councel call'd by night;
And in the midst thus undismai'd began.
   O now in danger tri'd, now known in Armes
Not to be overpowerd, Companions dear,
Found worthy not of Libertie alone,   420
Too mean pretense, but what we more affect,
Honour, Dominion, Glorie, and renown,
Who have sustaind one day in doubtful fight
(And if one day, why not Eternal dayes?)
What Heavens Lord had powerfullest to send   425
Against us from about his Throne, and judg'd
Sufficient to subdue us to his will,
But proves not so: then fallible, it seems,
Of future we may deem him, though till now
Omniscient thought. True is, less firmly arm'd,   430
Some disadvantage we endur'd and pain,
Till now not known, but known as soon contemn'd,
Since now we find this our Empyreal form
Incapable of mortal injurie
Imperishable, and though peirc'd with wound,   435
Soon closing, and by native vigour heal'd.
Of evil then so small as easie think
The remedie; perhaps more valid Armes,
Weapons more violent, when next we meet,
May serve to better us, and worse our foes,   440
Or equal what between us made the odds,
In Nature none: if other hidden cause
Left them Superiour, while we can preserve
Unhurt our minds, and understanding sound,
Due search and consultation will disclose.   445
   He sat; and in th' assembly next upstood
Nisroc,[23] of Principalities the prime;
As one he stood escap't from cruel fight,
Sore toild, his riv'n Armes to havoc hewn,
And cloudie in aspect thus answering spake.   450

[22] dominant, victorious.
[23] an Assyrian deity; see 2 Kings xix. 37.

Deliverer from new Lords, leader to free
Enjoyment of our right as Gods; yet hard
For Gods, and too unequal work we find
Against unequal armes to fight in pain,
Against unpaind, impassive;[24] from which evil   455
Ruin must needs ensue; for what avails
Valour or strength, though matchless, quell'd with pain
Which all subdues, and makes remiss the hands
Of Mightiest. Sense of pleasure we may well
Spare out of life perhaps, and not repine,   460
But live content, which is the calmest life:
But pain is perfet miserie, the worst
Of evils, and excessive, overturns
All patience. He who therefore can invent
With what more forcible we may offend   465
Our yet unwounded Enemies, or arm
Our selves with like defence, to me deserves
No less then for deliverance what we owe.
    Whereto with look compos'd *Satan* repli'd.
Not uninvented that, which thou aright   470
Beleivst so main to our success, I bring;
Which of us who beholds the bright surface
Of this Ethereous mould whereon we stand,
This continent of spacious Heav'n, adornd
With Plant, Fruit, Flowr Ambrosial, Gemms and Gold,   475
Whose Eye so superficially surveys
These things, as not to mind from whence they grow
Deep under ground, materials dark and crude,
Of spiritous and fierie spume,[25] till toucht
With Heav'ns ray, and temperd they shoot forth   480
So beauteous, op'ning to the ambient light.
These in thir dark Nativitie the Deep
Shall yeild us, pregnant with infernal flame,
Which into hollow Engins long and round
Thick-rammd, at th' other bore with touch of fire   485
Dilated and infuriate shall send forth
From far with thundring noise among our foes
Such implements of mischief as shall dash
To pieces, and orewhelm whatever stands
Adverse, that they shall fear we have disarmd   490
The Thunderer of his only dreaded bolt.
Nor long shall be our labour, yet ere dawn,

[24] incapable of feeling.
[25] foam of air and fire (acting below the earth); see l. 512.

Effect shall end our wish. Mean while revive;
Abandon fear; to strength and counsel joind
Think nothing hard, much less to be despaird.   495
He ended, and his words thir drooping chere[26]
Enlight'n'd, and thir languisht hope reviv'd.
Th' invention all admir'd, and each, how hee
To be th' inventer miss'd, so easie it seemd
Once found, which yet unfound most would have thought   500
Impossible: yet haply of thy Race
In future dayes, if Malice should abound,
Some one intent on mischief, or inspir'd
With dev'lish machination might devise
Like instrument to plague the Sons of men   505
For sin, on warr and mutual slaughter bent.
Forthwith from Councel to the work they flew,
None arguing stood, innumerable hands
Were ready, in a moment up they turnd
Wide the Celestial soil, and saw beneath   510
Th' originals of Nature in thir crude
Conception; Sulphurous and Nitrous Foam
They found, they mingl'd, and with suttle Art,
Concocted and adusted[27] they reduc'd
To blackest grain, and into store convey'd: 515
Part hidd'n veins digg'd up (nor hath this Earth
Entrails unlike) of Mineral and Stone,
Whereof to found thir Engins and thir Balls
Of missive ruin;[28] part incentive reed
Provide, pernicious with one touch to fire.   520
So all ere day-spring, under conscious Night
Secret they finish'd, and in order set,
With silent circumspection unespi'd.
Now when fair Morn Orient in Heav'n appeerd
Up rose the Victor Angels, and to Arms   525
The matin Trumpet Sung: in Arms they stood
Of Golden Panoplie, refulgent Host,
Soon banded; others from the dawning Hills
Look'd round, and Scouts each Coast light-armed scour,
Each quarter, to descrie the distant foe,   530
Where lodg'd, or whither fled, or if for fight,

[26] countenance.
[27] cooked together and burned.
[28] destruction from propelled matter; the "reed" is the match which will light
the fuse.

In motion or in alt:[29] him soon they met
Under spred Ensignes moving nigh, in slow
But firm Battalion; back with speediest Sail
Zophiel,[30] of Cherubim the swiftest wing,   535
Came flying, and in mid Air aloud thus cri'd.

    Arm, Warriours, Arm for fight, the foe at hand,
Whom fled we thought, will save us long pursuit
This day, fear not his flight; so thick a Cloud
He comes, and settl'd in his face I see   540
Sad[31] resolution and secure:[32] let each
His Adamantine coat gird well, and each
Fit well his Helm, gripe fast his orbed Shield,
Born eevn or high, for this day will pour down,
If I conjecture aught, no drizling showr,   545
But ratling storm of Arrows barb'd with fire.
So warnd he them aware themselves, and soon
In order, quit of all impediment;
Instant without disturb they took Allarm,
And onward move Embattell'd; when behold   550
Not distant far with heavie pace the Foe
Approaching gross and huge; in hollow Cube
Training his devilish Enginrie, impal'd[33]
On every side with shaddowing Squadrons Deep,
To hide the fraud. At interview both stood   555
A while, but suddenly at head appeerd
Satan: And thus was heard Commanding loud.

    Vanguard, to Right and Left the Front unfould;
That all may see who hate us, how we seek
Peace and composure,[34] and with open brest   560
Stand readie to receive them, if they like
Our overture, and turn not back perverse;
But that I doubt, however witness Heav'n,
Heav'n witness thou anon, while we discharge
Freely our part; yee who appointed stand   565
Do as you have in charge, and briefly touch
What we propound, and loud that all may hear.

    So scoffing in ambiguous words he scarce
Had ended; when to Right and Left the Front

[29] halt (NED cites only in phrase "to make alt"); most editors emend to
"halt."
[30] literally, "spy of God."
[31] firmly established.
[32] without anxiety.
[33] hemmed in.
[34] agreement.

Divided, and to either Flank retir'd.   570
Which to our eyes discoverd new and strange,
A triple-mounted row of Pillars laid
On Wheels (for like to Pillars most they seem'd
Or hollow'd bodies made of Oak or Firr
With branches lopt, in Wood or Mountain fell'd)   575
Brass, Iron, Stonie mould,[35] had not thir mouths
With hideous orifice gap't on us wide,
Portending hollow truce; at each behind
A Seraph stood, and in his hand a Reed
Stood waving tipt with fire; while we suspense,[36]   580
Collected stood within our thoughts amus'd,[37]
Not long, for sudden all at once thir Reeds
Put forth, and to a narrow vent appli'd
With nicest[38] touch. Immediate in a flame,
But soon obscur'd with smoak, all Heav'n appeerd,   585
From those deep-throated Engins belcht, whose roar
Emboweld[39] with outragious noise the Air,
And all her entrails tore, disgorging foul
Thir devilish glut, chaind Thunderbolts and Hail
Of Iron Globes, which on the Victor Host   590
Level'd, with such impetuous furie smote,
That whom they hit, none on thir feet might stand,
Though standing else as Rocks, but down they fell
By thousands, Angel on Arch-Angel rowl'd;
The sooner for thir Arms, unarm'd they might   595
Have easily as Spirits evaded swift
By quick contraction or remove; but now
Foul dissipation follow'd and forc't rout;
Nor serv'd it to relax thir serried files.
What should they do? if on they rusht, repulse   600
Repeated, and indecent overthrow
Doubl'd, would render them yet more despis'd,
And to thir foes a laughter; for in view
Stood rankt of Seraphim another row
In posture to displode thir second tire[40]   605
Of Thunder: back defeated to return
They worse abhorr'd. *Satan* beheld thir plight,
And to his Mates thus in derision call'd.

[35] material (of the earth).
[36] hanging in wonder and curiosity.
[37] wondering.
[38] most fastidious.
[39] filled.
[40] discharge.

O Friends, why come not on these Victors proud?
Ere while they fierce were coming, and when wee,   610
To entertain them fair with open Front
And Brest (what could we more?), propounded terms
Of composition,[41] strait they chang'd thir minds,
Flew off, and into strange vagaries fell,
As they would dance, yet for a dance they seemd   615
Somwhat extravagant and wild, perhaps
For joy of offerd peace: but I suppose
If our proposals once again were heard
We should compel them to a quick result.
To whom thus *Belial* in like gamesom mood.   620
Leader, the terms we sent were terms of weight,
Of hard contents, and full of force urg'd home,
Such as we might perceive amus'd them all,
And stumbl'd many, who receives them right,
Had need from head to foot well understand;   625
Not understood, this gift they have besides,
They shew us when our foes walk not upright.
So they among themselves in pleasant vein
Stood scoffing, highth'n'd in thir thoughts beyond
All doubt of Victorie, eternal might   630
To match with thir inventions they presum'd
So easie, and of his Thunder made a scorn,
And all his Host derided, while they stood
A while in trouble; but they stood not long,
Rage prompted them at length, and found them arms   635
Against such hellish mischief fit t' oppose.
Forthwith (behold the excellence, the power
Which God hath in his mighty Angels plac'd)
Thir Arms away they threw, and to the Hills
(For Earth hath this variety from Heav'n   640
Of pleasure situate in Hill and Dale)
Light as the Lightning glimps they ran, they flew,
From thir foundations loosning to and fro
They pluckt the seated Hills with all thir load,
Rocks, Waters, Woods, and by the shaggie tops   645
Up lifting bore them in thir hands:[42] Amaze,
Be sure, and terrour seis'd the rebel Host,
When coming towards them so dread they saw
The bottom of the Mountains upward turn'd,
Till on those cursed Engins triple-row   650

[41] unification, mutual agreement.
[42] Compare the piling of Mt. Pelion on Mt. Ossa by the Giants of earth.

They saw them whelm'd, and all thir confidence
Under the weight of Mountains buried deep,
Themselves invaded next, and on thir heads
Main Promontories flung, which in the Air
Came shadowing, and opprest whole Legions arm'd, 655
Thir armor help'd thir harm, crush't in and bruis'd
Into thir substance pent, which wrought them pain
Implacable, and many a dolorous groan,
Long strugling underneath, ere they could wind
Out of such prison, though Spirits of purest light, 660
Purest at first, now gross by sinning grown.
The rest in imitation to like Armes
Betook them, and the neighbouring Hills uptore;
So Hills amid the Air encounterd Hills
Hurl'd to and fro with jaculation dire, 665
That under ground they fought in dismal shade;
Infernal noise; Warr seem'd a civil[43] Game
To this uproar; horrid confusion heapt
Upon confusion rose: and now all Heav'n
Had gon to wrack, with ruin overspred, 670
Had not th' Almightie Father where he sits
Shrin'd in his Sanctuarie of Heav'n secure,
Consulting on the sum of things, foreseen
This tumult, and permitted all, advis'd:[44]
That his great purpose he might so fulfill, 675
To honour his Anointed Son aveng'd
Upon his enemies, and to declare
All power on him transferr'd: whence to his Son
Th' Assessor[45] of his Throne he thus began.
  Effulgence of my Glorie, Son belov'd, 680
Son in whose face invisible is beheld
Visibly, what by Deitie I am,
And in whose hand what by Decree I doe,
Second Omnipotence, two dayes are past,
Two dayes, as we compute the dayes of Heav'n, 685
Since *Michael* and his Powers went forth to tame
These disobedient; sore hath been thir fight,
As likeliest was, when two such Foes met arm'd;
For to themselves I left them, and thou knowst,
Equal in their Creation they were form'd, 690
Save what sin hath impaird, which yet hath wrought

---

[43] both nonmilitary and civilized.
[44] after having thought it out.
[45] sharer.

Insensibly, for I suspend thir doom;
Whence in perpetual fight they needs must last
Endless, and no solution will be found:
Warr wearied hath perform'd what Warr can do,   695
And to disorder'd rage let loose the reins,
With Mountains as with Weapons arm'd, which makes
Wild work in Heav'n, and dangerous to the main.
Two dayes are therefore past, the third is thine;
For thee I have ordain'd it, and thus farr   700
Have sufferd, that the Glorie may be thine
Of ending this great Warr, since none but Thou
Can end it. Into thee such Vertue and Grace
Immense I have transfus'd, that all may know
In Heav'n and Hell thy Power above compare,   705
And this perverse Commotion governd thus,
To manifest thee worthiest to be Heir
Of all things, to be Heir and to be King
By Sacred Unction,[46] thy deserved right.
Go then thou Mightiest in thy Fathers might,   710
Ascend my Chariot, guide the rapid Wheels
That shake Heav'ns basis, bring forth all my Warr,
My Bow and Thunder, my Almightie Arms
Gird on, and Sword upon thy puissant Thigh;
Pursue these sons of Darkness, drive them out   715
From all Heav'ns bounds into the utter Deep:
There let them learn, as likes them, to despise
God and *Messiah* his anointed King.
    He said, and on his Son with Rayes direct
Shon full, he all his Father full exprest   720
Ineffably into his face receiv'd,
And thus the filial Godhead answering spake.
    O Father, O Supream of heav'nly Thrones,
First, Highest, Holiest, Best, thou alwayes seekst
To glorifie thy Son, I alwayes thee,   725
As is most just; this I my Glorie account,
My exaltation, and my whole delight,
That thou in me well pleas'd, declarst thy will
Fulfill'd, which to fulfil is all my bliss.
Scepter and Power, thy giving, I assume,   730
And gladlier shall resign, when in the end
Thou shalt be All in All,[47] and I in thee
For ever, and in mee all whom thou lov'st:

[46] anointing; see *PL* III, 317.
[47] See *PL* III, n. 18.

But whom thou hat'st, I hate, and can put on
Thy terrors, as I put thy mildness on, 735
Image of thee in all things; and shall soon,
Armd with thy might, rid heav'n of these rebell'd,
To thir prepar'd ill Mansion driven down
To chains of darkness, and th' undying Worm,[48]
That from thy just obedience could revolt, 740
Whom to obey is happiness entire.
Then shall thy Saints unmixt, and from th' impure
Farr separate, circling thy holy Mount
Unfained *Halleluiahs* to thee sing,
Hymns of high praise, and I among them chief. 745
So said, he o're his Scepter bowing, rose
From the right hand of Glorie where he sate,
And the third sacred Morn began to shine
Dawning through Heav'n: forth rush'd with whirlwind sound
The Chariot[49] of Paternal Deitie, 750
Flashing thick flames, Wheel within Wheel undrawn,
It self instinct[50] with Spirit, but convoyd
By four Cherubic shapes, four Faces each
Had wondrous, as with Starrs thir bodies all
And Wings were set with Eyes, with Eyes the wheels 755
Of Beril, and careering[51] Fires between;
Over thir heads a chrystal Firmament,
Whereon a Saphir Throne, inlaid with pure
Amber, and colours of the showrie Arch.
Hee in Celestial Panoplie all armd 760
Of radiant *Urim*,[52] work divinely wrought,
Ascended, at his right hand Victorie
Sate Eagle-wing'd, beside him hung his Bow
And Quiver with three-bolted Thunder stor'd,
And from about him fierce Effusion rowld 765
Of smoak and bickering[53] flame, and sparkles dire;
Attended with ten thousand thousand Saints,
He onward came, farr off his coming shon,
And twentie thousand (I thir number heard)

[48] inward torment. Mark ix. 44: "Where their worm dieth not, and the fire is not quenched."
[49] See Ezek. i, a foreshadowing of the Last Day.
[50] imbued.
[51] running at full speed.
[52] the jewels of Aaron's breastplate (Exod. xxviii. 30); see n. to III, 598. Undoubtedly significant is the first word of the next line, "Ascended": it was the central word of the 1667 edition since 5275 lines precede it and follow it.
[53] quivering.

Chariots of God, half on each hand were seen: 770
Hee on the wings of Cherub rode sublime
On the Chrystallin Skie, in Saphir Thron'd.
Illustrious farr and wide, but by his own
First seen, them unexpected joy surpriz'd,
When the great Ensign of *Messiah* blaz'd   775
Aloft by Angels born, his Sign in Heav'n:[54]
Under whose conduct *Michael* soon reduc'd[55]
His Armie, circumfus'd[56] on either Wing,
Under thir Head imbodied all in one.
Before him Power Divine his way prepar'd;   780
At his command th' uprooted Hills retir'd
Each to his place, they heard his voice and went
Obsequious, Heav'n his wonted face renewd,
And with fresh Flowrets Hill and Valley smil'd.
This saw his hapless Foes but stood obdur'd,[57]   785
And to rebellious fight rallied thir Powers
Insensate, hope conceiving from despair.
In heav'nly Spirits could such perverseness dwell?
But to convince the proud what Signs avail,
Or Wonders move th' obdurate to relent?   790
They hard'n'd more by what might most reclame,
Grieving to see his Glorie, at the sight
Took envie, and aspiring to his highth,
Stood reimbattell'd fierce, by force or fraud
Weening to prosper, and at length prevail   795
Against God and *Messiah,* or to fall
In universal ruin last, and now
To final Battel drew, disdaining flight,
Or faint retreat; when the great Son of God
To all his Host on either hand thus spake.   800
    Stand still in bright array ye Saints, here stand
Ye Angels arm'd, this day from Battel rest;
Faithful hath been your warfare, and of God
Accepted, fearless in his righteous Cause,
And as ye have receiv'd, so have ye don   805
Invincibly; but of this cursed crew
The punishment to other hand belongs,
Vengeance is his, or whose he sole appoints;

---

[54] Compare Matt. xxiv. 30: "And then shall appear the sign of the Son of
man in heaven: and then shall all the tribes of the earth mourn, and they shall
see the Son of man coming in the clouds of heaven with power and great glory."
[55] led back.
[56] diffused around.
[57] intractable.

Number to this dayes work is not ordain'd
Nor multitude, stand onely and behold   810
Gods indignation on these Godless pourd
By mee; not you but mee they have despis'd,
Yet envied; against mee is all thir rage,
Because the Father, t' whom in Heav'n supream
Kingdom and Power and Glorie appertains,   815
Hath honourd me according to his will.
Therefore to mee thir doom he hath assign'd;
That they may have thir wish, to trie with mee
In Battel which the stronger proves, they all,
Or I alone against them, since by strength   820
They measure all, of other excellence
Not emulous, nor care who them excells;
Nor other strife with them do I voutsafe.
    So spake the Son, and into terrour chang'd
His count'nance too severe to be beheld   825
And full of wrauth bent on his Enemies.
At once the Four spred out thir Starrie wings
With dreadful shade contiguous, and the Orbs
Of his fierce Chariot rowl'd, as with the sound
Of torrent Floods, or of a numerous Host.   830
Hee on his impious Foes right onward drove,
Gloomie as Night; under his burning Wheels
The stedfast Empyrean shook throughout,
All but the Throne it self of God. Full soon
Among them he arriv'd; in his right hand   835
Grasping ten thousand Thunders, which he sent
Before him, such as in thir Souls infix'd
Plagues;[58] they astonisht all resistance lost,
All courage; down thir idle weapons drop'd;
O're Shields and Helmes, and helmed heads he rode   840
Of Thrones and mighty Seraphim prostrate,
That wisht the Mountains now might be again[59]
Thrown on them as a shelter from his ire.
Nor less on either side tempestuous fell
His arrows, from the fourfold-visag'd Four,   845
Distinct with eyes, and from the living Wheels,
Distinct alike with multitude of eyes,

[58] blows.
[59] Compare Hosea x. 8 ("The high places also of Aven, the sin of Israel,
shall be destroyed . . . and they shall say to the mountains, Cover us; and to
the hills, Fall on us") and Rev. vi. 16 ("And said to the mountains and rocks,
Fall on us, and hide us from the face of him that sitteth on the throne, and from
the wrath of the Lamb"), alluding to the Last Day.

One Spirit in them rul'd, and every eye
Glar'd lightning, and shot forth pernicious fire
Among th' accurst, that witherd all thir strength,   850
And of thir wonted vigour left them draind,
Exhausted, spiritless, afflicted, fall'n.
Yet half his strength he put not forth, but check'd
His Thunder in mid Volie, for he meant
Not to destroy, but root them out of Heav'n: 855
The overthrown he rais'd, and as a Heard
Of Goats or timerous flock⁶⁰ together throng'd
Drove them before him Thunder-struck, pursu'd
With terrors and with furies to the bounds
And Chrystal wall of Heav'n, which op'ning wide,   860
Rowl'd inward, and a spacious Gap disclos'd
Into the wastful Deep; the monstrous sight
Strook them with horror backward, but far worse
Urg'd them behind; headlong themselvs they threw
Down from the verge of Heav'n, Eternal wrauth   865
Burnt after them to the bottomless pit.
    Hell heard th' unsufferable noise, Hell saw
Heav'n ruining⁶¹ from Heav'n and would have fled
Affrighted; but strict Fate had cast too deep
Her dark foundations, and too fast had bound.   870
Nine dayes they fell; confounded *Chaos* roard,
And felt tenfold confusion in thir fall
Through his wild Anarchie, so huge a rout
Incumberd him with ruin; Hell at last
Yawning receav'd them whole, and on them clos'd,   875
Hell thir fit habitation fraught with fire
Unquenchable, the house of woe and pain.
Disburd'n'd Heav'n rejoic'd, and soon repaird
Her mural breach, returning whence it rowl'd.
Sole Victor from th' expulsion of his Foes   880
Messiah his triumphal Chariot turnd:
To meet him all his Saints, who silent stood
Eye witnesses of his Almightie Acts,
With Jubilie advanc'd; and as they went,
Shaded with branching Palm, each order bright,   885
Sung Triumph, and him sung Victorious King,
Son, Heir, and Lord, to him Dominion giv'n,
Worthiest to Reign: he celebrated rode

⁶⁰ a reference to the swine that perished with the devils expelled by Jesus
(Matt. viii. 28–34); see Mother M. Christopher Pecheux's discussion in *SEL*, III
(1963), 109–17.
⁶¹ falling.

Triumphant through mid Heav'n, into the Courts
And Temple of his mightie Father Thron'd   890
On high: who into Glorie him receav'd,
Where now he sits at the right hand of bliss.
    Thus measuring things in Heav'n by things on Earth
At thy request, and that thou maist beware
By what is past, to thee I have reveal'd   895
What might have else to human Race bin hid;
The discord which befell, and Warr in Heav'n
Among th' Angelic Powers, and the deep fall
Of those too high aspiring, who rebell'd
With *Satan*, hee who envies now thy state,   900
Who now is plotting how he may seduce
Thee also from obedience, that with him
Bereav'd of happiness thou maist partake
His punishment, Eternal miserie;
Which would be all his solace and revenge,   905
As a despite don against the most High,
Thee once to gain Companion of his woe.
But list'n not to his Temptations, warn
Thy weaker;[62] let it profit thee t' have heard
By terrible Example the reward   910
Of disobedience; firm they might have stood,
Yet fell; remember, and fear to transgress.

[62] Eve.

BOOK VII

THE ARGUMENT

Raphael at the request of *Adam* relates how and wherefore this world
was first created; that God, after the expelling of *Satan* and his Angels
out of Heaven, declar'd his pleasure to create another World and other
Creatures to dwell therein; sends his Son with Glory and attendance of
Angels to perform the work of Creation in six dayes: the Angels celebrate
with Hymns the performance thereof, and his reascention into Heaven.

    Descend from Heav'n *Urania*,[1] by that name
If rightly thou art call'd, whose Voice divine

[1] usually identified as the Muse of astronomy, the meaning of whose name
("heavenly") emphasizes Milton's invoking of divine inspiration. In Prov. viii
Wisdom, from "the top of high places," tells the sons of men of the Creation,
the subject of this book. But here the reference seems to be to the Spirit of God
as in the invocations in I, III, and IX.

Following, above th' *Olympian* Hill I soar,
Above the flight of *Pegasean*[2] wing.
The meaning, not the Name I call: for thou   5
Nor of the Muses nine, nor on the top
Of old *Olympus* dwell'st, but Heav'nlie born,
Before the Hills appeerd, or Fountain flow'd,
Thou with Eternal wisdom didst converse,[3]
Wisdom thy Sister, and with her didst play   10
In presence of th' Almightie Father, pleas'd
With thy Celestial Song. Up led by thee
Into the Heav'n of Heav'ns I have presum'd,
An Earthlie Guest, and drawn Empyreal Air,
Thy tempring; with like safetie guided down   15
Return me to my Native Element:
Least from this flying Steed unrein'd (as once
Bellerophon, though from a lower Clime),
Dismounted, on th' *Aleian* Field[4] I fall
Erroneous[5] there to wander and forlorn.   20
Half yet remains unsung but narrower bound
Within the visible Diurnal Sphear;[6]
Standing on Earth, not rapt above the Pole,[7]
More safe I sing with mortal voice, unchang'd
To hoarce or mute, though fall'n on evil dayes,   25
On evil dayes though fall'n, and evil tongues;[8]
In darkness, and with dangers compast round,
And solitude; yet not alone, while thou
Visit'st my slumbers Nightly, or when Morn
Purples the East: still govern thou my Song,   30
Urania, and fit audience find, though few.
But drive farr off the barbarous dissonance
Of *Bacchus* and his revellers, the Race
Of that wild Rout that tore the *Thracian* Bard[9]
In *Rhodope*, where Woods and Rocks had Eares   35
To rapture, till the savage clamor dround

---

[2] For Pegasus and Bellerophon (l. 18), see *Rouse*, n. 8.
[3] associate, live.
[4] the field on which Bellerophon landed.
[5] straying, wandering.
[6] as opposed to the first half of the poem dealing with the invisible, eternal, formless worlds of Heaven and Hell.
[7] not transported above the primum mobile.
[8] a temporal reference to the period of the Restoration (1660 and ff.); the "darkness" (l. 27) is his blindness. Eccles. xii. 1: "Remember now thy Creator in the days of thy youth, while the evil days come not, nor the years draw nigh. . . ."
[9] Orpheus; see *Lycidas*, n. 12.

Both Harp and Voice; nor could the Muse defend
Her Son. So fail not thou, who thee implores:
For thou art Heav'nlie, shee an empty dream.
   Say Goddess, what ensu'd when *Raphael*,   40
The affable Arch-Angel, had forewarn'd
Adam by dire example to beware
Apostasie, by what befell in Heav'n
To those Apostates, least the like befall
In Paradise to *Adam* or his Race,   45
Charg'd not to touch the interdicted Tree,
If they transgress, and slight that sole command,
So easily obeyd amid the choice
Of all tasts else to please thir appetite,
Though wandring. He with his consorted[10] *Eve*   50
The storie heard attentive, and was fill'd
With admiration, and deep Muse to hear
Of things so high and strange, things to thir thought
So unimaginable as hate in Heav'n,
And Warr so neer the Peace of God in bliss   55
With such confusion: but the evil soon
Driv'n back redounded[11] as a flood on those
From whom it sprung, impossible to mix
With Blessedness. Whence *Adam* soon repeal'd[12]
The doubts that in his heart arose: and now   60
Led on, yet sinless, with desire to know
What neerer might concern him, how this World
Of Heav'n and Earth conspicuous first began,
When, and whereof created, for what cause,
What within *Eden* or without was done   65
Before his memorie, as one whose drouth
Yet scarce allay'd still eyes the current stream,
Whose liquid murmur heard new thirst excites,
Proceeded thus to ask his Heav'nly Guest.
   Great things, and full of wonder in our eares,   70
Farr differing from this World, thou hast reveal'd
Divine interpreter, by favour sent
Down from the Empyrean to forewarn
Us timely of what might else have bin our loss,
Unknown, which human knowledge could not reach: 75
For which to th' infinitly Good we owe
Immortal thanks, and his admonishment

---

[10] marital partner (from "consortium").
[11] surged back.
[12] called back.

Receave with solemn purpose to observe
Immutably his sovran will, the end
Of what we are. But since thou hast voutsaf't   80
Gently for our instruction to impart
Things above Earthly thought, which yet concernd
Our knowing, as to highest wisdom seemd,
Deign to descend now lower, and relate
What may no less perhaps avail us known,   85
How first began this Heav'n which we behold
Distant so high, with moving Fires adornd
Innumerable, and this which yeelds or fills
All space, the ambient Air wide interfus'd
Imbracing round this florid[13] Earth, what cause   90
Mov'd the Creator in his holy Rest
Through all Eternitie so late to build
In *Chaos,* and the work begun, how soon
Absolv'd,[14] if unforbid thou maist unfould
What wee, not to explore the secrets ask   95
Of his Eternal Empire, but the more
To magnifie his works, the more we know.
And the great Light of Day yet wants to run
Much of his Race though steep, suspense in Heav'n
Held by thy voice, thy potent voice he heares,   100
And longer will delay to hear thee tell
His Generation, and the rising Birth
Of Nature from the unapparent[15] Deep:
Or if the Starr of Eevning and the Moon
Haste to thy audience, Night with her will bring   105
Silence, and Sleep listning to thee will watch,[16]
Or we can bid his absence, till thy Song
End, and dismiss thee ere the Morning shine.
   Thus *Adam* his illustrious Guest besought:
And thus the Godlike Angel answerd mild.   110
This also thy request with caution askt
Obtain: though to recount Almightie works
What words or tongue of Seraph can suffice,
Or heart of man suffice to comprehend?
Yet what thou canst attain, which best may serve   115
To glorifie the Maker, and inferr
Thee also happier, shall not be withheld

[13] both "red" with moving fires (hinting at its origin) and now "adorned with flourishing vegetation."
[14] finished.
[15] unseen (since it lies outside the primum mobile) and formless.
[16] keep watch.

Thy hearing, such Commission from above
I have receav'd, to answer thy desire
Of knowledge within bounds; beyond abstain   120
To ask, nor let thine own inventions hope
Things not reveal'd, which th' invisible King,
Onely Omniscient, hath supprest in Night,
To none communicable in Earth or Heaven:
Anough is left besides to search and know.   125
But Knowledge is as food, and needs no less
Her Temperance over Appetite, to know
In measure what the mind may well contain,
Oppresses else with Surfet, and soon turns
Wisdom to Folly, as Nourishment to Wind.   130
     Know then, that after *Lucifer* from Heav'n
(So call him, brighter once amidst the Host
Of Angels, then that Starr[17] the Starrs among)
Fell with his flaming Legions through the Deep
Into his place, and the great Son returnd   135
Victorious with his saints, th' Omnipotent
Eternal Father from his Throne beheld
Thir multitude, and to his Son thus spake.
     At least our envious Foe hath fail'd, who thought
All like himself rebellious, by whose aid   140
This inaccessible high strength, the seat
Of Deitie supream, us dispossest,
He trusted to have seis'd, and into fraud
Drew many, whom thir place knows here no more;[18]
Yet farr the greater part have kept, I see,   145
Thir station, Heav'n yet populous retains
Number sufficient to possess her Realmes
Though wide, and this high Temple to frequent
With Ministeries due and solemn Rites:
But least his heart exalt him in the harm   150
Already done, to have dispeopl'd Heav'n,
My damage fondly[19] deem'd, I can repair
That detriment, if such it be to lose
Self-lost, and in a moment will create
Another World, out of one man a Race   155
Of men innumerable, there to dwell,
Not here, till by degrees of merit rais'd
They open to themselves at length the way

---

[17] Venus, called Lucifer as the morning star.
[18] Job vii. 10: "Neither shall his place know him any more."
[19] foolishly.

Up hither, under long obedience tri'd,
And Earth be chang'd to Heav'n, and Heav'n to Earth,   160
One Kingdom, Joy and Union without end.
Mean while inhabit lax,[20] ye Powers of Heav'n,
And thou my Word, begotten Son, by thee
This I perform, speak thou, and be it don:
My overshadowing Spirit and might with thee   165
I send along, ride forth, and bid the Deep
Within appointed bounds be Heav'n and Earth,
Boundless the Deep, because I am who fill
Infinitude, nor vacuous the space.
Though I uncircumscrib'd my self retire,[21]   170
And put not forth my goodness, which is free
To act or not, Necessitie and Chance
Approach not mee, and what I will is Fate.
  So spake th' Almightie, and to what he spake
His Word, the filial Godhead, gave effect.   175
Immediate are the Acts of God, more swift
Then time or motion, but to human ears
Cannot without process of speech be told,
So told as earthly notion can receave.
Great triumph and rejoycing was in Heav'n   180
When such was heard declar'd th' Almightie's will;
Glorie they sung to the most High, good will
To future men, and in thir dwellings peace:
Glorie to him whose just avenging ire
Had driven out th' ungodly from his sight   185
And th' habitations of the just; to him
Glorie and praise, whose wisdom had ordain'd
Good out of evil to create, in stead
Of Spirits maligne a better Race to bring
Into thir vacant room, and thence diffuse   190
His good to Worlds and Ages infinite.
So sang the Hierarchies: Mean while the Son
On his great Expedition now appeer'd,
Girt with Omnipotence, with Radiance crown'd
Of Majestie Divine, Sapience and Love   195
Immense, and all his Father in him shon.
About his Chariot numberless were pour'd
Cherub and Seraph, Potentates and Thrones,

[20] scattered; "fill all those relinquished areas left uninhabited by those who joined Satan."
[21] God is not limited even though he withdraws his influence from part of infinitude, thus leaving Chaos.

And Vertues, winged Spirits, and Chariots wing'd,
From th' Armoury of God, where stand of old   200
Myriads between two brazen Mountains lodg'd
Against a solemn day, harnest at hand,
Celestial Equipage; and now came forth
Spontaneous, for within them Spirit liv'd,
Attendant on thir Lord: Heav'n op'n'd wide   205
Her ever during[22] Gates, Harmonious sound
On golden Hinges moving, to let forth
The King of Glorie in his powerful Word
And Spirit coming to create new Worlds.
On heav'nly ground they stood, and from the shore   210
They view'd the vast immeasurable Abyss
Outrageous as a Sea, dark, wasteful, wild,
Up from the bottom turn'd by furious winds
And surging waves, as Mountains to assault
Heav'ns highth, and with the Center mix the Pole.   215
   Silence, ye troubl'd waves, and thou Deep, peace,
Said then th' Omnific[23] Word, your discord end:
   Nor staid, but on the Wings of Cherubim
Uplifted, in Paternal Glorie rode
Farr into *Chaos,* and the World unborn;   220
For *Chaos* heard his voice: him all his Train
Follow'd in bright procession to behold
Creation, and the wonders of his might.
Then staid the fervid Wheels, and in his hand
He took the golden Compasses,[24] prepar'd   225
In Gods Eternal store, to circumscribe
This Universe, and all created things:
One foot he center'd, and the other turn'd
Round through the vast profunditie obscure,
And said, thus farr extend, thus farr thy bounds,   230
This be thy just Circumference, O World.
Thus God the Heav'n created, thus the Earth,
Matter unform'd and void: Darkness profound
Cover'd th' Abyss: but on the watrie calm
His brooding wings the Spirit of God outspred,   235
And vital vertue infus'd, and vital warmth
Throughout the fluid Mass, but downward purg'd

[22] everlasting.
[23] all-creating.
[24] Prov. viii. 27: "When he prepared the heavens, I was there: when he set a compass upon the face of the depth."

The black tartareous[25] cold infernal dregs
Adverse to life: then founded, then conglob'd[26]
Like things to like, the rest to several place   240
Disparted, and between spun out the Air,
And Earth self ballanc't on her Center hung.
    Let ther be Light, said God,[27] and forthwith Light
Ethereal, first of things, quintessence[28] pure
Sprung from the Deep, and from her Native East   245
To journie through the airie gloom began,
Sphear'd in a radiant Cloud, for yet the Sun
Was not; shee in a cloudie Tabernacle[29]
Sojourn'd the while. God saw the Light was good;
And light from darkness by the Hemisphere   250
Divided: Light the Day, and Darkness Night
He nam'd. Thus was the first Day Eev'n and Morn:
Nor past uncelebrated, nor unsung
By the Celestial Quires, when Orient Light
Exhaling first from Darkness they beheld;   255
Birth-day of Heav'n and Earth; with joy and shout
The hollow Universal Orb they fill'd,
And touch't thir Golden Harps, and hymning prais'd
God and his works, Creatour him they sung,
Both when first Eevning was, and when first Morn.   260
    Again, God said, let ther be Firmament[30]
Amid the Waters, and let it divide
The Waters from the Waters: and God made
The Firmament, expanse of liquid, pure,
Transparent, Elemental Air, diffus'd   265
In circuit to the uttermost convex
Of this great Round: partition firm and sure,
The Waters underneath from those above
Dividing: for as Earth, so he the World

---

[25] both hellish (from Tartarus) and sedimentary (from the incrustation of the residue from grapes in wine-making).
[26] formed them into a rounded mass (the Earth). Since the Earth is spherical at creation and composed of all things like, it conforms to concepts of perfection. First light (Day) is united and then each of the four elements: air, earth, water, and fire.
[27] Interwoven through l. 593 are quotations from Genesis (i. 3–31, ii. 1–9, 15–17).
[28] ether, the fifth or highest essence (element) of life.
[29] The Son ("That glorious Form, that Light unsufferable, / And that far-beaming blaze of Majesty," *Nativity Ode*, 8–9) came in a "Poor fleshly Tabernacle" (*Passion*, 17).
[30] the heavens stretching from the seas of the universe ("Round," l. 267) to the Crystalline (watery) Sphere ("Ocean," l. 271); see Gen. i. 6–7.

Built on circumfluous Waters calm, in wide   270
Crystallin Ocean, and the loud misrule
Of *Chaos* farr remov'd, least fierce extreams
Contiguous might distemper the whole frame:
And Heav'n he nam'd the Firmament: So Eev'n
And Morning *Chorus* sung the second Day.   275
   The Earth was form'd, but in the Womb as yet
Of Waters, Embryon immature involv'd,[31]
Appeer'd not: over all the face of Earth
Main[32] Ocean flow'd, not idle, but with warm
Prolific humour soft'ning all her Globe,   280
Fermented the great Mother to conceave,
Satiate with genial[33] moisture, when God said
Be gather'd now ye Waters under Heav'n
Into one place, and let dry Land appeer.
Immediately the Mountains huge appeer   285
Emergent, and thir broad bare backs upheave
Into the Clouds, thir tops ascend the Skie:
So high as heav'd the tumid Hills, so low
Down sunk a hollow bottom broad and deep,
Capacious bed of Waters: thither they   290
Hasted with glad precipitance,[34] uprowl'd
As drops on dust conglobing from the drie;
Part rise in crystal Wall, or ridge direct,
For haste; such flight the great command impress'd
On the swift flouds: as Armies at the call   295
Of Trumpet (for of Armies thou hast heard)
Troop to thir Standard, so the watrie throng,
Wave rowling after Wave, where way they found,
If steep, with torrent rapture,[35] if through Plain,
Soft-ebbing; nor withstood them Rock or Hill,   300
But they, or under ground, or circuit wide
With Serpent errour[36] wandring, found thir way,
And on the washie Oose deep Channels wore;
Easie, e're God had bid the ground be drie,
All but within those banks, where Rivers now   305
Stream, and perpetual draw thir humid train.[37]
The dry Land, Earth, and the great receptacle

[31] rolled up, infolded.
[32] both "expansive" and "essential."
[33] fertilizing.
[34] both "speed" and "drops of rain."
[35] carried along with great haste.
[36] erratic movement (like a serpent).
[37] watery course.

Of congregated Waters he call'd Seas:
And saw that it was good, and said, Let th' Earth
Put forth the verdant Grass, Herb yeilding Seed,   310
And Fruit Tree yeilding Fruit after her kind;
Whose Seed is in her self upon the Earth.
He scarce had said, when the bare Earth, till then
Desert and bare, unsightly, unadorn'd,
Brought forth the tender Grass, whose verdure clad   315
Her Universal Face with pleasant green,
Then Herbs of every leaf, that sudden flowr'd
Op'ning thir various colours, and made gay
Her bosom smelling sweet: and these scarce blown,
Forth flourish't thick the clustring Vine, forth crept   320
The smelling Gourd, up stood the cornie Reed
Embattell'd in her field: and the humble Shrub,
And Bush with frizl'd hair implicit:[38] last
Rose as in Dance the stately Trees, and spred
Thir branches hung with copious Fruit; or gemm'd[39]   325
Thir blossoms: with high woods the hills were crownd,
With tufts[40] the vallies and each fountain side,
With borders long the Rivers. That Earth now
Seemd like to Heav'n, a seat where Gods might dwell,
Or wander with delight, and love to haunt   330
Her sacred shades: though God had yet not rain'd
Upon the Earth, and man to till the ground
None was, but from the Earth a dewie Mist
Went up and waterd all the ground, and each
Plant of the field, which e're it was in th' Earth   335
God made, and every Herb, before it grew
On the green stemm; God saw that it was good.
So Eev'n and Morn recorded the Third Day.
    Again th' Almightie spake: Let there be Lights
High in th' expanse of Heaven to divide   340
The Day from Night; and let them be for Signes,
For Seasons, and for Dayes, and circling Years,
And let them be for Lights as I ordain
Thir Office in the Firmament of Heav'n
To give Light on the Earth; and it was so.   345
And God made two great Lights, great for thir use
To Man, the greater to have rule by Day,
The less by Night altern: and made the Starrs,

[38] entwined.
[39] budded.
[40] groups of trees or shrubbery.

And set them in the Firmament of Heav'n
T' illuminate the Earth, and rule the Day   350
In thir vicissitude, and rule the Night,
And Light from Darkness to divide. God saw,
Surveying his great Work, that it was good:
For of Celestial Bodies first the Sun
A mightie Sphear he fram'd, unlightsom first,   355
Though of Ethereal Mould: then form'd the Moon
Globose, and every magnitude of Starrs,
And sowd with Starrs the Heav'n thick as a field:
Of Light by farr the greater part he took,
Transplanted from her cloudie Shrine, and plac'd   360
In the Suns Orb, made porous to receive
And drink the liquid Light, firm to retain
Her gather'd beams, great Palace now of Light.
Hither as to thir Fountain other Starrs
Repairing, in thir gold'n Urns draw Light,   365
And hence the Morning Planet guilds her horns;⁴¹
By tincture⁴² or reflection they augment
Thir small peculiar, though from human sight
So farr remote, with diminution seen.
First in his East the glorious Lamp was seen,   370
Regent of Day, and all th' Horizon round
Invested with bright Rayes, jocond to run
His Longitude through Heav'ns high rode: the gray
Dawn, and the *Pleiades* before him danc'd
Shedding sweet influence: less bright the Moon,   375
But opposite in leveld West was set
His mirror, with full face borrowing her Light
From him, for other light she needed none
In that aspect, and still that distance keeps
Till night, then in the East her turn she shines,   380
Revolv'd on Heav'ns great Axle, and her Reign
With thousand lesser Lights dividual⁴³ holds,
With thousand thousand Starrs, that then appeer'd
Spangling the Hemisphere: then first adornd
With thir bright Luminaries that Set and Rose,   385
Glad Eevning and glad Morn crownd the fourth day.
      And God said, let the Waters generate
Reptil⁴⁴ with Spawn abundant, living Soul:
And let Fowl flie above the Earth, with wings

⁴¹ Galileo had discovered the phases of Venus.
⁴² absorption of the sun's light.
⁴³ divided (amongst the "thousand lesser Lights").
⁴⁴ any creeping thing (but including fish).

Displayd on th' op'n Firmament of Heav'n.   390
And God created the great Whales, and each
Soul living, each that crept, which plenteously
The waters generated by thir kinds,
And every Bird of wing after his kind;
And saw that it was good, and bless'd them, saying,   395
Be fruitful, multiply, and in the Seas
And Lakes and running Streams the waters fill;
And let the Fowl be multiply'd on th' Earth.
Forthwith the Sounds and Seas, each Creek and Bay
With Frie innumerable swarm, and Shoals   400
Of Fish that with thir Finns and shining Scales
Glide under the green Wave, in Sculls[45] that oft
Bank the mid Sea: part single or with mate
Graze the Sea weed thir pasture, and through Groves
Of Coral stray, or sporting with quick glance   405
Show to the Sun thir wav'd coats dropt[46] with Gold,
Or in thir Pearlie shells at ease, attend
Moist nutriment, or under Rocks thir food
In jointed Armour watch: on smooth[47] the Seal,
And bended Dolphins play: part huge of bulk   410
Wallowing unweildie, enormous in thir Gate
Tempest the Ocean: there Leviathan
Hugest of living Creatures, on the Deep
Stretcht like a Promontorie sleeps or swims,
And seems a moving Land, and at his Gills   415
Draws in, and at his Trunck spouts out a Sea.
Mean while the tepid Caves, and Fens and shoares
Thir Brood as numerous hatch, from th' Egg that soon
Bursting with kindly[48] rupture forth disclos'd
Thir callow young, but featherd soon and fledge   420
They summ'd thir Penns,[49] and soaring th' air sublime
With clang despis'd the ground, under a cloud
In prospect;[50] there the Eagle and the Stork
On Cliffs and Cedar tops thir Eyries build:
Part loosly[51] wing the Region, part more wise   425
In common, rang'd in figure wedge thir way,
Intelligent of seasons, and set forth

[45] schools of fish that make a shoal in the sea (l. 403).
[46] flecked.
[47] on the smooth sea.
[48] natural.
[49] fully feathered their wings.
[50] Seen from afar, the birds seemed to be a cloud.
[51] separately.

Thir Aerie Caravan high over Seas
Flying, and over Lands with mutual wing
Easing thir flight; so stears the prudent Crane   430
Her annual Voiage, born on Winds; the Air
Floats, as they pass, fann'd with unnumber'd plumes:
From Branch to Branch the smaller Birds with song
Solac'd the Woods, and spred thir painted wings
Till Ev'n, nor then the solemn Nightingale   435
Ceas'd warbling, but all night tun'd her soft layes:
Others on Silver Lakes and Rivers Bath'd
Thir downie Brest; the Swan with Arched neck
Between her white wings mantling[52] proudly, Rows
Her state with Oarie feet: yet oft they quit   440
The Dank, and rising on stiff Pennons, towr
The mid Aereal Skie: Others on ground
Walk'd firm; the crested Cock whose clarion sounds
The silent hours, and th' other whose gay Train
Adorns him, colour'd with the Florid hue   445
Of Rainbows and Starrie Eyes. The Waters thus
With Fish replenisht, and the Air with Fowl,
Ev'ning and Morn solemniz'd the Fift day.
    The Sixt, and of Creation last arose
With Eevning Harps and Mattin, when God said,   450
Let th' Earth bring forth Soul living in her kind,
Cattel and Creeping things, and Beast of th' Earth,
Each in their kind. The Earth obey'd, and strait
Op'ning her fertil Woomb teem'd at a Birth
Innumerous living Creatures, perfet formes,   455
Limb'd and full grown: out of the ground up rose
As from his Lair the wild Beast where he wonns[53]
In Forrest wild, in Thicket, Brake, or Den;
Among the Trees in Pairs they rose, they walk'd:
The Cattel in the Fields and Meddows green: 460
Those rare and solitarie, these in flocks
Pasturing at once, and in broad Herds upsprung.
The grassie Clods now Calv'd, now half appeer'd
The Tawnie Lion, pawing to get free
His hinder parts, then springs as broke from Bonds,   465
And Rampant shakes his Brinded[54] main; the Ounce,
The Libbard, and the Tyger, as the Moal
Rising, the crumbl'd Earth above them threw

---

[52] spreading out.
[53] lives.
[54] streaked with darker color.

In Hillocks; the swift Stag from under ground
Bore up his branching head: scarse from his mould   470
Behemoth[55] biggest born of Earth upheav'd
His vastness: Fleec't the Flocks and bleating rose,
As Plants: ambiguous between Sea and Land
The River Horse[56] and scalie Crocodile.
At once came forth whatever creeps the ground,   475
Insect or Worm; those wav'd thir limber fans
For wings, and smallest Lineaments exact
In all the Liveries dect of Summers pride
With spots of Gold and Purple, azure and green:
These as a line thir long dimension drew,   480
Streaking the ground with sinuous trace; not all
Minims of Nature; some of Serpent kind
Wondrous in length and corpulence[57] involv'd
Thir Snakie foulds, and added wings. First crept
The Parsimonious Emmet, provident   485
Of future, in small room large heart enclos'd,
Pattern of just equalitie perhaps
Hereafter, join'd in her popular Tribes
Of Commonaltie: swarming next appeer'd
The Female Bee that feeds her Husband Drone   490
Deliciously, and builds her waxen Cells
With Honey stor'd: the rest are numberless,
And thou thir Natures know'st, and gav'st them Names,
Needless to thee repeated; nor unknown
The Serpent suttl'st Beast of all the field,[58]   495
Of huge extent somtimes, with brazen Eyes
And hairie Main terrific, though to thee
Not noxious, but obedient at thy call.
Now Heav'n in all her Glorie shon, and rowl'd
Her motions, as the great first-Movers hand   500
First wheeld thir course; Earth in her rich attire
Consummate lovely smil'd; Air, Water, Earth,
By Fowl, Fish, Beast, was flown, was swum, was walkt
Frequent; and of the Sixt day yet remain'd;
There wanted yet the Master work, the end[59]   505
Of all yet don; a Creature who not prone
And Brute as other Creatures, but endu'd

[55] See Job xl. 15–24.
[56] hippopotamus.
[57] body; "involv'd": gathered in their folds to obscure them.
[58] Gen. iii. 1: "Now the serpent was more subtile than any beast of the field which the Lord God had made." The same line occurs as IX, 86, 560.
[59] the object.

With Sanctitie of Reason, might erect
His Stature, and upright with Front serene
Govern the rest, self-knowing, and from thence   510
Magnanimous to correspond with Heav'n,
But grateful to acknowledge whence his good
Descends, thither with heart and voice and eyes
Directed in Devotion, to adore
And worship God Supream, who made him chief   515
Of all his works: therefore th' Omnipotent
Eternal Father (for where is not hee
Present) thus to his Son audibly spake.
    Let us make now Man in our image, Man
In our similitude, and let them rule   520
Over the Fish and Fowl of Sea and Air,
Beast of the Field, and over all the Earth,
And every creeping thing that creeps the ground.
This said, he formd thee, *Adam*, thee O Man
Dust of the ground, and in thy nostrils breath'd   525
The breath of Life; in his own Image hee
Created thee, in the Image of God
Express, and thou becam'st a living Soul.
Male he created thee, but thy consort
Female for Race; then bless'd Mankind, and said,   530
Be fruitful, multiplie, and fill the Earth,
Subdue it, and throughout Dominion hold
Over Fish of the Sea, and Fowl of the Air,
And every living thing that moves on th' Earth.
Wherever thus created, for no place   535
Is yet distinct by name, thence, as thou know'st
He brought thee into this delicious Grove,
This Garden, planted with the Trees of God,
Delectable both to behold and taste;
And freely all thir pleasant fruit for food   540
Gave thee, all sorts are here that all th' Earth yeelds,
Varietie without end; but of the Tree
Which tasted works knowledge of Good and Evil,
Thou mai'st not; in the day thou eat'st, thou di'st;
Death is the penaltie impos'd, beware,   545
And govern well thy appetite, least sin
Surprise thee, and her black attendant Death.
Here finish'd hee, and all that he had made
View'd, and behold all was entirely good;
So Ev'n and Morn accomplish'd the Sixt day: 550
Yet not till the Creator from his work
Desisting, though unwearied, up returnd

Up to the Heav'n of Heav'ns his high abode,
Thence to behold this new created World
Th' addition of his Empire, how it shew'd   555
In prospect from his Throne, how good, how fair,
Answering his great Idea. Up he rode
Followd with acclamation and the sound
Symphonious of ten thousand Harps that tun'd
Angelic harmonies: the Earth, the Air   560
Resounded (thou remember'st, for thou heardst),
The Heav'ns and all the Constellations rung,
The Planets in thir stations list'ning stood,
While the bright Pomp ascended jubilant.
Open, ye everlasting Gates, they sung,   565
Open, ye Heav'ns, your living dores;[60] let in
The great Creator from his work returnd
Magnificent, his Six days work, a World;
Open, and henceforth oft; for God will deigne
To visit oft the dwellings of just Men   570
Delighted, and with frequent intercourse
Thither will send his winged Messengers
On errands of supernal Grace. So sung
The glorious Train ascending: He through Heav'n,
That open'd wide her blazing Portals, led   575
To Gods Eternal house direct the way,
A broad and ample rode, whose dust is Gold
And pavement Starrs, as Starrs to thee appeer,
Seen in the Galaxie, that Milkie way
Which nightly as a circling Zone thou seest   580
Powderd with Starrs. And now on Earth the Seventh
Eev'ning arose in *Eden*, for the Sun
Was set, and twilight from the East came on,
Forerunning Night; when at the holy mount
Of Heav'ns high-seated top, th' Impereal Throne   585
Of Godhead, fixt for ever firm and sure,
The Filial Power arriv'd, and sate him down
With his great Father, for he also went
Invisible, yet staid (such priviledge
Hath Omnipresence) and the work ordain'd,   590
Author and end of all things, and from work
Now resting, bless'd and hallowd the Seav'nth day,
As resting on that day from all his work,
But not in silence holy kept; the Harp

---

[60] Ps. xxiv. 7: "Lift up your heads, O ye gates; and be ye lift up, ye everlasting doors; and the King of glory shall come in."

Had work and rested not, the solemn Pipe,   595
And Dulcimer, all Organs of sweet stop,
All sounds on Fret[61] by String or Golden Wire
Temper'd soft Tunings, intermixt with Voice
Choral or Unison:[62] of incense Clouds
Fuming from Golden Censers hid the Mount.   600
Creation and the Six dayes acts they sung,
Great are thy works, *Jehovah,* infinite
Thy power; what thought can measure thee or tongue
Relate thee; greater now in thy return
Then from the Giant Angels; thee that day   605
Thy Thunders magnifi'd; but to create
Is greater then created to destroy.
Who can impair thee, mighty King, or bound
Thy Empire? easily the proud attempt
Of Spirits apostat and thir Counsels vain   610
Thou hast repeld, while impiously they thought
Thee to diminish, and from thee withdraw
The number of thy worshippers. Who seeks
To lessen thee, against his purpose serves
To manifest the more thy might: his evil   615
Thou usest, and from thence creat'st more good.
Witness this new-made World, another Heav'n
From Heaven Gate not farr, founded in view
On the cleer *Hyaline,* the Glassie Sea;[63]
Of amplitude almost immense,[64] with Starrs   620
Numerous, and every Starr perhaps a World
Of destind habitation; but thou know'st
Thir seasons: among these the seat of men,
Earth with her nether Ocean circumfus'd,
Thir pleasant dwelling place. Thrice happie men,   625
And sons of men, whom God hath thus advanc't,
Created in his Image, there to dwell
And worship him, and in reward to rule
Over his Works, on Earth, in Sea, or Air,
And multiply a Race of Worshippers   630

[61] a stop on a stringed instrument.
[62] solo.
[63] Gordon O'Brien discusses this recurrent image (in *Renaissance Poetics and the Problem of Power,* Chicago, 1956, especially pp. 113–15) as a correspondence between the mind of man (the "clear spirit" of *Lycidas,* 70) and the frame of heaven; derived from Rev. xv. 2, the figure embodies the concept of knowledge and the concept of power which come from God and are reflected back to Heaven.
[64] unmeasurable.

Holy and just: thrice happie if they know
Thir happiness, and persevere upright.
  So sung they, and the Empyrean rung,
With *Halleluiahs:* Thus was Sabbath kept.
And thy request think now fulfill'd, that ask'd   635
How first this World and face of things began,
And what before thy memorie was don
From the beginning, that posteritie
Informd by thee might know; if else thou seekst
Aught, not surpassing human measure, say.   640

BOOK VIII

THE ARGUMENT

Adam inquires concerning celestial Motions, is doubtfully answer'd, and
exhorted to search rather things more worthy of knowledge: *Adam* as-
sents, and still desirous to detain *Raphael,* relates to him what he re-
member'd since his own Creation, his placing in Paradise, his talk with
God concerning solitude and fit society, his first meeting and Nuptials
with *Eve,* his discourse with the Angel thereupon; who after admonitions
repeated departs.

  The Angel ended, and in *Adams* Ear
So Charming left his voice, that he a while
Thought him still speaking, still stood fixt to hear;
Then as new wak't thus gratefully repli'd.
What thanks sufficient, or what recompence   5
Equal have I to render thee, Divine
Hystorian, who thus largely hast allayd
The thirst I had of knowledge, and voutsaf't
This friendly condescention to relate
Things else by me unsearchable, now heard   10
With wonder, but delight, and, as is due,
With glorie attributed to the high
Creator; something yet of doubt remains,
Which onely thy solution can resolve.
When I behold this goodly Frame, this World[1]   15
Of Heav'n and Earth consisting, and compute,
Thir magnitudes, this Earth a spot, a grain,
An Atom, with the Firmament compar'd
And all her numberd Starrs, that seem to rowl
Spaces incomprehensible (for such   20

[1] Compare Milton's rendering of *Ps. 8,* 9–11.

Thir distance argues and thir swift return
Diurnal) meerly to officiate² light
Round this opacous³ Earth, this punctual⁴ spot,
One day and night; in all thir vast survey
Useless besides, reasoning I oft admire,⁵   25
How Nature wise and frugal could commit
Such disproportions, with superfluous hand
So many nobler Bodies to create,
Greater so manifold to this one use,
For aught appeers, and on thir Orbs impose   30
Such restless revolution day by day
Repeated, while the sedentarie Earth,
That better might with farr less compass move,
Serv'd by more noble then her self, attains
Her end without least motion, and receaves,   35
As Tribute such a sumless⁶ journey brought
Of incorporeal speed, her warmth and light;
Speed, to describe whose swiftness Number fails.
    So spake our Sire, and by his count'nance seemd
Entring on studious thoughts abstruse, which *Eve*   40
Perceaving where she sat retir'd in sight,
With lowliness Majestic from her seat,
And Grace that won who saw to wish her stay,
Rose, and went forth among her Fruits and Flowrs,
To visit how they prosper'd, bud and bloom,   45
Her Nurserie; they at her coming sprung
And toucht by her fair tendance gladlier grew.
Yet went she not, as not with such discourse
Delighted, or not capable her ear
Of what was high: such pleasure she reserv'd,   50
Adam relating, she sole Auditress;
Her Husband the Relater she preferr'd
Before the Angel, and of him to ask
Chose rather; hee, she knew would intermix
Grateful digressions, and solve high dispute   55
With conjugal Caresses, from his Lip
Not Words alone pleas'd her. O when meet now
Such pairs, in Love and mutual Honour joyn'd?
With Goddess-like demeanour forth she went;
Not unattended, for on her as Queen   60

² carry out their duty (of supplying); see also "officious," l. 99.
³ dark.
⁴ small and fixed in space (like a point).
⁵ regard with wonder.
⁶ immeasurable.

A pomp[7] of winning Graces waited still,
And from about her shot Darts of desire
Into all Eyes to wish her still in sight.
And *Raphael* now to *Adam*'s doubt propos'd
Benevolent and facil[8] thus repli'd.   65
  To ask or search I blame thee not, for Heav'n
Is as the Book of God before thee set,
Wherein to read his wondrous Works, and learn
His Seasons, Hours, or Dayes, or Months, or Yeares:
This to attain, whether Heav'n move or Earth,   70
Imports not, if thou reck'n right, the rest
From Man or Angel the great Architect
Did wisely to conceal, and not divulge
His secrets to be scann'd by them who ought
Rather admire; or if they list to try   75
Conjecture, he his Fabric of the Heav'ns
Hath left to thir disputes, perhaps to move
His laughter at thir quaint Opinions wide[9]
Hereafter, when they come to model Heav'n
And calculate the Starrs, how they will weild   80
The mightie frame, how build, unbuild, contrive
To save appeerances,[10] how gird the Sphear
With Centric and Eccentric scribl'd o're,
Cycle and Epicycle, Orb in Orb:
Alreadie by thy reasoning this I guess,   85
Who art to lead thy ofspring, and supposest
That bodies bright and greater should not serve
The less not bright, nor Heav'n such journies run,
Earth sitting still, when she alone receaves
The benefit: consider first, that Great   90
Or Bright inferrs not Excellence: the Earth
Though, in comparison of Heav'n, so small,
Nor glistering, may of solid good contain
More plenty then the Sun that barren shines,
Whose vertue on it self works no effect,   95
But in the fruitful Earth; there first receav'd
His beams, unactive else, thir vigour find.
Yet not to Earth are those bright Luminaries

---

[7] procession.
[8] mild of manner.
[9] far from the truth.
[10] invent theories to explain astronomical phenomena, such as the rotation of a sphere with the earth as center or not as center of the universe, moving in full orbit of itself or in a small circle whose center lay on the circumference of a large circle (orbit within an orbit).

Officious, but to thee Earths habitant.
And for the Heav'ns wide Circuit, let it speak   100
The Makers high magnificence, who built
So spacious, and his Line stretcht out so farr;
That Man may know he dwells not in his own;
An Edifice too large for him to fill,
Lodg'd in a small partition, and the rest   105
Ordain'd for uses to his Lord best known.
The swiftness of those Circles attribute,
Though numberless, to his Omnipotence,
That to corporeal substances could add
Speed almost Spiritual; mee thou thinkst not slow,   110
Who since the Morning hour set out from Heav'n
Where God resides, and ere mid-day arriv'd
In *Eden*, distance inexpressible
By Numbers that have name. But this I urge,
Admitting Motion in the Heav'ns, to shew   115
Invalid that which thee to doubt it mov'd;
Not that I so affirm, though so it seem
To thee who hast thy dwelling here on Earth.
God to remove his wayes from human sense,
Plac'd Heav'n from Earth so farr, that earthly sight,   120
If it presume, might err in things too high,
And no advantage gain. What if the Sun
Be Center to the World, and other Starrs
By his attractive vertue[11] and thir own
Incited, dance about him various rounds?   125
Thir wandring course now high, now low, then hid,
Progressive, retrograde, or standing still,
In six thou seest, and what if sev'nth to these
The Planet Earth, so stedfast though she seem,
Insensibly[12] three different Motions move?   130
Which else to several Sphears thou must ascribe,
Mov'd contrarie with thwart obliquities,[13]
Or save the Sun his labour, and that swift
Nocturnal and Diurnal rhomb[14] suppos'd,
Invisible else above all Starrs, the Wheel   135
Of Day and Night; which needs not thy beleef,

[11] magnetic attraction.
[12] imperceptibly; the three motions are rotation, revolution around the sun, and polar rotation around the ecliptic (the apparent path of the sun).
[13] the angles between the planes of the planets' equators and their orbits; each sphere's obliquity intersects another sphere's. That is, the movements of the spheres are transverse.
[14] the primum mobile.

If Earth industrious of her self fetch Day
Travelling East, and with her part averse
From the Suns beam meet Night, her other part
Still luminous by his ray. What if that light   140
Sent from her through the wide transpicuous air,
To the terrestrial Moon be as a Starr
Enlightning her by Day, as she by Night
This Earth? reciprocal, if Land be there,
Feilds and Inhabitants: Her spots thou seest   145
As Clouds, and Clouds may rain, and Rain produce
Fruits in her soft'n'd Soil, for some to eat
Allotted there; and other Suns perhaps
With thir attendant Moons thou wilt descrie
Communicating Male and Femal¹⁵ Light,   150
Which two great Sexes animate the World,
Stor'd in each Orb perhaps with some that live.
For such vast room in Nature unpossest
By living Soul, desert and desolate,
Onely to shine, yet scarce to contribute   155
Each Orb a glimps of Light, conveyd so farr
Down to this habitable, which returns
Light back to them, is obvious to dispute.¹⁶
But whether thus these things, or whether not,
Whether the Sun predominant in Heav'n   160
Rise on the Earth, or Earth rise on the Sun,
Hee from the East his flaming rode begin,
Or Shee from West her silent course advance
With inoffensive¹⁷ pace that spinning sleeps
On her soft Axle, while she paces Eev'n,   165
And beares thee soft with the smooth Air along,
Sollicit not thy thoughts with matters hid,
Leave them to God above, him serve and fear;
Of other Creatures, as him pleases best,
Wherever plac't, let him dispose: joy thou   170
In what he gives to thee, this Paradise
And thy fair *Eve;* Heav'n is for thee too high
To know what passes there; be lowlie wise:
Think onely what concerns thee and thy being;
Dream not of other Worlds, what Creatures there   175
Live, in what state, condition or degree,

¹⁵ of the sun (direct) and of the moon (reflected).
¹⁶ evidently disputable (since there are so many and they give off so little light).
¹⁷ unimpeded.

Contented that thus farr hath been reveal'd
Not of Earth onely but of highest Heav'n.
   To whom thus *Adam* cleerd of doubt, repli'd.
How fully hast thou satisfi'd mee, pure   180
Intelligence of Heav'n, Angel serene,
And freed from intricacies, taught to live,
The easiest way, nor with perplexing thoughts
To interrupt the sweet of Life, from which
God hath bid dwell farr off all anxious cares,   185
And not molest us, unless we our selves
Seek them with wandring thoughts, and notions vain.
But apt the Mind or Fancie is to roave
Uncheckt, and of her roaving is no end;
Till warn'd, or by experience taught, she learn,   190
That not to know at large of things remote
From use, obscure and suttle, but to know
That which before us lies in daily life,
Is the prime Wisdom; what is more, is fume,
Or emptiness, or fond impertinence,   195
And renders us in things that most concern
Unpractis'd, unprepar'd, and still to seek.
Therefore from this high pitch let us descend
A lower flight, and speak of things at hand
Useful, whence haply mention may arise   200
Of somthing not unseasonable to ask
By sufferance, and thy wonted favour deign'd.
Thee I have heard relating what was don
Ere my remembrance: now hear mee relate
My Storie, which perhaps thou hast not heard;   205
And Day is yet not spent; till then thou seest
How suttly to detain thee I devise,
Inviting thee to hear while I relate,
Fond, were it not in hope of thy reply:
For while I sit with thee, I seem in Heav'n,   210
And sweeter thy discourse is to my ear
Then Fruits of Palm-tree pleasantest to thirst
And hunger both, from[18] labour, at the hour
Of sweet repast; they satiate, and soon fill,
Though pleasant, but thy words with Grace Divine   215
Imbu'd, bring to thir sweetness no satietie.
   To whom thus *Raphael* answer'd heav'nly meek.
Nor are thy lips ungraceful, Sire of men,
Nor tongue ineloquent; for God on thee

[18] (which come) as a result of.

Abundantly his gifts hath also pour'd   220
Inward and outward both, his image fair:
Speaking or mute all comliness and grace
Attends thee, and each word, each motion formes.
Nor less think wee in Heav'n of thee on Earth
Then of our fellow servant, and inquire   225
Gladly into the wayes of God with Man:
For God we see hath honour'd thee, and set
On Man his equal Love: say therefore on;
For I that Day was absent, as befell,
Bound on a voyage uncouth[19] and obscure,   230
Farr on excursion toward the Gates of Hell;
Squar'd in full Legion (such command we had)
To see that none thence issu'd forth a spie,
Or enemie, while God was in his work,
Least hee incenst at such eruption bold,   235
Destruction with Creation might have mixt.
Not that they durst without his leave attempt,
But us he sends upon his high behests
For state, as Sovran King, and to enure[20]
Our prompt obedience. Fast we found, fast shut   240
The dismal Gates, and barricado'd strong;
But long ere our approaching heard within
Noise, other then the sound of Dance or Song,
Torment, and loud lament, and furious rage.
Glad we return'd up to the coasts of Light   245
Ere Sabbath Eev'ning: so we had in charge.
But thy relation now; for I attend,
Pleas'd with thy words no less then thou with mine.
    So spake the Godlike Power, and thus our Sire.
For Man to tell how human Life began   250
Is hard; for who himself beginning knew?
Desire with thee still longer to converse
Induc'd me. As new wak't from soundest sleep
Soft on the flowrie herb I found me laid
In Balmie Sweat, which with his Beames the Sun   255
Soon dri'd, and on the reaking moisture fed.
Strait toward Heav'n my wondring Eyes I turnd,
And gaz'd a while the ample Skie, till rais'd
By quick instinctive motion up I sprung,
As thitherward endevoring, and upright   260
Stood on my feet; about me round I saw

[19] unknown.
[20] make (obedience) a habit.

Hill, Dale, and shadie Woods, and sunnie Plains,
And liquid Lapse of murmuring Streams; by these,
Creatures that liv'd, and mov'd, and walk'd, or flew,
Birds on the branches warbling; all things smil'd,   265
With fragrance and with joy my heart oreflow'd.
My self I then perus'd, and Limb by Limb
Survey'd, and sometimes went,[21] and sometimes ran
With supple joints, as lively vigour led:
But who I was, or where, or from what cause,   270
Knew not; to speak I tri'd, and forthwith spake,
My Tongue obey'd and readily could name
What e're I saw. Thou Sun, said I, fair Light,
And thou enlight'n'd Earth, so fresh and gay,
Ye Hills and Dales, ye Rivers, Woods, and Plains,   275
And ye that live and move, fair Creatures, tell,
Tell, if ye saw, how came I thus, how here?
Not of my self; by some great Maker then,
In goodness and in power præeminent;
Tell me, how may I know him, how adore,   280
From whom I have that thus I move and live,
And feel that I am happier then I know.
While thus I call'd, and stray'd I knew not whither,
From where I first drew Air, and first beheld
This happie Light, when answer none return'd,   285
On a green shadie Bank profuse of Flowrs
Pensive I sate me down; there gentle sleep
First found me, and with soft oppression seis'd
My droused sense, untroubl'd, though I thought
I then was passing to my former state   290
Insensible, and forthwith to dissolve:
When suddenly stood at my Head a dream,
Whose inward apparition gently mov'd
My fancy to believe I yet had being,
And liv'd: One came, methought, of shape Divine,   295
And said, thy Mansion wants thee, *Adam*, rise,
First Man, of Men innumerable ordain'd
First Father, call'd by thee I come thy Guide
To the Garden of bliss, thy seat prepar'd.[22]
So saying, by the hand he took me rais'd,   300
And over Fields and Waters, as in Air
Smooth sliding without step, last led me up

---

[21] walked.
[22] The description of Eden (through l. 499) is drawn from Gen. ii. 8–9,
15–24.

A woodie Mountain; whose high top was plain,
A Circuit wide, enclos'd, with goodliest Trees
Planted, with Walks, and Bowers, that what I saw   305
Of Earth before scarse pleasant seemd. Each Tree
Load'n with fairest Fruit that hung to th' Eye
Tempting, stirr'd in me sudden appetite
To pluck and eat; whereat I wak'd, and found
Before mine Eyes all real, as the dream   310
Had lively shadowd:²³ Here had new begun
My wandring, had not hee who was my Guide
Up hither, from among the Trees appeer'd,
Presence Divine. Rejoycing, but with aw
In adoration at his feet I fell   315
Submiss:²⁴ he rear'd me, and Whom thou soughtst I am,
Said mildly, Author of all this thou seest
Above, or round about thee or beneath.
This Paradise I give thee, count it thine
To Till and keep, and of the Fruit to eat: 320
Of every Tree that in the Garden grows
Eat freely with glad heart; fear here no dearth:
But of the Tree whose operation²⁵ brings
Knowledge of good and ill, which I have set
The Pledge of thy Obedience and thy Faith,   325
Amid the Garden by the Tree of Life,
Remember what I warn thee, shun to taste,
And shun the bitter consequence: for know,
The day thou eat'st thereof, my sole command
Transgrest, inevitably thou shalt dye;²⁶   330
From that day mortal, and this happie State
Shalt loose, expell'd from hence into a World
Of woe and sorrow. Sternly he pronounc'd
The rigid interdiction, which resounds
Yet dreadful in mine ear, though in my choice   335
Not to incur; but soon his cleer aspect
Return'd and gracious purpose thus renew'd.
Not onely these fair bounds, but all the Earth
To thee and to thy Race I give; as Lords
Possess it, and all things that therein live,   340
Or live in Sea, or Air, Beast, Fish, and Fowl.
In signe whereof each Bird and Beast behold

²³ had shown a vision which seemed real.
²⁴ submissive.
²⁵ agency.
²⁶ explained by ll. 331-32.

After thir kinds; I bring them to receave
From thee thir Names, and pay thee fealtie
With low subjection; understand the same   345
Of Fish within thir watry residence,
Not hither summond, since they cannot change
Thir Element to draw the thinner Air.
As thus he spake, each Bird and Beast behold
Approaching two and two, these cowring low   350
With blandishment, each Bird stoop'd on his wing.
I nam'd them, as they pass'd, and understood
Thir Nature, with such knowledge God endu'd
My sudden apprehension: but in these
I found not what me thought I wanted still;   355
And to the Heav'nly vision thus presum'd.
    O by what Name, for thou above all these,
Above mankind, or aught then mankind higher,
Surpassest farr my naming, how may I
Adore thee, Author of this Universe,   360
And all this good to man, for whose well being
So amply, and with hands so liberal
Thou hast provided all things: but with mee
I see not who partakes. In solitude
What happiness, who can enjoy alone,   365
Or all enjoying, what contentment find?
Thus I presumptuous; and the vision bright,
As with a smile more bright'n'd, thus repli'd.
    What call'st thou solitude, is not the Earth
With various living creatures, and the Air   370
Replenisht, and all these at thy command
To come and play before thee, know'st thou not
Thir language and thir wayes, they also know,
And reason not contemptibly; with these
Find pastime, and bear rule; thy Realm is large.   375
So spake the Universal Lord, and seem'd
So ordering. I with leave of speech implor'd,
And humble deprecation thus repli'd.
    Let not my words offend thee, Heav'nly Power,
My Maker, be propitious while I speak.   380
Hast thou not made me here thy substitute,
And these inferiour farr beneath me set?
Among unequals what societie
Can sort,[27] what harmonie or true delight?
Which must be mutual, in proportion due   385

---

[27] be in harmony, be suitable.

Giv'n and receiv'd; but in disparitie
The one intense, the other still remiss[28]
Cannot well suit with either, but soon prove .
Tedious alike: Of fellowship I speak
Such as I seek, fit to participate   390
All rational delight, wherein the brute
Cannot be human consort; they rejoyce
Each with thir kind, Lion with Lioness;
So fitly them in pairs thou hast combin'd;
Much less can Bird with Beast, or Fish with Fowl   395
So well converse, nor with the Ox the Ape;
Wors then can Man with Beast, and least of all.
    Whereto th' Almighty answer'd, not displeas'd.
A nice[29] and suttle happiness I see
Thou to thy self proposest, in the choice   400
Of thy Associates, *Adam*, and wilt taste
No pleasure, though in pleasure, solitarie.
What thinkst thou then of mee, and this my State,
Seem I to thee sufficiently possest
Of happiness, or not? who am alone   405
From all Eternitie, for none I know
Second to me or like, equal much less.
How have I then with whom to hold converse
Save with the Creatures which I made, and those
To me inferiour, infinite descents   410
Beneath what other Creatures are to thee?
    He ceas'd, I lowly answer'd. To attain
The highth and depth of thy Eternal wayes
All human thoughts come short, Supream of things;
Thou in thy self art perfet, and in thee   415
Is no deficience found; not so is Man,
But in degree, the cause of his desire
By conversation with his like to help,
Or solace his defects. No need that thou
Shouldst propagat, already infinite;   420
And through all numbers absolute,[30] though One;
But Man by number is to manifest
His single imperfection, and beget
Like of his like, his Image multipli'd,
In unitie defective, which requires   425
Collateral love, and deerest amitie.

---

[28] the one deeply concerned (taut), the other always careless (slack).
[29] discriminating.
[30] in all things perfect.

Thou in thy secresie although alone,
Best with thy self accompanied, seek'st not
Social communication, yet so pleas'd,
Canst raise thy Creature to what highth thou wilt   430
Of Union or Communion, deifi'd;
I by conversing cannot these erect
From prone, nor in thir wayes complacence find.
Thus I embold'n'd spake, and freedom us'd
Permissive, and acceptance found, which gain'd   435
This answer from the gratious voice Divine.
    Thus farr to try thee, *Adam,* I was pleas'd,
And find thee knowing not of Beasts alone,
Which thou hast rightly nam'd, but of thy self,
Expressing well the spirit within thee free,   440
My Image, not imparted to the Brute,
Whose fellowship therefore unmeet for thee
Good reason was thou freely shouldst dislike,
And be so minded still; I, ere thou spak'st,
Knew it not good for Man to be alone,   445
And no such companie as then thou saw'st
Intended thee, for trial onely brought,
To see how thou could'st judge of fit and meet:
What next I bring shall please thee, be assur'd,
Thy likeness, thy fit help, thy other self,   450
Thy wish exactly to thy hearts desire.
    Hee ended, or I heard no more, for now
My earthly[31] by his Heav'nly overpowerd,
Which it had long stood under, streind to th' highth
In that celestial Colloquie sublime,   455
As with an object that excels the sense,
Dazl'd and spent, sunk down, and sought repair
Of sleep, which instantly fell on me, call'd
By Nature as in aid, and clos'd mine eyes.
Mine eyes he clos'd, but op'n left the Cell   460
Of Fancie my internal sight, by which
Abstract as in a transe methought I saw,
Though sleeping, where I lay, and saw the shape
Still glorious before whom awake I stood;
Who stooping op'n'd my left side, and took   465
From thence a Rib, with cordial spirits[32] warm,
And Life-blood streaming fresh; wide was the wound,
But suddenly with flesh fill'd up and heal'd:

[31] (nature).
[32] spirits of the heart.

The Rib he formd and fashiond with his hands;
Under his forming hands a Creature grew,   470
Manlike, but different sex, so lovely fair,
That what seemd fair in all the World, seemd now
Mean, or in her summ'd up, in her containd
And in her looks, which from that time infus'd
Sweetness into my heart, unfelt before,   475
And into all things from her Air inspir'd
The spirit of love and amorous delight.
Shee disappeerd, and left me dark, I wak'd
To find her, or for ever to deplore
Her loss, and other pleasures all abjure: 480
When out of hope, behold her, not farr off,
Such as I saw her in my dream, adornd
With what all Earth or Heaven could bestow
To make her amiable: On she came,
Led by her Heav'nly Maker, though unseen,   485
And guided by his voice, nor uninformd
Of nuptial Sanctitie and marriage Rites:
Grace was in all her steps, Heav'n in her Eye,
In every gesture dignitie and love.
I overjoyd could not forbear aloud.   490
    This turn hath made amends; thou hast fulfill'd
Thy words, Creator bounteous and benigne,
Giver of all things fair, but fairest this
Of all thy gifts, nor enviest. I now see
Bone of my Bone, Flesh of my Flesh, my Self   495
Before me; Woman is her Name, of Man
Extracted; for this cause he shall forgoe
Father and Mother, and to his Wife adhere;
And they shall be one Flesh, one Heart, one Soul.
    She heard me thus, and though divinely brought,   500
Yet Innocence and Virgin Modestie,
Her vertue and the conscience of her worth,
That would be woo'd, and not unsought be won,
Not obvious, not obtrusive, but retir'd,
The more desirable, or to say all,   505
Nature her self, though pure of sinful thought,
Wrought in her so, that seeing me, she turn'd;
I follow'd her, she what was Honour knew,
And with obsequious[33] Majestie approv'd
My pleaded reason. To the Nuptial Bowr   510
I led her blushing like the Morn: all Heav'n,

[33] compliant.

And happie Constellations on that hour
Shed thir selectest influence; the Earth
Gave sign of gratulation, and each Hill;
Joyous the Birds; fresh Gales and gentle Aires   515
Whisper'd it to the Woods, and from thir wings
Flung Rose, flung Odours from the spicie Shrub,
Disporting, till the amorous Bird of Night[34]
Sung Spousal, and bid haste the Eevning Starr
On his Hill top, to light the bridal Lamp.   520
Thus I have told thee all my State, and brought
My Storie to the sum of earthly bliss
Which I enjoy, and must confess to find
In all things else delight indeed, but such
As us'd or not, works in the mind no change,   525
Nor vehement desire, these delicacies
I mean of Taste, Sight, Smell, Herbs, Fruits, and Flowrs,
Walks, and the melodie of Birds; but here
Farr otherwise, transported I behold,
Transported touch; here passion first I felt,   530
Commotion strange, in all enjoyments else
Superiour and unmov'd, here onely weak
Against the charm of Beauties powerful glance.
Or Nature faild in mee, and left some part
Not proof enough such Object to sustain,   535
Or from my side subducting, took perhaps
More then enough; at least on her bestow'd
Too much of Ornament, in outward shew
Elaborate, of inward less exact.
For well I understand in the prime end   540
Of Nature her th' inferiour, in the mind
And inward Faculties, which most excell,
In outward also her resembling less
His Image who made both, and less expressing
The character of that Dominion giv'n   545
O're other Creatures; yet when I approach
Her loveliness, so absolute[35] she seems
And in her self compleat, so well to know
Her own, that what she wills to do or say,
Seems wisest, vertuousest, discreetest, best;   550
All higher knowledge in her presence falls
Degraded, Wisdom in discourse with her
Looses discount'nanc't, and like folly shews;

[34] the nightingale.
[35] perfect.

Authority and Reason on her wait,
As one intended first, not after made   555
Occasionally; and to consummate all,
Greatness of mind and nobleness thir seat
Build in her loveliest, and create an awe
About her, as a guard Angelic plac't.
To whom the Angel with contracted brow.   560
   Accuse not Nature, she hath don her part;
Do thou but thine, and be not diffident
Of Wisdom, she deserts thee not, if thou
Dismiss not her, when most thou needst her nigh,
By attributing overmuch to things   565
Less excellent, as thou thy self perceav'st.
For what admir'st thou, what transports thee so,
An outside? fair no doubt, and worthy well
Thy cherishing, thy honouring, and thy love,
Not thy subjection: weigh with her thy self;   570
Then value: Oft times nothing profits more
Then self-esteem, grounded on just and right
Well manag'd; of that skill[36] the more thou know'st,
The more she will acknowledge thee her Head,
And to realities yeild all her shows: 575
Made so adorn for thy delight the more,
So awful, that with honour thou maist love
Thy mate, who sees when thou art seen least wise.
But if the sense of touch whereby mankind
Is propagated seem such dear delight   580
Beyond all other, think the same voutsaf't
To Cattel and each Beast; which would not be
To them made common and divulg'd, if aught
Therein enjoy'd were worthy to subdue
The Soul of Man, or passion in him move.   585
What higher in her societie thou findst
Attractive, human, rational, love still;
In loving thou dost well, in passion not,
Wherein true Love consists not; love refines
The thoughts, and heart enlarges, hath his seat   590
In Reason, and is judicious, is the scale
By which to heav'nly Love thou maist ascend,
Not sunk in carnal pleasure, for which cause
Among the Beasts no Mate for thee was found.
   To whom thus half abash't *Adam* repli'd.   595
Neither her out-side formd so fair, nor aught

[36] self-esteem.

In procreation common to all kinds
(Though higher of the genial[37] Bed by far,
And with mysterious reverence I deem)
So much delights me as those graceful acts,   600
Those thousand decencies that daily flow
From all her words and actions mixt with Love
And sweet compliance, which declare unfeign'd
Union of Mind, or in us both one Soul;
Harmonie to behold in wedded pair   605
More grateful then harmonious sound to th' ear.
Yet these subject not; I to thee disclose
What inward thence I feel, not therefore foild,
Who meet with various objects, from the sense
Variously representing; yet still free   610
Approve the best, and follow what I approve.
To love thou blam'st me not, for love thou saist
Leads up to Heav'n, is both the way and guide;
Bear with me then, if lawful what I ask;
Love not the heav'nly Spirits, and how thir Love   615
Express they, by looks onely, or do they mix
Irradiance, virtual or immediate touch?
    To whom the Angel with a smile that glow'd
Celestial rosie red, Loves proper hue,
Answer'd. Let it suffice thee that thou know'st   620
Us happie, and without Love no happiness.
Whatever pure thou in the body enjoy'st
(And pure thou wert created) we enjoy
In eminence, and obstacle find none
Of membrane, joynt, or limb, exclusive barrs: 625
Easier then Air with Air, if Spirits embrace,
Total they mix, Union of Pure with Pure
Desiring; nor restrain'd conveyance need
As Flesh to mix with Flesh, or Soul with Soul.
But I can now no more; the parting Sun   630
Beyond the Earths green Cape and verdant Isles[38]
Hesperean[39] sets, my Signal to depart.
Be strong, live happie, and love, but first of all
Him whom to love is to obey, and keep
His great command; take heed least Passion sway   635
Thy Judgement to do aught, which else free Will
Would not admit; thine and of all thy Sons

[37] procreative.
[38] Cape Verde ("green") and the islands of the same name.
[39] in the West.

The weal or woe in thee is plac't; beware.
I in thy persevering shall rejoyce,
And all the Blest: stand fast; to stand or fall   640
Free in thine own Arbitrement it lies.
Perfet within, no outward aid require;
And all temptation to transgress repel.
    So saying, he arose; whom *Adam* thus
Follow'd with benediction. Since to part,   645
Go heav'nly Guest, Ethereal Messenger,
Sent from whose sovran goodness I adore.
Gentle to me and affable hath been
Thy condescension, and shall be honour'd ever
With grateful Memorie: thou to mankind   650
Be good and friendly still, and oft return.
    So parted they, the Angel up to Heav'n
From the thick shade, and *Adam* to his Bowr.

BOOK IX

THE ARGUMENT

Satan having compast the Earth, with meditated guile returns as a mist
by Night into Paradise, enters into the Serpent sleeping. *Adam* and *Eve*
in the Morning go forth to thir labours, which *Eve* proposes to divide in
several places, each labouring apart: *Adam* consents not, alledging the
danger, lest that Enemy, of whom they were forewarn'd, should attempt
her found alone: *Eve* loath to be thought not circumspect or firm enough,
urges her going apart, the rather desirous to make tryal of her strength;
Adam at last yields: The Serpent finds her alone; his subtle approach,
first gazing, then speaking, with much flattery extolling *Eve* above all
other Creatures. *Eve* wondring to hear the Serpent speak, asks how he
attain'd to human speech and such understanding not till now; the Ser-
pent answers, that by tasting of a certain Tree in the Garden he attain'd
both to Speech and Reason, till then void of both: *Eve* requires him to
bring her to that Tree, and finds it to be the Tree of Knowledge for-
bidden: The Serpent now grown bolder, with many wiles and arguments
induces her at length to eat; she pleas'd with the taste deliberates awhile
whether to impart thereof to *Adam* or not, at last brings him of the
Fruit, relates what perswaded her to eat thereof: *Adam* at first amaz'd,
but perceiving her lost, resolves through vehemence of love to perish
with her; and extenuating the trespass eats also of the Fruit: The Effects
thereof in them both; they seek to cover thir nakedness; then fall to
variance and accusation of one another.

No more of talk where God or Angel Guest
With Man, as with his Friend, familiar us'd
To sit indulgent, and with him partake
Rural repast, permitting him the while
Venial[1] discourse unblam'd: I now must change   5
Those Notes to Tragic; foul distrust, and breach
Disloyal on the part of Man, revolt,
And disobedience: On the part of Heav'n
Now alienated, distance and distaste,
Anger and just rebuke, and judgement giv'n,   10
That brought into this World a world of woe,
Sin and her shadow Death, and Miserie
Deaths Harbinger: Sad task, yet argument
Not less but more Heroic then the wrauth
Of stern *Achilles* on his Foe pursu'd[2]   15
Thrice Fugitive about *Troy* Wall; or rage
Of *Turnus* for *Lavinia* disespous'd,
Or *Neptun's* ire or *Juno's*, that so long
Perplex'd the *Greek* and *Cytherea's* Son;
If answerable style I can obtain   20
Of my Celestial Patroness,[3] who deignes
Her nightly visitation unimplor'd,
And dictates to me slumbring, or inspires
Easie my unpremeditated Verse:
Since first this Subject for Heroic Song   25
Pleas'd me long choosing, and beginning late;
Not sedulous by Nature to indite
Warrs, hitherto the onely Argument
Heroic deem'd, chief maistrie to dissect
With long and tedious havoc fabl'd Knights   30
In Battels feign'd; the better fortitude
Of Patience and Heroic Martyrdom
Unsung; or to describe Races and Games,
Or tilting Furniture,[4] emblazon'd Shields,
Impreses[5] quaint, Caparisons and Steeds;   35
Bases[6] and tinsel Trappings, gorgious Knights

[1] unobjectionable.
[2] referring to *Iliad*, XXII (Achilles' fighting Hector), *Aeneid*, XII (Turnus' competing with Aeneas), *Odyssey*, I (Neptune's avenging himself on Ulysses), and *Aeneid*, I (Juno's harassing Aeneas because of her anger and jealousy against his mother Venus).
[3] Urania; see VII, n. 1.
[4] furnishings.
[5] devices on shields.
[6] probably the lower parts of escutcheons; perhaps housings for horses.

At Joust and Torneament; then marshal'd Feast
Serv'd up in Hall with Sewers,[7] and Seneshals;
The skill of Artifice or Office mean,
Not that which justly gives Heroic name   40
To Person or to Poem. Mee of these
Nor skill'd nor studious, higher Argument
Remains, sufficient of it self to raise
That name, unless an age too late,[8] or cold
Climat,[9] or Years damp my intended wing   45
Deprest, and much they may, if all be mine,
Not Hers who brings it nightly to my Ear.
    The Sun was sunk, and after him the Starr
Of Hesperus, whose Office is to bring
Twilight upon the Earth, short Arbiter   50
Twixt Day and Night, and now from end to end
Nights Hemisphere had veild th' Horizon round:
When Satan who late fled before the threats
Of Gabriel out of Eden, now improv'd
In meditated fraud and malice, bent   55
On mans destruction, maugre what might hap
Of heavier on himself, fearless return'd.
By Night he fled, and at Midnight return'd
From compassing the Earth, cautious of day,
Since Uriel Regent of the Sun descri'd   60
His entrance, and forewarnd the Cherubim
That kept thir watch; thence full of anguish driv'n,
The space of seven continu'd Nights[10] he rode
With darkness, thrice the Equinoctial Line
He circl'd, four times cross'd the Carr of Night   65
From Pole to Pole, traversing each Colure;
On th' eighth return'd, and on the Coast averse
From entrance or Cherubic Watch, by stealth
Found unsuspected way. There was a place,
Now not, though Sin, not Time, first wraught the change,   70
Where Tigris at the foot of Paradise
Into a Gulf shot under ground, till part
Rose up a Fountain by the Tree of Life;
In with the River sunk, and with it rose

[7] butlers.
[8] referring to the decay of nature; see Nature does not suffer decay.
[9] The theory of the effects of cold climate is reviewed by T. B. Stroup in Modern Language Quarterly, IV (1943), 185–89; compare Z. S. Fink, MLQ, II (1941), 67–80.
[10] consisting of three days' flight around the equator and two days' each around two meridians of longitude at right angles with each other (each colure).

Satan involv'd in rising Mist, then sought   75
Where to lie hid; Sea he had searcht and Land
From *Eden* over *Pontus*,[11] and the Pool
Mæotis, up beyond the River *Ob;*
Downward as farr Antartic; and in length
West from *Orontes*[12] to the Ocean barr'd   80
At *Darien*,[13] thence to the Land where flows
Ganges and *Indus:* thus the Orb he roam'd
With narrow search; and with inspection deep
Consider'd every Creature, which of all
Most opportune might serve his Wiles, and found   85
The Serpent suttlest Beast of all the Field.
Him after long debate, irresolute
Of thoughts revolv'd,[14] his final sentence chose
Fit Vessel, fittest Imp of fraud, in whom
To enter, and his dark suggestions hide   90
From sharpest sight: for in the wilie Snake,
Whatever sleights none would suspicious mark,
As from his wit and native suttletie
Proceeding, which in other Beasts observ'd
Doubt might beget of Diabolic pow'r   95
Active within beyond the sense of brute.
Thus he resolv'd, but first from inward grief
His bursting passion into plaints thus pour'd:
   O Earth, how like to Heav'n, if not preferr'd
More justly, Seat worthier of Gods, as built   100
With second thoughts, reforming what was old!
For what God after better worse would build?
Terrestrial Heav'n, danc't round by other Heav'ns
That shine, yet bear thir bright officious Lamps,
Light above Light, for thee alone, as seems,   105
In thee concentring all thir precious beams
Of sacred influence: As God in Heav'n
Is Center, yet extends to all, so thou
Centring receav'st from all those Orbs; in thee,
Not in themselves, all thir known vertue appeers   110
Productive in Herb, Plant, and nobler birth
Of Creatures animate with gradual[15] life

---

[11] the Black Sea; Lake Maeotis is the Sea of Azov, and the Ob flows to the Arctic Sea.
[12] a river in Syria.
[13] the Isthmus of Panama on the Atlantic Ocean.
[14] wavering from mulling over thoughts; "his final sentence" is his decision to assume serpentine form.
[15] referring to links in the chain of being, upward to man.

Of Growth, Sense, Reason, all summ'd up in Man.
With what delight could I have walkt thee round,
If I could joy in aught, sweet interchange   115
Of Hill and Vallie, Rivers, Woods and Plains,
Now Land, now Sea, and Shores with Forrest crownd,
Rocks, Dens, and Caves; but I in none of these
Find place or refuge; and the more I see
Pleasures about me, so much more I feel   120
Torment within me, as from the hateful siege
Of contraries;[16] all good to me becomes
Bane, and in Heav'n much worse would be my state.
But neither here seek I, no nor in Heav'n
To dwell, unless by maistring Heav'ns Supream;   125
Nor hope to be my self less miserable
By what I seek, but others to make such
As I, though thereby worse to me redound:
For onely in destroying I find ease
To my relentless thoughts; and him destroyd,   130
Or won to what may work his utter loss,
For whom all this was made, all this will soon
Follow, as to him linkt in weal or woe,
In wo then; that destruction wide may range:
To mee shall be the glorie sole among   135
Th' infernal Powers, in one day to have marr'd
What he *Almightie* styl'd, six Nights and Days
Continu'd making, and who knows how long
Before had bin contriving, though perhaps
Not longer then since I in one Night freed   140
From servitude inglorious welnigh half
Th' Angelic Name, and thinner left the throng
Of his adorers: hee to be aveng'd,
And to repair his numbers thus impair'd,
Whether such vertue spent of old now faild   145
More Angels to Create, if they at least
Are his Created, or to spite us more,
Determin'd to advance into our room
A Creature form'd of Earth, and him endow,
Exalted from so base original,   150
With Heav'nly spoils, our spoils: What he decreed
He effected; Man he made, and for him built
Magnificent this World, and Earth his seat,
Him Lord pronounc'd, and, O indignitie!
Subjected to his service Angel wings,   155

[16] seat of conflicting feelings.

And flaming Ministers to watch and tend
Thir earthy Charge: Of these the vigilance
I dread, and to elude, thus wrapt in mist
Of midnight vapor glide obscure, and prie
In every Bush and Brake, where hap may find   160
The Serpent sleeping, in whose mazie foulds
To hide me, and the dark intent I bring.
O foul descent! that I who erst contended
With Gods to sit the highest, am now constraind[17]
Into a Beast, and mixt with bestial slime,   165
This essence to incarnate and imbrute,
That to the hight of Deitie aspir'd;
But what will not Ambition and Revenge
Descend to? who aspires must down as low
As high he soard, obnoxious[18] first or last   170
To basest things. Revenge, at first though sweet,
Bitter ere long back on it self recoils;
Let it; I reck not, so it light well aim'd,
Since higher I fall short, on him who next
Provokes my envie, this new Favorite   175
Of Heav'n, this Man of Clay, Son of despite,
Whom us the more to spite his Maker rais'd
From dust: spite then with spite is best repaid.
     So saying, through each Thicket Danck or Drie,
Like a black mist low creeping, he held on   180
His midnight search, where soonest he might find
The Serpent: him fast sleeping soon he found
In Labyrinth of many a round self-rowl'd,
His head the midst, well stor'd with suttle wiles:
Not yet in horrid Shade or dismal Den,   185
Nor nocent[19] yet, but on the grassie Herb
Fearless unfeard he slept: in at his Mouth
The Devil enterd, and his brutal sense,
In heart or head, possessing soon inspir'd
With act intelligential; but his sleep   190
Disturb'd not, waiting close[20] th' approach of Morn.
Now when as sacred Light began to dawn
In *Eden* on the humid Flowrs, that breath'd
Thir morning incense, when all things that breath,
From th' Earths great Altar send up silent praise   195

[17] both "compressed" and "forced."
[18] liable.
[19] harmful.
[20] hidden.

To the Creator, and his Nostrils fill
With grateful Smell, forth came the human pair
And joynd thir vocal Worship to the Quire
Of Creatures wanting voice, that done, partake
The season, prime for sweetest Scents and Aires: 200
Then commune how that day they best may ply
Thir growing work: for much thir work outgrew
The hands dispatch of two Gardning so wide.
And *Eve* first to her Husband thus began.
  Adam, well may we labour still to dress   205
This Garden, still to tend Plant, Herb and Flowr,
Our pleasant task enjoyn'd, but till more hands
Aid us, the work under our labour grows,
Luxurious by restraint; what we by day
Lop overgrown, or prune, or prop, or bind,   210
One night or two with wanton growth derides
Tending to wild. Thou therefore now advise
Or hear what to my mind first thoughts present,
Let us divide our labours, thou where choice
Leads thee, or where most needs, whether to wind   215
The Woodbine round this Arbour, or direct
The clasping Ivie where to climb, while I
In yonder Spring of Roses[21] intermixt
With Myrtle, find what to redress till Noon:
For while so near each other thus all day   220
Our task we choose, what wonder if so near
Looks intervene and smiles, or object new
Casual discourse draw on, which intermits
Our dayes work brought to little, though begun
Early, and th' hour of Supper comes unearn'd.   225
  To whom mild answer *Adam* thus return'd.
Sole *Eve,* Associate sole, to me beyond
Compare above all living Creatures dear,
Well hast thou motion'd, well thy thoughts imployd
How we might best fulfill the work which here   230
God hath assign'd us, nor of me shalt pass
Unprais'd: for nothing lovelier can be found
In Woman, then to studie houshold good,
And good works in her Husband to promote.
Yet not so strictly hath our Lord impos'd   235
Labour, as to debarr us when we need
Refreshment, whether food, or talk between,
Food of the mind, or this sweet intercourse

[21] cluster of new-blown roses.

Of looks and smiles, for smiles from Reason flow,
To brute deni'd, and are of Love the food,   240
Love not the lowest end of human life.
For not to irksom toil, but to delight
He made us, and delight to Reason joyn'd.
These paths and Bowers doubt not but our joynt hands
Will keep from Wilderness with ease, as wide   245
As we need walk, till younger hands ere long
Assist us: But if much converse perhaps
Thee satiate, to short absence I could yeild.
For solitude somtimes is best societie,
And short retirement urges sweet return.   250
But other doubt possesses me, least harm
Befall thee sever'd from me; for thou knowst
What hath bin warn'd us, what malicious Foe
Envying our happiness, and of his own
Despairing, seeks to work us woe and shame   255
By sly assault; and somwhere nigh at hand
Watches, no doubt, with greedy hope to find
His wish and best advantage, us asunder,
Hopeless to circumvent us joynd, where each
To other speedie aid might lend at need;   260
Whether his first design be to withdraw
Our fealtie from God, or to disturb
Conjugal Love, then which perhaps no bliss
Enjoy'd by us excites his envie more;
Or this, or worse, leave not the faithful side   265
That gave thee being, still shades thee and protects.
The Wife, where danger or dishonour lurks,
Safest and seemliest by her Husband staies,
Who guards her, or with her the worst endures.
    To whom the Virgin[22] Majestie of *Eve*,   270
As one who loves, and some unkindness meets,
With sweet austeer composure thus reply'd.
    Ofspring of Heav'n and Earth, and all Earths Lord,
That such an Enemie we have, who seeks
Our ruin, both by thee informd I learn,   275
And from the parting Angel over-heard
As in a shadie nook I stood behind,
Just then returnd at shut of Evening Flowrs.
But that thou shouldst my firmness therfore doubt
To God or thee, because we have a foe   280
May tempt it, I expected not to hear.

---

[22] innocent.

His violence thou fearst not, being such,
As wee, not capable of death or pain,
Can either not receave, or can repell.
His fraud is then thy fear, which plain inferrs   285
Thy equal fear that my firm Faith and Love
Can by his fraud be shak'n or seduc't;
Thoughts, which how found they harbour in thy brest,
Adam, misthought of her to thee so dear?
To whom with healing words Adam reply'd.   290
Daughter of God and Man, immortal Eve,
For such thou art, from sin and blame entire:[23]
Not diffident of thee do I dissuade
Thy absence from my sight, but to avoid
Th' attempt it self, intended by our Foe.   295
For hee who tempts, though in vain, at least asperses
The tempted with dishonour foul, suppos'd
Not incorruptible of Faith, not prooff
Against temptation: thou thy self with scorn
And anger wouldst resent the offer'd wrong,   300
Though ineffectual found: misdeem not then,
If such affront I labour to avert
From thee alone, which on us both at once
The Enemie, though bold, will hardly dare,
Or daring, first on mee th' assault shall light.   305
Nor thou his malice and false guile contemn;
Suttle he needs must be, who could seduce
Angels, nor think superfluous others aid.
I from the influence of thy looks receave
Access[24] in every Vertue, in thy sight   310
More wise, more watchful, stronger, if need were
Of outward strength; while shame, thou looking on,
Shame to be overcome or over-reacht
Would utmost vigor raise, and rais'd unite.
Why shouldst not thou like sense within thee feel   315
When I am present, and thy trial choose
With me, best witness of thy Vertue tri'd.
So spake domestick Adam in his care
And Matrimonial Love; but Eve, who thought
Less attributed to her Faith sincere,   320
Thus her reply with accent sweet renewd.
If this be our condition, thus to dwell
In narrow circuit strait'n'd by a Foe,

[23] untouched.
[24] accession, increase by addition.

Suttle or violent, we not endu'd
Single with like defence, wherever met,   325
How are we happie, still in fear of harm?
But harm precedes not sin: onely our Foe
Tempting affronts us with his foul esteem
Of our integritie: his foul esteem
Sticks no dishonor on our Front,[25] but turns   330
Foul on himself; then wherfore shund or feard
By us? who rather double honour gain
From his surmise prov'd false, find peace within,
Favour from Heav'n, our witness from th' event.
And what is Faith, Love, Vertue unassaid   335
Alone, without exterior help sustaind?
Let us not then suspect our happie State
Left so imperfet by the Maker wise,
As not secure to single or combin'd.
Frail is our happiness, if this be so,   340
And *Eden* were no *Eden* thus expos'd.
    To whom thus *Adam* fervently repli'd.
O Woman, best are all things as the will
Of God ordain'd them, his creating hand
Nothing imperfet or deficient left   345
Of all that he Created, much less Man,
Or aught that might his happie State secure,
Secure from outward force; within himself
The danger lies, yet lies within his power:
Against his will he can receave no harm.   350
But God left free the Will, for what obeys
Reason, is free, and Reason he made right,
But bid her well beware, and still erect,[26]
Least by some fair appeering good surpris'd
She dictate false, and misinform the Will   355
To do what God expresly hath forbid.
Not then mistrust, but tender love enjoyns,
That I should mind[27] thee oft, and mind thou me.
Firm we subsist, yet possible to swerve,
Since Reason not impossibly may meet   360
Some specious object by the Foe subornd,
And fall into deception unaware,
Not keeping strictest watch, as she was warnd.
Seek not temptation then, which to avoid

[25] forehead.
[26] always watchful.
[27] remind.

Were better, and most likelie if from mee   365
Thou sever not: Trial will come unsought.
Wouldst thou approve[28] thy constancie, approve
First thy obedience; th' other who can know,
Not seeing thee attempted, who attest?
But if thou think, trial unsought may find   370
Us both securer[29] then thus warnd thou seemst,
Go; for thy stay, not free, absents thee more;
Go in thy native innocence, relie
On what thou hast of vertue, summon all,
For God towards thee hath done his part, do thine.   375
    So spake the Patriarch of Mankind, but *Eve*
Persisted, yet submiss, though last, repli'd.
    With thy permission then, and thus forewarnd
Chiefly by what thy own last reasoning words
Touch'd onely, that our trial, when least sought,   380
May find us both perhaps farr less prepar'd,
The willinger I goe, not much expect
A Foe so proud will first the weaker seek,
So bent, the more shall shame him his repulse.
Thus saying, from her Husbands hand her hand   385
Soft she withdrew, and like a Wood-Nymph light
Oread or *Dryad*, or of *Delia's*[30] Train,
Betook her to the Groves, but *Delia's* self
In gate surpass'd and Goddess-like deport,
Though not as shee with Bow and Quiver armd,   390
But with such Gardning Tools as Art yet rude,
Guiltless of fire had formd, or Angels brought.
To *Pales*, or *Pomona*[31] thus adornd,
Likest she seemd, *Pomona* when she fled
Vertumnus, or to *Ceres* in her Prime,   395
Yet Virgin of *Proserpina* from *Jove*.
Her long with ardent look his Eye pursu'd
Delighted, but desiring more her stay.
Oft he to her his charge of quick return
Repeated, shee to him as oft engag'd   400
To be returnd by Noon amid the Bowr,
And all things in best order to invite
Noontide repast, or Afternoons repose.
O much deceav'd, much failing, hapless *Eve*,

[28] prove.
[29] more confident.
[30] Diana's. An oread was a mountain nymph; a dryad, a tree nymph.
[31] goddesses of flocks and herds, and of fruit. Vertumnus was god of the changing season, and Ceres, mother of Proserpina, taught men agriculture.

Of thy presum'd return! event perverse!   405
Thou never from that hour in Paradise
Foundst either sweet repast, or sound repose;
Such ambush hid among sweet Flowrs and Shades
Waited with hellish rancour imminent
To intercept thy way, or send thee back   410
Despoild of Innocence, of Faith, of Bliss.
For now, and since first break of dawn the Fiend,
Meer Serpent in appearance, forth was come,
And on his Quest, where likeliest he might find
The onely two of Mankind, but in them   415
The whole included Race, his purpos'd prey.
In Bowr and Field he sought, where any tuft
Of Grove or Garden-Plot more pleasant lay,
Thir tendance or Plantation for delight,
By Fountain or by shadie Rivulet   420
He sought them both, but wish'd his hap might find
Eve separate, he wish'd, but not with hope
Of what so seldom chanc'd, when to his wish,
Beyond his hope, *Eve* separate he spies,
Veild in a Cloud of Fragrance, where she stood,   425
Half spi'd, so thick the Roses bushing round
About her glowd, oft stooping to support
Each Flowr of slender stalk, whose head though gay
Carnation, Purple, Azure, or spect with Gold,
Hung drooping unsustaind, them she upstaies   430
Gently with Mirtle band, mindless the while,
Her self, though fairest unsupported Flowr,
From her best prop so farr, and storm so nigh.
Neerer he drew, and many a walk travers'd
Of stateliest Covert, Cedar, Pine, or Palm,   435
Then voluble[32] and bold, now hid, now seen
Among thick-wov'n Arborets and Flowrs
Imborderd on each Bank, the hand[33] of *Eve:*
Spot more delicious then those Gardens feign'd
Or of reviv'd *Adonis*, or renownd   440
Alcinous, host of old *Lærtes* Son,[34]
Or that, not Mystic,[35] where the Sapient King
Held dalliance with his fair *Egyptian* Spouse.
Much hee the Place admir'd, the Person more.

[32] easily turning in and out.
[33] handiwork.
[34] Ulysses.
[35] not mythological. The "sapient king" is Solomon, who married Pharaoh's daughter (1 Kings iii. 1).

As one who long in populous City pent,   445
Where Houses thick and Sewers annoy[36] the Air,
Forth issuing on a Summers Morn to breathe
Among the pleasant Villages and Farmes
Adjoynd, from each thing met conceaves delight,
The smell of Grain, or tedded Grass,[37] or Kine,   450
Or Dairie, each rural sight, each rural sound;
If chance with Nymphlike step fair Virgin pass,
What pleasing seemd, for her now pleases more,
She most, and in her look summs all Delight.
Such Pleasure took the Serpent to behold   455
This Flowrie Plat, the sweet recess of *Eve*
Thus earlie, thus alone; her Heav'nly form
Angelic, but more soft, and Feminine,
Her graceful Innocence, her every Air
Of gesture or lest action overawd   460
His Malice, and with rapine sweet bereav'd
His fierceness of the fierce intent it brought:
That space the Evil one abstracted stood
From his own evil, and for the time remain
Stupidly good, of enmitie disarm'd,   465
Of guile, of hate, of envie, of revenge;
But the hot Hell that always in him burns,
Though in mid Heav'n, soon ended his delight,
And tortures him now more, the more he sees
Of pleasure not for him ordain'd: then soon   470
Fierce hate he recollects, and all his thoughts
Of mischief, gratulating, thus excites.
     Thoughts, whither have ye led me, with what sweet
Compulsion thus transported to forget
What hither brought us, hate, not love, nor hope   475
Of Paradise for Hell, hope here to taste
Of pleasure, but all pleasure to destroy,
Save what is in destroying, other joy
To me is lost. Then let me not let pass
Occasion which now smiles, behold alone   480
The Woman, opportune to all attempts,
Her Husband, for I view far round, not nigh,
Whose higher intellectual more I shun,
And strength, of courage hautie, and of limb
Heroic built, though of terrestrial mould,   485
Foe not informidable, exempt from wound,

[36] pollute.
[37] grass spread out to make hay.

I not; so much hath Hell debas'd, and pain
Infeebl'd me, to what I was in Heav'n.
Shee fair, divinely fair, fit Love for Gods,
Not terrible, though terrour be in Love   490
And beautie, not approacht by stronger hate,
Hate stronger, under shew of Love well feign'd,
The way which to her ruin now I tend.
    So spake the Enemie of Mankind, enclos'd
In Serpent, Inmate bad, and toward *Eve*   495
Address'd his way, not with indented wave,
Prone on the ground, as since, but on his rear,
Circular base of rising foulds, that tour'd[38]
Fould above fould a surging Maze, his Head
Crested aloft, and Carbuncle his Eyes;   500
With burnisht Neck of verdant Gold, erect
Amidst his circling Spires,[39] that on the grass
Floted redundant: pleasing was his shape,
And lovely, never since of Serpent kind
Lovelier, not those that in *Illyria* chang'd[40]   505
Hermione and *Cadmus*, or the God[41]
In *Epidaurus;* nor to which transformd
Ammonian Jove, or *Capitoline* was seen,
Hee with *Olympias*, this with her who bore
Scipio the highth of *Rome*.[42] With tract oblique   510
At first, as one who sought access, but feard
To interrupt, side-long he works his way.
As when a Ship by skilful Stearsman wrought
Nigh Rivers mouth or Foreland, where the Wind
Veres oft, as oft so steers, and shifts her Sail;   515
So varied hee, and of his tortuous Train
Curld many a wanton wreath in sight of *Eve*,
To lure her Eye; shee busied heard the sound
Of rusling Leaves, but minded not, as us'd
To such disport before her through the Field,   520
From every Beast, more duteous at her call,
Then at *Circean* call the Herd disguis'd.[43]

[38] towered.
[39] coils.
[40] transformed (into serpents). When Pentheus revolted and acquired the
rule of Thebes from Cadmus, his grandfather, Cadmus and his wife Harmonia
(Hermione) were changed into dragons and carried off to the Elysian Fields.
[41] Aesculapius, depicted as a serpent (the caduceus being his symbol) in his
temple in Epidaurus.
[42] In the guise of a serpent Jove Ammon wooed Alexander the Great's mother
Olympias, and Roman Jove (Capitoline), Scipio's mother (Sempronia).
[43] Circe had turned Ulysses' men into swine.

Hee boulder now, uncall'd before her stood;
But as in gaze admiring: Oft he bowd
His turret Crest, and sleek enamel'd Neck,   525
Fawning, and lick'd the ground whereon she trod.
His gentle dumb expression turnd at length
The Eye of *Eve* to mark his play; he glad
Of her attention gaind, with Serpent Tongue
Organic, or impulse of vocal Air,[44]   530
His fraudulent temptation thus began.
    Wonder not, sovran Mistress, if perhaps
Thou canst, who art sole Wonder, much less arm
Thy looks, the Heav'n of mildness, with disdain,
Displeas'd that I approach thee thus, and gaze   535
Insatiate, I thus single, nor have feard
Thy awful brow, more awful thus retir'd.
Fairest resemblance of thy Maker fair,
Thee all things living gaze on, all things thine
By gift, and thy Celestial Beautie adore   540
With ravishment beheld, there best beheld
Where universally admir'd; but here
In this enclosure wild, these Beasts among,
Beholders rude, and shallow to discern
Half what in thee is fair, one man except,   545
Who sees thee? (and what is one?) who shouldst be seen
A Goddess among Gods, ador'd and serv'd
By Angels numberless, thy daily Train.
    So gloz'd the Tempter, and his Proem tun'd;
Into the Heart of *Eve* his words made way,   550
Though at the voice much marveling; at length
Not unamaz'd she thus in answer spake.
What may this mean? Language of Man pronounc't
By Tongue of Brute, and human sense exprest?
The first at lest of these I thought deni'd   555
To Beasts, whom God on thir Creation-Day
Created mute to all articulat sound;
The latter I demurr,[45] for in thir looks
Much reason, and in thir actions oft appeers.
Thee, Serpent, suttlest beast of all the field   560
I knew, but not with human voice endu'd;
Redouble then this miracle, and say,

---

[44] Satan spoke either by using the serpent's forked tongue or by vibrating the
air to create vocal sounds.
[45] doubt.

How cam'st thou speakable of mute,[46] and how
To me so friendly grown above the rest
Of brutal kind,[47] that daily are in sight?   565
Say, for such wonder claims attention due.
   To whom the guileful Tempter thus reply'd.
Empress of this fair World, resplendent *Eve*,
Easie to mee it is to tell thee all
What thou commandst, and right thou shouldst be obeyd: 570
I was at first as other Beasts that graze
The trodden Herb, of abject thoughts and low,
As was my food, nor aught but food discern'd
Or Sex, and apprehended nothing high:
Till on a day roaving the field, I chanc'd   575
A goodly Tree farr distant to behold
Loaden with fruit of fairest colours mixt,
Ruddie and Gold: I nearer drew to gaze;
When from the boughs a savorie odour blown,
Grateful to appetite, more pleas'd my sense   580
Then smell of sweetest Fenel, or the Teats
Of Ewe or Goat dropping with Milk at Eevn,
Unsuckt of Lamb or Kid, that tend thir play.
To satisfie the sharp desire I had
Of tasting those fair Apples, I resolv'd   585
Not to deferr; hunger and thirst at once,
Powerful perswaders, quick'n'd at the scent
Of that alluring fruit, urg'd me so keen.
About the mossie Trunk I wound me soon,
For high from ground the branches would require   590
Thy utmost reach or *Adams*: Round the Tree
All other Beasts that saw, with like desire
Longing and envying stood, but could not reach.
Amid the Tree now got, where plenty hung
Tempting so nigh, to pluck and eat my fill   595
I spar'd not, for such pleasure till that hour
At Feed or Fountain never had I found.
Sated at length, ere long I might perceave
Strange alteration in me, to degree
Of Reason in my inward Powers, and Speech   600
Wanted not long, though to this shape retain'd.
Thenceforth to Speculations high or deep
I turnd my thoughts, and with capacious mind

---

[46] How cam'st thou to be able to speak though otherwise incapable of human speech.
[47] "of the nature of a beast," with ironic overtones of the words' opposing connotations.

Considerd all things visible in Heav'n,
Or Earth, or Middle,[48] all things fair and good;   605
But all that fair and good in thy Divine
Semblance, and in thy Beauties heav'nly Ray
United I beheld; no Fair to thine
Equivalent or second, which compel'd
Mee thus, though importune perhaps, to come   610
And gaze, and worship thee of right declar'd
Sovran of Creatures, universal Dame.
   So talk'd the spirited[49] sly Snake; and *Eve*
Yet more amaz'd unwarie thus reply'd.
   Serpent, thy overpraising leaves in doubt   615
The vertue of that Fruit, in thee first prov'd:
But say, where grows the Tree, from hence how far?
For many are the Trees of God that grow
In Paradise, and various, yet unknown
To us, in such abundance lies our choice,   620
As leaves a greater store of Fruit untoucht,
Still hanging incorruptible, till men
Grow up to thir provision,[50] and more hands
Help to disburden Nature of her Birth.
   To whom the wilie Adder, blithe and glad.   625
Empress, the way is readie, and not long,
Beyond a row of Myrtles, on a Flat,
Fast by a Fountain, one small Thicket past
Of blowing Myrrh and Balm; if thou accept
My conduct, I can bring thee thither soon.   630
   Lead then, said *Eve*. Hee leading swiftly rowld
In tangles, and made intricate seem strait,
To mischief swift. Hope elevates, and joy
Bright'ns his Crest, as when a wandring Fire,
Compact of unctuous vapor, which the Night   635
Condenses, and the cold invirons round,
Kindl'd through agitation to a Flame,
Which oft, they say, some evil Spirit attends,
Hovering and blazing with delusive Light,
Misleads th' amaz'd Night-wanderer from his way   640
To Boggs and Mires, and oft through Pond or Pool,
There swallow'd up and lost, from succour farr.
So glister'd the dire Snake, and into fraud
Led *Eve* our credulous Mother, to the Tree
Of prohibition, root of all our woe;   645

---

   [48] the air.
   [49] embodying a spirit.
   [50] to the number of men provided for.

Which when she saw, thus to her guide she spake.
    Serpent, we might have spar'd our coming hither,
Fruitless to mee, though Fruit be here to excess,
The credit[51] of whose vertue rest with thee,
Wondrous indeed, if cause of such effects.   650
But of this Tree we may not taste nor touch;
God so commanded, and left that Command
Sole Daughter[52] of his voice; the rest, we live
Law to our selves, our Reason is our Law.
    To whom the Tempter guilefully repli'd.[53]   655
Indeed? hath God then said that of the Fruit
Of all these Garden Trees ye shall not eat,
Yet Lords declar'd of all in Earth or Air?
    To whom thus *Eve* yet sinless. Of the Fruit
Of each Tree in the Garden we may eat,   660
But of the Fruit of this fair Tree amidst
The Garden, God hath said, Ye shall not eat
Thereof, nor shall ye touch it, least ye die.
    She scarse had said, though brief, when now more bold
The Tempter, but with shew of Zeal and Love   665
To Man, and indignation at his wrong,
New part puts on, and as to passion mov'd,
Fluctuats disturb'd, yet comely, and in act
Rais'd, as of som great matter to begin.
As when of old som Orator renound   670
In *Athens* or free *Rome*, where Eloquence
Flourishd, since mute, to som great cause addrest,
Stood in himself collected, while each part,
Motion, each act won audience ere the tongue,
Somtimes in highth began, as no delay   675
Of Preface brooking through his Zeal of Right.
So standing, moving, or to highth upgrown
The Tempter all impassiond thus began.
    O Sacred, Wise, and Wisdom-giving Plant,
Mother of Science,[54] now I feel thy Power   680
Within me cleere, not onely to discern
Things in thir Causes,[55] but to trace the wayes

---

[51] trustworthiness.
[52] By this term (signifying a divine revelation) Eve makes the command less stringent.
[53] Eve's fall (through l. 781) is derived from Gen. iii. 1–6.
[54] knowledge.
[55] In the *Art of Logic* (Columbia, XI, 29), Milton defined a cause as: "that by the force of which a thing exists." Following Ramus, he talks of efficient

Of highest Agents, deemd however wise.
Queen of this Universe, doe not believe
Those rigid threats of Death; ye shall not Die: 685
How should ye? by the Fruit? it gives[56] you Life
To Knowledge; by the Threatner? look on mee,
Mee who have touch'd and tasted, yet both live,
And life more perfet have attaind then Fate
Meant mee, by ventring higher then my Lot.   690
Shall that be shut to Man, which to the Beast
Is open? or will God incense his ire
For such a petty Trespass, and not praise
Rather your dauntless vertue, whom the pain
Of Death denounc't,[57] whatever thing Death be,   695
Deterrd not from atchieving what might lead
To happier life, knowledge of Good and Evil;
Of good, how just? of evil, if what is evil
Be real, why not known, since easier shunnd?
God therefore cannot hurt ye, and be just;   700
Not just, not God; not feard then, nor obeyd:
Your fear it self of Death removes the fear.
Why then was this forbid? Why but to awe,
Why but to keep ye low and ignorant,
His worshippers; he knows that in the day   705
Ye Eat thereof, your Eyes that seem so cleer,
Yet are but dim, shall perfetly be then
Op'n'd and cleerd, and ye shall be as Gods,
Knowing both Good and Evil as they know.
That ye should be as Gods, since I as Man,   710
Internal Man, is but proportion meet,
I of brute human, yee of human Gods.
So ye shall die perhaps, by putting off
Human, to put on Gods, death to be wisht,
Though threat'n'd, which no worse then this can bring.   715
And what are Gods that Man may not become

---

causes (those by which a thing exists or is brought about) and helping causes.
Such discernment as Satan claims would recognize the slight dissent among
things when they seem to exhibit affinity with consentanies (things in agree-
ment). The "highest Agents" are those instruments (helping causes) through
which divine testimony operates. But since the procatarctic cause (that from
without) is powerless if there is no proegumenic cause (that from within),
Eve cannot duplicate the actions of such agents. Satan persuades that he,
as well as Eve if she partakes, has such power now within him from having eaten
the fruit.
[56] adds.
[57] whom the penalty of death threatened.

As they, participating God-like food?
The Gods are first, and that advantage use
On our belief, that all from them proceeds;
I question it, for this fair Earth I see,   720
Warm'd by the Sun, producing every kind,
Them nothing: If they all things, who enclos'd
Knowledge of Good and Evil in this Tree,
That whoso eats thereof, forthwith attains
Wisdom without their leave? and wherein lies   725
Th' offence, that Man should thus attain to know?
What can your knowledge hurt him, or this Tree
Impart against his will if all be his?
Or is it envie, and can envie dwell
In heav'nly brests? these, these and many more   730
Causes import your need of this fair Fruit.
Goddess humane,[58] reach then, and freely taste.

He ended, and his words replete with guile
Into her heart too easie entrance won:
Fixt on the Fruit she gaz'd, which to behold   735
Might tempt alone, and in her ears the sound
Yet rung of his perswasive words, impregn'd
With Reason, to her seeming, and with Truth;
Mean while the hour of Noon[59] drew on, and wak'd
An eager appetite, rais'd by the smell   740
So savorie of that Fruit, which with desire,
Inclinable now grown to touch or taste,
Sollicited her longing eye; yet first
Pausing a while, thus to her self she mus'd.

Great are thy Vertues, doubtless, best of Fruits,   745
Though kept from Man, and worthy to be admir'd,
Whose taste, too long forborn, at first assay
Gave elocution to the mute, and taught
The Tongue not made for Speech to speak thy praise:
Thy praise hee also who forbids thy use,   750
Conceals not from us, naming thee the Tree
Of Knowledge, knowledge both of good and evil;
Forbids us then to taste, but his forbidding
Commends thee more, while it inferrs the good
By thee communicated, and our want: 755
For good unknown, sure is not had, or had

[58] probably meaning only "human," since the received spelling is the common form for that word.
[59] The concept that the Noonday Devil is the most dangerous explains the time of occurrence of Eve's fall.

And yet unknown, is as not had at all.
In plain then, what forbids he but to know,
Forbids us good, forbids us to be wise?
Such prohibitions bind not. But if Death   760
Bind us with after-bands, what profits then
Our inward freedom? In the day we eat
Of this fair Fruit, our doom is, we shall die.
How dies the Serpent? hee hath eat'n and lives,
And knows, and speaks, and reasons, and discerns,   765
Irrational till then. For us alone
Was death invented? or to us deni'd
This intellectual food, for beasts reserv'd?
For Beasts it seems: yet that one Beast which first
Hath tasted, envies not, but brings with joy   770
The good befall'n him, Author unsuspect,[60]
Friendly to man, farr from deceit or guile.
What fear I then, rather what know to fear
Under this ignorance of Good and Evil,
Of God or Death, of Law or Penaltie?   775
Here grows the Cure of all, this Fruit Divine,
Fair to the Eye, inviting to the Taste,
Of vertue to make wise: what hinders then
To reach, and feed at once both Bodie and Mind?
    So saying, her rash hand in evil hour   780
Forth reaching to the Fruit, she pluck'd, she eat:[61]
Earth felt the wound, and Nature from her seat
Sighing through all her Works gave signs of woe,
That all was lost. Back to the Thicket slunk
The guiltie Serpent, and well might, for *Eve*   785
Intent now wholly on her taste, naught else
Regarded, such delight till then, as seemd,
In Fruit she never tasted, whether true
Or fansied so, through expectation high
Of knowledge, nor was God-head from her thought.   790
Greedily she ingorg'd without restraint,
And knew not eating Death:[62] Satiate at length,
And hight'n'd as with Wine, jocond and boon,[63]
Thus to her self she pleasingly began.
    O Sovran, vertuous, precious of all Trees   795
In Paradise, of operation blest

[60] with no suspicion of his truthfulness.
[61] the archaic preterite.
[62] knew not that she was eating Death.
[63] jovial.

To Sapience,[64] hitherto obscur'd, infam'd,[65]
And thy fair Fruit let hang, as to no end
Created; but henceforth my early care,
Not without Song, each Morning, and due praise   800
Shall tend thee, and the fertil burden ease
Of thy full branches offer'd free to all;
Till dieted by thee I grow mature
In knowledge, as the Gods who all things know;
Though others envie what they cannot give;   805
For had the gift bin theirs, it had not here
Thus grown. Experience, next to thee I owe,
Best guide; not following thee, I had remaind
In ignorance, thou op'nst Wisdoms way,
And giv'st access, though secret she retire.   810
And I perhaps am secret; Heav'n is high,
High and remote to see from thence distinct
Each thing on Earth; and other care perhaps
May have diverted from continual watch
Our great Forbidder, safe with all his Spies   815
About him. But to *Adam* in what sort
Shall I appeer? shall I to him make known
As yet my change, and give him to partake
Full happiness with me, or rather not,
But keep the odds of Knowledge in my power   820
Without Copartner? so to add what wants
In Femal Sex, the more to draw his Love,
And render me more equal, and perhaps,
A thing not undesirable, somtime
Superior; for inferior who is free?   825
This may be well: but what if God have seen,
And Death ensue? then I shall be no more,
And *Adam* wedded to another *Eve*,
Shall live with her enjoying, I extinct;
A death to think. Confirm'd then I resolve,   830
Adam shall share with me in bliss or woe:
So dear I love him, that with him all deaths
I could endure, without him live no life.

  So saying, from the Tree her step she turnd,
But first low Reverence don, as to the power   835
That dwelt within, whose presence had infus'd
Into the plant sciential[66] sap, deriv'd

---

[64] The word is derived from the Latin for "taste."
[65] subjected to infamy.
[66] having knowledge.

From Nectar, drink of Gods. *Adam* the while
Waiting desirous her return, had wove
Of choicest Flowrs a Garland to adorn   840
Her Tresses, and her rural labours crown,
As Reapers oft are wont thir Harvest Queen.
Great joy he promis'd to his thoughts, and new
Solace in her return, so long delay'd;
Yet oft his heart, divine[67] of somthing ill,   845
Misgave him; hee the faultring measure felt;
And forth to meet her went, the way she took
That Morn when first they parted; by the Tree
Of Knowledge he must pass, there he her met,
Scarse from the Tree returning; in her hand   850
A bough of fairest fruit that downie smil'd,
New gatherd, and ambrosial smell diffus'd.
To him she hasted, in her face excuse
Came Prologue, and Apologie to prompt,
Which with bland words at will she thus addrest.   855
    Hast thou not wonderd, *Adam*, at my stay?
Thee I have misst, and thought it long, depriv'd
Thy presence, agonie of love till now
Not felt, nor shall be twice, for never more
Mean I to trie, what rash untri'd I sought,   860
The pain of absence from thy sight. But strange
Hath bin the cause, and wonderful to hear:
This Tree is not as we are told, a Tree
Of danger tasted, nor to evil unknown
Op'ning the way, but of Divine effect   865
To open Eyes, and make them Gods who taste;
And hath bin tasted such: the Serpent wise,
Or not restraind as wee, or not obeying,
Hath eat'n of the fruit, and is become,
Not dead, as we are threat'n'd, but thenceforth   870
Endu'd with human voice and human sense,
Reasoning to admiration, and with mee
Perswasively hath so prevaild, that I
Have also tasted, and have also found
Th' effects to correspond, opener mine Eyes,   875
Dimm erst, dilated Spirits, ampler Heart,
And growing up to Godhead; which for thee
Chiefly I sought, without thee can despise.
For bliss, as thou hast part, to me is bliss,
Tedious, unshar'd with thee, and odious soon.   880

[67] portending.

Thou therfore also taste, that equal Lot
May joyn us, equal Joy, as equal Love;
Least thou not tasting, different degree
Disjoyn us, and I then too late renounce
Deitie for thee, when Fate will not permit.   885
    Thus *Eve* with Countnance blithe her storie told;
But in her Cheek distemper flushing glowd.
On th' other side, *Adam*, soon as he heard
The fatal Trespass don by *Eve*, amaz'd,
Astonied[68] stood and Blank, while horror chill   890
Ran through his veins, and all his joynts relax'd;
From his slack hand the Garland wreath'd for *Eve*
Down drop'd, and all the faded Roses shed:
Speechless he stood and pale, till thus at length
First to himself he inward silence broke.   895
    O fairest of Creation, last and best
Of all Gods works, Creature in whom excell'd
Whatever can to sight or thought be formd,
Holy, divine, good, amiable, or sweet!
How art thou lost, how on a sudden lost,   900
Defac't, deflowrd, and now to Death devote?[69]
Rather how hast thou yeelded to transgress
The strict forbiddance, how to violate
The sacred Fruit forbidd'n! som cursed fraud
Of Enemie hath beguil'd thee, yet unknown,   905
And mee with thee hath ruind, for with thee
Certain my resolution is to Die;
How can I live without thee, how forgoe
Thy sweet Converse and Love so dearly joyn'd,
To live again in these wild Woods forlorn?   910
Should Gcd create another *Eve*, and I
Another Rib afford, yet loss of thee
Would never from my heart; no no, I feel
The Link of Nature draw me: Flesh of Flesh,
Bone of my Bone thou art, and from thy State   915
Mine never shall be parted, bliss or woe.
    So having said, as one from sad dismay
Recomforted, and after thoughts disturb'd
Submitting to what seemd remediless,
Thus in calm mood his Words to *Eve* he turnd.   920
    Bold deed thou hast presum'd, adventrous *Eve*,
And peril great provok't, who thus hast dar'd

[68] dismayed.
[69] doomed.

Had it bin onely coveting to Eye
That sacred Fruit, sacred to abstinence,
Much more to taste it under bann to touch.   925
But past who can recall, or don undoe?
Not God Omnipotent, nor Fate, yet so
Perhaps thou shalt not Die, perhaps the Fact
Is not so hainous now, foretasted Fruit,
Profan'd first by the Serpent, by him first   930
Made common and unhallowd ere our taste;
Nor yet on him found deadly, he yet lives,
Lives, as thou saidst, and gains to live as Man
Higher degree of Life, inducement strong
To us, as likely tasting to attain   935
Proportional ascent, which cannot be
But to be Gods, or Angels Demi-gods.
Nor can I think that God, Creator wise,
Though threatning, will in earnest so destroy
Us his prime Creatures, dignifi'd so high,   940
Set over all his Works, which in our Fall,
For us created, needs with us must fail,
Dependent made; so God shall uncreate,
Be frustrate, do, undo, and labour loose,
Not well conceav'd of God, who though his Power   945
Creation could repeat, yet would be loath
Us to abolish, least the Adversary
Triumph and say; Fickle their State whom God
Most Favors, who can please him long; Mee first
He ruind, now Mankind; whom will he next?   950
Matter of scorn, not to be giv'n the Foe.
However I with thee have fixt my Lot,
Certain[70] to undergoe like doom, if Death
Consort with thee, Death is to mee as Life;
So forcible within my heart I feel   955
The Bond of Nature draw me to my own,
My own in thee, for what thou art is mine;
Our State cannot be severd, we are one,
One Flesh; to loose thee were to loose my self.
   So *Adam*, and thus *Eve* to him repli'd.   960
O glorious trial of exceeding Love,
Illustrious evidence, example high!
Ingaging me to emulate, but short
Of thy perfection, how shall I attain,
Adam, from whose dear side I boast me sprung,   965

[70] resolved.

And gladly of our Union hear thee speak,
One Heart, one Soul in both; whereof good prooff
This day affords, declaring thee resolv'd,
Rather then Death or aught then Death more dread
Shall separate us, linkt in Love so dear,   970
To undergoe with mee one Guilt, one Crime,
If any be, of tasting this fair Fruit,
Whose vertue, for of good still good proceeds,
Direct, or by occasion hath presented
This happie trial of thy Love, which else   975
So eminently never had bin known.
Were it I thought Death menac't would ensue
This my attempt, I would sustain alone
The worst, and not perswade thee, rather die
Deserted, then oblige thee with a fact[71]   980
Pernicious to thy Peace, chiefly assur'd
Remarkably so late of thy so true,
So faithful Love unequald; but I feel
Farr otherwise th' event, not Death, but Life
Augmented, op'n'd Eyes, new Hopes, new Joyes,   985
Taste so Divine, that what of sweet before
Hath toucht my sense, flat seems to this, and harsh.
On my experience, *Adam*, freely taste,
And fear of Death deliver to the Winds.
     So saying, she embrac'd him, and for joy   990
Tenderly wept, much won that he his Love
Had so enobl'd, as of choice t' incurr
Divine displeasure for her sake, or Death.
In recompence (for such compliance bad
Such recompence best merits) from the bough   995
She gave him of that fair enticing Fruit
With liberal hand: he scrupl'd not to eat
Against his better knowledge, not deceav'd,[72]
But fondly overcome with Femal charm.[73]
Earth trembl'd from her entrails, as again   1000
In pangs, and Nature gave a second groan,
Skie lowr'd, and muttering Thunder, som sad drops
Wept at compleating of the mortal Sin
Original; while *Adam* took no thought,
Eating his fill, nor *Eve* to iterate   1005

Fall is complete because reason has consented

[71] bind thee with a deed.
[72] Gen. iii. 12: "And the man said, The woman whom thou gavest to be with me, she gave me of the tree, and I did eat."
[73] Adam falls at l. 999, inverse number of the sign of the beast of Revelation (666), assigned in book II to Death.

Her former trespass fear'd, the more to soothe
Him with her lov'd societie, that now
As with new Wine intoxicated both
They swim in mirth, and fansie that they feel
Divinitie within them breeding wings   1010
Wherewith to scorn the Earth: but that false Fruit
Farr other operation first displaid,
Carnal desire enflaming, hee on *Eve*
Began to cast lascivious Eyes, she him
As wantonly repaid; in Lust they burn: 1015
Till *Adam* thus 'gan *Eve* to dalliance move.

    Eve, now I see thou art exact of taste,[74]
And elegant, of Sapience no small part,
Since to each meaning savour we apply,
And Palate call judicious; I the praise   1020
Yeild thee, so well this day thou hast purvey'd.
Much pleasure we have lost, while we abstain'd
From this delightful Fruit, nor known till now
True relish, tasting; if such pleasure be
In things to us forbidden, it might be wish'd,   1025
For this one Tree had bin forbidden ten.
But come, so well refresh't, now let us play,
As meet is, after such delicious Fare;
For never did thy Beautie since the day
I saw thee first and wedded thee, adorn'd   1030
With all perfections, so enflame my sense
With ardor to enjoy thee, fairer now
Then ever, bountie of this vertuous[75] Tree.

    So said he, and forbore not glance or toy
Of amorous intent, well understood   1035
Of *Eve*, whose Eye darted contagious Fire.
Her hand he seis'd, and to a shadie bank,
Thick overhead with verdant roof imbowr'd
He led her nothing loath; Flowrs were the Couch,
Pansies, and Violets, and Asphodel,   1040
And Hyacinth, Earths freshest softest lap.
There they thir fill of Love and Loves disport
Took largely, of thir mutual guilt the Seal,
The solace of thir sin,[76] till dewie sleep

---

[74] Since the word "savor" ("taste") derives from "Sapience," a pun is intended referring to the act of their disobedience.
[75] efficacious, but ironically pointing to the lack of chastity exhibited by their tasting of it.
[76] Prov. vii. 18: "Come, let us take our fill of love until the morning: let us solace ourselves with loves."

Oppress'd them, wearied with thir amorous play.   1045
Soon as the force of that fallacious Fruit,
That with exhilerating vapour bland
About thir spirits had plaid, and inmost powers
Made err, was now exhal'd, and grosser sleep
Bred of unkindly fumes, with conscious dreams   1050
Encumberd, now had left them, up they rose
As from unrest, and each the other viewing,
Soon found thir Eyes how op'n'd, and thir minds
How dark'n'd; innocence, that as a veil
Had shadow'd them from knowing ill, was gon,   1055
Just confidence, and native righteousness,
And honour from about them, naked left
To guiltie shame: hee cover'd, but his Robe
Uncover'd more. So rose the *Danite* strong
Herculean Samson from the Harlot-lap   1060
Of *Philistean Dalilah*, and wak'd
Shorn of his strength. They destitute and bare
Of all thir vertue: silent, and in face
Confounded long they sate, as struck'n mute,
Till *Adam*, though not less then *Eve* abash't,   1065
At length gave utterance to these words constraind.
    O *Eve*, in evil hour thou didst give ear
To that false Worm, of whomsoever taught
To counterfet Mans voice, true in our Fall,
False in our promis'd Rising; since our Eyes   1070
Op'n'd we find indeed, and find we know
Both Good and Evil, Good lost, and Evil got,
Bad Fruit of Knowledge, if this be to know,
Which leaves us naked thus, of Honour void,
Of Innocence, of Faith, of Puritie,   1075
Our wonted Ornaments now soild and staind,
And in our Faces evident the signes
Of foul concupiscence; whence evil store;
Ev'n shame, the last[77] of evils; of the first
Be sure then. How shall I behold the face   1080
Henceforth of God or Angel, earst with joy
And rapture so oft beheld? those heav'nly shapes
Will dazle now this earthly, with thir blaze
Insufferably bright. O might I here
In solitude live savage, in some glade   1085
Obscur'd, where highest Woods impenetrable
To Starr or Sun-light, spread thir umbrage broad

[77] worst.

And brown[78] as Evening: Cover me ye Pines,
Ye Cedars, with innumerable boughs
Hide me, where I may never see them more.   1090
But let us now, as in bad plight, devise
What best may for the present serve to hide
The Parts of each from other, that seem most
To shame obnoxious, and unseemliest seen,
Some Tree whose broad smooth Leaves together sowd,   1095
And girded on our loyns, may cover round
Those middle parts, that this new commer, Shame,
There sit not, and reproach us as unclean.
    So counsel'd hee, and both together went
Into the thickest Wood, there soon they chose   1100
The Figtree,[79] not that kind for Fruit renown'd,
But such as at this day to *Indians* known
In *Malabar* or *Decan* spreds her Armes
Braunching so broad and long, that in the ground
The bended Twigs take root, and Daughters grow   1105
About the Mother Tree, a Pillard shade
High overarch't, and echoing Walks between;
There oft the *Indian* Herdsman shunning heat
Shelters in cool, and tends his pasturing Herds
At Loopholes cut through thickest shade: Those Leaves   1110
They gatherd, broad as *Amazonian* Targe,[80]
And with what skill they had, together sowd,
To gird thir waste, vain Covering if to hide
Thir guilt and dreaded shame; O how unlike
To that first naked Glorie. Such of late   1115
Columbus found th' *American* so girt
With featherd Cincture, naked else and wild
Among the Trees on Iles and woodie Shores.
Thus fenc't, and as they thought, thir shame in part
Coverd, but not at rest or ease of Mind,   1120
They sate them down to weep, nor onely Teares
Raind at thir Eyes, but high Winds worse within
Began to rise, high Passions, Anger, Hate,
Mistrust, Suspicion, Discord, and shook sore
Thir inward State of Mind, calm Region once   1125
And full of Peace, now tost and turbulent:
For Understanding rul'd not, and the Will
Heard not her lore, both in subjection now

[78] dark.
[79] the banyan; its leaves are not broad (l. 1111), an error deriving from Pliny.
[80] shield.

To sensual Appetite, who from beneath
Usurping over sovran Reason claimd   1130
Superior sway: from thus distemperd brest,
Adam, estrang'd in look and alterd stile,
Speech intermitted thus to *Eve* renewd.
    Would thou hadst heark'n'd to my words, and stai'd
With me, as I besought thee, when that strange   1135
Desire of wandring this unhappie Morn,
I know not whence possess'd thee; we had then
Remaind still happie, not as now, despoild
Of all our good, sham'd, naked, miserable.
Let none henceforth seek needless cause t' approve   1140
The Faith they owe;[81] when earnestly they seek
Such proof, conclude, they then begin to fail.
    To whom soon mov'd with touch of blame thus *Eve.*
What words have past thy Lips, *Adam* severe,
Imput'st thou that to my default, or will   1145
Of wandring, as thou call'st it, which who knows
But might as ill have happ'n'd thou being by,
Or to thy self perhaps: hadst thou bin there,
Or here th' attempt, thou couldst not have discernd
Fraud in the Serpent, speaking as he spake;   1150
No ground of enmitie between us known,
Why hee should mean me ill, or seek to harm.
Was I t' have never parted from thy side?
As good have grown there still a liveless Rib.
Being as I am, why didst not thou the Head   1155
Command me absolutely not to go,
Going into such danger as thou saidst?
Too facil then thou didst not much gainsay,
Nay, didst permit, approve, and fair dismiss.
Hadst thou bin firm and fixt in thy dissent,   1160
Neither had I transgress'd, nor thou with mee.
    To whom then first incenst *Adam* repli'd.
Is this the Love, is this the recompence
Of mine to thee, ingrateful *Eve,* exprest
Immutable[82] when thou wert lost, not I,   1165
Who might have liv'd and joyd immortal bliss,
Yet willingly chose rather Death with thee:
And am I now upbraided, as the cause
Of thy transgressing? not enough severe,
It seems, in thy restraint: what could I more?   1170

[81] have.
[82] shown to be, unchangeable.

I warn'd thee, I admonish'd thee, foretold
The danger, and the lurking Enemie
That lay in wait; beyond this had bin force,
And force upon free will hath here no place.
But confidence then bore thee on, secure   1175
Either to meet no danger, or to find
Matter of glorious trial; and perhaps
I also err'd in overmuch admiring
What seemd in thee so perfet, that I thought
No evil durst attempt[83] thee, but I rue   1180
That errour now, which is become my crime,
And thou th' accuser. Thus it shall befall
Him who to worth in Woman overtrusting
Lets her will rule; restraint she will not brook,
And left t' her self, if evil thence ensue,   1185
Shee first his weak indulgence will accuse.
　　Thus they in mutual accusation spent
The fruitless hours, but neither self-condemning,
And of thir vain contest appeer'd no end.

[83] tempt.

BOOK X

THE ARGUMENT

Mans transgression known, the Guardian Angels forsake Paradise, and
return up to Heaven to approve thir vigilance, and are approv'd, God
declaring that the entrance of *Satan* could not be by them prevented.
He sends his Son to judge the Transgressors, who descends and gives
Sentence accordingly; then in pity cloaths them both, and reascends. *Sin*
and *Death* sitting till then at the Gates of Hell, by wondrous sympathie
feeling the success of *Satan* in this new World, and the sin by Man there
committed, resolve to sit no longer confin'd in Hell, but to follow *Satan*
thir Sire up to the place of Man: To make the way easier from Hell to
this World to and fro, they pave a broad Highway or Bridge over *Chaos*,
according to the Track that *Satan* first made; then preparing for Earth,
they meet him proud of his success returning to Hell; thir mutual gratu-
lation. *Satan* arrives at *Pandemonium*, in full assembly relates with boast-
ing his success against Man; instead of applause is entertained with a
general hiss by all his audience, transform'd with himself also suddenly
into Serpents, according to his doom giv'n in Paradise; then deluded
with a shew of the forbidden Tree springing up before them, they greed-
ily reaching to taste of the Fruit, chew dust and bitter ashes. The pro-
ceedings of *Sin* and *Death;* God foretells the final Victory of his Son over

them, and the renewing of all things; but for the present commands his Angels to make several alterations in the Heavens and Elements. *Adam* more and more perceiving his fall'n condition heavily bewails, rejects the condolement of *Eve;* she persists and at length appeases him: then to evade the Curse likely to fall on thir Ofspring, proposes to *Adam* violent wayes which he approves not, but conceiving better hope, puts her in mind of the late Promise made them, that her Seed should be reveng'd on the Serpent, and exhorts her with him to seek Peace of the offended Deity, by repentance and supplication.

Meanwhile the hainous and despightfull act
Of *Satan* done in Paradise, and how
Hee in the Serpent had perverted *Eve,*
Her Husband shee, to taste the fatall fruit,
Was known in Heav'n; for what can scape the Eye   5
Of God All-seeing, or deceave his Heart
Omniscient, who in all things wise and just,
Hinder'd not *Satan* to attempt the mind
Of Man, with strength entire, and free will arm'd,
Complete¹ to have discover'd and repulst   10
Whatever wiles of Foe or seeming Friend.
For still they knew, and ought t' have still remember'd
The high Injunction not to taste that Fruit,
Whoever tempted; which they not obeying,
Incurr'd, what could they less, the penaltie,   15
And manifold in sin, deserv'd to fall.
Up into Heav'n from Paradise in hast
Th' Angelic Guards ascended, mute and sad
For Man, for of his state by this they knew,
Much wondring how the suttle Fiend had stoln   20
Entrance unseen. Soon as th' unwelcome news
From Earth arriv'd at Heaven Gate, displeas'd
All were who heard, dim sadness did not spare
That time Celestial visages, yet mixt
With pitie, violated not thir bliss.   25
About the new-arriv'd, in multitudes
Th' ethereal People ran, to hear and know
How all befell: they towards the Throne Supream
Accountable made haste to make appear
With righteous plea, thir utmost vigilance,   30
And easily approv'd; when the most High
Eternal Father from his secret Cloud,
Amidst in Thunder utter'd thus his voice.

¹ perfectly equipped.

Assembl'd Angels, and ye Powers return'd
From unsuccessful charge, be not dismaid,   35
Nor troubl'd at these tidings from the Earth,
Which your sincerest care could not prevent,
Foretold so lately what would come to pass,
When first this Tempter cross'd the Gulf from Hell.
I told ye then he should prevail and speed[2]   40
On his bad Errand, Man should be seduc't
And flatter'd out of all, believing lies
Against his Maker; no Decree of mine
Concurring to necessitate his Fall,
Or touch with lightest moment[3] of impulse   45
His free Will, to her own inclining left
In eevn scale. But fall'n he is, and now
What rests,[4] but that the mortal Sentence pass
On his transgression, Death denounc't that day,
Which he presumes already vain and void,   50
Because not yet inflicted, as he fear'd,
By some immediate stroak; but soon shall find
Forbearance no acquittance ere day end.
Justice shall not return as bountie scorn'd.
But whom send I to judge them? whom but thee   55
Vicegerent Son, to thee I have transferr'd
All Judgement, whether in Heav'n, or Earth, or Hell.
Easie it may be seen that I intend
Mercie collegue with Justice, sending thee
Mans Friend, his Mediator, his design'd   60
Both Ransom and Redeemer voluntarie,
And destin'd Man himself to judge Man fall'n.
    So spake the Father, and unfoulding bright
Toward the right hand his Glorie, on the Son
Blaz'd forth unclouded Deitie; he full   65
Resplendent all his Father manifest
Express'd, and thus divinely answer'd mild.
    Father Eternal, thine is to decree,
Mine both in Heav'n and Earth to do thy will
Supream, that thou in mee thy Son belov'd   70
Mayst ever rest well pleas'd. I go to judge
On Earth these thy transgressors, but thou knowst,
Whoever judg'd, the worst on mee must light,
When time shall be, for so I undertook

    [2] succeed.
    [3] the force which tends to produce motion.
    [4] remains.

Before thee; and not repenting, this obtain   75
Of right, that I may mitigate thir doom
On me deriv'd,[5] yet I shall temper so
Justice with Mercie, as may illustrate[6] most
Them fully satisfied, and thee appease.
Attendance none shall need, nor Train, where none   80
Are to behold the Judgement, but the judg'd,
Those two; the third best absent is condemn'd,
Convict[7] by flight, and Rebel to all Law
Conviction to the Serpent none belongs.[8]
   Thus saying, from his radiant Seat he rose   85
Of high collateral glorie: him Thrones and Powers,
Princedoms, and Dominations ministrant
Accompanied to Heaven Gate, from whence
Eden and all the Coast[9] in prospect lay.
Down he descended strait; the speed of Gods   90
Time counts not, though with swiftest minutes wing'd.
Now was the Sun in Western cadence[10] low
From Noon, and gentle Aires due at thir hour
To fan the Earth now wak'd, and usher in
The Eevning cool when he from wrauth more cool   95
Came the mild Judge and Intercessor both
To sentence Man: the voice of God they heard
Now walking in the Garden, by soft winds
Brought to thir Ears, while day declin'd, they heard,
And from his presence hid themselves among   100
The thickest Trees, both Man and Wife, till God
Approaching, thus to *Adam* call'd aloud.
   Where art thou *Adam,* wont with joy to meet
My coming seen far off? I miss thee here,
Not pleas'd, thus entertaind with solitude,   105
Where obvious dutie[11] erewhile appear'd unsaught:
Or come I less conspicuous, or what change
Absents thee, or what chance detains? Come forth.
He came, and with him *Eve,* more loth, though first
T' offend, discount'nanc't both, and discompos'd;   110
Love was not in thir looks, either to God

[5] transferred.
[6] illuminate.
[7] proved guilty.
[8] that is, neither shall be bound to Satan as penalty.
[9] border, surrounding area.
[10] descent.
[11] duty to meet me.

Or to each other, but apparent[12] guilt,
And shame, and perturbation, and despair,
Anger, and obstinacie, and hate, and guile.
Whence *Adam* faultring long, thus answer'd brief.   115
  I heard thee in the Garden, and of thy voice
Affraid, being naked, hid my self. To whom
The gracious Judge without revile repli'd.
  My voice thou oft hast heard, and hast not fear'd,
But still rejoyc't, how is it now become   120
So dreadful to thee? that thou art naked, who
Hath told thee? hast thou eaten of the Tree
Whereof I gave thee charge thou shouldst not eat?
  To whom thus *Adam* sore beset repli'd.
O Heav'n! in evil strait this day I stand   125
Before my Judge, either to undergoe
My self the total Crime, or to accuse
My other self, the partner of my life;
Whose failing, while her Faith to me remains,
I should conceal, and not expose to blame   130
By my complaint; but strict necessitie
Subdues me, and calamitous constraint,
Least on my head both sin and punishment,
However insupportable, be all
Devolv'd; though should I hold my peace, yet thou   135
Wouldst easily detect what I conceal.
This Woman whom thou mad'st to be my help,
And gav'st me as thy perfet gift, so good,
So fit, so acceptable, so Divine,
That from her hand I could suspect no ill,   140
And what she did, whatever in it self,
Her doing seem'd to justifie the deed;
Shee gave me of the Tree, and I did eat.
  To whom the sovran Presence thus repli'd.
Was shee thy God, that her thou didst obey   145
Before his voice, or was shee made thy guide,
Superior, or but equal, that to her
Thou did'st resigne thy Manhood, and the Place
Wherein God set thee above her made of thee,
And for thee, whose perfection farr excell'd   150
Hers in all real dignitie: Adornd
Shee was indeed, and lovely to attract
Thy Love, not thy Subjection, and her Gifts
Were such as under Government well seem'd,

---

[12] easily seen.

Unseemly to bear rule, which was thy part   155
And person,[13] had'st thou known thy self aright.
   So having said, he thus to *Eve* in few:
Say Woman, what is this which thou hast done?
   To whom sad *Eve* with shame nigh overwhelm'd,
Confessing soon, yet not before her Judge   160
Bold or loquacious, thus abasht repli'd.
   The Serpent me beguil'd and I did eat.
   Which when the Lord God heard, without delay
To Judgement he proceeded on th' accus'd
Serpent though brute, unable to transferr   165
The Guilt on him who made him instrument
Of mischief, and polluted from the end
Of his Creation; justly then accurst,
As vitiated in Nature: more to know
Concern'd not Man (since he no further knew)   170
Nor alter'd his offence; yet God at last
To Satan first in sin his doom apply'd,
Though in mysterious terms, judg'd as then best:
And on the Serpent thus his curse let fall.
   Because thou hast done this, thou art accurst   175
Above all Cattel, each Beast of the Field;
Upon thy Belly groveling thou shalt goe,
And dust shalt eat all the dayes of thy Life.[14]
Between Thee and the Woman I will put
Enmitie, and between thine and her Seed;   180
Her Seed shall bruise thy head, thou bruise his heel.[15]
   So spake this Oracle, then verifi'd
When *Jesus* son of *Mary* second *Eve*,
Saw Satan fall like Lightning down from Heav'n,
Prince of the Air; then rising from his Grave   185
Spoild Principalities and Powers, triumpht
In open shew, and with ascention bright
Captivity led captive through the Air,
The Realm it self of Satan long usurpt,
Whom he shall tread at last under our feet;   190
Eevn hee who now foretold his fatal bruise,
And to the Woman thus his Sentence turn'd.
   Thy sorrow I will greatly multiplie
By thy Conception; Childern thou shalt bring

[13] role.
[14] Dust is, ironically, what constitutes Man; see l. 208.
[15] Lines 175–81 derive from Gen. iii. 14–15. Note that only bruising is involved, but its consequence for Satan will be more momentous than for the Son as man.

In sorrow forth, and to thy Husbands will   195
Thine shall submit, hee over thee shall rule.
    On *Adam* last thus judgement he pronounc'd.
Because thou hast heark'n'd to the voice of thy Wife,
And eaten of the Tree concerning which
I charg'd thee, saying: Thou shalt not eat thereof,   200
Curs'd is the ground for thy sake,[16] thou in sorrow
Shalt eat thereof all the days of thy Life;
Thorns also and Thistles it shall bring thee forth
Unbid, and thou shalt eat th' Herb of the Field,
In the sweat of thy Face shalt thou eat Bread,   205
Till thou return unto the ground, for thou
Out of the ground wast taken, know thy Birth,
For dust thou art, and shalt to dust return.
    So judg'd he Man, both Judge and Saviour sent,
And th' instant stroke of Death denounc't that day   210
Remov'd farr off; then pittying how they stood
Before him naked to the air, that now
Must suffer change, disdain'd not to begin
Thenceforth the form of servant to assume,
As when he wash'd his servants feet, so now   215
As Father of his Familie he clad
Thir nakedness with Skins of Beasts, or slain,
Or as the Snake with youthful Coat repaid;[17]
And thought not much[18] to cloath his Enemies:
Nor hee thir outward onely with the Skins   220
Of Beasts, but inward nakedness, much more
Opprobrious, with his Robe of righteousness,
Arraying cover'd from his Fathers sight.
To him with swift ascent he up returnd,
Into his blissful bosom reassum'd   225
In glory as of old, to him appeas'd
All, though all-knowing, what had past with Man
Recounted, mixing intercession sweet.
Meanwhile ere thus was sin'd and judg'd on Earth,
Within the Gates of Hell sate Sin and Death,   230
In counterview within the Gates, that now
Stood open wide, belching outrageous flame
Farr into *Chaos*, since the Fiend pass'd through,
Sin opening, who thus now to Death began.

[16] because of you (since also Adam is made of the dust).
[17] The skins come from beasts slain for that purpose or those recovered by
new skins after shedding the old, like the snake.
[18] did not object to.

O Son, why sit we here each other viewing   235
Idlely, while Satan our great Author thrives
In other Worlds, and happier Seat provides
For us his ofspring dear? It cannot be
But that success attends him; if mishap,
Ere this he had return'd, with fury driv'n   240
By his Avengers, since no place like this
Can fit his punishment, or their revenge.
Methinks I feel new strength within me rise,
Wings growing, and Dominion giv'n me large
Beyond this Deep; whatever draws me on,   245
Or sympathie,[19] or som connatural force
Powerful at greatest distance to unite
With secret amity things of like kind
By secretest conveyance. Thou my Shade
Inseparable must with mee along: 250
For Death from Sin no power can separate.
But least the difficultie of passing back
Stay his return perhaps over this Gulf
Impassable, impervious, let us try
Adventrous work, yet to thy power and mine   255
Not unagreeable, to found a path
Over this Main from Hell to that new World
Where Satan now prevails, a Monument
Of merit high to all th' infernal Host,
Easing thir passage hence, for intercourse,[20]   260
Or transmigration, as thir lot shall lead.
Nor can I miss the way, so strongly drawn
By this new felt attraction and instinct.
    Whom thus the meager Shadow answerd soon.
Goe whither Fate and inclination strong   265
Leads thee, I shall not lag behind, nor err
The way, thou leading, such a scent I draw
Of carnage, prey innumerable, and taste
The savour of Death from all things there that live:
Nor shall I to the work thou enterprisest   270
Be wanting, but afford thee equal aid.
    So saying, with delight he snuff'd the smell
Of mortal change on Earth. As when a flock
Of ravenous Fowl, though many a League remote,
Against the day of Battel, to a Field,   275

[19] attractive power.
[20] movement back and forth between, as opposed to "transmigration" (passage to one place only).

Where Armies lie encampt, come flying, lur'd
With scent of living Carcasses design'd
For death, the following day, in bloodie fight.
So scented the grim Feature, and upturn'd
His Nostril wide into the murkie Air,   280
Sagacious of his Quarry from so farr.
Then Both from out Hell Gates into the waste
Wide Anarchie of *Chaos* damp and dark
Flew divers, and with Power (thir Power was great)
Hovering upon the Waters; what they met   285
Solid or slimie, as in raging Sea
Tost up and down, together crowded drove
From each side shoaling²¹ towards the mouth of Hell.
As when two Polar Winds blowing adverse
Upon the *Cronian* Sea,²² together drive   290
Mountains of Ice, that stop th' imagin'd way²³
Beyond *Petsora* Eastward, to the rich
Cathaian Coast. The aggregated Soyl
Death with his Mace petrific, cold and dry,
As with a Trident smote, and fix't as firm   295
As *Delos*²⁴ floating once; the rest his look
Bound with *Gorgonian*²⁵ rigor not to move,
And with *Asphaltic* slime; broad as the Gate,
Deep to the Roots of Hell the gather'd beach
They fasten'd, and the Mole immense wraught on   300
Over the foaming deep high Archt, a Bridge
Of length prodigious joyning to the Wall²⁶
Immovable of this now fenceless²⁷ world
Forfeit to Death; from hence a passage broad,
Smooth, easie, inoffensive²⁸ down to Hell.   305
So, if great things to small may be compar'd,
Xerxes, the Libertie of *Greece* to yoke,
From *Susa*²⁹ his *Memnonian* Palace high
Came to the Sea, and over *Hellespont*
Bridging his way, *Europe* with *Asia* joyn'd,   310

²¹ making into a shoal.
²² the Arctic Ocean.
²³ the supposed passage to the east (Cathay) along the Siberian shore where
flows the Pechora.
²⁴ one of the Cyclades in the Aegean Sea created by Neptune with his trident
and firmly fixed in place by Zeus.
²⁵ petrifying.
²⁶ the outer shell of the created universe.
²⁷ both unenclosed (wide-extending) and defenseless.
²⁸ without impediments.
²⁹ the biblical Shushan, founded by Memnon's father Tithonus.

And scourg'd with many a stroak th' indignant waves.
Now had they brought the work by wondrous Art
Pontifical,[30] a ridge of pendent Rock
Over the vext Abyss, following the track
Of *Satan*, to the self-same place where hee   315
First lighted from his Wing, and landed safe
From out of *Chaos* to the outside bare
Of this round World: with Pinns of Adamant
And Chains they made all fast, too fast they made
And durable; and now in little space   320
The confines met[31] of Empyrean Heav'n
And of this World, and on the left hand Hell
With long reach interpos'd; three sev'ral wayes
In sight, to each of these three places led.
And now thir way to Earth they had descri'd,   325
To Paradise first tending, when behold
Satan in likeness of an Angel bright
Betwixt the *Centaur* and the *Scorpion* stearing
His *Zenith*, while the Sun in *Aries* rose:[32]
Disguis'd he came, but those his Childern dear   330
Thir Parent soon discern'd, though in disguise.
Hee, after *Eve* seduc't, unminded slunk
Into the Wood fast by, and changing shape
T' observe the sequel, saw his guileful act
By *Eve*, though all unweeting,[33] seconded   335
Upon her Husband, saw thir shame that sought
Vain covertures;[34] but when he saw descend
The Son of God to judge them, terrifi'd
Hee fled, not hoping to escape, but shun
The present, fearing guiltie what his wrauth   340
Might suddenly inflict; that past, return'd
By Night, and listning where the hapless Pair
Sate in thir sad discourse, and various plaint,
Thence gatherd his own doom, which understood
Not instant, but of future time. With joy   345

[30] pertaining to building bridges, and punning on "papal."
[31] The bridge to Hell joins the passage between Heaven and Earth (III, 510).
[32] Aries, under whose sign the Sun (Uriel) rises, lies opposite to Scorpio, near which is Centaurus; that is, Earth is placed between Satan and Uriel. Compare IV, n. 65. At this point, as Albert R. Cirillo shows (*ELH*, XXIX [1962], 372–95), the Sun (Son) and Satan each has reached his opposite noon / midnight; that is, at the Sun's rising has come Satan's fall (compare *PR* III, 201–2). The vernal equinox begins the year anew yielding hope and rebirth, and creating a metaphoric perpetual noon that is an image of eternity.
[33] unawares.
[34] the coverings of fig leaves.

And tidings fraught, to Hell he now return'd,
And at the brink of *Chaos*, neer the foot
Of this new wondrous Pontifice,[35] unhop't
Met who to meet him came, his Ofspring dear.
Great joy was at thir meeting, and at sight   350
Of that stupendious Bridge his joy encreas'd.
Long hee admiring stood, till Sin, his fair
Inchanting Daughter, thus the silence broke.
    O Parent, these are thy magnific deeds,
Thy Trophies, which thou view'st as not thine own,   355
Thou art thir Author and prime Architect:
For I no sooner in my Heart divin'd,
My Heart, which by a secret harmonie
Still moves with thine, joyn'd in connexion sweet,
That thou on Earth hadst prosper'd, which thy looks   360
Now also evidence, but straight I felt
Though distant from thee Worlds between, yet felt
That I must after thee with this thy Son;
Such fatal consequence[36] unites us three:
Hell could no longer hold us in her bounds,   365
Nor this unvoyageable Gulf obscure
Detain from following thy illustrious track.
Thou hast atchiev'd our libertie, confin'd
Within Hell Gates till now, thou us impow'rd
To fortifie thus farr, and overlay   370
With this portentous Bridge the dark Abyss.
Thine now is all this World, thy vertue hath won
What thy hands builded not, thy Wisdom gain'd
With odds what Warr hath lost, and fully aveng'd
Our foil in Heav'n; here thou shalt Monarch reign,   375
There didst not; there let him still Victor sway,
As Battel hath adjudg'd, from this new World
Retiring, by his own doom alienated,
And henceforth Monarchie with thee divide
Of all things, parted by th' Empyreal bounds,   380
His Quadrature, from thy Orbicular World,[37]
Or trie[38] thee now more dang'rous to his Throne.
    Whom thus the Prince of Darkness answerd glad.
Fair Daughter, and thou Son and Grandchild both,

[35] the bridge from hell.
[36] mutual dependence.
[37] Concepts of squareness and circularity are fallaciously contrasted: male,
female; imperfect, perfect; justice, mercy. Heaven was a square according to
Rev. xxi. 16.
[38] prove.

High proof ye now have giv'n to be the Race   385
Of *Satan* (for I glorie in the name,
Antagonist of Heav'ns Almightie King)
Amply have merited of me, of all
Th' Infernal Empire, that so neer Heav'ns dore
Triumphal with triumphal act have met,   390
Mine with this glorious Work, and made one Realm
Hell and this World, one Realm, one Continent
Of easie thorough-fare. Therefore while I
Descend through Darkness, on your Rode with ease
To my associate Powers, them to acquaint   395
With these successes, and with them rejoyce,
You two this way, among those numerous Orbs
All yours, right down to Paradise descend;
There dwell and Reign in bliss, thence on the Earth
Dominion exercise and in the Air,   400
Chiefly on Man, sole Lord of all declar'd,
Him first make sure your thrall, and lastly kill.
My Substitutes I send ye, and Create
Plenipotent on Earth, of matchless might
Issuing from mee: on your joynt vigor now   405
My hold of this new Kingdom all depends,
Through Sin to Death expos'd by my exploit.[39]
If your joynt power prevail, th' affaires of Hell
No detriment need fear, goe and be strong.
    So saying he dismiss'd them, they with speed   410
Thir course through thickest Constellations held
Spreading thir bane; the blasted Starrs lookt wan,
And Planets, Planet-strook,[40] real Eclips[41]
Then sufferd. Th' other way *Satan* went down
The Causey[42] to Hell Gate; on either side   415
Disparted *Chaos* over built exclaimd,
And with rebounding surge the barrs assaild,
That scorn'd his indignation: through the Gate,
Wide open and unguarded, *Satan* pass'd,
And all about found desolate; for those   420
Appointed to sit there, had left thir charge,
Flown to the upper World; the rest were all
Farr to the inland retir'd, about the walls

[39] Three meanings are intended: achievement; action for one's own advantage; and "unfolding" of his serpentine form at the temptation.
[40] unfavorably affected (as the planets themselves were considered to influence men).
[41] that is, of the Sun (Son), as at the crucifixion.
[42] causeway.

Of *Pandæmonium*, Citie and proud seat
Of *Lucifer*, so by allusion calld,   425
Of that bright Starr to *Satan* paragond.[43]
There kept thir Watch the Legions, while the Grand
In Council sate, sollicitous what chance
Might intercept thir Emperour sent, so hee
Departing gave command, and they observ'd.[44]   430
As when the *Tartar* from his *Russian* Foe
By *Astracan*[45] over the Snowie Plains
Retires, or *Bactrian* Sophi[46] from the horns
Of *Turkish* Crescent, leaves all waste beyond
The Realm of *Aladule*, in his retreat   435
To *Tauris* or *Casbeen*.[47] So these the late
Heav'n-banisht Host, left desert utmost Hell
Many a dark League, reduc't[48] in careful Watch
Round thir Metropolis, and now expecting
Each hour their great adventurer from the search   440
Of Forrein Worlds: he through the midst unmarkt,
In shew plebeian Angel militant
Of lowest order, past; and from the dore
Of that *Plutonian* Hall, invisible
Ascended his high Throne, which under state[49]   445
Of richest texture spred, at th' upper end
Was plac't in regal lustre. Down a while
He sate, and round about him saw unseen:
At last as from a Cloud his fulgent head
And shape Starr bright appeer'd, or brighter, clad   450
With what permissive glory since his fall
Was left him, or false glitter: All amaz'd
At that so sudden blaze the *Stygian* throng
Bent thir aspect, and whom they wish'd beheld,
Thir mighty Chief returnd: loud was th' acclaim: 455
Forth rush'd in haste the great consulting Peers,
Rais'd from thir dark *Divan*,[50] and with like joy
Congratulant approach'd him, who with hand
Silence, and with these words attention won.
    Thrones, Dominations, Princedoms, Vertues, Powers,   460

[43] compared.
[44] (his command).
[45] an outpost on the Volga.
[46] king of Persia.
[47] Tauris (Tabriz) and Casbeen were Persian cities ruled by Aladule.
[48] led back.
[49] canopy.
[50] council.

For in possession such, not onely of right,
I call ye and declare ye now, returnd
Successful beyond hope, to lead ye forth
Triumphant out of this infernal Pit
Abominable, accurst, the house of woe,   465
And Dungeon of our Tyrant: Now possess,
As Lords, a spacious World, t' our native Heav'n
Little inferiour, by my adventure hard
With peril great atchiev'd. Long were to tell
What I have don, what sufferd, with what pain   470
Voyag'd th' unreal, vast, unbounded deep
Of horrible confusion, over which
By Sin and Death a broad way now is pav'd
To expedite your glorious march; but I
Toild out my uncouth[51] passage, forc't to ride   475
Th' untractable Abyss, plung'd in the womb
Of unoriginal[52] *Night* and *Chaos* wild,
That jealous of thir secrets fiercely oppos'd
My journey strange, with clamorous uproar
Protesting Fate supream; thence how I found   480
The new created World, which fame in Heav'n
Long had foretold, a Fabrick wonderful
Of absolute perfection, therein Man
Plac't in a Paradise, by our exile
Made happie: Him by fraud I have seduc'd   485
From his Creator, and the more to increase
Your wonder, with an Apple; he thereat
Offended, worth your laughter,[53] hath giv'n up
Both his beloved Man and all his World,
To Sin and Death a prey, and so to us,   490
Without our hazard, labour, or allarm,
To range in, and to dwell, and over Man
To rule, as over all he should have rul'd.
True is, mee also he hath judg'd, or rather
Mee not, but the brute Serpent in whose shape   495
Man I deceav'd: that which to mee belongs,
Is enmity, which he will put between
Mee and Mankind; I am to bruise his heel;
His Seed, when is not set, shall bruise my head:
A World who would not purchase with a bruise,   500
Or much more grievous pain? Ye have th' account

[51] unknown.
[52] "unoriginated," since nothing existed before it.
[53] in parody of Ps. ii. 4; see II, 191 and n.

Of my performance: What remains, ye Gods,
But up and enter now into full bliss.
So having said, a while he stood, expecting
Thir universal shout and high applause   505
To fill his ear, when contrary he hears
On all sides, from innumerable tongues
A dismal universal hiss, the sound
Of public scorn; he wonderd, but not long
Had leasure, wondring at himself now more;   510
His Visage drawn he felt to sharp and spare,
His Armes clung to his Ribs, his Leggs entwining
Each other, till supplanted[54] down he fell
A monstrous Serpent on his Belly prone,
Reluctant, but in vain, a greater power   515
Now rul'd him, punisht in the shape he sin'd,
According to his doom: he would have spoke,
But hiss for hiss returnd with forked tongue
To forked tongue, for now were all transform'd
Alike, to Serpents all as accessories   520
To his bold Riot:[55] dreadful was the din
Of hissing through the Hall, thick swarming now
With complicated[56] monsters, head and tail,
Scorpion and Asp, and *Amphisbæna* dire,
Cerastes hornd, *Hydrus,* and *Ellops* drear,   525
And *Dipsas* (not so thick swarm'd once the Soil
Bedropt with blood of *Gorgon,* or the Isle
Ophiusa) but still greatest hee the midst,
Now Dragon grown, larger then whom the Sun
Ingenderd in the *Pythian* Vale on slime,   530
Huge *Python,* and his Power no less he seem'd
Above the rest still to retain; they all
Him follow'd issuing forth to th' open Field,
Where all yet left of that revolted Rout
Heav'n-fall'n, in station stood or just array,   535
Sublime[57] with expectation when to see
In Triumph issuing forth thir glorious Chief;
They saw, but other sight instead, a crowd

[54] tripped.
[55] revolt.
[56] twisted together. Among the fabulous serpents which follow are the amphisbaena, which had a head at both ends, the hydrus (a watersnake), the ellops (probably a swordfish), and the dipsas, whose bite provoked thirst. Serpents sprang from the blood of Medusa, and Ophiusa ("full of snakes") is one of the Balearic islands. Python was killed by Apollo at Delphi.
[57] upraised.

Of ugly Serpents; horror on them fell,
And horrid sympathie; for what they saw,   540
They felt themselvs now changing; down thir arms,
Down fell both Spear and Shield, down they as fast,
And the dire hiss renew'd, and the dire form
Catcht by Contagion, like in punishment,
As in thir crime. Thus was th' applause they meant,   545
Turnd to exploding hiss, triumph to shame
Cast on themselves from thir own mouths. There stood
A Grove hard by, sprung up with this thir change,
His will who reigns above, to aggravate
Thir penance, laden with fair Fruit like that   550
Which grew in Paradise, the bait of *Eve*
Us'd by the Tempter: on that prospect strange
Thir earnest eyes they fix'd, imagining
For one forbidden Tree a multitude
Now ris'n, to work them furder woe or shame;   555
Yet parcht with scalding thurst and hunger fierce,
Though to delude them sent, could not abstain,
But on they rould in heaps, and up the Trees
Climbing, sat thicker then the snakie locks
That curld *Megæra*:[58] greedily they pluck'd   560
The Fruitage fair to sight, like that which grew
Neer that bituminous Lake[59] where *Sodom* flam'd;
This more delusive, not the touch, but taste
Deceav'd; they fondly thinking to allay
Thir appetite with gust,[60] instead of Fruit   565
Chewd bitter Ashes, which th' offended taste
With spattering noise rejected: oft they assayd,
Hunger and thirst constraining, drug'd[61] as oft,
With hatefullest disrelish writh'd thir jaws
With soot and cinders fill'd; so oft they fell   570
Into the same illusion, not as Man
Whom they triumph'd once lapst. Thus were they plagu'd
And worn with Famin, long and ceasless hiss,
Till thir lost shape, permitted, they resum'd,
Yearly enjoynd, some say, to undergo   575
This annual humbling certain number'd days,
To dash thir pride, and joy for Man seduc't.
However some tradition they dispers'd
Among the Heathen of thir purchase got,

[58] one of the Furies.
[59] the Dead Sea. The fair apples of Sodom were but ashes inside.
[60] gusto, great relish.
[61] sickened.

THE COMPLETE POETRY OF JOHN MILTON

And Fabl'd how the Serpent, whom they calld   580
Ophion[62] with Eurynome, the wide-
Encroaching Eve perhaps, had first the rule
Of high Olympus, thence by Saturn driv'n
And Ops, ere yet Dictæan Jove was born.
Mean while in Paradise the hellish pair   585
Too soon arriv'd, Sin there in power before,
Once actual, now in body, and to dwell
Habitual habitant; behind her Death
Close following pace for pace, not mounted yet
On his pale Horse:[63] to whom Sin thus began.   590
    Second of Satan sprung, all conquering Death,
What thinkst thou of our Empire now, though earnd
With travail difficult, not better farr
Then still at Hells dark threshold to have sate watch,
Unnam'd, undreaded, and thy self half starv'd?[64]   595
    Whom thus the Sin-born Monster answerd soon.
To mee, who with eternal Famin pine,
Alike is Hell, or Paradise, or Heaven,
There best, where most with ravin I may meet;
Which here, though plenteous, all too little seems   600
To stuff this Maw, this vast unhide-bound[65] Corps.
    To whom th' incestuous Mother thus repli'd.
Thou therefore on these Herbs, and Fruits, and Flowrs
Feed first, on each Beast next, and Fish, and Fowl,
No homely morsels, and whatever thing   605
The Sithe of Time mows down, devour unspar'd,
Till I in Man residing through the Race,
His thoughts, his looks, words, actions all infect,
And season him thy last and sweetest prey.
    This said, they both betook them several wayes,   610
Both to destroy, or unimmortal make
All kinds, and for destruction to mature
Sooner or later; which th' Almightie seeing,
From his transcendent Seat the Saints among,
To those bright Orders utterd thus his voice.   615
    See with what heat these Dogs of Hell advance
To waste and havoc yonder World, which I
So fair and good created, and had still

[62] a Titan whose name means "serpent"; his wife was Eurynome, whose
name means "wide-encroaching." Jove, son of Saturn and Rhea (Ops), had a
shrine at Mount Dicte in Crete.
[63] from Rev. vi. 8.
[64] originally "to die."
[65] not bound by his hide.

Kept in that state, had not the folly of Man
Let in these wastful Furies, who impute   620
Folly to mee, so doth the Prince of Hell
And his Adherents, that with so much ease
I suffer them to enter and possess
A place so heav'nly, and conniving[66] seem
To gratifie my scornful Enemies,   625
That laugh, as if transported with some fit
Of Passion, I to them had quitted all,
At random yeilded up to their misrule;
And know not that I call'd and drew them thither
My Hell-hounds, to lick up the draff and filth   630
Which mans polluting Sin with taint hath shed
On what was pure, till cramm'd and gorg'd, nigh burst
With suckt and glutted offal, at one sling
Of thy victorious Arm, well-pleasing Son,
Both *Sin*, and *Death*, and yawning *Grave* at last   635
Through *Chaos* hurld, obstruct the mouth of Hell
For ever, and seal up his ravenous Jaws.
Then Heav'n and Earth renewd shall be made pure
To sanctitie that shall receive no stain:
Till then the Curse pronounc't on both precedes.   640
   He ended, and the heav'nly Audience loud
Sung *Halleluia*, as the sound of Seas,
Through multitude that sung: Just are thy ways,
Righteous are thy Decrees on all thy Works;[67]
Who can extenuate[68] thee? Next, to the Son,   645
Destin'd restorer of Mankind, by whom
New Heav'n and Earth shall to the Ages rise,
Or down from Heav'n descend. Such was thir song,
While the Creator calling forth by name
His mightie Angels gave them several charge,   650
As sorted[69] best with present things. The Sun
Had first his precept so to move, so shine,
As might affect the Earth with cold and heat
Scarce tollerable, and from the North to call
Decrepit Winter, from the South to bring   655
Solstitial summers heat. To the blanc Moon

[66] shutting the eyes.
[67] Rev. xv. 3: "And they sing the song of Moses the servant of God, and the song of the Lamb, saying, Great and marvellous are thy works, Lord, God Almighty; just and true are thy ways, thou King of Saints."
[68] disparage.
[69] harmonized.

Her office they prescrib'd, to th' other five[70]
Thir planetarie motions and aspects
In *Sextile*, *Square*, and *Trine*, and *Opposite*,[71]
Of noxious efficacie, and when to joyn   660
In Synod unbenigne, and taught the fixt
Thir influence malignant when to showr,
Which of them rising with the Sun, or falling,
Should prove tempestuous: To the Winds they set
Thir corners, when with bluster to confound   665
Sea, Air, and Shoar, the Thunder when to rowl
With terror through the dark Aereal Hall.
Some say he bid his Angels turn ascanse
The Poles of Earth twice ten degrees and more
From the Suns Axle;[72] they with labour push'd   670
Oblique the Centric Globe: Som say the Sun
Was bid turn Reins from th' Equinoctial Rode
Like distant breadth to *Taurus* with the Seav'n
Atlantick Sisters, and the *Spartan* Twins
Up to the *Tropic* Crab; thence down amain   675
By *Leo* and the *Virgin* and the *Scales*,
As deep as *Capricorn*, to bring in change
Of Seasons to each Clime; else had the Spring
Perpetual smil'd on Earth with vernant Flowrs,
Equal in Days and Nights, except to those   680
Beyond the Polar Circles; to them Day
Had unbenighted shon, while the low Sun
To recompence his distance, in thir sight
Had rounded still th' *Horizon*, and not known
Or East or West, which had forbid the Snow   685
From cold *Estotiland*,[73] and South as farr
Beneath *Magellan*. At that tasted Fruit
The Sun, as from *Thyestean* Banquet,[74] turn'd
His course intended; else how had the World
Inhabited, though sinless, more then now,   690
Avoided pinching cold and scorching heat?

[70] (planets).
[71] The planets are unbenign when their conjunction ("synod," l. 661) is at angles of 60 degrees, 90 degrees, 120 degrees, and 180 degrees.
[72] The tilting of the earth 23.5 degrees from the sun's course, which was the same as the celestial equator (Copernicus), or the alteration of the sun's course a like amount (l. 673; Ptolemy) created winter. The sun moves upward to the Tropic of Cancer (through the Bull and the Pleiades and then through Gemini) in Jan.–June, and southward to the Tropic of Capricorn (through Leo, Virgo, and Libra) in July–Dec.
[73] Labrador. "Magellan" means the Straits of Magellan.
[74] Atreus served his brother Thyestes his sons as food at a banquet of revenge.

These changes in the Heav'ns, though slow, produc'd
Like change on Sea and Land, sideral blast,[75]
Vapour, and Mist, and Exhalation hot,
Corrupt and Pestilent: Now from the North   695
Of *Norumbega*,[76] and the *Samoed* shoar
Bursting thir brazen Dungeon, armd with ice
And snow and hail and stormie gust and flaw,[77]
Boreas[78] and *Cæcias* and *Argestes* loud
And *Thrascias* rend the Woods and Seas upturn;   700
With adverse blast up-turns them from the South
Notus and *Afer* black with thundrous Clouds
From *Serraliona;* thwart of these as fierce
Forth rush the *Levant* and the *Ponent* Winds
Eurus and *Zephir* with thir lateral noise,   705
Sirocco, and *Libecchio*. Thus began
Outrage from liveless things; but Discord first
Daughter of Sin, among th' irrational,
Death introduc'd through fierce antipathie:[79]
Beast now with Beast gan war, and Fowl with Fowl,   710
And Fish with Fish; to graze the Herb all leaving,
Devourd each other; nor stood much in awe
Of Man, but fled him, or with count'nance grim
Glar'd on him passing: these were from without
The growing miseries, which *Adam* saw   715
Alreadie in part, though hid in gloomiest shade,
To sorrow abandond, but worse felt within,
And in a troubl'd Sea of passion tost,
Thus to disburd'n sought with sad complaint.
    O miserable of happie! is this the end   720
Of this new glorious World, and mee so late
The Glory of that Glory, who now becom
Accurst of blessed, hide me from the face
Of God, whom to behold was then my highth
Of happiness: yet well, if here would end   725
The miserie, I deserv'd it, and would bear
My own deservings; but this will not serve;
All that I eat or drink, or shall beget,

---

[75] malign influence from the stars.
[76] New England. The *"Samoed* shore" is Siberia.
[77] burst of wind.
[78] Boreas, Caecias, Argestes, and Thrascias were winds from the north; Notus and Afer (l. 702) from the south; Eurus (l. 705) from the east ("Levant"), and Zephyr from the west ("Ponent"); Sirocco (l. 706) from the southeast and Libecchio from the southwest.
[79] opposition.

Is propagated curse. O voice once heard
Delightfully, *Encrease and multiply*,   730
Now death to hear! for what can I encrease
Or multiplie, but curses on my head?
Who of all Ages to succeed, but feeling
The evil on him brought by me, will curse
My Head, Ill fare our Ancestor impure,   735
For this we may thank *Adam;* but his thanks
Shall be the execration; so besides
Mine own that bide upon me, all from mee
Shall with a fierce reflux on mee redound,[80]
On mee as on thir natural center light   740
Heavie, though in thir place. O fleeting joyes
Of Paradise, dear bought with lasting woes!
Did I request thee, Maker, from my Clay
To mould me Man, did I sollicite thee
From darkness to promote me, or here place   745
In this delicious Garden? as my Will
Concurd not to my being, it were but right
And equal to reduce me to my dust,
Desirous to resigne, and render back
All I receav'd, unable to perform   750
Thy terms too hard, by which I was to hold
The good I sought not. To the loss of that,
Sufficient penaltie, why hast thou added
The sense of endless woes? inexplicable
Thy Justice seems; yet to say truth, too late,   755
I thus contest; then should have been refus'd
Those terms whatever, when they were propos'd:
Thou didst accept them; wilt thou enjoy the good,
Then cavil the conditions? and though God
Made thee without thy leave, what if thy Son   760
Prove disobedient, and reprov'd, retort,
Wherefore didst thou beget me? I sought it not:
Wouldst thou admit for his contempt of thee
That proud excuse? yet him not thy election,
But Natural necessity begot.   765
God made thee of choice his own, and of his own
To serve him, thy reward was of his grace,
Thy punishment then justly is at his Will.
Be it so, for I submit, his doom is fair,
That dust I am, and shall to dust return:[81]   770

[80] flow back.
[81] Gen. iii. 19.

O welcom hour whenever! why delayes
His hand to execute what his Decree
Fix'd on this day? why do I overlive,
Why am I mockt with death, and length'n'd out
To deathless pain? how gladly would I meet   775
Mortalitie my sentence, and be Earth
Insensible, how glad would lay me down
As in my Mothers lap? there I should rest
And sleep secure; his dreadful voice no more
Would Thunder in my ears, no fear of worse   780
To mee and to my ofspring would torment me
With cruel expectation. Yet one doubt
Pursues me still, least all I cannot die,
Least that pure breath of Life, the Spirit of Man
Which God inspir'd, cannot together perish   785
With this corporeal Clod; then in the Grave,
Or in some other dismal place, who knows
But I shall die a living Death? O thought
Horrid, if true! yet why? it was but breath
Of Life that sinn'd; what dies but what had life   790
And sin? the Bodie properly hath neither.
All of me then shall die: let this appease
The doubt, since human reach no further knows.
For though the Lord of all be infinite,
Is his wrauth also? be it, man is not so,   795
But mortal doom'd. How can he exercise
Wrath without end on Man whom Death must end?
Can he make deathless Death? that were to make
Strange contradiction, which to God himself
Impossible is held, as Argument   800
Of weakness, not of Power. Will he draw out,
For angers sake, finite to infinite
In punisht man, to satisfie his rigour
Satisfi'd never; that were to extend
His Sentence beyond dust and Natures Law,   805
By which all Causes else according still
To the reception[82] of thir matter act,
Not to th' extent of thir own Sphear. But say
That Death be not one stroak, as I suppos'd,
Bereaving sense, but endless miserie   810
From this day onward, which I feel begun
Both in me, and without me, and so last

---

[82] The potentiality of matter is limited by that to which it is united; that is, God will not make man's punishment infinite though he himself is infinite.

To perpetuitie; Ay me, that fear
Comes thundring back with dreadful revolution
On my defensless head; both Death and I   815
Am found Eternal, and incorporate both,
Nor I on my part single, in mee all
Posteritie stands curst: Fair Patrimonie
That I must leave ye, Sons; O were I able
To waste it all my self, and leave ye none!   820
So disinherited how would ye bless
Me now your curse! Ah, why should all mankind
For one mans fault thus guiltless be condemn'd,
If guiltless? But from me what can proceed,
But all corrupt, both Mind and Will deprav'd,   825
Not to do onely,. but to will the same
With me? how can they then acquitted stand
In sight of God? Him after all Disputes
Forc't I absolve: all my evasions vain,
And reasonings, though through Mazes, lead me still   830
But to my own conviction: first and last
On mee, mee onely, as the sourse and spring
Of all corruption, all the blame lights due;
So might the wrauth. Fond wish! couldst thou support
That burden heavier then the Earth to bear,   835
Then all the World much heavier, though divided
With that bad Woman? Thus what thou desir'st
And what thou fearst, alike destroyes all hope
Of refuge, and concludes thee miserable
Beyond all past example and future,   840
To *Satan* only like both crime and doom.
O Conscience, into what Abyss of fears
And horrors hast thou driv'n me; out of which
I find no way, from deep to deeper plung'd!
    Thus *Adam* to himself lamented loud   845
Through the still Night, not now, as ere man fell,
Wholsom and cool, and mild, but with black Air
Accompanied, with damps and dreadful gloom,
Which to his evil Conscience represented
All things with double terror: On the ground   850
Outstretcht he lay, on the cold ground, and oft
Curs'd his Creation, Death as oft accus'd
Of tardie execution, since denounc't
The day of his offence. Why comes not Death,
Said hee, with one thrice acceptable stroke   855
To end me? Shall Truth fail to keep her word,
Justice Divine not hast'n to be just?

But Death comes not at call, Justice Divine
Mends not her slowest pace for prayers or cries.
O Woods, O Fountains, Hillocks, Dales and Bowrs,   860
With other echo late I taught your Shades
To answer, and resound farr other Song.
Whom thus afflicted when sad *Eve* beheld,
Desolate where she sate, approaching nigh,
Soft words to his fierce passion she assay'd: 865
But her with stern regard he thus repell'd.
    Out of my sight, thou Serpent,[83] that name best
Befits thee with him leagu'd, thy self as false
And hateful; nothing wants, but that thy shape,
Like his, and colour Serpentine[84] may shew   870
Thy inward fraud, to warn all Creatures from thee
Henceforth; least that too heav'nly form, pretended[85]
To hellish falshood, snare them. But for thee
I had persisted happie, had not thy pride
And wandring vanitie, when lest was safe,   875
Rejected my forewarning, and disdain'd
Not to be trusted, longing to be seen
Though by the Devil himself, him overweening
To over-reach, but with the Serpent meeting
Fool'd and beguil'd, by him thou, I by thee,   880
To trust thee from my side, imagin'd wise,
Constant, mature, proof against all assaults,
And understood not all was but a shew
Rather then solid vertu, all but a Rib
Crooked by nature, bent, as now appears,   885
More to the part sinister[86] from me drawn,
Well if thrown out, as supernumerarie
To my just number found. O why did God,
Creator wise, that peopl'd highest Heav'n
With Spirits Masculine, create at last   890
This noveltie on Earth, this fair defect
Of Nature, and not fill the World at once
With Men as Angels without Feminine,
Or find some other way to generate
Mankind? this mischief had not then befall'n,   895
And more that shall befall, innumerable
Disturbances on Earth through Femal snares,

---

[83] "Heva" was said to mean serpent, being an aspirated sound plus "Eve."
[84] a mottled, dull green.
[85] held before as a disguise.
[86] a pun of "left" side and "evil." Eve was traditionally considered morally defective because she was created from this bent rib.

And straight conjunction with this Sex: for either
He never shall find out fit Mate, but such
As some misfortune brings him, or mistake,   900
Or whom he wishes most shall seldom gain
Through her perversness, but shall see her gaind
By a farr worse, or if she love, withheld
By Parents, or his happiest choice too late
Shall meet, alreadie linkt and Wedlock-bound   905
To a fell Adversarie, his hate or shame:
Which infinite calamitie shall cause
To Human life, and houshold peace confound.
     He added not, and from her turn'd, but *Eve*
Not so repulst, with Tears that ceas'd not flowing,   910
And tresses all disorderd, at his feet
Fell humble, and imbracing them, besaught
His peace, and thus proceeded in her plaint.
     Forsake me not thus, *Adam*, witness Heav'n
What love sincere, and reverence in my heart   915
I bear thee, and unweeting have offended,
Unhappilie deceav'd; thy suppliant
I beg, and clasp thy knees; bereave me not,
Whereon I live, thy gentle looks, thy aid,
Thy counsel in this uttermost distress,   920
My onely strength and stay: forlorn of thee,
Whither shall I betake me, where subsist?
While yet we live, scarse one short hour perhaps,
Between us two let there be peace, both joyning,
As joyn'd in injuries, one enmitie   925
Against a Foe by doom express assign'd us,
That cruel Serpent: On me exercise not
Thy hatred for this miserie befall'n,
On me already lost, mee then thy self
More miserable; both have sin'd, but thou   930
Against God onely, I against God and thee,[87]
And to the place of judgment will return,
There with my cries importune Heav'n, that all
The sentence from thy head remov'd may light
On me, sole cause to thee of all this woe,   935
Mee mee onely just object of his ire.
     She ended weeping, and her lowlie plight,
Immoveable till peace obtain'd from fault
Acknowledg'd and deplor'd, in *Adam* wraught
Commiseration; soon his heart relented   940

[87] Compare IV, 299: "Hee for God only, shee for God in him."

Towards her, his life so late and sole delight,
Now at his feet submissive in distress,
Creature so fair his reconcilement seeking,
His counsel whom she had displeas'd, his aid;
As one disarm'd, his anger all he lost,   945
And thus with peaceful words uprais'd her soon.
    Unwarie, and too desirous, as before,
So now of what thou knowst not, who desir'st
The punishment all on thy self; alas,
Bear thine own first, ill able to sustain   950
His full wrauth whose thou feelst as yet lest part,
And my displeasure bearst so ill. If Prayers
Could alter high Decrees, I to that place
Would speed before thee, and be louder heard,
That on my head all might be visited,   955
Thy frailtie and infirmer Sex forgiv'n,
To me committed and by me expos'd.
But rise, let us no more contend, nor blame
Each other, blam'd enough elsewhere, but strive
In offices of Love, how we may light'n   960
Each others burden in our share of woe;
Since this days Death denounc't, if ought I see,
Will prove no sudden, but a slow-pac't evill,
A long days dying to augment our pain,
And to our Seed (O hapless Seed!) deriv'd.   965
    To whom thus *Eve*, recovering heart, repli'd.
Adam, by sad experiment I know
How little weight my words with thee can find,
Found so erroneous, thence by just event
Found so unfortunate; nevertheless,   970
Restor'd by thee, vile as I am, to place
Of new acceptance, hopeful to regain
Thy Love, the sole contentment of my heart,
Living or dying, from thee I will not hide
What thoughts in my unquiet brest are ris'n,   975
Tending to som relief of our extremes,
Or end, though sharp and sad, yet tolerable,
As in our evils,[88] and of easier choice.
If care of our descent perplex us most,
Which must be born to certain woe, devourd   980
By Death at last, and miserable it is
To be to others cause of misery,
Our own begotten, and of our Loins to bring

[88] in evils such as ours.

Into this cursed World a woful Race,
That after wretched Life must be at last   985
Food for so foul a Monster, in thy power
It lies, yet ere Conception to prevent
The Race unblest, to being yet unbegot.
Childless thou art, Childless remain: so Death
Shall be deceav'd his glut, and with us two   990
Be forc'd to satisfie his Rav'nous Maw.
But if thou judge it hard and difficult,
Conversing, looking, loving, to abstain
From Loves due Rites, Nuptial imbraces sweet,
And with desire to languish without hope,   995
Before the present object[89] languishing
With like desire, which would be miserie
And torment less then none of what we dread,
Then both our selves and Seed at once to free
From what we fear for both, let us make short,   1000
Let us seek Death, or he not found, supply
With our own hands his Office on our selves;
Why stand we longer shivering under feares,
That shew no end but Death, and have the power,
Of many ways to die the shortest choosing,   1005
Destruction with destruction to destroy.
     She ended heer, or vehement despair
Broke off the rest; so much of Death her thoughts
Had entertaind, as di'd her Cheeks with pale.
But *Adam* with such counsel nothing sway'd,   1010
To better hopes his more attentive mind
Labouring had rais'd, and thus to *Eve* repli'd.
     Eve, thy contempt of life and pleasure seems
To argue in thee somthing more sublime
And excellent then what thy mind contemns;   1015
But self-destruction therefore saught, refutes
That excellence thought in thee, and implies,
Not thy contempt, but anguish and regret
For loss of life and pleasure overlov'd.
Or if thou covet death, as utmost end   1020
Of miserie, so thinking to evade
The penaltie pronounc't, doubt not but God
Hath wiselier arm'd his vengeful ire then so
To be forestall'd; much more I fear least Death
So snatcht will not exempt us from the pain   1025
We are by doom to pay; rather such acts

[89] Eve.

Of contumacie will provoke the highest
To make death in us live: Then let us seek
Som safer resolution, which methinks
I have in view, calling to mind with heed   1030
Part of our Sentence, that thy Seed shall bruise
The Serpents head; piteous amends, unless
Be meant, whom I conjecture, our grand Foe
Satan, who in the Serpent hath contriv'd
Against us this deceit: to crush his head   1035
Would be revenge indeed; which will be lost
By death brought on our selves, or childless days
Resolv'd, as thou proposest; so our Foe
Shall scape his punishment ordain'd, and wee
Instead shall double ours upon our heads.   1040
No more be mention'd then of violence
Against our selves, and wilful barrenness,
That cuts us off from hope, and savours onely
Rancor and pride, impatience and despite,
Reluctance⁹⁰ against God and his just yoke   1045
Laid on our Necks. Remember with what mild
And gracious temper he both heard and judg'd
Without wrauth or reviling; wee expected
Immediate dissolution, which we thought
Was meant by Death that day, when lo, to thee   1050
Pains onely in Child-bearing were foretold,
And bringing forth, soon recompenc't with joy,
Fruit of thy Womb: On mee the Curse aslope
Glanc'd on the ground, with labour I must earn
My bread; what harm? Idleness had bin worse;   1055
My labour will sustain me; and least Cold
Or Heat should injure us, his timely care
Hath unbesaught provided, and his hands
Cloath'd us unworthie, pitying while he judg'd;
How much more, if we pray him, will his ear   1060
Be open, and his heart to pitie incline,
And teach us further by what means to shun
Th' inclement Seasons, Rain, Ice, Hail and Snow,
Which now the Skie with various Face begins
To shew us in this Mountain, while the Winds   1065
Blow moist and keen, shattering the graceful locks
Of these fair spreading Trees; which bids us seek
Som better shroud, som better warmth to cherish
Our Limbs benumm'd, ere this diurnal Starr

⁹⁰ struggle.

Leave cold the Night, how we his gather'd beams   1070
Reflected, may with matter sere foment,
Or by collision of two bodies grind
The Air attrite[91] to Fire, as late the Clouds
Justling or pusht with Winds rude in thir shock
Tine[92] the slant Lightning, whose thwart flame driv'n down   1075
Kindles the gummie bark of Firr or Pine,
And sends a comfortable heat from farr,
Which might supplie the Sun: such Fire to use,
And what may else be remedie or cure
To evils which our own misdeeds have wrought,   1080
Hee will instruct us praying, and of Grace
Beseeching him, so as we need not fear
To pass commodiously this life, sustain'd
By him with many comforts, till we end
In dust, our final rest and native home.   1085
What better can we do, then to the place
Repairing where he judg'd us, prostrate fall
Before him reverent, and there confess
Humbly our faults, and pardon beg, with tears
Watering the ground, and with our sighs the Air   1090
Frequenting, sent from hearts contrite, in sign
Of sorrow unfeign'd, and humiliation meek.
Undoubtedly he will relent and turn
From his displeasure; in whose look serene,
When angry most he seem'd and most severe,   1095
What else but favor, grace, and mercie shon?
   So spake our Father penitent, nor *Eve*
Felt less remorse: they forthwith to the place
Repairing where he judg'd them prostrate fell
Before him reverent, and both confess'd   1100
Humbly thir faults, and pardon beg'd, with tears
Watering the ground, and with thir sighs the Air
Frequenting, sent from hearts contrite, in sign
Of sorrow unfeign'd, and humiliation meek.

[91] The air is thought of as being "rubbed" by the collision, causing fire from friction.
[92] kindle.

BOOK XI

THE ARGUMENT

The Son of God presents to his Father the Prayers of our first Parents now repenting, and intercedes for them: God accepts them, but declares that they must no longer abide in Paradise; sends *Michael* with a Band of Cherubim to dispossess them; but first to reveal to *Adam* future things: *Michaels* coming down. *Adam* shews to *Eve* certain ominous signs; he discerns *Michaels* approach, goes out to meet him: the Angel denounces thir departure. *Eve's* Lamentation. *Adam* pleads, but submits: The Angel leads him up to a high Hill, sets before him in vision what shall happ'n till the Flood.

Thus they in lowliest plight repentant stood
Praying, for from the Mercie-seat[1] above
Prevenient Grace[2] descending had remov'd
The stonie[3] from thir hearts, and made new flesh
Regenerat grow instead, that sighs now breath'd   5
Unutterable, which the Spirit of prayer
Inspir'd, and wing'd for Heav'n with speedier flight
Then loudest Oratorie: yet thir port
Not of mean suiters, nor important less
Seem'd thir Petition, then when th' ancient Pair   10
In Fables old, less ancient yet then these,
Deucalion and chaste *Pyrrha* to restore
The Race of Mankind drownd, before the Shrine
Of *Themis*[4] stood devout. To Heav'n thir prayers
Flew up, nor miss'd the way, by envious winds   15
Blow'n vagabond or frustrate: in they pass'd
Dimentionless through Heav'nly dores; then clad
With incense, where the Golden Altar fum'd,
By thir great Intercessor, came in sight
Before the Fathers Throne: Them the glad Son   20
Presenting, thus to intercede began.
See Father, what first fruits on Earth are sprung
From thy implanted Grace in Man, these Sighs
And Prayers, which in this Golden Censer, mixt
With Incense, I thy Priest before thee bring,   25
Fruits of more pleasing savour from thy seed
Sow'n with contrition in his heart, then those
Which his own hand manuring[5] all the Trees
Of Paradise could have produc't, ere fall'n

[1] a plate on which was sprinkled the blood of sacrificed animals; thus, the throne of God.
[2] grace which precedes (repentance).
[3] Ezek. xi. 19: "and I will take the stony heart out of their flesh, and will give them an heart of flesh."
[4] goddess of justice. Deucalion and Pyrrha, surviving from the flood, cast stones to earth (compare l. 4) from which humans then sprang up.
[5] cultivating.

From innocence. Now therefore bend thine ear   30
To supplication, hear his sighs though mute;
Unskilful with what words to pray, let mee
Interpret for him, mee his Advocate
And propitiation, all his works on mee
Good or not good ingraft, my Merit those   35
Shall perfet, and for these my Death shall pay.
Accept me, and in mee from these receave
The smell of peace toward Mankind, let him live
Before thee reconcil'd, at least his days
Numberd, though sad, till Death, his doom (which I   40
To mitigate thus plead, not to reverse)
To better life shall yeeld him, where with mee
All my redeemd may dwell in joy and bliss,
Made one with me as I with thee am one.
    To whom the Father, without Cloud, serene.   45
All thy request for Man, accepted Son,
Obtain, all thy request was my Decree:
But longer in that Paradise to dwell,
The Law I gave to Nature him forbids:
Those pure immortal Elements that know   50
No gross, no unharmoneous mixture foul,
Eject him tainted now, and purge him off
As a distemper, gross to air as gross,
And mortal food, as may dispose him best
For dissolution wrought by Sin, that first   55
Distemperd all things, and of incorrupt
Corrupted. I at first with two fair gifts
Created him endowd, with Happiness
And Immortalitie: that fondly lost,
This other serv'd but to eternize woe;   60
Till I provided Death; so Death becomes
His final remedie, and after Life
Tri'd in sharp tribulation, and refin'd
By Faith and faithful works, to second Life,
Wak't in the renovation of the just,   65
Resignes him up with Heav'n and Earth renewd.
But let us call to Synod all the Blest
Through Heav'ns wide bounds; from them I will not hide
My judgments, how with Mankind I proceed,
As how with peccant Angels late they saw;   70
And in thir state, though firm, stood more confirmd.
    He ended, and the Son gave signal high
To the bright Minister that watch'd, hee blew

His Trumpet, heard in *Oreb*[6] since perhaps
When God descended, and perhaps once more 75
To sound at general Doom.[7] Th' Angelic blast
Fill'd all the Regions: from thir blissful Bowrs
Of *Amarantin*[8] Shade, Fountain or Spring,
By the waters of Life, where ere they sate
In fellowships of joy: the Sons of Light 80
Hasted, resorting to the Summons high,
And took thir Seats; till from his Throne supream
Th' Almighty thus pronounc'd his sovran Will.
    O Sons, like one of us Man is become
To know both Good and Evil, since his taste 85
Of that defended[9] Fruit; but let him boast
His knowledge of Good lost, and Evil got,
Happier, had it suffic'd him to have known
Good by it self, and Evil not at all.
He sorrows now, repents, and prayes contrite, 90
My motions in him, longer then they move,
His heart I know, how variable and vain
Self-left.[10] Least therefore his now bolder hand
Reach also of the Tree of Life, and eat,
And live for ever, dream at least to live 95
For ever, to remove him I decree,
And send him from the Garden forth to Till
The Ground whence he was taken, fitter soil.
    Michael, this my behest have thou in charge,
Take to thee from among the Cherubim 100
Thy choice of flaming Warriours, least the Fiend
Or in behalf of[11] Man, or to invade
Vacant possession som new trouble raise:
Hast thee, and from the Paradise of God
Without remorse[12] drive out the sinful Pair, 105
From hallowd ground th' unholie, and denounce
To them and to thir Progenie from thence
Perpetual banishment. Yet least they faint
At the sad Sentence rigorously urg'd,
For I behold them soft'n'd and with tears 110
Bewailing thir excess, all terror hide.

[6] Horeb or Mt. Sinai when Moses was given the Ten Commandments.
[7] Judgment Day.
[8] symbol of immortality.
[9] forbidden.
[10] left to itself.
[11] in regard to.
[12] pity.

If patiently thy bidding they obey,
Dismiss them not disconsolate; reveal
To *Adam* what shall come in future dayes,
As I shall thee enlighten, intermix   115
My Cov'nant in the womans seed renewd;
So send them forth, though sorrowing, yet in peace:
And on the East side of the Garden place,
Where entrance up from *Eden* easiest climbs,
Cherubic watch, and of a Sword the flame   120
Wide waving, all approach farr off to fright,
And guard all passage to the Tree of Life:
Least Paradise a receptacle prove
To Spirits foul, and all my Trees thir prey,
With whose stol'n Fruit Man once more to delude.   125
  He ceas'd; and th' Archangelic Power prepar'd
For swift descent, with him the Cohort bright
Of watchful Cherubim; four faces each
Had, like a double *Janus*, all thir shape
Spangl'd with eyes more numerous then those   130
Of *Argus*, and more wakeful then to drouze,
Charm'd with *Arcadian* Pipe, the Pastoral Reed
Of *Hermes*, or his opiate Rod.[13] Mean while
To resalute the World with sacred Light
Leucothea[14] wak'd, and with fresh dews imbalmd   135
The Earth, when *Adam* and first Matron *Eve*
Had ended now thir Orisons, and found
Strength added from above, new hope to spring
Out of despair, joy, but with fear yet linkt;
Which thus to *Eve* his welcome words renewd.   140
  Eve, easily may Faith admit, that all
The good which we enjoy, from Heav'n descends;
But that from us ought should ascend to Heav'n
So prevalent as to concern the mind
Of God high-blest, or to incline his will,   145
Hard to belief may seem; yet this will Prayer,
Or one short sigh of human breath, up-borne
Ev'n to the Seat of God. For since I saught
By Prayer th' offended Deitie to appease,
Kneel'd and before him humbl'd all my heart,   150
Methought I saw him placable and mild,

[13] The four faces of the cherubim, "full of eyes" (Ezek. i. 15, 18), command
the four quarters of the earth. Janus was the two-faced god of gates; Argus was
a monster with a hundred eyes, who guarded Io and who was put to sleep by
Hermes' reed and his caduceus.
[14] goddess of the dawn.

Bending his ear; perswasion in me grew
That I was heard with favour; peace returnd
Home to my brest, and to my memorie
His promise, that thy Seed shall bruise our Foe;   155
Which then not minded in dismay, yet now
Assures me that the bitterness of death
Is past, and we shall live. Whence Hail to thee,
Eve rightly call'd, Mother of all Mankind,[15]
Mother of all things living, since by thee   160
Man is to live, and all things live for Man.
    To whom thus Eve with sad[16] demeanour meek.
Ill worthie I such title should belong
To me transgressour, who for thee ordaind
A help, became thy snare; to mee reproach   165
Rather belongs, distrust and all dispraise:
But infinite in pardon was my Judge,
That I who first brought Death on all, am grac't
The sourse of life; next favourable thou,
Who highly thus to entitle me voutsaf'st,   170
Farr other name deserving. But the Field
To labour calls us now with sweat impos'd,
Though after sleepless Night; for see the Morn,
All unconcern'd with our unrest, begins
Her rosie progress smiling; let us forth,   175
I never from thy side henceforth to stray,
Wherere our days work lies, though now enjoind
Laborious, till day droop; while here we dwell,
What can be toilsom in these pleasant Walks?
Here let us live, though in fall'n state, content.   180
    So spake, so wish'd much-humbl'd Eve, but Fate
Subscrib'd not; Nature first gave Signs, imprest
On Bird, Beast, Air, Air suddenly eclips'd[17]
After short blush of Morn; nigh in her sight
The Bird of Jove,[18] stoopt from his aerie tour,   185
Two Birds of gayest plume before him drove:
Down from a Hill the Beast that reigns in Woods,[19]
First hunter then, pursu'd a gentle brace,
Goodliest of all the Forrest, Hart and Hind;
Direct to th' Eastern Gate was bent thir flight.   190

[15] Gen. iii. 20: "And Adam called his wife's name Eve; because she was the mother of all living."
[16] grave.
[17] darkened.
[18] the eagle, which swooped down ("stoopt") from its high nest.
[19] the lion.

Adam observ'd, and with his Eye the chase
Pursuing, not unmov'd to *Eve* thus spake.
   O *Eve*, some furder change awaits us nigh,
Which Heav'n by these mute signs in Nature shews
Forerunners of his purpose, or to warn   195
Us haply too secure of our discharge
From penaltie, because from death releast
Some days; how long, and what till then our life,
Who knows, or more then this, that we are dust,
And thither must return and be no more.   200
Why else this double object in our sight
Of flight pursu'd in th' Air and ore the ground
One way the self-same hour? why in the East
Darkness ere Dayes mid-course, and Morning light
More orient in yon Western Cloud that draws   205
O're the blew Firmament a radiant white,
And slow descends, with somthing heav'nly fraught.
   He err'd not, for by this the heav'nly Bands
Down from a Skie of Jasper lighted now
In Paradise, and on a Hill made alt,[20]   210
A glorious Apparition, had not doubt
And carnal fear that day dimm'd *Adams* eye.
Not that more glorious, when the Angels met
Jacob in *Mahanaim*, where he saw
The field Pavilion'd with his Guardians bright;[21]   215
Nor that which on the flaming Mount appeerd
In *Dothan*, cover'd with a Camp of Fire,
Against the *Syrian* King, who to surprize
One man, Assassin-like had levied Warr,
Warr unproclam'd.[22] The Princely Hierarch   220
In thir bright stand, there left his Powers to seise
Possession of the Garden; hee alone,
To find where *Adam* shelterd, took his way,
Not unperceav'd of *Adam*, who to *Eve*,
While the great Visitant approach'd, thus spake.   225
   Eve, now expect great tidings, which perhaps
Of us will soon determin, or impose
New Laws to be observ'd; for I descrie
From yonder blazing Cloud that veils the Hill
One of the heav'nly Host, and by his Gate   230

[20] halt.
[21] referring to Gen. xxxii. 1-2.
[22] The servant of Elisha saw a mountain full of horses and chariots, which
had been sent by the king of Syria to seize Elisha, besieged by fire (2 Kings vi.
13-17).

None of the meanest, some great Potentate
Or of the Thrones above, such Majestie
Invests him coming; yet not terrible,
That I should fear, nor sociably mild,
As *Raphael*, that I should much confide,   235
But solemn and sublime, whom not t' offend,
With reverence I must meet, and thou retire.
He ended; and th' Arch-Angel soon drew nigh,
Not in his shape Celestial, but as Man
Clad to meet Man; over his lucid Armes   240
A militarie Vest of purple flowd
Livelier then *Meliboean*,[23] or the grain
Of *Sarra*, worn by Kings and Heroes old
In time of Truce; *Iris* had dipt the wooff;
His starrie Helm unbuckl'd shew'd him prime   245
In Manhood where Youth ended; by his side
As in a glistering *Zodiac*[24] hung the Sword,
Satans dire dread, and in his hand the Spear.
Adam bowd low, hee Kingly from his State
Inclin'd not, but his coming thus declar'd.   250
    Adam, Heav'ns high behest no Preface needs:
Sufficient that thy Prayers are heard, and Death,
Then due by sentence when thou didst transgress,
Defeated of his seisure many dayes
Giv'n thee of Grace, wherein thou may'st repent,   255
And one bad act with many deeds well done
Mayst cover: well may then thy Lord appeas'd
Redeem thee quite from Deaths rapacious claim;
But longer in this Paradise to dwell
Permits not; to remove thee I am come,   260
And send thee from the Garden forth to till
The ground whence thou wast tak'n, fitter Soil.
    He added not, for *Adam* at the news
Heart-strook with chilling gripe of sorrow stood,
That all his senses bound; *Eve*, who unseen   265
Yet all had heard, with audible lament
Discover'd[25] soon the place of her retire.
    O unexpected stroke, worse then of Death!
Must I thus leave thee Paradise? thus leave
Thee Native Soil, these happie Walks and Shades,   270
Fit haunt of Gods? where I had hope to spend,

---

[23] of a town in Thessaly. Sarra is Tyre, famous for dyes.
[24] belt.
[25] revealed.

Quiet though sad, the respit of that day
That must be mortal to us both. O flowrs,
That never will in other Climate grow,
My early visitation, and my last   275
At Eev'n, which I bred up with tender hand
From the first op'ning bud, and gave ye Names,
Who now shall rear ye to the Sun, or rank[26]
Your Tribes, and water from th' ambrosial Fount?
Thee lastly nuptial Bowr, by mee adornd   280
With what to sight or smell was sweet; from thee
How shall I part, and whither wander down
Into a lower World, to this obscure
And wild, how shall we breath in other Air
Less pure, accustomd to immortal Fruits?   285
    Whom thus the Angel interrupted mild.
Lament not *Eve*, but patiently resigne
What justly thou hast lost; nor set thy heart,
Thus over-fond, on that which is not thine;
Thy going is not lonely, with thee goes   290
Thy Husband, him to follow thou art bound;
Where he abides, think there thy native soil.
    Adam by this from the cold sudden damp
Recovering, and his scatterd spirits returnd,
To *Michael* thus his humble words address'd.   295
    Celestial, whether among the Thrones, or nam'd
Of them the Highest, for such of shape may seem
Prince above Princes, gently hast thou tould
Thy message, which might else in telling wound,
And in performing end us; what besides   300
Of sorrow and dejection and despair
Our frailtie can sustain, thy tidings bring,
Departure from this happy place, our sweet
Recess, and onely consolation left
Familiar to our eyes, all places else   305
Inhospitable appeer and desolate,
Nor knowing us nor known: and if by prayer
Incessant I could hope to change the will
Of him who all things can, I would not cease
To wearie him with my assiduous cries: 310
But prayer against his absolute Decree
No more avails then breath against the wind,
Blown stifling back on him that breaths it forth:
Therefore to his great bidding I submit.

[26] put your plants into rows.

This most afflicts me, that departing hence,   315
As from his face I shall be hid, depriv'd
His blessed count'nance; here I could frequent,
With worship, place by place where he voutsaf'd
Presence Divine, and to my Sons relate;
On this Mount he appeerd, under this Tree   320
Stood visible, among these Pines his voice
I heard, here with him at this Fountain talk'd:
So many grateful Altars I would rear
Of grassie Terf, and pile up every Stone
Of lustre from the brook, in memorie,   325
Or monument to Ages, and thereon
Offer sweet smelling Gumms and Fruits and Flowrs:
In yonder nether World where shall I seek
His bright appearances, or footstep trace?
For though I fled him angrie, yet recall'd   330
To life prolong'd and promis'd Race, I now
Gladly behold though but his utmost skirts
Of glory, and farr off his steps adore.
     To whom thus *Michael* with regard benigne.
Adam, thou know'st Heav'n his, and all the Earth,   335
Not this Rock onely; his Omnipresence fills
Land, Sea, and Air, and every kind that lives,
Fomented[27] by his virtual[28] power and warmd:
All th' Earth he gave thee to possess and rule,
No despicable gift; surmise not then   340
His presence to these narrow bounds confin'd
Of Paradise or *Eden:* this had been
Perhaps thy Capital Seat, from whence had spred
All generations, and had hither come
From all the ends of th' Earth, to celebrate   345
And reverence thee thir great Progenitor.
But this præeminence thou hast lost, brought down
To dwell on eeven ground now with thy Sons:
Yet doubt not but in Vallie and in Plain
God is as here, and will be found alike   350
Present, and of his presence many a signe
Still following thee, still compassing thee round
With goodness and paternal Love, his Face
Express, and of his steps the track Divine.
Which that thou mayst beleeve, and be confirmd   355
Ere thou from hence depart, know I am sent

27 bathed (with warmth).
28 efficacious.

To shew thee what shall come in future dayes
To thee and to thy Ofspring; good with bad
Expect to hear, supernal Grace contending
With sinfulness of Men; thereby to learn   360
True patience, and to temper joy with fear
And pious sorrow, equally enur'd
By moderation either state to bear,
Prosperous or adverse: so shalt thou lead
Safest thy life, and best prepar'd endure   365
Thy mortal passage when it comes. Ascend
This Hill; let *Eve* (for I have drencht her eyes)
Here sleep below while thou to foresight wak'st,
As once thou slepst, while Shee to life was formd.
     To whom thus *Adam* gratefully repli'd.   370
Ascend, I follow thee, safe Guide, the path
Thou lead'st me, and to th' hand of Heav'n submit,
However chast'ning, to the evil turn
My obvious breast, arming to overcom
By suffering, and earn rest from labour won,   375
If so I may attain. So both ascend
In the Visions of God: It was a Hill
Of Paradise the highest, from whose top
The Hemisphere of Earth in cleerest Ken
Stretcht out to amplest reach of prospect lay.   380
Not higher that Hill nor wider looking round,
Whereon for different cause the Tempter set
Our second *Adam*[29] in the Wilderness,
To shew him all Earths Kingdoms and thir Glory.
His Eye might there command wherever stood   385
City of old or modern Fame, the Seat
Of mightiest Empire, from the destind Walls
Of *Cambalu*, seat of *Cathaian Can*[30]
And *Samarchand* by *Oxus, Temirs* Throne,[31]
To *Paquin* of *Sinæan* Kings,[32] and thence   390
To *Agra* and *Lahor* of great *Mogul*
Down to the golden *Chersonese*,[33] or where

[29] Christ.
[30] the Khan of China (Mongolia).
[31] the Mongolian conqueror Tamerlane's throne on the river Oxus.
[32] Peking of Chinese Kings.
[33] the Malay peninsula. The following geographic references include Persian
cities (Ecbatan, Hispahan), Turkish Byzantium (Bizance), Abyssinia (the
empire of the negus or king), coastal towns in eastern Africa (Ercoco, Mom-
baza, Quiloa, Melind, Sofala), and areas of northwestern Africa (ll. 403-4).
For rich Ophir, see 1 Kings ix. 28; Sofala trafficked in gold.

The *Persian* in *Ecbatan* sate, or since
In *Hispahan,* or where the *Russian Ksar*
In *Mosco,* or the Sultan in *Bizance,*   395
Turchestan-born; nor could his eye not ken
Th' Empire of *Negus* to his utmost Port
Ercoco and the less Maritime Kings
Mombaza, and *Quiloa,* and *Melind,*
And *Sofala* thought *Ophir,* to the Realm   400
Of *Congo,* and *Angola* fardest South;
Or thence from *Niger* Flood to *Atlas* Mount
The Kingdoms of *Almansor, Fez* and *Sus,*
Marocco and *Algiers,* and *Tremisen;*
On *Europe* thence, and where *Rome* was to sway   405
The World: in Spirit perhaps he also saw
Rich *Mexico* the seat of *Motezume,*
And *Cusco* in *Peru,* the richer seat
Of *Atabalipa,*[34] and yet unspoil'd
Guiana, whose great Citie *Geryons* Sons[35]   410
Call *El Dorado:* but to nobler sights
Michael from *Adams* eyes the Film remov'd
Which that false Fruit that promis'd clearer sight
Had bred; then purg'd with Euphrasie and Rue[36]
The visual Nerve, for he had much to see;   415
And from the Well of Life three drops instill'd.
So deep the power of these Ingredients pierc'd,
Eevn to the inmost seat of mental sight,
That *Adam* now enforc't to close his eyes,
Sunk down and all his Spirits became intranst: 420
But him the gentle Angel by the hand
Soon rais'd, and his attention thus recall'd.
  Adam, now ope thine eyes, and first behold
Th' effects which thy original crime hath wrought
In some to spring from thee, who never touch'd   425
Th' excepted Tree, nor with the Snake conspir'd,
Nor sinn'd thy sin, yet from that sin derive
Corruption to bring forth more violent deeds.
  His eyes he op'n'd, and beheld a field,
Part arable and tilth, whereon were Sheaves   430
New reapt, the other part sheep-walks and foulds;
Ith' midst an Altar as the Land-mark stood

[34] Atahualpa, the Inca king conquered by Pizarro.
[35] the Spaniards. El Dorado (the Gilded One) was a legendary king of South America, but here, a city of fabulous richness.
[36] herbs beneficial to eyesight.

Rustic, of grassie sord;[37] thither anon
A sweatie Reaper[38] from his Tillage brought
First Fruits, the green Ear, and the yellow Sheaf,   435
Uncull'd,[39] as came to hand; a Shepherd next
More meek came with the Firstlings of his Flock
Choicest and best; then sacrificing, laid
The Inwards and thir Fat, with Incense strew'd,
On the cleft Wood, and all due Rites perform'd.   440
His Offring soon propitious Fire from Heav'n
Consum'd with nimble glance, and grateful steam;
The others not, for his was not sincere;
Whereat hee inlie rag'd, and as they talk'd,
Smote him into the Midriff with a stone   445
That beat out life; he fell, and deadly pale
Groand out his Soul with gushing bloud effus'd.
Much at that sight was *Adam* in his heart
Dismai'd, and thus in haste to th' Angel cri'd.
    O Teacher, some great mischief hath befall'n   450
To that meek man, who well had sacrific'd;
Is Pietie thus and pure Devotion paid?
    T' whom *Michael* thus, hee also mov'd, repli'd.
These two are Brethren, *Adam*, and to come
Out of thy loyns; th' unjust the just hath slain,   455
For envie that his Brothers Offering found
From Heav'n acceptance; but the bloodie Fact
Will be aveng'd, and th' others Faith approv'd
Loose no reward, though here thou see him die,
Rowling in dust and gore. To which our Sire.   460
    Alas, both for the deed and for the cause!
But have I now seen Death? Is this the way
I must return to native dust? O sight
Of terrour, foul and ugly to behold,
Horrid to think, how horrible to feel!   465
    To whom thus *Michael*. Death thou hast seen
In his first shape on man; but many shapes
Of Death, and many are the wayes that lead
To his grim Cave, all dismal; yet to sense
More terrible at th' entrance then within.   470
Some, as thou saw'st, by violent stroke shall die,
By Fire, Flood, Famin, by Intemperance more
In Meats and Drinks, which on the Earth shall bring

[37] sward, turf.
[38] Cain, who envied his meek brother Abel (l. 436).
[39] unselected (to choose only the best).

Diseases dire, of which a monstrous crew
Before thee shall appear; that thou mayst know   475
What miserie th' inabstinence of *Eve*
Shall bring on men. Immediately a place
Before his eyes appeard, sad, noysom, dark,
A Lazar-house it seemd, wherein were laid
Numbers of all diseas'd, all maladies   480
Of gastly Spasm, or racking torture, qualmes
Of heart-sick Agonie, all feavourous kinds,'
Convulsions, Epilepsies, fierce Catarrhs,
Intestin Stone and Ulcer, Colic pangs,
Dæmoniac Phrenzie, moaping Melancholie   485
And Moon-struck madness, pining Atrophie,
Marasmus,[40] and wide-wasting Pestilence,
Dropsies, and Asthmas, and Joint-racking Rheums.
Dire was the tossing, deep the groans, despair
Tended the sick busiest from Couch to Couch;   490
And over them triumphant Death his Dart
Shook, but delaid to strike, though oft invok't
With vows, as thir chief good, and final hope.
Sight so deform what heart of Rock could long
Drie-ey'd behold? *Adam* could not, but wept,   495
Though not of Woman born; compassion quell'd
His best of Man, and gave him up to tears
A space, till firmer thoughts restraind excess,
And scarce recovering words his plaint renew'd.
    O miserable Mankind, to what fall   500
Degraded, to what wretched state reserv'd!
Better end heer unborn. Why is life giv'n
To be thus wrested from us? rather why
Obtruded on us thus? who if we knew
What we receive, would either not accept   505
Life offer'd, or soon beg to lay it down,
Glad to be so dismist in peace. Can thus
Th' Image of God in man created once
So goodly and erect, though faultie since,
To such unsightly sufferings be debas't   510
Under inhuman pains? Why should not Man,
Retaining still Divine similitude
In part, from such deformities be free,
And for his Makers Image sake exempt?
    Thir Makers Image, answerd *Michael*, then   515
Forsook them, when themselves they villifi'd

[40] consumption.

To serve ungovern'd appetite, and took
His Image[41] whom they serv'd, a brutish vice,
Inductive mainly to the sin of *Eve*.
Therefore so abject is thir punishment,   520
Disfiguring not Gods likeness, but thir own,
Or if his likeness, by themselves defac't
While they pervert pure Natures healthful rules
To loathsom sickness, worthily, since they
Gods Image did not reverence in themselves.   525
    I yeild it just, said *Adam*, and submit.
But is there yet no other way, besides
These painful passages, how we may come
To Death, and mix with our connatural dust?
    There is, said *Michael*, if thou well observe   530
The rule of not too much, by temperance taught
In what thou eatst and drinkst, seeking from thence
Due nourishment, not gluttonous delight,
Till many years over thy head return:
So maist thou live, till like ripe Fruit thou drop   535
Into thy Mothers lap, or be with ease
Gatherd, not harshly pluckt, for death mature:
This is old age; but then thou must outlive
Thy youth, thy strength, thy beauty, which will change
To witherd weak and gray; thy Senses then   540
Obtuse, all taste of pleasure must forgoe,
To what thou hast, and for the Air of youth
Hopeful and cheerful, in thy blood will reigne
A melancholly damp of cold and dry[42]
To waigh thy spirits down, and last consume   545
The Balm of Life. To whom our Ancestor.
    Henceforth I flie not Death, nor would prolong
Life much, bent rather how I may be quit
Fairest and easiest of this combrous charge,
Which I must keep till my appointed day   550
Of rendring up, and patiently attend[43]
My dissolution. *Michael* repli'd,
    Nor love thy Life, nor hate; but what thou liv'st
Live well, how long or short permit to Heav'n:
And now prepare thee for another sight.   555
    He look'd and saw a spacious Plain,[44] whereon

[41] Appetite (the image of Satan as Covetousness, Lust, and Gluttony); compare Phil. iii. 19: "whose God is their belly."
[42] See II, n. 44.
[43] await.
[44] See Gen. iv. 16 ff. for Cain's descendants.

Were Tents of various hue; by some were herds
Of Cattel grazing: others, whence the sound
Of Instruments that made melodious chime
Was heard, of Harp and Organ; and who moov'd   560
Thir stops and chords was seen: his volant touch
Instinct[45] through all proportions low and high
Fled and pursu'd transverse the resonant fugue.
In other part stood one who at the Forge
Labouring, two massie clods of Iron and Brass   565
Had melted (whether found where casual fire
Had wasted woods on Mountain or in Vale,
Down to the veins of Earth, thence gliding hot
To som Caves mouth, or whether washt by stream
From underground) the liquid Ore he dreind   570
Into fit moulds prepar'd; from which he formd
First his own Tools; then, what might else be wrought
Fusil[46] or grav'n in mettle. After these,
But on the hether side a different sort[47]
From the high neighbouring Hills, which was thir Seat,   575
Down to the Plain descended: by thir guise
Just men they seemd, and all thir study bent
To worship God aright, and know his works
Not hid, nor those things last which might preserve
Freedom and Peace to men: they on the Plain   580
Long had not walkt, when from the Tents behold
A Beavie of fair Women, richly gay
In Gems and wanton dress; to th' Harp they sung
Soft amorous Ditties, and in dance came on:
The Men though grave, ey'd them, and let thir eyes   585
Rove without rein, till in the amorous Net
Fast caught, they lik'd, and each his liking chose;
And now of love they treat till th' Eevning Star[48]
Loves Harbinger appeerd; then all in heat
They light the Nuptial Torch, and bid invoke   590
Hymen, then first to marriage Rites invok't;
With Feast and Musick all the Tents resound.
Such happy interview and fair event
Of love and youth not lost, Songs, Garlands, Flowrs,
And charming Symphonies attach'd the heart   595
Of *Adam,* soon enclin'd t' admit delight,
The bent of Nature; which he thus express'd.

---

[45] imbued (by the music of the spheres).
[46] fused or cast.
[47] See Gen. vi. 1–4 for Seth's descendants ("Sons of God," l. 622).
[48] Venus.

True opener of mine eyes, prime Angel blest,
Much better seems this Vision, and more hope
Of peaceful dayes portends, then those two past;   600
Those were of hate and death, or pain much worse,
Here Nature seems fulfill'd in all her ends.
    To whom thus *Michael.* Judge not what is best
By pleasure, though to Nature seeming meet,
Created, as thou art, to nobler end   605
Holie and pure, conformitie divine.
Those Tents thou sawst so pleasant, were the Tents
Of wickedness, wherein shall dwell his Race
Who slew his Brother; studious they appear
Of Arts that polish Life, Inventers rare,   610
Unmindful of thir Maker, though his Spirit
Taught them, but they his gifts acknowledg'd none.
Yet they a beauteous ofspring shall beget;
For that fair femal Troop thou sawst, that seemd
Of Goddesses, so blithe, so smooth, so gay,   615
Yet empty of all good wherein consists
Womans domestic honour and chief praise;
Bred onely and completed to the taste
Of lustful appetence, to sing, to dance,
To dress, and troul[49] the Tongue, and roul the Eye.   620
To these that sober Race of Men, whose lives
Religious titl'd them the Sons of God,
Shall yeild up all thir vertue, all thir fame
Ignobly, to the trains[50] and to the smiles
Of these fair Atheists, and now swim in joy,   625
(Erelong to swim at large) and laugh; for which
The world erelong a world of tears must weep.
    To whom thus *Adam* of short joy bereft.
O pittie and shame, that they who to live well
Enterd so fair, should turn aside to tread   630
Paths indirect, or in the mid way faint!
But still I see the tenor of Mans woe
Holds on the same, from Woman to begin.
    From Mans effeminate slackness it begins,
Said th' Angel, who should better hold his place   635
By wisdom, and superiour gifts receav'd.
But now prepare thee for another Scene.
    He look'd and saw wide Territorie spred

[49] wag.
[50] tricks.

Before him,[51] Towns, and rural works between,
Cities of Men with lofty Gates and Towrs,   640
Concours in Arms, fierce Faces threatning Warr,
Giants of mightie Bone, and bould emprise;
Part wield thir Arms, part courb the foaming Steed,
Single or in Array of Battel rang'd
Both Horse and Foot, nor idlely mustring stood;   645
One way a Band select from forage drives
A herd of Beeves, fair Oxen and fair Kine
From a fat Meddow ground; or fleecy Flock,
Ewes and thir bleating Lambs over the Plain,
Thir Bootie; scarce with Life the Shepherds flye,   650
But call in aid, which tacks[52] a bloody Fray;
With cruel Tournament the Squadrons join;
Where Cattel pastur'd late, now scatterd lies
With Carcasses and Arms th' ensanguind Field
Deserted: Others to a Citie strong   655
Lay Seige, encampt; by Batterie, Scale, and Mine,
Assaulting; others from the wall defend
With Dart and Jav'lin, Stones and sulfurous Fire;
On each hand slaughter and gigantic deeds.
In other part the scepter'd Haralds call   660
To Council in the Citie Gates: anon
Grey-headed men and grave, with Warriours mixt,
Assemble, and Harangues are heard, but soon
In factious opposition, till at last
Of middle Age one[53] rising, eminent   665
In wise deport, spake much of Right and Wrong,
Of Justice, of Religion, Truth and Peace,
And Judgement from above: him old and young
Exploded[54] and had seiz'd with violent hands,
Had not a Cloud descending snatch'd him thence   670
Unseen amid the throng: so violence
Proceeded, and Oppression, and Sword-Law
Through all the Plain, and refuge none was found.
Adam was all in tears, and to his guide
Lamenting turnd full sad; O what are these,   675
Deaths Ministers, not Men, who thus deal Death
Inhumanly to men, and multiply
Ten thousandfould the sin of him who slew

[51] What he sees owes much to the description of Achilles' shield in *Iliad*,
XVIII, 478 ff.
[52] rapidly diverges into.
[53] Enoch.
[54] assailed with contempt.

His Brother; for of whom such massacher
Make they but of thir Brethren, men of men?   680
But who was that Just Man, whom had not Heav'n
Rescu'd, had in his Righteousness bin lost?
  To whom thus *Michael.* These are the product
Of those ill-mated Marriages thou saw'st:
Where good with bad were matcht, who of themselves   685
Abhor to joyn; and by imprudence mixt,
Produce prodigious Births of bodie or mind.
Such were these Giants, men of high renown;[55]
For in those dayes Might onely shall be admir'd,
And Valour and Heroic Vertu call'd;   690
To overcome in Battel, and subdue
Nations, and bring home spoils with infinite
Man-slaughter, shall be held the highest pitch
Of human Glorie, and for Glorie done
Of triumph, to be styl'd great Conquerours,   695
Patrons of Mankind, Gods, and Sons of Gods,
Destroyers rightlier call'd and Plagues of men.
Thus Fame shall be atchiev'd, renown on Earth,
And what most merits fame in silence hid.
But hee the seventh from thee,[56] whom thou beheldst   700
The onely righteous in a World perverse,
And therefore hated, therefore so beset
With Foes for daring single to be just,
And utter odious Truth, that God would come
To judge them with his Saints: Him the most High   705
Rapt in a balmie Cloud with winged Steeds
Did, as thou sawst, receave, to walk with God
High in Salvation and the Climes of bliss,
Exempt from Death; to shew thee what reward
Awaits the good, the rest what punishment;   710
Which now direct thine eyes and soon behold.
  He look'd, and saw the face of things quite chang'd;
The brazen Throat of Warr had ceast to roar,
All now was turn'd to jollitie and game,
To luxurie and riot, feast and dance,   715
Marrying or prostituting, as befell,
Rape or Adulterie, where passing fair
Allurd them; thence from Cups to civil Broils.

[55] As John M. Steadman has pointed out (*PQ*, XL, 1961, 580–86), Milton's characterization of giants and the terminology of heroic virtue derives from the giants of Genesis; "might" is equated with "heroism."
[56] Enoch.

At length a Reverend Sire[57] among them came,
And of thir doings great dislike declar'd,   720
And testifi'd against thir wayes; hee oft
Frequented thir Assemblies, whereso met,
Triumphs[58] or Festivals, and to them preach'd
Conversion and Repentance, as to Souls
In Prison under Judgements imminent: 725
But all in vain: which when he saw, he ceas'd
Contending, and remov'd his Tents farr off;
Then from the Mountain hewing Timber tall,
Began to build a Vessel of huge bulk,
Measur'd by Cubit, length, and breadth, and highth,   730
Smeard round with Pitch, and in the side a dore
Contriv'd, and of provisions laid in large
For Man and Beast: when loe a wonder strange!
Of every Beast, and Bird, and Insect small
Came seavens, and pairs,[59] and enterd in, as taught   735
Thir order; last the Sire, and his three Sons
With thir four Wives; and God made fast the dore.
Meanwhile the Southwind rose, and with black wings
Wide hovering, all the Clouds together drove
From under Heav'n; the Hills to their supplie   740
Vapour, and Exhalation dusk and moist,
Sent up amain; and now the thick'n'd Skie
Like a dark Ceeling stood; down rush'd the Rain
Impetuous, and continu'd till the Earth
No more was seen; the floating Vessel swum   745
Uplifted; and secure with beaked prow
Rode tilting o're the Waves, all dwellings else
Flood overwhelmd, and them with all thir pomp
Deep under water rould; Sea cover'd Sea,
Sea without shoar; and in thir Palaces   750
Where luxurie late reign'd, Sea-monsters whelp'd
And stabl'd; of Mankind, so numerous late,
All left, in one small bottom swum imbark't.
How didst thou grieve then, *Adam*, to behold
The end of all thy Ofspring, end so sad,   755
Depopulation; thee another Floud,
Of tears and sorrow a Floud thee also drown'd,
And sunk thee as thy Sons; till gently reard

[57] Noah.
[58] processions.
[59] Gen. vii. 2: "Of every clean beast thou shalt take to thee by sevens, the male and his female: and of beasts that are not clean by two, the male and his female."

By th' Angel, on thy feet thou stoodst at last,
Though comfortless, as when a Father mourns   760
His Childern, all in view destroyd at once;
And scarce to th' Angel utterdst thus thy plaint.
    O Visions ill foreseen! better had I
Liv'd ignorant of future, so had borne
My part of evil onely, each dayes lot   765
Anough to bear; those now, that were dispenst[60]
The burd'n of many Ages, on me light
At once, by my foreknowledge gaining Birth
Abortive, to torment me ere thir being,
With thought that they must be. Let no man seek   770
Henceforth to be foretold what shall befall
Him or his Childern, evil he may be sure,
Which neither his foreknowing can prevent,
And hee the future evil shall no less
In apprehension then in substance feel   775
Grievous to bear: but that care now is past,
Man is not whom to warn: those few escap't
Famin and anguish will at last consume
Wandring that watrie Desert: I had hope
When violence was ceas't, and Warr on Earth,   780
All would have then gon well, peace would have crownd
With length of happy dayes the race of man;
But I was farr deceav'd; for now I see
Peace to corrupt no less then Warr to waste.
How comes it thus? unfould, Celestial Guide,   785
And whether here the Race of man will end.
    To whom thus *Michael*. Those whom last thou sawst
In triumph and luxurious wealth, are they
First seen in acts of prowess eminent
And great exploits, but of true vertu void;   790
Who having spilt much blood, and don much waste
Subduing Nations, and achiev'd thereby
Fame in the World, high titles, and rich prey,
Shall change thir course to pleasure, ease, and sloth,
Surfet, and lust, till wantonness and pride   795
Raise out of friendship hostil deeds in Peace.
The conquerd also, and enslav'd by Warr
Shall with thir freedom lost all vertu loose
And fear of God, from whom thir pietie feign'd
In sharp contest of Battel found no aid   800
Against invaders; therefore coold in zeal

[60] given.

Thenceforth shall practice how to live secure,
Worldlie or dissolute, on what thir Lords
Shall leave them to enjoy; for th' Earth shall bear
More then anough, that temperance may be tri'd: 805
So all shall turn degenerate, all deprav'd,
Justice and Temperance, Truth and Faith forgot;
One Man except, the onely Son of light
In a dark Age, against example good,
Against allurement, custom, and a World   810
Offended; fearless of reproach and scorn,
Or violence, hee of thir wicked wayes
Shall them admonish, and before them set
The paths of righteousness, how much more safe,
And full of peace, denouncing wrauth to come   815
On thir impenitence; and shall return
Of them derided, but of God observ'd
The one just Man alive; by his command
Shall build a wondrous Ark, as thou beheldst,
To save himself and houshold from amidst   820
A World devote to universal rack.
No sooner hee with them of Man and Beast
Select for life shall in the Ark be lodg'd,
And shelterd round, but all the Cataracts
Of Heav'n set open on the Earth shall powr   825
Rain day and night, all fountains of the Deep
Broke up, shall heave the Ocean to usurp
Beyond all bounds, till inundation rise
Above the highest Hills: then shall this Mount
Of Paradise by might of Waves be moov'd   830
Out of his place, pushd by the horned[61] floud,
With all his verdure spoil'd, and Trees adrift
Down the great River[62] to the op'ning Gulf,
And there take root an Iland salt and bare,
The haunt of Seals and Orcs,[63] and Sea-mews clang.[64]   835
To teach thee that God attributes to place
No sanctitie, if none be thither brought
By Men who there frequent, or therein dwell.
And now what further shall ensue, behold.
    He look'd, and saw the Ark hull[65] on the floud,   840
Which now abated, for the Clouds were fled,

[61] divided into branches.
[62] the Euphrates, which flows into the Persian Gulf.
[63] whales.
[64] noise of gulls.
[65] a verb, "loom up" and "float."

Drivn by a keen North-wind, that blowing drie
Wrinkl'd the face of Deluge, as decai'd;
And the cleer Sun on his wide watrie Glass
Gaz'd hot, and of the fresh Wave largely drew,   845
As after thirst, which made thir flowing shrink
From standing lake to tripping ebb, that stole
With soft foot towards the deep, who now had stopt
His Sluces, as the Heav'n his windows shut.
The Ark no more now flotes, but seems on ground   850
Fast on the top of som high mountain fixt.
And now the tops of Hills as Rocks appeer;
With clamor thence the rapid Currents drive
Towards the retreating Sea thir furious tyde.
Forthwith from out the Ark a Raven flies,   855
And after him, the surer messenger,
A Dove sent forth once and agen to spie
Green Tree or ground whereon his foot may light;
The second time returning, in his Bill
An Olive leaf he brings, pacific signe: 860
Anon drie ground appeers, and from his Ark
The ancient Sire descends with all his Train;
Then with uplifted hands, and eyes devout,
Grateful to Heav'n, over his head beholds
A dewie Cloud, and in the Cloud a Bow   865
Conspicuous with three listed⁶⁶ colours gay,
Betok'ning peace from God, and Cov'nant new.
Whereat the heart of *Adam* erst so sad
Greatly rejoyc'd, and thus his joy broke forth.
    O thou who future things canst represent   870
As present, Heav'nly instructer, I revive
At this last sight, assur'd that Man shall live
With all the Creatures, and thir seed preserve.
Farr less I now lament for one whole World
Of wicked Sons destroyd, then I rejoyce   875
For one Man found so perfet and so just,
That God voutsafes to raise another World
From him, and all his anger to forget.
But say, what mean those coloured streaks in Heavn,
Distended as the Brow of God appeas'd,   880
Or serve they as a flowrie verge to bind
The fluid skirts of that same watrie Cloud,
Least it again dissolve and showr the Earth?
    To whom th' Archangel. Dextrously thou aim'st;

⁶⁶ striped.

So willingly doth God remit his Ire,   885
Though late repenting him of Man deprav'd,
Griev'd at his heart, when looking down he saw
The whole Earth fill'd with violence, and all flesh
Corrupting each thir way; yet those remoov'd,
Such grace shall one just Man find in his sight,   890
That he relents, not to blot out mankind,
And makes a Covenant never to destroy
The Earth again by flood, nor let the Sea
Surpass his bounds, nor Rain to drown the World
With Man therein or Beast; but when he brings   895
Over the Earth a Cloud, will therein set
His triple-colour'd Bow, whereon to look
And call to mind his Cov'nant: Day and Night,
Seed time and Harvest, Heat and hoary Frost
Shall hold thir course, till fire purge all things new,   900
Both Heav'n and Earth, wherein the just shall dwell.[67]

[67] 2 Peter iii. 12–13: "Looking for and hasting unto the coming of the day
of God, wherein the heavens being on fire shall be dissolved, and the elements
shall melt with fervent heat? Nevertheless we, according to his promise, look
for new heavens and a new earth, wherein dwelleth righteousness." Compare
also *Naturam non pati senium.*

BOOK XII

THE ARGUMENT

The Angel *Michael* continues from the Flood to relate what shall suc-
ceed; then, in the mention of *Abraham,* comes by degrees to explain,
who that Seed of the Woman shall be, which was promised *Adam* and
Eve in the Fall; his Incarnation, Death, Resurrection, and Ascension;
the state of the Church till his second Coming. *Adam* greatly satisfied
and recomforted by these Relations and Promises descends the Hill with
Michael; wakens *Eve,* who all this while had slept, but with gentle
dreams compos'd to quietness of mind and submission. *Michael* in either
hand leads them out of Paradise, the fiery Sword waving behind them,
and the Cherubim taking thir Stations to guard the Place.

    As one who in his journey bates[1] at Noon,
Though bent on speed, so heer th' Archangel paus'd
Betwixt the world destroy'd and world restor'd,
If *Adam* aught perhaps might interpose;
Then with transition sweet new Speech resumes.   5

[1] pauses (to eat).

Thus thou hast seen one World begin and end;
And Man as from a second stock proceed.
Much thou hast yet to see, but I perceave
Thy mortal sight to fail; objects divine
Must needs impair and wearie human sense: 10
Henceforth what is to com I will relate,
Thou therefore give due audience, and attend.
This second sours of Men, while yet but few;
And while the dread of judgement past remains
Fresh in thir minds, fearing the Deitie,   15
With some regard to what is just and right
Shall lead thir lives, and multiplie apace,
Labouring the soil, and reaping plenteous crop,
Corn wine and oyl; and from the herd or flock,
Oft sacrificing Bullock, Lamb, or Kid,   20
With large Wine-offerings pour'd, and sacred Feast,
Shall spend thir dayes in joy unblam'd, and dwell
Long time in peace by Families and Tribes
Under paternal rule; till one² shall rise
Of proud ambitious heart, who not content   25
With fair equalitie, fraternal state,
Will arrogate Dominion undeserv'd
Over his brethren, and quite dispossess
Concord and law of Nature from the Earth,
Hunting (and Men not Beasts shall be his game)   30
With Warr and hostile snare such as refuse
Subjection to his Empire tyrannous:
A mightie Hunter thence he shall be styl'd
Before the Lord, as in despite of Heav'n,
Or from Heav'n claming second Sovrantie;   35
And from Rebellion shall derive his name,
Though of Rebellion others he accuse.
Hee with a crew, whom like Ambition joyns
With him or under him to tyrannize,
Marching from *Eden* towards the West, shall find   40
The Plain,³ wherein a black bituminous gurge
Boils out from under ground, the mouth of Hell;
Of Brick, and of that stuff they cast to build
A Citie and Towr, whose top may reach to Heav'n;
And get themselves a name, least far disperst   45
In foraign Lands thir memorie be lost,

² Nimrod ("rebel," l. 36), the mighty hunter (l. 33) who is fabled as the
founder of Babylon (Babel).
³ Shinar; a "gurge" is a whirlpool.

Regardless whether good or evil fame.
But God who oft descends to visit men
Unseen, and through thir habitations walks
To mark thir doings, them beholding soon,   50
Comes down to see thir Citie, ere the Tower
Obstruct Heav'n Towrs, and in derision sets
Upon thir Tongues a various⁴ Spirit to rase
Quite out thir Native Language, and instead
To sow a jangling noise of words unknown: 55
Forthwith a hideous gabble rises loud
Among the Builders; each to other calls
Not understood, till hoarse, and all in rage,
As mockt they storm; great laughter was in Heav'n
And looking down, to see the hubbub strange   60
And hear the din; thus was the building left
Ridiculous, and the work Confusion nam'd.⁵
    Whereto thus *Adam* fatherly displeas'd.
O execrable Son so to aspire
Above his Brethren, to himself assuming   65
Authoritie usurpt, from God not giv'n:
He gave us onely over Beast, Fish, Fowl
Dominion absolute; that right we hold
By his donation; but Man over men
He made not Lord; such title to himself   70
Reserving, human left from human free.
But this Usurper his encroachment proud
Stayes not on Man; to God his Tower intends
Siege and defiance: Wretched man! what food
Will he convey up thither to sustain   75
Himself and his rash Armie, where thin Air
Above the Clouds will pine his entrails gross,
And famish him of Breath, if not of Bread?
    To whom thus *Michael.* Justly thou abhorr'st
That Son, who on the quiet state of men   80
Such trouble brought, affecting to subdue
Rational Libertie; yet know withall,
Since thy original lapse, true Libertie
Is lost, which alwayes with right Reason dwells
Twinn'd, and from her hath no dividual being: 85
Reason in man obscur'd, or not obeyd,
Immediately inordinate desires
And upstart Passions catch the Government

⁴ quarrelsome, putting at variance.
⁵ that is, Babel.

From Reason, and to servitude reduce
Man till then free. Therefore since hee permits   90
Within himself unworthie Powers to reign
Over free Reason, God in Judgement just
Subjects him from without to violent Lords;
Who oft as undeservedly enthrall
His outward freedom: Tyrannie must be,   95
Though to the Tyrant thereby no excuse.
Yet somtimes Nations will decline so low
From vertue, which is reason, that no wrong,
But Justice, and some fatal curse annext
Deprives them of thir outward libertie,   100
Thir inward lost: Witness th' irreverent Son[6]
Of him who built the Ark, who for the shame
Don to his Father, heard this heavie curse,
Servant of Servants, on his vitious Race.[7]
Thus will this latter, as the former World,   105
Still tend from bad to worse, till God at last
Wearied with their iniquities, withdraw
His presence from among them, and avert
His holy Eyes; resolving from thenceforth
To leave them to thir own polluted wayes;   110
And one peculiar Nation to select
From all the rest, of whom to be invok'd,
A Nation from one faithful man[8] to spring:
Him on this side *Euphrates* yet residing,
Bred up in Idol-worship; O that men   115
(Canst thou believe?) should be so stupid grown,
While yet the Patriark liv'd, who scap'd the Flood,
As to forsake the living God, and fall
To worship thir own work in Wood and Stone
For Gods! yet him God the most High voutsafes   120
To call by Vision from his Fathers house,
His kindred and false Gods, into a Land
Which he will shew him, and from him will raise
A mightie Nation, and upon him showr
His benediction so, that in his Seed   125
All Nations shall be blest; he straight obeys,
Not knowing to what Land, yet firm believes:
I see him, but thou canst not, with what Faith

[6] Ham, father of Canaan.
[7] Ham saw his father naked, and Noah said, "Cursed be Canaan; a servant of servants shall he be unto his brethren" (Gen. ix. 25).
[8] Abraham.

He leaves his Gods, his Friends, and native Soil[9]
Ur of *Chaldæa*, passing now the Ford   130
To *Haran*, after him a cumbrous Train
Of Herds and Flocks, and numerous servitude;
Not wandring poor, but trusting all his wealth
With God, who call'd him, in a land unknown.
Canaan he now attains, I see his Tents   135
Pitcht about *Sechem*, and the neighbouring Plain
Of *Moreh;* there by promise he receaves
Gift to his Progenie of all that Land;
From *Hamath* Northward to the Desert South
(Things by thir names I call, though yet unnam'd)   140
From *Hermon* East to the great Western Sea,
Mount *Hermon*, yonder Sea, each place behold
In prospect, as I point them; on the shoar
Mount *Carmel;* here the double-founted stream
Jordan, true limit Eastward; but his Sons   145
Shall dwell to *Senir*, that long ridge of Hills.
This ponder, that all Nations of the Earth
Shall in his Seed be blessed; by that Seed
Is meant thy great deliverer, who shall bruise
The Serpents head; whereof to thee anon   150
Plainlier shall be reveald. This Patriarch blest,
Whom *faithful Abraham* due time shall call,
A Son,[10] and of his Son a Grand-child leaves,
Like him in faith, in wisdom, and renown;
The Grandchild with twelve Sons increast, departs   155
From *Canaan*, to a Land hereafter call'd
Egypt, divided by the River *Nile;*
See where it flows, disgorging at seaven mouths
Into the Sea: to sojourn in that Land
He comes invited by a yonger Son[11]   160
In time of dearth, a Son whose worthy deeds
Raise him to be the second in that Realm
Of *Pharao:* there he dies, and leaves his Race
Growing into a Nation, and now grown

[9] Ur was west and Haran east of the Euphrates. After travelling northwest, Abraham moves southwest into Canaan, then north to Hamath on the Orontes in Syria, to the west of which was the Great Desert. Mt. Hermon (and Senir in the same range) or more correctly (l. 145) the Jordan was considered the eastern boundary of Canaan, and the Mediterranean Sea bounded it on the west. Mt. Carmel was a promontory on the sea.

[10] Isaac, whose son was Jacob (later Israel, ll. 267–69), progenitor of the twelve tribes of Israel.

[11] Joseph.

Suspected to a sequent King,[12] who seeks   165
To stop thir overgrowth, as inmate guests
Too numerous; whence of guests he makes them slaves
Inhospitably, and kills thir infant Males:
Till by two brethren (those two brethren call
Moses and Aaron) sent from God to claim   170
His people from enthralment, they return
With glory and spoil back to thir promis'd Land.
But first the lawless Tyrant, who denies
To know thir God, or message to regard,
Must be compell'd by Signes and Judgements dire;   175
To blood unshed the Rivers must be turnd,
Frogs, Lice and Flies must all his Palace fill
With loath'd intrusion, and fill all the land;
His Cattel must of Rot and Murren die,
Botches and blains must all his flesh imboss,[13]   180
And all his people; Thunder mixt with Hail,
Hail mixt with fire must rend th' *Egyptian* Skie
And wheel on th' Earth, devouring where it rouls;
What it devours not, Herb, or Fruit, or Grain,
A darksom Cloud of Locusts swarming down   185
Must eat, and on the ground leave nothing green:
Darkness must overshadow all his bounds,
Palpable darkness, and blot out three dayes;
Last with one midnight stroke all the first-born
Of *Egypt* must lie dead. Thus with ten wounds   190
The River-dragon[14] tam'd at length submits
To let his sojourners depart, and oft
Humbles his stubborn heart, but still as Ice
More hard'n'd after thaw, till in his rage
Pursuing whom he late dismiss'd, the Sea   195
Swallows him with his Host, but them lets pass
As on drie land between two christal walls,
Aw'd by the rod of *Moses* so to stand
Divided, till his rescu'd gain thir shoar:
Such wondrous power God to his Saint will lend,   200
Though present in his Angel, who shall goe
Before them in a Cloud, and Pillar of Fire,
By day a Cloud, by night a Pillar of Fire,
To guide them in thir journey, and remove
Behind them, while th' obdurat King pursues: 205

[12] See Exod. i. 8.
[13] raise with swellings.
[14] Pharaoh; see Ezek. xxix. 3.

All night he will pursue, but his approach
Darkness defends[15] between till morning Watch;
Then through the Firey Pillar and the Cloud
God looking forth will trouble all his Host
And craze[16] thir Chariot wheels: when by command   210
Moses once more his potent Rod extends
Over the Sea; the Sea his Rod obeys;
On thir imbattell'd ranks the Waves return,
And overwhelm thir Warr: the Race elect
Safe towards *Canaan* from the shoar advance   215
Through the wild Desert, not the readiest way,
Least entring on the *Canaanite* allarmd
Warr terrifie them inexpert, and fear
Return them back to *Egypt,* choosing rather
Inglorious life with servitude; for life   220
To noble and ignoble is more sweet
Untraind in Armes, where rashness leads not on.
This also shall they gain by thir delay
In the wide Wilderness, there they shall found
Thir government, and thir great Senate[17] choose   225
Through the twelve Tribes, to rule by Laws ordaind:
God from the Mount of *Sinai,* whose gray top
Shall tremble, he descending, will himself
In Thunder Lightning and loud Trumpets sound
Ordain them Laws; part such as appertain   230
To civil Justice, part religious Rites
Of sacrifice, informing them, by types
And shadows, of that destind Seed to bruise
The Serpent, by what means he shall achieve
Mankinds deliverance. But the voice of God   235
To mortal ear is dreadful; they beseech
That *Moses* might report to them his will,
And terror cease; he grants what they besaught
Instructed that to God is no access
Without Mediator, whose high Office now   240
Moses in figure[18] beares, to introduce
One greater, of whose day he shall foretell,
And all the Prophets in thir Age the times
Of great *Messiah* shall sing. Thus Laws and Rites
Establisht, such delight hath God in Men   245

---

[15] prohibits (by lying between the Egyptians and the Israelites).
[16] shatter.
[17] the council of seventy elders chosen by Moses (Exod. xxiv. 1–9).
[18] as a type.

Obedient to his will, that he voutsafes
Among them to set up his Tabernacle,
The holy One with mortal Men to dwell:
By his prescript a Sanctuary is fram'd
Of Cedar, overlaid with Gold, therein   250
An Ark, and in the Ark his Testimony,
The Records of his Cov'nant, over these
A Mercie-seat[19] of Gold between the wings
Of two bright Cherubim, before him burn
Seaven Lamps[20] as in a Zodiac representing   255
The Heav'nly fires; over the Tent a Cloud
Shall rest by Day, a fiery gleam by Night,
Save when they journie, and at length they come,
Conducted by his Angel to the Land
Promis'd to *Abraham* and his Seed: the rest   260
Were long to tell, how many Battels fought,
How many Kings destroyd, and Kingdoms won,
Or how the Sun shall in mid Heav'n stand still
A day entire, and Nights due course adjourn,
Mans voice commanding,[21] Sun in *Gibeon* stand,   265
And thou Moon in the vale of *Aialon*,
Till *Israel* overcome; so call the third
From *Abraham*, Son of *Isaac*, and from him
His whole descent, who thus shall *Canaan* win.

    Here *Adam* interpos'd. O sent from Heav'n,   270
Enlightner of my darkness, gracious things
Thou hast reveald, those chiefly which concern
Just *Abraham* and his Seed: now first I find
Mine eyes true op'ning, and my heart much eas'd,
Erwhile perplext with thoughts what would becom   275
Of mee and all Mankind; but now I see
His day, in whom all Nations shall be blest,
Favour unmerited by me, who sought
Forbidd'n knowledge by forbidd'n means.
This yet I apprehend not, why to those   280
Among whom God will deigne to dwell on Earth
So many and so various Laws are giv'n;
So many Laws argue so many sins
Among them; how can God with such reside?
    To whom thus *Michael*. Doubt not but that sin   285

[19] See XI, n. 1.
[20] The candelabrum is likened to the seven planets shining throughout the universe.
[21] from Josh. x. 12.

Will reign among them, as of thee begot;
And therefore was Law giv'n them to evince
Thir natural pravitie,[22] by stirring up
Sin against Law to fight; that when they see
Law can discover sin, but not remove, 290
Save by those shadowie[23] expiations weak,
The bloud of Bulls and Goats, they may conclude
Some bloud more precious must be paid for Man,
Just for unjust, that in such righteousness
To them by Faith imputed, they may find 295
Justification towards God, and peace
Of Conscience, which the Law by Ceremonies
Cannot appease, nor Man the moral part
Perform, and not performing cannot live.
So Law appears imperfet, and but giv'n 300
With purpose to resign them in full time
Up to a better Cov'nant, disciplin'd
From shadowie Types to Truth, from Flesh to Spirit,
From imposition of strict Laws, to free
Acceptance of large Grace, from servil fear 305
To filial, works of Law to works of Faith.
And therefore shall not *Moses*, though of God
Highly belov'd, being but the Minister
Of Law, his people into *Canaan* lead;
But *Joshua* whom the Gentiles *Jesus* call,[24] 310
His Name and Office bearing, who shall quell
The adversarie Serpent, and bring back
Through the worlds wilderness long wanderd man
Safe to eternal Paradise of rest.
Meanwhile they in thir earthly *Canaan* plac't 315
Long time shall dwell and prosper, but when sins
National interrupt thir public peace,
Provoking God to raise them enemies:
From whom as oft he saves them penitent
By Judges first, then under Kings; of whom 320
The second,[25] both for pietie renownd
And puissant deeds, a promise shall receive
Irrevocable, that his Regal Throne
For ever shall endure; the like shall sing
All Prophecie, that of the Royal Stock 325

[22] depravity.
[23] The expiations are shadows (types) of Christ's expiation.
[24] Joshua is not only a type of Jesus; both words mean "savior."
[25] David.

Of *David* (so I name this King) shall rise
A Son, the Womans Seed to thee foretold,
Foretold to *Abraham*, as in whom shall trust
All Nations, and to Kings foretold, of Kings
The last, for of his Reign shall be no end.   330
But first a long succession must ensue,
And his next Son[26] for Wealth and Wisdom fam'd,
The clouded Ark of God till then in Tents
Wandring, shall in a glorious Temple enshrine.
Such follow him, as shall be registerd   335
Part good, part bad, of bad the longer scrowl,
Whose foul Idolatries, and other faults
Heapt to the popular sum, will so incense
God, as to leave them, and expose thir Land,
Thir Citie, his Temple, and his holy Ark   340
With all his sacred things, a scorn and prey
To that proud Citie, whose high Walls thou saw'st
Left in confusion, *Babylon* thence call'd.
There in captivitie he lets them dwell
The space of seventie years, then brings them back,   345
Remembring mercie, and his Cov'nant sworn
To *David*, stablisht as the dayes of Heav'n
Returnd from *Babylon* by leave of Kings[27]
Thir Lords, whom God dispos'd, the house of God
They first re-edifie, and for a while   350
In mean estate live moderate, till grown
In wealth and multitude, factious they grow;
But first among the Priests dissension springs,
Men who attend the Altar, and should most
Endeavour Peace: thir strife pollution brings   355
Upon the Temple it self: at last they[28] seise
The Scepter, and regard not *Davids* Sons,
Then loose it to a stranger,[29] that the true
Anointed King *Messiah* might be born
Barr'd of his right; yet at his Birth a Starr   360
Unseen before in Heav'n proclaims him com,
And guides the Eastern Sages, who enquire
His place, to offer Incense, Myrrh, and Gold;
His place of birth a solemn Angel tells
To simple Shepherds, keeping watch by night;   365

[26] Solomon.
[27] of Persia; that is, Cyrus, Cambyses, Darius, Xerxes, Artaxerxes.
[28] the Asmonean priest-princes, whose domination began with Jonathan in 153 B.C.
[29] Antipater, whose son Herod was ruling when Jesus was born.

They gladly thither[30] haste, and by a Quire
Of squadrond Angels hear his Carol sung.
A Virgin is his Mother, but his Sire
The Power of the most High; he shall ascend
The Throne hereditarie, and bound his Reign   370
With earths wide bounds, his glory with the Heav'ns.
    He ceas'd, discerning *Adam* with such joy
Surcharg'd, as had like grief bin dew'd in tears,
Without the vent of words, which these he breath'd.
    O Prophet of glad tidings, finisher   375
Of utmost hope! now clear I understand
What oft my steddiest thoughts have searcht in vain,
Why our great expectation should be call'd
The seed of Woman: Virgin Mother, Hail,
High in the love of Heav'n, yet from my Loyns   380
Thou shalt proceed, and from thy Womb the Son
Of God most High; so God with man unites.
Needs must the Serpent now his capital[31] bruise
Expect with mortal pain: say where and when
Thir fight, what stroke shall bruise the Victors heel.   385
    To whom thus *Michael*. Dream not of thir fight,
As of a Duel, or the local wounds
Of head or heel: not therefore joyns the Son
Manhood to God-head, with more strength to foil
Thy enemie; nor so is overcome   390
Satan, whose fall from Heav'n, a deadlier bruise,
Disabl'd not to give thee thy deaths wound:
Which hee, who comes thy Saviour, shall recure,
Not by destroying *Satan*, but his works
In thee and in thy Seed: nor can this be,   395
But by fulfilling that which thou didst want,
Obedience to the Law of God, impos'd
On penaltie of death, and suffering death,
The penaltie to thy transgression due,
And due to theirs which out of thine will grow: 400
So onely can high Justice rest appaid.[32]
The Law of God exact he shall fulfill
Both by obedience and by love, though love
Alone fulfill the Law; thy punishment
He shall endure by coming in the Flesh   405
To a reproachful life and cursed death,

[30] to Bethlehem.
[31] both "of the head" as prophesied and "fatal."
[32] satisfied.

Proclaiming Life to all who shall believe
In his redemption, and that his obedience
Imputed becomes theirs by Faith, his merits
To save them, not thir own, though legal works.   410
For this he shall live hated, be blasphem'd,
Seis'd on by force, judg'd, and to death condemnd
A shameful and accurst, naild to the Cross
By his own Nation, slain for bringing Life;
But to the Cross he nails thy Enemies,   415
The Law that is against thee, and the sins
Of all mankind, with him there crucifi'd,
Never to hurt them more who rightly trust
In this his satisfaction; so he dies,
But soon revives, Death over him no power   420
Shall long usurp; ere the third dawning light
Return, the Starrs of Morn shall see him rise
Out of his grave, fresh as the dawning light,
Thy ransom paid, which Man from death redeems,
His death for Man, as many as offerd Life   425
Neglect not, and the benefit imbrace
By Faith not void of works: this God-like act
Annuls thy doom, the death thou shouldst have dy'd,
In sin for ever lost from life; this act
Shall bruise the head of *Satan*, crush his strength   430
Defeating Sin and Death, his two main armes,[33]
And fix farr deeper in his head thir stings
Then temporal death shall bruise the Victors heel,
Or theirs whom he redeems, a death like sleep,
A gentle wafting to immortal Life.   435
Nor after resurrection shall he stay
Longer on Earth then certain times to appeer
To his Disciples, Men who in his Life
Still follow'd him; to them shall leave in charge
To teach all nations what of him they learn'd   440
And his Salvation, them who shall beleeve
Baptizing in the profluent[34] stream, the signe
Of washing them from guilt of sin to Life
Pure, and in mind prepar'd, if so befall,
For death, like that which the redeemer dy'd.   445
All Nations they shall teach; for from that day
Not onely to the Sons of *Abrahams* Loins

---

[33] In contrast the arms of Christ's warfare are Faith and Works; the arms of
war are Money and Iron (*Son. 17*).
[34] smoothly flowing.

Salvation shall be Preacht, but to the Sons
Of *Abrahams* Faith wherever through the world;
So in his seed all Nations shall be blest.   450
Then to the Heav'n of Heav'ns he shall ascend
With victory, triumphing through the air
Over his foes and thine; there shall surprise
The Serpent, Prince of air, and drag in Chains
Through all his Realm, and there confounded leave;   455
Then enter into glory, and resume
His Seat at Gods right hand, exalted high
Above all names in Heav'n; and thence shall come,
When this worlds dissolution shall be ripe,
With glory and power to judge both quick[35] and dead,   460
To judge th' unfaithful dead, but to reward
His faithful, and receave them into bliss,
Whether in Heav'n or Earth, for then the Earth
Shall all be Paradise, far happier place
Then this of *Eden*, and far happier daies.   465
    So spake th' Archangel *Michael*, then paus'd,
As at the Worlds great period; and our Sire
Replete with joy and wonder thus repli'd.
    O goodness infinite, goodness immense!
That all this good of evil shall produce,   470
And evil turn to good; more wonderful
Then that which by creation first brought forth
Light out of darkness! full of doubt I stand,
Whether I should repent me now of sin
By mee done and occasiond, or rejoyce   475
Much more, that much more good thereof shall spring,
To God more glory, more good will to Men
From God, and over wrauth grace shall abound.
But say, if our deliverer up to Heav'n
Must reascend, what will betide the few   480
His faithful, left among th' unfaithful herd,
The enemies of truth; who then shall guide
His people, who defend? will they not deal
Wors with his followers then with him they dealt?
    Be sure they will, said th' Angel; but from Heav'n   485
Hee to his own a Comforter[36] will send,
The promise of the Father, who shall dwell
His Spirit within them, and the Law of Faith
Working through love, upon thir hearts shall write,

[35] living.
[36] the Holy Spirit (John xv. 26).

To guide them in all truth, and also arm   490
With spiritual Armour, able to resist
Satans assaults, and quench his fierie darts,
What man can do against them, not affraid,
Though to the death, against such cruelties
With inward consolations recompenc't,   495
And oft supported so as shall amaze
Thir proudest persecuters: for the Spirit
Powrd first on his Apostles, whom he sends
T' evangelize the Nations, then on all
Baptiz'd, shall them with wondrous gifts endue   500
To speak all Tongues, and do all Miracles,
As did thir Lord before them. Thus they win
Great numbers of each Nation to receave
With joy the tidings brought from Heav'n: at length
Thir Ministry perform'd, and race well run,   505
Thir doctrine and thir story written left,
They die; but in thir room, as they forewarn,
Wolves shall succeed for teachers, grievous Wolves,
Who all the sacred mysteries of Heav'n
To thir own vile advantages shall turn   510
Of lucre and ambition, and the truth
With superstitions and traditions taint,
Left onely in those written Records pure,
Though not but by the Spirit understood.
Then shall they seek to avail themselves of names,   515
Places and titles, and with these to join
Secular power, though feigning still to act
By spiritual, to themselves appropriating
The Spirit of God, promis'd alike and giv'n
To all Beleevers; and from that pretense,   520
Spiritual Laws by carnal power shall force
On every conscience; Laws which none shall find
Left them inrould, or what the Spirit within
Shall on the heart engrave. What will they then
But force the Spirit of Grace it self, and bind   525
His consort Libertie; what, but unbuild
His living Temples, built by Faith to stand,
Thir own Faith not anothers: for on Earth
Who against Faith and Conscience can be heard
Infallible? yet many will presume: 530
Whence heavie persecution shall arise
On all who in the worship persevere
Of Spirit and Truth; the rest, farr greater part,
Will deem in outward Rites and specious formes

Religion satisfi'd; Truth shall retire   535
Bestuck with slandrous darts, and works of Faith
Rarely be found: so shall the World goe on,
To good malignant, to bad men benigne,
Under her own waight groaning, till the day
Appeer of respiration to the just,   540
And vengeance to the wicked, at return
Of him so lately promis'd to thy aid,
The Womans seed, obscurely then foretold,
Now amplier known thy Saviour and thy Lord,
Last in the Clouds from Heav'n to be reveald   545
In glory of the Father, to dissolve
Satan with his perverted World, then raise
From the conflagrant mass, purg'd and refin'd,
New Heav'ns, new Earth, Ages of endless date
Founded in righteousness and peace and love,   550
To bring forth fruits Joy and eternal Bliss.
    He ended; and thus *Adam* last reply'd.
How soon hath thy prediction, Seer blest,
Measur'd this transient World, the Race of time,
Till time stand fixt: beyond is all abyss,   555
Eternitie, whose end no eye can reach.
Greatly instructed I shall hence depart,
Greatly in peace of thought, and have my fill
Of knowledge, what this Vessel can contain;
Beyond which was my folly to aspire.   560
Henceforth I learn, that to obey is best,
And love with fear the onely God, to walk
As in his presence, ever to observe
His providence, and on him sole depend,
Mercifull over all his works, with good   565
Still overcoming evil, and by small
Accomplishing great things, by things deemd weak
Subverting worldly strong, and worldly wise
By simply meek; that suffering for Truths sake
Is fortitude to highest victorie,   570
And to the faithful Death the Gate of Life;
Taught this by his example whom I now
Acknowledge my Redeemer ever blest.
    To whom thus also th' Angel last repli'd:
This having learnt, thou hast attaind the sum   575
Of wisdom; hope no higher, though all the Starrs
Thou knewst by name, and all th' ethereal Powers,
All secrets of the deep, all Natures works,
Or works of God in Heav'n, Air, Earth, or Sea,

And all the riches of this World enjoydst,   580
And all the rule, one Empire; onely add
Deeds to thy knowledge answerable, add Faith,
Add Vertue, Patience, Temperance, add Love,
By name to come call'd Charitie, the soul
Of all the rest: then wilt thou not be loath   585
To leave this Paradise, but shalt possess
A Paradise within thee, happier farr.
Let us descend now therefore from this top
Of Speculation;[37] for the hour precise
Exacts our parting hence; and see the Guards,   590
By mee encampt on yonder Hill, expect[38]
Thir motion, at whose Front a flaming Sword,
In signal of remove, waves fiercely round;
We may no longer stay: go, waken *Eve*;
Her also I with gentle Dreams have calm'd   595
Portending good, and all her spirits compos'd
To meek submission: thou at season fit
Let her with thee partake what thou hast heard,
Chiefly what may concern her Faith to know,
The great deliverance by her Seed to come   600
(For by the Womans Seed) on all Mankind.
That ye may live, which will be many dayes,
Both in one Faith unanimous though sad,
With cause for evils past, yet much more cheer'd
With meditation on the happie end.   605
    He ended, and they both descend the Hill;
Descended, *Adam* to the Bowr where *Eve*
Lay sleeping ran before, but found her wak't;
And thus with words not sad she him receav'd.
    Whence thou returnst, and whither wentst, I know;   610
For God is also in sleep, and Dreams advise,
Which he hath sent propitious, some great good
Presaging, since with sorrow and hearts distress
Wearied I fell asleep: but now lead on;
In mee is no delay; with thee to goe,   615
Is to stay here; without thee here to stay,
Is to go hence unwilling; thou to mee
Art all things under Heav'n, all places thou,
Who for my wilful crime art banisht hence.
This further consolation yet secure   620
I carry hence; though all by mee is lost,

[37] contemplation, mental vision.
[38] await (their signal to move on).

Such favour I unworthie am voutsaft,
By mee the Promis'd Seed shall all restore.
  So spake our Mother *Eve*, and *Adam* heard
Well pleas'd, but answer'd not; for now too nigh   625
Th' Archangel stood, and from the other Hill
To thir fixt Station, all in bright array
The Cherubim descended; on the ground
Gliding meteorous, as Ev'ning Mist
Ris'n from a River o're the marish[39] glides,   630
And gathers ground fast at the Labourers heel
Homeward returning. High in Front advanc't,
The brandisht Sword of God before them blaz'd[40]
Fierce as a Comet; which with torrid heat,
And vapour as the *Libyan* Air adust,[41]   635
Began to parch that temperate Clime; whereat
In either hand the hastning Angel caught
Our lingring Parents, and to th' Eastern Gate
Led them direct, and down the Cliff as fast
To the subjected[42] Plain; then disappeer'd.   640
They looking back, all th' Eastern side beheld
Of Paradise, so late thir happie seat,
Wav'd over by that flaming Brand, the Gate
With dreadful Faces throng'd and fierie Armes:
Som natural tears they drop'd, but wip'd them soon;   645
The World was all before them, where to choose
Thir place of rest, and Providence thir guide:
They hand in hand with wandring steps and slow,
Through *Eden* took thir solitarie way.[43]

(1642?–1665?)

[39] marsh.
[40] Gen. iii. 24: "So he drove out the man; and he placed at the east of the Garden of Eden Cherubim and a flaming sword which turned every way, to keep the way of the tree of life."
[41] dried by heat.
[42] lying under (the cliff).
[43] Ps. cvii. 4: "They wandered in the wilderness in a solitary way."

Paradise Regain'd[1]

BOOK I

I who e're while the happy Garden sung,
By one mans disobedience lost, now sing
Recover'd Paradise to all mankind,
By one mans firm obedience fully tri'd
Through all temptation, and the Tempter foil'd   5
In all his wiles, defeated and repuls't,
And *Eden* rais'd in the wast Wilderness.
Thou Spirit who ledst this glorious Eremite
Into the Desert, his Victorious Field
Against the Spiritual Foe, and broughtst him thence   10
By proof th' undoubted Son of God, inspire,
As thou art wont, my prompted Song else mute,[2]
And bear through highth or depth of natures bounds
With prosperous wing full summ'd[3] to tell of deeds

---

[1] Drawn from Luke iv. 1–13 and Matt. iv. 1–11, the brief epic elaborates the three temptations in the wilderness: As Barbara Lewalski (*SP*, LVII, 1960, 186–220) views the poem, the first temptation (*concupiscentia carnis* or that of the flesh—hunger) explores Christ's role as prophet in I, 294–502; it is concerned with the opposition of truth and falsehood. The second temptation (*concupiscentia oculorum* or that of the world—kingdoms) explores Christ's role as king in II, 302–IV, 393; this extended assault on the virtues of temperance, contentment, magnanimity, and modesty is concerned with *voluptaria* (lures of sex, II, 153–234, and hunger, II, 302–405), *activa* (wealth, II, 406–86; glory, III, 108–44; and kingdom, III, 150–IV, 211) and *contemplativa* (poetry and philosophy, IV, 212–364). The third temptation (*superbia vitae* or that of the devil—the tower) explores Christ's role as priest in IV, 397–580; it involves imagery of the passion, sustained by patience and fortitude, leading to full identity as Son of God. The temptations to gluttony, avarice, and vainglory are arranged to move from necessity and limited bodily appeal, to fraud and man's relationships with the world, to violence and the pervasiveness of sin in all things, should the Son fall, through rejection of man's relationship with God. Christ is conceived as an example of Aristotelian magnanimity, as Merritt Y. Hughes illustrates in *SP*, XXXV (1938), 258–72; that is, a hero who whether accepting or refusing riches, advantages, or honors is actuated by a proper regard for his own dignity. Satan, on the other hand, is the antithesis of Christ: selfish, ambitious, devious, quibbling, and envious. As allegory, the poem points the way to achieve the kingdom of heaven: through virtuous obedience to God.

[2] probably referring to Thomas Ellwood's prompting after seeing the manuscript of *PL*: "but what hast thou to say of Paradise found?" (*The History of the Life of Thomas Ellwood* [London, 1714], p. 234).

[3] with fully grown feathers; i.e., with mature poetic powers.

Above Heroic, though in secret done,   15
And unrecorded left through many an Age,
Worthy t' have not remain'd so long unsung.
   Now had the great Proclaimer[4] with a voice
More awful then the sound of Trumpet, cri'd
Repentance, and Heav'ns Kingdom nigh at hand   20
To all Baptiz'd: to his great Baptism flock'd
With aw the Regions round, and with them came
From *Nazareth* the Son of *Joseph* deem'd
To the flood *Jordan*, came as then obscure,
Unmarkt, unknown; but him the Baptist soon   25
Descri'd, divinely warn'd, and witness bore
As to his worthier, and would have resign'd
To him his Heav'nly Office, nor was long
His witness unconfirm'd: on him baptiz'd
Heav'n open'd, and in likeness of a Dove   30
The Spirit descended, while the Fathers voice
From Heav'n pronounc'd him his beloved Son.
That heard the Adversary,[5] who roving still
About the world, at that assembly fam'd
Would not be last, and with the voice divine   35
Nigh Thunder-struck, th' exalted man, to whom
Such high attest was giv'n, a while survey'd
With wonder, then with envy fraught and rage
Flies to his place, nor rests, but in mid air
To Councel summons all high mighty Peers,   40
Within thick Clouds and dark ten-fold involv'd,
A gloomy Consistory; and them amidst
With looks agast and sad he thus bespake.
   O ancient Powers of Air and this wide world,
For much more willingly I mention Air,   45
This our old Conquest, then remember Hell
Our hated habitation; well ye know
How many Ages, as the years of men,
This Universe we have possest, and rul'd
In manner at our will th' affairs of Earth,   50
Since *Adam* and his facil consort *Eve*
Lost Paradise deceiv'd by me, though since
With dread attending when that fatal wound
Shall be inflicted by the Seed of *Eve*

---

[4] John the Baptist.
[5] Satan.

Upon my head.[6] Long the decrees of Heav'n   55
Delay, for longest time to him is short;
And now too soon for us the circling hours
This dreaded time have compast, wherein we
Must bide the stroak of that long threat'n'd wound,
At least if so we can, and by the head   60
Broken be not intended all our power
To be infring'd, our freedom and our being
In this fair Empire won of Earth and Air;
For this ill news I bring, the Womans seed
Destin'd to this, is late of woman born: 65
His birth to our just fear gave no small cause,
But his growth now to youths full flowr, displaying
All vertue, grace and wisdom to atchieve
Things highest, greatest, multiplies my fear.
Before him a great Prophet, to proclaim   70
His coming, is sent Harbinger, who all
Invites, and in the Consecrated stream
Pretends to wash off sin, and fit them so
Purified to receive him pure, or rather
To do him honour as their King; all come,   75
And he himself among them was baptiz'd,
Not thence to be more pure, but to receive
The testimony of Heav'n, that who he is
Thenceforth the Nations may not doubt; I saw
The Prophet do him reverence, on him rising   80
Out of the water, Heav'n above the Clouds
Unfold her Crystal Dores, thence on his head
A perfect Dove descend, what e're it meant,
And out of Heav'n the Sov'raign voice I heard,
This is my Son belov'd, in him am pleas'd.   85
His Mother then is mortal, but his Sire,
He who obtains[7] the Monarchy of Heav'n,
And what will he not do t' advance his Son?
His first-begot we know, and sore have felt,
When his fierce thunder drove us to the deep;   90
Who this is we must learn, for man he seems
In all his lineaments, though in his face
The glimpses of his Fathers glory shine.
Ye see our danger on the utmost edge

[6] Gen. iii. 15: "And I will put enmity between thee [the serpent] and the woman, and between thy seed and her seed; it shall bruise thy head . . . ."
[7] holds.

Of hazard, which admits no long debate,   95
But must with something sudden be oppos'd,
Not force, but well couch't fraud, well woven snares,
E're in the head of Nations he appear
Their King, their Leader, and Supream on Earth.
I, when no other durst, sole undertook   100
The dismal expedition to find out
And ruin *Adam*, and th' exploit perform'd
Successfully; a calmer voyage now
Will waft me; and the way found prosperous once
Induces best to hope of like success.   105
    He ended, and his words impression left
Of much amazement to th' infernal Crew,
Distracted and surpriz'd with deep dismay
At these sad tidings; but no time was then
For long indulgence to their fears or grief: 110
Unanimous they all commit the care
And management of this main enterprize
To him their great Dictator, whose attempt
At first against mankind so well had thriv'd
In *Adam*'s overthrow, and led thir march   115
From Hell's deep-vaulted Den to dwell in light,
Regents and Potentates, and Kings, yea gods
Of many a pleasant Realm and Province wide.
So to the Coast of *Jordan* he directs
His easie steps, girded with snaky wiles,   120
Where he might likeliest find this new-declar'd,
This man of men, attested Son of God,
Temptation and all guile on him to try;
So to subvert whom he suspected rais'd
To end his Raign on Earth so long enjoy'd: 125
But contrary unweeting[8] he fulfill'd
The purpos'd Counsel pre-ordain'd and fixt
Of the most High, who in full frequence[9] bright
Of Angels, thus to *Gabriel*[10] smiling spake.
    Gabriel this day by proof thou shalt behold,   130
Thou and all Angels conversant on Earth
With man or mens affairs, how I begin
To verifie that solemn message late,
On which I sent thee to the Virgin pure

    [8] unknowing.
    [9] attendance.
    [10] Gabriel, angel of comfort, heralded the coming of the Messiah (Dan. viii.
23–25, ix. 25–27), and made the annunciation to Mary (Luke i. 26–38).

PARADISE REGAIN'D (BOOK I) 523

In *Galilee*, that she should bear a Son 135
Great in Renown, and call'd the Son of God;
Then toldst her doubting how these things could be
To her a Virgin, that on her should come
The Holy Ghost, and the power of the highest
O're-shadow her: this man born and now up-grown, 140
To shew him worthy of his birth divine
And high prediction, henceforth I expose
To Satan; let him tempt and now assay
His utmost subtilty, because he boasts
And vaunts of his great cunning to the throng 145
Of his Apostasie; he might have learnt
Less over-weening, since he fail'd in *Job*,
Whose constant perseverance overcame
Whate're his cruel malice could invent.
He now shall know I can produce a man 150
Of female Seed, far abler to resist
All his sollicitations, and at length
All his vast force, and drive him back to Hell,
Winning by Conquest what the first man lost
By fallacy surpriz'd. But first I mean 155
To exercise him in the Wilderness;
There he shall first lay down the rudiments[11]
Of his great warfare, e're I send him forth
To conquer Sin and Death the two grand foes,
By Humiliation and strong Sufferance: 160
His weakness shall o'recome Satanic strength
And all the world, and mass of sinful flesh;
That all the Angels and Ætherial Powers,
They now, and men hereafter may discern,
From what consummate vertue I have chose 165
This perfect Man, by merit call'd my Son,
To earn Salvation for the Sons of men.
  So spake th' Eternal Father, and all Heav'n
Admiring stood a space, then into Hymns
Burst forth, and in Celestial measures mov'd, 170
Circling the Throne and Singing, while the hand
Sung with the voice, and this the argument.
  Victory and Triumph to the Son of God
Now entring his great duel, not of arms,

[11] The first principles of the Son's warfare constitute faith and obedience, to which are later added works (see *PL* XII, 427); these counter, respectively, the "two main arms" of Satan's warfare, Sin and Death.

But to vanquish by wisdom hellish wiles.   175
The Father knows the Son; therefore secure
Ventures his filial Vertue, though untri'd,
Against whate're may tempt, whate're seduce,
Allure, or terrifie, or undermine.
Be frustrate all ye stratagems of Hell,   180
And devilish machinations come to nought.
    So they in Heav'n their Odes and Vigils tun'd:
Mean while the Son of God, who yet some days
Lodg'd in *Bethabara* where *John* baptiz'd,
Musing and much revolving in his brest,   185
How best the mighty work he might begin
Of Saviour to mankind, and which way first
Publish his God-like office now mature,
One day forth walk'd alone, the Spirit leading;
And his deep thoughts, the better to converse   190
With solitude, till far from track of men,
Thought following thought, and step by step led on,
He enter'd now the bordering Desert wild,
And with dark shades and rocks environ'd round,
His holy Meditations thus persu'd.   195
    O what a multitude of thoughts at once
Awak'n'd in me swarm, while I consider
What from within I feel my self, and hear
What from without comes often to my ears,
Ill sorting with my present state compar'd.   200
When I was yet a child, no childish play
To me was pleasing, all my mind was set
Serious to learn and know, and thence to do
What might be publick good; my self I thought
Born to that end, born to promote all truth,   205
All righteous things: therefore above my years,
The Law of God I read, and found it sweet,
Made it my whole delight, and in it grew
To such perfection, that e're yet my age
Had measur'd twice six years, at our great Feast   210
I went into the Temple, there to hear
The Teachers of our Law, and to propose
What might improve my knowledge or their own;
And was admir'd[12] by all, yet this not all
To which my Spirit aspir'd, victorious deeds   215
Flam'd in my heart, heroic acts, one while

12 regarded with wonder.

To rescue *Israel* from the *Roman* yoke,
Then to subdue and quell o're all the earth
Brute violence and proud Tyrannick pow'r,
Till truth were freed, and equity restor'd: 220
Yet held it more humane, more heav'nly first
By winning words to conquer willing hearts,
And make perswasion do the work of fear;
At least to try, and teach the erring Soul
Not wilfully mis-doing, but unware   225
Misled; the stubborn only to subdue.
These growing thoughts my Mother soon perceiving
By words at times cast forth inly rejoyc'd,
And said to me apart, high are thy thoughts
O Son, but nourish them and let them soar   230
To what highth sacred vertue and true worth
Can raise them, though above example high;
By matchless Deeds express thy matchless Sire.
For know, thou art no Son of mortal man,
Though men esteem thee low of Parentage,   235
Thy Father is th' Eternal King, who rules
All Heav'n and Earth, Angels and Sons of men.
A messenger from God fore-told thy birth
Conceiv'd in me a Virgin, he fore-told
Thou shouldst be great and sit on *David*'s Throne,   240
And of thy Kingdom there should be no end.
At thy Nativity a glorious Quire
Of Angels in the fields of *Bethlehem* sung
To Shepherds watching at their folds by night,
And told them the Messiah now was born,   245
Where they might see him, and to thee they came;
Directed to the Manger where thou lais't,
For in the Inn was left no better room:
A Star, not seen before in Heav'n appearing
Guided the Wise Men thither from the East,   250
To honour thee with Incense, Myrrh, and Gold,
By whose bright course led on they found the place,
Affirming it thy Star new grav'n in Heav'n,
By which they knew thee King of *Israel* born.
Just *Simeon* and Prophetic *Anna*, warn'd   255
By Vision,[13] found thee in the Temple, and spake
Before the Altar and the vested Priest,
Like things of thee to all that present stood.

[13] See Luke ii. 25–38.

This having heard, strait I again revolv'd[14]
The Law and Prophets, searching what was writ   260
Concerning the Messiah, to our Scribes
Known partly, and soon found of whom they spake
I am; this chiefly, that my way must lie
Through many a hard assay ev'n to the death,
E're I the promis'd Kingdom can attain,   265
Or work Redemption for mankind, whose sins
Full weight must be transferr'd upon my head.
Yet neither thus disheart'n'd or dismay'd,
The time prefixt I waited, when behold
The Baptist (of whose birth I oft had heard,   270
Not knew by sight) now come, who was to come
Before Messiah and his way prepare.
I as all others to his Baptism came,
Which I believ'd was from above; but he
Strait knew me, and with loudest voice proclaim'd   275
Me him (for it was shew'n him so from Heav'n)
Me him whose Harbinger he was; and first
Refus'd on me his Baptism to confer,
As much his greater, and was hardly won;
But as I rose out of the laving stream,   280
Heav'n open'd her eternal doors, from whence
The Spirit descended on me like a Dove,
And last the sum of all, my Father's voice,
Audibly heard from Heav'n, pronounc'd me his,
Me his beloved Son, in whom alone   285
He was well pleas'd; by which I knew the time
Now full, that I no more should live obscure,
But openly begin, as best becomes
Th' Authority which I deriv'd from Heav'n.
And now by some strong motion I am led   290
Into this Wilderness, to what intent
I learn not yet, perhaps I need not know;
For what concerns my knowledge God reveals.
  So spake our Morning Star[15] then in his rise,
And looking round on every side beheld   295
A pathless Desert, dusk with horrid shades;
The way he came not having mark'd, return
Was difficult, by human steps untrod;
And he still on was led, but with such thoughts

---

[14] reflected upon.
[15] Rev. xxii. 16: "I am . . . the bright and morning star."

Accompanied of things past and to come   300
Lodg'd in his brest, as well might recommend
Such Solitude before choicest Society.
Full forty days he pass'd, whether on hill
Sometimes, anon in shady vale, each night
Under the covert of some ancient Oak,   305
Or Cedar, to defend him from the dew,
Or harbour'd in one Cave, is not reveal'd;
Nor tasted human food, nor hunger felt
Till those days ended, hunger'd then at last
Among wild Beasts: they at his sight grew mild,   310
Nor sleeping him nor waking harm'd, his walk
The fiery Serpent fled, and noxious Worm,[16]
The Lion and fierce Tiger glar'd aloof.
But now an aged man in Rural weeds,
Following, as seem'd, the quest of some stray Ewe,   315
Or wither'd sticks to gather; which might serve
Against a Winters day when winds blow keen,
To warm him wet return'd from field at Eve,
He saw approach, who first with curious eye
Perus'd him, then with words thus utter'd spake.   320
    Sir, what ill chance hath brought thee to this place
So far from path or road of men, who pass
In Troop or Caravan, for single none
Durst ever, who return'd, and dropt not here
His Carcass, pin'd with hunger and with droughth?   325
I ask the rather, and the more admire,
For that to me thou seem'st the man, whom late
Our new baptizing Prophet at the Ford
Of *Jordan* honour'd so, and call'd thee Son
Of God; I saw and heard, for we sometimes   330
Who dwell this wild, constrain'd by want, come forth
To Town or Village nigh (nighest is far)
Where aught we hear, and curious are to hear,
What happ'ns new; Fame also finds us out.
    To whom the Son of God. Who brought me hither   335
Will bring me hence, no other Guide I seek.
    By Miracle he may, reply'd the Swain,
What other way I see not, for we here
Live on tough roots and stubs, to thirst inur'd
More then the Camel, and to drink go far,   340
Men to much misery and hardship born;

[16] snake.

But if thou be the Son of God, command
That out of these hard stones be made thee bread;
So shalt thou save thy self and us relieve
With Food, whereof we wretched seldom taste.   345
    He ended, and the Son of God reply'd.
Think'st thou such force in Bread? is it not written
(For I discern thee other then thou seem'st)
Man lives not by Bread only, but each Word
Proceeding from the mouth of God; who fed   350
Our Fathers here with Manna; in the Mount
Moses was forty days,[17] nor eat nor drank,
And forty days *Eliah* without food
Wander'd this barren waste,[18] the same I now:
Why dost thou then suggest to me distrust,   355
Knowing who I am, as I know who thou art?
    Whom thus answer'd th' Arch Fiend now undisguis'd.
'Tis true, I am that Spirit unfortunate,
Who leagu'd with millions more in rash revolt
Kept not my happy Station, but was driv'n   360
With them from bliss to the bottomless deep,
Yet to that hideous place not so confin'd
By rigour unconniving,[19] but that oft
Leaving my dolorous Prison I enjoy
Large liberty to round this Globe of Earth,   365
Or range in th' Air, nor from the Heav'n of Heav'ns
Hath he excluded my resort sometimes.
I came among the Sons of God, when he
Gave up into my hands *Uzzean Job*
To prove him, and illustrate his high worth;   370
And when to all his Angels he propos'd
To draw the proud King *Ahab* into fraud
That he might fall in *Ramoth*, they demurring,
I undertook that office, and the tongues
Of all his flattering Prophets glibb'd with lies   375
To his destruction, as I had in charge.[20]
For what he bids I do; though I have lost
Much lustre of my native brightness, lost
To be belov'd of God, I have not lost
To love, at least contemplate and admire   380
What I see excellent in good, or fair,

[17] Exod. xxiv. 18.
[18] 1 Kings xix. 8.
[19] always alert (literally, "not closing its eyes").
[20] 1 Kings xxii. 19–23.

Or vertuous, I should so have lost all sense.
What can be then less in me then desire
To see thee and approach thee, whom I know
Declar'd the Son of God, to hear attent[21]   385
Thy wisdom, and behold thy God-like deeds?
Men generally think me much a foe
To all mankind: why should I? they to me
Never did wrong or violence, by them
I lost not what I lost, rather by them   390
I gain'd what I have gain'd, and with them dwell
Copartner in these Regions of the World,
If not disposer; lend them oft my aid,
Oft my advice by presages and signs,
And answers, oracles, portents and dreams,   395
Whereby they may direct their future life.
Envy they say excites me, thus to gain
Companions of my misery and wo.
At first it may be; but long since with wo
Nearer acquainted, now I feel by proof,   400
That fellowship in pain divides not smart,
Nor lightens aught each mans peculiar load.
Small consolation then, were Man adjoyn'd:
This wounds me most (what can it less) that Man,
Man fall'n shall be restor'd, I never more.   405
    To whom our Saviour sternly thus reply'd.
Deservedly thou griev'st, compos'd of lies
From the beginning, and in lies wilt end;
Who boast'st release from Hell, and leave to come
Into the Heav'n of Heav'ns; thou com'st indeed,   410
As a poor miserable captive thrall
Comes to the place where he before had sat
Among the Prime in Splendour, now depos'd,
Ejected, emptied, gaz'd, unpitied, shun'd,
A spectacle of ruin or of scorn   415
To all the Host of Heav'n; the happy place
Imparts to thee no happiness, no joy,
Rather inflames thy torment, representing
Lost bliss, to thee no more communicable,
So never more in Hell then when in Heav'n.   420
But thou art serviceable to Heav'ns King.
Wilt thou impute t' obedience what thy fear
Extorts, or pleasure to do ill excites?

[21] attentive.

What but thy malice mov'd thee to misdeem
Of righteous *Job*, then cruelly to afflict him   425
With all inflictions, but his patience won?
The other service was thy chosen task,
To be a liar in four hundred mouths;[22]
For lying is thy sustenance, thy food.[23]
Yet thou pretend'st to truth; all Oracles   430
By thee are giv'n, and what confest more true
Among the Nations? that hath been thy craft,
By mixing somewhat true to vent more lies.
But what have been thy answers, what but dark,
Ambiguous and with double sense deluding,   435
Which they who ask'd have seldom understood,
And not well understood as good not known?
Who ever by consulting at thy shrine
Return'd the wiser, or the more instruct
To fly or follow what concern'd him most,   440
And run not sooner to his fatal snare?
For God hath justly giv'n the Nations up
To thy Delusions; justly, since they fell
Idolatrous, but when his purpose is
Among them to declare his Providence   445
To thee not known, whence hast thou then thy truth,
But from him or his Angels President[24]
In every Province, who themselves disdaining
T' approach thy Temples, give thee in command
What to the smallest tittle thou shalt say   450
To thy Adorers; thou with trembling fear,
Or like a Fawning Parasite obey'st;
Then to thy self ascrib'st the truth fore-told.
But this thy glory shall be soon retrench'd;
No more shalt thou by oracling abuse   455
The Gentiles; henceforth Oracles are ceast,
And thou no more with Pomp and Sacrifice
Shalt be enquir'd at *Delphos* or elsewhere,
At least in vain, for they shall find thee mute.
God hath now sent his living Oracle   460

[22] referring to 1 Kings xxii. 6: "Then the king of Israel gathered the prophets together, about four hundred men."
[23] In "Food-Word Imagery in *PR*," *English Literary History*, XXVIII (1961), 225–43, Lee S. Cox shows that this metaphoric development marks a new stage of temptation in each book. The poem defines the nature of the Word Incarnate and, as here, the nature of Satan's word.
[24] presiding, occupying authoritative position.

Into the World, to teach his final will,
And sends his Spirit of Truth henceforth to dwell
In pious Hearts, an inward Oracle
To all truth requisite for men to know.
　　So spake our Saviour; but the subtle Fiend,   465
Though inly stung with anger and disdain,
Dissembl'd, and this Answer smooth return'd.
　　Sharply thou hast insisted on rebuke,
And urg'd me hard with doings, which not will
But misery hath wrested from me; where   470
Easily canst thou find one miserable,
And not inforc'd oft-times to part from truth;
If it may stand him more in stead to lie,
Say and unsay, feign, flatter, or abjure?
But thou art plac't above me, thou art Lord;   475
From thee I can and must submiss[25] endure
Check or reproof, and glad to scape so quit.
Hard are the ways of truth, and rough to walk,
Smooth on the tongue discourst, pleasing to th' ear,
And tuneable as Silvan Pipe or Song;   480
What wonder then if I delight to hear
Her dictates from thy mouth? most men admire
Vertue, who follow not her lore: permit me
To hear thee when I come (since no man comes)
And talk at least, though I despair t' attain.   485
Thy Father, who is holy, wise and pure,
Suffers the Hypocrite or Atheous Priest
To tread his Sacred Courts, and minister
About his Altar, handling holy things,
Praying or vowing, and vouchsaf'd his voice   490
To Balaam[26] Reprobate, a Prophet yet
Inspir'd; disdain not such access to me.
　　To whom our Saviour with unalter'd brow.
Thy coming hither, though I know thy scope,
I bid not or forbid; do as thou find'st   495
Permission from above; thou canst not more.
　　He added not; and Satan bowing low
His gray dissimulation, disappear'd
Into thin Air diffus'd: for now began
Night with her sullen wing to double-shade   500

[25] submissive.
[26] Though pressed by the king of Moab, Balaam could not curse the Israel-
ites, for the Lord had imposed on him the words to speak (Num. xxiii).

The Desert, Fowls in thir clay nests were couch't;
And now wild Beasts came forth the woods to roam.

BOOK II

Mean while the new-baptiz'd, who yet remain'd
At *Jordan* with the Baptist, and had seen
Him whom they heard so late expresly call'd
Jesus Messiah, Son of God declar'd,
And on that high Authority had believ'd,   5
And with him talkt, and with him lodg'd, I mean
Andrew and *Simon*, famous after known
With others though in Holy Writ not nam'd,
Now missing him thir joy so lately found,
So lately found, and so abruptly gone,   10
Began to doubt, and doubted many days,
And as the days increas'd, increas'd thir doubt:
Sometimes they thought he might be only shewn,
And for a time caught up to God, as once
Moses was in the Mount, and missing long;   15
And the great *Thisbite*[1] who on fiery wheels
Rode up to Heav'n, yet once again to come.
Therefore as those young Prophets then with care
Sought lost *Eliah*, so in each place these
Nigh to *Bethabara*; in *Jerico*   20
The City of Palms, *Ænon*, and *Salem* Old,
Machærus and each Town or City wall'd
On this side the broad lake *Genezaret*,
Or in *Perea*, but return'd in vain.
Then on the bank of *Jordan*, by a Creek: 25
Where winds with Reeds, and Osiers whisp'ring play
Plain Fishermen, no greater men them call,
Close in a Cottage low together got
Thir unexpected loss and plaints out breath'd.
Alas, from what high hope to what relapse   30
Unlook'd for are we fall'n, our eyes beheld
Messiah certainly now come, so long
Expected of our Fathers; we have heard
His words, his wisdom full of grace and truth,
Now, now, for sure, deliverance is at hand,   35
The Kingdom shall to *Israel* be restor'd:

[1] Elijah; see 2 Kings ii.

Thus we rejoyc'd, but soon our joy is turn'd
Into perplexity and new amaze:
For whither is he gone, what accident
Hath rapt him from us? will he now retire   40
After appearance, and again prolong
Our expectation? God of *Israel,*
Send thy Messiah forth, the time is come;
Behold the Kings of th' Earth how they oppress
Thy chosen, to what highth thir pow'r unjust   45
They have exalted, and behind them cast
All fear of thee, arise and vindicate
Thy Glory, free thy people from thir yoke,
But let us wait; thus far he hath perform'd,
Sent his Anointed, and to us reveal'd him,   50
By his great Prophet, pointed at and shown,
In publick, and with him we have convers'd;
Let us be glad of this, and all our fears
Lay on his Providence; he will not fail
Nor will withdraw him now, nor will recall,   55
Mock us with his blest sight, then snatch him hence,
Soon we shall see our hope, our joy return.
    Thus they out of their plaints new hope resume
To find whom at the first they found unsought:
But to his Mother *Mary,* when she saw   60
Others return'd from Baptism, not her Son,
Nor left at *Jordan,* tidings of him none;
Within her brest, though calm; her brest though pure,
Motherly cares and fears got head, and rais'd
Some troubl'd thoughts, which she in sighs thus clad.   65
    O what avails me now that honour high
To have conceiv'd of God, or that salute,[2]
Hail highly favour'd, among women blest;
While I to sorrows am no less advanc't,
And fears as eminent, above the lot   70
Of other women, by the birth I bore,
In such a season born when scarce a Shed
Could be obtain'd to shelter him or me
From the bleak air; a Stable was our warmth,
A Manger his, yet soon enforc't to fly   75
Thence into *Egypt,* till the Murd'rous King[3]
Were dead, who sought his life, and missing fill'd

[2] Gabriel's announcement to Mary that she would bear a son.
[3] Herod.

With Infant blood the streets of *Bethlehem;*
From *Egypt* home return'd, in *Nazareth*
Hath been our dwelling many years, his life   80
Private, unactive, calm, contemplative,
Little suspicious t' any King; but now
Full grown to Man, acknowledg'd, as I hear,
By *John* the Baptist, and in publick shown,
Son own'd from Heav'n by his Father's voice;   85
I look't for some great change; to Honour? no,
But trouble, as old *Simeon* plain fore-told,[4]
That to the fall and rising he should be
Of many in *Israel,* and to a sign
Spoken against, that through my very Soul   90
A sword shall pierce, this is my favour'd lot,
My Exaltation to Afflictions high;
Afflicted I may be, it seems, and blest;
I will not argue that, nor will repine.
But where delays he now? some great intent   95
Conceals him: when twelve years he scarce had seen,
I lost him, but so found, as well I saw
He could not lose himself; but went about
His Father's business;[5] what he meant I mus'd,
Since understand; much more his absence now   100
Thus long to some great purpose he obscures.
But I to wait with patience am inur'd;
My heart hath been a store-house long of things
And sayings laid up, portending strange events.
  Thus *Mary* pondering oft, and oft to mind   105
Recalling what remarkably had pass'd
Since first her Salutation heard, with thoughts
Meekly compos'd awaited the fulfilling:
The while her Son tracing the Desert wild,
Sole but with holiest Meditations fed,   110
Into himself descended, and at once
All his great work to come before him set;
How to begin, how to accomplish best
His end of being on Earth, and mission high:
For Satan with sly preface to return   115
Had left him vacant, and with speed was gon
Up to the middle Region of thick Air,
Where all his Potentates in Council sate;

[4] Luke ii. 34–35.
[5] Luke ii. 42–49.

There without sign of boast, or sign of joy,
Sollicitous and blank[6] he thus began.   120
    Princes, Heav'ns antient Sons, Æthereal Thrones,
Demonian Spirits now, from the Element
Each of his reign allotted, rightlier call'd,
Powers of Fire, Air, Water, and Earth beneath,
So may we hold our place and these mild seats   125
Without new trouble; such an Enemy
Is ris'n to invade us, who no less
Threat'ns then our expulsion down to Hell;
I, as I undertook, and with the vote
Consenting in full frequence[7] was impower'd,   130
Have found him, view'd him, tasted[8] him, but find
Far other labour to be undergon
Then when I dealt with *Adam* first of Men,
Though *Adam* by his Wives allurement fell,
However to this Man inferior far,   135
If he be Man by Mothers side at least,
With more then human gifts from Heav'n adorn'd,
Perfections absolute, Graces divine,
And amplitude of mind to greatest Deeds.
Therefore I am return'd, lest confidence   140
Of my success with *Eve* in Paradise
Deceive ye to perswasion over-sure
Of like succeeding here; I summon all
Rather to be in readiness, with hand
Or counsel to assist; lest I who erst   145
Thought none my equal, now be over-match'd.
    So spake th' old Serpent doubting, and from all
With clamour was assur'd thir utmost aid
At his command; when from amidst them rose
Belial[9] the dissolutest Spirit that fell,   150
The sensuallest, and after *Asmodai*[10]
The fleshliest Incubus,[11] and thus advis'd.
    Set women in his eye and in his walk,
Among daughters of men the fairest found;
Many are in each Region passing fair   155

[6] nonplused.
[7] crowded state.
[8] tested.
[9] The profligate Belial is described in *PL* I, 490–501.
[10] the demon lover in Tobit iii, vi, who killed Tobias' wife's first seven husbands.
[11] demonic seducer.

As the noon Skie; more like to Goddesses
Then Mortal Creatures, graceful and discreet,
Expert in amorous Arts, enchanting tongues
Perswasive, Virgin majesty with mild
And sweet allay'd, yet terrible to approach,   160
Skill'd to retire, and in retiring draw
Hearts after them tangl'd in Amorous Nets.
Such object hath the power to soft'n and tame
Severest temper,[12] smooth the rugged'st brow,
Enerve, and with voluptuous hope dissolve,   165
Draw out with credulous desire, and lead
At will the manliest, resolutest brest,
As the Magnetic[13] hardest Iron draws.
Women, when nothing else, beguil'd the heart
Of wisest *Solomon*, and made him build,   170
And made him bow to the Gods of his Wives.[14]
    To whom quick answer Satan thus return'd.
Belial, in much uneven scale thou weigh'st
All others by thy self; because of old
Thou thy self doat'st on womankind, admiring   175
Thir shape, thir colour, and attractive grace,
None are, thou think'st, but taken with such toys.
Before the Flood thou with thy lusty Crew,
False titl'd Sons of God, roaming the Earth
Cast wanton eyes on the daughters of men,   180
And coupl'd with them, and begot a race.
Have we not seen, or by relation heard,
In Courts and Regal Chambers how thou lurk'st,
In Wood or Grove by mossie Fountain side,
In Valley or Green Meadow to way-lay   185
Some beauty rare, *Calisto, Clymene,*
Daphne, or *Semele, Antiopa,*
Or *Amymone, Syrinx,* many more
Too long, then lay'st thy scapes on names ador'd,
Apollo, Neptune, Jupiter, or *Pan,*   190
Satyr, or Faun, or Silvan? But these haunts
Delight not all; among the Sons of Men,
How many have with a smile made small account
Of beauty and her lures, easily scorn'd
All her assaults, on worthier things intent?   195

12 temperament.
13 magnet.
14 See 1 Kings xi. 1–8.

Remember that *Pellean* Conquerour,[15]
A youth, how all the Beauties of the East
He slightly view'd, and slightly over-pass'd;
How hee sirnam'd of *Africa*[16] dismiss'd
In his prime youth the fair *Iberian* maid.   200
For *Solomon* he liv'd at ease, and full
Of honour, wealth, high fare, aim'd not beyond
Higher design then to enjoy his State;
Thence to the bait of Women lay expos'd;
But he whom we attempt is wiser far   205
Then *Solomon*, of more exalted mind,
Made and set wholly on th' accomplishment
Of greatest things; what woman will you find,
Though of this Age the wonder and the fame,
On whom his leisure will vouchsafe an eye   210
Of fond desire? or should she confident,
As sitting Queen ador'd on Beauties Throne,
Descend with all her winning charms begirt
T' enamour, as the Zone[17] of *Venus* once
Wrought that effect on *Jove*, so Fables tell;   215
How would one look from his Majestick brow
Seated as on the top of Vertues hill,[18]
Discount'nance her despis'd, and put to rout
All her array; her female pride deject,
Or turn to reverent awe? for Beauty stands   220
In th' admiration only of weak minds
Led captive; cease t' admire, and all her Plumes
Fall flat and shrink into a trivial toy,
At every sudden slighting quite abasht:
Therefore with manlier objects we must try   225
His constancy, with such as have more shew
Of worth, of honour, glory, and popular praise;
Rocks whereon greatest men have oftest wreck'd;
Or that which only seems to satisfie
Lawful desires of Nature, not beyond;   230
And now I know he hungers where no food
Is to be found, in the wide Wilderness;
The rest commit to me, I shall let pass
No advantage, and his strength as oft assay.

[15] Alexander the Great.
[16] Scipio Africanus.
[17] Venus' ornamented girdle which Juno wore to charm Jove (*Iliad*, XIV, 214–18).
[18] See *Son.* 9, n. 2.

He ceas'd, and heard thir grant in loud acclaim;   235
Then forthwith to him takes a chosen band
Of Spirits likest to himself in guile
To be at hand, and at his beck appear,
If cause were to unfold some active Scene
Of various persons each to know his part;   240
Then to the Desert takes with these his flight;
Where still from shade to shade the Son of God
After forty days fasting had remain'd,
Now hungring first, and to himself thus said.
    Where will this end? four times ten days I have pass'd   245
Wandring this woody maze, and human food
Nor tasted, nor had appetite; that Fast
To Vertue I impute not, or count part
Of what I suffer here; if Nature need not,
Or God support Nature without repast   250
Though needing, what praise is it to endure?
But now I feel I hunger, which declares,
Nature hath need of what she asks; yet God
Can satisfie that need some other way,
Though hunger still remain: so it remain   255
Without this bodies wasting, I content me,
And from the sting of Famine fear no harm,
Nor mind it, fed with better thoughts that feed
Mee hungring more to do my Fathers will.
    It was the hour of night, when thus the Son   260
Commun'd in silent walk, then laid him down
Under the hospitable covert nigh
Of Trees thick interwoven; there he slept,
And dream'd, as appetite is wont to dream,
Of meats and drinks, Natures refreshment sweet;   265
Him thought,[19] he by the Brook of *Cherith* stood
And saw the Ravens with their horny beaks
Food to *Elijah* bringing Even and Morn,
Though ravenous, taught t' abstain from what they brought:
He saw the Prophet also how he fled   270
Into the Desert, and how there he slept
Under a Juniper; then how awak't,
He found his Supper on the coals prepar'd,
And by the Angel was bid rise and eat,
And eat the second time after repose,   275
The strength whereof suffic'd him forty days;

[19] The accounts of Elijah here are found in 1 Kings xvii. 3-7, xix. 4-8.

Sometimes that with *Elijah* he partook,
Or as a guest with *Daniel* at his pulse.[20]
Thus wore out night, and now the Herald Lark
Left his ground-nest, high towring to descry   280
The morns approach, and greet her with his Song:
As lightly from his grassy Couch up rose
Our Saviour, and found all was but a dream,
Fasting he went to sleep, and fasting wak'd.
Up to a hill anon his steps he rear'd,   285
From whose high top to ken the prospect round,
If Cottage were in view, Sheep-cote or Herd;
But Cottage, Herd or Sheep-cote none he saw,
Only in a bottom saw a pleasant Grove,
With chaunt of tuneful Birds resounding loud;   290
Thither he bent his way, determin'd there
To rest at noon, and enter'd soon the shade
High rooft and walks beneath, and alleys brown
That open'd in the midst a woody Scene,
Natures own work it seem'd (Nature taught Art)   295
And to a Superstitious eye the haunt
Of Wood-Gods and Wood-Nymphs; he view'd it round,
When suddenly a man before him stood,
Not rustic as before, but seemlier clad,
As one in City, or Court, or Palace bred,   300
And with fair speech these words to him address'd.
    With granted leave officious I return,
But much more wonder that the Son of God
In this wild solitude so long should bide
Of all things destitute, and well I know,   305
Not without hunger. Others of some note,
As story tells, have trod this Wilderness;
The Fugitive Bond-woman[21] with her Son
Out cast *Nebaioth*, yet found he relief
By a providing Angel; all the race   310
Of *Israel* here had famish'd, had not God
Rain'd from Heav'n Manna,[22] and that Prophet[23] bold
Native of *Thebez* wandring here was fed
Twice by a voice inviting him to eat.

[20] peas, lentils, or beans; Dan. i. 8–16.
[21] Hagar (Gen. xxi. 14–19). However, her son was Ishmael; his son was Nebaioth.
[22] See Exod. xvi.
[23] Elijah.

Of thee these forty days none hath regard,   315
Forty and more deserted here indeed.
   To whom thus Jesus; what conclud'st thou hence?
They all had need, I as thou seest have none.
How hast thou hunger then? Satan reply'd,
Tell me if Food were now before thee set,   320
Would'st thou not eat? Thereafter as I like
The giver, answer'd Jesus. Why should that
Cause thy refusal, said the subtle Fiend,
Hast thou not right to all Created things,
Owe not all Creatures by just right to thee   325
Duty and Service, nor to stay till bid,
But tender all their power? nor mention I
Meats by the Law unclean, or offer'd first
To Idols, those young *Daniel* could refuse;
Nor proffer'd by an Enemy, though who   330
Would scruple that, with want opprest? behold
Nature asham'd, or better to express,
Troubl'd that thou shouldst hunger, hath purvey'd
From all the Elements her choicest store
To treat thee as beseems, and as her Lord   335
With honour, only deign to sit and eat.
   He spake no dream, for as his words had end,
Our Saviour lifting up his eyes beheld
In ample space under the broadest shade
A Table richly spred, in regal mode,   340
With dishes pil'd, and meats of noblest sort
And savour, Beasts of chase, or Fowl of game,
In pastry built, or from the spit, or boyl'd,
Gris-amber-steam'd; all Fish from Sea or Shore,
Freshet, or purling Brook, of shell or fin,   345
And exquisitest name, for which was drain'd
Pontus and *Lucrine* Bay,[24] and *Afric* Coast.
Alas how simple, to these Cates compar'd,
Was that crude Apple that diverted *Evel*
And at a stately side-board by the wine   350
That fragrant smell diffus'd, in order stood
Tall stripling youths rich clad, or fairer hew
Then *Ganymed* or *Hylas*,[25] distant more
Under the Trees now trip'd, now solemn stood
Nymphs of *Diana*'s train, and *Naiades*   355

[24] the Black Sea and the bay near Naples.
[25] See *El.* 7, n. 2, 3.

With fruits and flowers from *Amalthea*'s horn,[26]
And Ladies of th' *Hesperides*,[27] that seem'd
Fairer then feign'd of old, or fabl'd since
Of Fairy Damsels met in Forest wide
By Knights of *Logres*, or of *Lyones*,   360
Lancelot or *Pelleas*, or *Pellenore*,[28]
And all the while Harmonious Airs were heard
Of chiming strings, or charming pipes and winds
Of gentlest gale *Arabian* odors fann'd
From their soft wings, and *Flora*'s[29] earliest smells.   365
Such was the Splendour, and the Tempter now
His invitation earnestly renew'd.
    What doubts the Son of God to sit and eat?
These are not Fruits forbidd'n, no interdict
Defends[30] the touching of these viands pure,   370
Thir taste no knowledge works, at least of evil,
But life preserves, destroys life's enemy,
Hunger, with sweet restorative delight.
All these are Spirits of Air, and Woods, and Springs,
Thy gentle Ministers, who come to pay   375
Thee homage, and acknowledge thee thir Lord:
What doubt'st thou Son of God? sit down and eat.
    To whom thus Jesus temperately reply'd:
Said'st thou not that to all things I had right?
And who withholds my pow'r that right to use?   380
Shall I receive by gift what of my own,
When and where likes me best, I can command?
I can at will, doubt not, as soon as thou,
Command a Table in this Wilderness,
And call swift flights of Angels ministrant   385
Array'd in Glory on my cup t' attend:
Why shouldst thou then obtrude this diligence,
In vain, where no acceptance it can find,
And with my hunger what hast thou to do?
Thy pompous Delicacies I contemn,   390
And count thy specious gifts no gifts but guiles.
    To whom thus answer'd Satan malecontent:
That I have also power to give thou seest,

[26] horn of plenty.
[27] the guardians of the golden tree; see *Mask*, ll. 981–83.
[28] English geographic areas or knights, all connected with King Arthur.
[29] goddess of flowers.
[30] forbids. Satan dissembles, as Michael Fixler pointed out (*MLN*, LXX, 1955, 573–77), for certain meats and shellfish (ll. 342–45) were proscribed.

542   THE COMPLETE POETRY OF JOHN MILTON

If of that pow'r I bring thee voluntary
What I might have bestow'd on whom I pleas'd,   395
And rather opportunely in this place
Chose to impart to thy apparent need,
Why shouldst thou not accept it? but I see
What I can do or offer is suspect;
Of these things others quickly will dispose   400
Whose pains have earn'd the far-fet³¹ spoil. With that
Both Table and Provision vanish'd quite
With sound of Harpies wings, and Talons heard;
Only the importune Tempter still remain'd,
And with these words his temptation pursu'd.   405
    By hunger, that each other Creature tames,
Thou art not to be harm'd, therefore not mov'd;
Thy temperance invincible besides,
For no allurement yields to appetite,
And all thy heart is set on high designs,   410
High actions; but wherewith to be atchiev'd?
Great acts require great means of enterprise,
Thou art unknown, unfriended, low of birth,
A Carpenter thy Father known, thy self
Bred up in poverty and streights at home;   415
Lost in a Desert here and hunger-bit:
Which way or from what hope dost thou aspire
To greatness? whence Authority deriv'st,
What Followers, what Retinue canst thou gain,
Or at thy heels the dizzy Multitude,   420
Longer then thou canst feed them on thy cost?
Money brings Honour, Friends, Conquest, and Realms;
What rais'd *Antipater* the *Edomite*,
And his Son *Herod* plac'd on *Juda's* Throne;
(Thy throne) but gold that got him puissant friends?   425
Therefore, if at great things thou wouldst arrive,
Get Riches first, get Wealth, and Treasure heap,
Not difficult, if thou hearken to me,
Riches are mine, Fortune is in my hand;
They whom I favour thrive in wealth amain,   430
While Virtue, Valour, Wisdom sit in want.³²
    To whom thus Jesus patiently reply'd;
Yet Wealth without these three is impotent,
To gain dominion or to keep it gain'd.

³¹ far-fetched.
³² Compare the last lines of *Sonnet* 15.

Witness those antient Empires of the Earth,   435
In highth of all thir flowing wealth dissolv'd:
But men endu'd with these have oft attain'd
In lowest poverty to highest deeds;
Gideon and Jephtha, and the Shepherd lad,[33]
Whose off-spring on the Throne of Juda sat   440
So many Ages, and shall yet regain
That seat, and reign in Israel without end.
Among the Heathen (for throughout the World
To me is not unknown what hath been done
Worthy of Memorial) canst thou not remember   445
Quintius, Fabricius, Curius, Regulus?[34]
For I esteem those names of men so poor
Who could do mighty things, and could contemn
Riches though offer'd from the hand of Kings.
And what in me seems wanting, but that I   450
May also in this poverty as soon
Accomplish what they did, perhaps and more?
Extol not Riches then, the toyl[35] of Fools,
The wise mans cumbrance if not snare, more apt
To slacken Virtue, and abate her edge,   455
Then prompt her to do aught may merit praise.
What if with like aversion I reject
Riches and Realms; yet not for that a Crown,
Golden in shew, is but a wreath of thorns,
Brings dangers, troubles, cares, and sleepless nights   460
To him who wears the Regal Diadem,
When on his shoulders each mans burden lies;
For therein stands the office of a King,
His Honour, Vertue, Merit and chief Praise,
That for the Publick all this weight he bears.   465
Yet he who reigns within himself, and rules
Passions, Desires, and Fears, is more a King;
Which every wise and vertuous man attains:
And who attains not, ill aspire to rule
Cities of men, or head-strong Multitudes,   470
Subject himself to Anarchy within,
Or lawless passions in him which he serves.
But to guide Nations in the way of truth
By saving Doctrine, and from errour lead

[33] David; see Judges vi–viii, xi–xii, and 1 Sam. xvi–xvii.
[34] important early military leaders of Rome.
[35] snare.

To know, and knowing worship God aright,   475
Is yet more Kingly, this attracts the Soul,
Governs the inner man, the nobler part,
That other o're the body only reigns,
And oft by force, which to a generous mind
So reigning can be no sincere delight.   480
Besides to give a Kingdom hath been thought
Greater and nobler done, and to lay down
Far more magnanimous, then to assume.
Riches are needless then, both for themselves,
And for thy reason why they should be sought,   485
To gain a Scepter, oftest better miss't.

BOOK III

So spake the Son of God, and Satan stood
A while as mute confounded what to say,
What to reply, confuted and convinc't
Of his weak arguing, and fallacious drift;
At length collecting all his Serpent wiles,   5
With soothing words renew'd, him thus accosts.
I see thou know'st what is of use to know,
What best to say canst say, to do canst do;
Thy actions to thy words accord, thy words
To thy large heart give utterance due, thy heart   10
Conteins of good, wise, just, the perfect shape.
Should Kings and Nations from thy mouth consult,
Thy Counsel would be as the Oracle
Urim and Thummim,[1] those oraculous gems
On Aaron's breast: or tongue of Seers old   15
Infallible; or wert thou sought to deeds
That might require th' array of war, thy skill
Of conduct would be such, that all the world
Could not sustain thy Prowess, or subsist
In battel, though against thy few in arms.   20
These God-like Vertues wherefore dost thou hide?
Affecting private life, or more obscure
In savage Wilderness, wherefore deprive
All Earth her wonder at thy acts, thy self
The fame and glory, glory the reward   25
That sole excites to high attempts the flame

[1] See Lev. viii. 8, and compare PL VI, 762.

Of most erected Spirits, most temper'd pure
Ætherial, who all pleasures else despise,
All treasures and all gain esteem as dross,
And dignities and powers all but the highest?   30
Thy years are ripe, and over-ripe, the Son
Of *Macedonian Philip* had e're these
Won *Asia* and the Throne of *Cyrus*² held
At his dispose, young *Scipio* had brought down
The *Carthaginian* pride, young *Pompey* quell'd   35
The *Pontic* King³ and in triumph had rode.
Yet years, and to ripe years judgment mature,
Quench not the thirst of glory, but augment.
Great *Julius*, whom now all the world admires
The more he grew in years, the more inflam'd   40
With glory, wept that he had liv'd so long
Inglorious: but thou yet art not too late.
　　To whom our Saviour calmly thus reply'd.
Thou neither dost perswade me to seek wealth
For Empires sake, nor Empire to affect
For glories sake by all thy argument.   45
For what is glory but the blaze of fame,
The peoples praise, if always praise unmixt?
And what the people but a herd confus'd,
A miscellaneous rabble, who extol   50
Things vulgar, and well weigh'd, scarce worth the praise,
They praise and they admire they know not what;
And know not whom, but as one leads the other;
And what delight to be by such extoll'd,
To live upon thir tongues and be thir talk,   55
Of whom to be disprais'd were no small praise?
His lot who dares be singularly good.
Th' intelligent among them and the wise
Are few, and glory scarce of few is rais'd.
This is true glory and renown, when God   60
Looking on th' Earth, with approbation marks
The just man, and divulges him through Heav'n
To all his Angels, who with true applause
Recount his praises; thus he did to *Job*,
When to extend his fame through Heav'n and Earth,   65
As thou to thy reproach mayst well remember,
He ask'd thee, hast thou seen my servant *Job?*

---

² king of Persia, defeated by Alexander the Great.
³ Mithridates; Pompey was then (66 B.C.) forty years old.

Famous he was in Heav'n, on Earth less known;
Where glory is false glory, attributed
To things not glorious, men not worthy of fame.   70
They err who count it glorious to subdue
By Conquest far and wide, to over-run
Large Countries, and in field great Battels win,
Great Cities by assault: what do these Worthies,
But rob and spoil, burn, slaughter, and enslave   75
Peaceable Nations, neighbouring, or remote,
Made Captive, yet deserving freedom more
Then those thir Conquerours, who leave behind
Nothing but ruin wheresoe're they rove,
And all the flourishing works of peace destroy,   80
Then swell with pride, and must be titl'd Gods,
Great Benefactors of mankind, Deliverers,
Worship't with Temple, Priest and Sacrifice;
One is the Son of *Jove*, of *Mars* the other,[4]
Till Conquerour Death discover them scarce men,   85
Rowling in brutish vices, and deform'd,
Violent or shameful death thir due reward.
But if there be in glory aught of good,
It may by means far different be attain'd
Without ambition, war, or violence;   90
By deeds of peace, by wisdom eminent,
By patience, temperance; I mention still
Him whom thy wrongs with Saintly patience born,
Made famous in a Land and times obscure;
Who names not now with honour patient *Job*?   95
Poor *Socrates* (who next more memorable?)
By what he taught and suffer'd for so doing,
For truths sake suffering death unjust, lives now
Equal in fame to proudest Conquerours.
Yet if for fame and glory aught be done,   100
Aught suffer'd; if young *African*[5] for fame
His wasted Country freed from *Punic* rage,
The deed becomes unprais'd, the man at least,
And loses, though but verbal, his reward.
Shall I seek glory then, as vain men seek   105
Oft not deserv'd? I seek not mine, but his
Who sent me, and thereby witness whence I am.
   To whom the Tempter murmuring thus reply'd.

[4] Alexander was known as the son of Jove Ammon; Romulus, the son of Mars.
[5] Scipio.

Think not so slight of glory; therein least
Resembling thy great Father: he seeks glory,   110
And for his glory all things made, all things
Orders and governs, nor content in Heav'n
By all his Angels glorifi'd, requires
Glory from men, from all men good or bad,
Wise or unwise, no difference, no exemption;   115
Above all Sacrifice, or hallow'd gift
Glory he requires, and glory he receives
Promiscuous from all Nations, Jew, or Greek,
Or Barbarous, nor exception hath declar'd;
From us his foes pronounc't glory he exacts.   120
    To whom our Saviour fervently reply'd.
And reason; since his word all things produc'd,
Though chiefly not for glory as prime end,
But to shew forth his goodness, and impart
His good communicable to every soul   125
Freely; of whom what could he less expect
Then glory and benediction, that is thanks,
The slightest, easiest, readiest recompence
From them who could return him nothing else,
And not returning that would likeliest render   130
Contempt instead, dishonour, obloquy?
Hard recompence, unsutable return
For so much good, so much beneficence.
But why should man seek glory? who of his own
Hath nothing, and to whom nothing belongs   135
But condemnation, ignominy, and shame?
Who for so many benefits receiv'd
Turn'd recreant[6] to God, ingrate and false,
And so of all true good himself despoil'd,
Yet, sacrilegious, to himself would take   140
That which to God alone of right belongs;
Yet so much bounty is in God, such grace,
That who advance his glory, not thir own,
Them he himself to glory will advance.
    So spake the Son of God; and here again   145
Satan had not to answer, but stood struck
With guilt of his own sin, for he himself
Insatiable of glory had lost all,
Yet of another Plea bethought him soon.
    Of glory as thou wilt, said he, so deem,   150

---

[6] unfaithful.

Worth or not worth the seeking, let it pass:
But to a Kingdom thou art born, ordain'd
To sit upon thy Father *David*'s Throne;
By Mothers side thy Father, though thy right
Be now in powerful hands, that will not part   155
Easily from possession won with arms;
Judæa now and all the promis'd land
Reduc't a Province under *Roman* yoke,
Obeys *Tiberius;* nor is always rul'd
With temperate sway; oft have they violated   160
The Temple,[7] oft the Law with foul affronts,
Abominations rather, as did once
Antiochus:[8] and think'st thou to regain
Thy right by sitting still or thus retiring?
So did not *Machabeus:*[9] he indeed   165
Retir'd unto the Desert, but with arms;
And o're a mighty King so oft prevail'd,
That by strong hand his Family obtain'd,
Though Priests, the Crown, and *David*'s Throne usurp'd,
With *Modin* and her Suburbs once content.   170
If Kingdom move thee not, let move thee Zeal,
And Duty; Zeal and Duty are not slow;
But on Occasions forelock watchful wait.
They themselves rather are occasion best,
Zeal of thy Fathers house, Duty to free   175
Thy Country from her Heathen servitude;
So shalt thou best fullfil, best verifie
The Prophets old, who sung thy endless raign,
The happier raign the sooner it begins,
Raign then; what canst thou better do the while?   180
     To whom our Saviour answer thus return'd.
All things are best fullfil'd in their due time,
And time there is for all things, Truth hath said:[10]
If of my raign Prophetic Writ hath told,
That it shall never end, so when begin   185
The Father in his purpose hath decreed,
He in whose hand all times and seasons roul.
What if he hath decreed that I shall first
Be try'd in humble state, and things adverse,

[7] violation of the Holy of Holies by Pompey.
[8] See 1 Macc. i.
[9] Judas Maccabeus, born in Modin, won the throne of David after a long struggle with Antiochus.
[10] referring to Eccl. iii.

By tribulations, injuries, insults,   190
Contempts, and scorns, and snares, and violence,
Suffering, abstaining, quietly expecting
Without distrust or doubt, that he may know
What I can suffer, how obey? who best
Can suffer, best can do; best reign, who first   195
Well hath obey'd; just tryal e're I merit
My exaltation without change or end.
But what concerns it thee when I begin
My everlasting Kingdom, why art thou
Sollicitous, what moves thy inquisition?   200
Know'st thou not that my rising is thy fall,
And my promotion will be thy destruction?
    To whom the Tempter inly rackt reply'd.
Let that come when it comes; all hope is lost
Of my reception into grace; what worse?   205
For where no hope is left, is left no fear;
If there be worse, the expectation more
Of worse torments me then the feeling can.
I would be at the worst; worst is my Port,
My harbour and my ultimate repose,   210
The end I would attain, my final good.
My error was my error, and my crime
My crime; whatever for it self condemn'd,
And will alike be punish'd; whether thou
Raign or raign not; though to that gentle brow   215
Willingly I could fly, and hope thy raign,
From that placid aspect and meek regard,
Rather then aggravate my evil state,
Would stand between me and thy Fathers ire
(Whose ire I dread more then the fire of Hell),   220
A shelter and a kind of shading cool
Interposition, as a summers cloud.
If I then to the worst that can be hast,
Why move thy feet so slow to what is best,
Happiest both to thy self and all the world,   225
That thou who worthiest art should'st be thir King?
Perhaps thou linger'st in deep thoughts detain'd
Of the enterprize so hazardous and high;
No wonder, for though in thee be united
What of perfection can in man be found,   230
Or human nature can receive, consider
Thy life hath yet been private, most part spent
At home, scarce view'd the *Gallilean* Towns,

And once a year *Jerusalem,* few days
Short sojourn; and what thence could'st thou observe?   235
The world thou hast not seen, much less her glory,
Empires, and Monarchs, and thir radiant Courts,
Best school of best experience, quickest insight
In all things that to greatest actions lead.
The wisest, unexperienc't, will be ever   240
Timorous and loth, with novice modesty
(As he[11] who seeking Asses found a Kingdom),
Irresolute, unhardy, unadventrous:
But I will bring thee where thou soon shalt quit
Those rudiments,[12] and see before thine eyes   245
The Monarchies of th' Earth, thir pomp and state,
Sufficient introduction to inform
Thee, of thy self so apt, in regal Arts,
And regal Mysteries; that thou may'st know
How best their opposition to withstand.   250
    With that (such power was giv'n him then) he took
The Son of God up to a Mountain high.
It was a Mountain at whose verdant feet
A spatious plain out stretch't in circuit wide
Lay pleasant; from his side two rivers[13] flow'd,   255
Th' one winding, th' other strait and left between
Fair Champain with less rivers interveind,
Then meeting joyn'd thir tribute to the Sea:
Fertil of corn the glebe,[14] of oyl and wine,
With herds the pastures throng'd, with flocks the hills,   260
Huge Cities and high towr'd, that well might seem
The seats of mightiest Monarchs, and so large
The Prospect was, that here and there was room
For barren desert fountainless and dry.
To this high mountain top the Tempter brought   265
Our Saviour, and new train of words began.
    Well have we speeded, and o're hill and dale,
Forest and field, and flood, Temples and Towers
Cut shorter many a league; here thou behold'st
Assyria and her Empires antient bounds,   270

---

[11] Saul; see 1 Sam. ix–x.
[12] The rudiments to be discharged through Satan's help emphasize the word's connotation of ignorance in contrast to the Son's true rudiments (I, 157). The same misunderstanding of meaning lies in Satan's reference to "regal Mysteries" (l. 249).
[13] the Tigris and Euphrates.
[14] soil.

Araxes[15] and the *Caspian* lake, thence on
As far as *Indus* East, *Euphrates* West,
And oft beyond; to South the *Persian* Bay,
And inaccessible th' *Arabian* drouth:[16]
Here *Ninevee*, of length within her wall   275
Several days journey, built by *Ninus* old,
Of that first golden Monarchy the seat,
And seat of *Salmanassar*,[17] whose success
Israel in long captivity still mourns;
There *Babylon* the wonder of all tongues,   280
As antient, but rebuilt by him[18] who twice
Judah and all thy Father *David's* house
Led captive, and *Jerusalem* laid waste,
Till *Cyrus*[19] set them free; *Persepolis*
His City there thou seest, and *Bactra* there;   285
Ecbatana her structure vast there shews,
And *Hecatompylos* her hunderd gates,
There *Susa* by *Choaspes*, amber stream,
The drink of none but Kings; of later fame
Built by *Emathian*,[20] or by *Parthian*[21] hands,   290
The great *Seleucia*, *Nisibis*, and there
Artaxata, *Teredon*, *Ctesiphon*,
Turning with easie eye thou may'st behold.
All these the *Parthian*, now some Ages past,
By great *Arsaces* led, who founded first   295
That Empire, under his dominion holds
From the luxurious Kings of *Antioch*[22] won.
And just in time thou com'st to have a view
Of his great power; for now the *Parthian* King
In *Ctesiphon* hath gather'd all his Host   300
Against the *Scythian*,[23] whose incursions wild

---

[15] an Armenian river flowing into the Caspian. Satan surveys cities and provinces in the Persian, Mesopotamian, and Armenian complex.
[16] desert.
[17] Shalmaneser IV of Assyria captured the Israelites in 726 B.C. (see 2 Kings xvii. 3–4).
[18] Nebuchadnezzar; see Dan. iv. 30.
[19] king of Persia; see 2 Chron. xxxvi. 22–23.
[20] referring to Seleucus, general to Alexander the Great.
[21] Parthia formed an empire from conquests of Assyria, Persia, and later Seleucia. The Parthian method of fighting (ll. 305 ff.) was to turn one's horse swiftly upon discharging an arrow.
[22] seat of the Seleucid empire in Syria.
[23] an ancient people situated around the Black Sea, famed for savagery in battle; Sogdiana was a province of Persia.

Have wasted *Sogdiana;* to her aid
He marches now in hast; see, though from far,
His thousands, in what martial equipage
They issue forth, Steel Bows, and Shafts their arms   305
Of equal dread in flight, or in pursuit;
All Horsemen, in which fight they most excel;
See how in warlike muster they appear,
In Rhombs and wedges, and half moons, and wings.
   He look't and saw what numbers numberless   310
The City gates out powr'd, light armed Troops
In coats of Mail and military pride;
In Mail thir horses clad, yet fleet and strong,
Prauncing their riders bore, the flower and choice
Of many Provinces from bound to bound;   315
From *Arachosia,* from *Candaor* East,
And *Margiana* to the *Hyrcanian* cliffs
Of *Caucasus,* and dark *Iberian*[24] dales,
From *Atropatia* and the neighbouring plains
Of *Adiabene, Media,* and the South   320
Of *Susiana* to *Balsara's* hav'n.
He saw them in thir forms of battell rang'd,
How quick they wheel'd, and flying behind them shot
Sharp fleet of arrowie showers against the face
Of thir pursuers, and overcame by flight;   325
The field all iron cast a gleaming brown,
Not wanted clouds of foot, nor on each horn,
Cuirassiers all in steel for standing fight;
Chariots or Elephants endorst[25] with Towers
Of Archers, nor of labouring Pioners   330
A multitude with Spades and Axes arm'd
To lay hills plain, fell woods, or valleys fill,
Or where plain was raise hill, or over-lay
With bridges rivers proud, as with a yoke;
Mules after these, Camels and Dromedaries,   335
And Waggons fraught with Utensils of war.
Such forces met not, nor so wide a camp,
When *Agrican*[26] with all his Northern powers
Besieg'd *Albracca,* as Romances tell;

[24] an area in the Caucasus, not Spain.
[25] punning on the Latin word for "back" and referring to howdahs.
[26] king of Tartary and lover of Angelica, for whom he besieged Albracca, fortress of her father Gallophrone, king of Cathay. At the court of Charlemagne, she had won the hearts of Orlando, Rinaldo, and others, both Christians and pagans ("paynim"). (See Boiardo, *Orlando Innamorato,* I, x.)

The City of *Gallaphrone,* from thence to win 340
The fairest of her Sex *Angelica*
His daughter, sought by many Prowest[27] Knights,
Both *Paynim,* and the Peers of *Charlemane.*
Such and so numerous was thir Chivalrie;
At sight whereof the Fiend yet more presum'd, 345
And to our Saviour thus his words renew'd.
That thou may'st know I seek not to engage
Thy Vertue, and not every way secure
On no slight grounds thy safety; hear, and mark
To what end I have brought thee hither and shewn 350
All this fair sight; thy Kingdom though foretold
By Prophet or by Angel, unless thou
Endeavour, as thy Father *David* did,
Thou never shalt obtain; prediction still
In all things, and all men, supposes means, 355
Without means us'd, what it predicts revokes.
But say thou wert possess'd of *David's* Throne
By free consent of all, none opposite,
Samaritan or *Jew;*[28] how could'st thou hope
Long to enjoy it quiet and secure, 360
Between two such enclosing enemies
Roman and *Parthian?* therefore one of these
Thou must make sure thy own, the *Parthian* first
By my advice, as nearer and of late
Found able by invasion to annoy 365
Thy country, and captive lead away her Kings
Antigonus, and old *Hyrcanus* bound,
Maugre the *Roman:*[29] it shall be my task
To render thee the *Parthian* at dispose;
Chuse which thou wilt by conquest or by league. 370
By him thou shalt regain, without him not,
That which alone can truly reinstall thee
In *David's* royal seat, his true Successour,
Deliverance of thy brethren, those ten Tribes[30]
Whose off-spring in his Territory yet serve 375

[27] gallantest.
[28] who were generally opposed to each other.
[29] The Parthians helped Antigonus gain Judaea from Hyrcanus II, who had Roman aid, in 40 B.C. But note that Satan's advice for the Son to align himself with Parthia is specious since Parthia had already begun to decline after its defeat by Ventidius in 39–38 B.C.
[30] See 2 Kings xvii. 6; the "two of Joseph" (l. 377) were the tribes of Ephraim and Manasseh.

In *Habor,* and among the *Medes* dispers't,
Ten Sons of *Jacob,* two of *Joseph* lost
Thus long from *Israel;* serving as of old
Thir Fathers in the land of *Egypt* serv'd,
This offer sets before thee to deliver.   380
These if from servitude thou shalt restore
To thir inheritance, then, nor till then,
Thou on the Throne of *David* in full glory,
From *Egypt* to *Euphrates* and beyond
Shalt raign, and *Rome* or *Caesar* not need fear.   385
      To whom our Saviour answer'd thus unmov'd.
Much ostentation vain of fleshly arm,
And fragile arms, much instrument of war
Long in preparing, soon to nothing brought,
Before mine eyes thou hast set; and in my ear   390
Vented much policy,[31] and projects deep
Of enemies, of aids, battels and leagues,
Plausible[32] to the world, to me worth naught.
Means I must use thou say'st, prediction else
Will unpredict and fail me of the Throne: 395
My time I told thee (and that time for thee
Were better farthest off) is not yet come;[33]
When that comes think not thou to find me slack
On my part aught endeavouring, or to need
Thy politic maxims, or that cumbersome   400
Luggage of war there shewn me, argument
Of human weakness rather then of strength.
My brethren, as thou call'st them, those Ten Tribes
I must deliver, if I mean to raign
David's true heir, and his full Scepter sway   405
To just extent over all *Israel's* Sons;
But whence to thee this zeal, where was it then
For *Israel,* or for *David,* or his Throne,
When thou stood'st up his Tempter[34] to the pride
Of numbring *Israel,* which cost the lives   410
Of threescore and ten thousand *Israelites*
By three days Pestilence? such was thy zeal
To *Israel* then, the same that now to me.
As for those captive Tribes, themselves were they

[31] governmental shrewdness.
[32] worthy of applause.
[33] John vii. 6: "Then Jesus said unto them, My time is not yet come."
[34] See 1 Chron. xxi.

Who wrought their own captivity, fell off   415
From God to worship Calves, the Deities
Of *Egypt, Baal* next and *Ashtaroth,*[35]
And all th' Idolatries of Heathen round,
Besides thir other worse then heathenish crimes;
Nor in the land of their captivity   420
Humbled themselves, or penitent besought
The God of their fore-fathers; but so dy'd
Impenitent, and left a race behind
Like to themselves, distinguishable scarce
From Gentils, but by Circumcision vain,[36]   425
And God with Idols in their worship joyn'd.
Should I of these the liberty regard,
Who freed, as to their antient Patrimony,
Unhumbl'd, unrepentant, unreform'd,
Headlong would follow; and to thir Gods perhaps   430
Of *Bethel* and of *Dan?* no, let them serve
Thir enemies, who serve Idols with God.
Yet he at length, time to himself best known,
Remembring *Abraham* by some wond'rous call
May bring them back repentant and sincere,   435
And at their passing cleave th' *Assyrian* flood,
While to their native land with joy they hast,
As the Red Sea and *Jordan* once he cleft,
When to the promis'd land thir Fathers pass'd;
To his due time and providence I leave them.   440
  So spake *Israel's* true King, and to the Fiend
Made answer meet, that made void all his wiles.
So fares it when with truth falshood contends.

[35] deities of the Phoenicians.
[36] worthless and futile because the meaning of this great covenant has been
lost; see *Circumcision,* n. 6. Compare also ll. 433–35 below.

BOOK IV

  Perplex'd and troubl'd at his bad success
The Tempter stood, nor had what to reply,
Discover'd in his fraud, thrown from his hope,
So oft, and the perswasive Rhetoric
That sleek't his tongue, and won so much on *Eve,*   5
So little here, nay lost; but *Eve* was *Eve,*
This far his over-match, who self deceiv'd

And rash, before-hand had no better weigh'd
The strength he was to cope with, or his own:
But as a man who had been matchless held   10
In cunning, over-reach't where least he thought,
To salve his credit, and for very spight
Still will be tempting him who foyls him still,
And never cease, though to his shame the more;
Or as a swarm of flies in vintage time,   15
About the wine-press where sweet moust is powr'd,
Beat off, returns as oft with humming sound;
Or surging waves against a solid rock,
Though all to shivers dash't, th' assault renew,
Vain battry, and in froth or bubbles end;   20
So Satan, whom repulse upon repulse
Met ever; and to shameful silence brought,
Yet gives not o're though desperate of success,
And his vain importunity pursues.
He brought our Saviour to the western side   25
Of that high mountain, whence he might behold
Another plain,[1] long but in bredth not wide;
Wash'd by the Southern Sea, and on the North
To equal length back'd with a ridge of hills
That screen'd the fruits of th' earth and seats of men   30
From cold *Septentrion*[2] blasts, thence in the midst
Divided by a river, of whose banks
On each side an Imperial City stood,
With Towers and Temples proudly elevate
On seven small Hills, with Palaces adorn'd,   35
Porches and Theatres, Baths, Aqueducts,
Statues and Trophees, and Triumphal Arcs,
Gardens and Groves presented to his eyes,
Above the highth of Mountains interpos'd.
By what strange Parallax[3] or Optic skill   40
Of vision multiply'd through air, or glass
Of Telescope, were curious to enquire:
And now the Tempter thus his silence broke.
    The City which thou seest no other deem
Then great and glorious *Rome*, Queen of the Earth   45
So far renown'd, and with the spoils enricht
Of Nations; there the Capitol thou seest

---

[1] The central Italian plain, with the Tyrrhene Sea to the south and the Apennines to the northwest, is divided by the Tiber, on which lies Rome.
[2] northern.
[3] the apparent displacement of an object seen from two different positions.

Above the rest lifting his stately head
On the *Tarpeian* rock,[4] her Cittadel
Impregnable, and there Mount *Palatine*   50
Th' Imperial Palace, compass huge, and high
The Structure, skill of noblest Architects,
With gilded battlements, conspicuous far,
Turrets and Terrases, and glittering Spires.
Many a fair Edifice besides, more like   55
Houses of Gods (so well I have dispos'd
My Aerie Microscope) thou may'st behold
Outside and inside both, pillars and roofs
Carv'd work, the hand of fam'd Artificers
In Cedar, Marble, Ivory or Gold.   60
Thence to the gates cast round thine eye, and see
What conflux issuing forth, or entring in,
Pretors,[5] Proconsuls[6] to thir Provinces
Hasting or on return, in robes of State;
Lictors[7] and rods the ensigns of thir power,   65
Legions and Cohorts,[8] turmes of horse and wings:
Or Embassies from Regions far remote
In various habits on the *Appian* road,[9]
Or on th' *Æmilian*,[10] some from farthest South,
Syene,[11] and where the shadow both way falls,   70
Meroe Nilotic Isle, and more to West,
The Realm of *Bocchus* to the Black-moor Sea;
From th' *Asian* Kings and *Parthian* among these,
From *India* and the golden *Chersoness*,[12]
And utmost *Indian* Isle *Taprobane*,[13]   75
Dusk faces with white silken Turbants wreath'd:
From *Gallia*, *Gades*,[14] and the *Brittish* West,
Germans and *Scythians*, and *Sarmatians*[15] North

---

[4] See *El.* 1, n. 11.
[5] chiefly judicial magistrates, next in rank to consuls.
[6] provincial governors.
[7] officers, carrying fasces (a bundle of rods), who cleared the way for magistrates in public.
[8] tenth parts of a legion; a turme was a tenth part of a wing, a flank of the cavalry.
[9] lying between Rome and Brindisi.
[10] lying between Rome and the Adriatic Sea.
[11] a city on the Upper Nile. Bocchus was in northern Africa, and the Black-moor Sea means the Mediterranean along the northwestern African coast.
[12] the Malay peninsula.
[13] Ceylon.
[14] Cadiz.
[15] people of a region between the Vistula and Volga rivers.

Beyond *Danubius* to the *Tauric* Pool.[16]
All Nations now to *Rome* obedience pay,   80
To *Rome*'s great Emperour, whose wide domain
In ample Territory, wealth and power,
Civility of Manners, Arts, and Arms,
And long Renown thou justly may'st prefer
Before the *Parthian;* these two Thrones except,   85
The rest are barbarous, and scarce worth the sight,
Shar'd among petty Kings too far remov'd;
These having shewn thee, I have shewn thee all
The Kingdoms of the world, and all thir glory.
This Emperour[17] hath no Son, and now is old,   90
Old, and lascivious, and from *Rome* retir'd
To *Capreæ* an Island small but strong
On the *Campanian* shore, with purpose there
His horrid lusts in private to enjoy,
Committing to a wicked Favourite[18]   95
All publick cares, and yet of him suspicious,
Hated of all, and hating; with what ease
Indu'd with Regal Vertues as thou art,
Appearing, and beginning noble deeds,
Might'st thou expel this monster from his Throne   100
Now made a sty, and in his place ascending
A victor, people free from servile yoke!
And with my help thou may'st; to me the power
Is giv'n, and by that right I give it thee.
Aim therefore at no less then all the world,   105
Aim at the highest, without the highest attain'd
Will be for thee no sitting, or not long
On *David*'s Throne, be propheci'd what will.
    To whom the Son of God unmov'd reply'd.
Nor doth this grandeur and majestic show   110
Of luxury, though call'd magnificence,
More then of arms before, allure mine eye,
Much less my mind; though thou should'st add to tell
Thir sumptuous gluttonies, and gorgeous feasts
On *Cittron* tables or *Atlantic* stone;[19]   115
(For I have also heard, perhaps have read)
Their wines of *Setia, Cales,* and *Falerne,*

---

[16] the Sea of Azof.
[17] Tiberius.
[18] Sejanus.
[19] tables of fine wood from citrus trees or of marble.

Chios and *Creet*,[20] and how they quaff in Gold,
Crystal and Myrrhine[21] cups imboss'd with Gems
And studs of Pearl, to me should'st tell who thirst   120
And hunger still: then Embassies thou shew'st
From Nations far and nigh; what honour that,
But tedious wast of time to sit and hear
So many hollow compliments and lies,
Outlandish flatteries? then proceed'st to talk   125
Of the Emperour, how easily subdu'd,
How gloriously; I shall, thou say'st, expel
A brutish monster: what if I withal
Expel a Devil who first made him such?
Let his tormentor Conscience find him out,   130
For him I was not sent, nor yet to free
That people victor once, now vile and base,
Deservedly made vassal, who once just,
Frugal, and mild, and temperate, conquer'd well,
But govern ill the Nations under yoke,   135
Peeling[22] thir Provinces, exhausted all
By lust and rapine; first ambitious grown
Of triumph that insulting vanity;
Then cruel, by thir sports to blood enur'd
Of fighting beasts, and men to beasts expos'd,   140
Luxurious by thir wealth, and greedier still,
And from the daily Scene effeminate.
What wise and valiant man would seek to free
These thus degenerate, by themselves enslav'd,
Or could of inward slaves make outward free?   145
Know therefore when my season comes to sit
On *David's* Throne, it shall be like a tree
Spreading and over-shadowing all the Earth,
Or as a stone that shall to pieces dash
All Monarchies besides throughout the world,   150
And of my Kingdom there shall be no end:[23]
Means there shall be to this, but what the means,
Is not for thee to know, nor me to tell.
    To whom the Tempter impudent repli'd.
I see all offers made by me how slight   155

[20] The first three are Italian areas and the last two Greek islands all famous
for wines.
[21] made of a semiprecious stone; the glassware was transparent, showing
pieces of embedded colored glass (perhaps with gems).
[22] stripping.
[23] Luke i. 33.

Thou valu'st, because offer'd, and reject'st:
Nothing will please the difficult and nice,[24]
Or nothing more then still to contradict:
On th' other side know also thou, that I
On what I offer set as high esteem,   160
Nor what I part with mean to give for naught;
All these which in a moment thou behold'st,
The Kingdoms of the world to thee I give;
For giv'n to me, I give to whom I please,
No trifle; yet with this reserve, not else,   165
On this condition, if thou wilt fall down,
And worship me as thy superior Lord,
Easily done, and hold them all of me;
For what can less so great a gift deserve?
    Whom thus our Saviour answer'd with disdain.   170
I never lik'd thy talk, thy offers less,
Now both abhor, since thou hast dar'd to utter
Th' abominable terms, impious condition;
But I endure the time, till which expir'd,
Thou hast permission on me. It is written   175
The first of all Commandments, Thou shalt worship
The Lord thy God, and only him shalt serve;[25]
And dar'st thou to the Son of God propound
To worship thee accurst, now more accurst
For this attempt bolder then that on *Eve*,   180
And more blasphemous? which expect to rue.
The Kingdoms of the world to thee were giv'n,
Permitted rather, and by thee usurp't,
Other donation none thou canst produce:
If given, by whom but by the King of Kings,   185
God over all supreme? if giv'n to thee,
By thee how fairly is the Giver now
Repaid? But gratitude in thee is lost
Long since. Wert thou so void of fear or shame,
As offer them to me the Son of God,   190
To me my own, on such abhorred pact,
That I fall down and worship thee as God?
Get thee behind me; plain thou now appear'st
That Evil one, Satan for ever damn'd.
    To whom the Fiend with fear abasht reply'd.   195
Be not so sore offended, Son of God;

[24] fastidious.
[25] Matt. iv. 10; Luke iv. 8.

Though Sons of God both Angels are and Men,
If I to try whether in higher sort
Then these thou bear'st that title, have propos'd
What both from Men and Angels I receive,   200
Tetrarchs[26] of fire, air, flood, and on the earth
Nations besides from all the quarter'd winds,
God of this world invok't and world beneath;
Who then thou art, whose coming is foretold
To me so fatal, me it most concerns.   205
The tryal hath indamag'd thee no way,
Rather more honour left and more esteem;
Me naught advantag'd, missing what I aim'd.
Therefore let pass, as they are transitory,
The Kingdoms of this world; I shall no more   210
Advise thee, gain them as thou canst, or not.
And thou thy self seem'st otherwise inclin'd
Then to a worldly Crown, addicted more
To contemplation and profound dispute,
As by that early action may be judg'd,   215
When slipping from thy Mothers eye thou went'st
Alone into the Temple;[27] there wast found
Among the gravest Rabbies disputant
On points and questions fitting *Moses* Chair,
Teaching not taught; the childhood shews the man,   220
As morning shews the day. Be famous then
By wisdom; as thy Empire must extend,
So let extend thy mind o're all the world,
In knowledge, all things in it comprehend,
All knowledge is not couch't in *Moses* Law,   225
The *Pentateuch*[28] or what the Prophets wrote,
The *Gentiles* also know, and write, and teach
To admiration, led by Natures light;
And with the *Gentiles* much thou must converse,
Ruling them by perswasion as thou mean'st,   230
Without thir learning how wilt thou with them,
Or they with thee hold conversation meet?
How wilt thou reason with them, how refute
Thir Idolisms, Traditions, Paradoxes?
Error by his own arms is best evinc't.   235
Look once more e're we leave this specular Mount

[26] rulers of a quarter of the world (l. 202), but referring too to the four enumerated elements.
[27] See Luke ii. 42–47.
[28] the first five books of the Old Testament.

Westward, much nearer by Southwest, behold
Where on th' *Ægean* shore a City stands
Built nobly, pure the air, and light the soil,
Athens the eye of *Greece*, Mother of Arts   240
And Eloquence, native to famous wits
Or hospitable, in her sweet recess,
City or Suburban, studious walks and shades;
See there the Olive Grove of *Academe*,
Plato's retirement, where the *Attic* Bird[29]   245
Trills her thick-warbl'd notes the summer long,
There flowrie hill *Hymettus* with the sound
Of Bees industrious murmur oft invites
To studious musing; there *Ilissus* rouls
His whispering stream; within the walls then view   250
The schools of antient Sages; his[30] who bred
Great *Alexander* to subdue the world,
Lyceum there, and painted *Stoa*[31] next:
There thou shalt hear and learn the secret power
Of harmony in tones and numbers hit   255
By voice or hand, and various-measur'd verse,
Æolian charms and *Dorian Lyric* Odes,[32]
And his who gave them breath, but higher sung,
Blind *Melesigenes* thence *Homer* call'd,
Whose Poem *Phœbus* challeng'd for his own.   260
Thence what the lofty grave Tragœdians taught
In *Chorus* or *Iambic*, teachers best
Of moral prudence, with delight receiv'd
In brief sententious precepts, while they treat
Of fate, and chance, and change in human life;   265
High actions, and high passions best describing:
Thence to the famous Orators repair,
Those antient, whose resistless eloquence
Wielded at will that fierce Democratie,
Shook the Arsenal and fulmin'd over *Greece*,   270
To *Macedon*, and *Artaxerxes*[33] Throne;
To sage Philosophy next lend thine ear,
From Heav'n descended to the low-rooft house

[29] the nightingale.
[30] Aristotle.
[31] the "porch" in the marketplace of Athens where Zeno taught his Stoic philosophy.
[32] referring primarily to Sappho and Pindar.
[33] king of Persia, who sided with Sparta against Athens. The orators were Demosthenes and Pericles, respectively.

Of *Socrates*, see there his Tenement,
Whom well inspir'd the Oracle pronounc'd   275
Wisest of men; from whose mouth issu'd forth
Mellifluous streams that water'd all the schools
Of Academics old and new, with those
Sirnam'd *Peripatetics*,[34] and the Sect
Epicurean, and the *Stoic* severe;   280
These here revolve, or, as thou lik'st, at home,
Till time mature thee to a Kingdom's waight;
These rules will render thee a King compleat
Within thy self, much more with Empire joyn'd.
 To whom our Saviour sagely thus repli'd.   285
Think not but that I know these things, or think
I know them not; not therefore am I short
Of knowing what I ought: he who receives
Light from above, from the fountain of light,
No other doctrine needs, though granted true;   290
But these are false, or little else but dreams,
Conjectures, fancies, built on nothing firm.
The first and wisest of them all[35] profess'd
To know this only, that he nothing knew;
The next[36] to fabling fell and smooth conceits,   295
A third sort[37] doubted all things, though plain sence;
Others[38] in vertue plac'd felicity,
But vertue joyn'd with riches and long life,
In corporal pleasure he,[39] and careless ease,
The Stoic last in Philosophic pride,   300
By him call'd vertue; and his vertuous man,
Wise, perfect in himself, and all possessing
Equal to God, oft shames not to prefer,
As fearing God nor man, contemning all
Wealth, pleasure, pain or torment, death and life,   305
Which when he lists, he leaves, or boasts he can,
For all his tedious talk is but vain boast,
Or subtle shifts conviction to evade.
Alas what can they teach, and not mislead;
Ignorant of themselves, of God much more,   310

[34] followers of Aristotle.
[35] Socrates.
[36] Plato.
[37] Pyrrho, founder of the Sceptics.
[38] the Peripatetics.
[39] Epicurus.

And how the world began, and how man fell
Degraded by himself, on grace depending?
Much of the Soul they talk, but all awrie,
And in themselves seek vertue, and to themselves
All glory arrogate, to God give none,   315
Rather accuse him under usual names,
Fortune and Fate, as one regardless quite
Of mortal things. Who therefore seeks in these
True wisdom, finds her not, or by delusion
Far worse, her false resemblance only meets,   320
An empty cloud. However many books
Wise men have said are wearisom; who reads
Incessantly, and to his reading brings not
A spirit and judgment equal or superior,
(And what he brings, what needs he elsewhere seek)   325
Uncertain and unsettl'd still remains,
Deep verst in books and shallow in himself,
Crude or intoxicate, collecting toys,
And trifles for choice matters, worth a spunge;
As Children gathering pibles on the shore.   330
Or if I would delight my private hours
With Music or with Poem, where so soon
As in our native Language can I find
That solace? All our Law and Story strew'd
With Hymns, our Psalms with artful terms inscrib'd,   335
Our Hebrew Songs and Harps in *Babylon,*
That pleas'd so well our Victors ear, declare
That rather *Greece* from us these Arts deriv'd;
Ill imitated, while they loudest sing
The vices of thir Deities, and thir own   340
In Fable, Hymn, or Song, so personating
Thir Gods ridiculous, and themselves past shame.
Remove their swelling Epithetes thick laid
As varnish on a Harlots cheek, the rest,
Thin sown with aught of profit or delight,   345
Will far be found unworthy to compare
With *Sion*'s songs, to all true tasts excelling,
Where God is prais'd aright, and Godlike men,
The Holiest of Holies, and his Saints;
Such are from God inspir'd, not such from thee;   350
Unless where moral vertue is express't
By light of Nature not in all quite lost.
Thir Orators thou then extoll'st, as those

The top of Eloquence, Statists[40] indeed,
And lovers of thir Country, as may seem;   355
But herein to our Prophets far beneath,
As men divinely taught, and better teaching
The solid rules of Civil Government
In thir majestic unaffected stile
Then all the Oratory of *Greece* and *Rome*.   360
In them is plainest taught, and easiest learnt,
What makes a Nation happy, and keeps it so,
What ruins Kingdoms, and lays Cities flat;
These only with our Law best form a King.
  So spake the Son of God; but Satan now   365
Quite at a loss, for all his darts were spent,
Thus to our Saviour with stern brow reply'd.
  Since neither wealth, nor honour, arms nor arts,
Kingdom nor Empire pleases thee, nor aught
By me propos'd in life contemplative,   370
Or active, tended on by glory, or fame,
What dost thou in this World? the Wilderness
For thee is fittest place, I found thee there,
And thither will return thee, yet remember
What I foretell thee, soon thou shalt have cause   375
To wish thou never hadst rejected thus
Nicely or cautiously my offer'd aid,
Which would have set thee in short time with ease
On *David's* Throne; or Throne of all the world,
Now at full age, fulness of time, thy season,   380
When Prophesies of thee are best fullfill'd.
Now contrary, if I read aught in Heav'n,
Or Heav'n write aught of Fate, by what the Stars
Voluminous, or single characters,
In their conjunction met, give me to spell,   385
Sorrows, and labours, opposition, hate,
Attends thee, scorns, reproaches, injuries,
Violence and stripes, and lastly cruel death.
A Kingdom they portend thee, but what Kingdom,
Real or Allegoric I discern not,   390
Now when, eternal sure, as without end,
Without beginning; for no date prefixt
Directs me in the Starry Rubric set.
  So saying he took (for still he knew his power
Not yet expir'd) and to the Wilderness   395

---

[40] statesmen.

Brought back the Son of God, and left him there,
Feigning to disappear. Darkness now rose,
As day-light sunk, and brought in lowring night
Her shadowy off-spring unsubstantial both,
Privation meer of light and absent day.   400
Our Saviour meek and with untroubl'd mind
After his aerie jaunt, though hurried sore,
Hungry and cold betook him to his rest,
Wherever, under some concourse of shades
Whose branching arms thick intertwin'd might shield   405
From dews and damps of night his shelter'd head,
But shelter'd slept in vain, for at his head
The Tempter watch'd, and soon with ugly dreams
Disturb'd his sleep; and either Tropic now
'Gan thunder, and both ends of Heav'n, the Clouds   410
From many a horrid rift abortive pour'd
Fierce rain with lightning mixt, water with fire
In ruin reconcil'd: nor slept the winds
Within thir stony caves, but rush'd abroad
From the four hinges of the world, and fell   415
On the vext Wilderness, whose tallest Pines,
Though rooted deep as high, and sturdiest Oaks
Bow'd their Stiff necks, loaden with stormy blasts,
Or torn up sheer: ill wast thou shrouded then,
O patient Son of God, yet only stoodst   420
Unshaken; nor yet staid the terror there,
Infernal Ghosts, and Hellish Furies, round
Environ'd thee, some howl'd, some yell'd, some shriek'd,
Some bent at thee thir fiery darts, while thou
Sat'st unappall'd in calm and sinless peace.   425
Thus pass'd the night so foul till morning fair
Came forth with Pilgrim steps in amice[41] gray;
Who with her radiant finger still'd the roar
Of thunder, chas'd the clouds, and laid the winds,
And grisly Spectres, which the Fiend had rais'd   430
To tempt the Son of God with terrors dire.
And now the Sun with more effectual beams
Had chear'd the face of Earth, and dry'd the wet
From drooping plant, or dropping tree; the birds
Who all things now behold more fresh and green,   435
After a night of storm so ruinous,
Clear'd up their choicest notes in bush and spray

[41] a hood worn by the clergy.

To gratulate the sweet return of morn;
Nor yet amidst this joy and brightest morn
Was absent, after all his mischief done,   440
The Prince of darkness, glad would also seem
Of this fair change, and to our Saviour came,
Yet with no new device, they all were spent,
Rather by this his last affront resolv'd,
Desperate of better course, to vent his rage,   445
And mad despight to be so oft repell'd.
Him walking on a Sunny hill he found,
Back'd on the North and West by a thick wood,
Out of the wood he starts in wonted shape;
And in a careless mood thus to him said.   450
  Fair morning yet betides thee Son of God,
After a dismal night; I heard the rack
As Earth and Skie would mingle; but my self
Was distant; and these flaws, though mortals fear them
As dangerous to the pillard frame of Heav'n,   455
Or to the Earths dark basis underneath,
Are to the main[42] as inconsiderable,
And harmless, if not wholsom, as a sneeze[43]
To mans less universe, and soon are gone;
Yet as being oft times noxious where they light   460
On man, beast, plant, wastful and turbulent,
Like turbulencies in th' affairs of men,
Over whose heads they roar, and seem to point,
They oft fore-signifie and threaten ill:
This Tempest at this Desert most was bent;   465
Of men at thee, for only thou here dwell'st.
Did I not tell thee, if thou didst reject
The perfet season offer'd with my aid
To win thy destin'd seat, but wilt prolong
All to the push of Fate, persue thy way   470
Of gaining *David's* Throne no man knows when,
For both the when and how is no where told,
Thou shalt be what thou art ordain'd, no doubt;
For Angels have proclaim'd it, but concealing
The time and means: each act is rightliest done,   475
Not when it must, but when it may be best.
If thou observe not this, be sure to find,

---

[42] the universe.
[43] Svendsen (p. 39) points out that a sneeze was thought a benefit to health because it purged the brain ("mans less universe").

What I foretold thee, many a hard assay
Of dangers, and adversities and pains,
E're thou of *Israel*'s Scepter get fast hold;   480
Whereof this ominous night that clos'd thee round,
So many terrors, voices, prodigies
May warn thee, as a sure fore-going sign.
   So talk'd he, while the Son of God went on
And staid not, but in brief him answer'd thus.   485
   Mee worse then wet thou find'st not; other harm
Those terrors which thou speak'st of, did me none;
I never fear'd they could, though noising loud
And threatning nigh; what they can do as signs
Betok'ning, or ill boding, I contemn   490
As false portents, not sent from God, but thee;
Who knowing I shall raign past thy preventing,
Obtrud'st thy offer'd aid, that I accepting
At least might seem to hold all power of[44] thee,
Ambitious spirit, and wouldst be thought my God,   495
And storm'st refus'd, thinking to terrifie
Mee to thy will; desist, thou art discern'd
And toil'st in vain, nor me in vain molest.
   To whom the Fiend now swoln with rage reply'd:
Then hear, O Son of *David*, Virgin-born;   500
For Son of God to me is yet in doubt,
Of the Messiah I have heard foretold
By all the Prophets; of thy birth at length
Announc't by *Gabriel* with the first I knew,
And of th' Angelic Song in *Bethlehem* field,   505
On thy birth-night, that sung thee Saviour born.
From that time seldom have I ceas'd to eye
Thy infancy, thy childhood, and thy youth,
Thy manhood last, though yet in private bred;
Till at the Ford of *Jordan* wither all   510
Flock'd to the Baptist, I among the rest,
Though not to be Baptiz'd,[45] by voice from Heav'n
Heard thee pronounc'd the Son of God belov'd.
Thenceforth I thought thee worth my nearer view
And narrower Scrutiny, that I might learn   515
In what degree or meaning thou art call'd
The Son of God, which bears no single sence;

[44] from.
[45] not only because as an angel he was a fiery essence, but because such immersion absolved man of Adam and Eve's original sin. Though he had instigated that sin, he had not inherited it as had the descendants of Adam.

The Son of God I also am, or was,
And if I was, I am; relation stands;
All men are Sons of God; yet thee I thought   520
In some respect far higher so declar'd.
Therefore I watch'd thy footsteps from that hour,
And follow'd thee still on to this wast wild;
Where by all best conjectures I collect
Thou art to be my fatal enemy.   525
Good reason then, if I before-hand seek
To understand my Adversary,[46] who
And what he is; his wisdom, power, intent,
By parl, or composition, truce, or league
To win him, or win from him what I can.   530
And opportunity I here have had
To try thee, sift thee, and confess have found thee
Proof against all temptation as a rock
Of Adamant, and as a Center, firm;
To th' utmost of meer man both wise and good,   535
Not more; for Honours, Riches, Kingdoms, Glory
Have been before contemn'd, and may agen:
Therefore to know what more thou art then man,
Worth naming Son of God by voice from Heav'n,
Another method I must now begin.   540
    So saying he caught him up, and without wing
Of *Hippogrif*[47] bore through the Air sublime
Over the Wilderness and o're the Plain;
Till underneath them fair *Jerusalem*,
The holy City lifted high her Towers,   545
And higher yet the glorious Temple[48] rear'd
Her pile, far off appearing like a Mount
Of Alabaster, top't with Golden Spires:
There on the highest Pinacle he set
The Son of God; and added thus in scorn: 550
    There stand, if thou wilt stand;[49] to stand upright
Will ask thee skill; I to thy Fathers house
Have brought thee, and highest plac't, highest is best,

---

[46] Note that it is Satan who is called the "Adversary" in I, 33.
[47] a winged animal, half horse and half griffin.
[48] that built by Herod.
[49] both "stand up" rather than "fall down" and "remain steadfast in resistance." The Son is faced with the dilemma of remaining and not bringing God's command (ll. 556–59) to pass, or casting himself down and thus succumbing to Satan by putting God to the test. Thus should he cast himself down, his fall would be both literal and figurative.

Now shew thy Progeny;[50] if not to stand,
Cast thy self down; safely if Son of God: 555
For it is written,[51] He will give command
Concerning thee to his Angels, in thir hands
They shall up lift thee, lest at any time
Thou chance to dash thy foot against a stone.
    To whom thus Jesus: also it is written,   560
Tempt not the Lord thy God, he said and stood.
But Satan smitten with amazement fell
As when Earths Son *Antæus* (to compare
Small things with greatest) in *Irassa* strove
With *Joves Alcides*,[52] and oft foil'd still rose,   565
Receiving from his mother Earth new strength,
Fresh from his fall, and fiercer grapple joyn'd,
Throttl'd at length in th' Air, expir'd and fell;
So after many a foil the Tempter proud,
Renewing fresh assaults, amidst his pride   570
Fell whence he stood to see his Victor fall.
And as that *Theban* Monster[53] that propos'd
Her riddle, and him, who solv'd it not, devour'd;
That once found out and solv'd, for grief and spight
Cast her self headlong from th' *Ismenian* steep,   575
So strook with dread and anguish fell the Fiend,
And to his crew, that sat consulting, brought
Joyless triumphals of his hop't success,
Ruin, and desperation, and dismay,
Who durst so proudly tempt the Son of God.   580
So Satan fell and strait a fiery Globe
Of Angels on full sail of wing flew nigh,
Who on their plumy Vans[54] receiv'd him soft
From his uneasie station, and upbore
As on a floating couch through the blithe Air,[55]   585
Then in a flowry valley set him down
On a green bank, and set before him spred

[50] parentage.
[51] Matt. iv. 6–7, referring to Ps. xci. 11–12, which includes the significant
phrase "to keep thee in all thy ways."
[52] Hercules, who reasoned how to subdue the giant Antaeus.
[53] the Sphinx, who devoured those unable to solve her riddle; when Oedipus
gave the correct answer ("Man"), she flung herself from the acropolis into the
river Ismenus. The answer "Man" is symbolically meaningful at this point in
the Son's defeat of Satan.
[54] wings.
[55] Thus does God's command come to pass; the Son solved his dilemma
through faith.

A table of Celestial Food, Divine,
Ambrosial, Fruits fetcht from the tree of life,
And from the fount of life Ambrosial drink,   590
That soon refresh'd him wearied, and repair'd
What hunger, if aught hunger had impair'd,
Or thirst, and as he fed, Angelic Quires
Sung Heavenly Anthems of his victory
Over temptation, and the Tempter proud.   595
   True Image of the Father whether thron'd
In the bosom of bliss, and light of light
Conceiving, or remote from Heav'n, enshrin'd
In fleshly Tabernacle, and human form,
Wandring the Wilderness, whatever place,   600
Habit, or state, or motion, still expressing
The Son of God, with Godlike force indu'd
Against th' Attempter of thy Fathers Throne,
And Thief of Paradise; him long of old
Thou didst debel,[56] and down from Heav'n cast   605
With all his Army, now thou hast aveng'd
Supplanted *Adam*, and by vanquishing
Temptation, hast regain'd lost Paradise,
And frustrated the conquest fraudulent:
He never more henceforth will dare set foot   610
In Paradise to tempt; his snares are broke:
For though that seat of earthly bliss he fail'd,
A fairer Paradise is founded now
For *Adam* and his chosen Sons, whom thou
A Saviour art come down to re-install,   615
Where they shall dwell secure, when time shall be
Of Tempter and Temptation without fear.
But thou, Infernal Serpent, shalt not long
Rule in the Clouds; like an Autumnal Star
Or Lightning thou shalt fall from Heav'n trod down   620
Under his feet: for proof, e're this thou feel'st
Thy wound, yet not thy last and deadliest wound
By this repulse receiv'd, and hold'st in Hell
No triumph; in all her gates *Abaddon*[57] rues
Thy bold attempt; hereafter learn with awe   625
To dread the Son of God: he all unarm'd
Shall chase thee with the terror of his voice
From thy Demoniac holds, possession foul,

[56] subdue.
[57] Hell.

Thee and thy Legions, yelling they shall fly,
And beg to hide them in a herd of Swine,   630
Lest he command them down into the deep
Bound, and to torment sent before thir time.[58]
Hail Son of the most High, heir of both worlds,
Queller of Satan, on thy glorious work
Now enter, and begin to save mankind.   635
    Thus they the Son of God our Saviour meek
Sung Victor, and from Heav'nly Feast refresht
Brought on his way with joy; hee unobserv'd
Home to his Mothers house private return'd.

(1646–48 ?; revised or, according to some critics, written after 1665)[59]

[58] See *El.* 4, n. 20.

[59] The traditional dating of the entire epic after 1665 and before SA has been challenged by the editor in "Chronology of Milton's Major Poems" where these dates are conjectured. Parker, *Milton, A Biography*, II, 1140, suggests a date of c. 1656–58 for the first attempts at *PR*.

Samson Agonistes[1]

OF THAT SORT OF DRAMATIC POEM
WHICH IS CALL'D TRAGEDY

Tragedy, as it was antiently compos'd, hath been ever held the gravest, moralest, and most profitable of all other Poems: therefore said by *Aristotle* to be of power by raising pity and fear, or terror, to purge the mind of those and such like passions, that is to temper and reduce them to just measure with a kind of delight, stirr'd up by reading or seeing those passions well imitated.[2] Nor is Nature wanting in her own effects to make good his assertion: for so in Physic things of melancholic hue and quality are us'd against melancholy, sowr against sowr, salt to remove salt humours. Hence Philosophers and other gravest Writers, as *Cicero*, *Plutarch* and others, frequently cite out of Tragic Poets, both to adorn and illustrate thir discourse. The Apostle *Paul* himself thought it not unworthy to insert a verse of *Euripides* into the Text of Holy Scripture, 1 *Cor.* 15.33.[3] and *Paræus*[4] commenting on the *Revelation*, divides the whole Book as a Tragedy, into Acts distinguisht each by a Chorus of Heavenly Harpings and Song between. Heretofore Men in highest dignity

---

[1] Drawn from Hebraic material (Judges xiii–xvi) and Greek tragic structure, the drama reflects both Christian traditions (see Krouse's survey) and Hellenistic spirit (see Parker's study). In "SA and Milton in Old Age," p. 278, Hanford remarks, "by representing a clearly marked triumph of the human will over its own weakness, and by the substitution of Providence for blind fate as the power which overrules the action, the play provides material for a different understanding of catharsis from that contemplated by Aristotle." Based on Greek tragedy, Milton's drama consists of five episodes each followed by a chorus (stasimon) in addition to Samson's opening soliloquy (prologos) and a choral ode (parados) and a closing passage (exodos) in which is included a lament (kommos). As tragic hero, Samson has succumbed prior to the opening of the play to pride (hubris) and uxoriousness. His regeneration, the main "plot" of the play (although such regeneration is debated by critics), is developed through these five episodes, and thus forges the champion of truth indicated by the title. Samson must first overcome despair through fortitude in order to realize God's providential ways. "Agonistes" implies one engaged in a struggle as well as an actor (in the drama of life).

Biographical interpretations have been commonplace because of the element of blindness, but if the suggested earlier dating is correct, many allusions to contemporary and marital problems which have been inferred are invalidated.

[2] The principle of catharsis is described in *Poetics*, VI.

[3] "Evil communications corrupt good manners," attributed also to Menander.

[4] David Pareus (1548–1622), a Calvinist theologian, in his *Operum Theologicorum*.

have labour'd not a little to be thought able to compose a Tragedy. Of that honour *Dionysius* the elder[5] was no less ambitious, then before of his attaining to the Tyranny. *Augustus Cæsar* also had begun his *Ajax,* but unable to please his own judgment with what he had begun, left it unfinisht.[6] *Seneca* the Philosopher is by some thought the Author of those Tragedies (at least the best of them) that go under that name. *Gregory Nazianzen* a Father of the Church, thought it not unbeseeming the sanctity of his person to write a Tragedy, which he entitl'd, *Christ suffering.*[7] This is mention'd to vindicate Tragedy from the small esteem, or rather infamy, which in the account of many it undergoes at this day with other common Interludes; hap'ning through the Poets error of intermixing Comic stuff with Tragic sadness and gravity; or introducing trivial and vulgar persons, which by all judicious hath bin counted absurd; and brought in without discretion, corruptly to gratifie the people. And though antient Tragedy use no Prologue,[8] yet using sometimes, in case of self defence, or explanation, that which *Martial* calls an Epistle; in behalf of this Tragedy coming forth after the antient manner, much different from what among us passes for best, thus much before-hand may be Epistl'd; that *Chorus* is here introduc'd after the Greek manner, not antient only but modern, and still in use among the *Italians.* In the modelling therefore of this Poem, with good reason, the Antients and *Italians* are rather follow'd, as of much more authority and fame. The measure of Verse us'd in the Chorus is of all sorts, call'd by the Greeks *Monostrophic,*[9] or rather *Apolelymenon,* without regard had to *Strophe, Antistrophe* or *Epod,* which were a kind of Stanzas fram'd only for the Music, then us'd with the Chorus that sung; not essential to the Poem, and therefore not material; or being divided into Stanzas or Pauses, they may be call'd *Allæostropha.*[10] Division into Act and Scene referring chiefly to the Stage (to which this work never was intended) is here omitted. It suffices if the whole Drama be found not produc't beyond the fift Act.

Of the style and uniformitie, and that commonly call'd the Plot, whether intricate or explicit, which is nothing indeed but such œconomy, or disposition of the fable as may stand best with verisimilitude and decorum, they only will best judge who are not unacquainted with *Æschulus, Sophocles,* and *Euripides,* the three Tragic Poets unequall'd yet by any, and the best rule to all who endeavour to write Tragedy. The

[5] tyrant of Syracuse, who wrote numerous literary works.
[6] See Suetonius, II, lxxxv.
[7] This was a common ascription, though wrong.
[8] a "defense" of the writing of the play, not the passage preceding the entrance of the chorus.
[9] explained by the next phrase.
[10] strophes of varying lengths.

circumscription of time wherein the whole Drama begins and ends, is according to antient rule, and best example, within the space of 24 hours.

THE ARGUMENT

Samson made Captive, Blind, and now in the Prison at *Gaza*,[11] there to labour as in a common work-house, on a Festival day, in the general cessation from labour, comes forth into the open Air, to a place nigh, somewhat retir'd, there to sit a while and bemoan his condition. Where he happens at length to be visited by certain friends and equals of his tribe, which make the Chorus, who seek to comfort him what they can; then by his old Father *Manoa,* who endeavours the like, and withal tells him his purpose to procure his liberty by ransom; lastly, that this Feast was proclaim'd by the *Philistins* as a day of Thanksgiving for thir deliverance from the hands of *Samson,* which yet more troubles him. *Manoa* then departs to prosecute his endeavour with the *Philistian* Lords for *Samson's* redemption; who in the mean while is visited by other persons; and lastly by a publick Officer to require his coming to the Feast before the Lords and People, to play or shew his strength in thir presence; he at first refuses, dismissing the publick Officer with absolute denyal to come; at length perswaded inwardly that this was from God, he yields to go along with him, who came now the second time with great threatnings to fetch him; the Chorus yet remaining on the place, *Manoa* returns full of joyful hope, to procure e're long his Sons deliverance: in the midst of which discourse an Ebrew comes in haste, confusedly at first; and afterward more distinctly relating the Catastrophe, what *Samson* had done to the *Philistins,* and by accident to himself; wherewith the Tragedy ends.

[11] a principal city of the Philistines, lying on the eastern Mediterranean in Palestine.

THE PERSONS

Samson
Manoa *the Father of* Samson
Dalila *his Wife*
Harapha *of* Gath
Publick Officer
Messenger
Chorus *of* Danites

The Scene before the Prison in *Gaza*

Samson. A little onward lend thy guiding hand
To these dark steps, a little further on;
For yonder bank hath choice of Sun or shade,
There I am wont to sit, when any chance
Relieves me from my task of servile toyl,   5
Daily in the common Prison else enjoyn'd me,
Where I a Prisoner chain'd, scarce freely draw
The air imprison'd also, close and damp,
Unwholsom draught: but here I feel amends,
The breath of Heav'n fresh-blowing, pure and sweet,   10
With day-spring born; here leave me to respire.
This day a solemn Feast the people hold
To *Dagon*[12] thir Sea-Idol, and forbid
Laborious works, unwillingly this rest
Thir Superstition yields me; hence with leave   15
Retiring from the popular noise, I seek
This unfrequented place to find some ease;
Ease to the body some, none to the mind
From restless thoughts, that like a deadly swarm
Of Hornets arm'd, no sooner found alone,   20
But rush upon me thronging, and present
Times past, what once I was, and what am now.
O wherefore was my birth from Heav'n foretold
Twice by an Angel, who at last in sight
Of both my Parents all in flames ascended   25
From off the Altar, where an Off'ring burn'd,
As in a fiery column charioting
His Godlike presence, and from some great act
Or benefit reveal'd to *Abraham's* race?

[12] See *Nativity Ode*, n. 44.

Why was my breeding order'd and prescrib'd   30
As of a person separate to God,
Design'd for great exploits; if I must dye
Betray'd, Captiv'd, and both my Eyes put out,
Made of my Enemies the scorn and gaze;
To grind in Brazen Fetters under task   35
With this Heav'n-gifted strength? O glorious strength
Put to the labour of a Beast, debas't
Lower then bondslave! Promise was that I
Should *Israel* from *Philistian* yoke deliver;
Ask for this great Deliverer now, and find him   40
Eyeless in *Gaza* at the Mill with slaves,
Himself in bonds under *Philistian* yoke;
Yet stay, let me not rashly call in doubt
Divine Prediction; what if all foretold
Had been fulfill'd but through mine own default,   45
Whom have I to complain of but my self?
Who this high gift of strength committed to me,
In what part lodg'd, how easily bereft me,
Under the Seal of silence could not keep,
But weakly to a woman must reveal it,   50
O'recome with importunity and tears.
O impotence of mind, in body strong!
But what is strength without a double share
Of wisdom? Vast, unwieldy, burdensom,
Proudly secure, yet liable to fall   55
By weakest suttleties, not made to rule,
But to subserve where wisdom bears command.
God, when he gave me strength, to shew withal
How slight the gift was, hung it in my Hair.
But peace, I must not quarrel with the will   60
Of highest dispensation,[13] which herein
Happ'ly had ends above my reach to know:
Suffices that to me strength is my bane,
And proves the sourse of all my miseries;
So many, and so huge, that each apart   65
Would ask[14] a life to wail, but chief of all,
O loss of sight, of thee I most complain!
Blind among enemies, O worse then chains,
Dungeon, or beggery, or decrepit age!

[13] that which is appointed by God, but punning etymologically on its being "hung" in his hair (l. 59).
[14] require.

Light the prime work of God to me is extinct,   70
And all her various objects of delight
Annull'd, which might in part my grief have eas'd,
Inferiour to the vilest now become
Of man or worm; the vilest here excel me,
They creep, yet see, I dark in light expos'd   75
To daily fraud, contempt, abuse and wrong,
Within doors, or without, still as a fool,
In power of others, never in my own;
Scarce half I seem to live, dead more then half.
O dark, dark, dark, amid the blaze of noon,   80
Irrecoverably dark, total Eclipse
Without all hope of day!
O first created Beam, and thou great Word,
Let there be light, and light was over all;
Why am I thus bereav'd thy prime decree?   85
The Sun to me is dark
And silent as the Moon,
When she deserts the night
Hid in her vacant interlunar[15] cave.
Since light so necessary is to life,   90
And almost life it self, if it be true
That light is in the Soul,
She all in every part; why was the sight
To such a tender ball as th' eye confin'd?
So obvious and so easie to be quench't,   95
And not as feeling through all parts diffus'd,
That she might look at will through every pore?
Then had I not been thus exil'd from light;
As in the land of darkness yet in light,
To live a life half dead, a living death,   100
And buried; but O yet more miserable!
My self, my Sepulcher, a moving Grave,
Buried, yet not exempt
By priviledge of death and burial
From worst of other evils, pains and wrongs,   105
But made hereby obnoxious[16] more
To all the miseries of life,
Life in captivity

15 the interval between the old and the new moons; during this period the
moon was thought by the ancients to be "vacating" the night in a cave. The
etymologies of "cave" and "vacant" emphasize the "emptiness" of darkness.
16 susceptible (to something harmful).

Among inhuman foes.
But who are these? for with joint pace I hear   110
The tread of many feet stearing this way;
Perhaps my enemies who come to stare
At my affliction, and perhaps to insult,
Thir daily practice to afflict me more.
   Chorus. This, this is he; softly a while,   115
Let us not break in upon him;
O change beyond report, thought, or belief!
See how he lies at random, carelessly diffus'd,[17]
With languish't head unpropt,
As one past hope, abandon'd,   120
And by himself giv'n over;
In slavish habit, ill-fitted weeds
O're worn and soild;
Or do my eyes misrepresent? Can this be hee,
That Heroic, that Renown'd,   125
Irresistible[18] *Samson?* whom unarm'd
No strength of man, or fiercest wild beast could withstand;
Who tore the Lion, as the Lion tears the Kid,[19]
Ran on embattell'd Armies clad in Iron,
And weaponless himself,   130
Made Arms ridiculous, useless the forgery
Of brazen shield and spear, the hammer'd Cuirass,
Chalybean[20] temper'd steel, and frock of mail
Adamantean Proof;
But safest he who stood aloof,   135
When insupportably[21] his foot advanc't,
In scorn of thir proud arms and warlike tools,
Spurn'd them to death by Troops. The bold *Ascalonite*[22]
Fled from his Lion ramp,[23] old Warriors turn'd
Thir plated backs under his heel;   140
Or grovling soild thir crested helmets in the dust.
Then with what trivial[24] weapon came to hand,
The Jaw of a dead Ass, his sword of bone,

[17] spread in all directions.
[18] too powerful to be resisted.
[19] Judges xiv. 5-6: "a young lion roared against him . . . and he rent him as he would have rent a kid, and he had nothing in his hand."
[20] referring to natives of Pontus, on the Black Sea, known for their iron work.
[21] too powerful to be resisted.
[22] Ascalon was a Philistine coastal city; Judges xiv. 19.
[23] rage.
[24] also, "picked up at the crossroads."

A thousand fore-skins[25] fell, the flower of *Palestin*
In *Ramath-lechi* famous to this day: 145
Then by main force pull'd up, and on his shoulders bore
The Gates of *Azza*, Post, and massie Bar
Up to the Hill of *Hebron*, seat of Giants old,
No journey of a Sabbath day, and loaded so;
Like whom the Gentiles feign to bear up Heav'n.[26]   150
Which shall I first bewail,
Thy Bondage or lost Sight,
Prison within Prison
Inseparably dark?
Thou art become (O worst imprisonment!)   155
The Dungeon of thy self; thy Soul
(Which Men enjoying sight oft without cause complain)
Imprison'd now indeed,
In real darkness of the body dwells,
Shut up from outward light   160
T' incorporate with gloomy night;
For inward light alas
Puts forth no visual beam.
O mirror of our fickle state,[27]
Since man on earth unparallel'd!   165
The rarer thy example stands,
By how much from the top of wondrous glory,
Strongest of mortal men,
To lowest pitch of abject fortune thou art fall'n.
For him I reckon not in high estate   170
Whom long descent of birth
Or the sphear of fortune raises;
But thee whose strength, while vertue was her mate,
Might have subdu'd the Earth,
Universally crown'd with highest praises.   175
    Samson. I hear the sound of words, thir sense the air
Dissolves unjointed e're it reach my ear.
    Chorus. Hee speaks, let us draw nigh. Matchless in might,
The glory late of *Israel*, now the grief;
We come thy friends and neighbours not unknown   180

---

[25] uncircumcised Philistines; Judges xv. 15–17. The following exploit is found
in Judges xvi. 3; Azza is a variant of Gaza. The giants are the children of Anak
who were expelled from Hebron by Caleb (Judges i. 20).
[26] Atlas.
[27] example of decline through loss of virtue, l. 173, common to men and
government; Fortune's wheel, l. 172, does not bring true glory.

From *Eshtaol* and *Zora's* fruitful Vale[28]
To visit or bewail thee, or if better,
Counsel or Consolation we may bring,
Salve to thy Sores; apt words have power to swage
The tumors[29] of a troubl'd mind,   185
And are as Balm to fester'd wounds.
    Samson. Your coming, Friends, revives me, for I learn
Now of my own experience, not by talk,
How counterfeit a coin they are who friends
Bear in their Superscription[30] (of the most   190
I would be understood): in prosperous days
They swarm, but in adverse withdraw their head
Not to be found, though sought. Yee see, O friends,
How many evils have enclos'd me round;
Yet that which was the worst now least afflicts me,   195
Blindness, for had I sight, confus'd with shame,
How could I once look up, or heave the head,
Who like a foolish Pilot have shipwrack't
My Vessel trusted to me from above,
Gloriously rigg'd; and for a word, a tear,   200
Fool, have divulg'd the secret gift of God
To a deceitful Woman: tell me Friends,
Am I not sung and proverb'd for a Fool
In every street, do they not say, how well
Are come upon him his deserts? yet why?   205
Immeasurable strength they might behold
In me, of wisdom nothing more then mean;
This with the other should, at least, have paird,[31]
These two proportiond ill drove me transverse.[32]
    Chorus. Tax not divine disposal, wisest Men   210
Have err'd, and by bad Women been deceiv'd;
And shall again, pretend they ne're so wise.
Deject not then so overmuch thy self,
Who hast of sorrow thy full load besides;
Yet truth to say, I oft have heard men wonder   215
Why thou shouldst wed *Philistian* women rather
Then of thine own Tribe fairer, or as fair,
At least of thy own Nation, and as noble.

---

[28] cities from which Manoah came in the coastal valley of Sorec (l. 229).
[29] meaning "swellings," the word connotes the exaggeration or preoccupation arising from psychological disorder.
[30] an inscription on a coin.
[31] been equal.
[32] to thwart my intended use to God.

Samson. The first I saw at *Timna*,[33] and she pleas'd
Mee, not my Parents, that I sought to wed,   220
The daughter of an Infidel: they knew not
That what I motion'd was of God; I knew
From intimate impulse, and therefore urg'd
The Marriage on; that by occasion hence
I might begin *Israel's* Deliverance,   225
The work to which I was divinely call'd;
She proving false, the next I took to Wife
(O that I never had! fond wish too late)
Was in the Vale of *Sorec, Dalila,*
That specious Monster, my accomplisht snare.   230
I thought it lawful from my former act,
And the same end; still watching to oppress
Israel's oppressours: of what now I suffer
She was not the prime cause, but I my self,
Who vanquisht with a peal[34] of words (O weakness!)   235
Gave up my fort of silence to a Woman.
    Chorus. In seeking just occasion to provoke
The *Philistine*, thy Countries Enemy,
Thou never wast remiss, I bear thee witness:
Yet *Israel* still serves with all his Sons.[35]   240
    Samson. That fault I take not on me, but transfer
On *Israel's* Governours, and Heads of Tribes,
Who seeing those great acts which God had done
Singly by me against their Conquerours
Acknowledg'd not, or not at all consider'd   245
Deliverance offerd: I on th' other side
Us'd no ambition to commend my deeds,[36]
The deeds themselves, though mute, spoke loud the dooer;
But they persisted deaf, and would not seem
To count them things worth notice, till at length   250
Thir Lords the *Philistines* with gather'd powers
Enterd *Judea* seeking mee, who then
Safe to the rock of *Etham* was retir'd,
Not flying, but fore-casting in what place
To set upon them, what advantag'd best;   255
Mean while the men of *Judah* to prevent
The harrass of thir Land, beset me round;
I willingly on some conditions came

---

33 See Judges xiv. 1–4; his association with Dalila is told in Judges xvi. 4 ff.
34 a volley (as of gunfire).
35 The Israelites are still subjugated by the Philistines.
36 I did not walk about soliciting commendation for my deeds.

Into thir hands, and they as gladly yield me
To the uncircumcis'd a welcom prey,   260
Bound with two cords; but cords to me were threds
Toucht with the flame: on thir whole Host I flew
Unarm'd, and with a trivial weapon fell'd
Their choicest youth; they only liv'd who fled.
Had *Judah* that day join'd, or one whole Tribe,   265
They had by this possess'd the Towers of *Gath*,[37]
And lorded over them whom now they serve;
But what more oft in Nations grown corrupt,
And by thir vices brought to servitude,
Then to love Bondage more then Liberty,   270
Bondage with ease then strenuous liberty;[38]
And to despise, or envy, or suspect
Whom God hath of his special favour rais'd
As thir Deliverer; if he aught begin,
How frequent to desert him, and at last   275
To heap ingratitude on worthiest deeds?
  Chorus. Thy words to my remembrance bring
How *Succoth* and the Fort of *Penuel*
This great Deliverer contemn'd,
The matchless *Gideon* in pursuit   280
Of *Madian* and her vanquisht Kings:[39]
And how ingrateful *Ephraim*
Had dealt with *Jephtha*, who by argument,
Not worse then by his shield and spear
Defended *Israel* from the *Ammonite*,   285
Had not his prowess quell'd thir pride
In that sore battel when so many dy'd
Without Reprieve adjudg'd to death,
For want of well pronouncing *Shibboleth*.[40]
  Samson. Of such examples add mee to the roul,   290
Mee easily indeed mine[41] may neglect,
But Gods propos'd deliverance not so.
  Chorus. Just are the ways of God,[42]

---

[37] a principal city of Philistia, standing for the whole.
[38] Compare Mammon's words in *PL* II, 255–57.
[39] The cities of Succoth and Penuel refused to help the Hebrew general
Gideon when he was pursuing the kings of Midian (Judges vii. 4–9).
[40] Judges xi. 12–23, xii. 1–6. The Ephraimites were detected and slain by
Jephthah's Gileadites when they could not pronounce the first syllable of "Shib-
boleth" correctly.
[41] my nation.
[42] Rev. xv. 3: "And they sing the song of Moses the servant of God, and the

And justifiable to Men;
Unless there be who think not God at all, 295
If any be, they walk obscure;[43]
For of such Doctrine never was there School,
But the heart of the Fool,[44]
And no man therein Doctor but himself.

    Yet more there be who doubt his ways not just, 300
As to his own edicts, found contradicting,
Then give the rains to wandring thought,
Regardless of his glories diminution;
Till by thir own perplexities involv'd
They ravel more, still less resolv'd, 305
But never find self-satisfying solution.

    As if they would confine th' interminable,
And tie him to his own prescript,
Who made our Laws to bind us, not himself,
And hath full right t' exempt 310
Whom so it pleases him by choice
From National obstriction,[45] without taint
Of sin, or legal debt;
For with his own Laws he can best dispence.

    He would not else who never wanted means, 315
Nor in respect of th' enemy just cause
To set his people free,
Have prompted this Heroic *Nazarite*,
Against his vow of strictest purity,
To seek in marriage that fallacious[46] Bride, 320
Unclean, unchaste.

    Down[47] Reason then, at least vain reasonings down,
Though Reason here aver
That moral verdit quits her of unclean:
Unchaste was subsequent, her stain not his. 325

    But see here comes thy reverend Sire
With careful[48] step, Locks white as doune,
Old *Manoah*: advise[49]

---

song of the Lamb, saying, Great and marvellous are thy works, Lord, God Almighty; just and true are thy ways, thou King of saints."
[43] both "unknown" and "in the darkness of ignorance."
[44] Psalms xiv. 1: "The fool hath said in his heart, There is no God."
[45] the obligation of the Israelites not to marry outside their nation.
[46] deceitful.
[47] subordinate (to faith and revelation).
[48] full of concern.
[49] consider.

Forthwith how thou oughtst to receive him.
 Samson. Ay me, another inward grief awak't,   330
With mention of that name renews th' assault.
 Manoa. Brethren and men of *Dan,* for such ye seem,
Though in this uncouth[50] place; if old respect,
As I suppose, towards your once gloried friend,
My Son now Captive, hither hath inform'd[51]   335
Your younger feet, while mine cast back with age
Came lagging after; say if he be here.
 Chorus. As signal[52] now in low dejected state,
As earst in highest, behold him where he lies.
 Manoa. O miserable change! is this the man,   340
That invincible *Samson,* far renown'd,
The dread of *Israel's* foes, who with a strength
Equivalent to Angels walk'd thir streets,
None offering fight; who single combatant
Duell'd thir Armies rank't in proud array,   345
Himself an Army, now unequal match
To save himself against a coward arm'd
At one spears length. O ever failing trust
In mortal strength! and oh what not in man
Deceivable and vain! Nay what thing good   350
Pray'd for, but often proves our woe, our bane?
I pray'd for Children, and thought barrenness
In wedlock a reproach; I gain'd a Son,
And such a Son as all Men hail'd me happy;
Who would be now a Father in my stead?   355
O wherefore did God grant me my request,
And as a blessing with such pomp adorn'd?
Why are his gifts desirable, to tempt
Our earnest Prayers, then giv'n with solemn hand
As Graces, draw a Scorpions tail behind?   360
For this did th' Angel twice descend? for this
Ordain'd thy nurture holy, as of a Plant;
Select, and Sacred, Glorious for a while,
The miracle of men: then in an hour
Ensnar'd, assaulted, overcome, led bound,   365
Thy Foes derision, Captive, Poor, and Blind
Into a Dungeon thrust, to work with Slaves?
Alas methinks whom God hath chosen once

[50] strange.
[51] directed.
[52] That is, indicative of his present low state, he is lying down.

To worthiest deeds, if he through frailty err,
He should not so o'rewhelm, and as a thrall 370
Subject him to so foul indignities,
Be it but for honours sake of former deeds.
   Samson. Appoint[53] not heav'nly disposition, Father,
Nothing of all these evils hath befall'n me
But justly; I my self have brought them on, 375
Sole Author I, sole cause: if aught seem vile,
As vile hath been my folly, who have profan'd[54]
The mystery of God giv'n me under pledge
Of vow, and have betray'd it to a woman,
A *Canaanite*, my faithless enemy. 380
This well I knew, nor was at all surpris'd,
But warn'd by oft experience: did not she
Of *Timna* first betray me, and reveal
The secret[55] wrested from me in her highth
Of Nuptial Love profest, carrying it strait 385
To them who had corrupted her, my Spies,
And Rivals? In this other was there found
More Faith? who also in her prime of love,
Spousal embraces, vitiated with Gold,
Though offer'd only, by the scent conceiv'd 390
Her spurious first-born; Treason against me?
Thrice she assay'd with flattering prayers and sighs,
And amorous reproaches to win from me
My capital[56] secret, in what part my strength
Lay stor'd, in what part summ'd, that she might know: 395
Thrice I deluded her, and turn'd to sport
Her importunity, each time perceiving
How openly, and with what impudence
She purpos'd to betray me, and (which was worse
Then undissembl'd hate) with what contempt 400
She sought to make me Traytor to my self;
Yet the fourth time, when mustring all her wiles,
With blandisht parlies, feminine assaults,
Tongue-batteries, she surceas'd not day nor night
To storm me over-watch't,[57] and wearied out. 405
At times when men seek most repose and rest,
I yielded, and unlock'd her all my heart,

[53] arraign.
[54] impiously revealed.
[55] the answer to Samson's riddle (Judges xiv. 12–18).
[56] "major," "fatal," and connected with the head.
[57] tired from being vigilant.

Who with a grain of manhood well resolv'd
Might easily have shook off all her snares:
But foul effeminacy held me yok't   410
Her Bond-slave; O indignity, O blot
To Honour and Religion! servil mind
Rewarded well with servil punishment!
The base degree to which I now am fall'n,
These rags, this grinding, is not yet so base   415
As was my former servitude, ignoble,
Unmanly, ignominious, infamous,
True slavery, and that blindness worse then this,
That saw not how degeneratly I serv'd.

    Manoa. I cannot praise thy Marriage choises, Son,   420
Rather approv'd them not; but thou didst plead
Divine impulsion prompting how thou might'st
Find some occasion to infest our Foes.
I state not that; this I am sure; our Foes
Found soon occasion thereby to make thee   425
Thir Captive, and thir triumph; thou the sooner
Temptation found'st, or over-potent charms
To violate the sacred trust of silence
Deposited within thee; which t' have kept
Tacit, was in thy power; true; and thou bear'st   430
Enough, and more the burden of that fault;
Bitterly hast thou paid, and still art paying
That rigid score. A worse thing yet remains,
This day the *Philistines* a popular Feast
Here celebrate in *Gaza;* and proclaim   435
Great Pomp, and Sacrifice, and Praises loud
To *Dagon,* as their God who hath deliver'd
Thee *Samson,* bound and blind into thir hands,
Them out of thine, who slew'st them many a slain.
So *Dagon* shall be magnifi'd, and God,   440
Besides whom is no God, compar'd with Idols,
Disglorifi'd, blasphem'd, and had in scorn
By th' Idolatrous rout amidst thir wine;
Which to have come to pass by means of thee,
Samson, of all thy sufferings think the heaviest,   445
Of all reproach the most with shame that ever
Could have befall'n thee and thy Fathers house.
    Samson. Father, I do acknowledge and confess
That I this honour, I this pomp have brought
To *Dagon,* and advanc'd his praises high   450
Among the Heathen round; to God have brought

Dishonour, obloquie, and op't the mouths
Of Idolists, and Atheists; have brought scandal
To *Israel*, diffidence[58] of God, and doubt
In feeble hearts, propense anough before   455
To waver, or fall off and joyn with Idols;
Which is my chief affliction, shame and sorrow,
The anguish of my Soul, that suffers not
Mine eie to harbour sleep, or thoughts to rest.
This only hope relieves me, that the strife   460
With me hath end; all the contest is now
'Twixt God and *Dagon; Dagon* hath presum'd,
Me overthrown, to enter lists with God,
His Deity comparing and preferring
Before the God of *Abraham*. He, be sure,   465
Will not connive,[59] or linger, thus provok'd,
But will arise and his great name assert:
Dagon must stoop, and shall e're long receive
Such a discomfit, as shall quite despoil him
Of all these boasted Trophies won on me,   470
And with confusion blank his Worshippers.
    Manoa. With cause this hope relieves thee, and these words
I as a Prophecy receive: for God,
Nothing more certain, will not long defer
To vindicate the glory of his name   475
Against all competition, nor will long
Endure it, doubtful whether God be Lord,
Or *Dagon*. But for thee what shall be done?
Thou must not in the mean while here forgot
Lie in this miserable loathsom plight   480
Neglected. I already have made way
To some *Philistian* Lords, with whom to treat
About thy ransom: well they may by this
Have satisfi'd thir utmost of revenge
By pains and slaveries, worse then death inflicted   485
On thee, who now no more canst do them harm.
    Samson. Spare that proposal, Father, spare the trouble
Of that sollicitation; let me here,
As I deserve, pay on my punishment;
And expiate, if possible, my crime,   490
Shameful garrulity. To have reveal'd
Secrets of men, the secrets of a friend,

---

58 distrust.
59 shut his eyes.

How hainous had the fact been, how deserving
Contempt, and scorn of all, to be excluded
All friendship, and avoided as a blab, 495
The mark of fool set on his front![60] But I
Gods counsel have not kept, his holy secret
Presumptuously have publish'd, impiously,
Weakly at least, and shamefully: A sin
That Gentiles in thir Parables condemn 500
To thir abyss and horrid pains confin'd.[61]
   Manoa. Be penitent and for thy fault contrite,
But act not in thy own affliction, Son;
Repent the sin, but if the punishment
Thou canst avoid, self-preservation bids; 505
Or th' execution leave to high disposal,
And let another hand, not thine, exact
Thy penal forfeit from thy self; perhaps
God will relent, and quit thee all his debt;
Who evermore approves and more accepts 510
(Best pleas'd with humble and filial submission)
Him who imploring mercy sues for life,
Then who self-rigorous chooses death as due;
Which argues over-just, and self-displeas'd
For self-offence, more then for God offended. 515
Reject not then what offerd means, who knows
But God hath set before us, to return thee
Home to thy countrey and his sacred house,
Where thou mayst bring thy off'rings, to avert
His further ire, with praiers and vows renew'd. 520
   Samson. His pardon I implore; but as for life,
To what end should I seek it? when in strength
All mortals I excell'd, and great in hopes
With youthful courage and magnanimous[62] thoughts
Of birth from Heav'n foretold and high exploits, 525
Full of divine instinct, after some proof
Of acts indeed heroic, far beyond
The Sons of *Anac*, famous now and blaz'd,
Fearless of danger, like a petty God
I walk'd about admir'd of all and dreaded 530
On hostile ground, none daring my affront.
Then swoll'n with pride into the snare I fell

[60] forehead.
[61] referring to Tantalus who had divulged the secrets of the gods.
[62] heroic for God's greater glory.

Of fair fallacious looks, venereal trains,[63]
Soft'n'd with pleasure and voluptuous life;
At length to lay my head and hallow'd pledge   535
Of all my strength in the lascivious lap
Of a deceitful Concubine who shore me
Like a tame Weather, all my precious fleece,
Then turn'd me out ridiculous, despoil'd,
Shav'n, and disarm'd among my enemies.   540
    Chorus. Desire of wine and all delicious drinks,
Which many a famous Warriour overturns,
Thou couldst repress, nor did the dancing Rubie
Sparkling, out-pow'rd, the flavor, or the smell,
Or taste that cheers the heart of Gods and men,   545
Allure thee from the cool Crystalline stream.
    Samson. Where ever fountain or fresh current flow'd
Against the Eastern ray, translucent, pure,
With touch ætherial of Heav'ns fiery rod
I drank, from the clear milkie juice[64] allaying   550
Thirst, and refresht; nor envy'd them the grape
Whose heads that turbulent liquor fills with fumes.
    Chorus. O madness, to think use of strongest wines
And strongest drinks our chief support of health,
When God with these forbid'n made choice to rear   555
His mighty Champion, strong above compare,
Whose drink was only from the liquid brook.
    Samson. But what avail'd this temperance, not compleat
Against another object more enticing?
What boots it at one gate to make defence,   560
And at another to let in the foe
Effeminatly vanquish't? by which means,
Now blind, disheart'n'd, sham'd, dishonour'd, quell'd,
To what can I be useful, wherein serve
My Nation, and the work from Heav'n impos'd,   565
But to sit idle on the houshold hearth,
A burdenous drone; to visitants a gaze,
Or pitied object, these redundant locks
Robustious to no purpose clustring down,
Vain monument of strength; till length of years   570
And sedentary numness craze[65] my limbs
To a contemptible old age obscure.

---

[63] tricks of love (from Venus).
[64] fresh water.
[65] weaken.

Here rather let me drudge and earn my bread,
Till vermin or the draff[66] of servil food
Consume me, and oft-invocated death   575
Hast'n the welcom end of all my pains.
    Manoa. Wilt thou then serve the *Philistines* with that gift
Which was expresly giv'n thee to annoy them?
Better at home lie bed-rid, not only idle,
Inglorious, unimploy'd, with age out-worn.   580
But God who caus'd a fountain at thy prayer
From the dry ground to spring,[67] thy thirst t' allay
After the brunt of battel, can as easie
Cause light again within thy eies to spring,
Wherewith to serve him better then thou hast;   585
And I perswade me so; why else his strength
Miraculous yet remaining in those locks?
His might continues in thee not for naught,
Nor shall his wondrous gifts be frustrate thus.
    Samson. All otherwise to me my thoughts portend,   590
That these dark orbs no more shall treat with light,
Nor th' other light of life continue long,
But yield to double darkness nigh at hand:
So much I feel my genial[68] spirits droop,
My hopes all flat, nature within me seems   595
In all her functions weary of her self;
My race of glory run, and race of shame,
And I shall shortly be with them that rest.
    Manoa. Believe not these suggestions which proceed
From anguish of the mind and humours black,[69]   600
That mingle with thy fancy. I however
Must not omit a Fathers timely care
To prosecute the means of thy deliverance
By ransom or how else: mean while be calm,
And healing words from these thy friends admit.   605
    Samson. O that torment should not be confin'd
To the bodies wounds and sores
With maladies innumerable
In heart, head, brest, and reins;
But must secret passage find   610
To th' inmost mind,

[66] refuse or offal.
[67] at Ramath-lechi (Judges xv. 18–19).
[68] natural.
[69] melancholy.

There exercise all his fierce accidents,[70]
And on her purest spirits prey,
As on entrails, joints, and limbs,
With answerable pains, but more intense,   615
Though void of corporal sense.
    My griefs not only pain me
As a lingring disease,
But finding no redress, ferment and rage,
Nor less then wounds immedicable   620
Ranckle, and fester, and gangrene,
To black mortification.
Thoughts my Tormentors arm'd with deadly stings
Mangle my apprehensive tenderest parts,[71]
Exasperate, exulcerate, and raise   625
Dire inflammation which no cooling herb
Or medcinal liquor can asswage,
Nor breath of Vernal Air from snowy *Alp*.
Sleep hath forsook and giv'n me o're
To deaths benumming Opium as my only cure.   630
Thence faintings, swounings of despair,
And sense of Heav'ns desertion.
    I was his nursling once and choice delight,
His destin'd from the womb,
Promisd by Heav'nly message twice descending.   635
Under his special eie
Abstemious I grew up and thriv'd amain;
He led me on to mightiest deeds
Above the nerve of mortal arm
Against th' uncircumcis'd, our enemies.   640
But now hath cast me off as never known,
And to those cruel enemies,
Whom I by his appointment had provok't,
Left me all helpless with th' irreparable loss
Of sight, reserv'd alive to be repeated   645
The subject of thir cruelty, or scorn.
Nor am I in the list of them that hope;
Hopeless are all my evils, all remediless;
This one prayer yet remains, might I be heard,
No long petition, speedy death,   650
The close of all my miseries, and the balm.
    Chorus. Many are the sayings of the wise

[70] symptoms.
[71] the mind and the senses.

In antient and in modern books enroll'd;
Extolling Patience as the truest fortitude;
And to the bearing well of all calamities,   655
All chances incident to mans frail life
Consolatories writ
With studied argument, and much perswasion sought
Lenient[72] of grief and anxious thought,
But with th' afflicted in his pangs thir sound   660
Little prevails, or rather seems a tune,
Harsh, and of dissonant mood from his complaint,
Unless he feel within
Some sourse of consolation from above;
Secret refreshings, that repair his strength,   665
And fainting spirits uphold.
    God of our Fathers, what is man!
That thou towards him with hand so various,
Or might I say contrarious,
Temperst thy providence through his short course,   670
Not ev'nly, as thou rul'st
Th' Angelic orders and inferiour creatures mute,
Irrational and brute.
Nor do I name of men the common rout,
That wandring loose about   675
Grow up and perish, as the summer flie,
Heads without name no more rememberd,
But such as thou hast solemnly elected,
With gifts and graces eminently adorn'd
To some great work, thy glory,   680
And peoples safety, which in part they effect:
Yet toward these thus dignifi'd, thou oft
Amidst thir highth of noon,
Changest thy countenance, and thy hand with no regard
Of highest favours past   685
From thee on them, or them to thee of service.
    Nor only dost degrade them, or remit
To life obscur'd, which were a fair dismission,
But throw'st them lower then thou didst exalt them high,
Unseemly falls in human eie,   690
Too grievous for the trespass or omission,
Oft leav'st them to the hostile sword
Of Heathen and prophane, thir carkasses
To dogs and fowls a prey, or else captiv'd:

[72] soothing.

Or to th' unjust tribunals, under change of times,   695
And condemnation of th' ingrateful multitude.
If these they scape, perhaps in poverty
With sickness and disease thou bow'st them down,
Painful diseases and deform'd,
In crude[73] old age;   700
Though not disordinate, yet causless suffring
The punishment of dissolute days, in fine,
Just or unjust, alike seem miserable,
For oft alike, both come to evil end.
        So deal not with this once thy glorious Champion,   705
The Image of thy strength, and mighty minister.
What do I beg? how hast thou dealt already?
Behold him in this state calamitous, and turn
His labours, for thou canst, to peaceful end.
        But who is this, what thing of Sea or Land?   710
Femal of sex it seems,
That so bedeckt, ornate, and gay,
Comes this way sailing
Like a stately Ship
Of *Tarsus*, bound for th' Isles   715
Of *Javan* or *Gadier*[74]
With all her bravery on, and tackle trim,
Sails fill'd, and streamers waving,
Courted by all the winds that hold them play,
An Amber[75] scent of odorous perfume   720
Her harbinger, a damsel train behind;
Some rich *Philistian* Matron she may seem,
And now at nearer view, no other certain
Then *Dalila* thy wife.
        Samson. My Wife, my Traytress, let her not come near me. 725
        Chorus. Yet on she moves, now stands and eies thee fixt,
About t' have spoke, but now, with head declin'd
Like a fair flower surcharg'd with dew, she weeps
And words addrest seem into tears dissolv'd,
Wetting the borders of her silk'n veil: 730
But now again she makes address to speak.
        Dalila. With doubtful feet and wavering resolution
I came, still dreading thy displeasure, *Samson*,

[73] premature.
[74] Tarsus (now an area of Turkey) is here identified with the proud Biblical Tarshish; the isles of Noah's grandson are the isles of Greece, and Gadier is Cadiz. The ship was frequently used as a symbol of prostitution.
[75] ambergris.

Which to have merited, without excuse,
I cannot but acknowledge; yet if tears   735
May expiate (though the fact more evil drew
In the perverse event then I foresaw)
My penance hath not slack'n'd, though my pardon
No way assur'd. But conjugal affection
Prevailing over fear, and timerous doubt   740
Hath led me on desirous to behold
Once more thy face, and know of thy estate,
If aught in my ability may serve
To light'n what thou suffer'st, and appease
Thy mind with what amends is in my power,   745
Though late, yet in some part to recompense
My rash but more unfortunate misdeed.
    Samson. Out, out Hyæna;[76] these are thy wonted arts,
And arts of every woman false like thee,
To break all faith, all vows, deceive, betray,   750
Then as repentant to submit, beseech,
And reconcilement move[77] with feign'd remorse,
Confess, and promise wonders in her change,
Not truly penitent, but chief to try
Her husband, how far urg'd his patience bears,   755
His vertue or weakness which way t' assail:
Then with more cautious and instructed skill
Again transgresses, and again submits;
That wisest and best men full oft beguil'd
With goodness principl'd not to reject   760
The penitent, but ever to forgive,
Are drawn to wear out miserable days,
Entangl'd with a poysnous bosom snake,
If not by quick destruction soon cut off
As I by thee, to Ages an example.   765
    Dalila. Yet hear me *Samson;* not that I endeavour
To lessen or extenuate my offence,
But that on th' other side if it be weigh'd
By it self, with aggravations not surcharg'd,
Or else with just allowance counterpois'd,   770
I may, if possible, thy pardon find
The easier towards me, or thy hatred less.
First granting, as I do, it was a weakness

---

[76] The hyena was supposed to entice men by imitating man's voice in order
to devour them.
[77] propose.

In me, but incident to all our sex,
Curiosity, inquisitive, importune   775
Of secrets, then with like infirmity
To publish them, both common female faults:
Was it not weakness also to make known
For importunity, that is for naught,
Wherein consisted all thy strength and safety?   780
To what I did thou shewdst me first the way.
But I to enemies reveal'd, and should not.
Nor shouldst thou have trusted that to womans frailty:
E're I to thee, thou to thy self wast cruel.
Let weakness then with weakness come to parl   785
So near related, or the same of kind,
Thine forgive mine; that men may censure thine
The gentler, if severely thou exact not
More strength from me, then in thy self was found.
And what if Love, which thou interpret'st hate,   790
The jealousie of Love, powerful of sway
In human hearts, nor less in mine towards thee,
Caus'd what I did? I saw thee mutable
Of fancy, feard lest one day thou wouldst leave me
As her at *Timna*, sought by all means therefore   795
How to endear, and hold thee to me firmest:
No better way I saw then by importuning
To learn thy secrets, get into my power
Thy key of strength and safety: thou wilt say,
Why then reveal'd? I was assur'd by those   800
Who tempted me, that nothing was design'd
Against thee but safe custody, and hold:
That made for me, I knew that liberty
Would draw thee forth to perilous enterprises,
While I at home sate full of cares and fears   805
Wailing thy absence in my widow'd bed;
Here I should still enjoy thee day and night
Mine and Loves prisoner, not the *Philistines*,
Whole to my self, unhazarded abroad,
Fearless at home of partners in my love.   810
These reasons in Loves law have past for good,
Though fond and reasonless to some perhaps;
And Love hath oft, well meaning, wrought much wo,
Yet always pity or pardon hath obtain'd.
Be not unlike all others, not austere   815
As thou art strong, inflexible as steel.
If thou in strength all mortals dost exceed,

In uncompassionate anger do not so.
   Samson. How cunningly the sorceress displays
Her own transgressions, to upbraid me mine!   820
That malice not repentance brought thee hither,
By this appears: I gave, thou say'st, th' example,
I led the way; bitter reproach, but true,
I to my self was false e're thou to me;
Such pardon therefore as I give my folly,   825
Take to thy wicked deed: which when thou seest
Impartial, self-severe, inexorable,
Thou wilt renounce thy seeking, and much rather
Confess it feign'd, weakness is thy excuse,
And I believe it. Weakness to resist   830
Philistian gold: if weakness may excuse,
What Murtherer, what Traytor, Parricide,
Incestuous, Sacrilegious, but may plead it?
All wickedness is weakness: that plea therefore
With God or Man will gain thee no remission.   835
But Love constrain'd thee; call it furious rage
To satisfie thy lust: Love seeks to have Love;
My love how couldst thou hope, who tookst the way
To raise in me inexpiable hate,
Knowing, as needs I must, by thee betray'd?   840
In vain thou striv'st to cover shame with shame,
Or by evasions thy crime uncoverst more.
   Dalila. Since thou determinst weakness for no plea
In man or woman, though to thy own condemning,
Hear what assaults I had, what snares besides,   845
What sieges girt me round, e're I consented;
Which might have aw'd the best resolv'd of men,
The constantest t' have yielded without blame.
It was not gold, as to my charge thou lay'st,
That wrought with me: thou know'st the Magistrates   850
And Princes of my countrey came in person,
Sollicited, commanded, threat'n'd, urg'd,
Adjur'd by all the bonds of civil Duty
And of Religion, press'd how just it was,
How honourable, how glorious to entrap   855
A common enemy, who had destroy'd
Such numbers of our Nation: and the Priest
Was not behind, but ever at my ear,
Preaching how meritorious with the gods
It would be to ensnare an irreligious   860
Dishonourer of *Dagon:* what had I

T' oppose against such powerful arguments?
Only my love of thee held long debate;
And combated in silence all these reasons
With hard contest: at length that grounded maxim 865
So rife and celebrated in the mouths
Of wisest men; that to the public good
Private respects must yield; with grave authority
Took full possession of me and prevail'd;
Vertue, as I thought, truth, duty so enjoyning. 870
   Samson. I thought where all thy circling wiles would end;
In feign'd Religion, smooth hypocrisie.
But had thy love, still odiously pretended,
Bin, as it ought, sincere, it would have taught thee
Far other reasonings, brought forth other deeds. 875
I before all the daughters of my Tribe
And of my Nation chose thee from among
My enemies, lov'd thee, as too well thou knew'st,
Too well, unbosom'd all my secrets to thee,
Not only of levity, but over-power'd 880
By thy request, who could deny thee nothing;
Yet now am judg'd an enemy. Why then
Didst thou at first receive me for thy husband?
Then, as since then, thy countries foe profest:
Being once a wife, for me thou wast to leave 885
Parents and countrey; nor was I their subject,
Nor under their protection but my own,
Thou mine, not theirs: if aught against my life
Thy countrey sought of thee, it sought unjustly,
Against the law of nature, law of nations, 890
No more thy countrey, but an impious crew
Of men conspiring to uphold thir state
By worse then hostile deeds, violating th' ends
For which our countrey is a name so dear;
Not therefore to be obey'd. But zeal mov'd thee; 895
To please thy gods thou didst it; gods unable
To acquit themselves and prosecute their foes
But by ungodly deeds, the contradiction
Of their own deity, Gods cannot be:
Less therefore to be pleas'd, obey'd, or fear'd; 900
These false pretexts and varnish'd colours failing,
Bare in thy guilt how foul must thou appear!
   Dalila. In argument with men a woman ever
Goes by the worse, whatever be her cause.
   Samson. For want of words no doubt, or lack of breath, 905

Witness when I was worried with thy peals.[78]
   Dalila. I was a fool, too rash, and quite mistaken
In what I thought would have succeeded best.
Let me obtain forgiveness of thee, *Samson*,
Afford me place to shew what recompence   910
Towards thee I intend for what I have misdone,
Misguided; only what remains past cure
Bear not too sensibly,[79] nor still insist
T' afflict thy self in vain: though sight be lost,
Life yet hath many solaces, enjoy'd   915
Where other senses want[80] not their delights
At home in leisure and domestic ease,
Exempt from many a care and chance to which
Eye-sight exposes daily men abroad.
I to the Lords will intercede, not doubting   920
Thir favourable ear, that I may fetch thee
From forth this loathsom prison-house, t' abide
With me, where my redoubl'd love and care
With nursing diligence, to me glad office,
May ever tend about thee to old age   925
With all things grateful chear'd, and so suppli'd,
That what by me thou hast lost thou least shalt miss.
   Samson. No, no, of my condition take no care;
It fits not; thou and I long since are twain;
Nor think me so unwary or accurst   930
To bring my feet again into the snare
Where once I have been caught; I know thy trains
Though dearly to my cost, thy ginns, and toyls;[81]
Thy fair enchanted cup, and warbling charms
No more on me have power, their force is null'd,   935
So much of Adders wisdom I have learn't[82]
To fence my ear against thy sorceries.
If in my flower of youth and strength, when all men
Lov'd, honour'd, fear'd me, thou alone could hate me
Thy Husband, slight me, sell me, and forgo me;   940
How wouldst thou use me now, blind, and thereby
Deceiveable, in most things as a child
Helpless, thence easily contemn'd, and scorn'd,

[78] volleys of words (as of gunfire).
[79] passionately, sensitively.
[80] lack.
[81] snares, and nets to trap game.
[82] Adders were proverbially deaf, but Samson also means his knowledge now
of evil. Satan is called an adder in *PL* IX, 625.

And last neglected? How wouldst thou insult
When I must live uxorious to thy will   945
In perfet thraldom, how again betray me,
Bearing my words and doings to the Lords
To gloss upon, and censuring, frown or smile?
This Gaol I count the house of Liberty
To thine whose doors my feet shall never enter.   950
    Dalila. Let me approach at least, and touch thy hand.
    Samson. Not for thy life, lest fierce remembrance wake
My sudden rage to tear thee joint by joint.
At distance I forgive thee, go with that;
Bewail thy falshood, and the pious works   955
It hath brought forth to make thee memorable
Among illustrious women, faithful wives:
Cherish thy hast'n'd widowhood with the gold
Of Matrimonial treason: so farewel.
    Dalila. I see thou art implacable, more deaf   960
To prayers, then winds and seas, yet winds to seas
Are reconcil'd at length, and Sea to Shore:
Thy anger, unappeasable, still rages,
Eternal tempest never to be calm'd.
Why do I humble thus my self, and suing   965
For peace, reap nothing but repulse and hate?
Bid go with evil omen and the brand
Of infamy upon my name denounc't?
To mix with thy concernments I desist
Henceforth, nor too much disapprove my own.   970
Fame if not double-fac't is double-mouth'd,
And with contrary blast proclaims most deeds,
On both his wings, one black, the other white,
Bears greatest names in his wild aerie flight.
My name perhaps among the Circumcis'd   975
In *Dan,* in *Judah,* and the bordering Tribes,
To all posterity may stand defam'd,
With malediction mention'd, and the blot
Of falshood most unconjugal traduc't.
But in my countrey where I most desire,   980
In *Ecron, Gaza, Asdod,* and in *Gath*[83]
I shall be nam'd among the famousest
Of Women, sung at solemn festivals,
Living and dead recorded, who to save
Her countrey from a fierce destroyer, chose   985

[83] Philistine cities.

Above the faith of wedlock-bands, my tomb
With odours[84] visited and annual flowers,
Not less renown'd then in Mount *Ephraim*,
Jael, who with inhospitable guile
Smote *Sisera* sleeping through the Temples nail'd.[85]   990
Nor shall I count it hainous to enjoy
The public marks of honour and reward
Conferr'd upon me, for the piety
Which to my countrey I was judg'd t' have shewn.
At this who ever envies or repines   995
I leave him to his lot, and like my own.
    Chorus. She's gone, a manifest Serpent by her sting
Discover'd in the end, till now conceal'd.
    Samson. So let her go, God sent her to debase me,
And aggravate my folly who committed   1000
To such a viper his most sacred trust
Of secresie, my safety, and my life.
    Chorus. Yet beauty, though injurious, hath strange power,
After offence returning, to regain
Love once possest, nor can be easily   1005
Repuls't, without much inward passion felt
And secret sting of amorous remorse.
    Samson. Love-quarrels oft in pleasing concord end,
Not wedlock-trechery endangering life.
    Chorus. It is not vertue, wisdom, valour, wit,   1010
Strength, comliness of shape, or amplest merit
That womans love can win or long inherit;[86]
But what it is, hard is to say,
Harder to hit,
(Which way soever men refer it)   1015
Much like thy riddle, *Samson*, in one day
Or seven, though one should musing sit;
    If any of these or all, the *Timnian* bride
Had not so soon preferr'd
Thy Paranymph,[87] worthless to thee compar'd,   1020
Successour in thy bed,
Nor both so loosly disally'd
Thir nuptials, nor this last so trecherously
Had shorn the fatal harvest of thy head.

[84] spices burnt in ritual offerings.
[85] Jael struck a nail through the temples of the Canaanite leader Sisera (Judges v. 24–27).
[86] possess.
[87] Best Man, at a wedding.

Is it for that such outward ornament   1025
Was lavish't on thir Sex, that inward gifts
Were left for hast unfinish't, judgment scant,
Capacity not rais'd to apprehend
Or value what is best
In choice, but oftest to affect[88] the wrong?   1030
Or was too much of self-love mixt,
Of constancy no root infixt,
That either they love nothing, or not long?
   What e're it be, to wisest men and best
Seeming at first all heav'nly under virgin veil,   1035
Soft, modest, meek, demure,
Once join'd, the contrary she proves, a thorn
Intestin, far within defensive arms
A cleaving mischief, in his way to vertue
Adverse and turbulent, or by her charms   1040
Draws him awry enslav'd
With dotage, and his sense deprav'd
To folly and shameful deeds which ruin ends.
What Pilot so expert but needs must wreck
Embarqu'd with such a Stears-mate at the Helm?   1045
   Favour'd of Heav'n who finds
One vertuous rarely found,
That in domestic good combines:
Happy that house! his way to peace is smooth:
But vertue which breaks through all opposition,   1050
And all temptation can remove,
Most shines and most is acceptable above.
   Therefore Gods universal Law
Gave to the man despotic power
Over his female in due awe,   1055
Nor from that right to part an hour,
Smile she or lowr:
So shall he least confusion draw
On his whole life, not sway'd
By female usurpation, nor dismay'd.   1060
   But had we best retire, I see a storm?
Samson. Fair days have oft contracted[89] wind and rain.
Chorus. But this another kind of tempest brings.
Samson. Be less abstruse, my riddling days are past.
Chorus. Look now for no inchanting voice, nor fear   1065

---

[88] prefer.
[89] incurred, concentrated in intensity.

The bait of honied words; a rougher tongue
Draws hitherward, I know him by his stride,
The Giant *Harapha* of *Gath*, his look
Haughty as is his pile high-built and proud.
Comes he in peace? what wind hath blown him hither   1070
I less conjecture then when first I saw
The sumptuous *Dalila* floating this way:
His habit carries peace, his brow defiance.
    Samson. Or peace or not, alike to me he comes.
    Chorus. His fraught[90] we soon shall know, he now arrives.   1075
    Harapha. I come not *Samson,* to condole thy chance,[91]
As these perhaps, yet wish it had not been,
Though for no friendly intent. I am of *Gath,*
Men call me *Harapha,* of stock renown'd
As *Og* or *Anak* and the *Emims* old   1080
That *Kiriathaim* held; thou knowst me now
If thou at all art known. Much I have heard
Of thy prodigious might and feats perform'd
Incredible to me, in this displeas'd,
That I was never present on the place   1085
Of those encounters, where we might have tri'd
Each others force in camp or listed field:[92]
And now am come to see of whom such noise
Hath walk'd about, and each limb to survey,
If thy appearance answer loud report.   1090
    Samson. The way to know were not to see but taste.
    Harapha. Dost thou already single[93] me; I thought
Gyves and the Mill had tam'd thee? O that fortune
Had brought me to the field where thou art fam'd
T' have wrought such wonders with an Asses Jaw;   1095
I should have forc'd thee soon wish other arms,
Or left thy carkass where the Ass lay thrown:
So had the glory of Prowess been recover'd
To *Palestine,* won by a *Philistine*
From the unforeskinn'd race, of whom thou bear'st   1100
The highest name for valiant Acts; that honour
Certain t' have won by mortal duel from thee,
I lose, prevented by thy eyes put out.
    Samson. Boast not of what thou wouldst have done, but do
What then thou would'st, thou seest it in thy hand.   1105

[90] cargo, i.e., business.
[91] fate, mishap.
[92] plain of battle or tournament field.
[93] challenge to single combat.

Harapha. To combat with a blind man I disdain,
And thou hast need much washing to be toucht.
   Samson. Such usage as your honourable Lords
Afford me assassinated[94] and betray'd,
Who durst not with thir whole united powers   1110
In fight withstand me single and unarm'd,
Nor in the house with chamber Ambushes
Close-banded durst attaque me, no not sleeping,
Till they had hir'd a woman with their gold
Breaking her Marriage Faith to circumvent me.   1115
Therefore without feign'd shifts let be assign'd
Some narrow place enclos'd, where sight may give thee,
Or rather flight, no great advantage on me;
Then put on all thy gorgeous arms, thy Helmet
And Brigandine[95] of brass, thy broad Habergeon,[96]   1120
Vant-brass and Greves, and Gauntlet,[97] add thy Spear
A Weavers beam,[98] and seven-times-folded shield,
I only with an Oak'n staff will meet thee,
And raise such out-cries on thy clatter'd Iron,
Which long shall not with-hold mee from thy head,   1125
That in a little time while breath remains thee,
Thou oft shalt wish thy self at *Gath* to boast
Again in safety what thou wouldst have done
To *Samson,* but shalt never see *Gath* more.
   Harapha. Thou durst not thus disparage glorious arms   1130
Which greatest Heroes have in battel worn,
Thir ornament and safety, had not spells
And black enchantments, some Magicians Art
Arm'd thee or charm'd thee strong, which thou from Heav'n
Feign'dst at thy birth was giv'n thee in thy hair,   1135
Where strength can least abide, though all thy hairs
Were bristles rang'd like those that ridge the back
Of chaft wild Boars, or ruffl'd Porcupines.
   Samson. I know no Spells, use no forbidden Arts;
My trust is in the living God who gave me   1140
At my Nativity this strength, diffus'd
No less through all my sinews, joints and bones
Then thine, while I preserv'd these locks unshorn,
The pledge of my unviolated vow.

[94] treacherously attacked.
[95] plated body armor.
[96] jacket of mail.
[97] respectively, armor for the forearm, the legs, and the hand.
[98] The staff of Goliath's spear was also like a weaver's beam (1 Sam. xvii. 7).

For proof hereof, if *Dagon* be thy god,   1145
Go to his Temple, invocate his aid
With solemnest devotion, spread before him
How highly it concerns his glory now
To frustrate and dissolve these Magic spells,
Which I to be the power of *Israel's* God   1150
Avow, and challenge *Dagon* to the test,
Offering to combat thee his Champion bold,
With th' utmost of his Godhead seconded:
Then thou shalt see, or rather to thy sorrow
Soon feel, whose God is strongest, thine or mine.   1155
    Harapha. Presume not on thy God, what e're he be,
Thee he regards not, owns not, hath cut off
Quite from his people, and deliver'd up
Into thy Enemies hand, permitted them
To put out both thine eyes, and fetter'd send thee   1160
Into the common Prison, there to grind
Among the Slaves and Asses thy comrades,
As good for nothing else, no better service
With those thy boyst'rous[99] locks, no worthy match
For valour to assail, nor by the sword   1165
Of noble Warriour, so to stain his honour,
But by the Barbers razor best subdu'd.
    Samson. All these indignities, for such they are
From thine,[1] these evils I deserve and more,
Acknowledge them from God inflicted on me   1170
Justly, yet despair not of his final pardon
Whose ear is ever open; and his eye
Gracious to re-admit the suppliant;
In confidence whereof I once again
Defie thee to the trial of mortal fight,   1175
By combat to decide whose god is God,
Thine or whom I with *Israel's* Sons adore.
    Harapha. Fair honour that thou dost thy God, in trusting
He will accept thee to defend his cause,
A Murtherer, a Revolter, and a Robber.   1180
    Samson. Tongue-doughtie Giant, how dost thou prove me these?
    Harapha. Is not thy Nation subject to our Lords?
Thir Magistrates confest it, when they took thee
As a League-breaker and deliver'd bound

---

[99] coarse and strong.
[1] thy people.

Into our hands:[2] for hadst thou not committed   1185
Notorious murder on those thirty men
At *Askalon*, who never did thee harm,
Then like a Robber strip'dst them of thir robes?[3]
The *Philistines*, when thou hadst broke the league,
Went up with armed powers thee only seeking,   1190
To others did no violence nor spoil.
    Samson. Among the Daughters of the *Philistines*
I chose a Wife, which argu'd me no foe;
And in your City held my Nuptial Feast:
But your ill-meaning Politician Lords,   1195
Under pretence of Bridal friends and guests,
Appointed to await me thirty spies,
Who threatning cruel death constrain'd the bride
To wring from me and tell to them my secret,
That solv'd the riddle which I had propos'd.   1200
When I perceiv'd all set on enmity,
As on my enemies, where ever chanc'd,
I us'd hostility, and took thir spoil
To pay my underminers in thir coin.
My Nation was subjected to your Lords.   1205
It was the force of Conquest; force with force
Is well ejected when the Conquer'd can.
But I a private person, whom my Countrey
As a league-breaker gave up bound, presum'd
Single Rebellion and did Hostile Acts.   1210
I was no private but a person rais'd
With strength sufficient and command from Heav'n
To free my Countrey; if their servile minds
Me their Deliverer sent would not receive,
But to thir Masters gave me up for nought,   1215
Th' unworthier they; whence to this day they serve.
I was to do my part from Heav'n assign'd,
And had perform'd it if my known offence
Had not disabl'd me, not all your force:
These shifts refuted, answer thy appellant   1220
Though by his blindness maim'd for high attempts,
Who now defies thee thrice to single fight,
As a petty enterprise of small enforce.
    Harapha. With thee a Man condemn'd, a Slave enrol'd,
Due by the Law to capital punishment?   1225

[2] See ll. 256–64.
[3] See Judges xiv. 19.

To fight with thee no man of arms will deign.

    Samson. Cam'st thou for this, vain boaster, to survey me,
To descant on my strength, and give thy verdit?
Come nearer, part not hence so slight inform'd;
But take good heed my hand survey not thee.   1230

    Harapha. O *Baal-zebub!*[4] can my ears unus'd
Hear these dishonours, and not render death?

    Samson. No man with-holds thee, nothing from thy hand
Fear I incurable; bring up thy van,[5]
My heels are fetter'd, but my fist is free.   1235

    Harapha. This insolence other kind of answer fits.

    Samson. Go baffl'd[6] coward, lest I run upon thee,
Though in these chains, bulk without spirit vast,
And with one buffet lay thy structure low,
Or swing thee in the Air, then dash thee down   1240
To th' hazard of thy brains and shatter'd sides.

    Harapha. By *Astaroth*[7] e're long thou shalt lament
These braveries in Irons loaden on thee.

    Chorus. His Giantship is gone somewhat crest-fall'n,
Stalking with less unconsci'nable strides,   1245
And lower looks, but in a sultrie chafe.

    Samson. I dread him not, nor all his Giant-brood,
Though Fame divulge him Father of five Sons
All of Gigantic size, *Goliah* chief.[8]

    Chorus. He will directly to the Lords, I fear,   1250
And with malitious counsel stir them up
Some way or other yet further to afflict thee.

    Samson. He must allege some cause, and offer'd fight
Will not dare mention, lest a question rise
Whether he durst accept the offer or not,   1255
And that he durst not plain enough appear'd.
Much more affliction then already felt
They cannot well impose, nor I sustain;
If they intend advantage of my labours
The work of many hands, which earns my keeping   1260
With no small profit daily to my owners.
But come what will, my deadliest foe will prove
My speediest friend, by death to rid me hence,
The worst that he can give, to me the best.

    [4] sun god of the Philistines.
    [5] front line of battle.
    [6] disgraced and frustrated.
    [7] queen of heaven.
    [8] alluding to 2 Sam. xxi. 15–22.

Yet so it may fall out, because thir end   1265
Is hate, not help to me, it may with mine
Draw thir own ruin who attempt the deed.
   Chorus. Oh how comely it is and how reviving
To the Spirits of just men long opprest!
When God into the hands of thir deliverer   1270
Puts invincible might
To quell the mighty of the Earth, th' oppressour,
The brute and boist'rous force of violent men
Hardy and industrious to support
Tyrannic power, but raging to pursue   1275
The righteous and all such as honour Truth;
He all thir Ammunition
And feats of War defeats
With plain Heroic magnitude of mind
And celestial vigour arm'd,   1280
Thir Armories and Magazins contemns,
Renders them useless, while
With winged expedition
Swift as the lightning glance he executes
His errand on the wicked, who surpris'd   1285
Lose thir defence, distracted and amaz'd.
   But patience is more oft the exercise
Of Saints, the trial of thir fortitude,
Making them each his own Deliverer,
And Victor over all   1290
That tyrannie or fortune can inflict;
Either of these is in thy lot,
Samson, with might endu'd
Above the Sons of men; but sight bereav'd
May chance to number thee with those   1295
Whom Patience finally must crown.
This Idols day hath bin to thee no day of rest,
  Labouring thy mind
More then the working day thy hands,
And yet perhaps more trouble is behind.   1300
For I descry this way
Some other tending, in his hand
A Scepter or quaint[9] staff he bears,
Comes on amain, speed in his look.
By his habit I discern him now   1305
A Public Officer, and now at hand.

[9] skillfully wrought.

His message will be short and voluble.
Officer. *Ebrews*, the Pris'ner *Samson* here I seek.
Chorus. His manacles remark[10] him, there he sits.
Officer. *Samson*, to thee our Lords thus bid me say;   1310
This day to *Dagon* is a solemn Feast,
With Sacrifices, Triumph, Pomp, and Games;
Thy strength they know surpassing human rate,
And now some public proof thereof require
To honour this great Feast, and great Assembly;   1315
Rise therefore with all speed and come along,
Where I will see thee heart'n'd and fresh clad
T' appear as fits before th' illustrious Lords.
Samson. Thou knowst I am an *Ebrew*, therefore tell them,
Our Law forbids at thir Religious Rites   1320
My presence; for that cause I cannot come.
Officer. This answer, be assur'd, will not content them.
Samson. Have they not Sword-players, and ev'ry sort
Of Gymnic Artists, Wrestlers, Riders, Runners,
Juglers and Dancers, Antics, Mummers, Mimics,   1325
But they must pick me out with shackles tir'd,
And over-labour'd at thir publick Mill,
To make them sport with blind activity?
Do they not seek occasion of new quarrels
On my refusal to distress me more,   1330
Or make a game of my calamities?
Return the way thou cam'st, I will not come.
Officer. Regard thy self,[11] this will offend them highly.
Samson. My self? my conscience and internal peace.
Can they think me so broken, so debas'd   1335
With corporal servitude, that my mind ever
Will condescend to such absurd commands?
Although thir drudge, to be thir fool or jester,
And in my midst of sorrow and heart-grief
To shew them feats, and play before thir god,   1340
The worst of all indignities, yet on me
Joyn'd[12] with extream contempt? I will not come.
Officer. My message was impos'd on me with speed,
Brooks no delay: is this thy resolution?
Samson. So take it with what speed thy message needs.   1345
Officer. I am sorry what this stoutness[13] will produce.

[10] point him out.
[11] beware.
[12] imposed.
[13] courage.

Samson. Perhaps thou shalt have cause to sorrow indeed.

Chorus. Consider, *Samson;* matters now are strain'd
Up to the highth, whether to hold or break;
He's gone, and who knows how he may report   1350
Thy words by adding fuel to the flame?
Expect another message more imperious,
More Lordly thund'ring then thou well wilt bear.

Samson. Shall I abuse this Consecrated gift
Of strength, again returning with my hair   1355
After my great transgression, so requite
Favour renew'd, and add a greater sin
By prostituting holy things to Idols;
A *Nazarite* in place abominable
Vaunting my strength in honour to thir *Dagon?*   1360
Besides, how vile, contemptible, ridiculous,
What act more execrably unclean, prophane?

Chorus. Yet with this strength thou serv'st the *Philistines,*
Idolatrous, uncircumcis'd, unclean.

Samson. Not in thir Idol-worship, but by labour   1365
Honest and lawful to deserve my food
Of those who have me in thir civil power.

Chorus. Where the heart joins not, outward acts defile not.

Samson. Where outward force constrains, the sentence holds;
But who constrains me to the Temple of *Dagon,*   1370
Not dragging? the *Philistian* Lords command.
Commands are no constraints. If I obey them,
I do it freely; venturing to displease
God for the fear of Man, and Man prefer,
Set God behind: which in his jealousie   1375
Shall never, unrepented, find forgiveness.
Yet that he may dispense with[14] me or thee
Present in Temples at Idolatrous Rites
For some important cause, thou needst not doubt.

Chorus. How thou wilt here come off surmounts my reach.   1380

Samson. Be of good courage, I begin to feel
Some rouzing motions in me which dispose
To something extraordinary my thoughts.
I with this Messenger will go along,
Nothing to do, be sure, that may dishonour   1385
Our Law, or stain my vow of *Nazarite.*
If there be aught of presage in the mind,
This day will be remarkable in my life

---

[14] give a dispensation to.

By some great act, or of my days the last.
   Chorus. In time thou hast resolv'd, the man returns.   1390
   Officer. Samson, this second message from our Lords
To thee I am bid say. Art thou our Slave,
Our Captive, at the public Mill our drudge,
And dar'st thou at our sending and command
Dispute thy coming? come without delay;   1395
Or we shall find such Engines to assail
And hamper thee, as thou shalt come of force,
Though thou wert firmlier fast'n'd then a rock.
   Samson. I could be well content to try thir Art,
Which to no few of them would prove pernicious.   1400
Yet knowing thir advantages too many,
Because they shall not[15] trail me through thir streets
Like a wild Beast, I am content to go.
Masters commands come with a power resistless
To such as owe them absolute subjection;   1405
And for a life who will not change his purpose?
(So mutable are all the ways of men)
Yet this be sure, in nothing to comply
Scandalous or forbidden in our Law.
   Officer. I praise thy resolution, doff these links: 1410
By this compliance thou wilt win the Lords
To favour, and perhaps to set thee free.
   Samson. Brethren farewel, your company along
I will not wish, lest it perhaps offend them
To see me girt with Friends; and how the sight   1415
Of me as of a common Enemy,
So dreaded once, may now exasperate them
I know not. Lords are Lordliest in thir wine;
And the well-feasted Priest then soonest fir'd
With zeal, if aught Religion seem concern'd: 1420
No less the people on thir Holy-days
Impetuous, insolent, unquenchable;
Happ'n what may, of me expect to hear
Nothing dishonourable, impure, unworthy
Our God, our Law, my Nation, or my self,   1425
The last of me or no I cannot warrant.
   Chorus. Go, and the Holy One
Of *Israel* be thy guide
To what may serve his glory best, and spread his name
Great among the Heathen round: 1430

---

[15] because I do not desire them to.

Send thee the Angel of thy Birth, to stand
Fast by thy side, who from thy Fathers field
Rode up in flames after his message told
Of thy conception, and be now a shield
Of fire; that Spirit that first rusht on thee   1435
In the Camp of *Dan*
Be efficacious in thee now at need.
For never was from Heav'n imparted
Measure of strength so great to mortal seed,
As in thy wond'rous actions hath been seen.   1440
But wherefore comes old *Manoa* in such hast
With youthful steps? much livelier then e're while
He seems: supposing here to find his Son,
Or of him bringing to us some glad news?
    Manoa. Peace with you brethren; my inducement hither   1445
Was not at present here to find my Son,
By order of the Lords new parted hence
To come and play before them at thir Feast.
I heard all as I came, the City rings
And numbers thither flock; I had no will,   1450
Lest I should see him forc't to things unseemly.
But that which mov'd my coming now, was chiefly
To give ye part with me what hope I have
With good success to work his liberty.
    Chorus. That hope would much rejoyce us to partake   1455
With thee; say reverend Sire, we thirst to hear.
    Manoa. I have attempted[16] one by one the Lords
Either at home, or through the high street passing,
With supplication prone and Fathers tears
T' accept of ransom for my Son thir pris'ner;   1460
Some much averse I found and wondrous harsh,
Contemptuous, proud, set on revenge and spite;
That part most reverenc'd *Dagon* and his Priests;
Others more moderate seeming, but thir aim
Private reward, for which both God and State   1465
They easily would set to sale; a third
More generous far and civil, who confess'd
They had anough reveng'd, having reduc't
Thir foe to misery beneath thir fears;
The rest was magnanimity to remit,[17]   1470
If some convenient ransom were propos'd.

---

[16] tried to persuade.
[17] The rest of their revenge they would magnanimously remit.

What noise or shout was that? it tore the Skie.
  Chorus. Doubtless the people shouting to behold
Thir once great dread, captive, and blind before them,
Or at some proof of strength before them shown. 1475
  Manoa. His ransom, if my whole inheritance
May compass it, shall willingly be paid
And numberd down: much rather I shall chuse
To live the poorest in my Tribe, then richest,
And he in that calamitous prison left. 1480
No, I am fixt not to part hence without him.
For his redemption all my Patrimony,
If I need be, I am ready to forgo
And quit: not wanting him, I shall want nothing.
  Chorus. Fathers are wont to lay up for thir Sons, 1485
Thou for thy Son art bent to lay out all;
Sons wont to nurse thir Parents in old age,
Thou in old age car'st how to nurse thy Son,
Made older then thy age through eye-sight lost.
  Manoa. It shall be my delight to tend his eyes, 1490
And view him sitting in the house, ennobl'd
With all those high exploits by him atchiev'd,
And on his shoulders waving down those locks,
That of a Nation arm'd the strength contain'd:
And I perswade me God had not permitted 1495
His strength again to grow up with his hair
Garrison'd round about him like a Camp
Of faithful Souldiery, were not his purpose
To use him further yet in some great service,
Not to sit idle with so great a gift 1500
Useless, and thence ridiculous about him.
And since his strength with eye-sight was not lost,
God will restore him eye-sight to his strength.
  Chorus. Thy hopes are not ill founded nor seem vain
Of his delivery, and thy joy thereon 1505
Conceiv'd, agreeable to a Fathers love,
In both which we, as next[18] participate.
  Manoa. I know your friendly minds and—O what noise!
Mercy of Heav'n what hideous noise was that!
Horribly loud unlike the former shout. 1510
  Chorus. Noise call you it or universal groan
As if the whole inhabitation perish'd;
Blood, death, and deathful deeds are in that noise,

[18] as kinsmen.

Ruin, destruction at the utmost point.
 Manoa. Of ruin indeed methought I heard the noise,   1515
Oh it continues, they have slain my Son.
 Chorus. Thy Son is rather slaying them, that outcry
From slaughter of one foe could not ascend.
 Manoa. Some dismal accident it needs must be;
What shall we do, stay here or run and see?   1520
 Chorus. Best keep together here, lest running thither
We unawares run into dangers mouth.
This evil on the *Philistines* is fall'n,
From whom could else a general cry be heard?
The sufferers then will scarce molest us here,   1525
From other hands we need not much to fear.
What if his eye-sight (for to *Israels* God
Nothing is hard) by miracle restor'd,
He now be dealing dole[19] among his foes,
And over heaps of slaughter'd walk his way?   1530
 Manoa. That were a joy presumptuous to be thought.
 Chorus. Yet God hath wrought things as incredible
For his people of old; what hinders now?
 Manoa. He can I know, but doubt to think he will;
Yet Hope would fain subscribe, and tempts Belief.   1535
A little stay will bring some notice hither.
 Chorus. Of good or bad so great, of bad the sooner;
For evil news rides post, while good news baits.[20]
And to our wish I see one hither speeding,
An *Ebrew,* as I guess, and of our Tribe.   1540
 Messenger. O whither shall I run, or which way flie
The sight of this so horrid spectacle
Which earst my eyes beheld and yet behold;
For dire imagination still persues me?
But providence or instinct of nature seems,   1545
Or reason though disturb'd, and scarse consulted
T' have guided me aright, I know not how,
To thee first reverend *Manoa,* and to these
My Countreymen, whom here I knew remaining,
As at some distance from the place of horrour,   1550
So in the sad event too much concern'd.
 Manoa. The accident was loud, and here before thee
With rueful cry, yet what it was we hear not,
No Preface needs, thou seest we long to know.

[19] both "alms" and "pain."
[20] moves slowly.

Messenger. It would burst forth, but I recover breath   1555
And sense distract, to know well what I utter.
Manoa. Tell us the sum, the circumstance defer.
Messenger. Gaza yet stands, but all her Sons are fall'n,
All in a moment overwhelm'd and fall'n.
Manoa. Sad, but thou knowst to *Israelites* not saddest   1560
The desolation of a Hostile City.
Messenger. Feed on that first, there may in grief be surfet.
Manoa. Relate by whom.
Messenger.   By *Samson.*
Manoa.   That still lessens
The sorrow, and converts it nigh to joy.
Messenger. Ah *Manoa,* I refrain too suddenly   1565
To utter what will come at last too soon;
Lest evil tidings with too rude irruption
Hitting thy aged ear should pierce too deep.
Manoa. Suspense in news is torture, speak them out.
Messenger. Then take the worst in brief, *Samson* is dead.   1570
Manoa. The worst indeed, O all my hope's defeated
To free him hence! but death who sets all free
Hath paid his ransom now and full discharge.
What windy[21] joy this day had I conceiv'd
Hopeful of his Delivery, which now proves   1575
Abortive as the first-born bloom of spring
Nipt with the lagging rear of winters frost.
Yet e're I give the rains to grief, say first,
How dy'd he? death to life is crown or shame.
All by him fell thou say'st, by whom fell he,
What glorious hand gave *Samson* his deaths wound?   1580
Messenger. Unwounded of his enemies he fell.
Manoa. Wearied with slaughter then or how? explain.
Messenger. By his own hands.
Manoa.   Self-violence? what cause
Brought him so soon at variance with himself   1585
Among his foes?
Messenger.   Inevitable cause
At once both to destroy and be destroy'd;
The Edifice where all were met to see him
Upon thir heads and on his own he pull'd.
Manoa. O lastly over-strong against thy self!   1590
A dreadful way thou took'st to thy revenge.
More than anough we know; but while things yet

[21] empty.

Are in confusion, give us if thou canst,
Eye-witness of what first or last was done,
Relation more particular and distinct.   1595
    Messenger. Occasions drew me early to this City,
And as the gates I enter'd with Sun-rise,
The morning Trumpets Festival proclaim'd
Through each high street: little I had dispatch't
When all abroad was rumour'd that this day   1600
Samson should be brought forth to shew the people
Proof of his mighty strength in feats and games;
I sorrow'd at his captive state, but minded[22]
Not to be absent at that spectacle.
The building was a spacious Theatre   1605
Half round on two main Pillars vaulted high,
With seats where all the Lords and each degree
Of sort,[23] might sit in order to behold,
The other side was op'n, where the throng
On banks[24] and scaffolds under Skie might stand;   1610
I among these aloof obscurely stood.
The Feast and noon grew high, and Sacrifice
Had fill'd thir hearts with mirth, high chear, and wine,
When to thir sports they turn'd. Immediately
Was *Samson* as a public servant brought,   1615
In thir state Livery clad; before him Pipes
And Timbrels, on each side went armed guards,
Both horse and foot before him and behind,
Archers, and Slingers, Cataphracts and Spears.[25]
At sight of him the people with a shout   1620
Rifted the Air clamouring thir god with praise,
Who had made thir dreadful enemy thir thrall.
He patient but undaunted where they led him,
Came to the place, and what was set before him
Which without help of eye might be assay'd,   1625
To heave, pull, draw, or break, he still perform'd
All with incredible, stupendious force,
None daring to appear Antagonist.
At length for intermission sake they led him
Between the pillars; he his guide requested   1630
(For so from such as nearer stood we heard)

[22] resolved.
[23] quality.
[24] benches.
[25] men and horses clad in armor, and spearsmen.

As over-tir'd to let him lean a while
With both his arms on those two massie Pillars
That to the arched roof gave main support.
He unsuspitious led him; which when *Samson*   1635
Felt in his arms, with head a while enclin'd,
And eyes fast fixt he stood, as one who pray'd,
Or some great matter in his mind revolv'd.
At last with head erect thus cry'd aloud,
Hitherto, Lords, what your commands impos'd   1640
I have perform'd, as reason was, obeying,
Not without wonder or delight beheld.
Now of my own accord such other tryal
I mean to shew you of my strength, yet greater;
As with amaze shall strike all who behold.   1645
This utter'd, straining all his nerves he bow'd;
As with the force of winds and waters pent,
When Mountains tremble, those two massie Pillars
With horrible convulsion to and fro,
He tugg'd, he shook, till down they came and drew   1650
The whole roof after them, with burst of thunder
Upon the heads of all who sate beneath,
Lords, Ladies, Captains, Councellors, or Priests,
Thir choice nobility and flower, not only
Of this but each *Philistian* City round   1655
Met from all parts to solemnize this Feast.
Samson with these immixt, inevitably
Pull'd down the same destruction on himself;
The vulgar only scap'd who stood without.
    Chorus. O dearly-bought revenge, yet glorious!   1660
Living or dying thou hast fulfill'd
The work for which thou wast foretold
To *Israel*, and now ly'st victorious
Among thy slain self-kill'd
Not willingly, but tangl'd in the fold   1665
Of dire necessity, whose law in death conjoin'd
Thee with thy slaughter'd foes in number more
Then all thy life had slain before.
    Semichorus. While thir hearts were jocund and sublime,[26]
Drunk with Idolatry, drunk with Wine,   1670
And fat regorg'd of Bulls and Goats,
Chaunting thir Idol, and preferring
Before our living Dread who dwells

[26] elated.

In *Silo*[27] his bright Sanctuary:
Among them he a spirit of phrenzie sent,   1675
Who hurt thir minds,
And urg'd them on with mad desire
To call in hast for thir destroyer;
They only set on sport and play
Unweetingly importun'd   1680
Thir own destruction to come speedy upon them.
So fond[28] are mortal men
Fall'n into wrath divine,
As thir own ruin on themselves t' invite,
Insensate left, or to sense reprobate,[29]   1685
And with blindness internal struck.
    Semichorus. But he though blind of sight,
Despis'd and thought extinguish't quite,
With inward eyes illuminated
His fierie vertue rouz'd   1690
From under ashes into sudden flame,
And as an ev'ning Dragon[30] came,
Assailant on the perched roosts,
And nests in order rang'd
Of tame villatic[31] Fowl; but as an Eagle   1695
His cloudless thunder bolted on thir heads.[32]
So vertue giv'n for lost,
Deprest, and overthrown, as seem'd,
Like that self-begott'n bird[33]
In th' *Arabian* woods embost,[34]   1700
That no second knows nor third,
And lay e're while a Holocaust,
From out her ashie womb now teem'd,
Revives, reflourishes, then vigorous most
When most unactive deem'd,   1705
And though her body die, her fame survives,

---

[27] Shiloh.
[28] foolish.
[29] condemned.
[30] winged serpent emitting fire. Samuel S. Stollman (*English Language Notes*, VII [1970], 186–89) cites as allusion Gen. xlix. 16–18: "Dan shall judge his people, as one of the tribes of Israel. Dan shall be a serpent in the way, a horned snake in the path. . . . I wait for Thy salvation, O Lord."
[31] farmhouse.
[32] The lines refer the victory over the Philistines and their god to the Providence of God as comparison with *PL* VI, 762–64, shows.
[33] the Phoenix.
[34] sheltered.

A secular[35] bird ages of lives.
   Manoa. Come, come, no time for lamentation now,
Nor much more cause, *Samson* hath quit himself
Like *Samson,* and heroicly hath finish'd   1710
A life Heroic, on his Enemies
Fully reveng'd, hath left them years of mourning,
And lamentation to the Sons of *Caphtor*
Through all *Philistian* bounds. To *Israel*
Honour hath left, and freedom, let but them   1715
Find courage to lay hold on this occasion,
To himself and Fathers house eternal fame;
And which is best and happiest yet, all this
With God not parted from him, as was feard,
But favouring and assisting to the end.   1720
Nothing is here for tears, nothing to wail
Or knock the breast, no weakness, no contempt,
Dispraise, or blame, nothing but well and fair,
And what may quiet us in a death so noble.
Let us go find the body where it lies   1725
Soak't in his enemies blood, and from the stream
With lavers pure and cleansing herbs wash off
The clotted gore. I with what speed the while
(*Gaza* is not in plight[36] to say us nay)
Will send for all my kindred, all my friends   1730
To fetch him hence and solemnly attend
With silent obsequie and funeral train
Home to his Fathers house: there will I build him
A Monument, and plant it round with shade
Of Laurel ever green, and branching Palm,   1735
With all his Trophies hung, and Acts enroll'd
In copious Legend, or sweet Lyric Song.
Thither shall all the valiant youth resort,
And from his memory inflame thir breasts
To matchless valour, and adventures high: 1740
The Virgins also shall on feastful days
Visit his Tomb with flowers, only bewailing
His lot unfortunate in nuptial choice,
From whence captivity and loss of eyes.
   Chorus. All is best, though we oft doubt,   1745
What th' unsearchable dispose[37]

[35] living for (five) centuries.
[36] condition.
[37] ordering.

Of highest wisdom brings about,
And ever best found in the close.
Oft he seems to hide his face,[38]
But unexpectedly returns   1750
And to his faithful Champion hath in place
Bore witness gloriously; whence *Gaza* mourns
And all that band them to resist
His uncontroulable intent;
His servants he with new acquist[39]   1755
Of true experience from this great event
With peace and consolation hath dismist,
And calm of mind all passion spent.[40]

(*1646–48 ?; revised, 1653 or later ?*)[41]

[38] Compare Ps. xxvii. 9: "Hide not thy face far from me," and Ps. lxxxviii. 14: "Lord, why castest thou off my soul? why hidest thou thy face from me?"

[39] acquisition.

[40] As comparison with Milton's first sentence concerning tragedy indicates, complete catharsis has occurred.

[41] Traditional dating places *SA* last of Milton's poetic works (c. 1670), but this has been challenged by Parker, Gilbert, and the editor (see articles listed in the bibliography). The dates given here are those conjectured by Parker. See the introduction for an explanation of the order in which the poems are printed here.

Textual Notes

Collations of all known significant texts have been prepared for all poems. For brevity, however, only verbal variants in all texts and similar important differences are reported here. Manuscript readings which are not final are omitted, and abbreviations are generally expanded.

The basic text from which the present version of a poem is derived is marked by an asterisk. Milton's holograph copies best represent his intentions, though they contain some errors, lack full punctuation, and evidence spelling practices which were later abandoned. A basic manuscript text is altered in the direction of a basic printed text. Scribal copies and printed versions, however, are filled with idiosyncracies in mechanics. A text given in this edition follows the copy available which seems to have been closest to Milton; alterations are made when authority is found in another text, when (as with punctuation) they are necessary for easy understanding of a line, when an error seems certain, and when meter dictates. In addition a few spellings are changed to more standard (and Milton's later) forms: these include the dropping of most redundant final "e's." The result of these principles is, unfortunately, inconsistency; but it represents the kind of text offered the seventeenth-century reader without being an uncritical duplication of an original printing.

There were two collected editions of the minor poems during Milton's lifetime, one in 1645 and one in 1673; some poems appeared in separate publications or in other collected volumes, noted where pertinent. SA and PR were issued together in 1671, the only authoritative source; PL was first published in 1667 (reissued with introductory material in 1668 and 1669) and then revised for a second edition in 1674. Publication is referred to by date in the notes. Original copies in the New York Public Library are reported, compared with the facsimiles in Harris F. Fletcher's four-volume edition.

Aside from brief or incidental materials (corrections in presentation volumes, etc.) and copies with, apparently, no direct Miltonic connection, manuscript sources are the Trinity College MS (facsimile by William Aldis Wright, London, 1899), the Bridgewater MS of A Mask, the MS of the *Ode to Rouse*, and the MS of Book I of *PL*. These four important MSS are published in facsimile by Fletcher.

Evidence for the date of composition of each poem is cited as briefly as possible, since the researches of such men as Hanford, Parker, Tillyard, and Woodhouse have made it possible to record rather definite dates for most of the poems. For purposes of dating, the order of entry in the *TM* is obviously significant, but the arrangement within groups in the early editions is also informative, although errors or printing exigencies may have altered Milton's arrangement.

A PARAPHRASE ON PSALM 114
Date: 1624; composed, according to headnote, when Milton was fifteen.
Texts: 1645°, 1673.

PSALM 136
Date: 1624; composed, according to headnote for *Ps.* 114, when Milton was fifteen.
Texts: 1645°, 1673. A manuscript copy from the 1645 printing occurs in a poetic collection by William Sancroft (Bodleian Library, Tanner MS 466, pp. 34–35, ff. 20ᵛ–21); there are no verbal variants.
(7–8) *et al.* For &c. / For, &c. *and* For his, &c. *1645 and 1673 vacillate slightly differently between these two abbreviations.* (10, 13, 17, 21, 25) That / Who *1673.*

APOLOGUS DE RUSTICO ET HERO
Date: 1624–25; apparently written as a grammar school exercise.
Text: 1673°.

CARMINA ELEGIACA
Date: 1624–25; apparently a late grammar school exercise.
Text: MS in Netherby Hall, Longtown, Cumberland (autotype facsimile in PRO, catalogued: Autotypes / Milton &c. / Fac. 6 / Library / Shelf 156a; photograph° of autotype in British Museum, MS Add. 41063 I, f. 85; printed by A. J. Horwood, Camden Society, n.s. XVI (1876), xvi–xix, 62–63.
3 prænuncius ales. / p(　　　)le( ) *reading given is that recorded by Horwood.*

"IGNAVUS SATRAPAM DEDECET . . ."
Date: 1624–25; apparently a late grammar school exercise.
Text: photograph° of autotype of MS (see note to *Carmina Elegiaca*).
4 Stratus purpureo procubuit thoro / str(　)tus purp(　)eo p(　)buit
(　) *Horwood printed the first two words; Columbia Milton (XVIII.643) suggested last word.*

ELEGIA PRIMA
Date: early Apr. 1626; written during the spring vacation after his rustication
which occurred in the Lent term of 1626 (see ll. 9–12, 85–90). The Easter
term began on Apr. 19.
Texts: 1645°, 1673.
(13) molles, / *1645 shows three states: as given,* molles *without a comma,
and* molle *without* s *or a comma.* (29) auditur / *1673 is found in two states:*
auditor *and as given.* (40) Interdum / *1673 is found in two states:* Intredum
and as given.

ELEGIA SECUNDA
Date: Oct. ? 1626; composed, according to Latin note, when Milton was seven-
teen. Ridding's death occurred after Sept. 19 and before Nov. 28; Nov. is mere
conjecture. Since the term began on Oct. 11, this, *El.* 3, and *Eliensis* were prob-
ably written after that time.
Texts: 1645°, 1673.

ELEGIA TERTIA
Date: Oct. ? 1626; a Latin note says that this elegy was written when Milton
was seventeen. The reference in ll. 9–12 makes the month uncertain, but see
Bush, *Variorum* I, 65–68.
Texts: 1645°, 1673.

IN OBITUM PRÆSULIS ELIENSIS
Date: Oct. ? 1626; composed after *El.* 3 (see ll. 4–6). Felton died on Oct. 6,
and a Latin note places composition when Milton was seventeen.
Texts: 1645°, 1673.

IN OBITUM PROCANCELLARII MEDICI
Date: Oct.–Nov. 1626; Gostlin died Oct. 21, 1626. Milton's Latin note that the
poem was written when he was sixteen is in error. It precedes *Nov. 5* in 1645.
Texts: 1645°, 1673.

IN PRODITIONEM BOMBARDICAM
Date: Nov. 1626 ?; probably composed around the same time as *Nov. 5.*
Texts: 1645*, 1673.

IN EANDEM: "Thus did you strive . . ."
Date: Nov. 1626 ?; probably composed around the same time as *Nov. 5.*
Texts: 1645°, 1673.

IN EANDEM: "James derided . . ."
Date: Nov. 1626 ?; probably composed around the same time as *Nov. 5.*
Texts: 1645°, 1673.
(4) cornua / corona *1673.* (12) *not indented* 1673.

IN EANDEM: "Whom impious Rome . . ."
Date: Nov. 1626 ?; probably composed around the same time as *Nov. 5.*
Texts: 1645°, 1673.

IN INVENTOREM BOMBARDÆ
Date: Nov. 1626 ?; probably composed around the same time as *Nov. 5.*
Texts: 1645°, 1673.

IN QUINTUM NOVEMBRIS
Date: Nov. 1626; composed, according to Latin note, when Milton was seventeen.
Texts: 1645°, 1673.
(20) ceu / seu *1645, 1673.* (45) natat / notat *1673; erratum corrects.* (75) *indented 1673.* (125) casúmque *1673* / casúque *1645.* (143) præruptaque *1673* / semifractaque *1645.*

ELEGIA QUARTA
Date: late Mar. 1627; Latin note states that it was written when Milton was eighteen, from ll. 33–34 we know that it was written after Mar. 21, and it seems to be the verse epistle referred to in his letter of Mar. 26, 1627(?). (See Parker, *MLN,* LIII [1938], 399–407, for dating of the letter.) References to the war surrounding Hamburg are in agreement with this dating, and suggest no time later than the end of April. The elegy may have been composed before or after the letter, which apparently was written the day after Easter.
Texts: 1645°, 1673.
(89) fœtus; / fætus; *1645, 1673.*

ON THE DEATH OF A FAIR INFANT DYING OF A COUGH
Date: Jan.–Mar. 1628; Milton's niece was buried Jan. 22 and his second niece was born Apr. 9 (see last stanza). He notes in Latin that the poem was composed when he was seventeen. But since Milton was seventeen between Dec. 1625 and Dec. 1626, the printer or scribe may have simply misread "19" as "17."
Text: 1673°.
(53) Mercy *added to defective line.* (54) crown'd / cown'd *1673.*

AT A VACATION EXERCISE
Date: July 1628; Latin note that it was delivered when Milton was nineteen.
Text: 1673°.
Printed between the *Fifth Ode* and *Forcers of Conscience,* but an *erratum* repositions immediately after *Fair Infant.* (98) hallow'd / hollowed *1673.*

ELEGIA QUINTA
Date: spring 1629; written when Milton was twenty according to Latin note.
Texts: 1645°, 1673.
(30) perennis *1673* / quotannis *1645.* (115) Navita / Natvia *1673.*

ON THE MORNING OF CHRISTS NATIVITY
Date: Dec. 1629; year given in 1645.
Texts: 1645°, 1673. A manuscript copy from the 1645 printing occurs in a poetic collection by William Sancroft (Bodleian Library MS, Tanner 466, pp.

60–66, ff. 33ᵛ–36ᵛ); four verbal variants are noted: (52) Peace / Peace>
Calme (53) or / nor (86) dawn / Day (171) wrath / wroth.
(143–44) Th' enameld *Arras* of the Rainbow wearing, | And Mercy set be-
tween, *1645.* (171) wroth *1673* / wrath *1645.*

ELEGIA SEXTA
Date: Dec. 1629; reference to Diodati's letter of Dec. 13 (headnote) and to
Nativity Ode (ll. 79–90).
Texts: 1645°, 1673.

THE PASSION
Date: Mar. 1630; written, apparently, around Easter following the composition
of the *Nativity Ode.*
Texts: 1645°, 1673.
(22) latter / latest *1673.*

ELEGIA SEPTIMA
Date: May 1630; number of elegy and position after *El.* 6 in 1645. The printed
note "Anno ætatis undevigesimo" (at the age of nineteen) may have resulted,
as Parker has argued ("Notes," pp. 120–21), from a scribe's misreading of Mil-
ton's "uno et vigesimo" (twenty-one).
Texts: 1645°, 1673. A correction in Milton's hand is found in the Bodleian
Library copy of 1645 (catalogued 8° M168 Art, but kept as Arch G.f.17):
l. 21, "ærerno" is changed to "æterno".
(2) fuit. / suit. *1645, 1673.* (21) æterno *1673* / ærerno *1645.*

LINES APPENDED TO ELEGIA SEPTIMA (ELEGY 7)
Date: 1630 ? Most editors place this "renunciation" with *El.* 7, from which it is
separated by a thin line in 1645, 1673. However, it obviously postdates the
elegy and is separated in time from it ("formerly," l. 2); see also ll. 7–8. F. W.
Bateson (*English Poetry: a Critical Introduction* [New York, 1950], p. 161)
thinks 1635 the earliest possible date, though his basis is unsound; and others
have postulated the addition of the lines when the 1645 collection was being
conceived. The lines reflect the thought that produced both *Idea* and Platonic
references in other poems dated here in 1631.
Texts: 1645°, 1673.

SONG: ON MAY MORNING
Date: May 1630 ?; conjectural. Perhaps after Dec. 1629 (when Milton became
21) since, as Parker points out ("Notes," p. 115), he dated most of the poems
which we know were written prior to that time in terms of his age; *El.* 1, *El.* 6
(month but not the year), and the five epigrams on the Gunpowder Plot do not
carry notes concerning their compositional dates. The only poem which was
composed apparently later and which has a date in terms of age is *El.* 7 (May
1630); of later poems only *Shakespear, Lycidas,* and *Mask* carry year dates in
1645. It may be significant that *Song* precedes *Shakespear;* however, it follows

Epitaph on the Marchioness, which is clearly out of chronological order. Others have dated the poem from 1628 through 1632.
Texts: 1645°, 1673.

SONNET 1
Date: May 1630 ?; conjectural, but perhaps close to the Italian poems. See also textual note to *Song.* It may be significant that Milton purchased his copy of Giovanni della Casa's influential *Rime et prose* in Dec. 1629.
Texts: 1645°, 1673.

SONNET 2
Date: 1630 ?; uncertain, but perhaps sonnet group is dated by correspondences · with *El.* 7 (May 1630). Compare *Son.* 2 with the elegy; ll. 1–4 of *Son.* 4 with ll. 1–4 of the elegy; and ll. 8–14 of *Son.* 6 with ll. 89–90 of the elegy. The purchase of della Casa's *Rime et Prose* in Dec. 1629 likewise suggests composition after that date. *Son.* 5, addressed to Diodati, points to—but does not require— composition before mid-April when Diodati enrolled in the Academy of Geneva.
Texts: 1645°, 1673.
(5) mostrasi / mostra si *1645, 1673.*

SONNET 3
Date: 1630 ?; see textual note for *Son.* 2.
Texts: 1645°, 1673.

CANZONE
Date: 1630 ?; see textual note for *Son.* 2.
Texts: 1645°, 1673.

SONNET 4
Date: 1630 ?; see textual note for *Son.* 2.
Texts: 1645°, 1673.

SONNET 5
Date: 1630 ?; see textual note for *Son.* 2.
Texts: 1645°, 1673.
(2) sian / fian *1673.* (10) Scossomi / Scosso mi *1645, 1673.* (12) a trovar / e trovar *1673.*

SONNET 6
Date: 1630 ?; see textual note for *Son.* 2.
Texts: 1645°, 1673.
(6) Di / De *1645, 1673.* (8) e d'intero / d'intero *1673.*

ON SHAKESPEAR
Date: 1630; date given in 1645, in which it precedes the Hobson poems.
Texts: Shakespeare Second Folio (1632) in three states (Effigies A, B, and C); Shakespeare, *Poems* (1640); 1645°; Shakespeare Third Folio (1664); 1673.
Title An Epitaph on the admirable Dramaticke Poet W. SHAKESPEARE. A, B, C,

William *1640, 1664.* (4) Star-ypointing / starre-ypointed A. (6) weak / dull
A, B, C, *1664.* (8) live-long / lasting A, B, C, *1664.* (10) heart / part, A, B,
C, *1664.* (13) it / her A, B, C, *1664,* our *1640.* (15) dost / doth *1640.*

NATURAM NON PATI SENIUM
Date: June 1631 ?; precedes *Idea* (which see) in the editions, but was probably
written at the same general time. Frequently dated June 1628 (as, therefore, is
Idea) by those who suggest these as the verses mentioned in a letter to Alexan-
der Gill, July 2, 1628, but perhaps this date should be 1631.
Texts: 1645°, 1673.

DE IDEA PLATONICA
Date: June 1631 ? Since the poem is undated by Milton, it may lie after Dec.
1629 (see textual note to *Song*). Probably it was composed after the amatory
work of spring 1630, but certainly before Milton's graduation in July 1632.
Texts: 1645°, 1673.
(19) sedens *1673* / fedens *1645.* (23) diis / iis *1673.* (36) induxti / induxit
1673.

ON THE UNIVERSITY CARRIER
Date: early 1631; Hobson died Jan. 1, 1631.
Texts: 1645°, *Wit Restor'd* (1658), 1673, MS. 1.21, ff. 79ᵛ–80ʳ (Folger Li-
brary). A correction in Milton's hand is found in the Bodleian Library copy of
1645 (catalogued 8° M168 Art, but kept as Arch G.f.17): l. 2, "A" changed
to "And".
Title *Another.* 1658, On Hobson who dyed in the vacancy of his Carrage by
reason of the Sicknes att Cambridge. 1630. *MS.* (1) broke his girt, / his desire,
1658. (2) And *1673* / A *1645;* laid / left *1658;* dirt, / mire; *1658.* (6)
when / that *1658.* (7) had / hath *1658;* this / those MS. (8) Dodg'd /
Dog'dd *1658;* with him, / him *1658;* betwixt / 'twixt *1658,* MS; Bull. /
London-Bull. 1658. (14) In the kind office / Death in the likenesse *1658,* In
craftie likenes MS. (18) and's / and *1658.*

ANOTHER ON THE SAME
Date: early 1631; Hobson died Jan. 1, 1631.
Texts: Banquet of Jests (1640, 1657), 1645°, *Wit Restor'd* (1658), 1673;
Huntington Library MS, H.M. 116, pp. 100–1; Bodleian MS, Malone 21, f. 69ᵛ;
Bodleian MS, CCC.E.309, f. 48; St. John's College MS, S32, ff. 18ᵛ–19ʳ. As-
cribed to "Jo: Milton" by StJ MS.
Title *Upon old* Hobson *the Carrier of* Cambridge. *1640, 1657,* Vpon old Hob-
son Cambridge Carrier who dyed 1630 in yᵉ Vacation by reason of yᵉ Sick-
nesse yⁿ hot at Camb: *HMS,* On Hobson yᵉ Cambridge carrier who died 1630
in yᵉ vacancy of his carriage by reason of yᵉ sicknesse then hott at Cambridge
Malone, Hobson the Carrier *CCC,* Another of old Hobson who dyed in the
vacancie of his carriage the sicknes being breife in Cambridge. 1630. *StJ.* (1)
lieth one / Hobson lyes *1640, 1657, HMS, Malone, CCC, StJ.* (2) while /
whilst *1640, 1657, 1658, HMS, Malone, CCC, StJ;* could / did *1640, 1657,
HMS, CCC.* (3) hung / sung *1640, 1657, CCC.* (4) While / Whilst *1640,*

1657, 1658, CCC, So *HMS, Malone, StJ;* might / could *1658;* still / but
1658. (5) sphear-metal / spheares mettall *1640, 1657, CCC.* (6) revolution
/ resolution *1640, 1658, HMS, CCC, StJ;* was at / made of *1658.* (7) a / all
1640, 1657, CCC. (8) old truth / truth, 'twas *1640, 1657, CCC,* old truths
HMS. (9) an / some *1640, 1657, 1658, HMS, Malone, CCC, StJ;* with /
by *StJ;* wheel / wheeles *1658.* (10) being / once *1658,* when *StJ;* ceast /
seasd *1640, CCC.* (11) men / us *1640, 1657, CCC;* gave / giu's *HMS.*
(13–26, 29–34) *omitted 1658;* (15–20, 25–26) *omitted 1640, 1657, HMS,
Malone, CCC, StJ.* (13) Nor / No *HMS.* (14) hast'n'd / hasted *Malone.* (21)
chief / *omitted HMS, Malone;* right / aright *HMS, Malone.* (22) cart / carts
1640, 1657, CCC; went / were *1640, 1657, CCC,* was *HMS, Malone.* (23)
him / *omitted Malone. 27–28 given between l. 12 and l. 13 StJ.* (27) But /
For *1640, 1657, 1658, HMS, Malone, CCC, StJ;* doings / doing *HMS.* (28)
an / so sure an *HMS.* (30) had / *omitted HMS,* in *Malone.* (31) Linkt / Like
Malone; flowing / flowings *Malone.* (32) increase / disease *1640, 1657, CCC
with marginal emendation:* decease. (33) *indented 1640, 1657;* and / are
HMS. (34) *indented 1640, 1657;* this / his *StJ.*

HOBSONS EPITAPH
Date: early 1631; Hobson died on Jan. 1, 1631.

Texts:

Banquet of Jests (1640°)	A	Tanner 465, pp. 235–36	P
Witts Recreation (1640)	B	Folger Library MSS	
Banquet of Jests (1657)	C	1.27, f. 68ᵛ	Q
Wit Restor'd (1658)	D	452.1, p. 50	R
British Museum MSS		E.a.6, f. 4	S
Additional 5807, f. 2ᵛ	E	Harvard Univ. Library MS	
Additional 6400, f. 67ᵛ	F	Eng. 686, f. 78ᵛ	T
Additional 15227, f. 74ʳ	G	Huntington Library MS	
Additional 30982, f. 65	H	H.M. 116, p. 10	U
Harleian 791, f. 45ʳ	I	Rosenbach MS	
Harleian 6931, f. 24ᵛ	J	239/27, pp. 359–60	V
Sloane 542, f. 52ʳ	K	James H. Osborn Collection	
Bodleian Library MSS		Commonplace Book, Box 12,	
CCC, E.309, f. 48ᵛ	L	No. 5, pp. 225–26	W
Eng. Poet. f. 10, f. 101ᵛ	M	John Rylands Library MS	
Rawlinson Poet. 26, f. 64	N	Eng. 410, ff. 31ᵛ–32ʳ	X
Rawlinson Poet. 117, ff.		St. John's College Library MS	
105ᵛ–6ʳ	O	S.32, f. 18ᵛ	Y

This third poem on Hobson is included with qualification. Never published by
Milton, it has similarities to his acknowledged verses, which it follows in *Ban-
quet of Jests* and precedes in *Wit Restor'd.* William R. Parker, who first pro-
posed Milton's authorship (Columbia Milton, XVIII, 590–92), suggests that it
may have been omitted from 1645 because two poems in this vein may have
been considered sufficient. A poem in Harleian MS 6057, f. 15, with the title,
"On Hobson the Carrier," employs the first two lines; variants: amongst his

many / with some not his; not learned / vnlearned; yet of many / and yett a man of. S and T give alternate indentations of lines; and L copies as if this is the "Superscription" mentioned in the last line of the previous poem.
Title *On Hobson the Carrier*. B, *On the death of* Hobson, *the* Cambridge-*Carrier* D, V, *missing* E, F, L, In Hobsonum Architabellarium Cantabrigiensem. 1631. G, on hobson the Cambridge Carrier. H, An Other: I, O, An Epitaph on Hobson the Carrier of Cambridge K, On Chambridge Carrier M, Upon Thomas Hobson, yᵉ Carryer of Cambridge N, Upon Hobson the Carrier P, On Hobson died 1 Jan 1630 Q, Vpon Mr. Hobson, carryer of Cambridge. R, On Hobson the Carrier Buried in St Maryes in Cambrdige S, Hobsons Epitaph the Carrier of Cambredge T, Vpon Hobson yᵉ Cambridge Carrier. U, on the death of Hobson X. (1) Here *Hobson* lies amongst his many / Here lies Hobson amongst his many E, F, N, O, Here lies Hobson moungst his many H, Heere lies old Hobson among his P, Hobson lies heare amongst his many T; amongst / among X; many / *omitted* O; betters D / debters A, C, L, U. (2) A man / who though Q; not learned D / unlearned A, B, C, E, F, G, J, L, W; yet of many / yet a man of B, H, I, J, N, P, R, S, V, W, and yet of many E, F, and yet a man of G, Y, yet was a man of Q, but yet of many T. (3–4) *omitted* B, G, H, I, N, P, Q, R, S, V. (3) The / Yee U; well / all J, W; testify / justifie D. (4) That have / Who have D, X, But he E, F, That have oft O, That oft T; from / in E, F. (5–6) *reversed* Q. (5) it was well known hee many times had gone Q; was well / is well D, E, F, P, Y, well was T, X; oft / *omitted* L; hath he gon D / t'have begun A, C, L, haue he gon H, he hath gon V. (6) In Embassy / An Embassie D, E, F, In an embassage G, an Embassage H, On Embassies I, K, Y, On embassage J, N, O, R, S, In an Embassy L, On an embassage P, X, On Embassi T, His Embassy U; father / morning Y; the / a E, F, *omitted* G, P, X. (7) There's few in Cambridge, to his praise be it spoken B; in good time / to his praise G, H, I, J, N, P, Q, R, S, V, W, Y. (8) well remembreth / may remember B, I, K, P, will remember D, F, G, H, M, R, S, U, X, well remember E, L, N, Q, T, V, Y, do remember J, well remembers O, can remember W; som / a M; good / *missing* H. (9) thence / whence B, hence P, W; to *London* rode he / he rid to London B. (10) benighting D / benighted A, C, H, V, Y; he / nere V. (11–12) *missing* J, W. (11–18) *printed:* 13–14, 11–12, 17–18 B. (11) Then marueile not, though he soe soone is gone T; No / Nor B, D, M, N, S; wonder is it / is't a wonder B, wonder thinke yee G, wonder thinke it H, N, S, wonder thinks it R. (12) Since most men / Since all men B, K, P, For most G, For most men H, N, R, S, For all men T, V; knew / know D, E, F, H, I, M, N, P, Q, X, know, that G; long / still V. (13) Team / Terme U; of the best / very good J, W; could / would B, P, Q. (14) Bin mir'd in any ground / Bin mir'd in any way B, P, Q, V, Y, Them mir'd in any ground D, In any way beene mir'd G, beene mired any where H, Bin mir'd in any place I, R, S, Stucke fast in any ground J, W, Bin mir'd so M, Bin beemir'd any where N; the D / his A, C, E, F, J, L, V, a N, R, S, Y. (15–16) *omitted* B. (15) here K / there A, C, D, G, M, N, R, S, W, X; indeed, still / & still is G, indeed, and J, W, still P; like to D / at a A, C, L. (16) Until / Except J, Unles T, Till V; some / an J, some good V; lend / lens J, his D / a A, C, H, I, L, M, U, Y, some K, an X. (17–18) *indented* L. (17) So / Thus B, G, H, I, N, P, Q, R, S, V, Then M; rest / rests D, euʳ rest O; thou / the D; ever-toyling / everlasting B, dusty toyling G, toyling O. (18) to

Charls–wain / Charls his Waine *B, D, I, J, K, L, N, O, T, U, W, X,* Charles
Waine *H, M, Y,* Charlemaine *Q,* to Charles his wayne *R, S.*

AN EPITAPH ON THE MARCHIONESS OF WINCHESTER

Date: Apr. 1631; the Marchioness died on Apr. 15, 1631.
Texts: 1645°, 1673; British Museum MS, Sloane 1446, ff. 37b–38. The manu-
script has a note of authorship: "Jo Milton of Chr: Coll Cambr." ·
Title On the Marchionesse of Winchester whoe died in Child bedd. Ap: 15.
1631 *MS.* (15–23) *MS has:* Seauen times had the yeerlie starre | in euerie signe
sett vpp his carr | Since for her they did request | the god that sitts at marriage
feast | (when first the earlie Matrons runne |. (24) a / her *MS.* (27) whether /
whither *MS.* (40) vernall / a vernall *MS.* (42) on / one *MS.* (43) she / it *MS.*
(46) hast'ning / hastinge *MS.* (47) *indented* MS; thy / the *MS.* (49) thy /
they *MS.* (50) sease / ceaze *MS.* (52) thy / thine *MS.* (53) *indented* MS.
(61) Whilst / While *MS.* (64) Who / w^ch *MS.* (70) Light; / might *MS.*

L'ALLEGRO

Date: 1631 ?; conjectural, but later than the Hobson poems which it follows
in 1645. Ants Oras indicates (*NQ,* 198, 1953, 332–33) that the prosody of
L'Allegro and *Penseroso* is later than that of the *Epitaph on the Marchioness.*
The twin poems may have been written during the summer vacation.
Texts: 1645°, 1673.
(33) ye / you 1673. (104) he by / by the 1673.

IL PENSEROSO

Date: 1631 ?; conjectural, but later than the Hobson poems which it follows
in 1645. See note to *L'Allegro.*
Texts: 1645°, 1673. A correction in Milton's hand is found in the Bodleian
Library copy of 1645 (catalogued 8° M168 Art, but kept as Arch G.f.17):
l. 57, "Id" changed to "In".
(57) In 1673 / Id 1645.

SONNET 7

Date: Dec. 1632; l. 2 places the poem after the year during which he was
twenty-three (1631–32).
Texts: 1645°, 1673, TM°.
(2) twentith / twentieth 1673.

ARCADES

Date: 1633–34 ?; probably revised in 1637 (see Shawcross, "Speculations").
Date is very uncertain, but composition undoubtedly lies before that of *Mask.*
Texts: 1645°, 1673, TM°. A number of lines of TM have been damaged by
tearing. TM has early title "Part of a maske" which is replaced by "Part of an
Entertainment at . . . ." The first song is not labelled; therefore, the second
song is simply "Song" in TM, and the third, "2 Song".
(28) ye / you *TM.* (40) ye . . . ye / you . . . you *TM.* (47) With / in *TM,*
deleted. (49) or *TM* / and 1645, 1673. (81) ye / you *TM;* toward /
towards *TM.* (91) you / yee *TM.* (94) *aligned with lines 84, 85, etc.* 1645,

1673. (96) *not indented* 1645, 1673. (101) ye / you *TM*. (104) *not indented* 1645, 1673. (105) *not indented* 1645, 1673.

A MASK

Date: before Sept. 29, 1634, date of first performance; revised and enlarged c. Sept.–Dec. 1637.
Texts: 1637, 1645°, 1673; TM°, Bridgewater MS. Two mss of five songs written by Henry Lawes are extant: British Museum Add. MS 11,518 (in an unknown hand) and the Lawes MS (in Lawes' hand). The songs are: ll. 976–83, 992–95, 998–99 (Song 1); 230–43 (Song 2); 859–66 (Song 3); 958–75 (Song 4 in two parts); 1012–23 (Song 5). There are a number of musical differences between the two manuscripts. Verbal variants from the present text are as follows: (976) To the Ocean / From the Heav'ns *BMS, LMS*. (981) gardens / Garden *BMS, LMS*. (999) young *Adonis* soft / many'a Cherub oft *BMS, LMS*. (231) cell / shell *BMS, LMS*. (233) the / thy *BMS, LMS*. (241) Parly / Pity *BMS*. (242) translated / Transplanted *BMS, LMS*. (243) And give resounding grace / & hold a Counterpoint *BMS, LMS*. (859) Sabrina / Sabrina Sabrina *BMS, LMS*. (866) Listen / Listen Listen *BMS, LMS*. (965) On . . . on / o're . . . o're *BMS, LMS*. (967) ye / you *BMS, LMS*. (1012) But now / Now *BMS, LMS*. (1014) green earths / Earths green *BMS, LMS*. Lines 1021–22 also appear in Milton's hand in the album of Camillus Cardoyn, June 10, 1639. The Bridgewater presentation volume of 1637, in the Carl Pforzheimer Library, contains the following manuscript corrections in Milton's hand: (20) my / by; (49) comma after "Coasting" deleted; (73) in / is; (131) at / art; (223) sables / sable; (417) "you" inserted; (443) we / she; (474) sensualitie / sensualtie; (781) reproachfull / contemptuous
List of *dramatis personae* given only in 1645. Instead of *Spirit*, the MSS use *Dæmon;* the *Elder Brother* is frequently called 1 *Bro*. (dir.) *The . . . enters.* / A Guardian Spirit, or Dæmon. *TM*, then a guardian spiritt or demon descendes or enters. *BM*. (Lines 975–82, 987–94, 994A, 995, 997–98) *given as prologue before l. 1 in BM*. (2) shapes / shape 1673. (6) with / w^ch *BM*. (12) by / with *BM*. (18) *not indented* TM, BM. (20) by / my 1637. (26) gives / give *TM*. (43) you *TM* / ye 1637, 1645. (46) *not indented* TM; grape / Grapes *BM*. (58) Whom / w^ch *BM*. (62) shade *TM* / shades 1637, 1645, 1673, *BM*. (73) is / in 1637. (83) robes / webs *BM*. (dir., 92–93) Comus enters wth a charming rod & glasse of liquor with his rout all headed like some wild beasts thire garments some like mens & some like womens they come on in a wild & antick fashion *TM; his glass* / & a glass of liquor *BM; headed . . . women,* / like men & women but headed like wild beasts *BM*. (99) dusky / Northerne *BM*. (123) has *TM* / hath 1637, 1645, 1673. (131) art / at 1637. (132) spitts *TM* / spets 1637, 1645, 1673, *BM*. (dir., 144–45) *The Measure.* / the measure (in a wild rude & wanton antick) *TM, BM*. (161) glozing / gloweinge *BM*. (167) *omitted* 1673; thrift / thirst *TM, in scribe's hand*. (168) *reversed with l. 169* 1673. (169) *reversed with l. 168* 1673; heer. / hear *erratum for 1673*. (170) *Lady.* / *omitted* 1637, 1645, 1673, TM; mine / my *TM, BM*. (174) amongst *TM* / among 1637, 1645, 1673, *BM*. (188–90) *omitted* BM. (189) weeds *TM* / weed 1645, 1673. (195) stoln / stole 1645, 1673; els . . . night / *omitted* BM. (196–225) *omitted* BM. (201) the / *missing* TM.

(214) flittering *TM* / hovering *1645, 1673, TM in scribe's hand*. (223) sable / sables *1637*. (226) hallow / hollowe *BM*. (229) off. / hence *TM, BM*. (231) cell *TM* / shell *1637, 1645, 1673, BM*. (241) of / to *BM*. (243) *And give resounding grace* / And hould a Counterpoint *BM*. (dir., 243–44) Comus looks in and speaks *TM, BM*. (252) she *TM* / it *1645, 1673*. (270) prosperous / prosperinge *BM*. (291) Two such / Such tow *TM*. (294) 'em *TM* / them *1637, 1645, 1673*. (300) colours / cooleness *BM*. (304) To / *omitted, but given as catchword* BM. (312) wide *TM* / wilde *1645, 1673*, wild *TM in scribe's hand, 1637*. (317) roosted / rooster *BM*. (dir., 330–31) the tow brothers enter *TM*. (349) this close / lone *BM*. (356) What if / or els *BM*. (357–65) *missing* TM, BM; *three other lines are found:* so fares as did forsaken Proserpine | when the big rowling flakes of pitchie clowds | & darknesse wound her in. 1 bro. Peace, brother peace |. (370) trust / hope *BM*. (384) walks in black vapours, though the noone tyde brand *BM*. (385) blaze in the summer solstice *BM*. (390) a / an *1637, BM*. (399) treasure / treasures *BM*. (401) on / at *BM*. (402) let / she *BM*. (403) wild / wide *TM, BM*. (409) controversie: / question, no *TM, BM*. (409 ff.) *TM, BM give five additional undeleted lines:* I could be willing though now i'th darke to trie | a tough encounter wth the shaggiest ruffian | that lurks by hedge or lane of this dead circuit | to have her by my side, though I were sure | she might be free from perill were she is |. (410) Yet / but *TM, BM*. (413) banish gladly *TM* / gladly banish *1637, 1645, 1673, BM*. (415) imagine, / imagine brother *TM, BM*. (417) if you mean / if meane *1637*. (428) there, / even *TM, BM*. (432) Som say / naye more *BM*. (433) moorie *TM* / moorish *1637, 1645, 1673, BM*. (437) Has *TM* / Hath *1645, 1673*. (438) ye / you *BM*. (443) she / we *1637*. (444) naught *TM* / nought *1637, 1645, 1673, BM*. (448) That / the *BM*. (460) Begin / begins *BM*. (465) But / and *TM, BM*; lewd and lavish / lewde lascivious *BM*. (472) Hovering, *TM* / Lingering, *1645, 1673*. (474) sensualty / sensuality *1637, 1673, BM*. (481) off / of *1673, BM*; hallow / hollowe *BM*. (dir., 488–89) he hallows the guardian Dæmon hallows agen & enters in the habit of shepheard *TM*, he hallowes and is answered, the guardian dæmon comes in habited like a shepheard. *BM*. (493) fathers *TM* / father *1637, 1645, 1673*. (497) thou / *omitted* BM; Swain? / shepheard, *TM, BM*. (498) his *TM* / the *1637, 1645, 1673, BM*. (513) you. *TM* / ye, *1645, 1673*. (520) *not indented* TM. (547) mediate / mediate upon *1673*. (553) frighted / flighted *TM*. (555) soft / sweete, *BM*. (556) a / the softe *BM*; steam / stream *1673*; rich / *omitted* BM. (563) did / might *TM, BM*. (572) knew) / knowe) *BM*. (581) ye / yon *BM*. (605) buggs *TM* / forms *1645, 1673*. (608) and cleave his scalp *TM* / to a foul death, *1645, 1673*. (609) Down to the hipps. *TM* / Curs'd as his life. *1645, 1673*. (610) Thy / The *BM*. (616) thy self / *omitted* BM. (626) ope / open *BM*. (632–37) *missing* BM. (637) Which *TM* / That *1637, 1645, 1673, BM*. (657) Ile / I *TM, BM*. (dir., 657–58) *State 1 of l. 1 found in British Museum copy* (C.34.d.46) *of 1637; soft Musick, / missing* TM, BM; *appears / is discover'd* TM; *to whom . . . rise.* / she offers to rise *TM*. (678A) poore ladie thou hast neede of some refreshinge *BM*. (679–87) *missing* BM. (688) have / hast *BM*. (689) have / hast *BM;* but / heere *BM*. (697–700) *missing* BM. (698) forgeries *TM* / forgery *1637, 1645, 1673*. (709) sallow / shallow *BM*. (731) multitude / inultitude *1637*. (733, 734) *combined into one line in BM:* would soe emblaze with

starrs, that they belowe (737–55) *missing* BM. (743) a / an *TM*. (746) on *TM* / and 1637, 1645, 1673. (751) or *TM* / and 1637, 1645, 1673. (758) mine / my *BM*. (779, 806) *combined into one line in TM, BM:* cramms & blasphems his feeder. Come no more (779–806) *missing* TM, BM. (780) anough? / anow? 1673. (781) contemptuous / reproachfull 1637. (dir., 813–14) *with Swords* . . . *ground;* / strike his glasse downe *TM*, with swords . . . glasse of liquor out . . . ground *BM; his rout* . . . *resistance* / the shapes make as though they would resist *TM; The attendant* . . . *in.* / Dæmon enter wth them *TM*, the Demon is to come in with the brothers *BM*. (814) you / yee *BM;* let / left *BM*. (821) which / that *TM, BM*. (824) *not indented* TM. (828) That / whoe *BM*. (829) She / The 1673. (834) pearled / peackled *BM*. (846A) *undeleted line in TM:* and often takes our cattell wth strange pinches. (847) *omitted* BM. (857) besetting / distressed *TM*. (dir., 866–67) The verse to singe or not. *BM*. (871–72) *assigned to* El bro: *BM*. (873–74) *assigned to* 2 bro: *BM*. (875–76) *assigned to* El br: *BM*. (877–78) *assigned to* 2 br: *BM*. (879–82) *assigned to* El br: *BM*. (883) *song from this line onward assigned to* De: *BM*. (dir. 889–90) *by* / w^th *TM; water* / the water *TM, BM; and sings.* / Sings *TM*. (890–901) *indentations are inconsistent in texts; TM is followed in present version.* (897) *set* / rest *BM*. (898) *velvet* / *omitted* BM. (900–1) *given as part of song* 1637, 1645, 1673, *BM*. (911) thy / this *BM*. (dir., 921–22) and / *missing* TM. (927) tumble / tumbled 1673. (dir. 937–38) *song ends TM, BM; no line space* 1673. (938) Lady / sister *BM*. (938–43) *assigned to* El bro: *BM*. (944–55) *assigned to* De: *BM*. (951) there / neere *TM, BM*. (953) thir / this *BM*. (956) *assigned to* el br: *BM;* grow / are 1637, *BM*. (dir., 957–58) Exeunt. *TM; presenting* / and then is præsented *TM, BM; com in* / enter *TM; country-dancers* / countrie dances & such like gambols &c. *TM*, Countrie daunces, and the like &c., *BM; after them* / at those sports *TM*, towards the end of these sports *BM; Lady.* / Ladie enter *TM*, ladye come in. *BM; Song* / the Dæmon sings *TM*, the spiritt singes. *BM*. (dir., 965–66) 2 song. *TM*, 2 songe p^rsents . . . mother. *BM*. (972) *assays* / assaye Morgan copy of 1637. (dir., 975–76) they dance. the dances all ended the Dæmon sings. or sayes *TM, BM*. (976–83, 988–95, 995A, 996, 998–99) *given at beginning of BM*. (976) To the Ocean / ffrom the heavens *BM*. (984–87) *missing* BM. (988) that *deleted by* 1673 *erratum.* (995A) yellow, watchett, greene & blew *BM*. (996) with / oft with *BM; Elysian* / Manna *BM*. (997) *missing* BM. (999) young *Adonis* / many a Cherub *BM;* oft / soft *BM*. (1000–11) *missing* BM. (1012) *not indented* TM; But now / Now *BM*. (1014) green earths / earths greene *BM*. (1018) *not indented* TM, BM. (1020) ye / you *BM*.

PSALM 114

Date: end of Nov. 1634; from reference, apparently to this paraphrase, in a letter to Alexander Gill, dated Dec. 4.

Texts: 1645°, 1673.

15 σκαρθμοῖσιν/σκαφμοῖσιν 1673.

16 σφριγόωντες/σφριγόωντης 1673.

18 μητέρι/μητήρι 1673.

PHILOSOPHUS AD REGEM . . .
Date: Dec. 1634 ?; perhaps close to *Ps.* 114 which it follows in 1645.
Texts: 1645°, 1673.
Title insontem / in tem 1673, *two lines,* son *apparently cut off by right margin during printing.*
¹ τὸν/'τ' 1673.
⁴ Μάψ αὔτως/Μαψιδίως 1673
χρόνῳ μάλα πολλὸν/τεὸν πρὸς θυμόν 1673.
⁵ τοιόνδ'/τοιόν δ' 1645, 1673
πόλεως/πόλιος 1673.

ON TIME
Date: 1633–1637 ?; see textual note for *Solemn Musick.*
Texts: 1645, 1673, TM°; Bodleian MS, Ashmole 36, 37, f. 22ʳ.
Title (To be) set on a clock case *TM, deleted, replaced by present title,* Vpon a Clocke Case, or Dyall *BMS.* (2) stepping / sleepeinge *BMS.* (17) the / your *BMS.* (18) t'whose / whose *BMS.* (19–22) Shall heape our days with everlastinge store | When death and Chance, and thou O tyme shalbee noe more. *BMS.*

UPON THE CIRCUMCISION
Date: 1633–37 ?; see textual note for *Solemn Musick.*
Texts: 1645, 1673, TM°.
(1) *not indented* 1645, 1673, TM. (14) *double indentation* 1645, 1673. (15) *not indented* 1645, 1673. (27) *not indented* 1673. (28) *double indentation* 1645, 1673.

AT A SOLEMN MUSICK
Date: 1637. Date depends on when TM was begun, since the ode was worked out in it shortly afterward. Recent argument has suggested its first use in autumn 1637 (see Shawcross, "Speculations"). All previously dated in the early 1630's, *On Time* and *Upon the Circumcision* precede *Solemn Musick* in composition but lie apparently close to it. Unlike the early sonnets, the three odes evidence Italian prosody drawn directly from Tuscan poetry, as Prince shows (pp. 59–65); here Milton developed the "disciplined improvisation" which is basic to *Lycidas.*
Texts: 1645, 1673, TM 4°. There are two preliminary drafts of the full poem (TM 1, TM 2) and an additional revision (TM 3) of ll. 17–28; since they are superseded by TM 4, they are not collated. A correction in Milton's hand is found in the Bodleian Library copy of 1645 (catalogued 8° M168 Art, but kept as Arch G.f.17): l. 6, "content" changed to "concent".
(6) concent / content, *1645.* (28) *not indented* 1645, 1673; with him, and sing *1645* / and sing with him *TM 4.*

LYCIDAS
Date: Nov. 1637; date given in TM.
Texts: Justa Edovardo King naufrago (1638), 1645°, 1673, TM°. Corrections in Milton's hand occur in the Cambridge University copy of 1638 and in British Museum copy C.21.c.42: (10) he knew / he well knew *CM, BM.* (51) lord

/ lov'd *CM, BM.* (53) the old / your old *CM.* (67) do, / use *CM, BM.* (157) humming / whelming *CM, BM.* (175) oazie / oozie *CM;* oosie *also in margin of CM.* (177) in the blest kingdom[s meeke] of Joy, and Love. *added CM without comma and period, BM with bracketed section torn off.* A scrap of proof for p. 21 of 1638, ll. 23–58, was found pasted on the inner side of the back cover of *De Literis & Lingua Getarum,* 1597, in the Cambridge University Library (facsimile in Scolar ed.). Corrections, etc., are: (25, 27, 28, 29, 31, 41, 49) *corrections of letters.* (26) eye-lids *hyphen inserted.* (27) a-field, *hyphen inserted.* (31) wheel. *period inserted.* (32, 37, 52) *realignment of type.* Alterations made to the TM after 1640 are not, of course, found in 1638.

Headnote *missing* 1638 And . . . height. / *missing* TM. (10) he well knew / he knew *1638, 1645, 1673.* (15) *not indented* British Museum copy 1077.d.51 of 1638. (25) *not indented* 1638. (26) opening / glimmering *1638.* (30) Oft till the ev'n-starre bright *1638;* in / at *1645, 1673.* (31) westring / burnisht *1638.* (50) *not indented* 1638. (51) lov'd / lord *1638.* (53) your / the *1638.* (56) Ay / Ah *1638.* (64) *not indented* 1638; incessant / uncessant *1638, 1645, 1673.* (65) tend / end *1673.* (66) strictly / stridly *1638.* (67) use, / do, *1638.* (69) Or with / Hid in *1638.* (73) when / where *1638.* (85) *not indented* 1638. (103) *not indented* 1638. (105) Inwraught / Inwrought *1638, 1645, 1673.* (114) Anow / Enough *1638,* anough *TM.* (129) little / nothing *1645, 1673, not reinstated in TM.* (131) smite / smites *1638.* (149) beauties / beauty *1638, 1645, 1673.* (157) whelming / humming *1638, TM.* (177) *omitted* 1638.

AD PATREM

Date: Mar. 1638 ?; probably written about the time of publication of *Mask* (c. Feb.–Mar. 1638 ?), perhaps to accompany a gift copy. The poem may have been provoked by opposition to Milton's travelling abroad in preparation for a literary career. H. A. Barnett (*MLN,* LXXIII [1958], 82–83) has shown that the time of year of composition may be around Mar.
Texts: 1645°, 1673.
(8) possint / possunt *1673.*

AD SALSILLUM

Date: Nov. ? 1638; during first visit to Rome since it precedes *Mansus* in 1645.
Texts: 1645°, 1673.

MANSUS

Date: Dec. 1638; written and sent to Manso when Milton was in Naples.
Texts: 1645°, 1673.
(62) Peneium / Peceium *1645 Fletcher.* (82) Aut / Ant *1673.* (83) adsit) / ad sit) *1645, 1673.*

AD LEONORAM ROMÆ CANENTEM

Date: Feb. ? 1639; composed apparently during second visit to Rome.
Texts: 1645°, 1673.

AD EANDEM: "Another Leonora captured . . ."
Date: Feb. ? 1639; composed apparently during second visit to Rome.
Texts: 1645°, 1673.
(5) canentem / canentam *1673, erratum corrects.* (8) desipuisset / desipuiiset
1645, desipulisset *1673, erratum corrects.*

AD EANDEM: "Why, credulous Naples, . . ."
Date: Feb. ? 1639; composed apparently during second visit to Rome.
Texts: 1645°, 1673.

EPITAPHIUM DAMONIS
Date: autumn 1639; see headnote and ll. 58–61, 64, the notably rainy season of
England being Oct.–Nov. and the poem being written around harvest time.
Texts: 1640 (?), 1645°, 1673. At conclusion 1640 has: "Londini". *Headnote*
oriundus, / onundus, *1640.*

SONNET 8
Date: before Nov. 13, 1642, the date on which the Royalist army would have
reached London.
Texts: 1645, 1673, TM° (scribe).
Title On his dore when yᵉ Citty expected an assault *TM, scribe, deleted,* When
the assault was intended to yᵉ Citty 1642 *TM, Milton, date deleted.* (3) If
deed of honour did thee ever please, *1673.*

SONNET 9
Date: 1643–45; position in TM.
Texts: 1645, 1673, TM°.
(5) with *Ruth* / the *Ruth,* 1645. (13) of night, *1645* / ( ) night *TM.*

SONNET 10
Date: 1643–45; position in TM.
Texts: 1645, 1673, TM°.
Title To yᵉ Lady Margaret Ley *TM.*

IN EFFIGIEI EJUS SCULPTOREM
Date: 1645; written to accompany portrait, drawn in 1645 for the first collected
edition, though apparently based also on the Onslow portrait of 1629. In *Pro se
defensio* (p. 84) Milton indicates the execution of the portrait for the edition of
the poems.
Texts: 1645°, 1673. Given under portrait (frontispiece) in 1645, without title.
2 βλέπων' / βλόπων 1673.

SONNET 11
Date: autumn 1645 ?; traditional dating is 1646 ? since the poem follows *Son.*
13 in TM; however, its numbering and l. 3 suggest an earlier date of compo-
sition.
Texts: 1673, TM° 1 (Milton), TM 2 (scribe).
Numbered eleven by Milton and scribe, but transposed with *Son.* 12 by 1673
printer and erroneously titled to achieve topic reference.

Title *On the same.* 1673, On the detraction wch follow'd upon my writing certain treatises *TM 1, deleted; TM 2.* (4) cuckoes, *TM 2* / buzzards, *TM 1.*

SONNET 13
Date: c. Feb. 9, 1646; from TM.
Texts: Choice Psalmes put into Musick For Three Voices (1648), 1673, TM 2°
(Milton), TM 3 (scribe). A first draft (TM 1) in Milton's hand, being superseded by TM 2, is not collated except for its title, source of the 1648 title. Present lines 6 and 8 are not found in TM 1.
Title To my Friend M^r. Henry Lawes. 1648, To Mr. H. Lawes, on his Aires.
1673, TM 3 (as result of deletions), To my friend Mr Hen. Laws Feb. 9. 1645
TM 1, To M^r: Hen: Laws on the publishing of his Aires *TM 2* (scribe, in reference to 1653 publication), TM 3 (deleted to 1673 form with alteration to Lawes). (9) lend / send *1673.* (11) story. / °story. *1648, which has four lines in left margin:* "The story of Ariadne set by him in Music."

SONNET 14
Date: Dec. 1646; from TM.
Texts: 1673, TM 2° (Milton), TM 3 (scribe). A first draft (TM 1) in Milton's hand, being superseded by TM 2, is not collated except for its unique title.
Title On ye religious memorie of Mrs Catharine Thomason my christian freind deceas'd 16 Decem. 1646 *TM 1, deleted* (16, separately deleted, apparently was a false start of year). (1) thee / the TM 3. (12) in / on *1673, TM 3.*

AD JOANNEM ROÜSIUM
Date: Jan. 1647; printed date, perhaps of delivery, is Jan. 23.
Texts: 1673; Bodleian Library MS, Lat. misc. d. 77° (scribe, with a one-word correction by Milton).
Title *Ode.* / Ode. Joannis Miltonj *MS.*

THE FIFTH ODE OF HORACE. BOOK 1.
Date: 1646–48 ?; conjectural; appears before *Forcers of Conscience* in 1673, except for incorrectly placed *Vacation Exercise.* Dated by others from 1626 to 1655, but specific Latin text may not have been published before 1636.
Text: 1673°. All variants from 1673.
English Text: Title Book / Lib.
Latin Text: Three differences from modern versions are found: "munditie" and "quoties" in l. 5, and "Intentata" in l. 13. The text published by Milton, including these variants and not evidencing differences, is found in *Quinti Horatii Flacci poëmata scholiis siva annotationibus a I. Bond illustrata* (Amsterodami: G. J. Blaeuw, 1636).

SONNET 12
Date: Jan. 1647 ?; from position in TM.
Texts: 1673, TM 1° (Milton with revisions by scribe), TM 2 (scribe).
Numbered twelve by Milton and scribe, but transposed with *Son.* 11 by 1673 printer. (8) is it harder, / is harder *1673, erratum adds* it. (9) Colkitto, / Coliktto, *1673, corrected by erratum.*

ON THE FORCERS OF CONSCIENCE

Date: early 1647 ?; conjectured from intended position in TM. Two notes—one by Milton, one by a scribe—both place the poem between *Son.* 12 and *Son.* 15.

Texts: 1673, TM* (scribe, revisions by second scribe).

Title *On the new forcers of Conscience under the Long PARLIAMENT.* 1673. (1) off / of 1673. (17) bauk / bank 1673, *changed by erratum.*

PSALMS 80–88

Date: Apr. 1648; published note.

Text: 1673*. All variants from 1673.

Ps. 80: (77) *verse number omitted. Ps.* 81: *margin* (29) *Besether / *Be Sether;* (66) flour / flowr. *Ps.* 83: (8) high / hie.

SONNET 15

Date: Aug. 1648; on basis of TM title, before news of capture of Colchester (Aug. 27) reached London.

Texts: Letters of State (1694), TM*.

No lines are indented in 1694. In l. 8 TM reads "their" but the editor believes Milton's "her" was altered by an unknown hand; see note to ll. 7–8. "Warrs" in l. 10 has been mistranscribed as "Warr," in other editions.

Title To my Lord FAIRFAX. *1694,* On yᵉ Lord Gen. Fairfax at yᵉ seige of Colchester *TM, deleted.* (2) Filling each mouth / And fills all Mouths *1694.* (4) that / which *1694.* (5) vertue / Valour *1694.* (6) though / while *1694.* (8) her / their *TM.* (10) Warrs / War, *1694;* endless / Acts of *1694.* (11) Truth, and Right / injur'd Truth *1694.* (12) cleard from the shamefull brand / be rescu'd from the Brand *1694.* (14) share / shares *1694.*

VERSE FROM PRO POPULO ANGLICANO DEFENSIO

Date: 1650; ordered to answer Salmasius, Jan. 8, 1650, and *Defensio prima* published in Feb. 1651.

Texts: Madan #1 (1651)*, p. 154; Madan #2 (1651), p. 202; Madan #9 (1651), p. 249; Madan #13 (1652), p. 212; Madan #14 (1658), p. 127. See F. F. Madan, *The Library,* Ser. 4, IV (1923–24), 119–45, and Ser. 5, IX (1954), 112–21. The poem appears in Chapter 8.

SONNET 16

Date: May 1652; from TM.

Texts: Letters of State (1694), TM* (scribe, revisions by second scribe). No lines are indented in 1694.

Title To Oliver Cromwell. *1694,* To the Lord Generall Cromwell May 1652 On the proposalls of certaine ministers at yᵉ Commtee for Propagation of the Gospell *TM, deleted.* (1) who / that *1694;* cloud / Croud, *1694.* (2) detractions / distractions *1694.* (5) *omitted* 1694. (6) Hast reard Gods Trophies / And Fought God's Battels, *1694.* (7) stream / Streams *1694.* (8) resounds / resound *1694.* (11) renown'd then / than those of *1694.* (12) with / in *1694.*

SONNET 17
Date: June ? 1652; according to a statement in 1662 (p. 93), the sonnet was sent to Vane on July 3.
Texts: Life and Death of Sir Henry Vane (1662), *Letters of State* (1694), TM° (scribe).
Only l. 9 is indented in 1694. *Title* To Sir *HENRY VANE.* 1694, To Sr Henry Vane the younger *TM, deleted.* (7) best, / best be *1694.* (8) Move / Mann'd *1694.* (10) power / *omitted 1694.* (11) severs / serves *1694.* (13) firm / Right *1694.* (14) And reckons thee in chief her Eldest Son. *1694.*

PSALMS 1–8
Dates: Aug. 7–14, 1653; published note.
Text: 1673°.
Ps. 4: (14) *apart / a part 1673.*

VERSE FROM DEFENSIO SECUNDA
Date: 1654 ?; *Defensio secunda* was published in May 1654.
Texts: Ed. 1° (London, 1654), pp. 38–39; Ed. 2 (Hague, 1654), p. 28; Ed. 3 (Hague, 1654), p. 28.
(2) algentes / algentis *Edd. 2, 3.* (4) amicire / amiciri *Ed. 3.*

SONNET 18
Date: May ? 1655; date of state letters.
Text: 1673°.
Title *On the late Massacher in* Piemont. *1673.* (10) sow / so *1673, erratum corrects.*

SONNET 19
Date: Oct. ? 1655; position in 1673 edition. Date of composition is frequently given as 1652 because of l. 2 and the date of Milton's blindness; however, see n. to that line.
Text: 1673°.
(12) *indented 1673.*

SONNET 20
Date: Oct.–Nov. 1655; position in 1673 and ll. 2–5.
Text: 1673°.

SONNET 21
Date: Oct.–Nov. 1655; position in TM and 1673.
Texts: 1673°, TM°, ll. 5–14 (scribe). Lines 1–4 are missing in TM.
(2) with / with with *1673.* (8) intends / intend, *1673.*

SONNET 22
Date: Dec. 1655; position in TM and reference in l. 1 to total blindness (around beginning of 1652).
Texts: Letters of State (1694), TM° (scribe).
No lines are indented in 1694. *Title* To Mr. *Cyriac Skinner* Upon his Blindness.

1694. (3) light / Sight, *1694.* (4) sight / day *1694.* (5) Of / Or *1694.* (7) a / one *1694.* (12) talks / rings *1694.* (13) the / this *1694.* (14) better / other *1694.*

SONNET 23

Date: 1656–58 ?; date of composition may depend on the wife intended; however, the scribe is not known to have been employed by Milton before Jan. 1658.
Texts: 1673, TM* (scribe).

PARADISE LOST

Date: 1642 ?–1665 ?; early drafts probably date c. 1640, and Edward Phillips (Darbishire, pp. 72–73) read IV, 32–41, c. 1642.
Texts: 1667 (arguments, verse discussion, and errata added in reissues of 1668, 1669), 1674*; MS of I in Morgan Library (scribe, with corrections by various hands). Two different title pages exist for each issue of the first edition, the preliminary material being added with the second title page of 1668. There are two states of the first page of the first printing of this material: "The Printer to the Reader" appears in a four-line form and a six-line form. A second printing of the preliminary material, of sig. Z (VII.1–238), and of sig. Vv (X.1424–1541) was made at the time that the second title page of 1669 was produced. Two or three states exist in a number of signatures of 1667, two in the second printing of the verse, and three in the second printing of sig. Vv. The second edition of 1674 shows two states in sigs. A–D (Books I–II), alterations of three page numbers in later signatures, and a change of one word in the argument to X. A copy of this edition with a 1675 title page is found in the Univ. of Illinois Library; the copy shows a State 2 printing except for the recto of the B sig. in State 1. The MS apparently was the copy text for the first edition.

VERSE

and of *Virgil* / and *Virgil* 1669 printing.

BOOK I
(Argument) This / The *1668, 1669 printings.* (25) Eternal / th'Eternal *1667, corrected by erratum.* (159) aught MS / ought *1667, 1674.* (173) The / This MS. (377) thir / the *1667, 1674,* MS. (432) these MS / those *1667, 1674.* (504) th'hospitable dore / hospitable Dores *1667,* MS. (505) Expos'd a Matron to avoid / Yielded thir Matrons to prevent *1667,* MS. (530) fainting / fainted *1667,* MS. (603) courage, / valour, MS. (703) founded MS, *1667* / found out *1674.* (756) Capitol MS, *changed* / Capital *1667, 1674,* MS. (758) Band and / and Band *1667, reversed by erratum.*

BOOK II
(Argument) shall / should *1669 printing.* (282) where, *1667* / were, *1674.* (483) thir *1667* / her *1674.* (527) his *1667* / this *1674.* (881) grate / great *1667, corrected by erratum.*

BOOK III
(Argument) his right hand / the right hand *1669 printing;* plac't here, / plac't

there, *1669 printing.* (592) Mettal / Medal *1667, 1674.* (594) With / Which *1667.* (741) in / with *1667, State 1, corrected by erratum.*

BOOK IV

(Argument) find him / find him out *1668, 1669.* (451) on *1667* / of *1674.* (627) walk / walks *1667.* (705) shadier *1667* / shadie *1674.* (928) The *1667* / Thy *1674.*

BOOK V

(Argument) appearance / appearing *1669 printing.* (257) *indented* 1667, States 1, 2. (361) *indented 1667, 1674.* (616) *not indented* 1667, State 1. (627) now / *missing* 1667. (636–40) *text revised in 1674.* (636) *missing* 1667. (637) in communion / with refection *1667.* (638–39) *missing* 1667. (640) Excess, / Are fill'd, *1667.* (659) in / *missing* 1667, added by erratum. (830) one / our *1667, State 1.*

BOOK VII

(25) dayes, / tongues; *1669 printing.* (126) as / a *1669 printing.* (224) the / his *1669 printing.* (366) her / his *1667.* (451) Soul / Fowle *1667,* Foul *1674.*

BOOK VIII

Continued as VII.641–1290 in 1667; Argument is the last half of the Argument of VII. (Argument) *Adam* inquires / *Adam* then inquires *1668, 1669;* search / seek *1669 printing.* (1–3) *added 1674.* (4) To whom thus *Adam* gratefully repli'd. *1667.* (269) as *1667* / and *1674.* (398) *not indented 1674.*

BOOK IX

This is Book VIII in 1667. (92) sleights / fleights *1667.* (186) Nor / Not *1667.* (213) hear *1667* / bear *1674.* (347) aught / ought *1667.* (394) Likest *1667* / Likeliest *1674.* (632) made / make *1667.* (922) hast *1667* / hath *1674.* (1019) we *1667* / me *1674.* (1092) for *1667* / from *1674.* (1093) from *1667* / for *1674.* (1183) Woman / Women *1667, 1674.*

BOOK X

This is Book IX in 1667. (Argument) Son / Angels *1669 printing;* meet / met *1674, State 1;* full assembly *1668, 1669* / full of assembly *1674;* taste *1668, 1669* / take *1674.* (58) may *1667* / might *1674.* (241) Avengers, / Avenger, *1667.* (397) those *1667* / these *1674.* (408) prevail, *1667* / prevailes, *1674.* (550) fair *1667* / omitted *1674.* (827) then / omitted *1667.* (989–90) So Death *printed in l. 990 in 1667, 1674.*

BOOK XI

First half of Book X (ll. 1–897) and of Argument in 1667, 1668. (Argument) but declares / and declares *1669 printing;* Cherubim / Cherubims *1669 printing.* (380) to amplest *1667* / to the amplest *1674.* (427) sin derive *1667* / derive *1674.* (485–87) *added 1674.* (551–52) Of rendring up. *Michael* to him repli'd. *1667.* (579) last / lost *1667, corrected by erratum.* (651) tacks *1667* / makes *1674.* (870) who / that *1667.*

BOOK XII

Last half of Book X (ll. 898–1541) and of Argument in 1667, 1668. (Argument) The Angel . . . Fall; / thence from the Flood relates, and by degrees explains, who that Seed of the Woman shall be; *1668, 1669.* (1–5) *added 1674.* (6) *not indented* 1667. (191) The / This *1667.* (238) what they besaught / them thir desire, *1667.* (534) Will *1667* / Well *1674.*

PARADISE REGAIN'D

Date: c. 1646–48 ?; revised or, according to some critics, written after 1665; based on evidence of prosodic development (see Shawcross, "Chronology").
Text: 1671°.
All variants are from 1671. *BOOK I* (226) subdue. / destroy. *erratum replaces.* (333) aught / ought (400) Nearer / Never *erratum corrects.* (417) Imparts / Imports *erratum corrects.* (470) wrested / rested *BOOK II* (128) threat'ns then our / threat'ns our *erratum adds.* (341) pil'd, / pill'd, *erratum corrects.* BOOK *III* (238) insight / in sight (324) showers / shower *erratum corrects.* BOOK *IV* (124) compliments / complements (217) wast / was (288) ought / aught

SAMSON AGONISTES

Date: 1646–48 ?; revised, 1653 or later?; based on prosodic development (see Shawcross, "Chronology"); dates are those conjectured by Parker.
Text: 1671°.
All variants are from 1671. *Verse: paragraphed at "It suffices . . ." with no sentence break after "fift Act".* Drama: (157) complain) / complain'd) *changed by erratum.* (222) motion'd / mention'd *changed by erratum.* (306) indented State 1. (354) And such / Such *first word added by erratum.* (390) scent / sent (496) But I *misplaced on l.* 497. (660) with / to *changed by erratum.* (720) scent / sent (1248) divulge / divulg'd *changed by erratum.* (1313) rate, / race, *changed by erratum.* (1527–35, 1537) *added as* Omissa. (1552) here / heard *changed by erratum.*

Bibliography

WORKS

Bush, Douglas, J. E. Shaw, and A. Bartlett Giamatti, eds. *A Variorum Commentary on the Poems of John Milton*. New York: Columbia Univ. Press, 1970. Vol. 1.

Fletcher, Harris F., ed. *John Milton's Complete Poetical Works, Reproduced in Photographic Facsimile*. Urbana: Univ. of Illinois Press, 1943–48. Four vols.

Horwood, Alfred, ed. *A Common-Place Book of John Milton*. London: 1876. In facsimile.

Patrick, J. Max, gen. ed. *The Prose of John Milton*. Garden City: Doubleday & Co., Inc., 1967.

Patterson, Frank A., gen. ed. *The Works of John Milton*. New York: Columbia Univ. Press, 1931–38. Eighteen vols. in twenty-one.

Wolfe, Don M., gen. ed. *Complete Prose Works of John Milton*. New Haven: Yale Univ. Press, 1953–66. Four vols. in five to date.

REFERENCE

Bradshaw, John. *A Concordance to the Poetical Works of John Milton*. New York: Macmillan, 1894; reprinted, Hamden: Archon Books, 1965.

Le Comte, Edward S. *A Milton Dictionary*. New York: Philosophical Library, 1961.

BIBLIOGRAPHY

Fletcher, Harris F. *Contributions to a Milton Bibliography, 1800–1930*. Urbana: Univ. of Illinois Press, 1931; reprinted, New York: Russell and Russell, 1967. Addenda to Stevens.

Huckabay, Calvin. *John Milton: An Annotated Bibliography, 1929–1968*. Pittsburgh: Duquesne Univ. Press, 1969.

Stevens, David H. *Reference Guide to Milton from 1800 to the Present Day*. Chicago: Univ. of Chicago Press, 1930; reprinted, New York: Russell and Russell, 1967. Through 1928.

BIOGRAPHY

Clark, Donald L. *John Milton at St. Paul's School*. New York: Columbia Univ. Press, 1948; reprinted, Hamden: Shoe String Press, 1964.

Darbishire, Helen, ed. *The Early Lives of Milton*. London: Constable, 1932; reprinted, 1966.

Dorian, Donald C. *The English Diodatis*. New Brunswick: Rutgers Univ. Press, 1950.

Fletcher, Harris F. *The Intellectual Development of John Milton.* Urbana: Univ. of Illinois Press, 1956–62. Two vols. to date.

French, J. Milton, ed. *The Life Records of John Milton.* New Brunswick: Rutgers Univ. Press, 1949–58; reprinted, Stapleton, N.Y.: Gordian Press, 1966. Five vols.

Masson, David. *The Life of John Milton.* London: 1881–94; reprinted, New York: Peter Smith, 1946. Seven vols.

Parker, William R. *Milton: A Biography.* Oxford: Clarendon Press, 1968. Two vols.

Tillyard, E. M. W. *Milton.* London: Chatto and Windus, 1930; revised, 1966.

FAME AND INFLUENCE

Good, John W. *Studies in the Miltonic Tradition.* Urbana: Univ. of Illinois Press, 1915; reprinted, New York: Johnson Reprint Co., 1967.

Havens, Raymond D. *The Influence of Milton on English Poetry.* Cambridge, Mass.: Harvard Univ. Press, 1922; reprinted, London: Russell and Russell, 1961.

Nelson, James G. *The Sublime Puritan: Milton and the Victorians.* Madison: Univ. of Wisconsin Press, 1963.

Parker, William R. *Milton's Contemporary Reputation.* Columbus: Ohio State Univ. Press, 1940.

Sensabaugh, George. *Milton in Early America.* Princeton: Princeton Univ. Press, 1964.

Sensabaugh, George. *That Grand Whig, Milton.* Stanford: Stanford Univ. Press, 1952; reprinted, New York: Benjamin Blom, 1968.

Shawcross, John T., ed. *Milton: The Critical Heritage.* London: Routledge and Kegan Paul, 1970. Through 1731.

Wittreich, Joseph A., Jr., ed. *The Romantics on Milton.* Cleveland: Case Western Reserve Univ. Press, 1970.

STUDIES OF THE POETRY

Adams, Robert M. *Ikon: John Milton and the Modern Critics.* Ithaca: Cornell Univ. Press, 1955; reprinted, 1966.

Allen, Don Cameron. *The Harmonious Vision: Studies in Milton's Poetry.* Baltimore: Johns Hopkins Press, 1954.

Barker, Arthur, ed. *Milton: Modern Essays in Criticism.* New York: Oxford Univ. Press, 1965.

Daniells, Roy. *Milton, Mannerism and Baroque.* Toronto: Univ. of Toronto Press, 1963.

Grace, William. *Ideas in Milton.* Notre Dame: Univ. of Notre Dame Press, 1968.

Grierson, H. J. C. *Milton and Wordsworth: Poets and Prophets. A Study of Their Reactions to Political Events.* Cambridge: Cambridge Univ. Press, 1937; often reprinted.

Hanford, James Holly. *John Milton, Poet and Humanist.* Cleveland: Case Western Reserve Univ. Press, 1966.

Hughes, Merritt Y. *Ten Perspectives on Milton*. New Haven: Yale Univ. Press, 1965.

Hunter, William B., Jr., "The Sources of Milton's Prosody," *Philological Quarterly*, XXVIII (1949), 125–44.

Kermode, Frank, ed. *The Living Milton: Essays by Various Hands*. London: Routledge and Kegan Paul, 1960.

Lawry, Jon S. *The Shadow of Heaven: Matter and Stance in Milton's Poetry*. Ithaca: Cornell Univ. Press, 1968.

Madsen, William G. *From Shadowy Types to Truth: Studies in Milton's Symbolism*. New Haven: Yale Univ. Press, 1968.

Madsen, William G., "The Idea of Nature in Milton's Poetry," *Three Studies in the Renaissance*. New Haven: Yale Univ. Press, 1958. Pages 181–283.

Mahood, M. M. *Poetry and Humanism*. New Haven: Yale Univ. Press, 1950; reprinted, Port Washington, N.Y.: Kennikat Press, 1967.

Marilla, E. L. *Milton and Modern Man: Selected Essays*. University: Univ. of Alabama Press, 1968.

Milton Studies in Honor of Harris Francis Fletcher. Urbana: Univ. of Illinois Press, 1961.

Nicolson, Marjorie Hope. *John Milton: A Reader's Guide to His Poetry*. New York: Farrar, Straus, 1963.

Patrick, J. Max, ed. *SAMLA Studies in Milton*. Gainesville: Univ. of Florida Press, 1953.

Prince, F. T. *The Italian Element in Milton's Verse*. Oxford: Clarendon Press, 1954; reprinted, 1962.

Reesing, John. *Milton's Poetic Art: A Mask, Lycidas, and Paradise Lost*. Cambridge, Mass.: Harvard Univ. Press, 1968.

Rudrum, Alan, ed. *Milton: Modern Judgements*. London: Macmillan, 1968.

Schultz, Howard. *Milton and Forbidden Knowledge*. New York: Modern Language Association, 1955.

Sprott, S. Ernest. *Milton's Art of Prosody*. Oxford: Blackwell, 1953.

Thompson, E. N. S. *Essays on Milton*. New Haven: Yale Univ. Press, 1914; reprinted, New York: Russell and Russell, 1967.

Tillyard, E. M. W. *The Miltonic Setting: Past and Present*. Cambridge: Cambridge Univ. Press, 1938; often reprinted.

Tillyard, E. M. W. *Studies in Milton*. London: Chatto and Windus, 1951; often reprinted.

Watkins, Walter B. C. *An Anatomy of Milton's Verse*. Baton Rouge: Louisiana State Univ. Press, 1955; reprinted, Hamden: Shoe String Press, 1965.

Whiting, George. *Milton and This Pendant World*. Austin: Univ. of Texas Press, 1958; reprinted, New York: Octagon Books, 1967.

Whiting, George. *Milton's Literary Milieu*. Chapel Hill: Univ. of North Carolina Press, 1939; reprinted, London: Russell and Russell, 1964.

GENERAL CRITICISM

Banks, Theodore. *Milton's Imagery*. New York: Columbia Univ. Press, 1950.

Barker, Arthur. *Milton and the Puritan Dilemma, 1641–1660*. Toronto: Univ. of Toronto Press, 1942; reprinted, 1956.

Curry, Walter C. *Milton's Ontology, Cosmogony, and Physics.* Lexington: Univ. of Kentucky Press, 1957.

Eliot, T. S. *Milton.* Annual Lecture on a Master Mind (British Academy). Oxford: Oxford Univ. Press, 1947. Variously reprinted.

Eliot, T. S., "A Note on the Verse of John Milton," *Essays and Studies,* XXI (1936), 2–40. Variously reprinted.

Fink, Zera S. *The Classical Republicans.* Evanston: Northwestern Univ. Press, 1945, 1962.

Fixler, Michael. *Milton and the Kingdoms of God.* Evanston: Northwestern Univ. Press, 1964.

Hanford, James Holly, and James Taaffe. *A Milton Handbook.* Revised edition. New York: Appleton-Century-Crofts, 1970.

Kranidas, Thomas. *The Fierce Equation: A Study of Milton's Decorum.* The Hague: Mouton, 1965.

Le Comte, Edward S. *Yet Once More: Verbal and Psychological Pattern in Milton.* New York: Liberal Arts Press, 1954.

Patrides, C. A. *Milton and the Christian Tradition.* Oxford: Clarendon Press, 1966.

Samuel, Irene. *Plato and Milton.* Ithaca: Cornell Univ. Press, 1947; reprinted, 1965.

Saurat, Denis. *Milton: Man and Thinker.* Revised edition, London: Dent, 1944, 1946; reprinted, Hamden: Archon Books, 1964.

Shawcross, John T., "Speculations on the Dating of the Trinity MS of Milton's Poems," *Modern Language Notes,* LXXV (1960), 11–17.

Svendsen, Kester. *Milton and Science.* Cambridge, Mass.: Harvard Univ. Press, 1956.

Wolfe, Don M. *Milton in the Puritan Revolution.* New York: Thomas Nelson, 1941; reprinted, New York: Humanities Press, 1963.

MINOR POEMS

Arthos, John. *On "A Mask Presented at Ludlow-Castle".* Ann Arbor: Univ. of Michigan Press, 1954.

Brooks, Cleanth, and John E. Hardy, eds. *Poems of Mr. John Milton: The 1645 Edition with Essays in Analysis.* New York: Harcourt, Brace, 1951; reprinted, New York: Gordian Press, 1968.

Demaray, John G. *Milton and the Masque Tradition: The Early Poems, Arcades, and Comus.* Cambridge, Mass.: Harvard Univ. Press, 1968.

Diekhoff, John S., ed. *A Maske at Ludlow: Essays on Milton's Comus.* Cleveland: Case Western Reserve Univ. Press, 1968.

Elledge, Scott, ed. *Milton's Lycidas: Edited to Serve as an Introduction to Criticism.* New York: Harper & Row, 1966.

Honigmann, E. A. J., ed. *Milton's Sonnets.* London: Macmillan, 1966.

Parker, William R., "Notes on the Chronology of Milton's Latin Poems," *A Tribute to G. C. Taylor.* Chapel Hill: Univ. of North Carolina Press, 1952. Pages 113–31.

Patrides, C. A., ed. *Milton's Lycidas: The Tradition and the Poem.* New York: Holt, Rinehart & Winston, 1961.

Smart, John S., ed. *The Sonnets of John Milton.* Glasgow: Maclehose, Jackson, 1921; reprinted, Oxford: Clarendon Press, 1966.

Tuve, Rosemond. *Images and Themes in Five Poems by Milton.* Cambridge, Mass.: Harvard Univ. Press, 1957.

MAJOR POEMS

Broadbent, J. B. *Some Graver Subject: an Essay on Paradise Lost.* London: Chatto and Windus, 1960; reprinted, London: Schocken Books, 1967.

Burden, Dennis H. *The Logical Epic: A Study of the Argument of Paradise Lost.* London: Routledge and Kegan Paul, 1967.

Bush, Douglas. *Paradise Lost in Our Time.* Ithaca: Cornell Univ. Press, 1945; reprinted, New York: Peter Smith, 1948, 1957.

Chambers, A. B., "Chaos in *Paradise Lost,*" *Journal of the History of Ideas,* XXIV (1963), 55–84.

Cope, Jackson I. *The Metaphoric Structure of Paradise Lost.* Baltimore: Johns Hopkins Press, 1962.

Diekhoff, John. *Milton's Paradise Lost, a Commentary on the Argument.* New York: Columbia Univ. Press, 1946; reprinted, New York: Humanities Press, 1958.

Emma, Ronald David, and John T. Shawcross, eds. *Language and Style in Milton.* New York: Frederick Ungar, 1967.

Empson, William. *Milton's God.* London: Chatto and Windus, 1961; revised, 1965.

Evans, J. M. *Paradise Lost and the Genesis Tradition.* Oxford: Clarendon Press, 1968.

Ferry, Anne Davidson. *Milton's Epic Voice: The Narrator in Paradise Lost.* Cambridge, Mass.: Harvard Univ. Press, 1963.

Fish, Stanley E. *Surprised by Sin: the Reader in Paradise Lost.* London: Macmillan, 1967.

Frye, Northrop. *The Return of Eden.* Toronto: Univ. of Toronto Press, 1965.

Gardner, Helen. *A Reading of Paradise Lost.* Oxford: Oxford Univ. Press, 1965.

Gilbert, Allan H., "Is *Samson Agonistes* Unfinished?" *Philological Quarterly,* XXVIII (1949), 176–94.

Gilbert, Allan H. *On the Composition of Paradise Lost.* Chapel Hill: Univ. of North Carolina Press, 1947; reprinted, New York: Octagon Books, 1966.

Hägin, Peter. *The Epic Hero and the Decline of Heroic Poetry: A Study of the Neoclassical English Epic with special reference to Milton's Paradise Lost.* Bern: Francke, 1964.

Harding, Davis P. *The Club of Hercules: Studies in the Classical Background of Paradise Lost.* Urbana: Univ. of Illinois Press, 1962.

Jebb, Sir R. C. *Samson Agonistes and the Hellenic Drama.* London: H. Frowde, 1908.

Kelley, Maurice. *This Great Argument: a Study of Milton's De Doctrina Christiana as a Gloss upon Paradise Lost.* Princeton: Princeton Univ. Press, 1941; reprinted, Gloucester, Mass.: Peter Smith, 1962.

Kirkconnell, Watson. *The Celestial Cycle: The Theme of Paradise Lost in World*

Literature, with Translations of the Major Analogues. Toronto: Univ. of Toronto Press, 1952; reprinted, New York: Gordian Press, 1968.

Kirkconnell, Watson. *That Invincible Samson: The Theme of Samson Agonistes in World Literature with Translations of the Major Analogues.* Toronto: Univ. of Toronto Press, 1964.

Kranidas, Thomas, ed. *New Essays on Paradise Lost.* Berkeley: Univ. of California Press, 1969.

Krouse, F. Michael. *Milton's Samson and the Christian Tradition.* Princeton: Princeton Univ. Press, 1949; reprinted, Hamden: Shoe String Press, 1963.

Kurth, Burton O. *Milton and Christian Heroism.* Berkeley: Univ. of California Press, 1959; reprinted, Hamden, Shoe String Press, 1966.

Lewalski, Barbara K. *Milton's Brief Epic: The Genre, Meaning, and Art of Paradise Regained.* Providence: Brown Univ. Press, 1966.

Lewis, C. S. *A Preface to Paradise Lost.* Oxford: Oxford Univ. Press, 1942; frequently reprinted.

Lieb, Michael J. *The Dialectics of Creation: Patterns of Birth and Regeneration in Paradise Lost.* Amherst: Univ. of Massachusetts Press, 1970.

MacCaffrey, Isabel G. *Paradise Lost as 'Myth'.* Cambridge, Mass.: Harvard Univ. Press, 1959.

McColley, Grant. *Paradise Lost: An Account of Its Growth and Major Origins, with a Discussion of Milton's Use of Sources and Literary Patterns.* Chicago: Packard, 1940; reprinted, New York: Russell and Russell, 1963.

Parker, William R., "The Date of *Samson Agonistes,*" *Philological Quarterly,* XXVIII (1949), 145–66.

Parker, William R. *Milton's Debt to Greek Tragedy in Samson Agonistes.* Baltimore: Johns Hopkins Press, 1937; reprinted, Hamden: Archon Books, 1963.

Patrides, C. A., ed. *Milton's Epic Poetry: Essays on Paradise Lost and Paradise Regained.* Harmondsworth: Penguin Books, 1967.

Peter, John. *A Critique of Paradise Lost.* New York: Columbia Univ. Press, 1960.

Pope, Elizabeth M. *Paradise Regained: the Tradition and the Poem.* Baltimore: Johns Hopkins Press, 1947; reprinted, London: Russell and Russell, 1961.

Qvarnström, Gunnar. *The Enchanted Palace: Some Structural Aspects of Paradise Lost.* Stockholm: Almquist and Wiksell, 1967.

Rajan, B. *Paradise Lost and the Seventeenth Century Reader.* London: Chatto and Windus, 1947; frequently reprinted.

Ricks, Christopher. *Milton's Grand Style.* Oxford: Clarendon Press, 1963, 1968.

Ross, Malcolm M. *Milton's Royalism: A Study of the Conflict of Symbol and Idea in the Poems.* Ithaca: Cornell Univ. Press, 1943.

Samuel, Irene. *Dante and Milton: The Commedia and Paradise Lost.* Ithaca: Cornell Univ. Press, 1966.

Shawcross, John T., "The Balanced Structure of *Paradise Lost,*" *Studies in Philology,* LXII (1965), 696–718.

Shawcross, John T., "The Chronology of Milton's Major Poems," *PMLA,* LXXVI (1961), 45–58.

Sims, James H. *The Bible in Milton's Epics.* Gainesville: Univ. of Florida Press, 1962.

Steadman, John M. *Milton and the Renaissance Hero.* Oxford: Clarendon Press, 1967.

Steadman, John M. *Milton's Epic Characters: Image and Idol.* Chapel Hill: Univ. of North Carolina Press, 1968.

Stein, Arnold. *Answerable Style: Essays on Paradise Lost.* Minneapolis: Univ. of Minnesota Press, 1953; reprinted, Seattle: Univ. of Washington Press, 1967.

Stein, Arnold. *Heroic Knowledge: An Interpretation of Paradise Regained and Samson Agonistes.* Minneapolis: Univ. of Minnesota Press, 1957; reprinted, Hamden: Archon Books, 1965.

Summers, Joseph H. *The Muse's Method: An Introduction to Paradise Lost.* Cambridge, Mass.: Harvard Univ. Press, 1962.

Waldock, A. J. A. *Paradise Lost and Its Critics.* Cambridge: Cambridge Univ. Press, 1947; frequently reprinted.

West, Robert H. *Milton and the Angels.* Athens: Univ. of Georgia Press, 1955.

Whaler, James. *Counterpoint and Symbol. An Inquiry into the Rhythm of Milton's Epic Style.* Copenhagen: Rosenkilde and Bagger, 1956.

Wilkes, George A. *The Thesis of Paradise Lost.* Melbourne: Melbourne Univ. Press, 1961.

Wright, B. A. *Milton's Paradise Lost: A Reassessment of the Poem.* London: Methuen, 1962; reprinted, London: University Paperbacks, 1968.

Index of Titles and First Lines

ITALICIZED PAGE NUMBERS REFER TO TEXTUAL NOTES.